A *Backwoods Home* Anthology:

The Sixteenth Year

Published by
Backwoods Home Magazine
P. O. Box 712
Gold Beach, OR 97444
www.backwoodshome.com

ISBN: 0-9821577-9-7

Editor: *Dave Duffy*

Senior Editor: *John Silveira*

Art Director: *Don Childers*

Contributors:

Jeffrey R. Yago, Jackie Clay, David Lee, Claire Wolfe, Gary Gresh, Linda Gabris, Massad Ayoob, John Silveira, Mary Kenyon, Alice Brantley Yeager, James O. Yeager, Charles A. Sanders, Tom R. Kovach, Raymond Nones, Danny Fulks, Steven Gregersen, Jack Lintelmann, Dorothy Ainsworth, Kelly McCarthy, Gary F. Arnet, Gail Butler, Kathleen Sanderson, Julie Crist, Amy Peare, Sylvia Gist, Habeeb Salloum, Jarrett D. Kelly, Tom O'Toole, Joanne O'Toole

Introduction

This 16th Year Anthology joins our 15th Year Anthology on the printing press. We've published them at the same time to catch-up since we have not published an anthology for the last couple of years. We are now in our 21st year of publishing *Backwoods Home Magazine* so we have a bit more catch-up to do. While you're waiting, please enjoy this useful collection of self-reliance articles.

The years go by so quickly. When I started the magazine my daughter, Annie, was only seven years old. Now she is the 27-year-old managing editor of a magazine that gets better with age. My wife, Ilene, who has been the business manager of the magazine for many years, used to type in the articles directly from the author's manuscript. That was in a day before the scanning of text was invented. Now, of course, most of the authors submit their articles on CDROM or via the internet.

Good friends John Silveira and Don Childers, who have been with me since the first issue, are still with the magazine. Don is still a youngster at age 80. This issue also features many other knowledgeable authors, from Dorothy Ainsworth and Massad Ayoob to Jackie Clay and Claire Wolfe, and many more in between. Please enjoy them all and add this volume to your collection of *BHM* anthologies.

Dave Duffy
Publisher/Editor

Contents —

Issue Number 91

Issue Number 92

Issue Number 93

Issue Number 94

Issue Number 95

Issue Number 96

FREE COOKBOOK CD-ROM ♦ ♦ ♦ See page 99

Backwoods Home magazine

practical ideas for self-reliant living

Jan/Feb 2005
Issue #91
$4.95 US
$6.50 CAN

Chimney building

ce fishing
uild a trail
laple syrup recipes
rowing blueberries
olar water pumping
reparedness planning

ww.backwoodshome.com

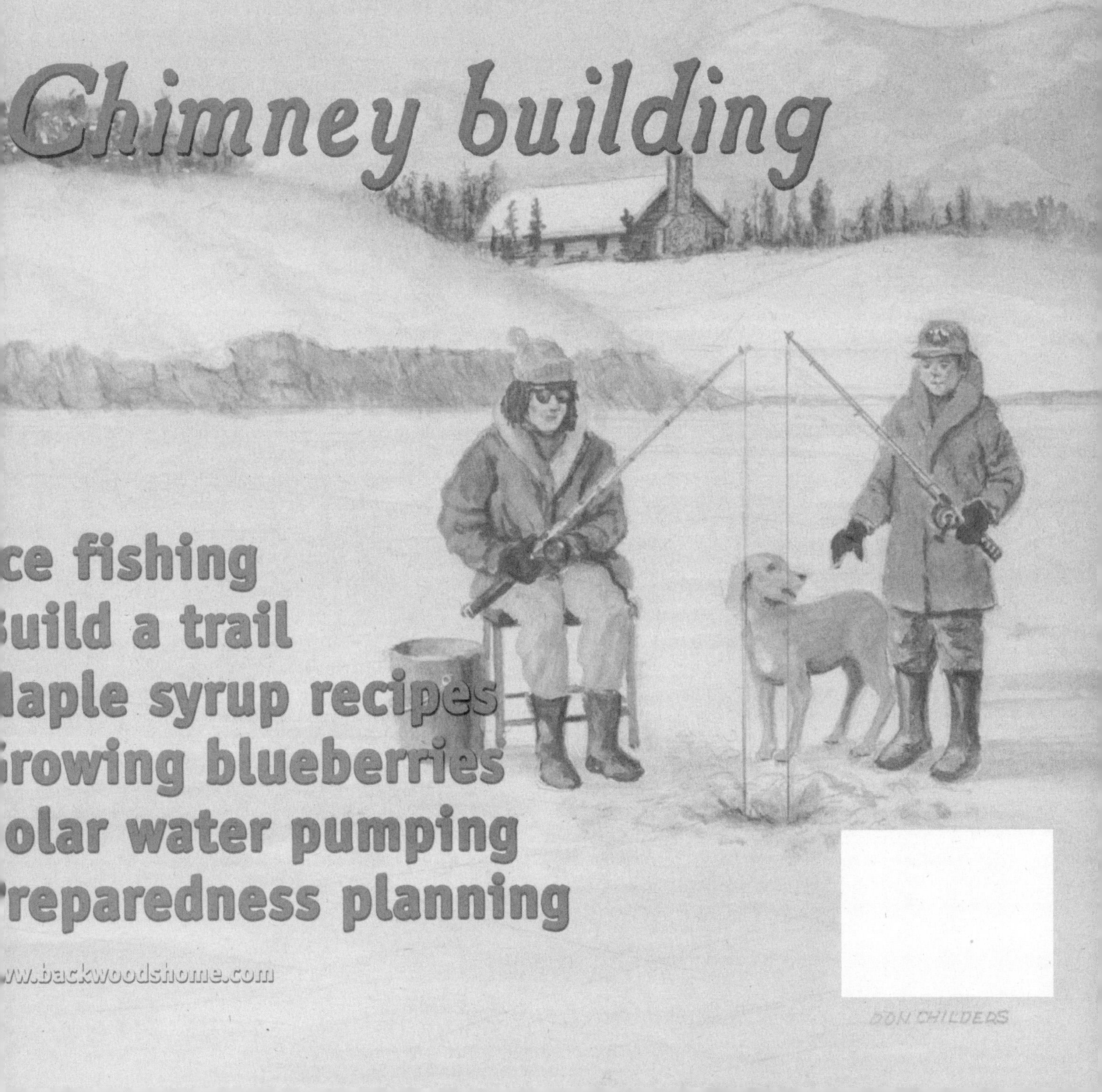

My view

That old survivalist mumbo jumbo and 10 reasons why it makes sense

I've got a suggestion for a sensible New Year's resolution for self-reliant types like myself, and I've got at least 10 good reasons to keep it. The resolution is to get prepared for any eventuality that could come down the highway in the future so that you and your family can survive it in comfort. Sounds like that old survivalist mumbo jumbo to some of you, but it makes more sense than ever these days for the following reasons:

1. Social Security and Medicare: I talked about this last issue. They're going to collapse. If you or any member of your family are connected with them, you'll be affected. The less you are dependent on any government program the better.

2. The economy: America is in debt up to its ears. If it continues, some economists predict foreigners may lose faith in the American dollar, pull their money out, and we'll be in an instant Depression. If you're near a large population center, you could be in for trouble from desperate people pouring into the countryside.

3. Terrorism: Terrorism could visit America again, possibly in the form of a biological attack which could require us to hunker down in our homes for months. A "dirty bomb" may require us to evacuate for an extended period. A chemical attack would be less severe, unless it happened right in our town.

4. Rising crime in the country: It may be down in the cities, but it's rising in the countryside because a lot of city scumbags have moved into our neighborhoods. The farther out you live, the safer you'll be, but there are lots of self defense measures you can take, including being properly trained in the use of a gun.

5. Inflation: It'll probably be the government's choice weapon to battle the coming insolvency of Social Security and Medicare, mentioned in number 1 above. If inflation reaches 21%, as it did in the Carter years, you're going to look pretty smart with a garage full of survivalist items like a generator and a year's worth of food and other supplies. Inflation is already affecting selected items, such as plywood which jumped by $7 a sheet a few months ago. Hard to build a home, addition, or anything else without plywood.

6. Illness: What if a deadly epidemic like the 1918 flu came back, and there is no vaccine available (Sound familiar?) to protect your family? You might have to stay home to avoid becoming contaminated with the deadly illness. Do you have enough food and supplies to do that? On a personal basis, if your breadwinner falls ill, who or what keeps the family going? If the main wood chopper falls ill, who cuts the wood for your wood stove? It's tough having a sick family member, but it's much tougher having it complicated by having too little food and other necessities in the house.

7. A personal economic meltdown: You personally could fall on temporary hard times with the loss of your income. Are you ready to weather such an event until you can get the income flowing again? If you're making good money now, pay off your debt, and put some money away, either in a bank or in a drawer. (These days your drawer pays you almost as much interest as a bank.) Maybe even pay up your mortgage, if you have one, a few months in advance. That'll also cut down on your interest payments. Stock up on food. Not only is it like having money in the bank, but it's a good hedge against rising food prices.

8. A severe winter: No one knows where the price of oil and gas are going, so it's a good idea to keep extra fuel on hand. I don't keep a big tank of gas because even with a gas stabilizer added it tends to get stale. But I do keep my vehicles full of gas and I have several 5-gallon cans of Stabil-treated gas, plus oil and lubricants to take care of my chain saw and other 2-stroke implements. I also have about a three year supply of wood for my wood stoves, and backup propane heat. If there is an electric blackout I have backup propane lights in several rooms. One of the best ways to deal with a fuel shortage in a cold winter is to simply stay home with your ample supplies and enjoy the wood stove.

9. It's healthy and fun: Preparedness, at least the way my family practices it, is cost effective, convenient, healthy, and fun. There's nothing like coming home from Costco with a truck load of food and supplies you've bought at the much cheaper bulk rate prices. We seldom run out of anything no matter what my wife decides is for dinner. I date everything and rotate it with the new supplies, so it is very unusual for us to have to throw anything away. We've also got lots of frozen kale (I love kale soup...) and stored pumpkins (...and pumpkin pie) put away from this year's garden. We have a big garden and a bunch of chickens, so we eat lots of pesticide-free food and phytochemical-rich eggs.

I've left the 10th reason blank because I haven't even come close to covering all the reasons to practice preparedness, or all the ways you can do it and have fun doing it. Plug in your own reason. Preparedness is really a way of life, just like losing weight or staying in shape. You have to want to do it. If you just store a bunch of stuff, it's going to eventually go bad and you'll end up throwing it out. Look around at the uncertainties in the world, and see if practicing preparedness in some form might be a good idea for your family. ***— Dave Duffy***

Build your own solar-powered water pumping station

By Jeffrey R. Yago, P.E., CEM

In the last issue, there was an excellent article by Dorothy Ainsworth on water pumping using mechanical windmills. In this issue I will address another form of "free" water pumping. There are many remote applications where a solar-powered water pump is more cost effective than installing a conventional grid-connected AC pump.

I recently designed a solar-powered pumping system for a local farmer wanting to pump water from a lake up to a watering trough for cattle in a distant fenced field. We have also designed larger systems to pump directly from drilled wells up to elevated storage tanks, which provide gravity-fed water back down to remote ranch buildings.

Local residents enjoying the "solar water supply" at the open top drinking tank.

Basic system description

These solar applications made economic sense because the location was too remote to run a long power line. A solar-powered water system is one of the easiest solar power systems to install, since you will not need a battery or battery charging equipment. When the sun is shining, the system is pumping, when the sun is not shining, the system is off—simple.

By adding a storage tank and increasing the size of the pumping system, excess pumped water can be stored, which can continue to supply water during the night or when it's cloudy and the pump is off.

Low voltage DC pumps designed to operate on solar power are not designed like 220-volt AC water pumps. A DC water pump is designed to pump using the absolute minimum of electrical power. Unfortunately, this also usually means a very low flow rate, so having a storage tank or open trough is essential.

Although the flow rate can be less than one gallon per minute (GPM) for the smaller pump sizes, this small flow will be fairly constant throughout the solar day (9 AM to 3 PM for most locations). This low flow rate can still provide over 350 gallons of water per day from all but the deepest well applications.

A solar module can be mounted almost anywhere, but should face in a southerly direction (for North America). Most farm and ranch applications should have the modules and pump controller mounted on a raised pole to stay above snow drifts and potential damage from animals.

A pole mount also allows easier adjustment of module tilt and east-west orientation during initial setup to achieve the best overall year-round performance. For most applications the tilt will be equal to your latitude.

Pump controller

Your solar powered pumping system should include a pump controller such as the one in the photo on page 37. Although it is possible to connect the pump leads directly to the output terminals of the solar module, a controller provides much better pump performance and start/stop control. It will also avoid trying to operate the pump in a stalled condition when solar output is too low.

Each residential-size solar module will produce a fairly constant 17-volts output at almost any level of sunlight. However, the current output (amps) will be directly proportional to sun intensity. The pump will have

A 24-volt DC SolarJack pump for a 4-inch well casing

a minimum current draw when stalled and no pumping is taking place. As the voltage is increased, pump rotation and water pumping is increased as long as enough current is available. During less than ideal solar periods, the current output of the solar module(s) can be below the amp draw required for the pump to begin pumping. A solar pump controller will convert any excess voltage of the solar array to more output current.

The resulting lower voltage will not provide the normal flow output from the slower turning pump, but it will allow reduced flow during those hours the pump will normally be "stalled." In addition to matching the voltage and current load of the pump with the charging current and voltage output of the solar module, a solar-pump controller also includes wiring terminals for normally open (n.o.) and normally closed (n.c.) switch contacts. This makes it easy to add a high and low level float switch to the storage tank, or a low-limit float switch for the well or pond providing the water source.

The following information is taken from my book titled, *Achieving Energy Independence—One Step at a Time*. You might find this book helpful if you are considering installing your own solar power system, and it goes into much more detail than space allows here.

Table 1 will get you started by estimating how much water you will need per day. Since your pump will not work during cloudy weather, be sure to have a tank or trough that can hold several days' usage.

Pumping basics

Any well or pressure pump is designed to provide a given flow of water (GPM) for a given pressure or lift (head). Pumping "head" is measured in feet, and represents the total lift the pump can raise water from a low point to a high point. When measuring the distance a submerged pump must raise water, you do not start with how far down the pump is in the well. You start by measuring from the above ground surface down to the lowest level the well water will be during pumping.

For example, let's say we want to fill an open water tank (no pressure) that is on the top of a small hill. We estimate that the water level in this tank will be 3 feet high above ground level, but the hill top is 50-feet higher than where the well is going to be drilled. The well will be 100 feet deep and the pump will be positioned 80 feet down. We notice the water level is only 30 feet below the surface, but will probably drop considerably when the pumping starts unless it is a very fast refilling well.

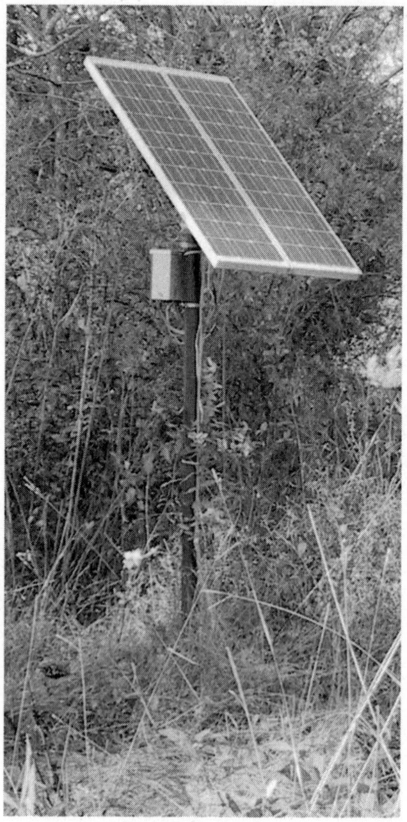

Pole-mounted solar array during initial setup

If your well driller cannot provide this information, you will need to estimate how much "draw-down" the well will have during pumping. For a fairly fast recharging well, let's add another 20 feet for this estimated draw-down. For our example, the

Table 1: Water usage *

Per Person (incl. washing)	75 gallons per day
Bath	30 gallons per day
Toilet	3 gallons per flush
Shower	3 gallons per minute
Horse or Cow (drinking)	12 gallons per day
Water Weight	8.33 pounds per gallon
Convert Head (ft) to PSI	Divide by 2.31

* From *Achieving Energy Independence—One Step at a Time*

pump would need to have a minimum lift of (30 feet + 20 feet to lowest water level) + 50 feet elevation of the tank + 3 feet tank water depth = 103 feet total pumping head. If you want to convert feet head to pounds per square inch (PSI) pressure, divide by 2.31 which equals 45 PSI (103/2.31). If your tank will be closed and pressurized, you will need to add the desired tank water pressure to this pump's head pressure.

Instead of a deep well, you may need to pump from a lake or pond at a lower level up to a storage tank. The pump lift estimating procedures we used in the above deep well example also applies. However, you measure from the lake's surface level, regardless of how deep the pump will be below the surface.

When using a large body of water as a water source, you will want to suspend the pump off the bottom using an underwater support or surface floats to avoid plugging the pump intake with mud from the bottom.

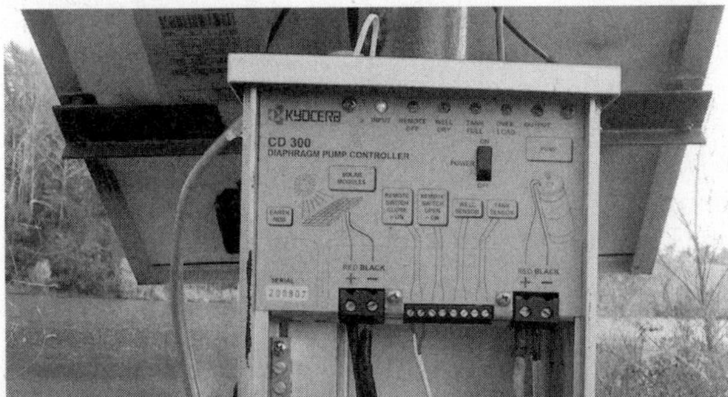

Kyocera solar pump controller (cover removed)

Another common mistake to avoid, is do not oversize the piping. For most applications, you will be pumping less than two GPM, and at this low flow rate, these low flow solar pumps will not provide enough water velocity through a large pipe to keep suspended solids from settling out onto the bottom of the piping. A typical residential size ½-HP deep well pump can pump over six GPM, which produces a much higher velocity. For these larger flow AC pumps, larger pipe sizing is used to keep flow resistance low on long piping runs. However, for a low-flow solar pump for applications requiring less than 100 feet of piping, a ½-inch PVC pipe size will probably work just fine. For runs over 100 feet, I suggest using ¾-inch PVC piping. If you need to pump water over 300 feet, a 1-inch pipe size will lower the high pressure drop of the smaller pipe, but you may have problems with sediment settling in the bottom of the pipe due to the low flow rates involved.

Float switch in the tank to turn off the pump when tank is filled

Remember, the purpose of the storage tank or drinking trough is to allow a very slow water flow constantly pumping throughout the day, to build up a large volume of water to supply brief periods of high water usage.

Solar module sizing

You may want to consult the DC pump distributor to determine the size of solar array that will be required for your specific application. For high pumping heads (feet of lift) or high flow rates, you may want to consider buying a higher voltage DC pump instead of a smaller 12-volt DC pump. This will require using two or more nominal 12-volt solar modules to provide the higher voltage.

To get you started with solar array sizing, it is rare that any solar-pumping application can get by with less than a 75-watt solar module, and larger applications will require two modules for acceptable pump performance. A 48-volt DC pump will require a minimum of four nominal 12-volt solar modules (4x12).

The installation shown in this article supplies water to a cattle drinking trough located 75 feet higher than a nearby lake, which is 300 feet away. We used a 24-volt DC Solar Jack TM pump, two Kyocera 60-watt solar modules, and 320 feet of ¾-inch PVC pipe. The photos were taken in late October after 6 p.m. and the panels were no longer facing the setting sun, yet there was still almost ½-gallon per minute flow of fresh water up to the trough.

Piping head loss

In addition to the elevation head (feet) your pump must lift the water from a low pond or drilled well up to a storage tank, it also must overcome

TABLE 2: PVC piping head loss (feet) for each 100 feet of pipe

FLOW GPM	½-INCH	¾-INCH	1-INCH
0.5	0.27	X	X
1.0	0.99	X	X
1.5	2.09	X	X
2.0	3.56	0.90	X
2.5	5.38	1.37	X
3.0	X	1.92	X
4.0	X	3.26	1.01
5.0	X	4.93	1.52
6.0	X	X	2.13
8.0	X	X	3.64

Note: "X" not recommended due to low velocity or high pressure drop.

the resistance to flow of the pipe. As I stated earlier, for small-flow DC pumping applications, if you oversize the piping to reduce friction loss, you could increase sediment problems at these low flow data rates. Table 2 provides piping resistance to flow in terms of head (feet). This makes it easy to calculate total pump size, by adding this pipe friction head loss to the lift head we estimated earlier.

As an example, let's say you need to calculate the piping pressure loss for a 2-gallon per minute flow through 250 feet of pipe. If we use ½-inch PVC pipe, the loss would be 8.9 feet head (3.56 x 250/100). If we increased the pipe size to ¾-inch PVC, the loss would be 2.3 feet head (0.90 x 250/100). At this low flow rate either pipe size will work, unless your pump cannot handle the additional pressure loss of the smaller pipe. As flow rates increase, a larger pipe may be unavoidable on longer pipe runs.

Pump selection

Table 3 provides a size comparison of several popular models of smaller DC pumps, and the relationship of pump flow (GPM) to pump head (feet). Notice how the same pump will have a substantially reduced flow rate as this head pressure is increased. Since this is only a very limited list of pump models and brands available, please consult the dealer for more specific sizing information.

The manufacturers listed in Table 3 offer many other pump models having many different combinations of DC voltage, flow rate, and head or lift. Selecting the right pump for your specific application can reduce the size and cost of the solar array that will be required to provide the power. Buying a low cost pump with poor efficiency will require a much more expensive solar array.

Jeff Yago is a licensed professional engineer and certified energy manager with over 25-years experience in the energy conservation field. He is also certified by the North American Board of Certified Energy Practitioners as a licensed solar installer. He has extensive solar thermal and solar photovoltaic system design experience and has authored numerous articles and texts. Δ

Solar pump suppliers

Dankoff Solar Pumps
www.dankoffsolar.com

Backwoods Solar
www.backwoodssolar.com

Real Goods
www.realgoods.com

TABLE 3: DC pump flow vs. head

PUMP MODEL	DC Volts	25 ft. head	100 ft. head	200 ft. head
ShurFlo #9300	12	0.98 GPM	0.86 GPM	X
	24	1.9 GPM	1.72 GPM	X
SolarJack SCS	30	6.5 GPM	X	X
	60	X	5.1 GPM	X
	75	X	X	3.0 GPM
Dankoff #5218	48	2.7 GPM	2.1 GPM	1.8 GPM
Dankoff #5226	48	3.6 GPM	3.2 GPM	2.7 GPM

Note: Some DC pumps are designed to operate at several different voltages, producing higher flow as you add more solar modules.

Starting over — again Part 2

"You can only do so many things in a day's work. Period. You may want to do this or that so badly that you can taste it. You wake up at night trying to figure out how to work more. But the fact is you can do what you can do. No more."

By Jackie Clay

Spring breakup had finished here in northern Minnesota, and the remnants of huge snowbanks poured rivers of melting water onto the mile-long trail as the warm April sun beat down. Having been only a logging road used during the winter, there were puddles big enough to float our canoe, so our first priority was to do some heavy duty road work with old-fashioned equipment. A couple shovels, a hoe, and a pick completed our manual tools. The good old four-wheeler worked to haul trailer load after trailer load of rock and gravel into the worst clay holes.

Repairing the road

We had done remote road work a lot before this in the mountains of Montana. There, too, we lived a long, long way from a maintained road.

We have learned a lot and still have much to learn about keeping roads driveable with little pocket cash. First off, we worked hard to drain off any water standing or running onto the road. There is usually a higher side to a trail and a lower side. The trick is to channel the water down onto the lower side, then find a place to trench it off into the woods or a marsh. This was not done once, but many times, as the water in holes lowered, requiring more work to get them as dry as possible. We are still always alert for puddles on the road that need help draining. Our little ditches get

A poor man's culvert; a dip to drain off water lined with large stones.

plugged up with silt and leaves, and mud from passing vehicles can create a dam, blocking water flow.

Depending on the soil, some wet spots need only draining and fill. Others, with clay or muck bottoms, need large rocks for a bed, then loads of gravel on top of the rocks to raise the roadbed. Water will not stand on higher ground. Only low spots will *retain* water, no matter how long it rains.

Our son, David, loves to do road work. (Don't we all like to create little channels and watch water flowing?) He dug and filled many, many low spots, channeling the water off at every opportunity. It gave him an excuse to run the ATV and do road building at the same time. We were still leaving our Suburban out near the road and running in gas, feed, supplies, and spring water with the four-wheeler to avoid tearing ruts into our soft road. Once you make huge ruts, they are with you for a long, long time. And they get worse and worse. We really didn't mind the so-called isolation and inconvenience of not driving in and out. And slowly the road got drier and the worst holes became more solid.

We learned to create a "poor man's culvert," too. In several spots, the original trail builders had used a backhoe to dig fill out of one side of the trail and build it up. Unfortunately, in several spots, they picked the uphill side of the trail. During snow melt or heavy rains, these little ponds fill up and seep out onto the trail. Working for two days, we dug out a little dip about two feet wide and a foot deep to the downhill side. Now, this drained the pond pretty well, but it would also tear up our vehicles when we drove the trail. Not to mention what the propane truck driver would say. So we lined the ditch with fist-sized round rocks. This let the water flow through, but gave the vehicles a good bed to drive over, with little bumping to deal with.

The "big" garden spot, lest you think it's going to be easy.

Our road building really picked up when my oldest son, Bill, was finished with his tractor the first of May and told us to come on down and pick it up for the summer. Glory be! That Ford tractor has a gravel bucket that holds three times as much gravel as David's little trailer does. And it scoops it up, too. We also picked up Bill's cement mixer to begin our footings and foundation on the new house.

It was an exciting time, watching the leaves and blooms come out on the trees, berry bushes, and wild flowers, knowing that we were finally getting ready to really get to work on our new homestead.

Our poor goat barn was only about half done, but it held the critters well

Whacking brush in the new garden. Surprisingly, the Troy Bilt tiller turned under fearsome brush.

out of reach of predators. In the daytime, they ranged about happily grazing and browsing on grass, tree leaves, and brush. At night, they were shut in their pens. But we had to leave it undone, in order to get on with other projects. If there is one thing I've learned: *you can only do so many things in a day's work.* Period. You may want to do this or that so badly that you can taste it. You wake up at night trying to figure out how to work more. But the fact is you can do what you can do. No more.

Spring was great. We had four goat kids born from two does, four long-eared, wonderfully spotted, cuter-than-heck, silky bundles of bounce. I traded off the first two for some sheeting for the goat barn, giving us a milking doe and a gallon of goat milk a day for the house. I could hardly wait to make yogurt, cheese, and ice cream again. The second set of twins I left on the doe, who also milked a good gallon of sweet milk. I wanted to keep the doe kid and I didn't want to be milking two does with everything else I had to do.

We needed to get a garden started, the road improved, and get our house under way. Winter comes too quickly on spring's heels in the North. With the tractor, the house site was easily leveled. First I scraped the top foot of good topsoil off to one side, digging out all the tree stumps I could. This left only two solid pine stumps, which would end up under the house in the crawl space, but out of the way. The benefits were that I didn't have to work for many days, and taking the stumps out would have left a soft spot near the footing that might weaken the foundation. It seemed the best option.

All of the other rock and gravel was sorted as best as I could. Any that seemed fine enough for cement went around the outside of our site to be used when we mixed the cement. The large rocks went in another pile, as we were going to use those in the foundation, using slip forms and stacking the nice round granite rocks artistically. The rough, in-between gravel was hauled out onto the worst holes in our trail. There are advantages to building on a gravel ridge.

Most days, I averaged about eight loads on the road a day and much of that time was spent in travel. It would have been nice to have a dump truck, but we didn't. Then there were chores, cooking, house chores, and water hauling. The days went by fast. Too fast.

While we worked, our tomatoes grew.

Putting in the gardens

When I got tired of hauling gravel, we hacked at the new garden spots. I had trays of tomato plants in the window of the fish house that I started back in late March. They were lusty and large by the end of April, begging to go out into the soil in their cozy Wall'o Water tipis. (See Jackie's article on these garden gadgets in Issue #79, Jan/Feb 2003—editor.) So we worked hard at getting the new garden roughed in.

Now, some folks figure that because we've been homesteading for decades that everything just naturally comes easier for us. Sigh. Sometimes I wish it were so. Unfortunately, we have to work just as hard to accomplish most things as the next person. And, no, we don't have perfect, fluffy black garden soil, either. I feel somewhat like Jackie Appleseed, having carved innumerable gardens out of clay, rock, and tree roots, only to move onward in the quest for a better homestead that we owed less money for.

Here, as we began working on the garden, we decided on two garden spots. One, on the slope downhill from our building site, had beautiful soil and faced the south. It was also quite close to the creek and small beaver pond, should we have to pump water on the plants during dry spells. The other was downslope from the goat barn, right smack in the middle of small popple trees and hazelnut brush. But there was the possibility of tripling the size of this garden in the following years, due to the lay of the land. This site also faced south and east.

So the small spot below our future house was tilled and made into three beds which measured four feet by twenty feet each. And this is the spot we chose for our baby tomato plants. We dug out the rocks, roots, and grass clumps. Blueberry plants were pulled out, brush was dug out and hauled off. It made us feel like murderers pulling up all those lusty blueberry bushes, with their little pink buds, when in the catalogs, the same bushes cost $7.99 and up. But on our land, there are millions of blueberry bushes, and these were, in effect, weeds. And weeds are simply strong growing plants, growing in the wrong place for a person's convenience.

I worked in some lime, as the soil here is acidic, along with some of the rotted manure out of our stock trailer. We worked these beds extremely well, then planted 32 tomato plants of four varieties which I liked in cold climates. These were Early Goliath, Early Cascade, Oregon Spring, and Stupice.

First we laid down red plastic mulch to increase the soil temperature. Then in a few days, we began planting, cutting "X"s in the center of the plastic to receive our plants. After planting each plant very deeply, which grows nice strong roots along the stem, we set a five-gallon plastic bucket down over it, upside down, and placed a Wall'o Water around the bucket to hold the Wall'o Water in place while we filled the cells with water, then we removed the bucket. We had to haul our water to the site in five-gallon water jugs, so we were only able to plant a dozen plants a day, filling each empty tipi with sun-warmed water. Even though the night time temperatures dipped into the high teens, our little baby tomatoes took right off in their little individual greenhouses.

We had left enough room on the bottom sides of the beds to plant green beans and wax beans. This area we kept worked up with our handy little Mantis tiller until the danger of frost was past and it was safe to plant these frost-sensitive crops.

The batter boards and string to keep things square and level. The inner string has been removed for ease of pouring cement.

While we waited, we worked like mad on the big garden. Big? Ha! The best we could do was an area about 20 by 75 feet. We were right in the brush, and we tilled, hacked, dug, and chopped with axe and grub hoe trying to get out as many runners and roots as we could, fearing the whole garden would pop right back to brush again. Then there were the rocks, logs, stumps, and tree roots. We kept the garden cart and a couple of five-gallon plastic buckets on hand to receive this "trash." The rocks went out onto our trail and the wood went back into the low corner of our horse pasture. My, did we work for that spot for our large garden, even though it was half the size of my smallest garden out of *four* in Montana. But it was a start and it was all we could do right then.

In this spot, we planted onions, carrots, and radishes, and later on, when it had warmed up, sweet corn, melons, and squash. The weather was warm, and very soon, we had a garden. If only the deer would let it be.

Spending less time in the garden than I had ever done in my life, I turned my focus to the house and resumed hauling gravel and leveling the hillside.

It was about this time that my youngest sister called from Michigan asking me if I would come get my elderly parents, whom she was living near and helping out, so as to give her a break. She had been super-stressed with a business, his and her parents, among other things, and needed to breathe.

So we shifted our focus and prepared to have house guests in our little travel trailer and fish house shack. My sister, Sue, who lives in a suburb of Duluth, an hour and a half south of us, and I readied for a trip to Michigan. Right in the middle of the best building weather in Minnesota. But, like I've said, you do what you can do.

My husband, Bob, is a great guy but doesn't have the drive that I do. Okay, so I'm obsessed with getting things done. Can't help it. And David is only 13. So I was not surprised to find the place just as I left it a week later, when I drove into the yard in Mom and Dad's station wagon. Oh well, the animals were happy and the place hadn't burned down.

My son, Bill, had found a loaner oldie travel trailer for us to "camp" in while Mom and Dad were there visiting. Five people and three dogs are just too much for one shack. So I cooked in our old shack and spent the day in and out of there, not wanting to leave Mom and Dad alone, as they both have health issues, including Mom's recent heart attack.

The building site

When the trail was driveable with Mom and Dad's car (it was hard for them to get in and out of our big four-wheel drive vehicles), we finished leveling the building site. We were having trouble getting it right because of the slope both ways, and were very happy to have Bill drive up with a transit on the front seat of his truck.

Like a pro, he set things up and had me hold the pole. We had cut batter boards, which are simply two sturdy wooden stakes with a 1x4, about two feet long, screwed to the top. You pound in the stakes outside each corner, making a 90° corner on which to fasten strings to mark the ends and sides of the foundation. We needed two of these for each corner, making eight in all to mark the corners and string all four sides so we could dig footings correctly. I wanted two feet of rock foundation above the footings on the downhill side, so with the transit, we slowly worked the batter boards which were about two feet outside of the actual corners, and strings, which crossed at the actual corners, until things seemed right.

Of course, on measuring, the rectangle was out of square, measuring first the sides and ends, then across the diagonal, making an X. Both sides of the X need to be the same length, and of course, both sides and both ends needed to be correct, as well.

It took most of the afternoon, adjusting the screws which were on top of the 1x4s to wind the strings tightly on, but slowly, our adjustments were minute and the measurements were accurate. When we had the outside four cords nearly perfect, we added the inside set, making the double markings with which to gauge our footing's width.

When we had all the cords stretched tightly, I only had to measure 16 inches down from the strings to the top of the footing trench, which would be the top of the cement, to find level. When we dug, we had a stick with a black mark at one foot and we only had to stick that in our trench to find out if it was deep enough.

We are building on a very firm old rock and gravel point and dug our footings out a foot deep and a foot wide. This we did by hand with a pick, shovel, and pointed hoe. And like our other "waste" from the site, we hauled the not so good stuff out onto the trail, saved the finer gravel for cement work, and sorted out the large rocks to go into the foundation.

And the preliminary work was even more fun because Mom and Dad were there to share it with us. Even though having them entailed more work for us, it was a real treat to have Mom thrill to each new-blooming wild flower and to look up from cement work, and to see my 92-year-old father driving the riding lawn mower down the foot path to see how we were doing. After all, it was they who took me away to the woods when I was real little, and frequently all the time I was growing up. It only seemed right to have them there with us while we were starting our wilderness homestead.

Bob and David free the new apple tree from the pot.

Fruit trees

Taking a break from digging the footings, we began to plant the four apple trees that my sister, Sue, and my parents gave me as a pre-birthday present. We had been very short of cash and I had not been able to buy new fruit trees this spring, even though I considered it a near-necessity. So with those great potted trees in the stock trailer (to protect them from the goats), we began to ready a spot for them.

By then, David was using Bill's tractor (with permission, of course), and doing a darned good job, too. Not only was he scraping up gravel and hauling it to the trail, but he had learned to ditch and dig holes with the gravel bucket. So I had him scrape the brush and logs from our new little orchard spot and then dig four widely spaced holes for the trees.

It's best to dig a hole at least twice as big as the root ball of the tree. We did better than that with the tractor. Each tree had a hole four feet long, two feet deep, and three feet wide. And each hole was dug in about 10 minutes. With a shovel, you couldn't have dug half that hole in a whole day.

He tipped the bottom lip of the bucket, which has power down, then drove forward. This caused the bucket to dig in well. As he went forward, he lifted

After a 90° day of cement pouring we are cement spattered and tired.

the bucket to level, then raised it when the hole was wide enough. Driving forward a few more feet, he dumped the dirt and repeated the process several more times, each time, working deeper and deeper. When we had a good hole, he went back to the yard and got a bucket full of old rotted manure from the stock trailer pile. Then we carried the first young tree to its spot.

When you plant potted trees, you don't want to disturb their roots. So, instead of just dumping the tree out, we carefully cut away the plastic pot with a sharp knife, being careful not to cut the roots too badly. Then, gently, we peeled the plastic away, with the tree in the hole. While one of us held the trunk gently upright, the other shoveled topsoil and gravel into the hole next to the tree. Filling each hole took longer than digging it because we had to do it by hand. We certainly didn't want to risk damaging those trees by using the tractor.

After the tree was planted to the level it had been in the pot, leaving the graft well out of the soil, we wrapped wire screen around the trunk several times. Mice, rabbits, and voles will completely girdle a young tree by eating the tender bark during the winter. So the screening was a must. We applied it right down below the soil so that when we mulched the trees, the rodents couldn't get under the mulch to nibble on the tree. We protected the trees up to three feet, as the snow does get deep here. We were extra happy, as that screen came from the dump out of discarded window screens.

The screen was tied with twine to hold it in place, but not so tightly that it would impair future growth.

After the tree's trunk was protected, we forked a good layer of strawy-mulch around it for at least four feet in diameter. Not only would the mulch help hold in moisture during the hot, dry months, but it would prevent any grass or weeds from competing with the young tree and protect it from intense cold during the winter. As a bonus, the manure would slowly feed the little trees into winter and beyond.

We pounded in four six-foot steel fence posts outside the ring of mulch so the goaties and deer couldn't munch on the trees, which they most certainly would. Even moose delight in crunching up tender young fruit trees. So we made a stout fence out of wire stock fencing around each tree as it was planted. We made our circles five feet in diameter. (We should have made them ten feet, as we found creative goats could stand on the wire and nibble leaves, bending over after a rain.)

When the trees were snugly in their little corrals, I went around and tied a soft twine here and there, to help straighten up a couple of tops that were growing a little crooked. Ahhh, almost done.

While I was fastening the twine, David hauled out a big barrel of water and the little gasoline Homelite water pump. We pumped ten gallons of water on each tree, completely flooding the little basin it was rooted in. This helps settle the soil, reducing the possibility of any air pockets around the roots. If it had been dry weather, we would have gently watered in a whole 55-gallon barrel on each tree. But it had been raining and the soil was already moist.

Once a week, unless it had rained well, we watered our new little orchard and delighted in watching the leaves spread out and bask in the spring and summer sun.

Garden pests

In the mornings, even with Mom and Dad to care for now, I enjoyed walking down to my little gardens and watching the plants grow. Now in June, I could see eight long rows of sweet corn four inches high and growing, beans with three sets of leaves, onions reaching for the sun, and tomatoes coming to the top of their snug Wall'o Waters. The gardens were little, but things were really growing well. The good, virgin soil was fertile.

But one morning, the garden didn't look so good. Around each place a corn plant had been was a little hole and although the wilting plant was there, the kernel of corn was gone. As we had no crows yet, we figured the culprits were either chipmunks or ground squirrels, which we have in abundance. And, darn it, we enjoy watching the cheerful little critters. (They kind of remind me of me, the way they pack away food for the winter.) Traps and poison are out. We couldn't fence them out, so I just had to watch as they destroyed all but the last three corn plants. I did find out that they don't relish beans or any other garden crops. So I tilled up the corn plot and planted extra beans. We could always use more beans.

Then I planted six more tomato plants in this "big" garden, as I now had the space for them.

The footings got dug, but we were slow. Part of that was the extra time it took to care for Mom and Dad. And Dad, because of his damaged lungs, needed to participate in a pulmonary rehab twice a week. You can't build house and drive to town at the same time. But my son Bill told me that if we could get the footings and foundation in and floor it over, he and his friends would come up for a weekend and frame up our little story and a half house for us. I was worried, but comforted.

Then, nearly to the end of my parents' visit, my youngest sister called again and said that if Mom and Dad wanted to, they could stay in Minnesota with us. Again, we were happy to hear this, but the timing stunk. But, then, when is timing right? It would have been easier if we could have gotten the house finished first. Summer was under way, and we were still digging footings.

But finally they were finished, including the two support pillars in the center of the house to support the cross beams which would stiffen the floor joists.

In each trench, we laid two lengths of steel reinforcing rod to strengthen the cement footings and help prevent cracking. These were supported by laying large rocks at each end and every five feet, all the way around. Where rods were "spliced," the ends were simply overlapped by a foot or so and supported with rocks. We held the rods up six inches from the bottoms of the trenches to get the most strength we could from the rods.

And we began to mix cement. We hauled the water to the site in 55-gallon barrels in the pickup, started the siphon with the water pump, then just folded the hose and stuck it in the back truck pocket when we wanted to shut off the water flow.

Using the handy, clean, on-site gravel, we were able to save time and money. The gravel was a good mixture of coarse sand and rock, so we used a mixture of six shovels of gravel to each shovelful of Portland cement. First we'd pour a little water into the rotating mixer, which worked off our generator hauled to the site. Then gravel was added, then cement and enough water to make a pourable mix.

We found that two batches could be mixed together, and we could still easily handle it in a wheelbarrow. Bob and David mixed cement and hauled it to the trench and I would shovel it into place around the reinforcing rod. Then they would dump the remainder. I was in charge of running the shovel down into the cement to make sure air bubbles and vacant spots were removed, leveling the cement and measuring exactly 16 inches from the top of the cement to the taut string above, run from our batter boards.

We tried to pour at least half a side at a time but the weather did not cooperate. This year we've had a *lot* of rain. That slowed down our already snail's pace. I do the best that I can. It may not be someone else's best, but it's mine and it'll have to do.

The "free" trailer

About this time, we *knew* we could not get the house in move-in condition before cold weather hit in October. I was getting unsettled and couldn't sleep at night. There had to be *something* we could do differently.

Once again, my son, Bill, had the answer. "Why don't you pick up a free older mobile home and have that hauled up? You could use that to camp in for the winter and get at the house in the spring."

Now I absolutely hate everything about mobile homes—*except* that they are bigger than a travel trailer and it would be instant (or almost instant) housing for the five of us and our pets. I gritted my teeth and told him to see if he could find us one. Mom and Dad were quite happy about the prospect, not having the intense feelings about trailers that I do.

In a few days, Bill called to say that he'd found us a freebie; a 14 by 70-foot, three-bedroom trailer in good shape "for a free trailer." And a fellow that worked near him would haul it up to our land for about $600. "You can shove it way back into the trees," Bill said, "so it won't show later on. You can always use it for storage..."

But that much living space for $600 struck the Scotch in me, and I did feel a sense of impending doom lift from my shoulders. Yes, we could start the house again in the spring. I knew that we couldn't fix up the old trailer and get it ready for winter and keep on working on our new house.

Something I've learned in life is that everything doesn't have to happen when you want it to. Sometimes it just has to wait until later. It's like when you live way remote and plan a trip to town during the winter. You wake up and the storm clouds look ugly over to the West. No use in fighting the way things are. There are other days. It's just how it is in the backwoods. Δ

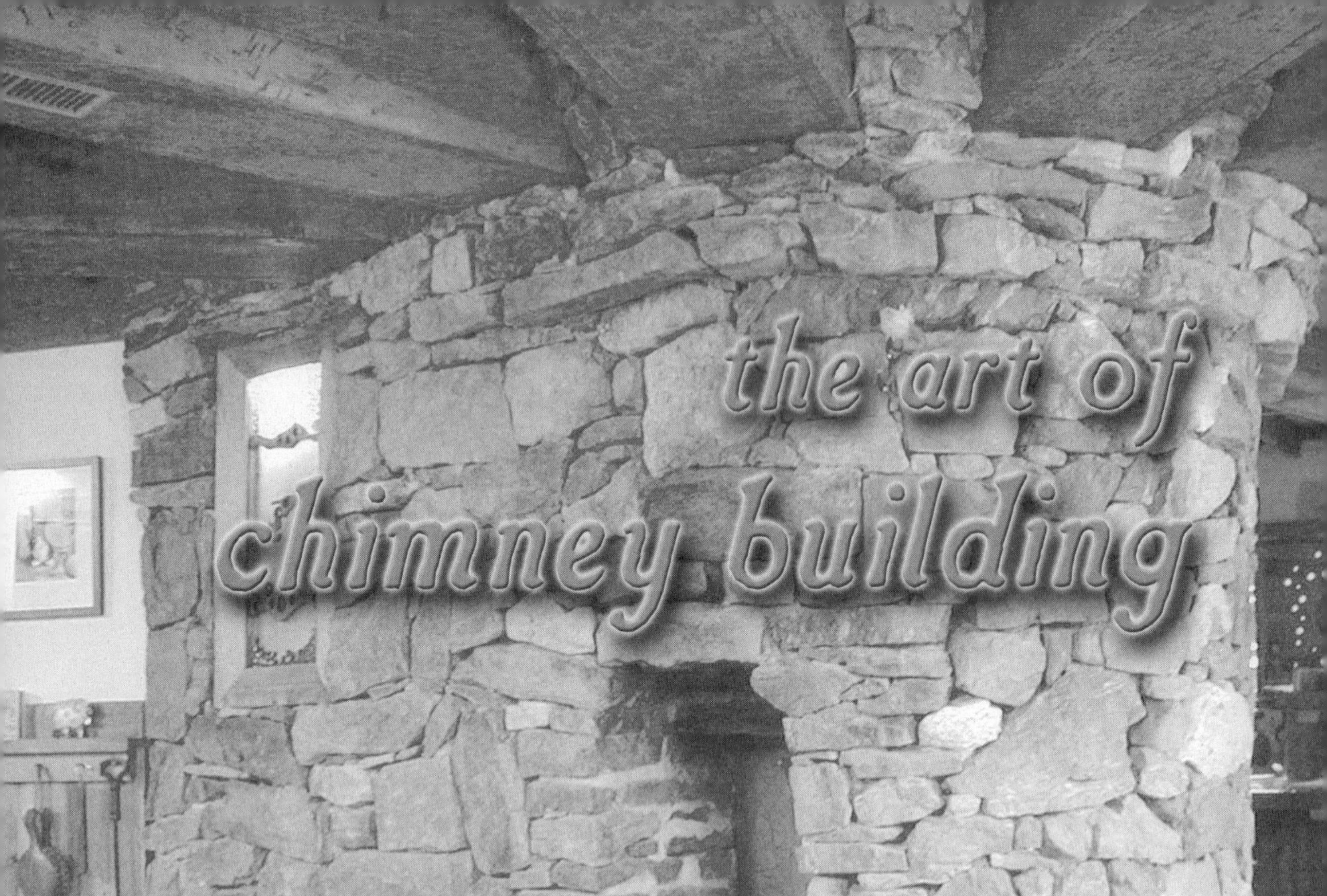

Fifteen ton central chimney that incorporates a fireplace/furnace combination, a shower stall, stained glass windows, and light fixtures. It supports the second and third floors and roof while supplying heat to all three levels for several days between firings. It also cools the home in summer and provides a solid anchoring base for the whole structure.

Winter is coming and, as usual, the price of heating oil has gone up again along with the price of propane, natural gas, and firewood. In my last article I wrote about ways to get more heat out of the firewood you work so hard, or pay so much, to acquire. This article gives you another project to increase the efficiency of a wood burning heating system—a well-designed chimney.

The chimney is an improvement over the old smoke disposal method of leaving a hole in the top of the tipi or lodge to let the smoke escape from the hearth fire. But it is not much of an improvement. Back then you burned wood because it was plentiful and about the only fuel available. Taxing your brain with the technicalities of efficient wood burning was less important than other distractions like fighting off the indigenous native population, acquiring food enough to stay alive, and trying to get at least half your children to adulthood to care for you in your old age, thus allowing you to live to the advanced age of 50 or so. Things are, thankfully, different now. These days, fighting the effects of indigenous inflation, avoiding obesity, and accumulating a few valuables to pass on to your children are important goals for many people. Fortunately, this allows time to research technical wood burning with fewer distractions.

This is where a chimney becomes important. Granted, I am exaggerating a little but bear with me. An efficient chimney extracts more heat from your firewood. This is important and has value, but a chimney can do much more.

In my 30 odd years of building occupant-friendly homes, the chimney has become a project worthy of more attention than you would at first realize. The work involved in building a chimney is significant no matter how basic it may be. A simple smoke expeller made of flue tile and chimney block takes several days of work to build. If you are ambitious enough to take on a chimney project, could you be motivated sufficiently to consider making it a bigger endeavor if the result brought you significant benefits? If so, read on and see just how much a chimney can do for you.

Second level of three story, 47-ton heating system. This level includes two flue chimney, fireplace, two dioramas, windows, lighting, supports two floors, and part of the roof, plus it is a wall between two rooms.

My passion for not leaving well enough alone in home design led to exploring chimney construction projects other builders have shunned. However, good things came from these adventures in designing and you will learn about them here.

Basic masonry chimneys

A basic masonry chimney that accepts the exhaust from a woodstove or other heating device is built of heat-treated flue tiles enclosed within a casing of chimney blocks and is generally located outside of the home. A through the wall fireproof receptacle for the exhaust pipe and an ash cleanout door are built into it. The chimney sits on a foundation of sufficient substance to support it. It costs about $1000 and lasts perhaps 15 years with proper maintenance.

Upgrades from the basic model add a veneer of brick or stone around the chimney and most often accommodate a fireplace inside the structure. Examples of these chimney types can be seen by the hundreds of thousands, even millions, all over the country. The former are plain basic, the latter more attractive but both are wasteful and inefficient.

There are two main reasons for this. First, the location of the chimney outside the building means that every BTU of heat entering the chimney is lost to the outdoors. Second, the construction method of such chimneys further insures total loss of heat to the outdoors. This is just sad. It does simplify the construction work for such projects, since it is built outside the house, but attractive outdoor chimneys cost from $5,000 to more money than God would pay.

So, let's adjust for our own personal reality. The most basic purpose of a chimney is to safely exhaust the smoke from your woodstove or wood furnace to the outside. I am limiting this discussion to wood heaters because other heating devices have somewhat different issues and I can make another $50 or so writing an article about them another time.

Chimney location

The first consideration is where to locate your chimney. Since the primary purpose of this chimney is to be an efficient heat transferring mechanism, the optimal place for it is the center of your home. Planning the location in a new home is fairly easy. For an existing home, planning is more complex but read on. Other factors discussed later make where to put it more obvious and explain why the extra work has merit.

Once you have chosen the location for the new chimney, build a good foundation for it. If you have a poured floor in your basement, it very likely is firm enough for most chimney projects. If you are building a home from scratch, or working in an existing home without a poured basement floor, and a pad for the chimney is needed, do the extra details. Add reinforcing metal bars in the six inches or more of concrete to prevent cracking. Add insulation in the form of two-inch Styrofoam under the concrete where the chimney will sit to limit heat loss through the floor. A vapor barrier of plastic sheeting is a good thing to add. A 30-foot tall chimney of the kind I will describe should have at least a 10-foot by 10-foot by 6-inch reinforced and insulated foundation. Additional design elements or existing problems may require a more elaborate foundation but let's worry about that later.

Building a chimney

What follows is the skimpiest efficient chimney you can build. It is done almost the same way as the plain ugly ones you see all over the place. It consists of a column of eight-inch-square, two-foot-long, heat-treated flue tiles surrounded by chimney blocks to the height you need. Common chimney blocks come in two varieties. The full block is 8 inches high and 16 inches square with a 9-inch square hole in the middle to accommodate the flue tiles and weighs enough to risk a hernia if you use them for the whole height of the chimney. The other common chimney block is called a half lift. It is a U-shaped block, two of which make the equivalent of a full chimney block, but half as likely to cause a groin pull during construction. They have another advantage I will point out later.

Existing chimney boxed and insulated to prevent creosote build up and improve flue draft. It is much more attractive than the plain tile and block version it covered up.

How these components are assembled is pretty obvious but there are details you must attend to during construction. Mortar joints should be about ½ inch or less wide and fully packed with mortar. Each course must be square and level, horizontally and vertically. An ash cleanout door should be installed near the bottom. A six-inch thimble must be built in at an appropriate height to receive the pipe from the wood heater. I use high temperature silicone to seal the joints of the flue tiles. Stagger the joints of the chimney blocks in relation to the joints of the flue tiles. Regular concrete blocks, 8 inches by 8 inches by 16 inches, can be used from the foundation to just below the ash cleanout door for economy. Fill the hollow cavities with sand and leave at least a one-inch clearance (I like two or more) from any wood structure for the whole height of the chimney.

Unless you have serious experience mixing mortar I recommend you use commercial mortar mix. Use no metal, other than the thimble and ash cleanout door, during construction of the chimney in order to lessen the possibility of fracturing the chimney blocks from expansion of the metal when heated. Leave four to six inches of the last flue tile extending above the chimney blocks. Form a cap of mortar around the flue tile that slants down and out over the chimney blocks to shed water. Let the chimney cure two or three days minimum before using.

Wear gloves to protect your skin. It is important not to let mortar or cement come in contact with any cuts or abrasions or you may acquire some interesting scars like the one I have. Wear good shoes, preferably with steel toes. Wash your tools often and be very careful. There are numerous masonry technique details I am omitting but space is limited and I think each project should have a few little mysteries. It builds character.

Boxed, insulated chimney top with faux stone facade. Note poured concrete cap. This project incorporates a hatch allowing access to the roof as well as two flues. It is 50 inches wide and 48 inches high.

Before I show you the secrets to building an efficient chimney you need to know why regular ones are not. There is a little air space between the flue tiles and the surrounding chimney blocks that acts as a thermal break, preventing the transfer of heat from flues to blocks. This is a good thing and a bad thing.

It is a good thing for the flue tiles to absorb enough heat from the wood smoke to promote a strong upward draft in the chimney. If the heat were conducted directly through the flue tiles to the blocks, the chimney would dissipate it quickly to the outside air, slowing the draft, causing back drafts and creating creosote.

Outside chimneys tend to absorb moisture. When damp chimney blocks are exposed to repeated heating and cooling, cracks develop. This is unavoidable near the chimney top, which allows even more moisture to invade the blocks, eventually ruining the chimney. When you add freezing weather to the equation it is easy to see why outside chimneys fail. When this happens to a beautiful and expensive brick or stone chimney adorning the outside wall of a home it is just sad. That little airspace is important.

Professional masons know all this. I am not certain but I think it is one of the hot topics down at the Masonic Lodge secret meetings. The bad thing is all the heat lost by having an outside chimney. If you have a grand fireplace that *is* the wall of your house, all that masonry is absorbing heat from your warm home and conducting it outside in winter and vice versa in summer. Having a fire in your fireplace in winter actually cools your home because it pulls warm air right up the chimney. All you get is some radiant heat that doesn't last very long. It is depressing.

Cheer up, because I know a way to make the physics of all this work for you. Some of it borders on rocket science and is quite exciting.

You have probably figured it out already. The little airspace has to be filled and the chimney must be inside the house. These changes make the chimney absorb much more heat and radiate it into the living space rather than outdoors. Before you drop this magazine and charge off to build one of these wonder chimneys there is more you need to know. Each of these changes requires a different method of chimney construction.

Consider the airspace between the flue tiles and chimney blocks. Filling it solid with mortar accomplishes the feat of allowing conduction of heat to the chimney blocks. However, repeated heating and subsequent cooling of the mortar fill and the chimney blocks causes them to develop fractures, especially in the area around the connection of the stovepipe and

Stone cave shower stall. Part of the mass of the chimney. Warm all winter, cool in summer.

chimney where it is hottest. This is not necessarily bad. The fractures mean that the block has expanded as much as it can and is now stable. When this happens you can seal the fracture with silicone and leave it alone.

On the other hand if fractures bother you, as they do me, there is something you can do. Instead of stuffing the airspace with regular mortar make a batch of 50% mortar mix and 50% fine sand with enough clean water to produce a mixture about the consistency of gravy (with no lumps). Pour this into the airspaces as you build. It cures to a relatively soft but conductive stratum that does the job of transferring heat and it compresses just enough to prevent most cracking. Do not be tempted to use just sand or other loose fill in the airspaces. It conducts the heat but sifts into any cracks, heats, cools, sifts some more and eventually ruins the chimney or settles enough to restore the airspaces. Don't ask me how I know.

"Flying Saucer" chimney top cover in open position. Note pivot point location. Rope control is hidden by wooden structure on left. Also note simulated white stonework and poured mortar cap of chimney.

Before going further let's explore the potential of what we just learned. Heat that the chimney is now able to extract from flue gases is radically increased. The best way to make use of this new circumstance is to add mass to the chimney. A four to twelve-or-more-inch veneer of brick or stone mortared into place around it (in full contact, of course) holds lots of the additional BTUs. It also lessens or eliminates any fracturing that may occur in the chimney blocks.

When I build a chimney like this I wrap six-inch mesh reinforcing screen twice around the chimney blocks before adding a veneer of rock or brick. The screen is far enough away from the hot flue gasses so expansion does not crack any masonry but it is close enough to make metal's superior conductive capacity spread the heat faster and more evenly through the masonry mass. Cutting strands of this wire and curling them into the mortar between bricks or stones as you build provides a reinforcing matrix that strengthens the whole structure. When finished you have a two by two-foot, or more, chimney that is a prominent and practical improvement to your heating system and home while lowering fuel costs. I think it is well worth the work and money.

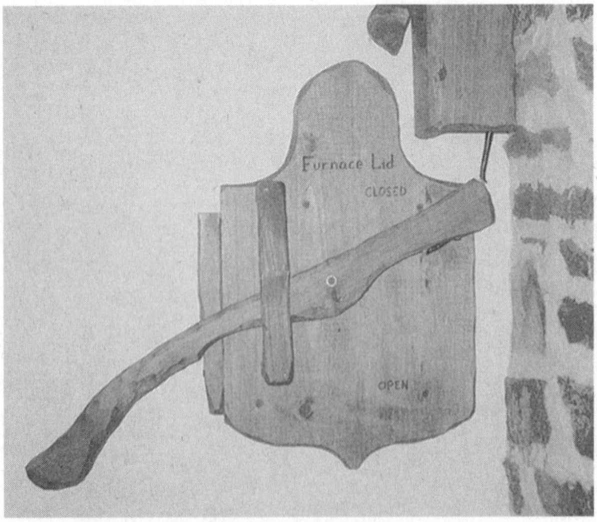

This is a control handle that opens and closes the chimney top cover of an efficiency enhanced masonry mass chimney. One of many designs.

To get the most from this new chimney it should be in the center of the space you are planning to heat. If you have a two-story home with a basement, the chimney can serve all three levels. When I have a choice in planning I make the chimney serve two rooms on each floor by building it as part of the wall between the rooms. Don't do this if you are building the basic flue tile and chimney block version because it gets too hot, often too hot to touch. The flue tile, chimney block and veneer version is more massive, holds more heat at lower temperatures and presents less danger of overheating the things around it. Even so, do not allow any wood or flammable building material to actually touch the masonry.

When I build a wall with a chimney in it I stud the wall to

two inches short of the masonry. Then I bring the drywall to within a quarter inch of the masonry and use joint compound and fiberglass tape to finish the wall tight to the chimney. Each room is comfortably warmed and private.

I built a chimney some years ago that used a veneer layer of regular concrete blocks (cores filled with sand for maximum mass). One side of the chimney was built through a wall less one half inch. Drywall took up the half inch and was in contact with the warm masonry. The wall looked just like you would expect but contributed lots of radiant heat to the room. This kind of designing verges on magic.

I think you get the idea. Oversized, reinforced, carefully built, heat radiating chimney of great beauty near the center of your home on an adequate foundation being fed by one of the wood heaters I described in my last article. An ambitious project I admit but we use less than half the wood we used to and in the present market that saves us about $700 a year and a lot of labor. Seven hundred dollars goes a long way in paying for the materials needed for this home improvement, too.

A couple of bonuses come with this project. In winter your home stays warm a long time after the fire has gone out. In summer the large masonry mass air-conditions your home by absorbing heat in your house and conducting it into the cooler earth under its foundation. Not only that but think of all the compliments you will graciously receive for building it.

Other options

Do not get too comfortable though because now we move on to Advanced Upgrade Options. If you like playing with those masonry tools and equipment you bought or borrowed, here are some more possibilities. Also, a little further on I will show you a couple of necessary utilities for these chimneys that have (drum roll, please) artistic possibilities.

When I said these chimneys are oversized at two feet by two feet I was being modest. The one in our house now, a small part of which you can see in one of the pictures, is 14 feet by 6 feet at the base, rises three stories and weighs 47 tons. When heated it keeps our home warm for a week or more. I don't recommend you take on a project this huge on your first try. I built this big boy because when we bought our property there was so much rock laying around I had to do something with it in self-defense.

When you have acquired piles of rock and concrete products it will occur to you how much weight that stuff would support if you let it. In fact it could not only warm your house better if bigger but also hold up floors and roofs by having joists and rafters resting on it.

My houses use a central stonework core that contains a furnace or fireplace plus provides support for each floor and the roof. Big beams resting on a stone structure gives a nice sensation of strength to a home. The tons of stone, block, and mortar provide a stabilizing anchor for the home too. That shudder some homes exhibit in a strong wind never bothers a home with a backbone of stone.

Think about the potential of an oversized chimney in your building plans. There are some things to keep in mind. For safety, always reinforce any masonry that you build. Keep at least 12 inches, preferably more, of solid masonry plus an inch or two of air between the hot flue gases and flammable building materials. Be certain that any place where a joist, beam, or rafter rests on masonry is solid under it, right down to the foundation. If you promise to look up and thoroughly understand what a corbel is, you can alter this rule. Just remember, solid masonry will support about a bazillion tons under compression but it does not bend or flex one little bit. Don't put it in a structural position where that might happen.

You can have a plan that uses an oversized chimney to hold up the house, heats several levels and rooms, provides a wall in a few places and does it beautifully. With all that masonry you could also add a fireplace or two and have several flues enclosed in the chimney. We did that in our house. In the basement a wood furnace does the general heating and has its own flue. On the second level, which is the first floor of our living quarters, we have a fireplace with a sunken hearth and it, too, has its own flue. Each flue warms the chimney mass but the fireplace is cozier to sit by on cool evenings when the big furnace would be too much. We also use the fireplace to cook meat, fish, and marshmallows for special dinners. The sunken hearth allows the warmth to rise up into the room, heating the space more efficiently and keeping sparks from flying too far from the hearth.

I have built small windows, diorama art works, and light fixtures into the stonework of several chimneys. However, the best option is a shower stall built into the stonework. It is warmed by the chimney during winter and cool in summer. It looks like a cave and is the most pleasant place to shower, ever.

Speaking of caves, stonework is a good location for little niches to display stuff. A loose stone with a cavity behind it is an excellent and fireproof hiding place. How you use the mortar in the joints of your stonework is worth a whole book. Speaking of books related to this subject, find some by Ken Kern at your library and enjoy.

These little or large details influence the style and character of your stonework and that is good. Take plenty of time and thought while building these projects. Each one could and probably will out last you by many lifetimes. Don't forget to sign your work.

I have saved one important segment of this project for last. The part of the chimney that protrudes up out of the roof encompasses several issues to consider. First is to safely get the smoke out of your house. Second is to extract more heat from your fuel wood. There are other issues too. I will deal with those in a little while.

When you reach the roof exit point as you are mortaring the flue tiles and chimney blocks together, stop filling the little airspace we talked about earlier. This slows the transfer of heat from flue to blocks. You can probably figure out why. This partially solves issues one and two.

Even with this detail attended to, a great quantity of heat gets conducted from the warm masonry inside the house to the part of the chimney protruding into the cold winds and frigid temperatures up there on the roof. This situation is another reason why masonry chimneys, even ones located mostly inside a home, are inefficient. Heat moves from where it is warm to where it is cold. The greater the difference in temperature between your living room and the outdoors, the higher the rate of heat lost through the chimney structure. That is just basic rocket science. You can look it up. There is a very simple, or a very elegant, way to fix all that.

Build a box around the part of the chimney exposed above the roof with 2x4 lumber and plywood covered on the outside with 90 pound rolled roofing. Make the roofing material blend into the roof shingles, or whatever is on the roof, to shed rainwater. Leave at least six inches between the chimney and the box walls and stuff the cavity with fiberglass insulation.

Build a temporary form around the top of the box and fill with mortar and steel mesh to a thickness of at least three inches. Form the mortar around the top of the last flue tile and out over the chimney blocks and the box you built. It is a little tricky to do but build the temporary form so that when it is removed the mortar slab overhangs the box. You don't want water leaking into the box onto the insulation. Extra protection is accomplished by sealing that joint with silicone after the mortar has cured. Study the picture of the simple chimney top box to understand this project better.

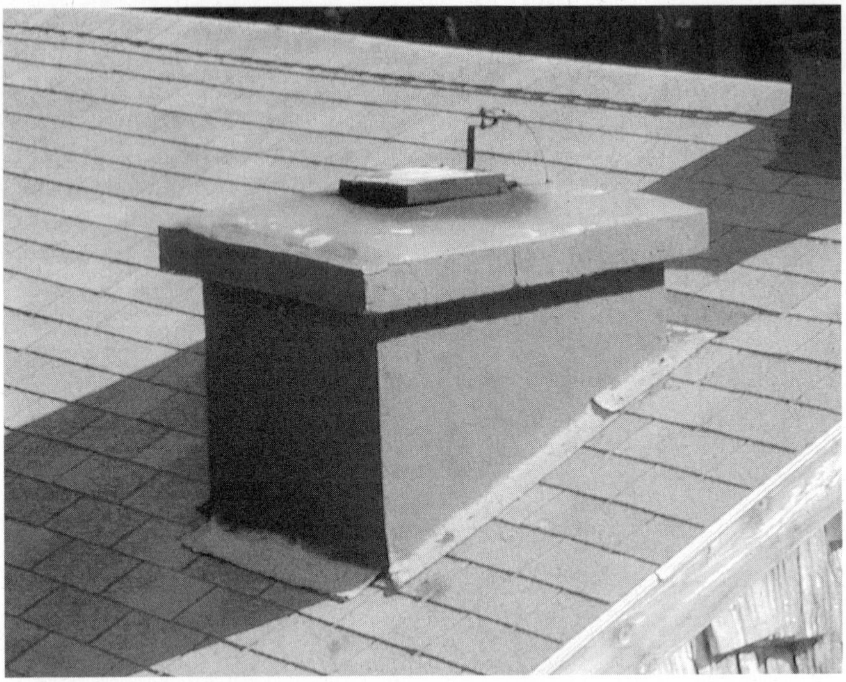

Simple boxed, insulated chimney with concrete top and concrete hatch cover which is operated from inside the building with sleeve in cable mechanism

The picture of the more elaborate chimney top gives you an idea of what these chimney top boxes can look like if you are an overachiever. (See page 11) This one was covered with black 90 pound roofing material and appliquéd with faux stone made of pine boards cut, carved, and colored to imitate the real thing and attached with screws. From a distance it looks absolutely real, maybe even surreal. I have done many chimney boxes in various styles with faux brick and simulated stone facades.

Regulations exist regarding chimney height in relation to roof height, inclusion of catalytic converters, and other rules inflicted by government agencies and insurance companies that can actually inhibit the efficiency and safety of these types of chimney and heater systems. Dealing with that is a whole other issue and I don't have time for political criticism just now. However, I suggest you give this aspect some attention.

The section of chimney showing above a house is a strong, eye-catching feature significantly increasing the individuality, beauty, and character of a home. Consider the chimney top box a work of art and give it the thought and attention to detail it deserves. You will feel a sense of pride each time you look at it.

After all of the planning and work of building one of these chimneys, it should be topped off with something clever. Make a cover, not just a damper, to close off the opening right at the top of the chimney. Probably about 90% of the time during the year your chimney is dormant. A cover keeps out rain and critters. But more importantly, it stops the draft, trapping the heat absorbed by the mass and forcing it to warm your home rather than escape into space.

You can buy commercial covers that cost around $150 which are generally intended to be used with fireplaces. But you can make your own. I have built many different ones based on what I had available at the time. My favorite is what I call the Flying Saucer. It is a twelve-inch diameter domed steel cover that once protected the valve on a large propane tank. I attached a four-foot by half-inch diameter steel rod to the center of the cap with a U bolt so it was suspended like a bell. About two and a half feet along the rod I made a pivot point attached to the roof. Raising and lowering the end of the rod makes the cover lift to open the chimney, or drop into place over the hole to close the chimney. Note the photograph on page 12 for a better understanding of this device. From the ground the rod is almost invisible and the cover looks like a flying saucer hovering in the smoke above the chimney. That one still shocks people. Speaking of shock, ground any metal on the roof to your lightning protection system for safety.

The best method of actuating any of these systems is a sleeve of one-inch diameter black plastic water pipe containing a weatherproof quarter inch rope built into the structure of the house. The upper end is located near the chimney to accommodate the cover mechanism of your choice. The lower end should be convenient to the furnace or wood heater and include a way to hold the rope that keeps the cover either open or closed. I use a loop in the rope and a peg on the wall to secure it but there are a variety of ways to do this. The flexibility of this cable and sleeve device allows you to route it through the house structure relatively easily. The weight of the cover closes the chimney. Pulling the rope opens it. I would like to discuss many more details about these projects but, alas, there are only so many pages in the magazine.

There is a safety note you must be aware of. Closing the chimney before the fire is dead out forces smoke and gases in the chimney to find another exit. If you have provided your wood heater with a ducted source of outside air to the combustion chamber, as I recommended in my last article, and your heater is tightly built, this is less of a worry. However, put a sign by the control rope warning everyone to close the chimney flue only after the fire is dead out. This is important! People die from misdirected wood smoke. Keep your smoke detectors working and, for more protection, install CO_2 detectors.

This heater and chimney system is less likely to cause problems for five reasons:

1) A hot fire of short duration consumes more of the fuel, leaving less material to form as creosote on the inner flue tile walls and avoiding the danger of a chimney fire. Our chimney has been in operation for over ten years and has produced less than a pint of creosote.
2) This system uses no dampers. The strong draft inherent in this system does not allow the smoke to linger and leak into the home.
3) The short burn time most often takes place during the day when household members are awake and aware. A good habit to adopt with other heaters too.
4) Most of this system is inert carefree masonry. The other parts are simple to maintain and repair. If it is simple to do, it is less likely be ignored.
5) Increased efficiency means burning less wood, making less smoke, producing less pollution, tolerating less risk, creating less work, and costing less money. Truly, less is more in this case.

Just when you thought this article must be finished here comes another idea. Imagine one of these special chimneys containing a small fireplace custom built to accommodate a tipi. When you get the urge to go camping for an extended time you just climb the chimney, attach the top of the tipi to anchor hooks embedded up there. Connect the skirt of the tipi to more hooks embedded in the ground and you have, potentially, a year round home in half an hour. No poles to deal with, constant warmth, no nasty smoke stains on your canvas, and even if you don't put up the tipi it makes a great camp fireplace without the smoky eyes syndrome. I guess you could do this with other tent designs too. I just have an affinity for tipi living.

Okay, I am done for now. I hope this article will stimulate some new thoughts about how home building designs can evolve. Δ

Claire goes to the movies

Reviewed by Claire Wolfe

With this issue we start a new feature—mini movie reviews. Our chosen films will feature themes of self-reliance, independence, individual courage, and freedom and will usually be available on DVD or VHS for backwoods home viewing.

Boys will be men

There are a lot of people these days who want to turn us all into perpetual infants—forever dependent, forever docile, and forever sheltered from both the harsh realities and great adventures of life. That's sad for everyone, but its particularly unhealthy for our boy children. Boys need to take crazy risks, make big booms, land in big messes, and sometimes get their butts kicked on the way to becoming responsible grown men.

This month, we've picked two movies—one recent and one almost-classic—about teenaged boys beginning that long process of growing up.

Secondhand Lions (2003), rated PG, 111 minutes

Walter (Haley Joel Osment) is a shy teenager without much personality or gumption. His mother Mae (Kyra Sedgwick) is a vixen, more interested in money and men than in her sad-eyed son. With both those passions in her flighty head, she dumps Walter on his great uncles' scary and decrepit ranch. Chasing off after a new man, she assigns Walter a job: Find the cash. The two uncles, Garth and Hub, have mysteriously reappeared after decades among the missing, and they're rumored to be sitting on millions and millions of dollars of treasure.

What ensues is both comedy and drama, adventure and romance, as Walter and his eccentric old uncles (wonderfully played by Robert Duvall and Michael Caine) work wonders on each other.

Where have the uncles really been all those decades? Do they honestly have hidden treasure? At first, when their story begins to emerge, it seems like pure fantasy. Surely no one outside of an Indiana Jones or Errol Flynn movie could have lived such lives! But then we begin to see that they...well, see and decide for yourself.

Whatever their earlier adventures, however, Garth and Hub have become old and resigned. They're doing little more than waiting to die. Their only entertainment is shooting at the dozens of salesmen who drive up to their door, having heard rumors of the treasure and being determined to earn a bit of it for their own pockets.

As the uncles' tales of their heroic past begin to awaken Walter to the glorious possibilities of life, Walter in turn RE-awakens them—with a little help from a lion named Jasmine (not to mention a savvy salesman who finally figures out which item two men who keep shooting at him might like to buy).

Secondhand Lions was sneered at by the critics (perhaps in part because of its frequent and sympathetic, although humorous, use of firearms) and it disappeared out of theaters almost before it appeared. But it's become a big seller on video and DVD. Rent it or buy it and you'll see why.

Stand By Me (1986), rated R, 89 minutes

At the end of the 1950s, four misfit adolescent boys from a small Oregon town head cross-country on an overnight trek. Their aim: to look at the body of a missing boy who died in the woods. Their quest becomes a competition to get there ahead of the older, meaner boys who also know the body's location, and thus to claim the "glory" of the find.

This unpromising premise (based on a non-supernatural Stephen King story) was so offputting I waited years to watch it, despite being told repeatedly how good this Rob Reiner-directed film is. To focus on the boys' grim, childish goal is to miss the real gold—their journey toward maturity.

As the tale begins the four are bosom pals despite their differences: sensitive writer wannabe Gordie (Wil Wheaton); tough reject Chris (River Phoenix); insanely macho Teddy (Corey Feldman); and chubby geek Vern (Jerry O'Connell). But the overland journey, through swamps, dark nights, wild tales, goofy play, and real perils reveals the deeper—and sometimes darker—side of each boy. By the end of this "adolescent Deliverance," alliances and friendships have shifted. Some of the four have grown and some have failed to grow.

The movie is a charmer. Its incredible cast also includes Richard Dreyfuss, a very young John Cusak, and handsome villain Kiefer Sutherland. Great period music keeps it lively and authentic (especially the scene where the boys bop along the trail to the tune of "Lollipop"). And anybody who values firearms for self defense and as a symbol of grown-up responsibility will cheer a certain climactic scene.

The R rating is for unfortunate and anachronistic foul language, and for a few gross-out scenes (which are actually very well done). Δ

PRACTICAL PREPAREDNESS PLANNING

By Jeffrey R. Yago

In light of recent terrorist attacks around the world, it's time to renew our preparedness and readiness to cope with such an attack. And don't think you won't be a terrorist target if you live in rural America. It is the belief of some terrorist analysts that Al-Qaeda and other terrorist groups will change its tactics and begin targeting America's rural communities.

A catastrophe caused by a terrorist attack would be similar, in many respects, to a catastrophe caused by a natural event such as a hurricane, earthquake, or flood, so we can start our preparedness review by going through the many back issues of *BHM* that have dealt in detail with such preparations. Fortunately, they have been bound together into nine anthologies and come with a detailed index (See pages 2-3 and 94). *BHM* also puts out an excellent preparedness primer, *Emergency Preparedness and Survival Guide*.

There are some very easy and low-cost things we can all do today, whether at home or travelling through a large town or city, and whether the catastrophe is caused by terrorists or nature.

There are three critical areas of potential danger we need to address:

1. How do we prepare and where is safe if caught in a large city during a terrorist attack, blackout, building fire, or civil unrest?
2. How do we prepare and where is safe if caught in a vehicle during traffic gridlock, a multi-car pileup, rising water, or road closure?
3. How do we prepare a home for extended power outages?

Flee or fight

The first question to address in any major disruption to your normal life is: Should I stay put, or leave? Although each situation is different, staying on the upper floor of a high-rise building, on a congested highway or bridge, or continuing to approach an obviously barricaded road is not smart. In almost every major disaster, the people who did not pay attention to initial warnings, or thought they should wait for help to arrive, are no longer with us.

Most of the time you will be safer in your own home, especially if you

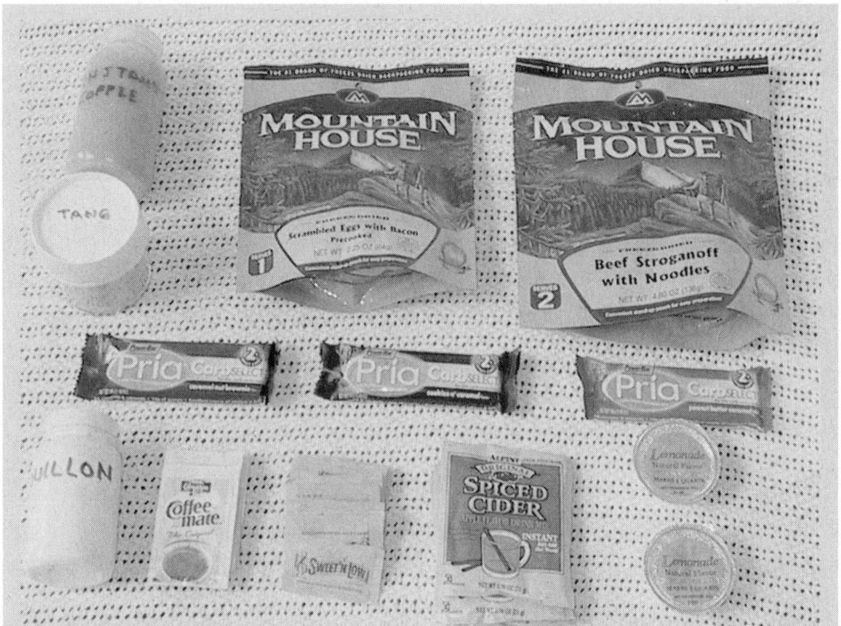

Ready-to-eat food: this includes repackaged items like Tang™, instant coffee, and bouillon to make chemically-purified water more palatable, along with dehydrated, precooked meals and high-energy bars.

live in a rural area and have made some initial emergency preparations. But anywhere there are large concentrations of people, such as high-rise apartment complexes, stadium events, and major traffic jams, is not where you want to be when there is a power outage, earthquake, or terrorist attack.

Staying in your car during a snowstorm may be safer than trying to hike through a blizzard, but being blocked in the third car back, of what will soon be a 50-car pileup in the fog, is not safer than hiking up to the nearest embankment. A full size vehicle can be washed away, with you in it, while stalled in less than two feet of fast moving and rising water.

Almost anything can cause major traffic gridlock in a large city even during "normal" days, so don't assume cabs, buses, or trains will always be there to whisk you safely away when things are not normal. If you live in a rural area, you still may need to walk miles in the dark after your truck decided to die. The bottom line is, walking 10-miles might be your only form of transportation during the early stages of almost any emergency.

You may have 14 pairs of shoes at home, but if you visit a large city and normally wear dress shoes or high heels, always keep a really comfortable pair of walking shoes and athletic socks in your car, office, and suitcase. If you are visiting in a large city area, know that during power outages, darkness attracts rioters, muggers, and thieves. If you do need to travel on foot, the safest time is during very early daylight hours when most of last night's rioters are still sleeping it off!

Being downhill or downwind from almost anything is not smart. Whether smoke from fires, gas from broken pipes, or discharge from a bioterrorist attack, stay upwind and out of low areas and dead-end streets. If you are on an island (Manhattan, for example), head for the water, not the bridges and tunnels which will quickly come to a standstill.

Communication

Your second dilemma to address, after resolving the first "flee-or-fight" question, is contacting family and friends. Whether you just survived a major traffic pileup, earthquake, or civil unrest, you want to let others know you are okay, and you want to know they are okay.

Do not expect your home phone or e-mail system to function, at least not initially. Cell phones and pagers may work, assuming you have an alternate method of keeping the battery charged. Extended power outages have resulted in loss of cell phone service when a power outage lasted longer than the cell tower's backup generator fuel supply. Also, tall cell towers do not always survive hurricane force winds.

There are several easy ways to address this communications issue, and all families should devise their own plan, but it needs to be done in advance. The following is a suggested outline to follow:

1. Discuss who calls whom, and what phone numbers to use for local day and night emergency contacts. It's good to also agree on an alternate "check-in" person out-of-state, if local contact cannot be established. A prepaid phone card usually works with pay phones that may not allow you to enter a home phone access-pin number. Also agree on what action to take if communication cannot be established in a reasonable time.

2. Agree on a specific meeting point, if several family members live in the same area and would be affected by the same emergency. Check out in advance a safe area that is easy for everyone to reach, even when roads are impassable and the power is out.

3. Agree on who leaves to pick up the others, and who stays put. It makes no sense for everyone to head out for the home of someone else, when they have already left for another destination. Someone needs to be "home-base."

4. Purchase a solar powered cell phone charger and cigarette lighter adapter, both for under $40.00. Keep these with you in your car and when traveling. Radio Shack™ and your cellular phone store sell several types of alternative battery chargers for cell phones, pagers, and rechargeable flashlights. Newer digital color-dis-

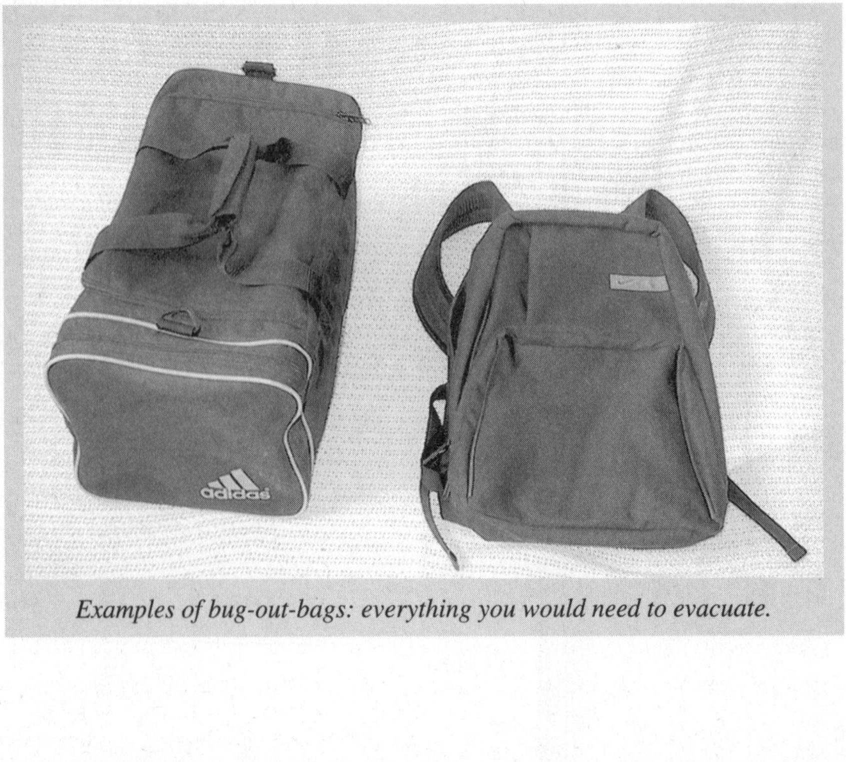

Examples of bug-out-bags: everything you would need to evacuate.

play cell phones are great for emergencies, since you can view TV news channels, weather channels, and download e-mail, but they also use more battery power and will not operate long without recharging. Remember, your regular chargers will not operate without utility power.

Emergency planning — while traveling

When traveling, especially to large cities, there are several items you should always have with you. Although the more restrictive security measures at airports now limit what you carry on your person, the following useful items are still allowed in your checked luggage:

1. Have two flashlights when traveling anywhere. You need a small LED style key ring flashlight for initial emergency lighting to find your way in a suddenly dark hallway or parking lot. These not only are tiny, but their light is very bright in a totally dark room, and the LED style will operate for many hours on a tiny hearing-aid battery.

You should always travel with a penlight-size flashlight, in addition to the key ring light. Although these may be larger than you would want in your pocket, they are still small and those with the new LED bulbs will operate for many hours on one set of batteries. These can easily fit into a purse, briefcase, glove compartment, or travel luggage.

2. It is very important to carry some cash, safely hidden on your person when traveling. I realize in this day of credit cards for gas, credit cards for meals, credit cards for clothing, and credit cards for cash machines, we have gotten away from carrying more than a few dollars in change in our pockets. However, during power outages and emergencies, money machines and credit card cash registers will not operate, and without cash you will not be able to buy gas, take a cab, buy a ticket, purchase food, or rent a hotel room.

3. You should always have a few high-energy snack bars and bottled water with you when traveling. These also fit easily in the glove compartment of your car, in a purse, or your carry-on luggage. Although this is not a steak dinner, people have lived for days with just a few of these to eat and water to drink.

4. Always keep a small portable earphone-type AM radio with you when traveling. The smaller earphone AM radios are much easier to carry, and can operate for weeks on one battery. All local emergency and weather warnings will be communicated by AM radio. Remember, larger AC powered radios and televisions do not work without utility power.

5. Obtain an up-to-date state highway map and an enlarged city street map before traveling to a state or city that is not familiar, and keep these with you. This may be your only source for alternate route information during a crisis, since running the same direction as everyone else, is not always smart.

6. Locate the nearest exit, and a back-up alternate exit point as soon as you arrive at a hotel, restaurant, or coliseum event. Head that direction at the very first sign of trouble, before you suddenly find all escape routes blocked. Commercial building codes require emergency exits and stairwell construction to be fire-rated, and these are there for your safety, even if we are too lazy to use them.

Emergency planning — at home

There have been numerous articles related to emergency planning and long-term food storage, and I have listed several excellent sources for more free information at the end of this article.

Are you a person who purchases today only what you will eat tonight or tomorrow morning, and have almost nothing (except beer) in the refrigerator? Many of us practically live out of our cars, and mealtime means it's time to look for the next

Travel clothing: well broken-in shoes, hat, compact sleeping bag, and vacuum-packed raincoat, socks, and underwear to save space and keep them dry.

drive-through window. When we think about emergency foods, we need to think both short-term and long-term, and we should keep both types on hand. If your home or apartment has limited space, you can still store over a week's worth of food and water under a bed, in a closet, or in your car trunk.

Short-term: I define short-term as a three-day-long power outage, when roads may be blocked by storm damage limiting vehicle travel. Short-term foods need to be similar to what you would normally eat, but easier to prepare without electricity or heat, and take up minimum storage space. Some suggestions include small cans of pre-cooked meat and tuna, crackers, peanut butter, canned spaghetti, beef stew, and a few candy bars to keep your spirits up.

Instant tea or coffee, lemonade, Tang™, and bouillon cubes take up almost no room, have a very long shelf life, and will taste really good when hungry, as long as you have water and a way to heat it. Remember, most frozen or refrigerated foods will need to be eaten immediately or they will spoil when the power goes out. You may not have a functioning stove or microwave to cook these heavy meals, so don't depend on what is in your freezer to keep you from starving.

You will need a hand operated can opener, paper towels and plates, plastic trash bags, and lots of bottled water. During a power outage, city water quickly becomes contaminated, or does not flow at all when the pressure pumps fail. Rural well pumps also do not work without electricity. We take for granted all the water we use each day to drink, wash dishes, wash clothes, prepare meals, and bathe, but without it, things can get ugly really fast.

I recommend using empty 2-liter soft drink bottles, as these are easy to store and carry, and are free. An adult requires an absolute minimum of a two-liter bottle of water each day, with one gallon per day even better. Avoid gallon-size water and milk jugs, as their thin-plastic wall construction and snap-on top are not designed for long-term storage.

The 2-liter plastic soft drink bottles with screw caps have a heavier wall thickness since they are designed to hold pressure, and are usually darker in color. Adding a few drops of Clorox™ to each bottle of water before resealing will reduce algae growth and kill harmful bacteria. Mark all food and drink containers with date purchased, and rotate at least once each year.

Long-term: Although probably not practical for people living in a city or small apartment, long-term food storage requires a large storage space, lots of planning, and a long-term commitment. Long-term food storage is intended for those of you living in more rural areas, or where weeklong power outages and storm damage is a fact of life.

First, you definitely need a large pantry or storeroom, with lots of large, sturdy, easy-to-access shelves. It should be located in an area of your home that does not get too hot or too cold. A dry basement is a good location if there is no chance of water damage or flooding. Families into long-term food storage have a backup means to pump water and cook food; and they purchase specially-packaged bulk foods with long shelf life.

In addition to the easy-to-prepare short-term food items, long-term pantries are used to store bulk cases of pasta, powdered milk, canned vegetables, sugar, rice, coffee, peanut butter, and honey. You will want

Communications equipment including a car adapter and solar charger for your cell phone, a digital AM radio with comfortable earphone, a headband type LED flashlight, a rugged mini-flashlight, vacuum-packed extra-long life batteries, plus CD-RW disks to preserve valuable records and photographs.

freeze-dried instant potatoes, eggs, butter, and cheese in #10 cans. Below these shelves you can store wheat, popcorn, oats, and a variety of dried beans in large 6-gallon nitrogen-packed plastic pails to reduce spoilage and discourage rodents. Each item should be carefully dated, and anything approaching its shelf-life should be rotated out. You will need additional cooking supplies including shortening, olive oil, baking powder, baking soda, dry yeast, and spices.

Long-term storage also means more than food. Being able to go several weeks or months on your own requires plenty of non-food items also.

You will need extra batteries for radios and flashlights, strike-anywhere matches, cases of paper towels, toilet paper, napkins, paper plates, and plastic garbage bags. Poor disposal of waste during emergency conditions will result in a rapid increase in the local insect and rodent population.

Skin problems are common when daily bathing is substantially reduced due to water shortages, and skin lotions, bacteria-fighting soaps, sunscreen, extra medications, vitamins, tooth and hair care products, and a good first-aid kit are a must.

Bug-out bag

If your current lifestyle or living arrangement makes it impractical to follow any of the emergency preparations I have recommended so far, there is still hope.

Although the idea originally began with hobos and undercover agents, a "bug-out-bag" is actually a very good idea for today's fast-paced lifestyle. The concept is to be able to keep a backpack for each person near the door, that has everything each would need if they only had minutes to evacuate and may not be able to return. Keep in mind, this happens to people like you everyday through no fault of their own. Fast moving forest fires, tornados, earthquakes, hurricanes, gas explosions, floods, and accidental toxic spills are in the news everyday and cause massive evacuations and total destruction of entire towns.

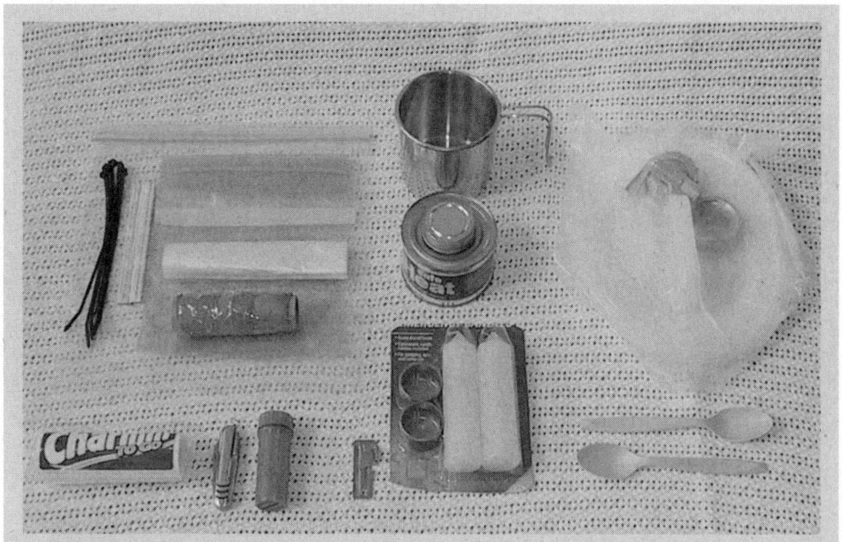

Equipment required to prepare food and other items such as: stainless-steel drinking cup, candles, "canned heat," utensils, knife, can opener, matches, Ziploc bags, trash bags, cable-ties, twist-ties, and toilet tissue. On the right is a vacuum-packed fold-up five-gallon jug with spout-cap.

A bug-out-bag needs to be sturdy, water resistant, not too big, and easy-to-carry long distances. A backpack is fairly small, but you will not want to lug 50-pounds around all day, so packing takes a little planning. First, you want some food, but it must be lightweight and not require any preparation. A few well-sealed energy bars, and several "meals ready-to-eat" (MRE) are a must. These are available from any camping or sporting goods store.

A bug-out-bag is the perfect place to keep the LED flashlight and portable AM radio I mentioned earlier. Try to select radios and flashlights that use the same size batteries, and keep extra batteries with them. A change of dry socks and underwear makes travel a little more bearable, and there are lightweight hooded raincoats and thermal blankets that fold up to the size of your fist. These are really handy, since most evacuation emergencies do not occur on sunny days.

Many of us never walk long distances, and rarely walk any distance outside at night, especially between April and July, when the mosquitoes and black flies take over. If you are forced to evacuate at night and on foot, a good quality rub-on bug repellent (large spray cans are too bulky) is a must to have handy.

Remember, a bug-out-bag may be the only item you ever get out of your home or apartment. Since almost everyone now has access to computers, your bug-out-bag should also include an emergency backup CD and key-chain size portable memory card or jump-drive. One CD can store copies of all-important historic records.

A single CD can hold copies of all your family photos, insurance policies, bank and stock records, medical records, address lists, phone numbers, and personal inventory information. These are things you will need after an emergency is over, and are considered irreplaceable.

Since financial records change daily or weekly, these files can be stored on a tiny jump-drive that you can carry on a key ring for regular backup of these files. We can worry about finding another computer later, and be sure to use the encryption code feature on these backup devices for any files you need to keep private.

Some better backpacks have several exterior pockets that are perfect to hold bottled water. On the floor in the closet, and just below your bug-out-bag is the perfect place to keep that extra pair of walking shoes and sweat socks I mentioned earlier. Remember, these should not be new. An unplanned 10-mile walk under duress is not a good time to break in brand new boots.

A bug-out-bag does not have to be expensive to make, and some people I know have duplicate bug-out-bags. They keep one in the front closet at home, and one at work or in their car trunk. Don't forget to keep cash for travel in a safe place, but still easy to grab on your way out the door.

Remember the pictures of the 1993 World Trade Center bombing, the Oklahoma Federal Building bombing, and the 9/11 World Trade Center and Pentagon bombings? Remember all the people running through clouds of dust, holding anything available over their nose and mouth? Many had to walk miles to reach clean air.

You can buy a soft disposable #N95 respirator for under $2.00 at any building supply or drug store. These are extremely lightweight, can be folded, and are 95% effective against most airborne particles. Several of these are a must for your bug-out-bag, but remember, these are dust and infectious disease masks. However, these dust masks will not protect you from poison gas.

Packing a bug-out-bag is not like packing for vacation, and probably unlike any packing you have ever done. The odds are, if you ever need it, you will be on foot and may need to carry it for miles. Every ounce of weight must be for only what is absolutely necessary to keep you alive.

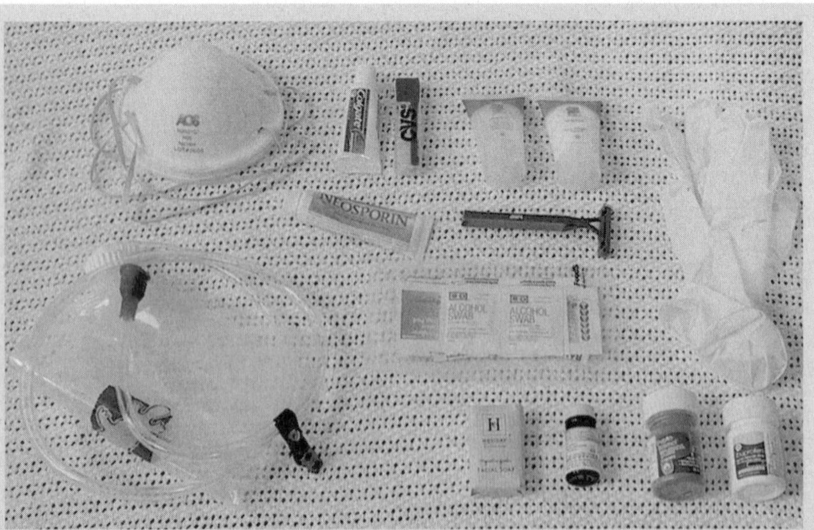

Medical supplies including dust mask, toothbrush, toothpaste, shampoo, lotion, Neosporin, throwaway razor, Pepto-Bismol, Ibuprofen, hard hand soap, bandages, water purification tablets, latex gloves, and bug repellent. The tubing on the bottom left is attached to a fold-up plastic water bottle and bite valve so you can drink water without stopping to remove the bottle from your backpack.

Pack hard-surfaced items toward the outside, place soft items like clothing toward the inside against your back. Put items you need often like energy bars, a flashlight, radio, and water bottle, in the smaller exterior pockets.

To make it a little easier for you to get started, I have divided everything you will need into seven groups. You can add items to each group, but I strongly recommend that you do not delete any item shown, as these have been identified as the most-needed items to have during extreme situations.

Group 1 — the bag itself: The advantage of using a simple book-bag during an emergency or when walking miles through unfriendly areas, is how non-threatening and worthless it appears. Most people around you will assume it is just books and maybe a change of clothes, and would never realize its survival value.

I recommend a quality-made gym bag or student-size book bag. A rectangular gym bag fits nicely in a car trunk or office filing cabinet, but the book bag is easier to carry long distances since it has padded shoulder straps. Stay with a name brand bag having double stitched and sealed joints, and support straps that are strong and comfortable. I do not recommend large camping backpacks designed to carry tents and sleeping bags, as you are not going camping! You are trying to stay alive for several days and may be walking a long distance. You only have room for the basics.

Group 2 — ready-to-eat food: Any food you carry must be highly concentrated or dehydrated, and very lightweight. Meals ready-to-eat (MRE) come in foil packs that only require tearing off the top seal and pouring in a cup of preferably hot water. I recommend buying small empty plastic storage bottles from a camping or sporting goods store, as these are un-breakable, and have wide-mouth openings with waterproof lids.

This group includes:

- Two or three dehydrated precooked meals.
- Three or four high-energy bars. (Avoid chocolate bars that usually melt in your pocket.)
- Repackage instant coffee into a small camping style plastic bottle.
- Repackage Tang™ into a small camping style plastic bottle.
- Repackage chicken and beef bullion cubes into a small camping style plastic bottle.
- Coffee and tea drinkers may want to include a few individual foil-wrapped creamers and sugar substitutes.
- Highly concentrated pre-sweetened lemonade drink mixes. A matchbox size container can make 2-quarts.

Group 3 — travel clothing: As I stated earlier, if you need a bug-out-bag, you will most likely be walking many miles to safety. It is also likely that this will be in poor weather conditions. At a minimum, you should have:

- A good quality pair of waterproof hiking boots (broken in)
- Two or three pairs of heavy hiking sweat socks
- Fold-up soft hat with a large sun and rain blocking brim
- Fold-up extra-long raincoat with built-in hood
- Fold-up thermal space blanket

The small pouch in the photo on page 20 contains an adult-size sleeping bag made from a thermal space blanket, which retains 80% of all body heat. This yellow pouch is the size of a softball.

I vacuum packed the hooded raincoat, extra socks, and change of underwear to save space and keep everything dry.

Group 4 — communication: This group will keep you in touch with the world while on the move. CD-RW disks can preserve valuable records and family photographs. This group includes:

- Car adapter for your cell phone
- Solar charger adapter for your cell phone and radio
- Digital AM radio with comfortable earphone
- Headband type LED flashlight for walking outdoors in the dark
- Rugged mini-flashlight for walking down dark hallways and stairwells
- Vacuum-packed extra long-life batteries for radio and flashlights
- CD-RW disk and portable jump-drive

Group 5 — food preparation: This group includes the minimum equipment required to heat and prepare food, and other several items you will need.

- Stainless-steel long-handled drinking cup for holding over open-flame for heating
- Long-life emergency candles and a canned heat
- Unbreakable plastic camping utensils
- Quality Swiss Army style knife
- Fold-up Army-style can opener
- Strike anywhere matches in a waterproof container
- Miscellaneous sizes of Ziploc™ bags, plastic trash bags, nylon cable-ties, wire twist-ties, and extra-strong nylon string
- Camping size roll of toilet tissue

On the right side of the photo with the food preparation supplies is a fold-up 5-gallon jug with spout-cap, that I vacuum-packed down to the size of a small dinner plate! When expanded, it will allow you to carry 5-full gallons of drinking water, gasoline, diesel fuel, or bathing water. This will also come in handy if stranded and out of gas.

Group 6 — medical supplies: Most of us have never had to walk really long distances, especially just after a traumatic event. Long hikes can also mean blisters, headaches, and dehydration. Your bug-out-bag needs a few medical supplies.

- Two or more fold-up dust masks with a 95% efficiency rating
- One or two fold-up toothbrushes and travel-size toothpaste
- Highly concentrated shampoo in well-sealed plastic tube
- Highly concentrated skin lotion in well-sealed plastic tube
- Plastic tube of NeosporinTM
- Lightweight throwaway razor
- Small plastic bottles of Pepto-BismolTM and Ibuprofen
- Small bar of quality hard hand soap
- Assorted sizes of flat stick-on bandages (no room for roll bandages or tape)
- Water purification tablets in waterproof bottle
- Latex gloves
- Rub-on bug repellent

The tubing on the bottom left of the photo with the medical supplies is attached to a fold-up plastic water bottle and bite valve. These are designed to allow backpackers on

Resources

Emergency Preparedness and Survival Guide by *Backwoods Home Magazine.*
Making the Best of Basics—A Family Preparedness Handbook by James Talmage
No Such Thing as Doomsday by Phillip and Arlene Hoag
When Every Moment Counts—What You Need to Know About Bio-terrorism by Senator Bill Frist, M.D.
www.ready.gov — Department of Homeland Security
www.bt.cdc.gov — Center for Disease Control
www.fema.gov/areyouready — Federal Emergency Management Agency
www.nlm.nih.gov/medlineplus — National Institute for Health
www.open.gov/emergency

long hikes to drink water without stopping or removing the bottle from the backpack.

Clean water is very heavy to carry long distances, and having camping style water-purification equipment and hand-operated filter pumps are nice, but too bulky for our needs here. For short-term needs, water purification tablets and fold-up plastic containers can be used to convert rainwater, river water, or water runoff into safe drinking water, although it may have a chemical taste. Adding powered drink flavorings will mask any bad taste from the purification tablets.

Group 7 — Personal items: Even with all of the above groups, your bag will still have room for at least one change of clothes and extra medications. The book bag on the right in the photo on page 19 held everything shown in all photographs, and still weighed less than 13 pounds.

Emergency clothing should be made of lightweight cotton and very durable. One pair of quality jeans and a casual shirt will provide the most use. Be sure they have been washed several times and are now soft with a relaxed fit. It is assumed if it is winter, you will already have a coat with you. Extra medications should be repackaged in waterproof plastic bottles.

Everyone should be prepared to survive on their own for a few days, and not assume the government is prepared to instantly house and feed an entire city in tents. Emergency assistance can take days or weeks to arrive and get organized, so you need to take care of your own family until you can get to a safer area, or until help does arrive.

Lastly, emergency preparations and food storage are like having a fire extinguisher hanging in your kitchen: you hope you are buying something you will never need, but someday you may be really glad you did. Δ

The supermarket bait shop

By Gary Gresh

Purists' protests aside, bait remains the best way to catch many species of fish. Despite its seeming popularity, the problem with bait is that it may not always be available when you need it most. You might be traveling or camping and not have the slightest idea where to purchase bait. Limited space on trips might prevent you from taking along those 89 tackle boxes full of you favorite lures. You may find that your six-year-old prefers using bait to dry flies. And with bait costs escalating, savvy fishermen need to know how to keep bait costs to a minimum and still catch fish. One of the best ways to do this is to scavenge the pantry at home or visit the nearest supermarket.

Many anglers now shop at the local grocery store, and not just for snacks and beverages. Your supermarket may be the best stocked bait shop in town. And if the fish don't eat it, you can. With the exception of wilderness areas, there's usually a food store somewhere nearby, even in very rural areas. If not, then raid the pantry.

Trout are the number one quarry of many anglers, and bait fishing is probably the most popular method of catching stocked trout and even wild trout. Many trout fishermen have whole kernel corn on their shopping list. Rig one or more kernels on a hook for a deadly trout bait. It can also be used to bait a hole for carp and is deadly on the big goldfish. Thread several kernels on the bend and shank of the hook for carp. You can even chum for carp with it. Throw a few handfuls into known carp holes to get them feeding. It will catch suckers and panfish as well.

Kept in a closed container, corn will keep fairly well in a fridge or cooler. Some anglers maintain that certain brands outperform others. Other trout fishermen swear by soaking their kernel corn in beer overnight. They claim that the beverage flavor really attracts trout. Party trout, no doubt. Another favorite vegetable, frozen green peas, will also catch carp.

Channel cats are exceptionally fond of both natural and supermarket baits including worms, minnows, dead crawfish, chicken livers, and a variety of homemade stink baits.

Another effective (and tasty) trout, bluegill, and sunfish bait is tiny marshmallows. They come in different flavors and colors and you may find that some colors outproduce others on a given day. A bag usually contains a variety of colors and will supply plenty of baits. You can use them whole or cut them in half and mold them around your hook.

Don't forget the cheese. Velveeta cheese is a popular trout bait. Cut it into tiny squares and place it on a hook or roll it in a ball around the hook. A little cotton may help keep it on. Garlic cheese is an increasingly popular bait. Cheese will also attract panfish, carp and catfish. Use bigger cheeseballs for carp, and catfish. It may hold better on a treble hook. All cheeses will keep well in a refrigerator or cooler. You can even add your own scents.

Small pieces of hot dog or bacon can also be used to catch trout and catfish. Cut them up before fishing and store in a covered container. Slice strips of uncooked bacon and skitter it among lily pads for bass and pickerel, just as you would some more expensive "pork" baits.

And an even cheaper bait is cooked elbow macaroni, which can be threaded on a hook to catch trout or panfish. Boil macaroni until it softens a bit and store it in a plastic container. Some anglers color it with red or yellow food dye. Thread two or three elbows on a long shank hook for catfish, carp and even bass. When using macaroni for trout, bass, or panfish, give it some action or drift it in the current. For bullhead, catfish, and carp, let the macaroni lie still on the bottom.

White bread is another thrifty and effective bait. You can mold it into big doughballs for carp or small doughballs for trout and sunnies. Really tiny doughballs, on hooks to match, will catch minnows and other small baitfish. This will keep the kids

bacon

entertained, and provide live bait as well.

Boiled pearl tapioca has been successfully used to catch bluegills. You can even dye it red to make imitation salmon eggs that can be drifted for trout.

In the cereal aisle, carp baits abound. Grab a box of Shredded Wheat, take a piece of large shredded wheat biscuit, clench it in your hand and dip it into water for a few seconds. Knead it into a sticky lump and mold it around your hook. You can also do the same thing with oatmeal but adding a little sugar makes it much more effective.

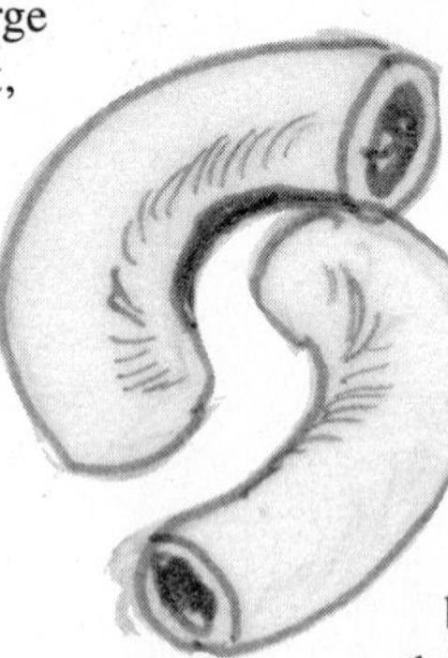

elbow macaroni

Many carp fishermen have a favorite doughball recipe. Common ingredients include cornmeal, breakfast cereals, sugar, molasses, flavored gelatin, fruit flavored sodas (strawberry has its adherents), flour, oil, honey, cotton, and even bourbon whiskey. The trick is to add substances that will toughen it and give it flavor. Smelly baits are not necessary for carp.

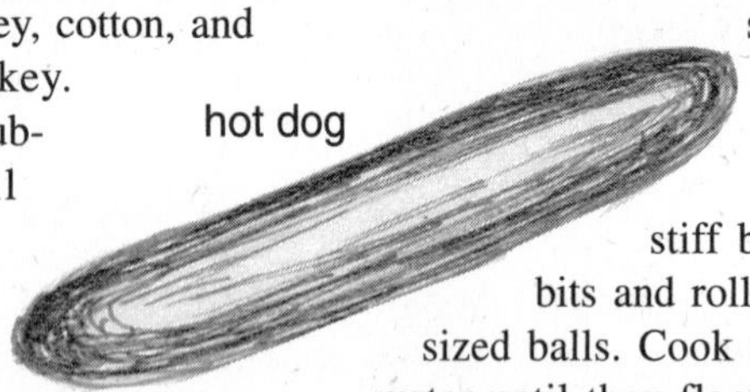

hot dog

Here's a popular recipe. Bring a pint of water to boil. While the water is heating, mix together two cups of cornmeal and one cup of flour. When the water begins to boil, turn the heat to low. Add half a package of flavored gelatin and stir well. Add two tablespoons of sugar and a tablespoon of pure vanilla extract to the pan. Add the dry mix carefully using a large soup spoon. Add enough mix to cover the surface of the water. When a bubble of water seeps through, cover the bubble with more dry mix. Continue covering the bubbles with dry mix until all the cornmeal/flour mix has been added. Then stir the dough for about thirty seconds. Remove the pan from the heat and empty the contents onto a piece of aluminum foil. As soon as the mixture is cool enough, knead it and roll it into a ball. Wrap the dough in foil so that no air gets into it. It can be stored in the refrigerator for about a week.

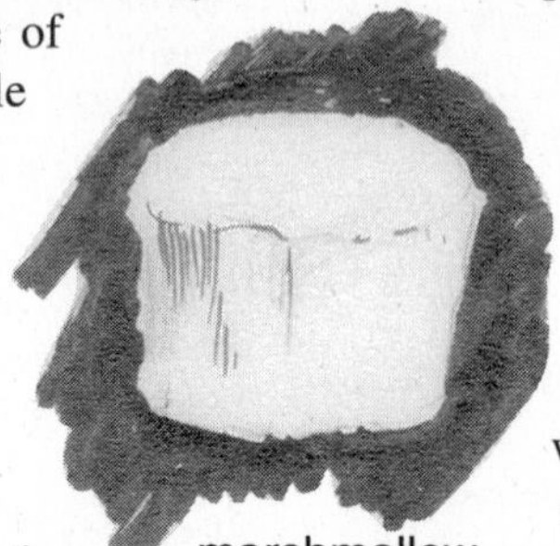

marshmallow

Is there any food item more common than the potato? Peel and grate a large potato or two or three small ones. Add two tablespoons of cornmeal, about half a teaspoon of salt, and enough flour and shredded cotton to make a stiff batter. Pinch off bits and roll them into bait-sized balls. Cook these in boiling water until they float. Dip them out and dry them on paper towels. Carry them in a plastic bag. You can also add a grated onion, or two tablespoons of sweet syrup, molasses or sugar, or both. Carp seem to prefer sweet baits. Instead of shredded cotton, you can use cornstarch or egg white as a binder. These may not be needed if the dough is stiff enough.

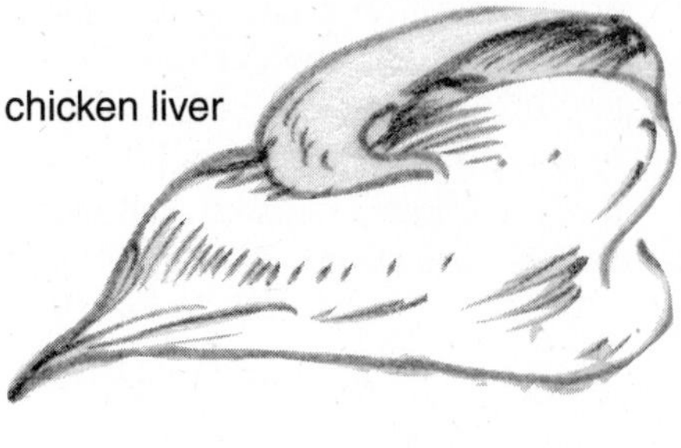

chicken liver

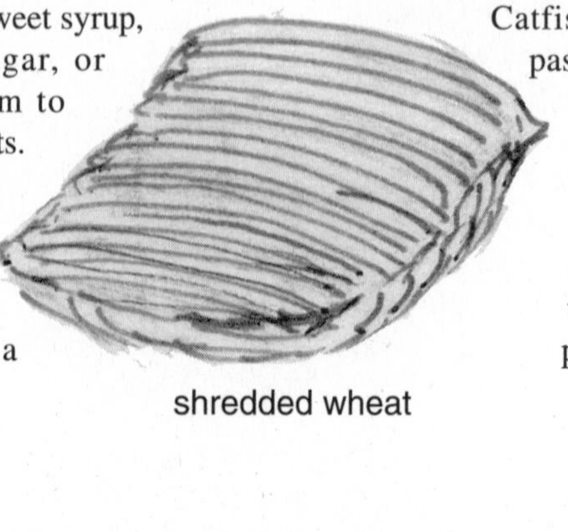

shredded wheat

One basic recipe mixes equal parts bread, oatmeal, cereal, and sugar with enough water to make a stiff dough. You can carry it as one ball and pinch off pieces as needed.

All catfish will eagerly respond to supermarket baits. Liver—especially chicken liver, but also pork and beef—makes great catfish bait. Fish guts will also take plenty of cats, if you can find a cooperative fishmonger, or save some from another fish you have cleaned. Bad clams are another good bait. Bullheads will even hit pieces of soap.

Many anglers add oil of anise to increase the odor. Stink baits are sometimes toughened with cotton, sponges, or similar substances. Cut red, pink, yellow, or white plastic sponges into cubes and soak them in anything odoriferous. Work cheese spread, the smellier the better, into them. Supplies of stink bait can often be prepared ahead of time and then frozen. On a much more appetizing note, salami, and the aforementioned hot dog, and bacon will entice both catfish and catfishermen.

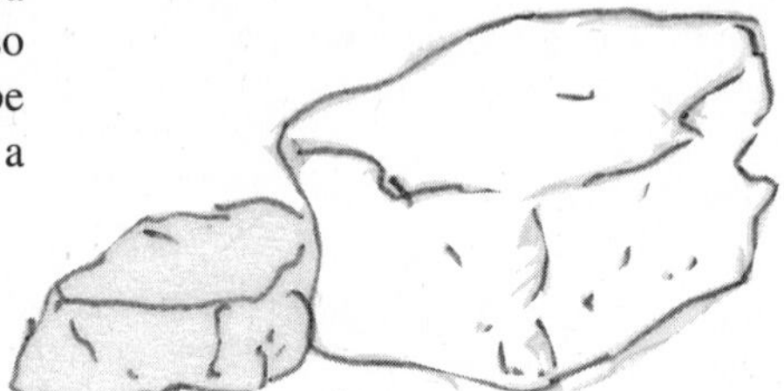

cheese

Catfishermen should not pass by the spice rack. Mix two tablespoons of anise seed and two tablespoons of vanilla extract in a cup of water, pour it in a pan, and let it simmer

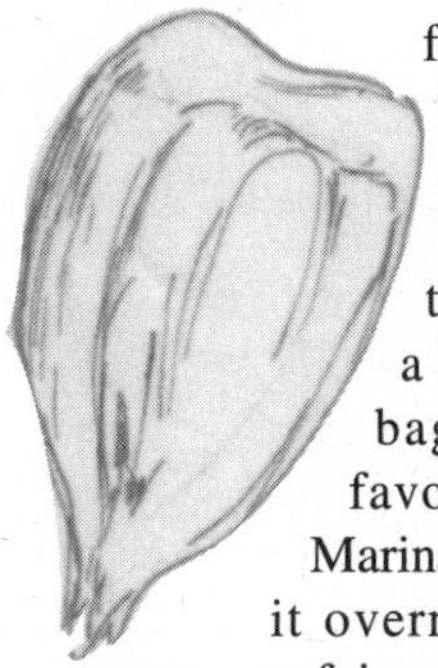

kernel corn

for a few minutes. Allow the mixture to cool and then place it in a sealed plastic bag with your favorite cut bait. Marinate cut bait in it overnight in your refrigerator before using or freezing it.

A simple dough bait that appeals to bottom feeders mixes flour and any kind of cheese into a firm ball. An even tastier combination mixes equal parts of hamburger and cheese with enough flour to make a stiff paste.

Every locality seems to have its own favorite supermarket baits. If fishing in a new area, don't be afraid to ask local anglers about their most effective baits. You just might be in for a few surprises.

With a little effort, you can have your cake—er, bait—and, in some cases, eat it, too.

Editor's Note: Before trying out these baits in your area please contact your local Fish and Game Office for the regulations for your state. Δ

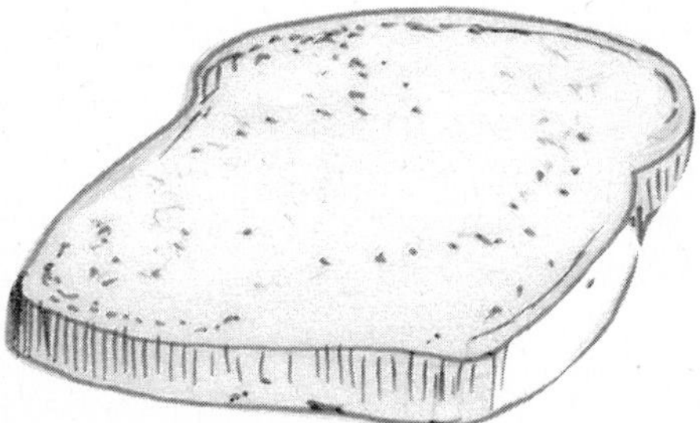

bread

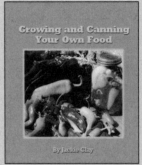

Catch your own bait

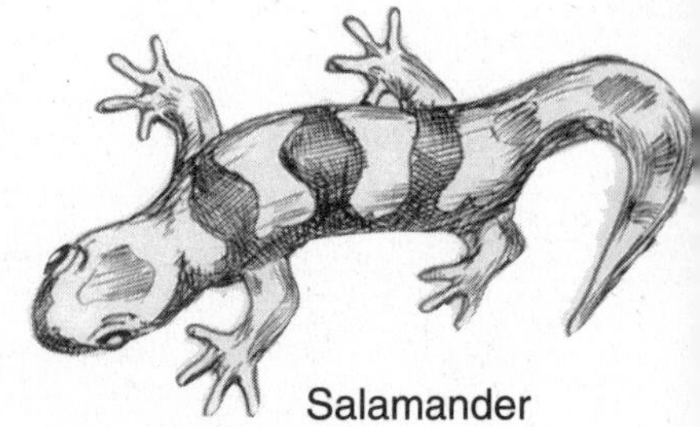
Salamander

By Gary Gresh

Expensive lures and pricey tackle shop baits can sometimes make fishing an expensive proposition, raising the cost of the intended fish fry to that of a gourmet dinner. So why not look at some of the cheaper alternatives—and they work just as well when no bait shop is around, or if you run out of bait.

Worms

Most anglers can usually scrounge up some live bait in the backyard or at streamside. Dig in the garden or compost heap or under stones for worms. They can also be found on the sidewalk or pavement after a rainy night. Small redworms (one to three inches) are usually found in manure, compost, humus, or other organic debris. Medium-sized garden worms (three to six inches) are most abundant in rich moist dirt. Big nightcrawlers (up to 12 inches) are usually found on the surface in sodded areas. Keep your worms in wet moss or soil in a cool, dark place. Properly cared for, they should last the duration of your trip.

All three sizes of worms should catch fish. Depending on the size of the worms and the fish you are after, worms can be fished singly, several to a hook, or cut into pieces. For a lifelike wiggle, insert the hook under the worm's yellowish collar. Run the hook through the worm twice to make the worm secure. Let the end of the worm dangle.

Night crawlers and wigglers are great bait for many species of game fish. They are especially deadly on trout when waters are running high and dirty due to heavy rains. Channel cats, white catfish, and bullheads will readily strike a worm bait.

They're a top bait for most species of panfish. They remain a premier natural bait for game fish such as walleyes, and largemouth, smallmouth, and white bass. In the spring, before trout season gets underway, try them for cold water suckers.

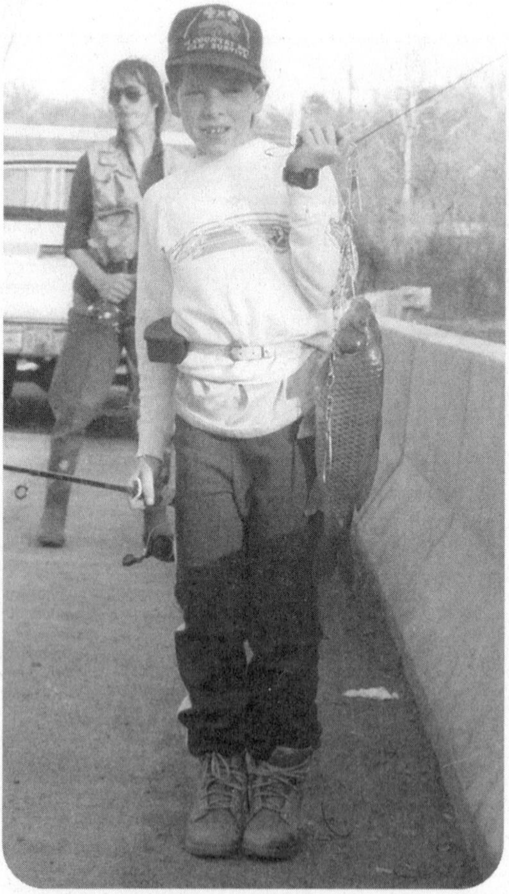
Carp are attracted to a vast number of supermarket baits including kernel corn, cheese, doughbaits, and even elbow macaroni. This small carp was taken on corn.

Worms will live indefinitely in damp soil, if kept away from the sun. They can be fed cracker crumbs, mash, or similar foods. On fishing trips, don't crowd them. Carry them in a can or bait bucket filled with damp soil or moss.

Minnows

Minnows are another great all-round bait that will catch almost anything. Small minnows are a great trout bait. Minnows, alive or dead, will also catch bullheads, white catfish, and channel cats. Minnows are another great panfish bait. They're always a top bait for sunfish, crappies, and perch. Is there a better natural bait for largemouths, smallmouths, white bass, walleyes and saugers than live minnows?

Minnows may be caught in nets, seines, and traps. Bait traps with bread or cornmeal. Very large minnows can sometimes be caught on small hooks baited with bread, dough, or "moss." Those taken from still or slow moving waters will live longer.

Portable, battery powered air pumps will keep them alive in a minnow bucket when it is not flowing in water. A tablespoon or so of peroxide will also help oxygenate the water. So will occasional splashes of seltzer or 7-UP.

Minnows kept too long in a bucket will die from lack of oxygen. If the minnows begin to turn on their sides, stir or slosh the water or blow air into the water with a hose. Porous "breather" bait buckets help to keep water cool so that minnows are less

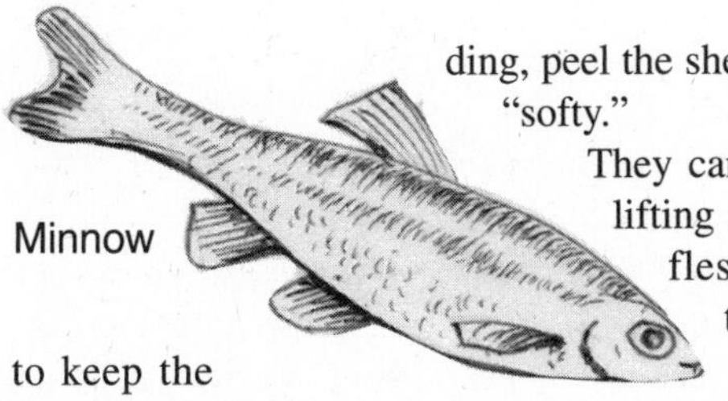

active and hence use oxygen less rapidly. Ice placed on the bucket's lid so that the water drips in as the ice melts helps to keep the water cool. Use a floating bait bucket so you can keep it in the water while you fish.

Minnows may also be kept alive on a wet towel on a tray in your cooler. They will last all day or more when kept in this manner. It actually works better than just keeping them in a minnow bucket all day.

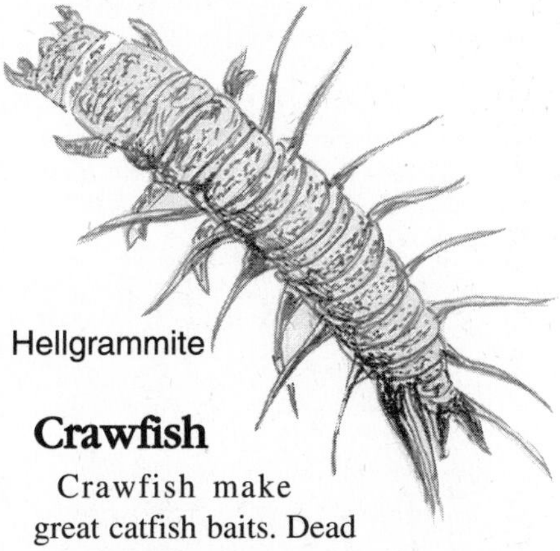

Crawfish

Crawfish make great catfish baits. Dead crayfish, threaded on a hook, are good for catfish. Channel cats, white cats, and bullheads all inhale crawfish. Flatheads prefer crawfish tails. Crawfish are another good panfish bait. For panfish, use the tail meat, either squeezing out the meat or cracking the shell to partially strip it off. The meat from large pincers can also be used for panfish.

Crawfish are also great smallmouth bait. For smallmouths, use crawfish whole and alive, hooked through the tail. Dead crawdads can be threaded on a hook and fished as an artificial lure for bass. The hard shell is shed periodically. The soft shell stage is best for bait. Just before shedding, peel the shell off to make a "softy."

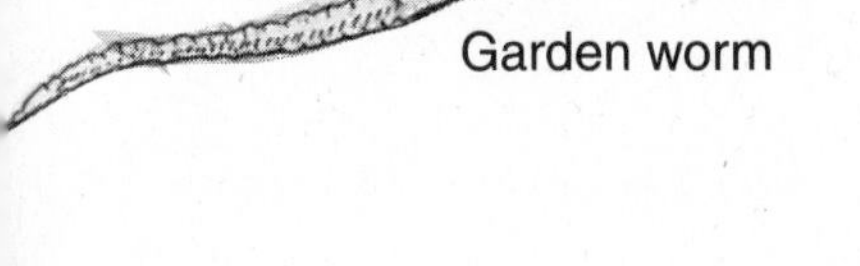

They can be caught by lifting rocks in riffles and letting the current wash them into a net. They may also be caught in modified minnow traps. Simply enlarge the openings so they are large enough for the crawfish to enter. Bait the trap with meat.

Crawfish can also be captured in plastic milk jugs buried in the creek bottom. Cut the top off so the jug is completely open at the top. Place it in a hole so the top of the jug is flush with the creek bottom. Bait the jugs. Crawfish enter the jug, go to the bottom and have difficulty escaping. Use several jugs in different sections of the creek so you don't fish it out. If kept wet and cool, they will stay alive for a day.

Larvae

In many weed fields, trout and panfish anglers can spot weeds with galls. These marble-sized growths resulted when insects laid eggs in the plants. Inside the gall is a small larva that can be used for trout bait. Due to the small size of the larva, more than one can be used. You can either fish the larva on a plain hook or use it to dress a small jig or other lure.

Bee or wasp larvae, catalpa worms, mealworms, or nymphs of water insects all are good trout and panfish bait and are sometimes effective on smallmouths. Caddisworms can either be removed from the case or have the case lightly crushed.

Amphibians

Best known as live baits for largemouth bass and other game fish, dead frogs, salamanders, and tadpoles in the two to three-inch range are great catfish bait. Simply string them on a hook. To fish them alive, hook them through the lips or leg muscle, leaving them free to swim. Tadpoles are also good bait and can be hooked through the thick tail. String dead ones on a hook. Salamanders are best hooked under the backbone in front of the tail. Keep them cool and damp.

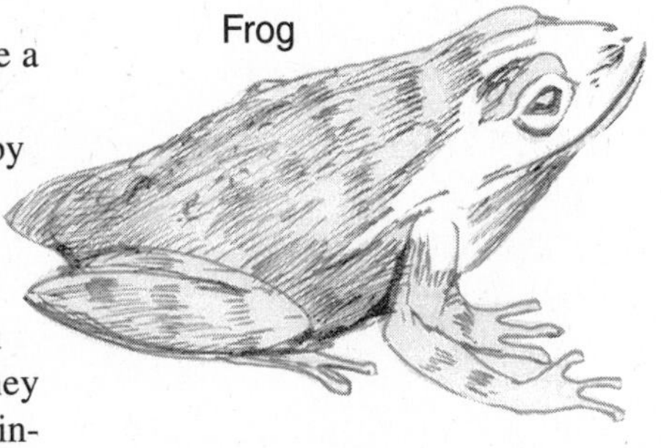

Leeches, crickets, grasshoppers, and hellgrammites

Leeches live in the litter on the bottom in still waters. Very hardy, they should be hooked like worms and used for catfish and bass. They are very hardy.

Crickets can be attracted with baits such as bread but can be difficult to keep on the hook. Keep them alive in large cans with damp sand on the bottom. Feed them mash or cornmeal. Crickets are great bait for crappies and large sunnies.

Largemouth bass are fond of grasshoppers. They are usually abundant in late summer or fall and are easy to catch, especially by kids. They are tougher than crickets and easier to keep alive.

Hellgrammites, the pincer-jawed larvae of the dobson fly, live under rocks in swift water. They are deadly on smallmouth bass. Hook them through the tail or collar.

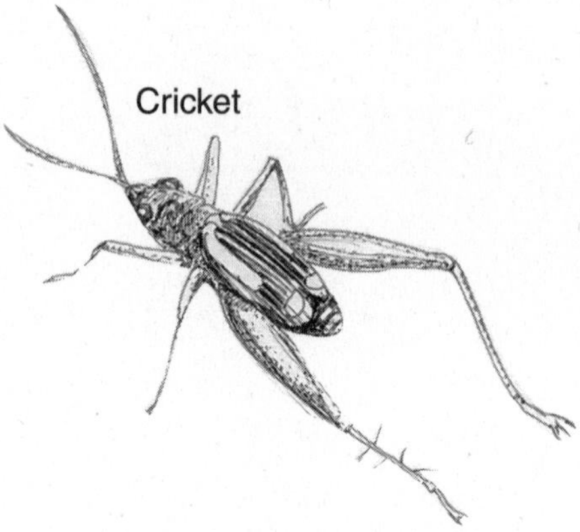
Cricket

Live chubs, suckers, and small perch are among the top natural baits for muskellunge and large northerns. Fly fishing with small wet or dry flies and still fishing with worms are the best ways to put some chubs in the livewell. For suckers, still fish on the bottom with worms. Night fishing is usually best, but they will certainly bedevil trout fishermen during the day as well.

Still fishing for perch works well with live minnows in the winter or

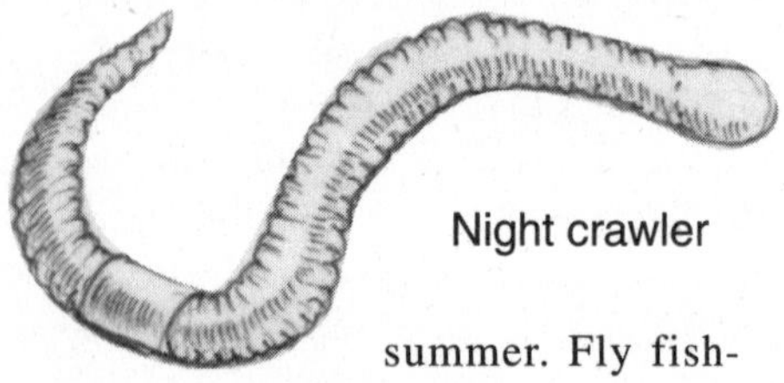
Night crawler

summer. Fly fishing with streamers, spinner flies, or spoons is very effective in spring or fall. Spinning with small spoons or jigs is equally effective. Jigging spoons are deadly when ice fishing for perch.

Mealworms

Mealworms are excellent trout and panfish bait and can easily be raised at home. All you need are some mason jars, uncooked oatmeal, stockings and some live mealworms from the bait shop or pet shop.

Clean and dry the mason jars and fill them halfway with oats. Add some mealworms to each jar and cover the mouth with the stocking to allow air to circulate and to prevent escapes. For food, place two pieces of potato peel in each jar. A friend of

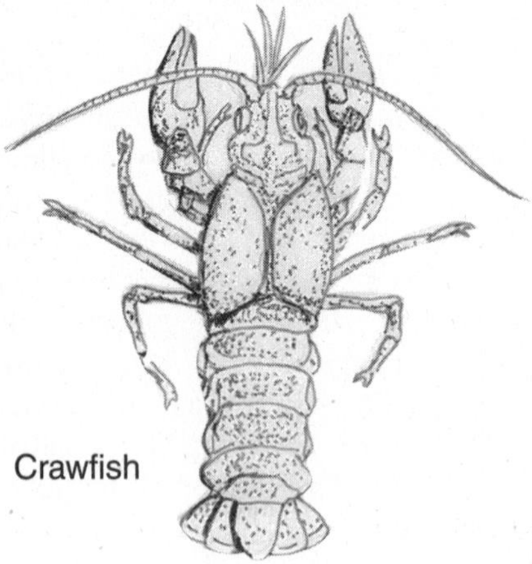
Crawfish

mine saves used tea bags, dries them out, and feeds the dried tea to his mealworms. The mealworms do not eat the oats. Place the jars in a cool, dark place such as a shed, barn, or garage so escapees don't infest your house. Replace the potato peels every two weeks.

Within a few weeks, the worms will pupate and emerge as small, black beetles that will mate and lay hundreds of eggs in the oat flakes. When the beetles die, you'll see hundreds of small worms creeping around the oats that will grow into mealworms in a few weeks.

Mealworms grow faster and enter the beetle stage faster in warm temperatures than in cold. This allows you to refrigerate some whole letting the others mature faster, delaying the beetle stage for some so you have a constant supply of mealworms.

Excessive heat will kill them. Fungus destroys them too if the jars get too

Perch

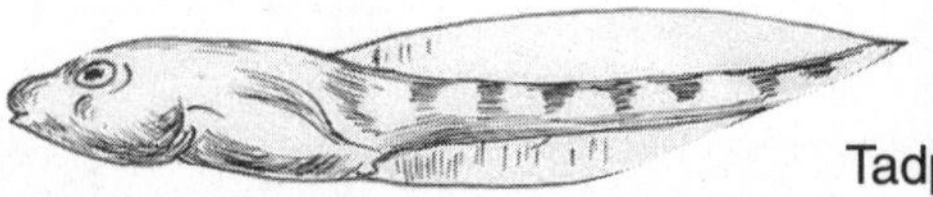
Tadp

moist. To avoid this, limit the number of potato peels per jar and use the stocking as a cover to allow air to circulate freely. Throw away any contaminated jars so the fungus doesn't spread to others.

So, as you can see, there is a veritable cornucopia of baits that anglers can catch, collect, or even raise themselves.

Heck, the most fun might be in gathering the bait. You'll keep the kids busy, save some money, and never be without the deadliest fresh baits.

Editor's Note: Before trying out these baits in your area please contact your local Fish and Game Office for the regulations for your state. Δ

Helpful hints with lures

If you prefer using lures when you are fishing, here are a few helpful hints:

- Fish that live in murky water, such as ponds and lakes that have rotting vegetation clouding them up, see primarily red and green colors. Largemouth bass, for example, have only red and green photoreceptors in their eyes. Artificial lures that have a lot of other colors have them primarily to attract the attention of fishermen, not fish.
- Bigger lures are often better than smaller ones. Studies with fish suggest they pass up bait under a certain size in favor of larger bait. Largemouth bass, for example, prefer bait at least half the size of their mouth. When hungry, they'll strike at prey larger than their mouths.
- Fish go after injured fish before going after healthy fish. So a lure with action that imitates an injured fish is best.
- Feeding stimulants work. Lab tests with fish show significantly more hits when a feeding stimulant such as pureed shrimp or minced fish has been added to a bait. Even a tiny bit of stimulant produced results.

Source: Science News, www.sciencenews.org

Breaking ice on hard water fishing
a cool introduction to a fun sport

By Linda Gabris

Only thing hard about hard water fishing is the ice. Once you've broken through that obstacle, the rest is easy gliding. Ice fishing is great sport for the whole family and there's good news: You don't have to take out a loan to outfit your party, regardless of number, since novice gear is pretty basic stuff.

In order to enjoy brisk days on frozen lakes, you need to be dressed properly, as nothing ruins fun faster than chattering teeth. Warm winter boots, proven waterproof, are a must as sometimes lakes are slushy. Follow the old "dress in layers" rule which allows peeling when too hot. Regardless of what's underneath, your outer layer is most important and should be insulated, water and wind proof. Top with wool caps or toques and enough mitts to go around twice. Goggles protect eyes against blustery winds and sun glasses should be worn on bright days when lakes are glaring.

Breaking the obstacle

When I was a kid, dad would cuss a blue streak while chiseling holes in our backyard lake with a primitive tool known as a spud. Once opened, we guarded the holes from freezing over by covering with layers of cardboard and snow when not in use. You'll be able to hack a family's worth of holes with an ice chisel in early winter when ice is relatively thin (see guidelines for safe ice) but as the season progresses and ice grows to depths of a foot or more, the job with a spud becomes a dreadful thought.

An ice auger is a fascinating tool that no space-age fisherman should be without, for it drills holes quickly with ease allowing freedom to test the whole lake rather than being confined to one spot. Manual augers are least expensive models but you can go all out with smooth-cutting power tools that bore up to 10-inch holes through two-foot ice with amazing speed.

Linda Gabris with a couple of great trout for supper. Ice fishing is a delightful way to cash in on winter fun.

The only thing hard about hard water fishing is the ice. Warm wear, a stick, line, sinker, and bell and you're ready to roll.

Here's something to smile about: When it comes to rods, you can go without, for in the old days almost everyone used willow twigs and I can vouch they work fine. If you're crafty, you can recycle a broken fly or light spinning rod tip into an ice rod, for it only needs to be about a quarter the length of a regular pole. Refit the handle or plop on a cork and you've got it made. There are inexpensive contraptions called tip-ups for ice fishing or better yet, outfit the gang

Ice safety

Check with authorities for updated ice conditions before venturing on any lake. A general guideline calls for 4 inches of ice to hold a person, 6 to 8 inches for a snowmobile and 12 inches for a vehicle. Areas around beaver dams can sport thinner ice than normal and spring fed lakes and river mouths should be treated with extra caution.

with store-bought ice rods and you'll still be smiling since they are surprisingly reasonable compared to other types of rods.

You'll need line

Black braided line used to be the norm, but today monofilament line is more popular. When fishing smaller or stocked lakes with average-sized populations, you can go with lighter tests. For larger lakes with bigger possibilities, increase test accordingly. If word has it that monsters inhabit the lake, use line that'll pass the test.

If you don't have a tackle box full of basics, get leaders. I like nickel wound with interlock snaps and crane swivels. You'll need hooks and sinkers. When choosing hook size remember the old saying: it's easier to catch a big fish on a small hook than a small fish on a big hook. You'll also need a dipper or skimmer for keeping holes free of ice buildup, a fish bonker to put down keepers, and a basket to hold and carry catch. Most importantly, ensure everyone in your party who requires one by law, pockets a valid fishing license.

So what tickles the appetite of fish under ice? In lakes where I've had warm weather luck with worms, I've had winter luck as well. Same seems to holds true for other bait. Most tackle shops supply worms year-round along with an assortment of appetizers like creel (shrimp) and bottled roe. Be sure to check regulations regarding bait restrictions and read up on quotas, size, and species limits before heading out.

One way to find out what fish in local lakes fancy is to ask your dealer to recommend what's hot. These folks are tuned in to what's happening and will be happy to help you make a good selection. Bright, flashy spoons and lures that offer lively action when jigged (worked up and down to attract fish) are sure bets. There's tons of tackle like scented power bait, lures that glow under water, and synthetic worms and minnows that "swim" like the real thing, so let your partners have fun helping to choose. Of course, nothing beats striking up a conversation with other fishermen to see what they've been having luck with.

Where to drill

In early winter under first ice, rainbow and brook trout in smaller, stocked waters are noted for hanging out in shallows in search of feed. Fishing the shoreline with worms, creel, or roe is the way to go. As ice thickens fish are forced into deeper realms.

Larger trout are roamers and in bigger lakes can be found in middle depths in earlier parts of the season, moving down as ice grows. River inlets where incoming oxygenated water carries and churns up food are promising spots. Bays, points, or islands with sudden drop-offs are interesting places to check for activity and nothing attracts quicker than jigging a flashy lure.

Any lure with good action is worth trying when the goal is a predacious fish with a ravenous appetite like lake trout. Deep-dwelling char need lots of coaxing with big colorful spoons. Smaller-mouthed whitefish fancy worms and roe above all else. If you're targeting burbot, which bite best in late afternoon, fish the mud

Ethics on ice

Remember it's your legal responsibility to leave markings on holes. A firmly planted stick directly above hole alerts others of its presence.

Be considerate. Space holes thoughtfully away from other fishermen, leaving plenty of elbow room.

Never leave garbage, dead fish or entrails on the ice. Wasting unwanted catch and littering are against the law. Fish that aren't intended for the table must be released quickly and gently, head first, back into the hole.

Don't build fires on the ice. Remains are unsightly and pollute the water in the spring.

The author caught this nice supper trout through the ice using just some line, a sinker, a hook, and a worm tied onto a willow stick.

where they will be rooting along with suckers and other bottom feeders.

Patterns vary from lake to lake due to cover, oxygen, weather, food, and fishing traffic, so hot spots are only hot when you find them. Some swear calm, overcast days are more prospective than windy days with bright sun. It's said that deep water fish see best during bright sun and shallow dwellers have better vision in early and late afternoon light. I figure fish strike when they're hungry and like any mode of angling, success depends heavily on patience and luck.

When testing your luck with a baited hook, drop your sinkered line to the bottom. Wind in to the desired starting depth and secure. Plant twig, rod, or tip-up firmly in the snow with tip centered directly over hole so line is not rubbing on ice which can cause wearing. You can attach a little bell to alert nibbling or watch the flag on your tip-up for action. When a fish strikes, you get your chance at catching.

If there are no bites at the expected depth, try lowering or raising line. Fish may be hovering a few feet off the bottom or scouring just below the ice surface. Keep exploring depths until you reach action.

Jigging is the most productive method of catching big fish under ice. Any spoon that can be worked to resemble lively minnow action is ideal for jigging. Lower your lure to desired starting depth. Secure the line around your mitten or gloved hand or jig with rod by slowly raising and lowing the lure. Start out by making short, sharp jerks. If this doesn't generate interest, try swinging the lure back and forth. If you still aren't drawing attention, alternate action by making exaggerated moves—long, swift pulls followed by shorter, slower ones. This kind of action can be seen underwater for miles. A trick worth trying is to drop a lure to the bottom and work it to stir up mud. This muddy action resembles a

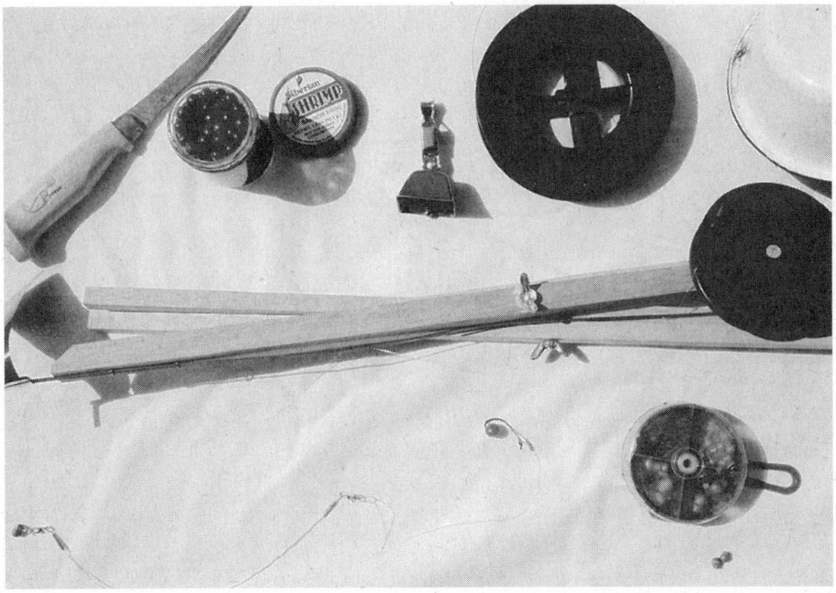

The basics for ice fishing are no more than a tip-up (for propping up your line), line, leader, sinker, hook, and bait such as roe. The addition of a bell to sound an alarm and a handy knife for dressing out your catch is nice, too.

My pick of hard water lures that offer good action for jigging and lots of underwater flash—clockwise from the top: Red Gold Gibbs, Two Eye Lucky Strike, Gibbs One Eye Wiggler, Gibbs Kit-a-mat, Jumbo Kamlooper, Gold Williams Wabler, Silver One Eye Lucky Strike, Green-yellow Ruby Eye.

Trout—or any catch—in cornmeal jackets with almonds

There are as many great ways to cook a fish as there are to catch one, but if I had to pick a favorite recipe, this would have to be it.

Nothing beats fresh caught trout fried up crispy in a golden jacket of cornmeal and topped with crunchy toasted almonds. It's so elegant yet incredibly simple that it's a perfect pick for a quick supper after an invigorating day on the ice. And don't fret if your party's catch isn't enough to go around to everyone as a full course, dish what you caught up as an appetizer and enjoy while swapping tales of the day. Once your fishin' partners taste fish done in this fashion, they'll be hungerin' to hit the ice again.

Take your catch of fresh cleaned trout and wash and pat dry with paper towels. Put one cup cornmeal (enough for two fish of about a pound each—or more or less depending on amount of fish to be coated) into a paper bag and add 4 teaspoons of flour, ¼ teaspoon each of salt and pepper, and a pinch of paprika.

Heat 2 tablespoons fat (bacon grease, butter, or oil) into heavy cast iron frying pan until sizzling.

Break 1 large or 2 small eggs onto plate and beat lightly with a fork. Dip fish into egg, then drop into paper bag. Shake until thoroughly coated with the cornmeal.

Slide fish into hot pan and fry until crisp and golden on one side. Turn and cook the other side.

Remove fish from pan. Drain on paper towels and hold hot.

Add 1 cup slivered almonds to the pan and toast until golden. Top the fish with the almonds. Serve with lemon wedges or tartar sauce. A glass of white wine pays highest compliment to this meal.

bottom-feeder rooting for food. Since bottom feeders often make a trophy's meal, this trickery could whet the appetite of a prize.

There's nothing more thrilling than sight-fishing—watching action below ice. The old-fashioned way is to lay on your belly, hood head with a scarf to block light, and peer into the hole to watch fish approaching and see their reaction to your offering. Today you can buy a portable fabric dark house for sight-fishing or build your own. Just take a cardboard box, paint the inside black, cut a hole in the side for your head to fit in, and you're ready to roll.

If you want to go high-tech, there are underwater cameras that are truly unbelievable and depth and fish finders that work like a charm. Not to mention portable ice huts with comfy seats, heaters that'll keep you cozy, sleighs and sleds to tote your gear, and oodles of other newfangled things that lifts a great old sport to exciting new heights.

Whether you go basic or high tech, sharing a thermos of hot chocolate with your loved ones on a snow-sparkling lake is the ultimate pleasure of winter. Fun that's simply hard to beat. Δ

Pickled fish and rollmops

White fleshed fillets are being rolled into rollmops ready for poaching then pickling.

By Linda Gabris

The zesty creations called rollmops (those mouthwatering appetizers that you buy in jars at the supermarket or by bulk in a deli) have deep European roots, but there's a lot more to pickled fish than just herring.

Traditional rollmops, herring fillets wrapped around a small sour pickle and cured in brine, are as old as history dates. The term comes from *rollen*, meaning "to roll up" in German, and *moppen*, meaning "sour face" in Dutch.

Once considered an everyday staple, pickled fish today is ranked high on the list of gourmet delights. Commercial rollmops are rather pricey, but the good news is that any fish can be pickled and anglers who haven't yet landed a catch in the crock don't know what they're missing.

Pickling is a safe and easy method of putting up fish for short term storage. Often when I have a fresh fish that doesn't fit into the immediate menu or net a good buy at the fish market, I get out my crock and pickle the prize. This makes a delicious appetizer that saves up to a month, allowing it to be enjoyed in several settings.

Small fish are ideal for pickling in traditional rollmop fashion and nothing makes a better "mock" rollmop than plentiful smelt or other small pan fish. Larger catch including whitefish, perch, walleye, bass, and trout are succulent when pickled. Since skin is tougher on larger fish and flesh is usually too thick for rolling, the fish is best skinned, filleted, and cut into serving-sized chunks before pickling because acid in the brine helps break down and dissolve bones. Even the most discriminate can't resist spicy suckers in the pickle jar.

Rollmops fresh out of the crock

There are two basic methods of pickling fish.

The old-fashioned way involves packing salted-down fish into a crock or jar and covering with boiling brine. If this method is practiced, modern day home-picklers are advised to freeze fish first for at least 48 hours in case tapeworms are present in the flesh. This method works great for previously frozen catch or store-bought frozen buys.

The other method, which was handed down to me from my grandmother, calls for gently poaching fish in boiling brine before putting into crock. This eliminates the need of freezing first, which allows fish to be pickled at prime. In the unlikely event that flesh contains parasites, heat will destroy them. I use this method for pickling fresh catch.

When pickling fish, use only high-grade distilled vinegar, coarse pickling salt, fresh spices, and earthen crock or glass jars as metal containers may cause discoloration or "tinny" taste.

Here are some interesting recipes to try.

Spicy pickled fish chunks:

2 to 3 pounds previously frozen fish, thawed (any kind of white or light fleshed fish fillets, head, tail, and skin removed and cut into one-inch pieces) Whitefish, perch, bass, catfish, walleye, suckers can be used. Lake trout is good pickled and even though other trout is usually pinker or redder fleshed, they can also be used in this recipe.
8 cups of white vinegar
1 cup pickling salt
3 medium onions, thinly sliced
1 cup red wine
2 cups sugar
¼ cup mixed pickling spice
3 whole bay leaves
1 tablespoon hot crushed chilies
3 whole cloves of garlic (if desired)

In a glass bowl, combine 4 cups of vinegar and the salt and stir until dissolved. Submerge the prepared fish. Cover and put in fridge for at least 24 hours or up to three days. Remove from fridge, drain, and discard liquid. Rinse fish well under cold running water.

Put the fish chunks into an earthen crock or jars, layering with onion rings. In a saucepan, bring the remaining vinegar, wine, sugar, spices, and garlic to a boil. Taste and adjust seasoning, if needed. Let simmer 5 minutes.

Pour a bit of boiling pickling liquid over the fish, enough to take chill out of crock. Slowly add remaining liquid. Put a lid on the crock or seal jars and cool to room temperature. Refrigerate for at least five days before serving. Store under refrigeration for no longer than a month.

Serve pickled fish as an appetizer accompanied with thin slices of black bread, sour cream, and pickled baby onions. A glass of white wine and you've got it made.

Mock rollmops:

2 pounds thin white-fleshed fish fillets (or 2 pounds butterfly-slit smelt with skin left on and tail snipped)
1 or 2 jars of gherkin pickles
4 cups vinegar
1 cup dry white wine
¼ cup salt
1 cup sugar
4 Tbsp. pickling spice
5 dried chili peppers (if you like it hot)
3 medium onions, thinly sliced

Pat the fillets with paper towels to remove moisture. Lay a gherkin on the tail end of fillet or smelt, roll up tightly and fasten with a toothpick. Proceed until all pieces of fish are wrapped around a pickle.

In a pot, combine all the ingredients except the fish and bring to a boil. Reduce the heat and simmer 10 minutes.

Gently ease fish into the brine. Bring back to a boil. Reduce heat and poach 8 minutes.

Remove from heat and cool. Pour into crock or ladle into jars and cover or seal. Refrigerate for at least 3 days before serving in order for flavors to draw.

Serve rollmops with crusty bread sticks for a hearty snack.

Once rolled up and secured with a toothpick, the rollmops are quickly poached.

Old-fashioned pickled salmon: Here's a wonderful, updated recipe for pickled salmon. You can process fresh catch or frozen buys.

4 to 5 pounds of salmon, skin removed
1½ cups pickling salt
2 cups cider vinegar
4 cups white vinegar
3 cups sugar
½ cup pickling spice
2 lemons, sliced
1 cup white wine (or cider vinegar)
2 onions, thinly sliced

If the fish is fresh, freeze 48 hours before processing. If frozen, you're ready to roll. Cut into two-inch pieces. Place the fish in large glass bowl and set aside. In medium mixing bowl, combine the salt and cider vinegar and stir until the salt is dissolved. Pour over the fish. Refrigerate for eight days, stirring every day.

Drain and discard the brine. Rinse the fish in cold water to remove excess salt. Cover with cold water and put in fridge for three hours.

In a large pan, combine the white vinegar, sugar, spices, and lemon. Heat until the sugar is dissolved. Don't boil. Cool then add the wine.

Drain fish and discard the soaking water. Pack fish into crock or jars, layering with the onion. Pour the pickling liquid over the fish. Seal the jars and store in the fridge. Let set for at least a week before serving. This saves up to one month under refrigeration. Makes about 4 quarts.

Note: In the olden days grandmother "put down" salmon and other fish in a crock without the use of a refrigerator and it sat in the cellar under brine for many months on end. However, home preservers today are strongly advised not to do it in the way of the olden days as spoilage could occur if cellar temperatures are not kept constant. Δ

Ayoob on Firearms

Firearms: tools of rural living

So, editor Dave Duffy and I got to talking about guns. We agreed that for some people they are sporting equipment like a Spaulding racquet or a Big Bertha golf club, and for others they are *objets d'art* like Patek-Phillipe wristwatches or Waterford crystal. For most of us, though, they are tools.

And, very definitely, power tools. Remote control drills, with the width and depth of the hole adjusted by the choice of bore size and ammunition. Tools of survival, in many ways.

Countless working ranchers have used guns to save their lives from stock animals gone rogue. The legendary Elmer Keith was an early 20th century cattleman when a bronc went wild, and Keith would have been dragged to death with his foot caught in the stirrup if he hadn't been able to unholster the single action Colt revolver he carried and fire upward, killing the animal and saving his life. On another day, a fast draw with his ranch revolver saved him from being bitten by a rattlesnake.

More commonly, the "survival" element involves food. The high powered rifle in the pickup, the .22 or shotgun on the tractor, or that holstered handgun can turn a random sighting of a meat animal on the property into food on the table. It can also eradicate the fox that raids the henhouse, the coyote that has been stalking the family cats, or the wolf that is licking its chops for the newly-birthed lamb. Not to mention keeping the bounty of the produce garden for the family's bellies instead of those of the varmints.

There is also the protection factor. An Alaskan backwoodsman, about to be mauled by a huge brown bear, kills it with his Ruger .357 Magnum revolver. Fishing in the same state, a sportsman and his partner are attacked by a great bruin. The shaken partner fumbles and drops his slug-loaded 12 gauge shotgun in the water, but the first man empties a 16 shot Taurus 9mm semiautomatic pistol into the huge ursine head, killing the beast and saving two human lives. In the lower 48, a game ranger's Smith & Wesson .357 kills a mountain lion poised to spring on him, and a young boy's .22 rifle stops a maddened dog from ripping his baby sister apart. Camping in the wilderness, a man is set upon by a gang of thugs who must have thought "Deliverance" was a training film. But, the camper has a Ruger Mini-14 .223 caliber semiautomatic rifle with him, and this leads to an acceptable outcome.

There are different tools for different jobs. Durability is an important factor in selection, of course, but so is power level. So is portability. And so is ease of use, in the hands of every dweller in that particular backwoods home who may need to use that particular tool.

Shotguns

The smoothbore musket was the weapon of the Pilgrims, and the "blunderbuss" remains an icon of Thanksgiving imagery as a result. Historians tell us that when the wagon trains bore the pioneers westward in the 19th Century, each Conestoga wagon was more likely to bear a "scattergun" than a rifle. The shotgun has the longest and richest history of any American firearm, and it remains a cornerstone of the back-

Massad Ayoob

woods home gun rack. In many farm households, the shotgun is the only firearm the family finds necessary.

Supremely versatile, the shotgun can fire birdshot to capture the fowl of the air and rabbits and squirrels, or single-projectile slug loads for the beasts of the field, accurate enough to slay the deer and powerful enough to kill the marauding bear. The 20-gauge is ample for most needs, but the more powerful 12-gauge is more versatile, and is by far the most popular choice among farmers and homesteaders. The shotgun is a useful tool in all its forms, but the two most commonly seen as heavy-duty working guns are the single-barrel and the slide-action.

The single-shot break open shotgun is cheap and easy to manufacture in a sturdy and functional form. The Harrington & Richardson seems to be the most popular brand, one rich in

Author's rural "car gun" is this Remington 870 12-gauge pump shotgun. It features rifle sights, extended magazine....

history as a workingman's gun, but there are many others on the market, all very affordable. Very safe to handle in that it can be kept unloaded, then quickly "broken" open and a shell inserted into its barrel, the "single" demands careful one-shot, one-kill discipline since it will take so long to reload a follow-up round if the first shotgun blast does not accomplish the necessary task.

The slide-action repeater, with several shells in the tubular magazine beneath its barrel, is more forgiving of error in aim, and altogether more practical when there might be multiple targets or one determined creature which must be shot multiple times. The most affordable of the sophisticated shotguns, this "pump gun" is also the most rugged and the least demanding of maintenance, and hence particularly well suited to the rough working "life" of a tool on a farm or a ranch. Now that I'm finally living in the boonies instead of just working there, the gun I keep behind my front seat is a Remington Model 870 12-gauge pump, with short, handy 20-inch barrel and folding stock. This makes it extremely short overall, easy to discreetly cover with a jacket as it lies on the floor behind the driver's seat, and therefore easy to grab and exit with from the driver's

...and folding stock, which makes the gun much more compact for readily accessible storage...

door. It's a moment's work to flip the stock open, simultaneously pumping a shell into the chamber, and bring it to the shoulder to aim with Remington's optional rifle type sights. Loaded with Federal full power one-ounce rifled slugs, it has crushing power at close range, and the accuracy of a Kalashnikov battle rifle out to 100 yards, a perfect range of versatility for my particular needs.

Rifles

I would venture to guess that the humble .22 is the most popular of backwoods home rifles. It's the right size for the varmints who plague the vegetable garden, and the right size for stewpot rabbits and squirrels. When butchering livestock, it's powerful enough to slaughter instantly and humanely with a brain shot placed with surgical precision at very close range. Trappers like .22s for humanely euthanizing captured animals, because they make only a tiny hole in the pelt. The ammunition is cheap, the sound of the shot is soft, and recoil is nonexistent, all of which encourage shooting practice, which is a helluva lot of fun and hugely practical when you live in the boondocks.

The typical .22 farm rifle may be an old Mossberg, a fine vintage Remington or Winchester, the ubiquitous Marlin, or the hugely popular modern Ruger 10/22, or any of several others. It may be bolt action or lever action, slide action or semiautomatic. It will, however, be too light in

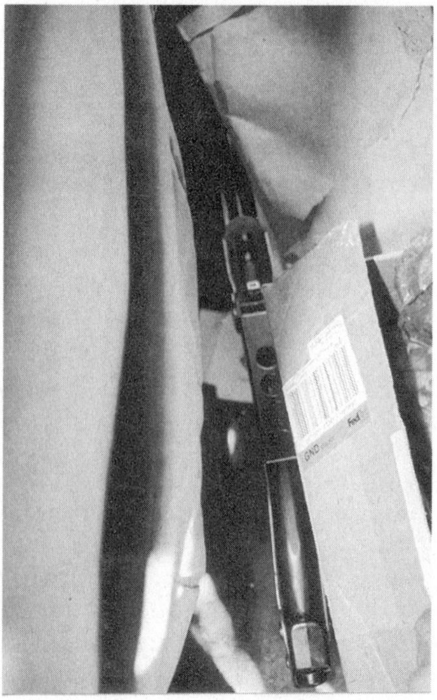

...such as this, discreetly concealed behind the driver's seat of his vehicle.

Simple, rugged, and cheap, single-shot break-open shotguns remain popular as rural working guns. This one is from Stoeger, selling for $130 new.

This old Mossberg .22 rifle has served generations as a farm rifle for work and recreational needs.

power to handle large creatures efficiently, particularly under the widely varying conditions of the real world, which can make accurate shot placement difficult.

In the larger caliber guns, the .30/30 is probably the most popular everyday "working rifle" of the hinterlands, and has been so since its introduction in the late 19th century. Flat in silhouette and usually weighing under seven pounds, your classic .30/30s, like the Winchester Model 94 and the Marlin Model 336, are easy to carry and easy to scabbard alongside your horse, your ATV, your tractor, or even your snowmobile. Millions of both have been produced. Their "cowboy style" lever action design allows efficiently fast shooting, and is evocative of a classic time in rural American history.

Often overlooked but uniquely suitable for use as a heavy-duty farm tool is the surplus military rifle, particularly the bolt action guns of WWII and even WWI vintage. Designed to work in the mud of the trenches and the sands of Pacific islands, and to function even when there is no time to clean or lubricate them, these guns were built to be dropped and kicked around and keep on working and shooting straight. The ugly full-length wooden stocks and upper wooden handguard of the typical military rifle was there to protect its barrel.

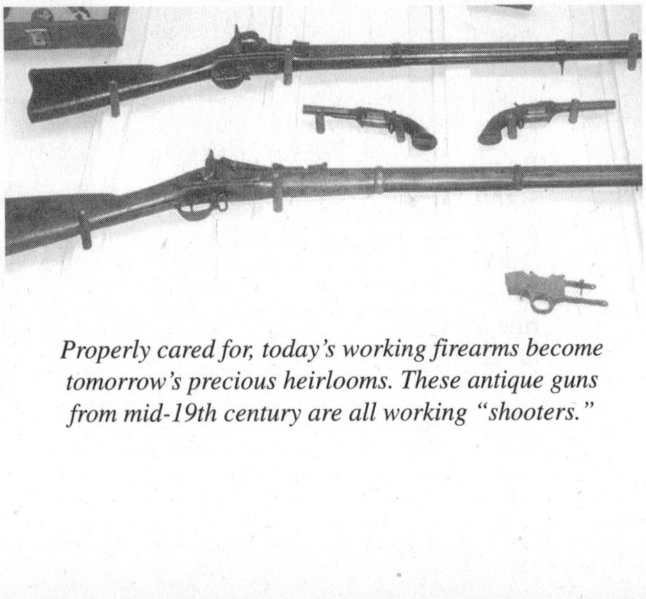

Properly cared for, today's working firearms become tomorrow's precious heirlooms. These antique guns from mid-19th century are all working "shooters."

Among the best are the classic Springfield ('03) and American Enfield (P-14 and P-17); among the best and most affordable are the Mauser and the British Short Magazine Lee Enfield (SMLE). The Springfield and the P-17 fire America's most loved hunting rifle cartridge, the .30/06; the P-14 and the SMLEs are chambered for the .303 British round, still popular among Canadian hunters. The Mausers can be had in a variety of calibers, perhaps the most useful being the 7mm Mauser, aka 7X57. This load is great for deer, and with its long, narrow 175 grain soft nose hunting bullet offers enough penetration to be adequate for moose and black bear, yet its soft recoil reminds you more of a .30/30.

It used to be in vogue to "sporterize" these old guns with lighter, sleeker stocks, more modern sights, and so on. But that was in a time when a commercially made Winchester or Marlin .30/30 cost about $70, and a Winchester Model 70 maybe a C-note or a little more, but the surplus bolt guns went for $25 to $30 each in good condition. Today, you're looking at about $250 for one of the more usefully sized surplus bolt actions, such as the Enfield Jungle Carbine or the short Spanish Mauser 7mm carbine, which is the same or a little more than a used .30/30 in the same condition. The economic advantage of the surplus rifle has been lost, though its rugged durability under the most extreme conditions remains.

In semiautomatics, the military style guns tend to be a bit too clumsy in the large caliber range, but that's also true of the bolt actions. Also, any military-style semi-auto will tend to be expensive, and you have to remember that in most states, the game laws prohibit hunting with any semiautomatic rifle having a greater

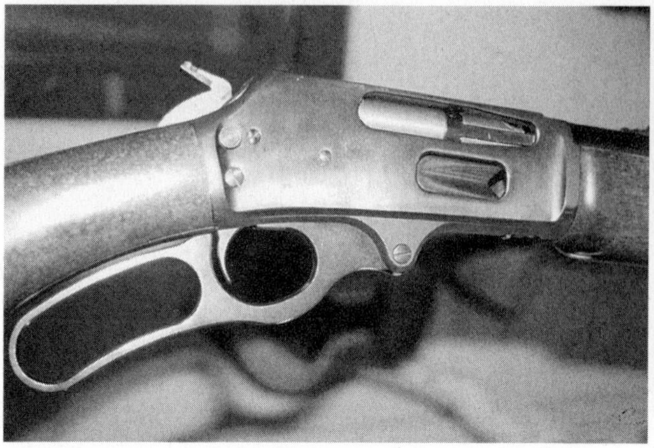

Lever action .30/30s like this Marlin Model 336 have served as working rifles in millions of backwoods homes.

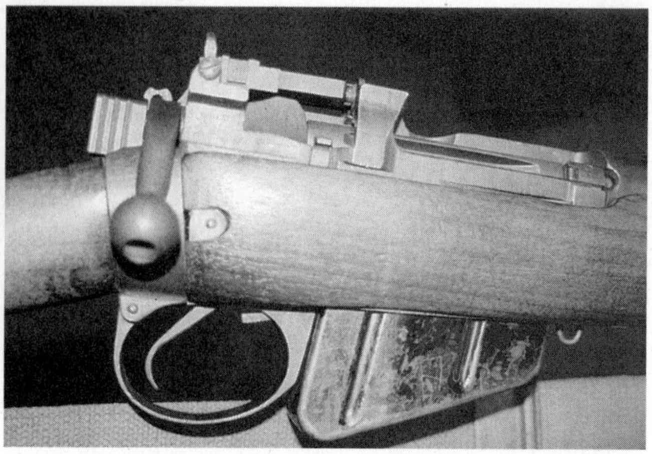

The rugged old Lee-Enfield .303, built for combat in mid-20th century, can withstand the rigors of farm work.

than five-cartridge magazine capacity. They're also pretty expensive. For farm work as opposed to hunting, the most logical choice in terms of both economy and functionality is the SKS, in surplus or newly manufactured form. Still available for under $200 if you shop carefully, they fire the 7.62X39 mm military cartridge of the AK47. With soft nose hunting ammunition, this cartridge gives you practical ballistics that can best be described as ".30/30 Lite."

Handguns

As with rifles, the .22 is particularly popular and particularly useful for rural home and farm handgun needs. Semiautomatic pistols like the Ruger or the old, classic, and aptly named Colt Woodsman, are popular choices. However, a revolver will give you more versatility. The auto will cycle only with conventional .22 Long Rifle ammunition. With the revolver you can use mild .22 Shorts or even lighter .22 BB and CB caps to shoot mice and pest birds in the barn without tearing up the walls and floors too badly; you can use .22 "ratshot" loads for close up, reactive shooting at snakes; and of course, you have the full range of .22 Long Rifle options. At my current backwoods digs, the handgun that gets the most use is a Smith & Wesson K-22 target revolver. On rainy days, I can sit under the porch roof and plink at a little steel Birchwood-Casey target set against the range backstop 50 yards away. The .22 will do nicely for that damn possum that tore up the neighbor's cat, and similar chores. If you think you're a good enough a marksman, the .22 handgun is an extremely sporting tool for hunting rabbits and squirrels.

The .22 is generally considered too light for defensive use against dangerous animals, whether they approach you on two legs or four. A .38 Special revolver or 9mm pistol is generally considered to be the minimum power floor for defensive handguns. Where is the handgun's place on the working farm's gun rack? The answer is, its place is not on the rack at all. It's called a "sidearm" because its place is at your side. Lacking the range and easily delivered marksmanship of a shoulder gun, the handgun is "the emergency reaction tool that is always there." My friend Clint Smith, Vietnam combat vet and ex-SWAT cop, founded the famous Thunder Ranch training school in Texas and the new School of Arms in Oregon. He's famous for explaining, "The handgun is what you use to fight your way back to the shotgun or rifle you shouldn't have left behind in the first place." Words to live by, especially when you're extremely remote from

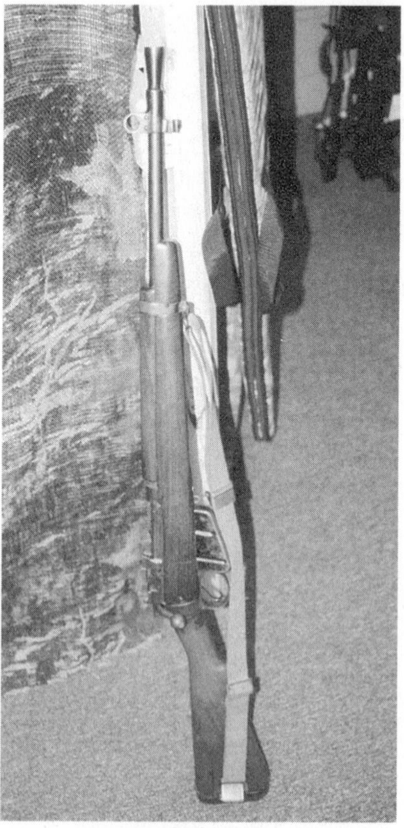

British military surplus SMLE Jungle Carbine is a heavy-duty working rifle for backwoods home needs.

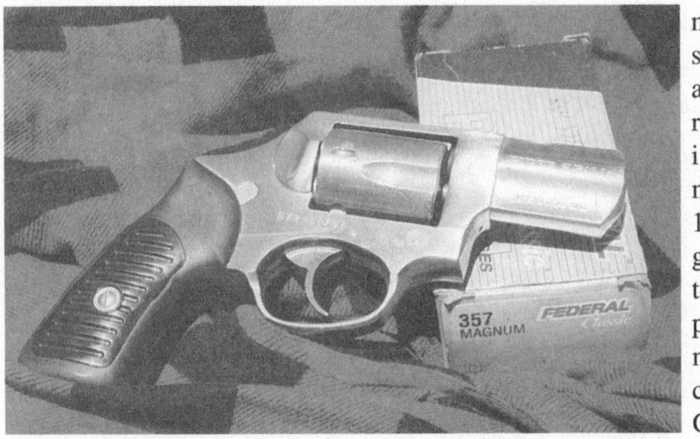

Ruger SP101 is author's choice for an easily concealable, powerful handgun for all-the-time carry.

assistance from cops and game wardens.

Choice of handgun? In a semiautomatic, as with a rifle, it makes sense to pick a military design expressly created to endure the rigors of heavy duty with minimal maintenance. The Beretta 92 9mm, known as the M9/M10 in American military circles, is a good example. Much more popular, however, is the GI pistol the Beretta replaced, the 1911 .45, which is more powerful and therefore much more suitable for shooting larger creatures. The single action Frontier style revolver is the traditional weapon of the movie cowboy, and is in fact seen in abundance among today's working cowboys, but I have to say that I've seen more carrying modern double action Magnum revolvers, and even more with .45 automatics in their pickup trucks or at their sides.

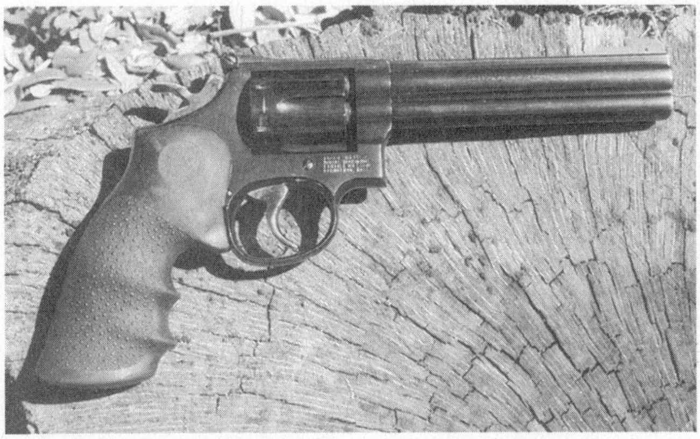

This durable, superbly accurate Smith & Wesson K-22 revolver gets more actual firing use at the author's place than any other gun.

The Glock pistol should be strongly considered for this application. No semiautomatic is less demanding in terms of maintenance and lubrication. That is, they work well even if they've unavoidably become dirty. The Glock 21 .45 is big but light and very accurate; the Glock 30 .45 is much smaller, still very light and very accurate. For shooting large animals, though, the 10mm Glock's greater penetration with full power ammo makes it a better choice. The big Glock 20 in this caliber was the backwoods choice of gun expert Chuck Karwan, who determined that with all 15 rounds in its preban magazine and a 16th in its firing chamber, it carried more potential foot-pounds of energy on board when fully loaded than any Magnum revolver. Paco Kelly, an experienced street cop and highly accomplished handgun hunter, has had good luck in the latter pursuit with the compact, 11-shot Glock 29, which is to the larger 10mm as the Glock 30 is to the Glock 21 in .45s. If you want something a little smaller, Glock's standard frame guns are made in compact and subcompact sizes in 9mm Luger, .40 S&W, or .357 SIG. A subcompact Glock 27 in .40 or Glock 33 in .357 will approximate the power level of a .357 Magnum revolver if you choose the right ammo, and will be the same size "package" to carry as a small frame Magnum, but with lighter weight and ten shot cartridge capacity instead of five or six. A friend of mine in the South had his Glock 27 on when an alligator approached his small rowboat; he put a .40 slug in the critter's head, and it thrashed into a death roll and sank beneath the surface before it could reach the boat.

If wearing a gun visibly on the property is not in keeping with your family values, lifestyle, or local social conventions, you might want something smaller for all day wear with discreet concealment. A small .357 Magnum

Suitable for all-the-time carry, the light and compact baby Glock is available in powerful calibers like .40 S&W. One of the author's friends used a little .40 cal. Glock 27 like this one to stop an attacking 'gator with one shot.

Military pistols like this Beretta 9mm offer high durability and minimal maintenance needs.

revolver is the ticket here. Rossi, Ruger, Smith & Wesson, and Taurus all produce short barrel, five shot .357s which are suitable for this application. My own choice in this category, hands down, would be the Ruger SP101 with two and a quarter inch barrel, loaded with 125 grain hollow point .357 Magnum ammo. The little Ruger snubby is as accurate at 25 yards as a much larger service revolver, and is by far the most rugged of the small frame .357s, as well as the most comfortable to shoot.

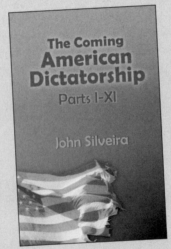

If concealment is not a factor, my choice for all day wear on the belt if a powerful handgun was needed would be a .44 Magnum. I'm partial to the Smith & Wesson Model 629 with four-inch barrel. We owe the concept of this particular S&W, and the .44 Mag cartridge itself, to the aforementioned Elmer Keith. The recoil is notoriously vicious, but if you've paid your dues in training and practice, there is no more practical high-powered handgun for all day carry, whether you're talking dangerous game or large farm animals that turn ugly on you.

General advice

Backwoods life, whether on the farm or in the woods, can be hard. Hard on the people, hard on the clothing, and hard on the equipment. That's why a true backwoodsman's pants are more likely to wear the Carhartt label than Tommy Hilfiger or Gucci. It's also why the backwoods firearm needs to be a rugged, heavy-duty design.

You don't want a gun that requires constant maintenance. At the same time, you always want to take care of your tools. That goes double for tools whose mission can include emergency rescue, which is definitely the job description of backwoods household firearms. Wipe them down regularly, and lubricate your autoloading guns monthly, even if they haven't been fired. A semiautomatic's parts have long bearing surfaces, and won't work well if not lubricated. Lubricant is generally liquid: it can evaporate or drain out of the gun, irrespective of whether it is actually fired.

Firearms are the ultimate durable consumer goods. Many people get pleasure from hunting and shooting with their parents' or grandparents' guns. Few of us use Dad's old clothes washer or drive Grandpa's old car. The maintenance you give your firearms will preserve them for generations to come, who will cherish these functional heirlooms.

Don't neglect safe storage issues. The gun wants to be where you can reach it immediately, but unauthorized persons cannot reach it and activate it at all.

It ain't easy. It's about being responsible. But, hey, if you weren't into that, you wouldn't be into backwoods living. Δ

Ask Jackie

Jackie Clay

If you have a question about rural living, send it in to Jackie Clay and she'll try to answer it. Address your letter to *Ask Jackie*, PO Box 712, Gold Beach, OR 97444. Questions will only be answered in this column. — Editor

How long to hang meat?

Hi, I was just wondering the reason for hanging meat for a period of time and for how long? For example, moose meat.

Rob Gibeault
legroslk@hotmail.com

The reason for hanging meat is that the enzymes in the meat begin to break down tougher fibers in the meat, making it more tender. In effect, this is the pre-spoilage stage; if the meat hangs too long, it will begin to decay. This is why you hear so many reports of "gamey" tasting meat. It has simply hung too long, often with little or no care. You can't hang an animal in a tree out in the sun, especially when the temperatures fluctuate to the 40s or even 50s during the day, then dip lower at night, for days on end. This is even worse when the animal was not properly cleaned out and skinned. (You sure wouldn't go buy a nice roast from the store and do that, huh?)

Another reason we hang our meat is so that I can cut it into workable chunks to jerk and can. For instance, I've found that I can quarter a deer or moose and process one forequarter, plus the backstrap in one day, a hind quarter in another day, the neck and tenderloins another day, and so on.

In optimum conditions, say in a locker plant, meat can be hung for 14 days. We don't have these conditions at home, so we try to get our meat to hang about seven days before processing. But that is with the weather cooperating, of course. If it turns unexpectedly warm, we process that meat right *now*, rather than risk having off-flavored meat or spoilage.

For this reason, we also hunt only when the weather is favorable. I've passed up many a game animal because the day was getting too warm for good meat handling, no matter how fast I field dressed it and got ice into the body cavity.

In really cold weather, your meat can hang longer, but it is hard to cut up frozen carcasses unless you use a chain saw, axe, or good hand saw.

— Jackie

Canned potatoes

Canned some new potatoes. Is it ok if the bottom of the jars have white sediment on them? Is it from the starch in the potatoes? Thanks.

Carol Raup
C_Raup@hotmail.com

Yes, this sediment is perfectly natural. It is partly starch and partly just fine potato particles. If you are making soup or stew, just dump in the whole jar. Or if this is too much water in the recipe, pour out some then use the sediment. It is also a great ingredient for bread, making the bread rise better and taste naturally sweeter. Love those home canned potatoes.

— Jackie

Freezer-burned meat

I was given lots of pork ribs, beef, and chicken with bits of freezer burn on it What a shame. I would like to know if I can cook with it and is it safe to eat?

Alice Costa
mawicker@rcn.com

Sorry, Alice. I, too have been given lots and lots of freezer burned meat in my time and, try as I might, I just have never found a way to use it that I couldn't taste the nasty, clawing taste of freezer burn in the resulting food. And I have used some really spicy recipes, too.

While it is safe to eat, it just doesn't taste good.

What I've done is to cook up a big pot of this meat, along with vegetables and rice, and after removing the bones, made stew for our dogs. They love it and at least you get some benefit from all that lost meat.

— Jackie

Acidic tomato sauce

In issue 89, on page 71, a letter on acidic tomatoes—the solution is simple. Instead of sugar, and depending on the quantity of the tomato sauce, use a half teaspoon to a teaspoon of baking soda (sodium bicarbonate) and mix. It is a simple chemical reaction of neutralizing the acidity of the tomato sauce. But if you use too much baking soda you will ruin the taste of the sauce, so try a little at a time until it tastes right.

Robert D'Andrea
Spring Lake, NJ.
modena@optonline.net

Yes, Robert, you're right. You can use the baking soda instead of sugar. I've found that most folks prefer the additional sugar to the sauce with the baking soda, but it's probably not good for us.

— Jackie

Swinging gate

I am looking for plans to build a gate in a fence that a rider can push down while he's on the horse and the gate swings open. As the rider passes through, the rider pulls a rope on the other side and the gate swings closed. I've seen these on trails but can't figure out how to build one.

David Zimmerman
zimaxinc@cinci.rr.com

You've got me, David. I've ridden all my life and have never seen such a gate. Sounds better than dismounting, then remounting on the other side every time you pass through the gate. Especially with my bad bones. Any readers who are horsemen have an idea to help us all?

— Jackie

When I was young my dad used to buy sausage making supplies (spices & seasonings) from Sedro's Industries in Rochester, NY. I found an old catalog from them but do not know what happened to the company. I am trying to purchase the same spices & seasonings we used. Hopefully you can help. The reason I am contacting you is Phyllis Hobson advertised in the catalog so maybe someone knows what happen to them?

Steve Shanley
Stillwater, MN
sshanley@comcast.net

Chicken feed

Thanks for the scratch-feed idea in issue 88. I didn't know that was an option, and have been feeding chick starter for new chicks, grower for the older chicks, and mash for the laying hens. I have found a mash without meat by-products in it, although it has fish meal. Is that any better than what you have seen produced? I've become frustrated this season trying to keep separate all the different ages of birds and their respective feeds, seeing as the older birds would rather steal in and eat the baby food. I've wondered what farmers 100 years ago fed their chicks. What do you feed yours? Do you grind up the scratch feed so that it's easier for the babies, or do you feed starter and the like? I'm ready to switch to one feed for all ages, but don't want to short-change anybody. As we live in north-central Minnesota, would you recommend adding anything to the scratch (other than vegetable scraps) for the chickens in the winter?

Faye Lilyerd
lilyerd@ncis.com

I start my hatchery baby chicks on commercial chick starter, but as soon as they feather out and become more active, I switch them to scratch feed. To boost up the protein, they also get lots of goat milk and whey from cheese making. They have a pan of it in front of them, just as they do water. It does attract flies in the summer, but the chicks snap them up for dessert.

In the old days, farmers would start their chicks on coarsely ground grains soaked in milk, buttermilk, and whey, along with mashed hard boiled eggs. This works fine. I've done it but it is labor intensive.

My northern Minnesota chickens got scratch feed for 20 years, summer and winter. And they still do. But I do supplement it with vegetable scraps, soaked alfalfa pellets (or fine hay leaves), and milk. They come through the winter in fine shape. If you are pushing for egg production, as do commercial flocks, this will not make copious eggs. But it will supply a homestead nicely.

— Jackie

Chinese chestnuts

After reading everything you have shared with BHM for the last three years I can't find an article on what to do with Chinese chestnuts a neighbor planted 40 years ago and are now abandoned for all, but the deer and me.

Carl and Inge Harmon
bullseye10@wfeca.net

Lucky you! Chinese chestnuts are large, sweet, and the trees are very hardy. Also a bonus is the fact that the burrs in which the nuts grow are squirrel-proof until the nut ripens and they split open. Then you'd better hurry or the little buggers will beat you to the harvest. After you harvest your nuts, let them dry in a single layer somewhere out of the weather where the squirrels can't get to them. This increases their sweetness and prevents molding.

Once the nuts are dry, you can store them in a burlap sack, stirring them around once in a while, in a dry location until you have time to peel them to use. As you know, chestnuts have a relatively thin shell with a large, sweet nutmeat.

You can shell your harvest by either roasting or boiling which makes the shell easier to penetrate. To roast them (unless you want to roast chestnuts by an open fire...), simply lay a layer of them on a cookie sheet and bake in your oven at about 350° F for about 15 minutes. Stir once or twice to make sure they roast evenly. Then cut the shell open with a sharp knife and peel.

To boil them, cut an X on the flat side of the shell of the chestnuts, then drop them in water and simmer for 17 minutes. (Any bad nuts will float to the top right away after you drop them in.) Then take the nuts out of the water, drain and peel, removing any clinging skins with a knife.

You can then puree the boiled nuts to use in a variety of recipes, using them as a vegetable, such as in stir fries, soups, breads, cakes, etc. The Indians of several tribes combined mashed chestnuts with squash for use in little cakes.

The roasted nuts can be laid out in a single layer after peeling, then salted and re-roasted for just long enough to make the oil in them hold the salt. They are pretty darned good that way. Eat hearty.

— *Jackie*

Squash and spaghetti sauce

Hi Jackie...HELLLLLLP! Have been searching through all my back issues of BHM for your recipe for making and canning spaghetti sauce, but still haven't found it. I remember you added summer squash among other veggies, and since our garden has been very prolific this year, I'm trying to get everything I can in the freezer, canned, or dehydrated.

What is the best way to preserve winter squash? We like it on the dry side like mashed potatoes with butter and a little brown sugar. I've frozen it before but found it soupy. We live in a mobile home on 1.1 acre (in Michigan) without a root cellar to keep veggies through the winter.

Alice
agwlco@yahoo.com

You know, Alice, I don't remember writing a recipe for making spaghetti sauce with summer squash and other veggies in it. I'll tell you this, I incorporate squash in a heck of a lot of recipes that it's not "supposed" to be in, though. What I usually do, regarding spaghetti sauce and squash, is to bake a spaghetti squash, then cut it in half on a cookie sheet. Remove any seeds and fluff up the strings. Then I dump a quart of home canned spaghetti sauce over it, sprinkle liberally with grated Mozzarella cheese and bake until the cheese is lightly tan in spots. That tastes divine.

You can chop up your summer squash and add it to about anything, from pickles to your spaghetti sauce and no one will be the wiser, as it doesn't have much of a taste until you do something with it. I even slice it thin and add to my cucumber and onions with sour cream.

I can chunks of squash to use if we should run out of fresh squash. I don't have a root cellar either, and simply store my squash under the bed, next to the cold wall and out of the light. To can it this way, just cut up two-inch chunks of raw squash, place it in your wide mouth canning jar, add a teaspoon full of salt if you want, and cover the squash to within an inch of the top of the jar with boiling water. Then process the jars for 90 minutes at 10 pounds of pressure (unless you live at an altitude above 2,000 feet, then check your canning manual for instructions).

When you use the home canned squash, drain off the water, place in a baking dish in the oven, pat with butter and sprinkle with brown sugar. Bake until done or as dry as you like. We, too, don't like mushy squash.

Don't forget to use your squash in "pumpkin" pies for the best pies imaginable, in breads, bars, casseroles, and egg nog. Get creative. It's more versatile than most people realize. I dry quite a bit of squash, then grind it to flour and add it to my whole wheat bread. No one ever guesses, and I sure don't tell 'em.

— *Jackie*

Purple eyed pea jelly?

I am searching for a recipe for Purple Eyed Pea Jelly for home canning purposes. Can you help me?

Charlene Evans
cen89311@centurytel.net

I can't help you on this one, Charlene. I've never even *heard* of Purple Eyed Pea Jelly. Can anyone out there give Charlene a hand? And, please let me know, too.

— *Jackie*

Horseradish recipe

I can't find a recipe for horseradish. Do you have one or know of someone who may have one I could get? I have one plant I planted this summer. I would love to make relish from it next year. Thank you for your time.

Joe
JC0320@aol.com

Your plant may, or may not have roots large enough to grate for horseradish this fall. To use the root, dig the plant carefully and deeply. The roots are quite long. Then wash the root well and trim the top and little side roots off. Carefully peel the root. You may want to process the horseradish outside as it is very strong and your eyes and nose will run like no onion has every made them run.

Simply grate the root with a vegetable grater or give it a whiz in your old blender. I say "old" blender, because you sometimes can't get the taste and smell of the horseradish out of a blender jar. I've got an old one I got at the dump and I use it for chopping dehydrated onions and horseradish, as well as garlic. I don't want my terrific smoothies and milk shakes tasting like those strong vegetables.

You can mix the grated root with vinegar if you like really strong horseradish. Then simply keep this in the refrigerator in a closed jar. Or you can mix the vinegared horseradish with mayonnaise for a milder, smoother version of this pungent condiment. I can't imagine a roast without it. Good eating.

— Jackie

Canning cabbage

I am trying to find how to can cabbage.

Chris Watts
chrisw348@comcast.net

Cabbage is very easy to can. It does get a bit strong when put up that way, but I just dump out the water in which it was canned and simmer it in fresh water or milk.

To can cabbage, cut it into smaller chunks with the heart removed or slice it. Cover the cabbage with boiling water in a large pot and simmer for three minutes to wilt down the cabbage and make more fit into a jar. Dip the cabbage out and pack into jars, packing tightly. Add a teaspoon full of salt to each quart, if desired. Add hot liquid that the cabbage was boiled in to cover the cabbage to one inch of the top. Process the jars for 30 minutes at 10 pounds of pressure (unless you live at an altitude above 2,000 feet; consult your canning manual for directions).

This cabbage works well in boiled dinners, stews, soups, and other mixed dishes. A favorite way to use it at our house is to drain it well, rinse, then lightly fry in just a little butter. When it is lightly browned, add fresh milk and simmer. It's simple and very good.

— Jackie

Dangers of water bath canning

I am trying to find my mom a recipe for water bath canning for green beans.

She's looking for just a basic recipe that uses some type of acid, lemon juice, etc.

She canned like this years ago but has forgotten how.

She does not own a pressure cooker and has no intentions of buying one.

Vera
verarob@netnitco.net

Sorry Vera, but there's just no safe recipe for water bath canning green beans unless she pickles them. For instance she could make dilly beans, mustard yellow bean pickles, etc. Many, many people used to water bath process their bean, corn, and even meat. But it just is not safe. One of the biggest dangers is *botulism*, a sure killer that is both odorless and tasteless. Using a water bath to can low-acid items like green beans is the same as letting your children play with a loaded gun.

I'm sorry your mom is not interested in buying a pressure canner. They are *so easy and safe to use*. And the canning takes much less time, too.

— Jackie

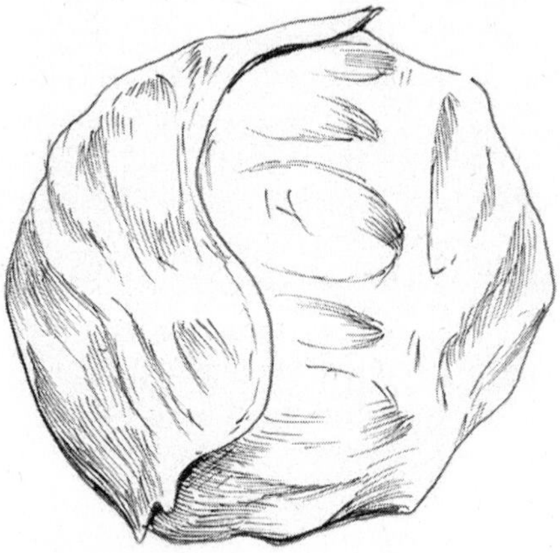

An excess of zucchini

I don't know why, but I can only manage to get zucchini by the bushel. I plant "just a little" and it all dies. I plant too much and every single seed sprouts and flourishes with no bugs. This year I tried to strike a balance by planting several different kinds of squash. Guess what prevailed?

Anyway, I need to know what to do with it all. I remember my mother canning summer squash one year and it was an awful mushy mess. I've noticed that if you fry apples before canning, they will stay "sliced apples" instead of turning to applesauce. Would the same thing work for summer squash? I've tried pickling it, and didn't really care for the results. I've had some success sneaking limited quantities into soups, sauces, etc.

Secondarily, what about animal feed? Will cows and pigs eat this stuff? My chickens won't—not even the very small ones. A number of years ago, a neighbor had cows in the field adjacent to me and I tossed the very large zucchinis to them. They wouldn't touch them, but these were some pretty huge zucchini (they didn't bust when you threw them).

Charlotte
CPatrick@washgas.com

Ahhh, the zucchini story! Here in Minnesota, the only time you lock your truck is during zucchini season; if you come out of church, your truck cab will be full of canoe-sized squash.

Okay, what does one do with all that squash? Everything! My dearest and best friend, Gloria makes the *best* bread and butter pickles from guess what? Substitute it for any cuke in a pickle recipe and your family will love you.

Gee, I can apples all the time, and don't have them turn to applesauce. I either halve the little ones or slice them to bake in pies and other desserts and they come out very nice. But I do not use Macintosh apples. My folks had an apple orchard and we kiddies called them "Mackinquashes" because they cooked down to mush quickly.

To can your summer squash, wash and slice. Don't remove the skin unless the squash is old and the skin is tough. The skin helps the squash hold its shape. Slice into half-inch slices, then halve or quarter them to fit into the jar. Pack tightly in jars and cover with boiling water to within an inch of the top. Process the jars for 25 minutes for pints and 30 minutes for quarts.

Yes! Cows and pigs will eat squash. So will chickens. You might have to train them at first, by whacking a few of them up. I used to work on a ranch where the owner raised corn and squash for his animals. One of my jobs was to rope shocks of corn and drag them out to spread out over the fence for the stock. Then I dragged a big canvas back to the shock and loaded it with squash, kept under the shock to keep it from freezing. They all ate the big squash with relish. And my own animals now also munch squash of all kinds down happily. The skins may turn your animals off if they have never eaten it before.

David likes to jump on squash to "help" the critters get at them. He calls it "hop squash."

— Jackie

Canning mistake?

I have just started canning and I think I made a mistake and I am wondering how crucial a mistake it is. I made pickles on the weekend and I water bathed them but I did not cover the jars with water (I got confused and thought that I should keep water from going over the tops). I sterilized the jars and lids before filling them, the brine boiled up nice and hot and all of my jars sealed perfectly. Is this a terrible problem? I don't want to poison my family.

Deana Lehmann Mooers
deana.lehmannmooers@stackpole.ca

It's probably just fine. Certainly not a terrible problem. And you will not poison your family with your pickles.

The absolute worst thing that could happen is that the seals could fail. Unnoticed, any pickles that are not in the vinegar might turn dark or go soft. But pickles are *so acidic* that some recipes for pickles do not even require water bath processing. The reason that the water should go over the jars is so you ensure that all of the food and the complete jar is equally heated. Just look at your pickles before serving them. If they look good, smell good, and are not gooshy soft, they will make you proud.

— Jackie

Pressure canner advice

I am looking into buying a pressure canner and would like your input as to whether the weighted type or the gauged type is better. Thanks.

Matt Stone
ms191@hotmail.com
Hyde Park, NY

I much prefer the pressure canners with a gauge over the weighted types. In that way, you can see exactly what is going on—before it happens and surprises you. But both types work fine. Mom has used a weighted jiggly vent canner for years and years. And who do you suppose taught me to can?

— Jackie

Gardening in Alaska

I thought I would bring to your attention something I have learned since I started gardening in Alaska. According to a book, Alaska Gardening Guide, by Ann Roberts, on page 182/183 there is chapter and verse re: the use of clear plastic vs. black plastic.

In a nutshell, clear is better because it lets the light through to the soil. The weed seeds that germinate do not set seed and lift the plastic for a 'greenhouse effect' and then they can be tilled back for green manure. We have a different sun angle that needs the magnification the clear can also provide.

There is lots more in that chapter and better said than my paraphrase.

Everything else you suggested to the lady in Tok was dead on. I have raised beds and some of them have a layer of Styrofoam insulation in the bottom (also suggested by the book). My tomatoes were happy to have warm toes. Happy gardening,

DeNise
info@remotewatersystems.com

Milk and canning soup

Can you can potato soup with the milk already added? Thanks,

Merlin
Merlin461@aol.com

You can home can potato soup with the milk added to it, but I don't think you'll like the results. The milk gives a curdled appearance to the soup which we find unappetizing. It is so easy to just can chunks of potato, then when you're ready to make soup, just make a white sauce using two tablespoons of margarine melted in a saucepan to which you add two tablespoons of flour stirred in to make a paste. Then you should slowly add milk until you get a thickness to the sauce that you like. Finally, add a quart jar of *drained* potatoes for a nice pot of potato soup.

— Jackie

A goat vs. a cow

I'm so glad to hear you've moved to Minnesota! I could tell by your letters in Backwoods Home Magazine that you really wanted to move back there.

I too am a misplaced Minnesota girl. I live by Hot Springs, SD. In the country to be sure! It's very arid here. We have no well. That really bothers me, as I too like to depend on no one else other than ourselves.

We built a house and garage. No animals at the time except pets. I can't wait to get milk animals and chickens. The chickens will come this fall, as my mother-in-law will give me her old ones. First I have to get the chicken house built. Then a milk animal. I would prefer goats, but alas my husband hates them. I've had both goats and milk cows in the past. Which is actually the best most efficient animal? Personally I think the goat can't be beat for food to milk production, but is it drastically different between them?

Also do you grow sweet corn for your masa harina or something else?

Also, how do you store your grains from year to year? I know I'm full of questions, but if you were visiting me we would talk for hours! Thanks and I love to read your articles. Wish we were neighbors!

Christine Stabnow
chrimar2@gwtc.net

You're right, Christine, we *would* talk for hours, as I really love talking with fellow homesteaders. To answer your question about a milk animal; I would say your best option, with a goat hating husband, is to get a milk cow. Some spouses can change their minds about certain animals, but you've got to face facts. Many do not. You *might* try taking him to a goat dairy in your area where he can see for himself that goats are really clean, friendly, delightful creatures that *do not smell*. Sometimes a person, such as your husband, has some preconceived ideas about goats. "They eat everything. They climb on the car. They give milk that tastes like a goat. They have long horns and butt your backside." Sound familiar?

Goats are versatile eaters, preferring to browse on twigs and leaves, to only grazing on grass. But they will not touch hay on which you have walked, will not drink water that is the slightest bit dirty, and will never, never eat from an apple which you have taken a bite out of first.

But if your husband is resolved, you'll have to choose a cow to save peace in the family. And a cow is a wonderful addition to a homestead, too. Besides they give so much milk that you can feed a pig to butcher in addition to making butter, cheese, ice cream, and all the rest.

Where a good dairy goat doe will produce a gallon or more every day, a decent cow will give you five or six gallons. That's a lot of milk. Just think of what you can do with it. The down side is that she will have to be milked every day, morning and night. Friends may be happy to feed and water your animals while you are on a trip or sick, but it takes a special friend, indeed, to come milk for you twice a day.

To get out of this predicament, you can keep the calf your cow gives birth to and both bottle feed it and let it suck from his mother. What I do is keep them separate at first while he is small. During that time, I bottle feed him, occasionally letting him out of his pen to suck his mom after I've milked. This keeps the cow letting her milk down for you, but remembering that the calf is her baby. Then when he is larger and will not overeat and get scours (loose stools) from the milk, let him spend the night with her after you have milked. This prevents gorging on milk and teaches them to pasture together. Then, when you have to be away at milking or have a bad case of the flu, you can let mother and child stay together. He will "milk" your cow and do it happily.

You can't do this too often, as his milky slobber will cause her teats to chap and crack painfully. But it is a pretty good temporary fix for a perplexing problem.

Masa harina (corn flour made from hominy), is best made from a flint corn which is shiny, rounded, and hard. Most sweet corns have very small kernels which are dented and soft textured. Sweet corn does, however, make great cornmeal. Most commercial cornmeal is made from flint corn, but meal ground from sweet corn has a less gritty texture and much sweeter taste.

— Jackie

Morning glories as weeds

My garden did great this year. Lots of tomatoes and pumpkins. But I also have morning glory crawling and spreading throughout one of my raised beds. I don't want it to spread any further and I'd love to get rid of it for next year's garden. Any ideas as to how to prepare my soil during the winter as well as in the spring to get rid of this creepy stuff?

Ilene Duffy
Gold Beach, OR

Glad your garden did so well this year. Ahhh, morning glories. Wild ones and tame can sometimes raise heck when they're where you don't want them. If they're in a raised bed you use for annual vegetables, the easiest way to get rid of them is to cover that bed with a chunk of old carpet from the dump. Do it right now and leave it in place until spring is about done with. I've seen nothing that will kill out stubborn weeds like your morning glories like that old carpet. In effect, it cooks the soil with the sun on it and prevents any seeds from germinating. A piece of heavy black plastic will do almost as well. Water the ground if it is not moist, then lay your killer mulch in place. And don't take it up until late spring. Use that bed for your later crops; make another, if you need the space early.

Morning glories or bind weed can get out of hand if not nipped in the bud. Bind weed roots run down over two feet sometimes, and if one little piece is left you've got a new crop. Now why can't sweet corn be that way?

When you plant that previously weedy bed, be on the lookout every couple of days for a sprouting new plant of your enemy and dig it out deeply. If you keep this war up, you'll get rid of it. I promise.

— Jackie

Standing near the top of the trail, looking down. The bright sunny spot in the middle distance will be the site of my future camping "pagoda;" it will have a small view. This portion of the trail, the first we completed, taught us one lesson: Use more steps. The slope here is graceful looking, but it isn't fun to walk on, up or down.

You can turn a "useless" piece of land into a useful one and create something beautiful by building a trail in your backyard. It doesn't even matter whether you have a lot of land or just a small scrap of nature.

In my case, my useless patch was a mere half acre choked with blackberry brambles and other largely impenetrable weed species. Only a few tall trees (all that was left after a 10-year-old clear-cut) poked above the brush. To make it even more useless, the whole area ran so steeply downhill from my cabin that in places you couldn't stand on it.

The original idea was simply to cut a swath through the blackberries to be able to harvest more of them. But as we ground through the brush, small views began to emerge, along with little niches that cried out to have benches, sculpture gardens, or picnic shelters placed in them.

The result—still very much a work in progress—is a steep, winding trail just under a quarter mile long that presents both challenges and surprising beauties.

Opening the trail

Any book on trail building will admonish you to survey carefully before cutting your trail. This is great theory, but not much good when you can't see or walk on the terrain you're working with. In my case, surveying meant standing at the top of the hill, pointing, and saying, "Around that big cedar tree, then over there toward those two pines poking up. Within that area, do whatever works."

Mitsu the golden retriever helped by fetching back every stick or branch we tossed off the trail. Here she sits with a pile of our step-building supplies.

Using a chainsaw, brush-cutter, and a ho-dad (a grubbing hoe), a friend who spent years building fire trails for a local timber company bulled his way into the bramble. I chickened out on doing that part myself, and I'm glad I did. His instinct for which turn to take or which terrain to cross was uncanny, especially given that he couldn't even see most of my landmarks once he was down in the brush.

The trick was to be flexible, to be ready to change our minds, and to consult often about where the path was heading.

It would have been nice to have a loop trail, but we ended up with a one-way path (you have to come back up the hill to the cabin the same way you went down) because there was only one route that worked.

On the upper slopes, we cut openings through the brambles about six feet wide, using the brush cutter and chain saw. Then within that opening we used the ho-dad to level a walking surface (treadway) 30 to 36 inches wide. Lower, where the trail winds its way through more obstacles, our treadway narrowed to as little as 18 inches.

It took about 18 hours to open the trail and to cut (and brace with treated 2x8s) the 30 steps required to get us through the steepest stretches.

Surfacing the trail

Because my soil is a mixture of slick clay, year-round mud, and only a bit of good, dry loam, I decided to surface the trail with gravel. If you live in a place with dryer conditions or more sandy soils, you might not

The steps leading up from the "Godzilla" footbridge. This staircase incorporates several happy accidents. First is the natural handrail on the right, courtesy of a conveniently fallen log. Second is the artsy construction of steps necessitated by the discovery of an old car right in our intended path.

need to surface the entire course. But almost every trail needs rock or gravel fill along some portion.

I chose ¾-minus rock—that is gravel whose largest pieces are ¾-inches, but whose smallest bits are just grit. This turned out to be a great choice; the gritty "minus" part enables the rock to pack down into a stable surface, and the ¾-inch maximum is kind to the feet. This rock was also inexpensive, costing about $5.50 per ton.

The standard calculation says one ton of gravel equals 90 square feet of coverage, 2 inches deep. But there was nothing standard on this project. Depth of the gravel varies from about 1½ inches over good soils to as much as 6 inches in swampy areas, in hollows around tree roots, and at the base of bridges. I bought 12 tons—a full dump-truck load. What doesn't go on the trail will patch my driveway.

One of the experts around the local pot-bellied stove recommended that I start graveling at the farthest end of the trail and work back up, reasoning that if I worked from the trailhead downward repeated trips with the wheelbarrow would tear up the newly graveled surface. That was another good piece of theory that didn't fit the reality. Once we'd grubbed the vegetation out of the treadway with the ho-dad, the exposed clay slopes near the top of the trail became impassibly slippery and had to be graveled ASAP.

Yes, the wheelbarrow did tear up the surface a bit, requiring minor repairs (particularly since I used the barrow's legs as brakes in steep patches). But all the back-and-forthing also helped pack the surface down. Simple fact: If I hadn't graveled the top of the trail first I'd have never made it to the bottom—at least not on my feet.

The "Godzilla" footbridge just after we carried it down from the cabin. I built the framework for this bridge on my deck, figuring that would make it easier to level and square up. I'm about to nail on the decking as my helper Ken trims away a little more of the dense brush that surrounds the trail.

One of several small footbridges. This one crosses a muddy trickle that might someday be a miniature fern-banked streamlet.

Graveling is without a doubt the most time-consuming, labor-intensive part of trail building. In my case, the truckload of rock had to be dumped 100 feet from the trailhead, then carried by wheelbarrow down the very steep upper slopes. Half-way down, the trail becomes too steep, narrow, and twisty for the wheelbarrow. From that spot I had to carry the rest of the gravel in plastic buckets.

I paced myself by hauling a couple of barrow or bucket loads down, then stopping to spread the gravel using the back (not the tines) of a metal rake.

Before I started the bucket portion of the job, the prospect of such primitive, time-consuming donkey-work seemed mind-boggling. My lazy brain had fantasies of hiring a helicopter to ferry scoops of gravel to the otherwise inaccessible trail. But carrying small amounts of rock in buckets actually turned out to be easier and far more relaxing than having my 130-pound self pulled downhill by a heavy, unstable wheelbarrow. The slow-paced work was almost contemplative.

Building bridges and turnpikes

Midway down the slope, we discovered a surprisingly flat area about 150 feet wide. You'd think this was a good thing. But no; it turned out to be far and away the most difficult part of the project (and a portion of the project I'm still working on). This whole area was one giant, muddy seep—so gooey that in places it would suck your shoes off.

It took various tricks to get through Mudville.

Over well-defined rills, or in places where the sucking mud was only a few feet across, I constructed a series of small footbridges. I built them with 2x6 pressure-treated decking screwed onto stringers—no handrails or complex understructures required. (Official trail builders call these simple bridges "puncheons.") I used pressure-treated 4x4s for the stringers.

Some very useful trail-building books (especially *Lightly on the Land: The SCA Trail-Building and Maintenance Manual*, published by The Mountaineers, Seattle, Washington) show how to carve flat-surfaced stringers and make planking out of native logs. If you have a lot of trees, that could save you money and give a nice, natural look.

In my case, however, since I was working in a 10-year-old clear-cut, most of the trees were too young to be useful, the few mature trees were too precious to cut, and any logs lying around were already rotting. I had lots of 4x4s from an old building project, and they were a good choice for stringers. Even in the deep woods, commercial decking is commonly used on puncheons—and it was certainly easier than any alternative.

Trail-building manuals recommend 36-inch-wide bridges for hiking trails (wider for ski or equestrian trails). But with this trail being strictly for personal use, I made my first bridge

This area of the trail was steep and solid clay. The combination made it hard to walk on in the best of times, and really bad after a rainstorm. We graveled this area early to make it passable and built in lots of steps both for comfort and erosion control.

A diagram of one type of turnpike. Essentially, a turnpike is a box made of logs, lumber, or stones. You fill it with pourous materials, top it with gravel or good soil, and rise over soggy spots.

Mudville. This is what the worst section of the trail looks like at the driest time of year. The mud will suck your shoes right off. Temporary boards give us passage while I wait to build a raised turnpike and drainage system.

This is the "Godzilla" footbridge—the first and largest I built. It's 10 feet long and 30 inches across. Although trail-building books recommend at least a 36 inch width for bridges on hiking trails, even 30 was overkill in this case.

30 inches wide—then quickly decided even that was overkill. My remaining bridges were all just 20 inches wide. Since none of them had to cross any vertigo-inducing gullies, and none were more than 10 feet long, they were fine. My 30-inch bridge now looks like the Godzilla of puncheons to me.

Ken, my helper, uses the blunt end of a ho-dad (a grubbing hoe) to hammer the stakes that anchor the stair risers. He used the sharp end of the ho-dad to scalp the vegetation from the treadway.

Generally, I built the framework for the bridges up at my cabin, then carried them down the hill and decked them, using 2½-inch decking screws and a cordless drill with a Phillips screwdriver bit. I figured framing them at the cabin would make it easier to get them both level and square. But it made very little difference. I built one bridge in place and had no difficulties with it.

To anchor the bridges, I laid down several inches of well-tamped gravel at each of the four corners, set the bridge in place, then built up more gravel around the ends of the structure. Where the mud was particularly oozy, or where one corner of the bridge needed to be raised, I set 2x8x16-inch concrete blocks (another leftover from an old construction project) on top of the gravel pad, pressed them in firmly, laid the end of the bridge on them, and built up more gravel around them.

The bridges are quite stable, even in areas where the mud was most soupy.

One muddy stretch was too long and too awful for a footbridge. In that patch I'm in the process of building a turnpike. A turnpike is a raised course which, in conjunction with drainage ditches, lifts the surface of the trail above the seepage.

To build a turnpike, you border the muddy area with a "box" of logs, treated lumber (e.g. 6x6s), railroad ties, or very large (100-pound plus) rocks, anchored well into the ground. Fill the box with more large rocks (if they're available) and spread gravel or good soil on top of those. If rocks aren't available, you can fill your "box" with gravel or good mineral soil. It's very labor-intensive, heavy work. But it gives you a dry trail.

The book *Lightly on the Land* describes other options for coping with wet passages, including simpler options (like a waterbar, which uses a log or line of stones to direct flowing water off the trail). The turnpike is not the easiest option, but it was the most suitable one in this spot.

Coping with surprises

Finding Mudville was only one of many surprises we discovered on this short trail—some pleasant, some not-so-pleasant, and some that caused us to shake our heads before we decided to turn them into opportunities.

For example, one of the "features" beside my trail is the rusted, broken body of a 1950-vintage sedan that someone pushed off the road decades ago. I'd already decided the twisted relic was going to become a trailside "sculpture." (It was easier to call it art than to move it.) What I didn't know was that another part of that old wreck lay directly under the planned trail bed.

We needed to cut a set of steps right in that spot. But with metal buried in the ground, we couldn't drive stakes to hold our 2x8 step supports. So we narrowed and turned the steps so they went around the car's rusted old springs. And I laid concrete blocks, embedded in gravel, instead of staked wooden steps. The effect was quite artsy.

This was a lazy person's solution. A more ambitious trail builder would have found a way to winch the old car body out of there. But now I've got a real conversation piece.

Being flexible and creative was definitely part of the fun of the project. In another case, a tree that was growing nearly horizontal above the trail became a leafy arbor to sit under on hot days.

Cost & fantasies

The total cost of the trail so far has been just over $400—and that's with paying my friend to open the path:

- ✓ $180 — Opening the trail, cutting and bracing the steps
- ✓ $105 — 12 tons of gravel, including delivery
- ✓ $132 — Treated decking, treated lumber for steps, deck screws

That covers all the basics. Once the trail is fully graveled and bridged, though, that's when my fantasies kick in and things could get more expensive. In addition to creating quiet sitting areas and sculpture gardens, there are two spots that simply demand more, more, more. I plan to construct a 6 by 8-foot pagoda near the upper end of the trail for picnicking and sleep-outs. And at the very bottom—where we discovered a dark, peaceful glade with a small, crystal rill babbling through it, a tiny screen-house/meditation chamber with a copper firepit is on my wish list.

This will all cost money. And labor. The sheer effort of getting building materials into these places will be . . .

I built this 7-foot by 20-inch footbridge in place above a tiny hollow where a spring emerges from the hillside. Note the way the 4 x 4 stringer extends beyond the bridge. This was done to create a well for piling up an extra-thick load of gravel. The extra gravel made the bridge more solid and also filled hollows in some tree roots that crossed the path at that spot.

interesting. But that's part of the pleasure of the trail. Like the man who gets warmth from his firewood twice—once when he cuts it and once when he burns it—I'll get years of creative pleasure from building my trail, then years more as I relax and relish what I've created. Δ

A more hard-working trail builder might have found some way to get this ancient car spring out of the treadway. But I thought it made an interesting "feature." It definitely makes a conversation piece. Because part of the old car's steel body was also in this area, I had to go from wooden steps and stakes to concrete block steps.

The last word

The impact of firearms on crime, business, and politics

The other day a news item stated that for the last 10 years the crime rate in the United States has been dropping, but the "experts" don't seem to know why.

Nothing in society is simple, and there are all kinds of factors operating at any one time, but one of the things the media and the so-called experts have apparently overlooked, consciously or unconsciously, is the plethora of new laws that allow law-abiding citizens to carry concealed weapons. Just a few decades ago, there were almost none, but today 37 states have "right-to-carry" laws on their lawbooks. Nine others, plus Washington, D.C., allow carrying with restrictions, and in the remaining four the right is denied.

In the meantime, as state after state considered easing carrying restrictions, gun phobics marched out their sordid descriptions of gunfights in bars and shootouts at traffic accidents. They never materialized. Still, they marched them out, again and again, every time another state considered a right-to-carry law despite the drop in crime that followed the passage of such laws in other states.

Why does right to carry result in reduced crime? In surveys of violent criminals, the number one thing they say they fear is not the police, who almost always get to the scene of a crime after it's over, but an armed citizen. And in his book, *More Guns, Less Crime*, economist John Lott pointed out that in a county-by-county study of all 3,054 counties in the U.S., wherever gun restrictions are relaxed violent crime rates have dropped, with the greatest drops in the counties that had had the most crime. In adjoining states where right to carry was instituted in one state and not the other, crime in the counties in the right-to-carry states went down while, right across the border, crime in the state with restrictions generally went up.

Business and guns

Americans love their guns; and criminals, politicians, and businesses should beware—perhaps with good cause. The number of gun owners is significant. The website for *Reason Magazine* (www.reason.com) cites a Gallup poll taken in the year 2000. About 40 percent of Americans report having guns in their homes. This amounts to as many as 90 million gun owners, and the average gun owner owns about four guns.

When K-Mart hired Rosie O'Donnell as a spokesperson, one of the first things I and several people I know did was to decide not to shop there anymore. A movement materialized on the Internet calling for a K-Mart boycott. Stores like K-Mart work on a very thin profit margin; it doesn't take a large percentage of their shoppers staying away or switching to a competitor to affect their profitability. In the United States, gun ownership is higher in rural rather than urban areas. It may not be coincidental that the least profitable of K-Mart's stores became the rural ones and those are the ones K-Mart's management decided to close on their way to bankruptcy.

In a country where 47 percent of men reported owning guns in their homes, Ace Hardware was committing economic suicide by having O'Donnell as a spokesperson. I stopped shopping at the local Ace as did the publisher of this magazine, and a call on the Internet came out to boycott them until Ace suddenly dropped her. No reason was given, but the protest from customers—men, gun owners—was likely the reason. Ace, at least, didn't have to confront bankruptcy.

Smith & Wesson, the gun manufacturer, caved in to the Clinton trigger locks and saw sales dramatically plunge as a boycott began and they, too, went bankrupt. The company now has new ownership and gun buyers have more or less forgiven the company. But the market reaction by gun owners was clear: "Don't fool with our guns."

Politics and guns

George W. Bush is wishy-washy on guns, but John Kerry never saw an antigun bill he wouldn't sign. Nearing the end of the 2004 campaign, John Kerry's advisors saw the writing on the wall, but just a little too late. They saw he had to pick up some votes in the so-called "red" states and they suddenly had Kerry do a photo shoot looking for all the world like a hunter. But few were fooled and, just as it's hard to tell how much of K-Mart's bankruptcy was caused by gun owner boycotts, it's difficult to tell how many voters that would have voted for Kerry either stayed home or voted for Bush just because of his antigun stance.

In the 2000 election, in several states where gun ownership was high, including Al Gore's home state of Tennessee, Bush eked out victories over antigunner Gore by the slimmest of margins. We'll never know how many votes Gore lost because of his antigun stance, but just a few percent in any one of at least five states would have swung the election to him.

Just as politicians, entertainers, and media types woefully underestimate the number of people who believe in God, despite the number of churches that dot the American landscape, they and many businesses continue to underestimate the number of Americans who believe in the *Second Amendment* and their right to bear arms and want the option to defend their families and themselves. They are blind to this despite the fact that there are more guns in this country than there are people. And these shortsighted people will continue to pay the price for their lack of vision in the future. Δ — **John Silveira**

March/April 2005
Issue #92
$4.95 US
$6.50 CAN
Backwoods Home magazine
practical ideas for self-reliant living
The art of living in small spaces
Cool weather greens
A solar-powered light
Build a germination bed
The painted forever floor
Get a start on spring crops
www.backwoodshome.com
DON CHILDERS

My view

Training for the Boston Marathon

Ever get a wild idea in your head that just won't go away, and you start working on it like crazy? It happens to me all the time. For the past three months I've been in training for the *Boston Marathon* because while jogging on my treadmill one day I got the idea that I should run a marathon, and what better marathon than the most famous of them all. Of course I have to qualify for it first by running a lesser known marathon under a specified time. I'll qualify at the *Portland Marathon* in Oregon in October so I can run the *Boston Marathon* in April, 2006.

Some people think I'm crazy. After all, I have no history of road racing, but have a history of back and neck problems, including a broken back and some fused disks. I've even lost an inch and a half of height as an aging adult. And I've had a mild hernia for a few years. But I'm not deterred; a good idea is a good idea.

Not all of my past ideas have been as good as this one. When I went to Las Vegas to make a living playing blackjack, I went broke quickly and ended up having to take a job as a newspaper reporter to pay the rent. Another time I hurriedly built a second story onto my house without any plans, only to have to tear it off a year later. And in my twenties I made detailed plans to row a boat across the Atlantic Ocean. Fellow *BHM* editor, John Silveira, was in on that one, but another *BHM* editor, Richard Blunt, talked us out of it. It's no wonder that I've developed a reputation among family and long time acquaintances as someone with a lot of wild, screwy ideas.

This marathon idea was off to a good start for the first three months. I steadily increased my time and speed on the treadmill from a half hour to an hour. Between it and light weights and working on a heavy bag, I got my weight down to a solid 160 pounds. But then I felt a tweak in my right ankle. It may have been just pain from the scar tissue left from a couple of broken ankles of years ago, but I apparently overcompensated with my running style and that led to my knee getting sore until finally, and suddenly, my back turned to rubber. I'm now back to walking slowly, and carefully, on the treadmill.

I haven't given up. Far from it. I've just begun to tame this idea. But a lot of other people think I'm nuts, and believe it's another manifestation of my off kilter ideas.

Wild ideas bother a lot of people, especially people who never seem to get any wild ideas. But not all wild ideas are as bad as the ones I've mentioned above. When I was 20, John Silveira and I decided to hitchhike around the country, from coast to coast and border to border. Our families were upset with us and insisted we should be out earning college tuition, but three months later we finished a 9,000-mile hitchhiking trip that we still talk about 40 years later. We rate it as one of the best things we've ever done.

Dave Duffy

And don't forget, this magazine comes from my wild idea to quit my well paying job, move to the wilderness, and live simply and satisfactorily beyond the clutches and problems of mainstream society.

People like me who consistently conceive of wild ideas and try to carry them out are in the minority in the world. I suspect many of *BHM's* readership share my wild idea mentality because they have taken, or contemplate taking, great risks with their lives by moving into the country. Some have even thrown off their high salaried corporate jobs and begun risky home businesses.

But the majority of people in America would consider such moves foolish. They take no chances and they act on no wild ideas that pass their way. In fact, most advocate against them, preferring instead that everyone do as they do, namely follow a safe and "sensible" path through life.

Having wild ideas is, I think, part of a philosophical view of life that says you can do anything you want with your life, no matter what the obstacles are, no matter who says you can't. You just put one foot in front of the other and your idea, or your dream, will become reality sooner or later. Giving up is not an option, but failure is acceptable so long as you go on to another equally ambitious idea.

Life is full of naysayers who say you can't move way out into the country, cut wood, grow a garden, store food, and take care of yourself and family without any help from the outside world. They've never done it, so why should you.

If you've got a good idea, whether it involves moving to the country, running a marathon, or anything else you want to do, give it a try. If you fail, learn the lesson of that failure and try again. If you realize only one of your "wild" dreams, that'll be one more than those who played it safe and never pursued their dreams at all. ***— Dave Duffy***

Couponing, refunding, and stockpiling will make your money stretch

By Mary Kenyon

Seven years ago, when my brother John helped us move into our current country home, he commented wryly, "If you ever fill those cupboards upstairs I don't want to help you move again." Once a sickroom in the older brick home, someone had converted it into wall to wall cupboards and drawers. Now, seven years later, not only are the cupboards full, but I've managed to fill each and every nook and cranny of our spacious home and the stockpiling has spilled into our hallways.

Open one of the cupboards and you'd see neatly stacked gift items waiting for Christmas or one of the birthdays of my eight children, son-in-law, or my granddaughter. I add to this stash year-round as I find gifts on clearance or at sidewalk sales. Open any of the other cupboards and you'd think you had just stepped into a discount store; dozens of deodorants, toothpaste, body washes, and bottles of shampoo are stored inside. Drawers hold toothbrushes, razors, and band-aids. Packages of toilet paper are stacked neatly behind the closet door, and in a pyramid in the hallway. Kitchen cupboards are packed with canned goods and bagged cereal.

Y2K fanatic? Compulsive shopper? No, this is something more insidious, something I have been doing since getting married as a college student, 25 years ago, and that has become more of a necessity since the births of eight children. In a home where it is not unusual to go through a tube of toothpaste and a bottle of shampoo each week, my method of stockpiling using coupons has become a defense mechanism against the high cost of living. While my country living female peers spend hours laboring over their hot stoves in the August heat to preserve their harvest I would more likely be found in an air-conditioned store clearance aisle. While other women might be sewing their own clothing or making their own soap, I am just as likely to be finding clothing for my family at a 25-cents thrift store tag sale and getting my soap free during my weekly trip into town. As a busy homeschooler, freelance writer, and book seller, I choose to spend at least one day a week combining my usual book hunt with shopping sprees at discount stores and thrift stores. And I've found a different way to fill my shelves with very little money invested. I use coupons!

The Kenyons insulate their hallway with the toilet paper packages Mary purchased for 75 cents a package after coupons, vs. the usual retail price of $2.89 each in her area. Daughters Emily, age 7, and Katie, age 4, enjoyed a game of stacking the packages in a pyramid.

I started using coupons when I got married in 1979 and wanted to save money on our paltry $20 a week grocery bill. My use of coupons has increased exponentially with the births of each of our children. By child number four I wasn't just saving 40 percent off at the grocery store with coupons, I was also sending in for nearly $100 a month on refunds on the products I bought. For years I had access to double couponing and started stockpiling the products I was getting for free or nearly free with coupons. I replenished my supply of coupon inserts weekly at the local recycling center. For a few years, most of my Christmas shopping consisted of free premiums from refund offers and my files of UPCs and product packaging. My children loved their free tee shirts, stuffed animals, radios, and balls.

Those were the heyday years for refunders and couponers alike. Refund offers now require specifically dated receipts and it has been several years since I lived near a friendly recycling center or a store that doubled coupons. In the past few years my greatest savings have come through combining clearance or sale prices with high-value coupons. Each time I enter a discount or grocery store I search for clearance shelves or baskets. As a homeschooling family we attend a lot of book sales in towns within a 50-mile radius. We often stop at local discount stores in those towns and search their clearance aisles with my large coupon box in tow. It is not unusual for me to empty a shelf of clearance deodorant and walk out of a store paying only the tax or a few cents for my cart-full.

Stockpiling is smart shopping, especially if you have a large family as I do, and you might already be doing it on a small-scale, buying several of a product when it goes on sale. But stockpiling is even smarter when you are combining coupon savings with those sale prices. Getting started in couponing, refunding, and stockpiling is easy, and you can get as involved as you want, using a few coupons a week, or doing it as a part-time hobby as I do. My job as a stay-at-home mother is to make sure our meager budget stretches as far as possible.

Getting organized

Some advice to get you started in couponing and stockpiling;

1) ***Clip and save every high-value coupon, even if it is for something you don't normally use.***

Buy a Sunday paper and clip the coupon inserts faithfully. If there is a coupon on a product you always use or a high-value coupon on something you often see on sale, ask for extra coupon inserts from neighbors, friends, relatives or co-workers. Ask the librarian at your local library if you can have the inserts from their papers. You can even go online and order more of the coupons on eBay.com or sites such as www.couponclippers.com. Never pay more than 10 cents on the dollar for your coupons or it just defeats the purpose of using coupons to save money in the first place. I have paid as much as a dollar for a coupon worth $7.99, but normally pay a 10-cent fee per $1 coupon. There are also websites for couponers to trade coupons, such as www.Kachinaweb.com or www.Refundcents.com. One area of the country might have a $1 coupon available, whereas another might have a "Buy One, Get One Free" coupon out. I've traded $2 dishwasher detergent coupons for $1 dish soap coupons since I don't have a dishwasher, so now I have shelves of the dish soap I can use. And the 40 bottles stored away were free because of trading.

The reason for buying or trading for multiples of coupons you would use? You never know when you might stumble across a clearance aisle or sale on an item marked down low enough to get it free or for pennies with the coupon. Or, if it is a product you use a lot of, you will want more than one coupon so you can buy several when it is on sale.

2) ***Keep your coupons organized.***

All that clipping and sorting into categories isn't going to do you any good if you forget to bring your coupons with you when you go to the store. Most discount stores sell coupon holders with built-in dividers and these are wonderful when you are just starting out. You will soon outgrow that size, though, and want to invest in something bigger, like a large plastic shoebox holder with index cards between the categories. Some coupon users like to organize their coupons in school binders with the clear sports card holders for organizing their coupons. You can also buy a plastic box made specifically for coupons. My favorite is sold at www.RefundCents.com. This site also has information about using the binder method of coupon organization, as well as trading boards and information on saving money in other ways.

3) ***Keep an eye on weekly sale ads.***

Besides the coupon inserts, the ads section are the first thing I read each Sunday. When my favorite razors go on sale for half-price and I have 20 $2-off coupons, that's the time to use my coupons. Learn which stores price-match and take all your ads to that store so you don't have to run all over town bagging your bargains. Watch for Free After Rebate (FAR) items, and don't forget to use your coupon on those, and send for the rebate, too. Stores like Walgreens and Rite-Aid have monthly rebate booklets and if you shop right you should be able to make a monthly profit by using coupons on their FAR items. Some stores let you use your manufacturer's coupons along with their store coupons for even more savings. I recently stocked up on a particular brand of shampoo the store had a $1.50 coupon for, and for which I also had $1 manufacturer's coupons. Final tally? 20 bottles of shampoo for tax only!

4) ***Always check clearance aisles and reduced bins.***

I have gotten some of my best deals on marked down health and beauty items, getting products for free or for a few pennies each using coupons on clearanced products. While my family might prefer one brand of deodorant, I'm not going to pass up 10-cent deodorant and can always sell some at a garage sale, donate to a food pantry or shelter (they don't ever get enough of that kind of product), or allow my adult children to raid my closet once in awhile. Last year I filled a big basket with extra items as one of their Christmas gifts. After filing her own cupboards last year with my gifts, my oldest daughter, Elizabeth, decided she, too, wanted to start stockpiling and has started her own coupon file.

5) ***Stock up on the cheapest items and find a place for storage of stockpiled items.***

If you find shampoo marked down to $1 a bottle, and you have 20 $1-off coupons in your coupon box, buy 20 bottles. If you don't have extra cupboard or closet space, you can store Rubbermaid-type containers full of shampoo in your own closet or even under your bed. If you are worried about the shelf life of some of the stored products, call the toll-free numbers listed on the packages for information on expected shelf life. I rotate my stockpile of things like toothpaste, making sure we use the oldest tubes first.

I will admit my children got tired of a brand of bagged cereal when I came home with 30-plus bags for free with my coupons several months ago. I still have some left and while they don't want it for breakfast anymore, I am sure that after another week or two of hot cereal or muffins they will be happy to enjoy the treat of cold cereal again.

6) *Don't forget the rebates.*

Coupon inserts have refund forms amongst the coupons and you can often find FAR offers directly on the products and packaging, especially on the new products that come out. Good coupons in the inserts on a new product will come out about the same time a rebate does, so a wise use of your coupon combined with the refund sometimes means you actually make money on the product. Send for your refund immediately when you get home from the store so you don't forget, and don't forget to ask for a separate receipt if you are buying more than one product for a refund because you will need separate receipts for each.

7) *Think outside of the box regarding uses for your stockpiles.*

I recently traded a box full of soaps, cleaners, and toothpaste for a goat for my daughter. I let the owner of the goat raid my cupboards and choose what she estimated was worth the $25 goat price to her. I have also filled baskets with extra bath soaps and deodorants as Christmas gifts. My siblings were thrilled last year to get a new shower puff along with 10 bottles of shower soap. My cost for the gift? Only $1.59 for the body puff.

Does this sound like too much work? That's the complaint I most often hear when I share the details of my couponing/refunding lifestyle. "It's just pennies," one sister commented, "I don't have time for that." Maybe so, but I regularly save 2000 to 3000 pennies at the grocery store each week and even more at the discount stores with my coupons. Those "pennies" really add up. And my family knows if they run out of something liked deodorant, toothpaste, or shampoo, there's more where that came from in a cupboard just a few steps away. And the best thing of all? It was either free or nearly free. Δ

The forever floor

By David Lee

It is pretty devious starting off an article with an exaggeration but now that I have your attention let me tell you about a floor surfacing method I have been using over the years that performs better than what you are used to. It is waterproof for outside applications. It is easily repaired when damaged. It is slip resistant and easy to clean. It can be fitted into difficult or complicated locations. It comes in any color or style you can imagine and can be redecorated easily at any time. Best of all, it allows you to express your artistic talent. Plus this surfacing method isn't limited to being used only on a floor. With proper care it could quite possibly last forever.

A good, long lasting floor needs a solid, fairly smooth subfloor. Concrete certainly qualifies but the most likely surfaces are plywood or

Three background colors are used on this floor. Repainting the various colored "tiles" does not have to be done all at the same time, nor do they need to be repainted the same color. Floor colors can gradually be changed over time.

an old floor that needs refinishing. When I show you how this system is applied you can decide what will be involved in preparing the surface for your individual project. I have had some interesting results covering less than uniform floors by using this method.

Once the floor is stable, dry, clean, and all holes larger than .30 caliber have been filled with wood putty you can begin. This system uses Plastic Roof Cement (PRC) to bond 90# roll roofing to the floor. I know, you're shocked. Before you turn the page muttering something about 'tar paper shacks' just bear with me a few more minutes.

The roofing material for this job must have complete mineral coverage. Some manufacturers leave a two-inch lap strip. You don't want that. Be sure to check each roll in order to get the right stuff. Exchanging heavy rolls of roofing annoys everyone involved. The color you buy does not matter.

Putting the floor down

Measure and accurately cut a length of 90# roofing that just fits the room from wall to wall. Using a measuring tape, tee square, and a sharp utility knife, cut the roofing material on the backside, not the mineral side. Lay it down on the floor on one side of the room. Be sure it lays flat. If you have mopboards, and even if you don't, be very accurate with your cuts and placement. Now roll up four or five feet of the piece of roofing so that the mineral side is inside the rolled up part.

Use a small hand brush or a large paint brush to remove the last bits of dirt and dust. Then, with a large putty knife, trowel, or similar tool, extract some PRC (Plastic Roofing Cement) from a five-gallon bucket and place blobs of it on the part of the floor you just uncovered. Spread the PRC with a serrated trowel. I use a 3/8-inch serrated trowel for most projects. Work slowly and apply an even thickness (3/8 inch) to completely cover the work area. Small indentations, nail holes, floor seams, and other minor imperfections should be filled with PRC.

Flooring being applied showing tools and a 5-gallon PRC bucket

Roll the roofing back down onto the floor. Go to the other end of the piece of roofing and roll it up to where the PRC is just beginning to be exposed. Put yourself and your bucket of PRC on the covered section of floor behind the roll. Blob and spread PRC ahead of the roll and work your way across the room unrolling the material as you go. Take your time doing this part of the job. Too much PRC makes a lumpy floor that won't last. Too little is better than too much. A firm continuous bond is imperative. Don't use any nails or staples.

After the first piece of material is glued down it can be "slipped" around slightly if it is not perfectly straight and flat. One foot on the material and one on the bare floor or both feet on the material and pushing against the wall with your hands is enough leverage to adjust the position of the piece. Do this slowly and carefully because I think you can imagine the laughs you will get if the slipping part goes wrong.

Cut the second piece of material and repeat the procedure. This time, however, you have the added task of making sure the seam is exactly aligned. Careful trowel work is necessary to get the seam securely bonded without too much oozing of PRC, or too little PRC in order to stick it down. Remember, go slow and be meticulous. This is a Forever Floor and worth the trouble.

The temperature during this installation has an effect on how well the job proceeds. Warm is better. PRC spreads best when it is from a freshly opened bucket and the temperature is above 70° F. Higher temperatures extend 'slippage' time. I have not kept track of how much coverage a bucket of PRC gets. It varies with the volume of voids it has to avert. (Sorry.)

Be aware that PRC takes a few days to cure. Some circumstances may require putting weights on parts of the floor where bonding is reluctant. Concrete blocks, extra cans of paint, lumber, brothers-in-law, sacks of cement, or whatever you have for ballast will work. Just be prepared to leave the items in place for a couple of days. Most times this won't be a problem if the temperature is right and the PRC thickness is uniform. During installation, wear good, thick knee pads to preserve your knee joints for old age.

Cleaning up

If, like me, you have the occasional dufus moment and get PRC where it should not be, clean it up right away because it has the ability to travel. Blot up PRC with a rag if it gets on the mineral side of the roofing. Leaving a little discoloration on the minerals is okay. It will be fixed later. Clean tools and their handles with paint thinner or spray degreaser and a rag. Don't let it linger on your hands. I think it may be what melted my fingernails one time.

WD-40 and a rag are best for skin, shoe sole, and kneepad cleaning so keep these items handy. Don't hesitate when some PRC escapes. Deal with it immediately. It will save you a lot of trouble in the long run.

To keep the person responsible for laundry happy, wear clothes from, or about to go to, the rag pile. Then burn them after the job, if necessary.

Let's recap. Prepare the floor by nailing down loose parts. Fill large holes. Get it fairly smooth and clean it well. Accurately cut the roofing pieces and bond them to the floor with Plastic Roof Cement.

Painting

Before we start the next step I am going to tell you a secret you must protect with the same self-discipline you guard your source of...ginseng plants. Customers of the local paint supply store often return or reject paint that for some reason turned out to be the wrong color. Many stores throw it away. Can you believe that? But they'll sell it cheap if you know it exists, they like you, and you ask for it. I've gotten some of the finest quality paints for...well, very cheap. Get all you can. I have acquired as much as 35 gallons at a time. For our purpose here, use only latex paint. Any color, gallons, quarts, gloss, flat, exterior, interior—it doesn't matter. They all work. You can understand that if everyone knew about this secret there wouldn't be any when you need it so stifle the urge to share this knowledge.

Applying the first coat of paint

You probably have guessed that the roll roofing floor is going to get painted. Before we talk about that, let's examine an advantage of this method. Often, when a building is going up, a new floor is exposed to the weather for many days, maybe weeks. Covering it with bonded roll roofing prevents damage caused by dew, rain, and hot sun. I apply roofing material right out to the perimeter of the floor as soon as it is built, then erect the walls on top of it. This creates a gasket-like seal between the floor and wall plates. And doing it at this time, in this way, is easier than working up to the wall later. Damage is minimized during construction and throughout the life of the building when water is prevented from soaking through the floor.

Now let's appreciate the reasons for all that latex paint. If you simply cemented down the roofing material and started walking on it, the minerals would become dislodged and the floor would wear out quickly. You may have seen roll roofing nailed to docks and piers at marinas. It doesn't last long and needs replacing often, but it makes a pretty good non-slip walking surface.

Latex is not just paint. It is good glue, too. Two or three coats of it

You can create interesting patterns on your floors using a variety of latex paints.

encapsulate the minerals on the roofing material and hold them in place like they were welded there. More importantly, latex paint absorbs the wear the floor receives. When the minerals start to show, you paint the floor again. And that is the key to the superiority of the forever floor.

Let's get back to that fresh new floor covered with roll roofing. Sweep away the few loose mineral granules and get the first two coats of paint applied as soon as possible. It's easy. If you are working up to a wall, use a brush to cut in around the perimeter of the room. Then just pour the paint from the can onto the floor and spread it with a long handled paint roller. If there are no walls yet, just pour and spread. Play nice music while you paint and it is a wonderful, almost Zen-like, experience.

Be smart. Use the most repulsive color paint for the first few coats and save your favorite for last. When I am doing a floor that will be exposed to weather I apply two coats right away before it rains. Latex dries in an hour or two so the job can be done in one day. Two coats give me a good work surface while I build. Later, when all else is done, I can touch up and do the finish painting. If your floor project is outdoors, put two additional coats down for a finished surface that lasts years before needing a recoat. Indoor floors do fine with only three coats since the weather is usually not so harsh inside your house.

You may have access to oil paint but I do not recommend it for your floors because dust and cat paw prints

The floor colors add interest to this sunny office.

get on it before it has a chance to dry. Even under the most favorable conditions oil paint can take days to cure enough to allow foot traffic. If you cannot live without that certain color that only comes in oil...well, don't say I didn't warn you.

If you still think this is just glorified tarpaper, get a magnifying glass, lie down on the floor and scrutinize it. The latex has covered and filled in between all the granules and holds them forcefully in place. The granules combined with the latex makes a surface almost as hard as rock. The bumpy texture creates a non-slip surface, yet it is smooth enough for easy sweeping and mopping.

Repairing your floor

Forever is a long time and some calamity may occur which pokes a hole or gash in your floor, necessitating a repair. Compared to vinyl or wood, this floor is a cinch to fix. Cut a new piece of roll roofing in a football shape just large enough to cover the mishap. Use a magic marker and trace around the football shape. Use a sharp utility knife, perhaps a chisel, and cut on the lines you traced. Scrape away the old roofing material inside the lines and down to the sub floor. This isn't easy so persist carefully. Make sure the new piece fits into the cutout closely. Cement the new piece in place with you-know-what and paint over it with latex. Sit on a chair over the repair to guard it while the paint dries. Enjoy the beverage of your choice and feel proud of yourself.

Sometimes you might have a particularly difficult location that needs floor covering. Perhaps your architect, in a fit of artistic flair, designed a really complicated hallway, niche, staircase, or something. Ordinarily it would be carpeted because carpet is easy to carve into odd shapes and tack into place. Maybe vinyl was chosen, or hardwood flooring. These are good but expensive solutions, not so much in materials, but skilled labor. Plus they all have to be refinished or replaced after a few years because of wear or boredom.

This floor excels in these places. When applied during construction the job is done inexpensively. If done by you in an existing building it still keeps the floor covering budget in check.

Sections of roofing material can be cut and installed like puzzle pieces once you become adept at doing the geometry and aligning seams. This advantage makes the roofing material method easier than trying to install one really complex hunk of carpet or vinyl and with less waste.

Remember, once in place, this floor does not wear out. As for preventing floor covering replacement on account of boredom...well, just read on.

Artistic expression

Now comes my favorite subject: artistic expression. After your two or three coats of inexpensively acquired latex paint have been applied and your floor is up to its potential in the matter of wear, you are going to look at it and wonder how you will ever get comfortable with that Turkey Trot Teal, or whatever that last color was called.

Fortunately, you can fix all that. Push the budget limits and go buy some colors you really like, at retail prices, to decorate the floor. This endears you to the paint dealer and he will be inclined to let you have more of his mis-mixed paints later.

Study the pictures accompanying this article and you'll notice I get carried away a little bit with colors. I do have a method however.

Step 1: Use a background color, or two or three. If you use only one background color just do the whole floor with it and proceed to the next step. If you use two or more backgrounds, divide the floor into sections, relevant only to you, and use separate colors for each. Use background colors that contrast or complement, but do not clash with, the finish colors.

Step 2: Put on the finish colors. You'll notice I paint the floors in a mosaic pattern. This is easy and my favorite method but you can conjure up your own style. Limited only by your imagination, the possibilities are infinite. The fact that latex comes in gloss, semi-gloss, and flat provides you with another design element to play with.

I do my finish painting in stages and this is how it works. Each night about an hour before bedtime I take my color of the day and a two-inch brush and paint a number of individual, various sized, spots on the floor. They are dry by morning and do not disturb our daily activities. Next night I use another color and add more spots, keeping a margin between them, allowing the background color to show. Eventually the whole floor gets done.

I don't clean the paintbrush between sessions. I just store it in a plastic bag to prevent the paint from drying and use it again during the next session. Intermingled coloring is a technique I use, so for me a clean brush is not necessary. This work is so pleasant that it is tempting to just

An easy to clean and maintain bathroom floor

go right out the door and paint the pavement in the driveway. In fact, I have done that.

You can make the floor look like patio stones. You can paint "carpets" or scenes on the floor. This technique is called trompe l'oeil (pardon my French). Trompe l'oeil means "fool the eye." In case you would like to study up on it, books have been written about painting floors as art. You can help bring this art form back with your own forever floor if you are so inclined. What's really cool is, even if you screw up or change your mind, it's okay. Just paint over it.

Repainting is what keeps your forever floor dear to you. Tired of it? Repaint. An accomplished artist comes for a visit? Make him or her work for their keep. Each layer of paint makes the floor last longer. Artwork makes it more valuable and attractive.

You could paint any old floor made of concrete or wood. I have done both but there are problems. Concrete tends to slough off paint with changes in humidity and temperature. There is a way to pour concrete so it accepts paint effectively but that is another story. Concrete has sort of an evil mystical power to make a person's legs tired if they have to stand on it too long. A layer of something between you and the concrete breaks that spell. Don't ask me why. It just does. And the local Masonic Lodge guys aren't letting loose the secret reason for this phenomenon. I asked.

Painted wood just looks like...well, painted wood, which is okay if you like it. By adding bonded roll roofing and paint you give the floor a new dimension and longevity. Old wood plank floors should be saved and restored with reverence. But if you have a fairly recent hard or soft wood floor with little gaps, dents, dings and such, covering it with this system turns it into a very interesting new floor. If, later on, carpet or wood must be added, either can be installed over this material.

Other applications

Now that you know about the forever floor, imagine the constant counter. I have built several of these in kitchens and bathrooms. It is easy to make a large, long countertop with no seams.

Imagine a few more applications. How about the eternal tabletop, continual seat and ceaseless shelf? All are good projects for using this method. I have used it to create non-slip walkways or, as I call them, permanent pathways, on the boat I am building. When I build a counter, shelf, tabletop, or stairs I add a perimeter of hardwood molding to protect the edges of the roofing material. Other than that it is the same process as the floor. There are better adhesives than PRC for these non-floor projects if you want to try them. Various construction glues work okay.

People who have seen the forever floor often don't believe their eyes, or me, when I tell them what it is. Other than certain grades of vinyl, there are no closely comparable floor coverings, which make real estate appraisers apprehensive. But once you see how inexpensive, durable, and beautiful this floor is, I think you'll agree that the forever floor is worth it. Δ

Removing mold

By Tom Kovach

Mold is a type of microscopic fungus. There are many types and they are present throughout the environment, indoors and out. Mold spores germinate and grow in a moist environment. Indoor mold can cause allergies or allergy-like symptoms affecting the upper respiratory system. Here are some tips on how homeowners can clean up and remove mold in their homes:

1. Identify and remove any sources of moisture. This can include flooding, roof leaks, firewood stored indoors, plumbing leaks, condensation, watering house plants, etc.

2. Begin drying any materials that got wet. Do this as soon as possible. For severe moisture problems, use fans and dehumidifiers and move wet items away from walls and off floors.

3. Remove and dispose of mold-contaminated materials. Look for mold on porous items that may have absorbed moisture. This would include sheet rock, insulation, plaster, carpet, ceiling tiles, wood (other than solid wood), and paper products. Items with mold should be removed, bagged, and thrown out. Porous material that may have been in contact with sewage should also be bagged and thrown out. Non-porous materials can be saved if they are properly cleaned and dried and kept that way.

4. Clean non-porous or semi-porous items. Mold can grow on materials like hard plastic, concrete, glass, or metal. But it can be removed with careful cleaning. Scrub them thoroughly with a stiff brush, hot water, and a non-ammonia soap or detergent or commercial cleaner. For heavily contaminated items, use a HEPA vacuum (not a conventional household vacuum or shop vac). If you can't get a HEPA vacuum, wipe the item carefully, removing as much surface contamination as possible. Rinse wipes often with clean water and dispose of your wipes and rinse water frequently and properly.

5. Mix ¼ to ½ cup bleach per gallon of water and apply to surfaces where mold growth was visible before cleaning. Apply with a spray bottle, garden sprayer, sponge, or some other suitable method. Collect any run-off of the bleach solution with a wet/dry vacuum, sponge, or mop. Do not rinse or wipe the bleach solution from items or surfaces being treated...allow it to dry on the surface.

Always handle bleach with caution. Never mix bleach with ammonia ... toxic chlorine gas may result. Bleach can irritate the eyes, nose, throat and skin. Make sure a door or window is open while you are working and protect the eyes and skin from contact with bleach. Because bleach is so corrosive, test a small area of the surface you are cleaning before you proceed on the whole thing. Remember, bleach alone is not an effective way to combat mold. It won't reliably kill mold, especially if organic contamination (dirt, dust, mold growth, etc.) has not been cleaned away first.

6. Stay alert for problems. Continue to look for signs of moisture or new mold growth. Pay special attention to areas where mold grew previously. If the mold returns, repeat the cleaning process and consider using a stronger disinfecting solution. New mold growth may mean that the contaminated material should be removed, or that you still have a moisture problem. Be patient about rebuilding your home or getting new furnishings. Wait until everything has been completely cleaned and dried. Drying out wet building materials can take a long time. Δ

Delicious crisp cool weather greens are easy to grow

By Alice Brantley Yeager
Photos by James O. Yeager

A good example of fresh flavor is the taste of homegrown greens—turnip, collard, mustard, spinach, and others. These plants are known as cool weather crops—plants you grow during the spring and fall seasons. Contrast the fresh crispness of newly picked leaves with the somewhat tough ones in the markets and there's simply no contest. After all, what can be expected of greens that have sometimes traveled hundreds of miles to reach the produce bins? It's the same with edible roots such as turnips. Cook some turnips just pulled from the garden and notice the prime flavor.

Southern gardeners, having a longer growing season, can take advantage of both spring and fall to raise greens, whereas folks living in colder areas need to allow more time for their ground to warm up in spring and, by the same reasoning, sow the fall crop before soil cools too much to let seeds germinate properly. After really cold weather begins in any area, the quality of usable greens will go down. Forget about sowing seeds after the "right time" has passed.

If you have plenty of garden space for growing greens, so much the better, but greens can be raised almost anywhere. Seeds can even be sown in flower beds where summer flowers have run their course. Just remove the spent plants from the beds and put them in the compost pile. Cultivate the beds, add some well decomposed compost and plant your turnips, etc. If you have successfully grown flowers, chances are that you can now have some nice fall greens.

Florida Broad Leaf Mustard will add a peppery taste to most greens mixtures.

After the greens have passed their prime, continue the cycle by either digging them into the soil or putting them in the compost bin. If you live in a part of the country where winters are mild and plants will winter over 'til spring, leave the plants alone and they will produce some tender new leaves in the spring, bolt, and produce nectar for many beneficial insects including honeybees. Bright yellow flowers from these plants can even be used as fillers in bouquets where their sweet smell will perfume a room.

One thing about raising greens—it is easy to do and it pays off in a delicious way. Most greens will thrive in ordinary garden soil with a pH factor of 6.0 - 8.0. If you haven't raised these food plants before and want to be absolutely sure about your soil, take a sample to your local county extension agent and ask to have it checked out. You can then add whatever is needed to improve the soil or leave it as is.

Greens might be classified as a lazy person's kind of plants. They don't require constant attention. Mainly, they need a well drained and sunny location, a fair amount of moisture and good loose garden soil free of weeds. Sandy loam is best for raising greens as well as many other garden crops. If you have access to poultry litter, try liberally mixing some into your soil during the fall and see what it does for your spring garden and those spring greens.

If soil is heavy, such as where quite a bit of clay is present, improve it by working organic matter (pine needles, grass clippings, compost, etc.) into the area to gradually loosen it up and enrich it. Periodic applications of organic mulch around plants are always beneficial, as the mulch will break down adding humus to the soil. Not many gardens succeed where plant roots have to fight heavy poor soil for their existence.

Whenever I plant greens, I prefer to plant in rows rather than broadcast seeds in beds. Rows give easy access to the plants and they are easy to mulch. A good mulch put down alongside rows will prevent soil from washing away and deter weeds. Moreover, roots of young plants will not be exposed when heavy rains occur. If additional mulch is applied as plants grow, it is unlikely that much dirt will splash up on leaves making them hard to clean. Although green tops may suffer some damage from freezing weather, root crops such as rutabagas will stay in good condition for several weeks when protected by a good mulch.

Whether sowing seeds in spring or fall, they should never be sown thickly as that is only going to lead to a lot of unnecessary work in the form of thinning. Crowded seedlings will not produce a good crop of leaves *or* roots, whereas plants with plenty of room to grow will develop both nutritious tops and roots.

As winter advances, in order to maintain the best quality, it is advisable to harvest the plants. Cut off the tops and either store the roots in a cool room or refrigerate them. Some will keep indefinitely if refrigerated.

When greens bolt (go to flower) in spring, they not only provide a sweet scent in the garden, but honeybees are quick to start gathering nectar.

Leaving the plants in the ground too long in the fall may cause the roots to become woody and strong flavored. If the leaves haven't sustained too much damage, sort through them and have one last good meal of fresh fall greens.

There are many varieties of "greens," each with its own particular growth habit and flavor. Some plants produce edible roots and some do not. Many folks favor a single variety cooked alone and some like a mixture of greens. It's all up to the individual. My husband, James, and I like a mixed blend of flavors such as turnip greens, mustard, collards, etc. Also, one should not overlook tender radish, beet, and poke salad greens depending on the time of year you are gathering greens. If French sorrel is available, mix in some of those leaves as their sour flavor will further enhance the blend of flavors. Considering all, you can come up with some downright delicious combinations.

Tokyo Cross turnips

Tokyo Cross is one of our favorite varieties of turnips. It's a hybrid and far surpasses the old Purple Top still preferred by many gardeners. Tokyo Cross has a smooth crisp texture, good mild flavor and is delicious cooked or sliced raw and eaten with dips. It's earlier maturing than some of the older varieties and holds its quality longer than other turnips. Green tops stay tender until really hard freezes occur.

No one likes to encounter bits of sand or grit when eating greens, so be sure to thoroughly wash greens in cool water (more than once, if necessary) before using. If there are any tough stems, just grasp the stem about a third of the way into the leaf and strip away the tough part and discard it. Pay attention to greens before cooking and you can be sure they will be perfect in texture as well as taste. (If you raise rabbits, give them the discarded stems. They won't turn them down.)

Pot-likker

The water in which greens are cooked should not be discarded, as this is a fringe benefit. The thin consomme type liquid is formally known as pot-likker and is abundant in flavor and vitamins. Lift the greens from the pot, place them in a serving dish and treat folks to bowls of pot-likker, with hot pieces of cornbread for dunking. (See basic recipe for cooking greens.)

A house filled with the aroma of greens cooking mingled with that of cornbread baking transports many of us back to a time when a great portion of our food came directly from home gardens. Who could ask for more—except maybe a sweet potato pie for dessert?

Basically, the following will produce a very good pot of greens that no one will turn down.

Cooked greens:

greens
turnips, peeled and diced
green onions or a medium onion, chopped
bacon or other cured meat
salt (optional)
chili pepper hot sauce (optional)

Greens cook down considerably, so gather a substantial amount of them—turnip greens, mustard, collards, beet, sorrel, radish—whatever is available and tender. Cook in a porcelain or stainless pot—no aluminum.

Inspect greens for any insects and remove tough stems. This is easily done by stripping the stems from the leaves wherever the tough stems begin. Discard stems and wash greens thoroughly in cool water and drain. (Wash more than once if necessary.)

If using salt bacon, boil meat for a few minutes in plain water to remove most of salt. Drain and set aside. If using cured meat, boiling before combining with greens is unnecessary. Cut any seasoning meat into small pieces. A quick method is to fry several pieces of sliced, cured bacon, cut in small pieces, and cook with greens along with some of the drippings.

Put salt bacon or cured meat in pot along with 3-4 cups of water. Bring to a boil and simmer about 10 minutes. This is to assure that at the end of the cooking process, meat will be thoroughly cooked and tender. (It's not necessary to pre-boil the fried bacon.) Add the greens, turnips, and onions and bring to a boil. Cut back the heat to simmer and cook until greens are tender. Stir occasionally to keep greens from clinging together in a mass.

Twenty to twenty-five minutes cooking time should be sufficient to produce a delectable pot of greens.

Our favorite turnip—Tokyo Cross. It is medium sized, has a mild flavor and crisp texture (great sliced for dips), and yields plenty of greens.

Seed sources:

Tokyo Cross Hybrid
Pinetree Garden Seeds
P.O. Box 300
New Gloucester, ME 04260
Fax 1-888-52-seeds
Phone 1-207-926-3400

W. Atlee Burpee & Co.
Warminster, PA 18974
Fax 1-800-487-5530
Phone 1-800-888-1447

J.W. Jung Seed Co.
335 S. High Street
Randolph, WI 53957-0001
Fax 1-800-692-5864
Phone 1-800-247-5864

Florida Broad Leaf Mustard
W. Atlee Burpee & Co.
Warminster, PA 18974
Fax 1-800-487-5530
Phone 1-800-888-1447

Purple Top Turnip
Carried by most seed companies.

French Sorrel
Territorial Seed Co.
P.O. Box 158
Cottage Grove, OR 97424-0061
Fax 1-888-657-3131
Phone 1-541-942-9547

Rutabaga
Any seed company offering turnip seeds will usually have rutabaga seeds.

A pot of mixed greens complete with bits of turnips and salt bacon

Taste-test to see if you might like a bit of salt added.

Put the greens in a hot serving dish and reserve the liquid to enjoy as pot likker soup. At the start of cooking, put in some extra cups of water if several pot likker lovers are present.

Always have a bottle of hot sauce handy to dash on a serving of greens. Some folks like it more than others, but almost everyone likes a bit of hot sauce. You might say it livens up the conversation.

Caution: Be sure to serve greens with your favorite hot cornbread with plenty of butter available. (We prefer cornbread made with yellow home-ground meal.) No other bread will do.

Rutabaga casserole:

- 6 cups mashed rutabagas (approx. 2 fairly large rutabagas)
- 2 cups canned cream
- 3 eggs, beaten
- 1 stick oleo, cut in small pieces
- 1 medium onion, minced
- 1 tsp. salt (optional)

Peel and steam (or boil) rutabagas until tender enough to mash as you would potatoes. Combine rest of items with rutabagas and put in well buttered casserole. Bake at 350° for 45 minutes and then lower heat to 300° and bake about 30 minutes longer. Good served with pork roast.

Sweet potato pie:

- 3 eggs, beaten
- 1 cup light brown sugar
- 1 tsp. salt (optional)
- ½ tsp. ground nutmeg
- ¼ tsp. ground ginger
- ½ tsp. ground cinnamon
- 2 cups mashed, cooked sweet potatoes
- 1 cup evaporated milk
- 1 unbaked 9 inch pie shell

Combine first six ingredients. Add sweet potatoes, milk and mix well. Pour into pie shell and bake at 350° for an hour and 15 minutes or until table knife inserted in center comes out clean. Check on doneness a few minutes before time is up to be sure that pie does not overcook.

Sweet potatoes—the old timey way: Have at least one medium size sweet potato per person and maybe a couple of extra ones just in case someone is extra hungry. Be sure your fireplace is well supplied with ashes and plenty of live coals.

Before the days of aluminum foil, it was customary to bury sweet potatoes in ashes with a liberal supply of glowing coals on top of the ashes. There the potatoes would stay for about an hour or until done depending on size of the potatoes and heat from the embers.

The sweet potatoes were gingerly extracted from the coals by using a poker and allowed to rest on the hearth for a few minutes until they could be handled. Ashes were shaken off as much as possible and then began the process of either peeling the potatoes or splitting them down the middle and putting on as much butter as allowed.

What a mouth watering delicacy! Even more so if the weather was bone-chilling outside and the day's chores completed.

If you don't have a fireplace to carry you back to less complicated times, there's still a fair copy of this tasty treat to be had. Wrap your sweet potatoes in aluminum foil, place them on a cookie sheet or shallow pan and bake them for about an hour at 350°. Using a hot pad, test for doneness by gently squeezing the potatoes. If they feel somewhat firm, they need to bake a bit longer. Enjoy! Δ

Ask Jackie

Jackie Clay

If you have a question about rural living, send it in to Jackie Clay and she'll try to answer it. Address your letter to *Ask Jackie*, PO Box 712, Gold Beach, OR 97444. Questions will only be answered in this column. — Editor

Powdered egg shelf life

Back in '98-'99 I was really into preparing for Y2K going so far as to visit a Mormon Cannery with friends and use there facilities to can. (They really have the right idea, always staying prepared). I also visited a local distributor of bulk food and canned a lot of their stuff. At the cannery I sealed the tin cans and threw in the moisture absorbing packages, and with the stuff I canned at home (in five-gallon pails) I used moisture absorbing bags and diatomaceous earth to control bugs. My question is, the egg powder that I canned at the cannery, what's the shelf life? The first three years I was near the ocean, cool temps. The past three years have been in the desert, hot during the summer, but the containers were all inside the house in cool temps.

jason mays
jdmays1@earthlink.net

Most preparedness companies give egg powder a seven-year "shelf life." Of course it's prudent to rotate all long term storage foods so that everything stays as fresh and nutritious as possible.

But sometimes something sneaks past you and you have, say, 10-year-old powdered eggs. Open a can and give her the sniff test. If it looks fine and smells fine, it probably is just fine. Make up a small batch of scrambled eggs or something and give it a taste. Now powdered eggs don't taste just like fresh eggs do, but they should be edible with no "funny" taste, which sometimes indicates they have become rancid. This is not common, however, and I'd guess your powdered eggs are just fine. I just opened a 1998 can of my own and am now using *old* powdered eggs which are just as nice as they were back when.

Don't give up on preparedness because the Y2K was a nonevent. There are plenty of reasons that it is essential that everyone have at least a year's worth of food and essential supplies stored up. Few emergencies announce themselves with the fanfare of Y2K. Most just sneak up on you.

— Jackie

Dry goods storage and battling meal weevils

I am trying to get together a one-year food storage program. I have found two-gallon buckets that I have purchased for the storing of beans, rice, sugar, wheat, and anything else that I can find to store in them. I am storing my food in food saver bags in the two-gallon buckets. I am placing bags from my food saver in the buckets and sucking the air out of them before I put on the lids, label, and place into storage. My questions:

1. Do I get enough of the air out of the bags with the food saver to protect the rice, beans, etc., or should I be purchasing the oxygen remover packets?

2. Should I have put in a moisture remover also?

3. How will I know that I blew it with my storage?

4. And last question. When I bought this home I was left the gift of weevils from the family that was here. How do I get rid of them so they don't get into my wheat, rice, and flour in my food storage?

Phyllis Pettigrew
ppettigr@mtaonline.net

Good for you, Phyllis. I'm so glad to hear from folks that are still involved in long-term food storage. Preparedness is *always* a good idea.

To answer your questions: Yes, you get enough air out of the bags to keep your rice, beans, and other dry goods with the food saver vacuum. I have stored such things for years and years without even this handy helper. The key is to keep the foods totally dry and out of the reach of insects, moisture, or rodents. Everyone should rotate their long-term food storage, replacing the older food with fresher. Once in a while, you may have one food go rancid, but this is really rare.

I have been keeping a long-term pantry for many decades and have lost very, very little food. And that which was lost usually happened due to breaching of the container for some reason or another. (Dropping off a shelf is one that comes to mind.) The old adage, "Don't keep all your eggs in one basket," applies here, meaning don't store all your food in one container or one spot. I have mine placed in three areas, in many containers, just in case.

Meal weevils or pantry moths are a devilish problem. Drastic measures are required. First, get rid of all opened flour, corn meal, or baking mixes. Ditch any mixes or bags of flours or mixes that have trickling leaks, indicating weevils. (Signs of weevil activity are foul smell in the flour, webs at the top of the bags, little whitish, long moths in the house, and of course, the presence of "bugs" in your flour or corn meal.)

I've had good luck using pantry moth traps in the kitchen and pantry. I've bought mine from Gardens Alive. You can also buy them from Gardener's Supply Company, 128 Intervale Rd., Burlington VT, 05401 or www.gardeners.com. These are little "tents" with a lure scent inside. The moths fly in, but get stuck in the sticky inner surface and don't fly out. You'll be amazed at how many moths you can catch in a week. When you don't catch any more, you're out of moths and if you've done your work cleaning your pantry, you should have no reinfestation. Take care when buying new grain products; often you bring them home. Do not buy leaking bags of flours or mixes. If flour can sift out, moths can get in and lay their eggs.

Putting a few bay leaves in the bags with your flours will repel the moths, should any be left around. Also, keep all your flours in an airtight container and you should be in the clear.

— ***Jackie***

Drying lemons

How do I dehydrate whole fruits, i.e. whole lemons?

Jay
rugby.dogs@verizon.net

Whole lemons are easy to dehydrate, although, obviously you must slice the whole lemon in order to dehydrate it. I buy them whenever I can get a good deal, then dehydrate them and make a great lemon powder that I use in a huge variety of recipes, from baked goods to Chinese food.

Wash the lemons with hot water to remove any insect spray or other noxious chemicals. Pat them dry, then slice about a quarter of an inch thick. Remove and discard any seeds from the lemon rounds and place the rounds in a single layer on a dehydrator screen or on a cookie sheet, if you don't have a dehydrator. Dehydrate at about 145° F until they are dry. The oven of your gas kitchen range, with only a pilot light on, will dry your cookie sheet trays of lemons. Or you can leave them in the backseat of your car on a warm, sunny day. They dry quickly.

Once they are dry, the pulp is crispy and the rind tough and leathery. What I do is whiz them in the old blender that I got at the dump, until the whole lemon is a granular powder. This is *excellent* in pies, all baked goods, and a ton of other recipes. It is very lemony in fragrance and taste.

— ***Jackie***

Mincemeat recipes

My grandfather speaks fondly of the mincemeat his mother used to make—"much better than the stuff they sell in the store now." He remembered it the most in sandwiches, not the typical pie. I would like to mince meat for him, but after looking at several recipes, I have several questions.

Did mincemeat originally have (or is it necessary to have) alcohol in it in some form? Some recipes call for brandy, and others cider, and some use a combination. My grandfather didn't remember his mother keeping brandy on hand, but then, he never really watched her make mincemeat, either. At first I was just going to use cider, but almost all cider you can buy has been pasteurized. Wouldn't that affect the taste? And if she never canned it, wouldn't the unpasteurized eventually have some alcohol? Or is it possible that she used vinegar instead? I did find one recipe that called for cider and cider vinegar, and then it was "seasoned to taste" with brandy right before serving. I find it odd to think of alcohol in a child's sandwich, but maybe no one did back then. Any suggestions?

Also, what would be the best way of storing it? The meat is cooked ahead of time. I know a lot of people used to (and maybe still do) just leave it in the crock, or else seal it with "greased paper and twine" or paraffin. Some recipes told me to can it for 20 minutes at 15 pounds for pints (I was going to do half pints). And I know I've read you're supposed to can meat for 70 minutes, but isn't that for raw meat, not precooked? Would it be better for the taste and texture if I just froze it instead?

A lot of the recipes call for Citron, but if that used to be easy to find it sure isn't now. Do you think they usually used fresh citron or candied citron? Is there any chance you could help clear things up for me, or should I just experiment?

Talitha Purdy
talithap@gmail.com

I can understand your confusion, as there are *so* many recipes for "mincemeat." Most of the old recipes for mincemeat did call for brandy. This was both for flavoring and for the preserving qualities. With the sugars and other preservatives, the mincemeat was packed in a crock and kept in a cold place all winter. Today, I would recommend freezing the resultant mincemeat, if it is a mincemeat with minced meat in it.

The brandy was put in at the end of the cooking down time and the boiling cooked off most of the alcohol, so the children weren't being fed alcohol.

The citron was candied citron. Folks often grew citron melon and candied the peel as you do watermelon rind pickle to use in different recipes. Store bought candied citron will be fine.

Some of my recipes use cider or cider and vinegar. I don't think the pasteurized cider would make a difference, especially if you freeze the mincemeat. (Many women used the brandy, but didn't advertise it.)

Here are two good Amish recipes for mincemeat, one which is a great way to have nonmeat mincemeat from green summer tomatoes.

Abigail Troyer's mincemeat:

1 lb. lean beef, cubed
2/3 cup water
6 cups chopped apples
1 cup raisins
2 cups currants
½ cup chopped orange peel
2 Tbsp. grated lemon peel
¼ cup orange juice
2 Tbsp. lemon juice
2 cups sugar
1 tsp. cinnamon
½ tsp. ground cloves
½ tsp. ground nutmeg
½ tsp. mace
1 tsp. salt
2 cups apple cider
1 cup brandy

In a sauce pan bring the water to a boil and cook beef cubes covered for an hour. When the meat has cooled, put it through a food chopper. Combine all the ingredients, except the brandy, in a large sauce pan and cook uncovered for two hours, stirring occasionally. When the mixture begins to thicken, add the brandy and cook five minutes longer. Seal in hot, sterilized jars.

Summertime mincemeat:

3 cups chopped green tomatoes
3 cups chopped apples
1 cup vinegar
1 cup molasses
3 cups brown sugar
½ cup butter
1 Tbsp. salt
2 cups raisins
1 tsp. cinnamon
½ tsp. ground cloves
½ tsp. ground ginger

Combine all the ingredients in large kettle. Boil five minutes and seal in hot sterilized jars for pie filling.

Personally, I would recommend either freezing the mincemeats or processing the tomato version in a hot water bath canner for 15 minutes, but these are the original recipes.

— *Jackie*

Potato scab

We live in the Copper River Basin in south central Alaska and Valdez. We probably rate as "part time homesteaders" because our land and home are 90 miles from work across a pass that can get 900 inches of snow in a bad winter. We have a trailer in town near work so we do not have livestock yet. Currently our main garden is only 50 feet by 80 feet. This has been cleared up over the last 10 years. Because of limited space we are using a short rotation: potatoes every other year on about half of the ground and everything else on the rest. We are using commercial fertilizer in moderation as well as some compost that is sometimes supplemented with well rotted horse manure and waste fish food (I work at a fish hatchery). We have also spread wood ashes (mostly spruce and willow). Water is supplied with drip irrigation tape. Our problem is that over the last two years we have started getting significant scab on the potatoes. We do save our own seed but last year the new variety we ordered was as bad as any. Is the wood ash making the ground too "sweet." Any suggestions to cope with this problem would be very helpful. Eventually we will clear up more ground to allow a longer rotation and some fallow time, but this is slow work.

Howard and Sue Brewi
Alaska

The most frequent cause of scab in potatoes is too much fertilizer. I would give your garden a rest from the fertilizer, in the area you will be growing potatoes at any rate. If possible, try growing them in a new, freshly cleared section of garden that hasn't seen fertilizer or potatoes before. Potatoes usually love fresh ground and will reward you with scab-free potatoes. It's often a temptation to overfertilize the garden, especially when it is a smaller garden and the fertilizer is available. We just love our gardens to death, so to speak. Planting a variety of potato that has some resistance to scab is also a help. Lighten up on the watering after blooming will also help give better results.

— *Jackie*

Canning winter squash

I've frozen winter squash and it is in my opinion horrible. I've found recipes for canning it but I've read it doesn't taste good either.

Our basement isn't cool enough to keep it and it will get too cold in the garage by February and freeze.

Welcome to Minnesota.I live here too.

Sherry Morse
Minnesota

Thanks for your welcome, Sherry. We are enjoying our new northern Minnesota homestead a bunch. I also hate frozen winter squash. It is *great*, canned, though. Don't believe everything you read. When I serve my own canned squash, I chunk it up and cook it as little as possible. Also, I often bake it, before serving, to dry off some of the liquid and get a consistency my family likes. I do not puree it. That would be yucky, unless you used it in baking. Squash makes a great "pumpkin" pie.

Don't give up on your basement. Get a big cardboard box, put it in the coolest corner of your basement, and stack a few squash in there. Throw an old quilt over the box and check on the temperature. You'll be surprised at how much difference that makes. Any good keeping variety of winter squash should do just fine for several months.

— Jackie

"Hot seal" canning question

How safe is the "hot seal" canning method for preserving barbecue sauce? I'm cooking my sauce over 170 degrees for about an hour and boiling my lids. Most of the sauce doesn't last more than 2-3 weeks before being consumed by family and friends.

The sauce has a lot of sugar, vinegar, and ketchup in it—no tomatoes.

Gary Hairlson
fotobro@charter.net

Your method of canning your barbecue sauce is probably just fine. Without seeing your recipe I can't be positive, but I wouldn't be afraid to take second helpings. The sugar, vinegar, and ketchup (which does have tomatoes, obviously, but also sugar and vinegar to preserve it) would not cause food poisoning or mold problems.

— Jackie

Canning chili peppers

I would like to can chili peppers. I had an overabundance of them this year. My family likes to make things with them in. But I have only found pickle peppers. There has to be a recipe for them.

Kammi VanderZiel
kjv@frontiernet.net

Sure you can home can chili peppers. I can them every time I have enough, as I use the canned roasted peppers in a lot of recipes. My favorite is scrambled eggs with chilies in them, topped with melted cheddar and crunchy toast. To can them, first roast them for best taste. This is easily done by laying the peppers on your grill over hot coals, not flames, until the skins blister and begin to blacken. Roll them over and do the other side. You can also roast them in your oven on a cookie sheet at 400° F, but the grill tastes best (especially if you use mesquite or fruit tree wood). After they are roasted, quickly place them in a paper sack and roll the top shut. Leave them in it until they are cool. This helps the skins peel off easily. Remove the skins and seeds, if desired. Removing the seeds reduces somewhat the fire of the chili. Wear rubber gloves or the area under your finger nails will burn like heck for days. I don't, and mine do.

Pack the chilies in half pint jars, then fill the jar to within half an inch of the top with boiling water. Half a teaspoon of salt may be added, if desired. Process the jars in a pressure canner for 35 minutes at 10 pounds pressure, unless you live at an altitude above 2,000 feet, in which case, consult your canning manual for directions on adjusting your pressure to correspond with your altitude.

— Jackie

Canning pumpkin

I would like to know why I can't find directions for hot water bath canning of fresh pumpkin. I need to know how long to process quart jars in a hot water canner? Can you help? I do not want to use a pressure canner. I have done this before and had no problems but I forgot how long to process the jars. What is the time table for hot water canning to the timetable for the pressure cooker method?

Gloria Broadwater
mrsbigo@earthlink.net

It is not safe to water bath process pumpkin. I know that lots of people have done it, but to be safe, pumpkin and **all other vegetables and all meats, must be home canned in a pressure canner**.

Fruits (and tomatoes are technically a fruit) can be hot water canned.

Pressure canning is very easy to do, believe me. It is scarcely more difficult than boiling water in the water bath canner. But if you are dead set against canning pumpkin with a pressure canner, either freeze your pureed pumpkin or dehydrate it in quarter inch thick slices.

— Jackie

Giving mild/sweet peppers a "bite"

I purchased mild/sweet peppers in error. I have just cut and cleaned a bushel and I want to can them and give them a bite. What can I do with them to make them have a bite? I normally can Hungarian mild/leaning toward hot and try to mellow them. I am now faced with trying to make them hotter. I could try adding some pepper chips but I do not want to waste the whole lot. Please advise.

Mary Hulewicz
mary@yourbranchlender.com

If you want a real zing in those oh-so-mild peppers, try canning them with two or three habaneros in each pint. These little dandies are so hot that they'll fire up everything they come in contact with. If you don't want that much heat, drop one or two dried hot peppers in each jar, as you would hot dill pickles. We don't want you to catch fire.

— Jackie

Chiltipine question

I am trying to grow chiltipine via aquaponics, and they are just sprouts. Just in case they do not produce hot peppers, I will plant them in potting soil. Do you know what type of soil to use? I live in the Dallas, Texas area where soil is mostly clay base and I don't think it will support the chiltipine plant very well. I assume I will need to purchase various types of potting soil and soil supplements to make their native soil mixture. Please advise.

Larry Zavala
Dallas, TX

I'll bet your peppers will produce those tiny round firecrackers they're famous for under your conditions. But, should you decide to plant them in soil, I would simply mix some of your clay soil with some sharp sand for drainage and perhaps a little compost for tilth and fertility and watch them grow. You might even plant one or two in the flower bed of your house.

One of my husband, Bob's, friends invited him to spend the weekend at his parents home in south Texas. Bob was surprised when his mother picked some "little pepper berries" from a big plant next to her front door to chop up on their breakfast eggs. These were chiltipines and they really woke the "boys" up.

These little native wild chiles grow from Arizona and New Mexico, down into Mexico throughout the desert canyons. Mockingbirds like to pick the berry-like peppers for a midday snack. And they are thought to spread the crop through their droppings, bringing seed and fertilizer to a new area.

— Jackie

Blackberries

I have 60 lbs. of blackberries and if it don't frost I might get more than 100 lbs. of them. Other then jam what is the best way to keep them?

Rich
RichaOw9@aol.com

Wow, Rich, you've hit a gold mine. Oh my, what can you do with all of them? Well you could freeze them to use as fresh. I don't generally like to freeze things, but berries freeze so well and taste amazingly like fresh, it's a good way to go. Simply spread them out on a cookie sheet and drop them in the freezer. Just as soon as they're frozen, bag them up, making sure most of the air is out of the bag. You can sprinkle them with sugar as you bag them, if you'd like. They won't keep but about six months, but I doubt if you will have them that long.

Or you can dehydrate them. This is easy, too. Just spread them out in a single layer on a dehydrator tray or cookie sheet. Dehydrate at about 150° F until they are like tough raisins. If you use the cookie sheet, you can use your gas oven with only the pilot light on. It's best to scrape them around about halfway through, so the entire berry dries. You can even use the backseat of your car on a warm sunny day to dry the berries.

These are great in muffins or pancakes. Just toss a handful in the batter and bake. Or for a pie, simply soak for about an hour in warm water, drain, and use as fresh.

Blackberries can up quite nicely, too. Simply fix a syrup mixture of water and as much or little sugar as you prefer and boil that. Then add the berries to a jar, gently thumping the jar down to settle the berries snugly without mashing them, to within half an inch of the top of the jar. Then fill the jar to within half an inch of the top with the hot, boiled syrup. Process the jars 15 minutes for pints and 20 minutes for quarts in a boiling water bath.

Or you can make blackberry pancake and ice cream syrup from the blackberries. In a large kettle pour enough water to cover the bottom an inch or so deep. Add the berries and begin to heat, mashing the berries with a potato masher. Stir well as you juice the berries. Strain off juice, either overnight with a jelly bag, or through a strainer, removing the seeds and pulp. Then add four cups of juice to one cup of sugar and cook until as thick as you want. Pour into hot pint jars and process 15 minutes in a boiling water bath. This is excellent and also makes a tasty treat when you've got a sore throat.

— Jackie

Is Montana changing?

Just finished reading the article "Starting Over—Again," and I have a question about your opinion of Montana. Is the political climate in Montana changing from the influx of well-heeled California types? I have read and heard that the people moving to the northwest are generally very liberal and unfriendly to those of us who prefer less government and less regulation.

My wife and I were planning to eventually visit the area with a vague idea of scouting out property for the day when we can retire and hopefully enjoy a somewhat quieter more peaceful existence. Is Montana a likely place or have movie stars bought up everything worth considering?

Bruce Ruzicka
Mount Washington, KY

Montana has changed a whole lot in the last 10 or 15 years. Parts have become the "Vail" lifestyle, after that part of Colorado was full to the gills. The prettiest spots in Montana, the Bitterroot Valley, Gallatin Valley, Flathead Valley, and others are *expensive* and full of multimillion dollar homes. And of course, many people who can afford that don't have time for you or me. Even ranching areas have changed. There are fewer and fewer family ranches and more ranch managers for millionaire owners.

Ranch land has gone sky high and there are very few small parcels of land available for sale at anywhere near reasonable prices. The small acreages are usually either in a "remote subdivision" (20-acre mountain parcels) which have little useable land and many neighbors or mining claims which are usually in remote mountainous areas. This is great, but you will be snowed in for at least five months out of the year. We lived on one and it was *great*, but we snowmobiled in and out seven miles from December till the middle of May.

I'm not saying it is not possible to find a great small Montana homestead at an affordable price, but it grows harder and harder every day as people's incomes go up and up (or so it seems by all those new huge log homes).

Write to Steve Murphy, our realtor friend who works for Bill Walker Real Estate, 75 E. Lyndale, Helena, MT (406) 443-3424. He's a great guy and can give you the latest list of smaller pieces of land in the best (we think) area of Montana for homesteaders.

— Jackie

Canning cheese

I read somewhere about you canning cheese. Now I can't find out how. Can you tell me where to look or better yet, how to do it?

Cathy Adams
Camden, OH

You won't find this one in a canning manual, but I experimented around and found something that works for me. One day I was canning tomatoes while whacking a chunk of cheddar cheese for "lunch." Mmmm, I wondered. Tomatoes are acid. Cheese is acid. So I cut up cubes of cheese, sitting a wide-mouthed pint jar in a pan of water, on the wood stove. Slowly cubes of cheese melted and I added more until the jar was full to within half an inch of the top. Then I put a hot, previously boiled lid on the jar, screwed down the ring firmly tight and added the cheese to a batch of jars in the boiling water bath canner to process. It sealed on removal, right along with the jars of tomatoes. Two years later, I opened it and it was great. Perhaps a little sharper than before, but *great*. So I started canning cheese of all types (but not soft cheeses) and, so far, they've all been successful. To take the cheeses out of the jar, dip the jar in a pan of boiling water for a few minutes, then take a knife and go around the jar, gently prying the cheese out. Store it in a plastic zip lock bag.

— Jackie

Tomatillo jam

I work at a public library and recently had a patron looking for a recipe for tomatillo jam. Believe it or not, I couldn't find one in any of our recipe books. Of course, by that time I was determined to come up with a recipe for this woodsy-looking gentleman. So I thought who better to ask than Jackie Clay? Do you have anything related to tomatillo jam, jelly, or preserves?

Richda McNutt
alan.mcnutt@worldnet.att.net.

One recipe for tomatillo jam calls for 4½ cups husked tomatillos run through a food grinder with a coarse knife. Add 2 cups of sugar, ½ teaspoon ground cinnamon, and ½ teaspoon ground cloves. Bring to a boil stirring constantly until thickened. It should sheet off a cool teaspoon, not run off in drops. Pour into hot, sterilized jars to within half an inch of the top. Wipe the rim of the jar clean. Place hot, previously boiled lids on the jars and screw the rings down firmly tight. Process in boiling water bath for 10 minutes. Or just pour into jars, cool, then refrigerate. This is very good.

You can also add chopped walnuts for a conserve, instead of a jam.

— Jackie

Build a heated germination bed

By Charles A. Sanders

The heated germination bed in the author's home greenhouse. The covers can be lowered at night to provide even more warmth.

Many of us who garden have learned the benefits of starting our own vegetable and flower plants. There are several benefits to having a spot to start your own plants:

- Getting a jump on the normal growing season.
- Not having to wait on commercial plant growers.
- Growing uncommon or unique varieties that you particularly like but are hard to find.
- Economics—once you have everything in place, you can grow your plants for little or no cost.

First, I'll describe the construction of our germination bed we use in our greenhouse. Our small greenhouse is built onto the side of our workshop. We have started thousands of plants in this homemade structure over the years. To get the seeds sprouted and growing, I built a heated germination bed on one of the benches in the greenhouse. It is at a convenient work height and really gets the plants going. The big advantage—and something to keep in mind when starting your plants—is that it is heated from the bottom. Regardless of how you construct your germination bed, the secret is to provide gentle heat from beneath the starting flats or trays. There are electrically heated rubber mats available, but I have not been able to justify the high prices asked for the mats offered in the growing supply catalogs. Also, being somewhat of a do-it-yourselfer, I thought that the way to go would be to make my own to fit my needs.

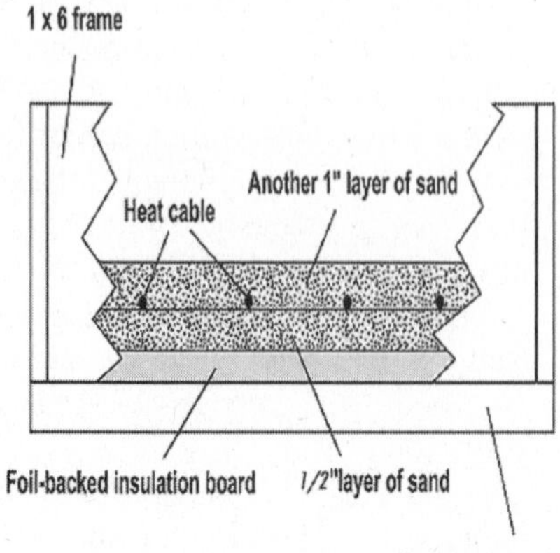

Details of a heated germination bed

On the bench

The heated germination bed that I constructed in our greenhouse is simple and works very well. I began by framing in an area of one of the greenhouse benches with some old 1 x 6 lumber. The measurements were not critical, but I did allow space for several of the black plastic seedling trays that we had recycled from a local grocery store that was selling commercial plants. The accompanying illustration pretty well describes the sizing and most of the construction details.

Once I had the frame built, I cut a piece of foil-backed insulation board to fit snuggly inside the frame. Any cracks were then sealed with a squirt of expandable foam insulation that is available at any hardware store.

Next, a ½-inch layer of clean sand was added and spread evenly over the insulation board. I then arranged a heat cable as evenly as possible on top of the sand. After it was in place, I added another layer of sand and spread it evenly over the cable.

Here's an important note about the heat cable. The cables used in this project and those mentioned below are not the type used to keep pipes from freezing. I purchased them from a commercial grower's supply

Resources

Heat cables:
Charlie's Garden and Greenhouse, 17979 State Rt. 536, Mt. Vernon, WA 98273.

Greenhouse covering:
Northern Greenhouse Sales, P.O. Box 42, Neche, ND 58265.

company. They are made just for the purpose we are using them for and keep the soil at about 70° F.

Another trick I added was the covers, or lids, for the germination beds that you can see in the photograph. I simply made these from 1 x 2 stock of a convenient length. I covered them with the same woven plastic material that the greenhouse is covered with. They can be raised or lowered as temperatures dictate. Even in the greenhouse, the covers can help to get plants sprouted more quickly.

Making a "hot bed"

One of the old standby methods of creating a heated germination bed, or simply a "hot bed," is to make the structure right on the ground from some concrete blocks or treated lumber. It can be built against the garden wall, against an outbuilding, or freestanding. It can have a sloped covering or can be flat. I prefer to make it higher in the back than in the front to allow for a sloped covering and runoff of rain. The covering can be in the form of some old window sashes, used storm windows, homemade frames covered with plastic or glass, or anything else you come up with to do the job. The difference in this structure and an ordinary cold frame is that for germinating seeds, we will again be providing bottom heat. This can be done most easily in two ways.

The first method for heating your hot bed is as described above, using a heat cable. Arrange it evenly in the bottom of the bed, being sure that the wire does not cross itself. Doing so can cause the cable to overheat, burn out and possibly cause a fire.

The second method is the "old-fashioned way." As you might already know, decomposing plant material can create a good amount of heat. This is especially true if the plant material has been processed through some type of livestock first! To utilize the benefits of this decomposition, remove enough soil from your planting bed so that you can replace it with about a foot of fresh livestock manure. As the manure decomposes, it will create steady even heat for your sprouting seeds. It's a good idea to keep the bed in the 75-85 degree range. A cheap outdoor thermometer will help you keep tabs on the temperature. Monitor the temperature in the bed, covering it at night and on cool cloudy days, and raising the cover during the day as conditions warrant. The sun will heat things up even on cool days, so keep an eye on it. It is easy to "cook" young plants if they don't get some ventilation. Δ

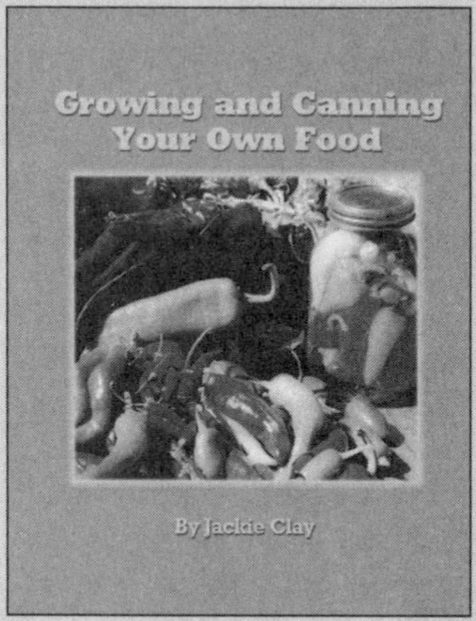

Butcher-block restoration

By Tom R. Kovach

Some homes, especially some older ones, have butcher-block counters. They can have a rustic appeal and can also be quite handy. However, if they have not been attended to for some time they can start to crack or separate as the wood begins to dry out.

The moisture in the wood should be replenished on a regular basis to prevent drying and cracking.

When a butcher-block counter starts to show a lot of cut marks it should be sanded with fine sandpaper. Butcher-block oil or thin mineral oil should be applied to treat the wood. Cooking oils, such as vegetable or olive oil, should *not* be used as they will turn rancid. The best commercial products are moisturizers and protectants made with a blend of oils and beeswax. Read the labels.

The butcher-block counter should be treated with a light oil once a day for a week, then once a week for a month. After that it should be treated with oil about once a month to prevent additional drying and cracking. Δ

Some tips for aging gardeners

By Tom R. Kovach

As we get older and find we have more time to do things we enjoy such as gardening, we also discover that with age comes aches, pains and other problems that slow us down a bit. But that doesn't mean we still can't keep gardening. We just have to scale back a bit and face up to the realization that we can only do so much.

My father still worked in his vegetable garden when he was in his eighties. I remember him putting pads on his knees and always keeping plenty of water nearby and taking regular rests in the shade.

Here are some tips for older gardeners:

- If it becomes too hard or painful, cut back on your gardening. Consider raised beds and containers where you won't have to bend or kneel so much. Try growing flowers and other plants that are less demanding, plants that do well with less human care.

- Do some warm-up exercises before working in the garden. Vary what you do so that the same joints and muscles are not always doing the work. And as my father did, take plenty of breaks in a shaded area. In fact, try working in the early or later parts of the day when the temperature is cooler and you're not constantly in the heat of the sun. Protect yourself with loose fitting, light colored clothes. Wear a wide brimmed hat and long pants and long sleeved shirt. Sunburn and overly long exposure to the sun can lead to skin cancer. For the exposed parts of your body, face, hands, neck, etc., use a fragrance-free sunscreen with an SPF of 15 or more.

- Make sure you consume plenty of fluids. When my father gardened, he carried an old army canteen full of water with him. Don't drink ice-cold water. Have some liquid before and while you're gardening, especially on hot days.

- Always protect your eyes with proper sunglasses. Use polarized ones with UV-blocking filters. Make sure these glasses fit well so that you will be comfortable and don't have to keep pushing them up. Remember, if the glasses are too dark your pupils will dilate and allow more damaging UV light to enter.

- You shouldn't try to skimp on buying proper sunglasses and neither should you try to cut corners when buying garden tools. Your tools should be sharp and in good working order. If you look around at gardening stores, you'll find there are tools to fit every gardener. This includes people with smaller hands or who are shorter. Find tools that have padded grips or handles that are adjustable to fit your needs. If they're lightweight and still do the job, all the better. These tools will involve less stress. You can also find some tools that are designed to be used standing up, and these will eliminate extra bending over.

- If you garden sitting down, or on your knees like my father did, look for products that will help you work from a sitting position. There are kneeling devices that flip over to form small seats, and short carts will work as both a low stool and a means of carrying plants, tools, etc.

My father used leather mittens with liners to protect his knees. But now there are high-density foam kneeling pads or strap-on knee pads such as carpet layers and roofers use.

- While it is nice to garden around dusk when the air is cooler, it's also the time the bugs are out. To protect yourself from mosquitoes or other biting creatures, use repellents containing DEET. This is especially effective against mosquitoes. Also, remember that the scent of soaps, shampoos, etc., attracts insects. So take your bath or shower when the gardening is done for the day.

Younger gardeners

Younger gardeners also need to be safety conscious.

About 10 years ago the *Physicians and Sportsmedicine Journal* included gardeners on its list of 10 occupations with the highest rates of carpal tunnel syndrome, a painful and sometimes disabling inflammation near the base of the hand at the wrist.

So besides warming up first, take plenty of breaks, at least one every hour, or engage in a different activity to prevent repetitive motions. If you're raking for a long time, for example, switch to something like hauling with a wheelbarrow or planting something.

If you use wide-handled tools with padded or thicker handles, you protect the smaller joints in your hands. Working with your wrist in a more neutral or straight position will help to prevent injuries in the wrist and forearm.

It is best not to sit back on your knees, because bending your knees this far is not only a tough position for the joints, but requires you to push most of your body weight up with your hands and wrists, placing increased pressure on these joints. Try to get used to using some sort of bench or a short gardening stool.

And, of course, limit gardening in extreme heat. Δ

Build a simple solar powered outdoor light

By Jeffrey R. Yago, P.E., CEM

In our last issue, I discussed how to use solar energy to power a remote well pump. In this issue, I will describe how you can build a simple solar powered light. This is not one of those inexpensive solar walk lights sold in garden supply stores. This is a commercial quality light that can easily illuminate a parking area, remote outbuilding, dark driveway, or large road sign. Figure 1 shows the pole lamp version of this lighting system.

Figure 1. Pole-mounted street light showing a front view of the solar light

Main components

There are four components required to build any solar powered light: the solar array, high efficiency D.C. lamp, charge controller, and a battery. The solar array will be the most expensive component required, and these are now available in many different sizes and wattage ratings.

Figure 2 shows the rear view of a solar pole light. The solar array includes an adjustable pole mount which allows facing the solar array toward the south (in northern latitudes), with a tilt angle approximately equal to the latitude (30 to 40 degrees for most parts of the central United States). The weatherproof light fixture is mounted at a height and tilt that best illuminates the area desired.

Just under the solar array is a weatherproof, but vented, enclosure to house all electrical components. This will include a sealed no-maintenance battery and a solar charge controller. The charge controller protects the battery from over-charging, maximizes the charging voltage and current output of the solar array, and controls when the light operates.

Figure 2. Rear view of a pole-mounted solar light

Lighting fixture types

Figures 3 and 4 show one of the newest types of low-voltage DC light fixtures available. This is a 35-watt low-pressure sodium street light that includes built-in time controls. A standard plug-in photocell is mounted on the top, and the protective fixture housing includes switch controls to adjust the lamp start delay time and operating times.

Low-pressure sodium lighting appears brownish in color and is normally used to illuminate large parking areas and highways due to its long lamp life and very low energy requirements. This type of fixture is usually mounted on a tall pole to illuminate a large area when low light level and a non-white color spectrum is acceptable.

Figure 5 shows a 13-watt compact fluorescent fixture in an aluminum housing, now available for 12-volt DC operation. This fixture is commonly used for ground level mounting to illuminate up towards a sign or wall area.

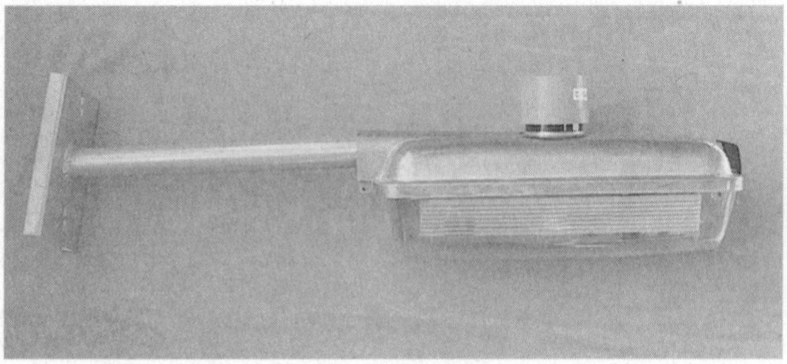

Figure 3. 12-volt D.C. low-pressure sodium fixture by Orgatech-Omegalux Corp.

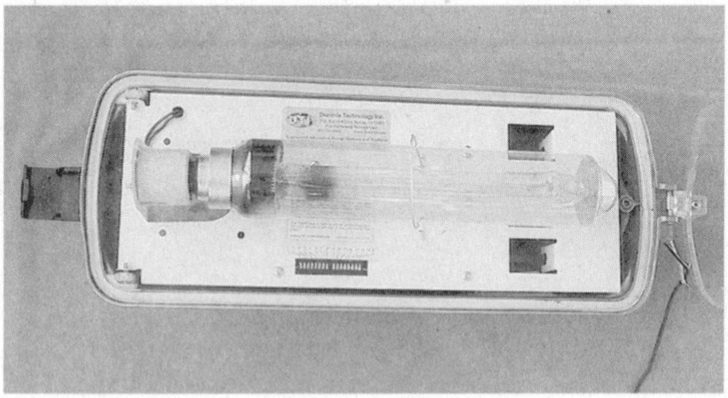

Figure 4. Low-pressure sodium fixture with lens removed. Note timer program control dip switches.

Figure 6 shows a low-voltage compact fluorescent fixture with a nonmetallic housing that includes a photocell. This fixture and lens design is intended to mount on the side of a wall to illuminate the ground area next to a building or over an entry. Both fixtures use a two-pin base, compact fluorescent twin-tube lamp, typically in the 9 or 13-watt size. Fixtures designed for use with very low wattage lamps maximize the light output by using a highly polished reflector behind the lamp, and a clear plastic focusing lens in front of the lamp.

System controls

Unlike most dusk-to-dawn photocell controls used with AC grid connected outdoor lights, most solar powered lighting applications do not operate the light continuously all night, as a way to reduce the solar array size and extend battery life.

In many northern latitudes, it is not unusual during cloudy winter months for a conventional photocell controlled outdoor light to turn on around 4 p.m. in the evening, and stay on until 7 a.m. the next morning.

Since short winter days may only provide four hours of solar energy collection time, it's difficult to fully recharge a battery in this short period and then expect it to power a lighting load continuously for the next 15 hours.

Figure 7 shows two brands of solar battery charge controllers that include built-in lighting timer controls. The Trace C12 controller on the left of the photo provides good three-stage battery charging, plus provides on/off light control using the solar array as a photocell to signal when it gets dark.

For more sophisticated applications, the MorningStar Sunlight solar control on the right of the photo is an excellent choice. This controller is available in 10 and 20-amp versions, and for 12 and 24-volt DC applications. In addition to being a three-stage battery charge controller, an adjustable dial allows programming the light to stay "on" from 2 to 10 hours after sunset, to turn "off" then back "on" for 1 to 2 hours before sunrise, or simply to provide dusk-to-dawn operation. Some solar controllers also include a jumper to select between a flooded and sealed battery to maximize charging efficiency and extend battery life.

Putting it all together

Figure 8 shows a complete solar-powered sign lighting system we recently designed for an industrial park. The main entrance sign was located over a half mile from the nearest office building, which would have required trenching a long distance under a parking lot, street, and sidewalk.

The installation costs to run a conventional underground AC power line this far were higher than the cost of a self-contained solar powered lighting system. This installation has a 13-watt fluorescent fixture (see Figure 5) located in the planter box on each side of the sign, a pole-mounted solar array mounted next to the sign, and a weatherproof box located behind the sign which contains the charge controller and 12-volt gel-cell battery.

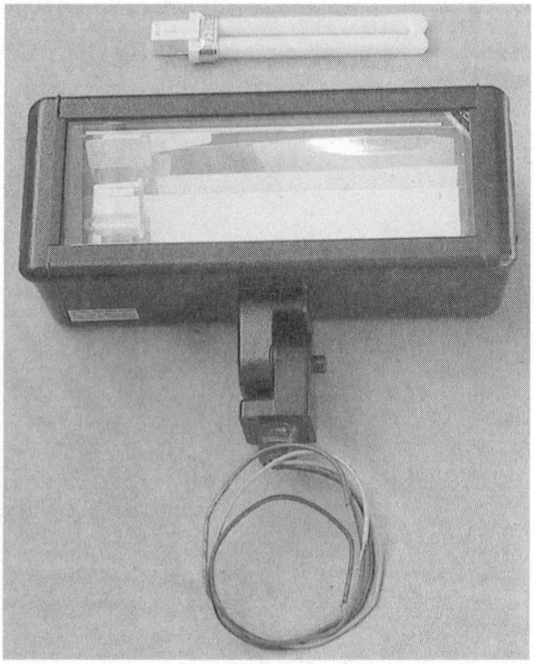

Figure 5. 12-volt DC compact fluorescent ground-mounted fixture

The sizing of the solar array, battery, and charge controller will depend on the wattage of lamp you choose, and how many hours you want it to operate each night. If your location is subject to frequent periods of cloudy weather, your battery needs to store energy for more than one day of lighting operation.

For example, let's say you want to power a 13-watt fluorescent fixture an average of 4 hours each night. **(13 watts x 4 hours)/ 12 volts = 4.33 amp-hour/day**

Since there will be an efficiency loss during both the battery charging and battery discharging process, and additional efficiency losses for the fluorescent ballast, charge controller, and wiring, we need to add at least 30 percent more to our initial calculation. **(4.3 amp-hour) x (1.3) = 5.8 amp-hour/day**

If you want three days of continued operation during cloudy weather when there will be no solar charging, you will need a solar charged battery that can store three times this daily amp-hour value.

I strongly recommend buying a good quality sealed or gel-cell battery designed for daily deep discharge cycling. In addition, since the enclosure must be vented for safety in case of battery out-gassing, the battery life will be reduced due to the high and low outdoor temperatures it will experience. For these applications, most batteries will need replacement every three years.

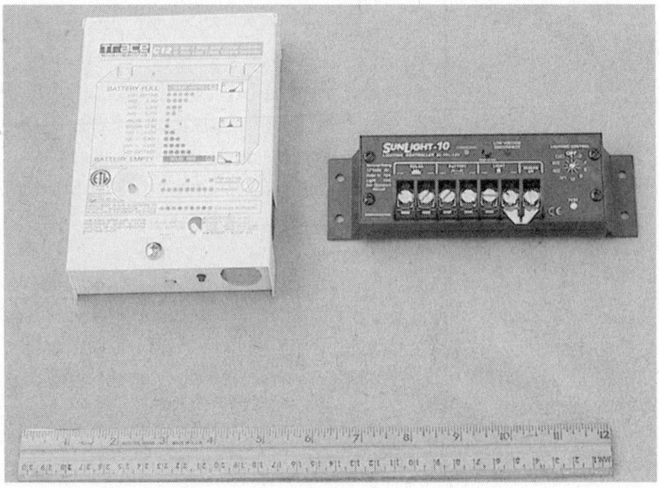

Figure 7. Low-voltage charge controllers with built-in lighting controls

Array sizing

Like the battery, the size of the solar array also depends on the lamp wattage and daily operating hours. Unless you live in a very southern or desert climate, a fixed south facing solar array will receive direct sunlight only from an average of 9 a.m. to 3 p.m. during summer months, and 10 a.m. to 2 p.m. during winter months.

This means a solar array having a 40-watt nameplate rating could generate 240-watt hours (40 watt x 6 hours) of power during a very sunny day. A 13-watt fluorescent lamp would operate 18 hours on this energy (240 watt-hour/13 watts), assuming no efficiency losses.

However, solar module nameplate ratings are based on lab testing under perfect solar conditions. Actual power output will vary for each hour of the day for different module orientations, and for constantly changing cloud cover and air temperature. If your lighting application is more demanding, you may need more than one solar module, or use a larger battery to guarantee the light will always be able to operate the hours required.

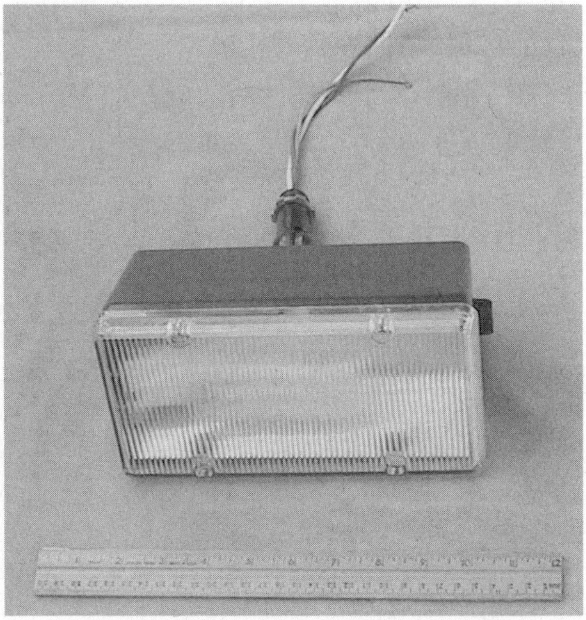
Figure 6. 12-volt D.C. compact fluorescent wall-mounted fixture by Thin-Lite Corp.

Wiring diagram

The wiring diagram I have included in Figure 9 shows a typical circuit to connect a solar array, battery, charge controller, and light fixture. Due to the lower 12-volt operation, the operating currents will be 10 times higher than the current required if this was a 120 volt AC light fixture having the same wattage lamp.

Therefore, I recommend using a minimum of 10-gauge stranded copper wire. Any wire exposed to sunlight and moisture needs to be rated for this type of service. In addition, since a solar module can be extremely hot during the summer, any wire used to connect to its rear terminals must also have a high temperature rating. A single conductor type "USE" cable is an excellent choice for solar applications and should meet all UL code requirements.

Also note that I have included a separate fuse to protect the battery and load side of this circuit. Keep all

Figure 8. Solar powered street signage that includes: ground-mounted light fixtures located in the planter box on each side of the sign, a pole-mounted solar array mounted next to the sign, and a weather-proof box located behind the sign which contains the charge controller and 12-volt gel-cell battery.

wiring runs short and use "crimp" type copper terminals to reduce voltage loss and improve long-term connector reliability. Be sure to use a #6 or larger solid copper wire to connect the solar module frame, light fixture, and mounting rack to a ground rod.

Conclusions

For estimating purposes, I recommend using a 40-watt solar array and 50 amp-hour capacity battery to power a 13-watt lamp five hours per night. For a 35-watt lighting load, you will need an 80 amp-hour or larger battery, and at least two 50-watt solar modules. Some parts of the United States may require higher values than these estimates. These values should provide at least three days of standby operation during cloudy weather without discharging the battery below its safe operating limit. Remember, repeated discharging of any battery below a 50 percent discharge level will significantly reduce battery life, and automotive type batteries cannot take this daily deep discharge cycling.

Finally, due to significant differences in weather conditions and solar availability in each area of the country, you may need to experiment with the light's start and stop operating times to avoid excessive battery discharge.

If you like the idea of a solar powered outdoor light, but would prefer not to do-it-yourself, there are many packaged systems now available that are pre-sized for your specific location and lighting requirements. Δ

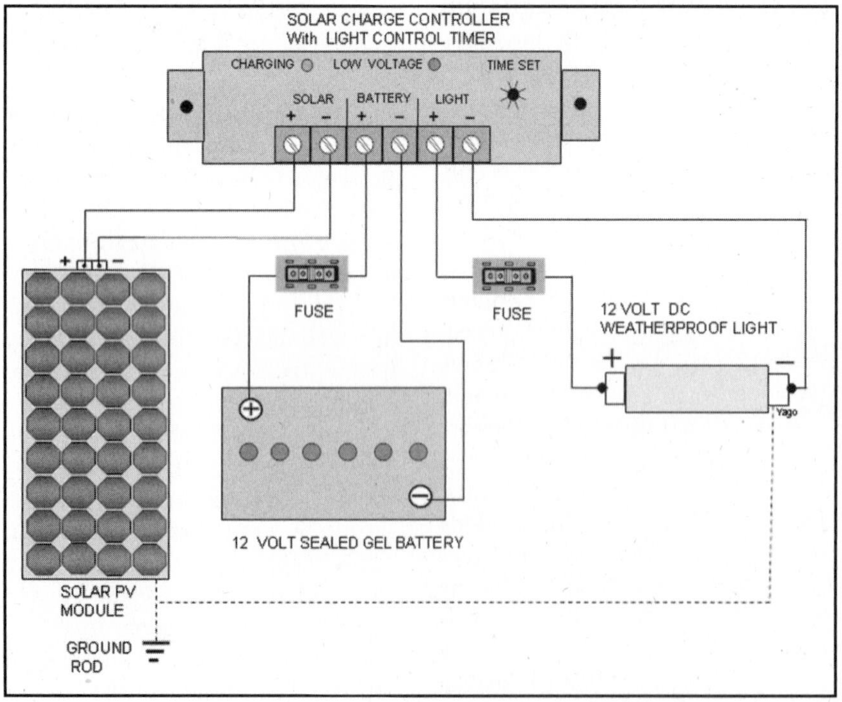

Figure 9. A solar powered light wiring diagram

Resources

DC Light Fixtures

Thin-Lite Corp
www.thinlite.com
805-987-5021

Solar Components

National Solar Supply
www.nationalsolarsupply.com
866-255-1829

Kansas Wind Power
www.kansaswindpower.net
785-364-4407

Backwoods Solar Electric Systems
www.backwoodssolar.com
208-263-4290

Complete systems

Power Pod Corp
www.powerpod.com
888-786-3374

Swiss chard

the leaf vegetable that keeps on giving!

By Raymond Nones

For years every spring I planted spinach in my garden. For those who have never tasted home grown spinach, there is a world of difference between its taste and that of store bought. However, although home grown tastes great, its downside is that it is not an easy crop to grow. A heavy feeder, it quickly bolts to seed as soon as the days begin to lengthen. I was getting very little in return for a lot of effort. I decided to look for a spinach substitute.

Of all of the crops I considered, Swiss chard stood out. From its first sowing I have never looked back. It was everything I wanted and more. It's the only plant I know of that gives a continuous harvest starting in the cool spring, right through a hot summer, and far into cool late fall. What's more, if covered with a shredded leaf mulch, it will overwinter, then can continue to be harvested in the following season up to summer when it will go to seed.

My garden is a modular form, three 4x8-foot framed raised beds. At sowing time, in the bed where the Swiss chard is to go, I prepare the soil by raking it smooth, then spreading a thin layer of fine compost over the area. Since rows are planted across the bed, I use a four-foot length of 1x2 furring strip as a "planting stick." The stick is painted white with the face being marked off in increments of one inch.

Markings on the planting stick make seed spacing quick and easy.

You can make furrows by laying the stick across the bed and then tilting it to a 45° angle so that the edge in contact with the soil forms a "V" when worked back and forth. Then place the stick flat next to the furrow and using the markings on its face, sow a seed at every inch mark. Hold the seed in the palm of one hand and pick it up with the thumb and forefinger of the other. After the furrow is sown, curl the forefinger and, with that part between the first and second joints, press the seed into the soil.

Like beets, each seed ball contains more than one seed. When seedlings come up, thin any clumps so that only one seedling stands every one inch. When they are big enough to use, as needed, thin to two inches apart. Use thinnings in salads. As plants grow bigger, again thin as needed, this time to four inches. Once that phase is finished, finally thin the plants so they are spaced out to eight inches.

For these remaining plants, harvesting is done by plucking (not cutting) the outer leaves together with their stalks leaving the heart of the plant intact. New stalks and leaves will grow back rather quickly. Grasp the stalk at its base right at the ground level and either snap off with a twisting motion or by pulling downward with a sharp tug. Take a few leaves at a time from each plant so they will continue to produce.

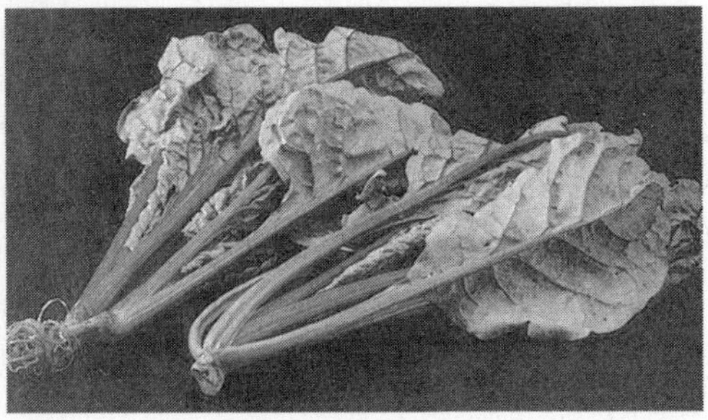

Red Swiss chard

At maturity the entire plant can be harvested leaving only the center heart. It will re-grow, in effect giving you a new plant. Swiss chard is one of the few vegetables that provides a continuous harvest without successive plantings.

Besides being extremely productive, it is also a beautiful plant and is often used as an ornamental. But it excels as a leaf crop. The leaves can be eaten raw in salads or cooked like spinach. Stalks can be chopped up and also eaten uncooked in salads or can be left intact and cooked like asparagus. As for food value, it is one of the best vegetables for vitamin A and is an excellent source of calcium and iron.

The plant comes in a variety of colored stalks; red, white, or shades of yellow. Take your pick or grow them all by buying a rainbow seed assortment. The most widely grown varieties are: *Fordhook Giant, Lucullus, Rhubarb Chard,* and *Bright Lights.*

I am a dyed in the wool Swiss chard fan. I heartily recommend reserving a place for it in your garden. Δ

Starting over again

Part 3

An unexpected freeze and a bigger temporary home

By Jackie Clay

Spring had changed to summer, seemingly overnight. The first of the blueberries were already getting ripe and the wild red raspberries hung heavy on their brambles, scattered here and there across the long hill on our new backwoods homestead in northern Minnesota. The goats ran wild across the clearings during the day, constantly snacking on popple twigs, berry tips, and wildflowers. But there was plenty for all of us, and we didn't mind sharing. Our goats and sheep seemed to delight in their new home, almost as much as we did.

But summer in northern Minnesota is way, way too short, especially when you're trying to establish the bare bones for your new homestead, as we are. It didn't help that this past summer was the coldest summer on record in Minnesota history.

I had gotten up early the 26th of July, intent on visiting our two gardens on the edge of the wilderness, which we had hacked out of small openings in the trees. Somehow, just walking among the growing plants that looked so vital and healthy encouraged and uplifted me.

The tomatoes were already two feet tall, having had their cozy Wall 'O Water tipis removed two weeks ago. They had plenty of tomatoes set on their vines, some of which were already starting to turn color. The Early Cascade and Oregon Spring tomatoes both set fruit even when the weather is cool, so at least a dozen plants offered fresh tomatoes in a week or less.

David gives Grandpa a tour of our new Minnesota homestead

We had been running around like the proverbial chickens with their heads cut off last summer, trying to do too many things all at the same time. We were immensely enjoying having Mom and Dad living with us and being able to tap into the vast storehouse of knowledge they have. But with Mom in a wheelchair and Dad able to get around with a cane and helper, I was spending a lot of time doing other things than pouring cement and nailing nails.

I was not frustrated with the care giving, but with not getting things done I wanted to. After we had finally decided we would get the old, free mobile home that my son, Bill, found for us to use as temporary housing while we built the house, our efforts had switched from finishing our rock foundation to cleaning up the place the mobile would be put when it arrived.

I had been kind of avoiding my tomato beds below the now-abandoned house site, as it was just too depressing. Although I know we'll pick up the construction again in the spring, the home site looks dismal and sad. I'll admit that a few mornings I went out there and sat down and cried.

But after giving myself a pep talk on that sunny, clear, cool morning, I set off with our old three legged Labrador retriever, Pup, to check the garden. All the way out there, I marveled at how well the blueberries looked, hanging heavy with green, luscious fruit, bending the branches down with the bounty. It was going to be a very good blueberry year. And we have about a quarter mile of hillside, covered in blueberries.

When I reached the tomato beds, I stopped stock still, not believing my eyes. Every tomato plant, every pepper, and the rows of bush beans in front of the tomatoes were black and drooping dismally. It had *frozen* last night. On the 26th of *July*! Not frosted lightly—frozen. I couldn't breathe for a long minute. The backbone of our garden was gone; perhaps the tomatoes were not dead, but would sprout from the roots, but it would be too late to produce a crop. There was just nothing to do about it.

Unfortunately, gardening is like love. Sometimes it is wonderful, sometimes it smacks you in the face. But if you don't run the risk, you don't find the joy. This disaster totally enforces the reason for keeping at least a year's worth of food on hand. Luckily, I still had boxes and boxes of home canned tomatoes, tomato sauces, salsa, peppers, green beans, and more stacked neatly in our storage building in town. Without this, our loss would have been more of a disaster.

And likewise, it just goes to show you that those folks who laugh at establishing a good garden as a guard against future emergencies, saying if something happens, they'll grow a garden are in for a rude shock. You don't always *get* a crop when you plant your plants or seeds. A first-year garden is that much more of a gamble as the soil is not enriched and is full of roots, grass, and weeds. I've had more than one garden that took three or four years to hit excellent productivity.

Two weeks before the killing freeze, my tomatoes were snug in their Wall O' Waters and doing fine.

But nothing would have saved our garden this past summer. We had no warning of a freeze. (And who would expect one near the end of July?) I cried a bit and walked home to tell the family.

A used mobile home

But bad times don't last, and a day or so later Bill called to say our not-so-new mobile home would be hauled in a week. Were we ready? Well, pretty much so. I had been cutting the gravel hill down, hauling the excess down the trail, filling in bad spots that we had trouble with during spring breakup.

We had chosen a site for our trailer, about 300 feet from where our new home was to be built, as we didn't want to view the trailer from our new log home. Yet we wanted it fairly close so we could share a water line from the well when that was drilled later on.

Fixing a tractor

David asked if he could haul gravel with the tractor. I hesitated. He had been riding with me on most of the trips and carefully watching me scrape dirt, move piles of old logs, and dig stumps with the bucket of Bill's Ford tractor. I finally let him run the hydraulics, dumping the gravel on the road and start the tractor in the morning. But I told him that he would have to have permission from his older brother to actually run the tractor by himself.

David was nearly 14 and has worked with us and equipment of all sorts since he could handle it, but I would never turn him loose with someone else's equipment without permission. (It helped his cause that Bill had also grown up with farm equipment and had driven tractors since he was about 11.)

I've always stressed safety, safety, and more safety with the kids, and David is no exception. So I caved and asked Bill if he could use the tractor.

My tomatoes froze, dead. I was in shock.

The blueberry crop was great this summer. We used them fresh every day for yogurt, ice cream, on cereal, and in desserts.

"Yeah, sure. If he breaks it, he fixes it," he answered.

So David began learning more about the tractor. First I loaded the bucket and he hauled it down the road to spread. Then he began digging gravel and leveling the trailer site. This freed me to help Bob pick up other roots, lengths of rotten logs, and dig rocks that were in the way.

Actually, it was *I* who "broke" the tractor, rupturing a hydraulic hose. And, yes, I did fix it. But, boy, was that a chore. That fitting must have been on the tractor since it was built in 1951. We bent a wrench on it and it wouldn't budge. There wasn't room enough to get a large pipe wrench on it. We were stumped.

I called Bill and he suggested getting a map gas torch. A what? It's like a propane torch, but burns much hotter. You know, the *yellow* tank. Okay. Off we went to town. After a lengthy search, we finally came home with a new hydraulic hose and a map gas torch and tank. We cooked the fitting considerably, and it did finally loosen with another wrench with a pipe slid over the end to lengthen it for extra leverage. If you do this, remember that there *is* a risk that you could bend or break the wrench. But most times, you will not and the added length will get that fitting to turn.

Then we tried to put on the new hydraulic hose and found that we couldn't because both ends turned the opposite direction. Again I called Bill, who suggested getting a union fitting to put on one end. This would allow the joint to swivel. Yep, that worked just fine. Then, later, I looked at another of the hydraulic hoses and found a union on that one. Someone else must have had the same problem in the past. Now I'm smarter than I was.

The trailer is delivered

So we spent a week measuring the trailer site, leveling it, and shoving back the old logs even further into the trees, trying for a relatively flat spot on the gentle east-facing slope. After a couple of holdups, Bill called and told us that the trailer would come up the next day and that he had borrowed his friend, Andy's, larger tractor to help haul in the trailer in the event that Dale Sandberg, the driver and a family acquaintance, couldn't get it down our mile-long trail.

We had gone down the trail and cut out any leaning trees or ones that were too close to the road, hoping that our judgment was good. We didn't want our trailer ripped up or stuck part way home. A 14-foot wide trailer would take up every bit of our trail. It had rained, but the trail seemed pretty solid. Would the rig get stuck somewhere? And if it did, would we be able to get it out?

Later that day, David on his four wheeler and me leading the way, Dale and Bill started down the trail with the, seemingly, *huge* trailer. It filled the entire trail, crashing over small trees and brush on both sides as it went. We all held our breath as it came on...and on. In about 10 minutes, the trailer was backed into its resting place in our yard. Bill was right. Shoved way back in the trees, you didn't notice it too much. And look at all that *room*. After living for six months in a 28-foot travel trailer and attached fish house, a 70-foot trailer looked simply *huge*.

Bill, Bob, and David blocked up the tongue and wheels very well to prevent our temporary home from rolling down the slope and we were in business. As the trailer had been used only for a hunting shack and weekender, the care it had received was not the best. The inside was basically solid, but there were rotten spots in the hall and bedroom floors, squirrel holes in the ceiling, mouse you-know-whats everywhere, and plenty of cleaning to do. Besides that, the insulation under the trailer was pretty much gone and the roof had leaked. Yep, a fixer-upper. But that's what we do best, it seems.

We had bought several rolls of fiberglass insulation and had them sitting next to the site. So while Mom and Dad sat in lawn chairs, Bill, Bob, and David crawled under the trailer and began the horrible job of tearing out the old insulation and stapling new insulation between the floor joists. I acted as the gofer, opening bags of insulation and handing the appropriate sized batts. In this trailer, there were three sizes of openings between the floor joists, 15 inches, 22 inches, and 25 inches. This made things more difficult. A 16-inch batt would work for the 15-inch openings, and a 24-inch batt could be compressed to fit in the 22-inch opening, but we had to tape part of a 15-inch batt to another to make the 25-inch openings. This slowed things down considerably.

It took several weeks to get it mostly insulated, but the next week Bill came with a large air powered hydraulic jack and he jacked the trailer up just enough to get the wheels off that he had borrowed from his wife's uncle. About that time, a friend rolled in to remove the axles we said he could have if he took them off. We have no plans on ever moving that trailer again so getting the axles off made it easier to insulate and block the trailer up on its cement block piers. When our new house is done and we move in, we will use the mobile home as a guest house and storage for our "too much stuff."

Like a hive of bees, we clustered around the trailer, Bill jacking and leveling, David, Bob, and I carrying cement blocks, handing a shovel to Bill under the trailer to level the spot each pier sat on, finding blocks of two-inch planks to finish out piers to be perfectly level, and other gofer jobs. We worked very carefully, as that trailer weighs several tons and we had no desire to end up squashed under our home like the witch in *The Wizard of Oz*.

David escorts the new free-for-the-hauling mobile up our mile-long trail.

Flooring and doors

As soon as we had the trailer squared in as low as it could possibly sit, Bill packed up his equipment and got ready to head home. About that time, Mom and Dad wanted to see the inside of their new temporary home. So we lifted Mom's wheelchair up through the front door and Dad climbed gingerly up the cement blocks we'd piled as temporary steps in front. Aided by three of us, they were in. Inspecting the unit, front to back, both were full of ideas for remodeling. Like I said, the five of us in our little travel trailer was cozy. This seemed to be a battleship.

But so much work to do. First off was to shore up the rotten spots in the floor. That turned out to be easier than we thought. Most rotten spots were at the edges of the trailer due to water leaks. We just had to sandwich one or more two-inch planks along the floor joists to support a new piece of plywood under the flooring. This we screwed snugly, using a battery powered power screw driver.

This is one of the handiest tools we own on the homestead. We have two, one a 9-volt and the other a 12-volt. Bill uses an 18-volt unit, which has much more power and lasts longer between recharges. We use ours for some job nearly every day of the week. The big bonus over using nails is that you can later remove something, without damaging the building material. It seems that we're in a constant state of changing from temporary to permanent, building to rebuilding, and the screws save time and material.

In front of the front door was a large rotten spot, due to the door being fit incorrectly. The previous owner had added an exterior storm door, which had no flashing. The water poured off the roof, down in between the doors and ran into the house. Pretty soon, the flooring had rotted. To fix that, we used a stud finder to locate the floor joists on each side of the rotten spot. Then carefully adjusting our circular saw to

Bob, Bill, and Dale Sandberg set the new trailer into its site.

The floor was rotten by the front door. We cut out a four by four-foot piece and replaced it.

cut just a tiny bit deeper than the flooring was thick, we marked out a four foot square to remove the bad flooring.

The lines were drawn down the center of each floor joist, then across them at right angles. Carefully holding the saw down firmly in front, with the rear elevated and the guard held very gingerly open, I started sawing, slowly lowering the saw to meet the line and moving forward as I did so. This neatly cut through the flooring to the wall. Then I turned around and finished the cut past where I had started. Repeating this on two other cuts, we were ready to remove the flooring. David got under the trailer and with a hammer and pry bar, he loosened the chunk until we were able to pry it loose above. Being rotten, it broke up in several pieces, but it came off, leaving nice straight edges.

While I measured and cut a new piece (which we'd scrounged at the dump), Bob and David nailed in short pieces of header (2x6) to support where we'd cut across the floor joists, as the flooring had to be supported all the way around.

It only took a few minutes to nail the new flooring into place. Now you don't fall through the floor when you come into the door!

Speaking of the door, the Mickey Mouse storm door fell off in my hand the first day we had the trailer home. It's lucky it didn't fall off on the highway. Our friend, Tom, who got the trailer axles, saw the bad state of our front door. The frame had pretty much rotted away due to the same water leak that had done in the floor. Tom's a pretty handy guy, doing carpentry, roofing, and all manner of other fixer upper jobs for a living.

A day later, here came Tom with a complete door and frame he'd taken out on a job. Grabbing a saw, tape measure, and hammer, he, Bob, and David set about tearing out the old door and installing the new one. Whew, could that man work! In an hour, they'd completely installed the door and he hung the curtain that came with it. And the door actually closed all the way.

He did more or less what we did with the floor. He cut out all the rotted wood, carefully saving the inside paneling and outside aluminum, cut studs to replace the vertical studs that had supported the door frame, tacked the sheeting back onto it, and slid in the door frame.

Once we could keep heat inside the trailer and critters out, we set about getting it ready to live in it as soon as possible. Mom and Dad's bedroom floor had been sheeted with plywood underlayment, as it wasn't rotten, but was weak in spots. They bought a roll of vinyl flooring to cover it so it was my job to get it ready to put down.

This was a little tricky to cut as there was a built-in set of drawers, a closet, and one wall was two inches off square when the trailer was built. Using a large square, I determined that the outside walls were nearly square. Then, using them as a starting point, I very carefully took measurements for everything. Two days later, I measured it again and checked my figures. All were correct but one, which I remeasured and changed. You know the old adage "measure twice, cut once?" It is so true.

We have no flat, smooth place to lay out linoleum, so we hauled it to a grassy meadow half a mile down our trail and unrolled it carefully. Then with a permanent marker, a straight, 10-foot long 1x3, and a yardstick, I marked the cuts, praying they were right. Again, checking everything

David screwing down the decking

over, I was satisfied they were correct. Sweating mightily, Bob and I cut the flooring, using a pair of straight tin snips and a linoleum knife.

Rolling it up again, we were off for home. Preparation of the floor consisted of covering a hole where a floor vent had been, filling cracks where pieces of plywood had joined and sanding them, vacuuming, and covering the areas with a few sheets of newspaper to prevent any possible wearing.

To do the job right, we should have used mastic, but this flooring may be taken up later to use in a bedroom in the house, so we just laid it without cement. Carefully starting with the roll in the square corner without a closet or other cutout, we unrolled and kept tugging the flooring perfectly straight. So far, so good. Then came the closet and its cutouts. Bob has more patience, so he crawled in there and puttered around with a linoleum knife for perfection. Not bad. Then we fit it around the drawers. Ouch, we were two inches shy. How could that have happened?

I was frantic until Bob pulled the side of the cabinet back out. It was poorly built and someone had pushed it in during the work. Whew!

We were done and it actually *fit.*

I spent a lot of time scrubbing, painting, and fixing. Here, I was painting over horrible orange striped paneling in the kitchen.

I cut carpet bars for the bathroom door and the hall doorway, to keep our feet from ripping up the edges of the vinyl. Add some trim to the walls, and we're in business. Not perfect, but suited to our purpose. And the room looks a hundred times brighter and much cleaner.

Angel, our goat, supervises deck construction.

Heating

Okay, now they had a bedroom. But the nights were getting cool and Mom freezes when it's 75°. We needed heat in the trailer before we could move in. And you can't use a mobile home furnace without electricity. Running the generator 24/7 is not an option.

Dad has bad lungs and cannot tolerate wood smoke or even aftershave lotion. So we couldn't use a wood stove, which isn't safe in a mobile home anyway. Our other option was to install a vented propane heater in their bedroom, and plan on adding another one before real cold weather hit in the living room. They are expensive, but with elderly parents, we had no choice.

Dad bought a smaller unit at our local Fleet Supply store and Bill, who is a certified gas technician, installed it. We could move in without having popsicle parents.

Being located on top of a hill, with the surrounding land relatively clear due to a clearcut timber sale 10 years ago, we get quite a bit of wind. And we didn't want the mobile rocked off its piers in a strong gust. So to stabilize it further, we set about to start skirting the trailer. This prevents wind from getting under it and lifting. It also keeps it warmer in the winter. We just used pieces of plywood siding that we had scavenged at the dump and cleaned up. I screwed the top to the outside floor joist of the trailer and where the pieces joined I screwed them to vertical pieces of 2x4. As Bob and David insulated a section of the trailer I added the skirting on both sides. The front I beam sat right on the ground.

Building an access

Two days after getting the mobile set up on our site, we celebrated Dad's 93rd birthday (and my nephew, Sean's 15th birthday) in the barebones trailer. To get in, we carried Mom's wheelchair up through the door and helped Dad, with his cane, climb the rickety stack of cement blocks we were using for a temporary stairway. That was scary, but Dad is stubborn and wanted in.

So, to avoid future problems, we set about to add a deck and handicap ramp to our new, temporary home. Measuring eight feet out from the trailer, we dug two three-foot-deep holes with a post hole digger. (To get them square, we also measured 10 feet apart, then measured diagonally, like an X. When both measurements were exact, we had the marks for our holes.) Then we tamped in the two

Mom in her new home

treated 4x4 posts that were eight feet long. Using a level on both sides of each post, I made sure that they were straight, all ways as they were set.

Then we screwed a 2x6 onto the outside floor joist of the trailer. To make sure this was the right height (so the deck would be exactly level with the mobile's floor), I held a scrap of decking on top of the 2x6. I screwed the end near the door first, with Bob and David holding the 2x6 and a level. Then we did the other end and center.

Holding a piece of decking on this plank, we held a level on it, establishing where another 2x6 would be screwed to the outside of the posts we had set. Then we leveled this one, which would support the outside edge of the 8-by-10-foot deck. We also ran other 2x6s from the posts to the 2x6 on the trailer to box in the bottom of the deck, then every two feet, from one end of the 10-foot deck, to the other. This would securely support the decking.

After this was done, we simply screwed down the decking. David loves helping on such projects. He got his start back in New Mexico. At five years of age, he helped Grandpa make two other decks, using a power screwdriver before he could ride a bicycle.

We had the deck complete in two hours, and then started the ramp. I screwed a piece of 2x6 down across the top of what would be the head of the ramp, holding it down ¾ of an inch, so the ramp would end up flush with the deck. Then we screwed a 16-foot 2x6 against the trailer, on a gentle slope, with the bottom resting on a piece of patio block, flush with the ground. The bottom of this plank was beveled, to sit flush with the ground. We did this kind of trial and error, but finally got it right, cutting two to match.

The second formed up the outside of the ramp. We dug in three more posts, which would support the cross pieces under the ramp and would also hold the hand rails. We found scraps of 2x6 here and there, cutting them to fit every two feet across the ramp, and especially from post to inside (trailer side) of the frame.

Then all that was left to do was to screw down the ¾-inch treated plywood, making a solid, gentle access ramp for wheelchairs, canes, and walkers.

This ramp was completed in less than a day, including the hand rails. But I will admit that at the end of the afternoon, we were all pooped. Bob opted for a nap and I asked David if he wanted to go with me in the canoe out on the big beaver pond.

He seldom turns down canoeing, and minutes later we were paddling across the still water. We had not been on the big beaver pond since spring as there were many waterfowl nests that we did not wish to disturb. We were especially interested in what had become of the Canada goose nest on a hummock near the beaver lodge. The last time we'd been on the pond, there had been six eggs clustered in a batch of goose down. Had they hatched or had a predator gotten the eggs?

Quietly we paddled to the nest and found the remains of six hatched eggs. The babies were hatched. And by now we knew they were not babies any longer. Geese grow quickly.

We sat on the pond for quite some time, as the sun went down over the pines. Beaver swam curiously around us, trying to find out what *that* strange creature was on their pond. They came very close and looked us in the eyes. Then *whack*! Their tails would smack the water in the alarm signal. But in a few minutes they were back, scarcely able to contain their curiosity.

It was nearly dark when we began paddling slowly for home and there in the flooded, dead trees, we saw the family of geese, all in a line moving slowly on the golden water. Mom, Pop, and all six babies. Only the babies were colored the same as the adults, and very nearly as big. Months pass quickly here in the backwoods. Δ

David and I check out the big beaver pond after work.

Start spring off early with

potatoes, English peas, green onions, lettuce, & radishes

By Alice Brantley Yeager
Photos by James O. Yeager

Fresh green onions are the epitome of early garden goodness.

Snow and ice in the North and occasionally the same in the South plus torrential rains all add up to a lesson in patience. Gardens everywhere eventually lose their mud-like texture, the soil becomes workable, and we gardeners can dig in. It's spring!

First crops will no doubt include potatoes. To be assured of a bountiful harvest, one must plant potato pieces during cool weather. Some folks swear by February 14 as the main planting date no matter what the weather conditions. Ironically, February 14, 2004, dumped four to five inches of snow on our area of Southwestern Arkansas. There were no potato planters seen working on that date.

By the time mid-spring occurs, we expect the potato crop to be showing promise. Some gardeners like to carefully dig under the plants for young potatoes about the size of a half dollar and cook them with the first English peas of the season. This is as tasty a dish as ever comes out of an early garden.

If a gardener consistently has problems raising potatoes, there are several things that could be wrong. Potatoes require a well-drained, sunny location. Boggy conditions will not produce a decent crop, if any. Ideally, soil should be loose and loamy with pH factor of 4.8 - 6.5, but the good news is that almost any well-worked, fertile garden soil will produce potatoes.

Oak Leaf lettuce ready to be thinned and enjoyed in fresh, green salads.

If your soil has a tendency to pack, as with clay dirt, dig in plenty of humus, compost, aged manure, etc., as far ahead of planting time as possible. Fall would be good, thus giving the organic matter some time to condition the clay and form a better soil texture by planting time. A good policy for home gardens is to continue to mulch plants with organic matter during growing or dry seasons. Mulch will gradually break down, thus maintaining good soil and giving a continuous supply of nutrients for other plants raised in the same location after potatoes are dug. No plants producing crops of tubers or roots should be cramped for space to develop.

Never plant potato pieces as soon as they are cut. It's better to let them lie a day or so to give them a chance to dry out a bit. Then put a couple of tablespoons of powdered sulphur in a sack with the potato pieces and shake to coat the pieces. This will help prevent problems with soil fungi. (You can find sulphur at most plant supply stores.)

If you're a beginning gardener and don't have an experienced gardener

Early in the season, before potatoes mature to this size, carefully remove a few small ones from beneath their parent plants to enjoy cooked with English peas.

to guide you, it would be well worth your time to go by your local county extension agent's office and get information on a soil test. The agent will have plenty of advice and pamphlets, and they're *free*.

English peas

Another delicious early crop is English peas. We southerners have to plant them early—as soon as soil can be worked in late January or February. Waiting until the weather warms up is a no-no as far as the peas are concerned. They are strictly a cool weather crop and their vines wilt away with the coming of summer. If you live in an area where it's feasible to plant English peas, consider yourself lucky. The flavor of fresh peas from the early garden is in a class by itself. Enjoy some right off the vine while you are picking a supply for the kitchen.

Most of us don't think much about health benefits when we're enjoying a nice day in our gardens harvesting one thing or another. Munching on snap peas or larger shelling varieties is a tasty diversion—a boon of gardening. Locked away in those delicious peas are plenty of vitamins and minerals including vitamin A and potassium. Another plus—fresh peas are not high in calories.

Peas should be planted according to packet directions in well-worked, loose soil containing plenty of humus. Peas, like potatoes, will grow in almost any good garden soil. If the pH is 6.0 to 8.0, so much the better.

The vines of most peas do require some support, but whether you put up trellis netting, stick down twiggy sticks, or make a twine support is all up to you. Putting up the support right after planting is a good idea. Shortly after those seedlings appear, they are going to be producing tendrils and looking for a way up. That's also the time to lay down a good thick mulch of pine needles or other organic material to keep dirt from being washed away from roots by heavy rains.

If you are harvesting more peas than you can use at the moment, put some away for later—particularly for use in gloomy winter weather when you need both a nutritious lift and a pleasant memory of a nice day in the garden. English peas freeze well and I believe they hold their flavor better when frozen than when canned. To freeze, shell freshly picked peas and get some use from the pods by composting them. One or two minutes blanching in boiling water is sufficient for peas. To stop the cooking process, immediately drain peas, put them in ice water for 30 seconds or so and drain again. (Don't let them become overdone from boiling.) Store in air tight containers in the freezer and don't forget to date the containers. Peas are best when used before the end of the following winter.

Cleaned snap peas and snow peas may be processed the same way. Be sure to get rid of any strings or blemished pods before freezing and don't overdo the blanching. Like shelled English peas, the pods need to retain some crispness.

Green onions

What would an early spring garden be without some tender green onions? Almost any store handling garden plants will have bunches of green onions for sale and, believe me, there are usually more plants in those bunches than you think. Show me a garden that won't grow onions and you'll be showing me a plot that won't grow anything.

As with most garden plants, soil needs to be workable. Planting is easy. Take a broom handle or hoe handle and press down to make holes about 1½ to 2 inches deep in rows about 6 inches apart. Drop one plant in each hole, replace the earth and water to settle the soil. When plants begin to grow and are of a size to use, harvest by pulling out every other plant as needed. This gives room for the others to grow and you may want to leave some plants in the ground to mature and use later.

Spring onions not only come in bunches, but sets, seeds, and bulbs may be purchased, too. There are lots of different types, so enjoy experimenting. I like the bunches as they are easy to plant and they grow fast.

Easter Egg radishes are full-flavored and give added color to salads.

I like to use mulch around any leafy crop as it protects leaves from dirt being splashed up by showers. Cleaning leaves is a lot easier when grit is not a problem.

Who doesn't love a crisp green salad made with a main ingredient of fresh garden lettuce? Mixed with radishes, green onions, carrots, or other early edibles, a salad served with one's favorite crackers is a meal within itself. If one is trying to lose weight, this is a nutritious way to do it.

ers to mature. This stretches the season and makes good use of space, particularly in a small garden.

There are so many good things from the early garden that it's hard to confine comments to just a few. There are the wild plants, too. Wild onions may be a bit tedious to clean, but what a flavor! Lamb's quarters, with a taste similar to asparagus, is a real treat. Poke salad, parboiled, and garnished with hard boiled eggs—just super good. Wild strawberries don't produce well here and we envy the folks who can go out and gather them to eat fresh or make preserves, etc. Our earliest wild berry is the dewberry and, like other wild berries, it's packed with flavor that tame berries don't have.

As weather predictions have become more reliable through advanced technology, we have also seen lots of changes in the vegetables we grow. Many years ago, who would have thought we'd have so many varieties? If one type fails us because of growing conditions, we

Not only are green onions delicious to use cut-up in salads, gravies, etc., but they give flavor and color when chopped and sprinkled as a garnish over bowls of potato soup, clam chowder, and other light colored soups. Try placing a dish of just-cleaned, whole green onions on the dinner table with other victuals. The tasty onions won't last long unless you have some mighty finicky guests.

Lettuce

Fresh garden lettuce is great whether used in salads or on sandwiches. The best variety of loose-leaf for our garden is one called Oak Leaf. It is heat-resistant and we usually have better luck with this lettuce than any other.

Like other early vegetables, lettuce needs a sunny spot, fertile and loose soil. Plant according to packet directions. If you want to get a head start, plant seeds indoors in peat pots and transplant to the garden when danger of hard freezes are no longer a threat.

Radishes

How about something to add to salads that not only gives them a zippy taste, but also has eye appeal? Easter egg radishes have a delightful range of colors—pink, white, red, and even purple.

Radishes need loose soil, too, so that their roots may reach their potential. There are some of us who like to broadcast lettuce and radish seeds together in a bed. As the plants grow, they may be thinned so as to leave room for oth-

Peas are at the peak of their flavor when first shelled.

can choose another that is more suited to our area. This is particularly true when it comes to early crops. I am always attracted to varieties in catalogs that are listed as being able to take heat and humidity. I avoid the ones that are recommended for northern gardens, as those are going to go downhill as soon as they get a sampling of our climate. Not much we can do about the climate, but I appreciate the companies that give warnings.

Early harvests come and go too soon. I have only touched on a few that almost anyone can grow. Domestic varieties or wild ones, they're here to use and enjoy. Make the most of it.

Fresh English peas with new potatoes

6-8 new potatoes, no larger than a half-dollar
2 cups freshly shelled English peas
1 medium sized green onion, cleaned and chopped
¼ stick butter
salt and pepper to taste

Long before the potato crop is ready to harvest, carefully select some small new potatoes from beneath the parent plants. Wash the potatoes and remove skins by scraping with a paring knife or by rubbing the tubers between your fingers. (Skins are usually very tender at this stage of growth.) Boil cleaned potatoes in a stainless steel or porcelain pot using just enough water to cover them. When potatoes are about half done, put in the peas and onion, lower heat to a simmer and cook until potatoes are done and peas are still a bit firm. Season to taste with butter, salt, and pepper and have a sampling of some of the good things of spring.

While cooking, some folks like to add a sprig of peppermint or sweet marjoram to the pot, removing the sprigs when cooking has finished. It's fun to experiment with various culinary herbs, but don't use any that will override the wonderful flavor of the peas and potatoes.

Plump English peas ready to be shelled

English pea salad

2 cups freshly shelled English peas
2 celery ribs, strings removed and coarsely chopped
1 green onion, cleaned and chopped
½ tsp. coarsely ground peppercorns
1/8 tsp. garlic powder
1/3 cup mayonnaise
¾ cup cubed OR coarsely grated cheese
loose-leaf lettuce (optional)

Cook peas in enough water to cover. When just tender, drain peas and cool by putting them in cold water for a minute or two. Drain well and mix all ingredients together in a large bowl. Cover with lid or plastic wrap and refrigerate for several hours to achieve a nice blend of flavors.

Regarding cheese—select a favorite such as a sharp cheddar. Amount can vary depending on strength of cheese flavor, as that should not dominate other flavors in the salad.

This salad has both eye and taste appeal when servings are nested on freshly washed and drained loose-leaf lettuce such as Oak Leaf.

Wild onion dip

8 - 10 wild onions
½ cup sour cream
¼ tsp. salt
¼ tsp. coarsely ground peppercorns
1/3 cup cooked summer sausage, finely chopped (You may substitute any cooked, flavorful crumbly-type sausage.)
dash of paprika (optional)

Seek out some wild onions and strip away tough parts. Wash thoroughly and finely chop. Avoid onions that are past their prime with flower heads beginning to discolor, as they are not worth cleaning.

Mix wild onions with rest of ingredients and refrigerate in a covered bowl for a few hours to allow flavors to blend. When ready to use, sprinkle some paprika over the mixture for color.

This is one of those dips that doesn't last long when served with crisp veggies—Jerusalem artichokes, carrots, cauliflower florets, celery, snap peas, and so on.

Seed sources:

Most seed catalogs list a variety of English peas including the snap and snow types. Just pay attention to ones recommended for your climate.

Potatoes are usually available at your local plant stores. Be sure to ask for seed potatoes. Don't try to raise potatoes from those obtained from supermarket bins.

The following company is one of the few still carrying the Oak Leaf variety of loose-leaf lettuce.

R. H. Shumway's
334 W. Stroud Street
Randolph, WI 53956-1274 Δ

The art of living in SMALL SPACES

Photos by Jay Shafer

By Claire Wolfe

Long ago, I read that to live in the country you must have the soul of a poet, the dedication of a saint, and a good station wagon.

Today I suppose you'd have to update the station wagon to an SUV, but the fact remains: To live successfully anywhere outside the mainstream of life you must have an unconventional spirit coupled with down-to-earth practicality—a combo that can be hard to find and harder still to balance.

I live in the country, but my latest life choices have also involved living in miniature spaces—which presents an additional set of challenges, both to the soul and to practicality. For the last three years I've shared a one-room cabin with a pack of dogs and one outnumbered but boldly unflappable cat. The cabin has an exterior footprint of 409 square feet—nine feet above the minimum my county requires for a residence. Its interior space is about 360 square feet, including closets and cabinet space.

I work as well as live here, so I'm in this one room 24 hours a day, except when the critters and I are out dog walking, running errands, picking blackberries, or otherwise adventuring.

On winter days, when I'm tripping over tails, wiping up muddy pawprints for the umpteenth time, and having accusatory canine noses stuck into my computer ("Mom, we're booooored!") the cabin sometimes feels as small as a shoebox. On summer afternoons, it's luxuriously spacious with its glass door thrown open to sunlight and all its denizens sprawled on the deck.

In fact it seems so large that I'm currently contemplating spending part of my year in a structure about one third this size. Think dollhouse (or rather, converted garden shed).

I'm hardly alone. Even as the size of the average new American house has more than doubled (from 1,100 square feet during the post-WWII housing boom to more than 2,225 by 1999), more and more people are also exploring small-space living. These include, most visibly, RVers spending months in their cleverly designed rolling homelets, simple-living advocates wanting to use fewer resources, homeless camper-dwellers, folks living on boats, and country newcomers (like many readers of this magazine) who are camping out in garages, trailers, cabins, or sheds while building their dream homes. Finally you've got people like me who'd rather have 409 paid-for square feet than 2,225 square feet of mortgaged luxury.

RVers and boat dwellers have built-in advantages. Literally built-in. RVs and boats, with their endless crannies, hidden storage spaces, and double-purpose furnishings (like tables that turn into beds) provide the construction model for the rest of us.

But there's more to small-space living than just clever design. Living well in tiny spaces has four parts:

- Coping
- Building
- Gadgeting
- Decorating

Let's take a brief look at all four. Oh, and before we do, I'll confess that a lot of my knowledge comes from what I-didn't-anticipate, or

The structures pictured were made by Tumbleweed Tiny House Co. at www.tumbleweedhouses.com.

I-didn't-do when I built my cabin. It was a learning experience.

Successful coping

Coping—the actual art of getting along in that tiny space—is logically the fourth thing to consider, since after all, you can't do it until you've built and furnished. But unless you're interested in doing what it takes to "live small," there's no point in even thinking about the other three steps.

Living small inevitably brings some surprises.

For instance, most people automatically assume that a smaller house requires less housework than a big one. First learning experience: In small spaces, every dirty dish left on the counter, every pile of bills you set on a tabletop upon return from the Post Office, becomes—proportionally—a big mess. Unlike in a large house, they're right there in your face. They might be taking up your only work space or eating area. Also, when all your activities are confined to one small space, that space will get dusty and dirty more quickly than when your activities are spread around 2,000 square feet.

So ...

• **Plan to cultivate** neatnik habits. Find a place for everything and put everything in its place as soon as you're done with it.

• **If you can't** immediately put things away, then have a transitional junk drawer or cabinet where you stash stuff until you can file, fold, sort, or dispose of it. (This is in addition to your usual junk drawer where you keep odds and ends on a long-term basis. I know you have one; everybody does.)

• **Above all, banish clutter** from your kitchen countertops. Eliminate small appliances you don't need. Stash those you do need inside cabinets. Buy the under-cabinet mounting types of appliances where feasible. Buy or construct a countertop "appliance garage." An uncluttered kitchen is the biggest step toward small-space sanity.

• **Don't own** a lot of stuff. If you can do without it, do without it.

• **If you can't do without** it, cheat. Build yourself a small garden shed, rent a storage bin, or purchase one of those $350 Rubbermaid instant-sheds at your local garden supply, and use that for your extra possessions.

• **Resolve** that you will never again go on mad acquistion binges, host your entire family reunion, or have giant parties—unless you have them outdoors during nice weather.

Designing and building for living small

Before tackling any small-space building or remodeling project, take a look at the interiors of boats and RVs. Make note of their space-saving design features—like underbed storage, dual-purpose furnishings, fold-up tables, compact water heaters, and especially the way they turn every bit of "useless" space into a cabinet.

Also look at what boat and RV builders *do wrong*. My friend, Charles Curley, who spent much of his youth ocean sailing, remembers a table whose swing-up leaf kept everybody on one side of the table from being able to reach the kitchen during meals. He recalls another table whose similar leaf had to be folded down every time anyone wanted to get into the refrigerator. Bad design.

Just as small spaces can actually be harder to keep clean than large ones, they can also be harder to design because they require more clever attention to picky detail. Some tips:

• **Don't underestimate** the amount of storage you need. This is the biggest mistake I made in planning my cabin. I figured one clothes closet, one linen closet, and the kitchen cabinets were enough for my simple life. I now wish I'd built in at least one entire wall of miscellaneous closets, cabinets, and drawers. Cabinets and drawers are a lot more expensive to construct than simple open space. But don't scrimp on them. You can never have too much storage.

• **Open shelves** are a budget-minded substitute for cabinets and drawers, but having all your stuff out in the open can be ugly. It's a terrible dust-collector, besides. If you must use open shelving, get some cheap cafe-curtain rods and plain cotton fabric and make yourself curtains you can pull tight over the face of the shelves to keep out dust and keep from having to look at heaps of stuff all the time.

• **Use pocket doors** that slide into the wall; that way you don't have to leave lots of space for doors to swing open.

• **Consider constructing** (or buying) a platform bed with big storage drawers underneath.

This built-in desk has plenty of storage and light.

• **Consider a Roman-style** bathtub, again with a platform underneath. Design it cleverly with a hidden, spring-latch operated panel and you can even use this as your top-secret storage space.

• **Build with good attic access** or an easily accessible storage loft. The typical hatch-in-the-ceiling access discourages us from using that space above our heads. A generous-sized hatch with a ship's ladder (or specially constructed folding ladder) encourages use by making access less formidable.

• **If you live in tornado country** where basements are a necessity, or if you live elsewhere and your budget allows a basement, then you're ahead of the rest of us. But even if a real basement isn't in your future, you might have what I call the Thoreau option. In his famous cabin at Walden Pond, Henry David Thoreau had a crude dug-out partial basement where he stored fruits and vegetables. In part of the country where I once lived, very few houses had real basements, but many inexpensive worker's houses had their water heaters and central heating units placed in similar, crudely dug spaces under the floorboards. (The code bureaucrats may freak—or may require at least a concrete pad.)

• **If you heat or cook with wood,** a pass-through bin for firewood will save space and mess. Build the bin on the outside wall of your house, with a door to insert wood from the outdoors and another, next to your woodstove, to pull the wood inside.

• **If you're building your own kitchen cabinets** or having them custom-built, extend them all the way to the ceiling. You may have to use a step-ladder to access the top shelves, but you'll avoid the maddening waste of standard-height (30-inch) cabinets, which end a foot below the standard 8-foot ceiling. If you must have 30-inch cabinets, then don't enclose the above-cabinet space with the traditional soffit. Leave the above-cabinet space open and use it to display attractive, seldom-used kitchen items.

• **Where feasible,** replace traditional walls with half-height walls, pass-throughs, or movable screens. The bigger area you can see, the less cramped you'll feel. (This has a drawback, though. The more you see, the less easy it is to avoid looking at those dishes on the counter or bills on the table.)

• **If you're really into simple,** inexpensive design, and you don't require insulation in all your walls, then consider leaving an open stud wall for small-item storage. You can install extra cross-braces for shelves and use better-than-stud-quality 2x4s or 2x6s for the uprights. Done poorly, this would be a tacky-looking solution to any storage problem. But when going for a rustic or artsy look, it could be done quite cleverly, augmented with attractive stain or paint.

• **Design with multiple use** in mind. A built-in fold-down workbench can double as a kitchen table. A kitchen countertop with a knee hole under it becomes a desk.

This kitchen has extra storage near the ceiling, and hooks, instead of cabinet space, for frequently used items like pots.

• **Build in bins** for dry dog food. Or for bulk human foods like wheat or split peas.

• **Build niches** to hold your TV and electronic gear. Electronics not only take up a lot of space when sitting out on countertops or tabletops; they take up a lot of visual space. They're always in your face, wherever you turn. And they're not pretty. Tuck them into a cabinet-wall and they'll be easier to live with.

• **Whatever else you do,** be sure to let in lots of light using glass doors, big windows, skylights, or (depending on your climate) big doors that can stand wide open in summertime. No matter how tiny your interior space, the entire outdoors can still be part of your design.

Helpful gadgets for saving space

Having just touted a relatively "stuffless" existence, it's a little ironic—oh, but so much fun—to delve into space-saving gadgets. It's also ironic that so many small gadgets are more expensive than their larger work-alikes. So to keep the budget down, we'll look at only a few.

• **Check out under-counter refrigerators,** 20-inch-wide ranges, counter-top dishwashers, and small European washer-dryer all-in-ones. (See them at www.compactappliance.com)

• **If the exotic washer-dryer** combos are beyond your budget (or you worry about getting parts for them), then of course a stacking washer-dryer pair is your friend. I looked at apartment-sized versions but ultimately realized the full-sized models didn't take up much more space and were a much better buy.

• **Replace your desktop computer** with a laptop. The traditional problem of the laptop keyboard being too small and cramped for comfortable use is being solved by the new widescreen laptop models. And you can usually attach an external keyboard. They even have folding keyboards if you really want to save space.

• **Another computer solution:** Charles Curley, Tech Geek Supreme, suggests buying a rack-mounted computer rather than your standard consumer off-the-shelf desktop model. Rack-mounted computers are more expensive, but they're usually higher quality. And the thing that makes them perfect for small spaces is that they can bolt to the underside of a table, inside a cabinet (if well-ventilated), or in storage space under a platform bed. Then the only space-consuming item you need to worry about is your monitor. And with flat-panel LCD monitors now becoming affordable (under $300), no problem.

• **Consider getting rid of your range** altogether if you don't cook much. You can replace it with a microwave and a two-burner hotplate. Or cook on your wood stove. Or cook outdoors on a handy, folding stainless-steel Pyromid (which you'll have to purchase from eBay.com, since these wonderful little devices aren't currently being manufactured any more.)

• **Get a TV** with a built-in DVD player. Or get a TV card and use your computer as your TV/DVD player. Or consider your TV among the excess stuff you can get rid of.

Decorating to make small look bigger

Finally, when you're ready to move your furniture in:

• **Use light colors;** they make rooms look bigger. Go for white or brushed-metal appliances, white or light wood cabinets, painted (instead of wood) walls.

• **Avoid wildly patterned upholstery,** bedspreads, or carpets. Muted is good.

• **Put nice, big mirrors** on your walls, or even a whole wall of mirrored squares.

• **Have glass,** Plexiglass, or Lucite tabletops.

• **Have a tabletop** or workbench that folds up against the wall. Use small tables with big leaves.

• **Use futons,** sofa-beds, or other furniture that can go quickly from compact to full-size as you need it.

To people who've never done it, small-space living often sounds cramped and uncomfortable. Certainly it can become that way in a structure that's poorly designed or if you get sloppy in your living habits.

But be clever and conscientious and you can have a very nice little life while saving a bundle, not only on construction, but on heating, air conditioning, maintenance, and furnishing. Oh yes, and on top of everything else, you'll be giving the taxers a whole lot less to tax than your neighbors who're building those 2,225 square-foot palaces. Δ

Ayoob on Firearms

Winchester '94: the classic backwoods home deer rifle

The Winchester '94 may be the most iconic firearm in American history, and is certainly so in rural America. In constant production for 110 years, save for when Winchester small arms manufacturing capability was diverted to military weapons for two world wars, it was produced under the aegis of USRAC (the United States Repeating Arms Corporation), and then and now by Browning USA after Winchester's parent company, Olin, got out of the gun-making business. More than five million of these classically American rifles have been produced.

Most have been in the form of carbines, or short rifles, with 20-inch barrels. They've been made with 26-inch and longer barrels, and in many calibers. In the year of their introduction, 1894, they were produced for two then-very-popular black powder cartridges, the .32-40 and the .38-55. With each, the first number stood for caliber—bore diameter in hundredths of an inch—and the second number stood for how many grains of black powder it would be loaded with.

Ayoob with Steve Denney's 16-inch barrel Winchester .30-30. It's a short, light, well-balanced package, soft in recoil, and easy to carry in the woods all day.

The '94 was the latest evolution of "the gun that won the West," Winchester's Model 1873, chambered for cartridges so weak—such as the .38-40 and .44-40—that handguns could fire them. But in 1895, Winchester set a benchmark in the history of hunting rifles. They chambered the Model '94 for the first hunting cartridge to use smokeless gunpowder. The .30-30 Winchester spat a bullet weighing 165 grains, .30 caliber, propelled by 30 grains of high-pressure smokeless gunpowder, at the then astonishing muzzle velocity of 1970 feet per second.

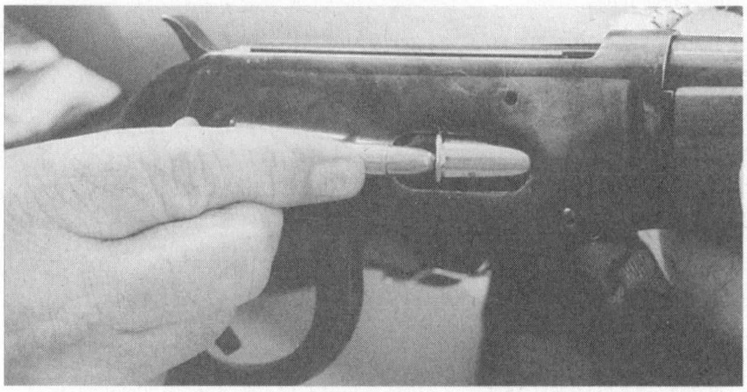

Tip for easy loading: Instead of letting the loading gate close behind each cartridge, load the first partway in and push the next in behind it. It's smoother and easier. ***NEVER*** *use pointed nose ammunition with these guns; note how bullet nose of rear cartridge directly contacts primer of the one forward.*

Sporting riflery had just turned a major corner. At what then seemed lightning fast velocity, the bullet didn't drop as much in its travel, allowing effective game-killing accuracy at distances previously beyond the reach of any but the professional hunter. Instantly, the .30-30 was a best seller. It would remain so for the next 110 years.

A brief history

As time went on, the .30-30 warmed up, power-wise. The most popular factory formats for .30-30 hunting ammunition are a 170-grain bullet at 2200 feet per second, and a 150-grain projectile at around 2400 feet per second. However, in his authoritative textbook, *Ammo and Ballistics*, Bob Forker notes, "There is a little something to remember when looking at the performance data for the .30-30 Winchester. The velocity specifications are measured in a 24-inch barrel and a lot of guns that are chambered for the .30-30 have 20-inch barrels.

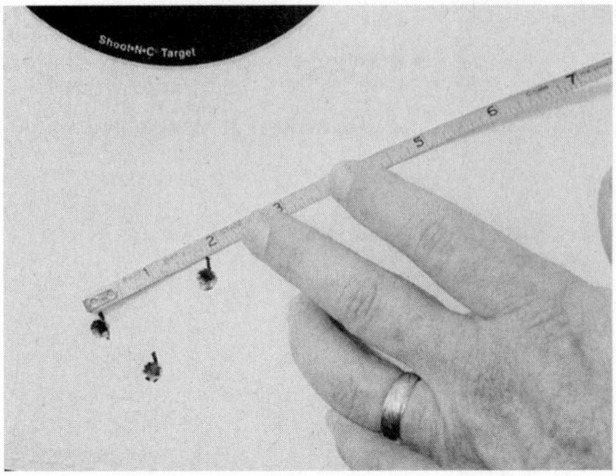

Measured center to center, 3-shot group fired at 100 yards with open sight, 16-inch Winchester 94 is $1\frac{5}{8}$ inches. The ammo was 170-grain Remington soft point .30-30.

This will cost about 100-150 fps in the short barrel. Time has proved that this doesn't make much difference because .30-30s are seldom used where long shots are required."

Untold millions of deer have been killed with this lever-action rifle, most commonly with the 20-inch barrel, spanning the late 19th, entire 20th, and early 21st centuries. According to gun expert Sam Fadala, it has also been used in military conflict, most notably by the followers of Pancho Villa who found its lever action made it faster to shoot than the bolt action 7mm Mauser it replaced in many of their hands. "Called the treinta y treinta in Mexico, the round and its '94 rifle are an institution. No vaquero would turn down a chance to own a '94 .30-30," said Fadala.

In defensive use, the .30-30 turned out to be a formidable manstopper. Its forensic history in the United States is one of substantial and quickly debilitating wounds on human targets. For many years, it was a popular gun in the law enforcement armory, and there are reportedly still some correctional institutions carrying them, and there are definitely some street cops carrying them. This writer knows an Indiana detective who keeps a Model '94 in the trunk of his patrol car, though it's chambered for the .44 Magnum cartridge, not the .30-30.

The Winchester '94 is an almost totally ambidextrous rifle, as Steve Denney demonstrates shooting southpaw.

Over the years, the Winchester '94 was chambered for many rounds. Some as light as the .25-20, some as powerful as the .307 Winchester, which approached the truly high-power rifle ballistics of the .308, and roughly equaled those of another old favorite, the .300 Savage. At about the same time came the .356 Winchester and the .375 Winchester. The former caliber load was little more than a honked-up .35 Remington, and the latter, a resurrected .38-55 on steroids. The .307, .356, and .375 Winchester were offered in a beefed-up rifle Winchester called the Big Bore '94. It was an ugly caricature of the slim .30-30; no one liked the new heavy duty '94 or its three new cartridges, and all three calibers eventually slipped into obscurity. The Big Bore '94 remains, in the mighty .444 Marlin caliber, favored by some who fear very large bears at very close range.

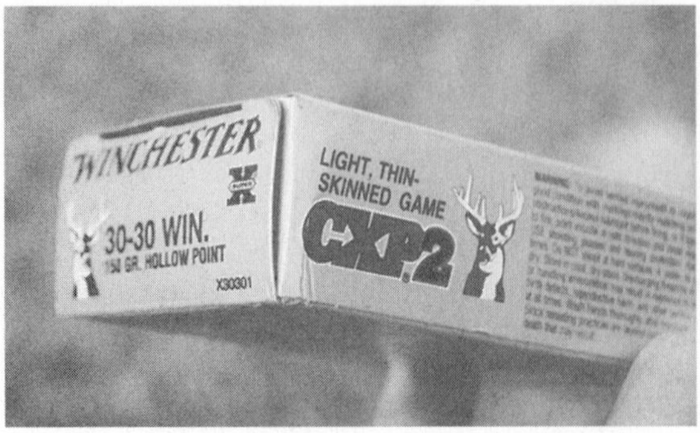

Note that Winchester, originators of the .30-30 cartridge, suggest it for "light, thin-skinned game."

When cowboy action shooting became popular, instead of resurrecting the old pistol caliber carbines (which reached their zenith of development with the 1892 model Winchester), the company decided to just chamber the .30-30 size rifle for rounds like the .44 Magnum and the .45 Colt. The Model 94 in .44 Magnum turned out to be a pretty decent little thick-woods deer rifle on its own account. On the other hand, every one I shot in the .45 Colt caliber had extraction problems. That round has a very small rim, not enough for the Winchester's extractor to reliably grab. This is probably why the '94's predecessor, the 1973 model, was never made in that caliber back in the Wild West days, when having revolvers and rifles of the same caliber first caught on.

The second most popular caliber in the 1894 model was the .32 Special. Introduced in 1895, according to Forker, the .32 Winchester Special fired a .321" diameter 170-grain bullet at 2250 feet per second, with perhaps sixty foot-pounds more energy than an equivalent .30-30 load. Legend has it that it was designed for those who liked the .30-30 but didn't trust anything but black powder yet (it was effective when loaded with that), and that it was a fallback for those around the turn of the 20th century who feared that modern smokeless powder might "burn out" the barrel of a .30-30. The reasoning went that if such a barrel burned out, the rifle could simply be re-bored out to .32 Special dimensions. I doubt that this ever happened, but such are the apocryphal stories in the world of the firearm. Expert Forker observes that no rifle in caliber .32 Special has been manufactured since 1960, but you'll notice that any gun shop, and indeed most sporting goods stores, keep .32 Special ammo on hand. This demonstrates the popularity and longevity of the Winchester 94, by far the most common gun to be found in .32 Special caliber.

Learn to keep the butt at the shoulder and work the lever crisply. Action has already closed on a fresh round as ejected spent casing from last shot cartwheels over Ayoob's head.

But the .30-30 was the round that defined the Winchester 94. Jackie Clay has mentioned in the pages of *Backwoods Home* that she uses a Winchester .30-30 to harvest her annual venison supply. It's a safe bet that four-plus million of those five million Winchester '94s were made for this cartridge.

It's generally accepted that the outside limit of the .30-30 for distance should be about 150 yards. Beyond that, the velocity drops off and both the probability of a vital hit and the power of the projectile take a precipitous dive. But, as Forker noted, that's OK: the .30-30 is in its element in tight cover: heavy timber, heavy brush, terrain where the shot is more likely to be 150 feet than 150 yards.

Wrapping the fingers outside the lever works for some, such as petite Terri Strayer.

At mid-20th century, writers in gun and hunting periodicals began suggesting that the .30-30 was inadequate for deer, compared to more powerful calibers. A couple of million hunters just smiled and kept on bagging their annual venison with a single 170-grain bullet. Where the .30-30 got the bad rap was from folks trying to shoot big Western mule deer with them at 200 to 300 yards. At that distance both power and trajectory were falling off, and deer that got away were the victims of bad hits by hunters who overextended their short-range rifles. On the biggest whitetails in the Midwest and the East, at reasonable distances, the .30-30 was always a reliable game-getter.

The '94 is a slim, flat rifle. It carries naturally in a saddle scabbard on horseback, or in a rack in the pickup, and especially, in the human hand. It balances just ahead of its lever and trigger guard assembly, and with the carbine-length barrel, it weighs seven pounds or a little less. That makes it an easy burden when trekking over rough terrain. Polar expeditions have brought Winchester '94s with them. They were, and I'm told still are, a

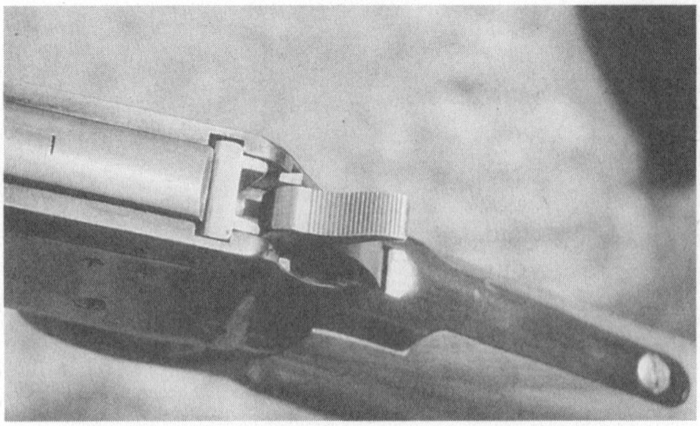

In days of yore, woodsmen carried live rounds in the chamber with hammer at half cock notch as shown. Today, more collectively experienced, smart shooters carry it with the firing chamber empty.

favorite among the Inuit peoples of Alaska. "Eskimos" know the importance of traveling light. The .30-30 is ample for seals and walrus, and while no hunter from the Lower 48 would ever go after a large brown bear with something that feeble, the Inuits have been laying the big bruins low with Winchester '94s for more than a century, relying on cool confidence in their marksmanship skill to put the 170-grain bullets in exactly the right place.

Picking the '94

Multiple books have been written about the classic lever-action Winchester. There have been enough variations of the Model '94 alone to sustain such books, filled with arcane information for the most committed gun enthusiast. Long barrels and short, plain and fancy, and so on.

My own first deer rifle was a Winchester 1894, in the original .38-55 caliber, with a 26-inch barrel. I own it still. Loaded, it weighed between eight and nine pounds. For a little kid, that was about the same as an Army BAR man lugging a 20-something-pound Browning Automatic Rifle through the Pacific jungles in WWII. Yet, it says something about the inherently good human engineering that John Browning put into the Winchester '94 when he designed it, when that little kid of long ago—and countless other little rural kids of so many generations—could manage to carry it thanks to its good balance. Could manage to work its mechanism, thanks to the famous smoothness of its action. And could hit what they shot at, thanks to its inherent accuracy.

Fadala notes in his excellent book on the Winchester '94 that it could often group its shots in an inch and a half at a hundred yards. He was not exaggerating. "Been there, seen that."

The long-barreled '94 was, and is, an elegant rifle. That said, it can also be cumbersome. This is why the 20-inch carbine barrel became the paradigm.

And you don't have to stop there.

It its early days, before the National Firearms Act of 1934 that severely restricted ownership of machine guns, "sawed off shotguns," and rifles with barrels shorter than sixteen inches, Winchester produced their first "Trapper" version of the Model 1894. Its barrel was only 14 inches. Those guns are now expensive collectors' items. In the latter half of the 20th century, the company experimented with 16-inch barrels, barely the legal limit. These turned out to be modestly successful. The 16-inch Win-chester '94 is produced today as the youth model, with a short stock. This is proportional to smaller folks, as its name implies, but also works very well with thick, heavy winter clothing.

Taking a fifth of the length off the already-short 20-inch barrel makes the little lever gun an absolute joy to carry. It's now much easier to deploy from a saddle scabbard or the rack of an ATV, or to jerk out of the pickup truck when you're driving on the farm and spot a coyote.

With four inches less barrel in which burning powder can build pressure, you lose some velocity. However, it's unlikely that the deer will know the difference.

You're certainly not giving up accuracy with the 16-inch barrel. My buddy Steve Denney liked the concept, but didn't care for the tinny-looking front sight Winchester was putting on the very short .30-30s. He took his 20-inch model to the gunsmith instead, and had it cut to 16 inches and fitted with a Marble gold bead front sight. Using that with the old- fashioned "buckhorn" rear notch sight on the barrel, Steve fired a 100-yard group in front of me and some friends that measured one and five-eighths inches. The ammo was store-bought Remington 170-grain soft point.

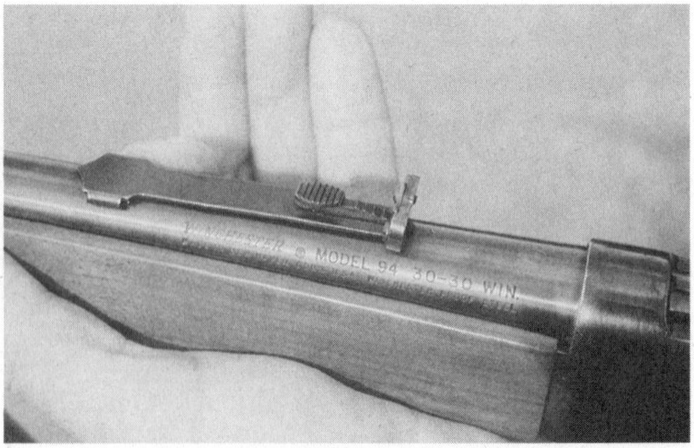

Most Model 94 Winchesters were made in .30-30, and most were equipped with these rudimentary "buckhorn" rear sights.

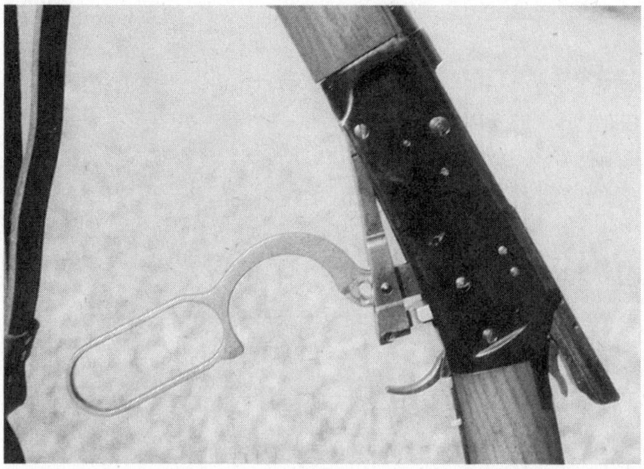

Be sure you work the action all the way forward, or the next cartridge will fail to come up on its internal carrier to feed into the firing chamber.

Using the '94

For most of the period of its production, the Winchester '94 was probably unsafe to carry with a live cartridge in the firing chamber. In theory, it was safe if you kept its exposed hammer on the half-cock notch, but in practice, some rifles were so worn that a pull of the trigger could drop the hammer from that "safety point" with enough momentum to discharge the rifle. Moreover, it was discovered that a sharp slap of the lever or a sharp blow to the butt could cause the firing pin to slam forward inside the mechanism and fire the gun, the so-called "inertia discharge."

Such a case in New Hampshire, in which two hunters were wounded by the accidentally fired bullet, resulted in a Federal court case in which Winchester paid out big bucks to the plaintiffs. *Croteau v. Olin* resulted in a redesign of the rifle. A lighter firing pin with a heavier spring was incorporated to reduce the chance of an inertia fire, and a manual safety in the form of a push-button cross bolt was installed through the firing mechanism. This allowed the gun to safely be carried "cocked and locked," which absolutely creeped out every one of us old hunters who saw someone in the woods with a Winchester '94 in that condition. In our world, the hammer was only eared back when you had venison in your sights. Moreover, setting the rifle down on one side could push the safety "off," and setting it down on the other side could push the safety "on," rendering it unshootable when you needed it in a hurry. The new design was almost universally hated. A couple of years ago, the Winchester '94 was offered with a new, improved safety, a sliding type on the tang of the rifle behind the hammer. It works like those on double-barrel shotguns, and is much handier and more efficient.

Still, the best rule with these guns is to load the tubular magazine under the barrel, and leave the chamber empty. When you see something you want to shoot, lever the action to chamber a round. This is the only way to carry one loaded in a backwoods vehicle or on horseback.

The lever action design makes these rifles very fast for a follow-up shot, but only if you know how to properly work the mechanism. Keep the butt at your shoulder and the sights on the target, and move only the operating hand to cycle the gun. You need to work it sharply and crisply. The shell lifter that brings the next cartridge up in line with the firing chamber doesn't rise until the very end of the forward lever stroke, and if you short-stroke the lever action, your next pull of the trigger will result in a "click" instead of a "bang." When you work the lever, make sure you take your finger out of the trigger guard, or it could get a nasty pinch against the trigger as the action closes. Leave your thumb out to the side instead of wrapping it over the tang of the rifle when you shoot, and you'll be much faster on the lever for the next shot.

Some of these millions of rifles came out of the factory smoother than others. Some have a sharp edge along the inside of the lever that can chew up the hand in practice and make the hand hesitant when the levering movement is needed for something serious. A Dremel Moto-tool and a light touch can solve this problem for you. Some of the cowboy-style shooters tie rawhide around the outside of the lever loop to make it softer on the fingers, but this also reduces the amount of space inside. The resulting "latigo look" does have a certain Western cachet, but it's not amenable to large or gloved hands. A third option is to wrap the fingers around the outside of the lever loop. I did this as a kid, and found it worked better with big gloves on in deep cold. However, you're now pulling the lever forward instead of pushing it, and will need to relearn the lever action stroke. The arc of the lever's swing will feel slightly longer, and with your hand farther forward on it, you'll need a little more range of movement.

Caliber? If you inherited a .38-55, as I did, or got a good deal on a used .32 Special, go with it. You may have to look harder for ammo, but it'll get the job done. If you're setting out to buy one, your main choice these days is .30/30 or .44 Magnum. The .44 cartridge, designed for a revolver, is shorter and you can load eleven of them in a 20-inch barrel gun, nine in the shorter magazine tube of the 16-inch Trapper. If most of your shooting is under 100 yards, it will drop Bambi with authority. With .44 Special ammo, it's a light-kicking plinker and a useful gun for cowboy re-enactment shooting, where your rifle can't fire high-powered ammunition. If you think the range might extend to 150 yards, the flatter-shooting .30-30 makes more sense; the 20-inch carbine will only hold six of these longer cartridges, but hopefully, that'll be five more than you need.

Being by far the most popular cartridge for the rifle, .30-30 is the caliber in which you'll most likely encounter it on the used gun market. It's no trick to find one in decent shape for about $200. Suggested retail on a new one is in the low $400 range.

The buckhorn sights they come with have proven adequate for generations, but serious hunters find that a good peep sight like the Williams or Redfield, with the aperture removed to give a large "ghost ring" view, is faster and more accurate. Most of these guns eject through the top of the action, so a scope has to be set to the side, though Winchester has produced their "angle eject" version expressly to allow a telescopic sight on top. Most purists think this breaks up the classic lines and easy handling of the '94, but it does allow more precise shooting, and the telescope's magnification is a safety factor in that it helps the woodsman identify the target.

The bottom line is, the Winchester '94 has been the quintessential backwoods home rifle for 11 decades, and shows no signs of fading away. The first two and a half million were sold between 1894 and 1963. The next two and a half million were sold in the shorter time span since, which indicates that it's getting even more popular as it goes along.

For further good reading on the Winchester '94, I recommend:

Winchester's .30-30 Model '94 by Sam Fadala, Stackpole Books, 1986.

Ammo and Ballistics by Bob Forker, Safari Press, 2000. Δ

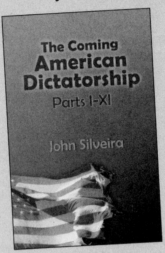

Perfect Dread

By Danny Fulks

Danny Fulks, 71, is one of those rare writers capable of painting a vivid picture of life back in another time. His stories focus on the 20s, 30s, and 40s of Ohio, Kentucky, and West Virginia, which were areas much like greater Appalachia and the South. Fulks is Professor Emeritus, Marshall University in West Virginia, and an adjunct professor at Ohio University. He is the author of Tragedy on Greasy Ridge: True Stories from Appalachian Ohio, available from amazon.com, danny.fulks@adelphia.net, and the Jesse Stuart Foundation, Ashland, KY, (606) 326-1667.

— Dave Duffy

Guyan Valley, Olive, Good Hope, Bethel, Palestine, Old Baptist. Little, white one-room churches, bell towers, spires pointing to the sky, big time centers of social life in Indian Guyan Creek Valley, southern Ohio. Names invoked peace, love, Bible lands. Early Sunday, winter mornings, janitors stoked pot-bellied coal stoves. Came summer, opened windows. Inside, rows of wooden pews, no cushions, no kneeling pads. Pulpit up front, higher level, wooden chairs for preacher, guests, musicians. The message was stark: two kinds of people: saved, unsaved. Preacher talked slow, easy rhythm, rising tone, sweat, gave urgent message. Unsaved: burn in hell, an everlasting, eternal punishment. Saved: live forever with loved ones in Heaven, a place with streets of gold. Emotions rose. Mothers testified, in tears, asked for prayers for

Photo courtesy Fern Lewis collection

The man second from the right is Junius Fulks, the author's great-uncle.

Photo courtesy Gallia County Historical Society

Public school teacher and class, Gallia County, Ohio, circa 1930. Third row center: Child smiling, not getting caught. And, by the way, don't hit on this teacher.

their children, sinners, lost. You could be saved, alright, on your knees up front, righteous saints praying over you, loud voices, tears, sad hymns coming from the choir: *Oh, why not tonight?/ Wilt thou be saved?/ Oh, why not tonight.* Through warm months, there was a revival or special singing going on somewhere. Groups got together, drove Model As, went to special singing, feet washing at Tick Ridge Methodist.

Martin Luther's idea, once saved, always saved. Simple: don't drink, cuss, commit adultery, lie, work on Sunday except to milk, hang out in beer joints. No dancing, please. Join a church, give money, work on building repairs, help the poor, take communion with grape juice. Be leery of science. Preachers told stories of World War I doughboys, lives saved by bullets stuck in shirt-pocket Bibles. If a bullet lodged in a pack of Fatimas saved a life, no story. God doesn't work like that. Don't vex Him. If you backslide, confess again. Anything you did was known by others. If it

Photo courtesy Duane Null Collection

Spring plowing, Greasy Ridge, Ohio. Circa 1920

Photo courtesy Duane Null Collection

Short on gas? Ride your bike to church at Siloam Baptist.

Pleasure, fun, must be sin. A few people in the valley were beyond hope. They swore with abandon, stole chickens, went on drunks for weeks, got free gas with a siphon hose, milked their neighbor's cow through a hole in the fence. Homegrown irony: Elmer Chambers, young man lived so far back up a hollow he had papers on him instead of a birth certificate, was bad to start fights at Good Hope during summer revival meetings. A deacon went into town, swore out a warrant. On the stand, the prosecutor asked Elmer if he believed in God. He goes, "Do I look like a goddamned atheist?" A couple of character witnesses spoke, judge let him off free to start more fights. Life was sober, unpretentious. A few happened out of sight, at night, it was known by God. It would get out, too. Men, women known by whether their word was good. No need to write it out. Offer to sell a neighbor a horse for 50 dollars, a stranger came along before the buyer picked it up, offered more? No deal. Borrowers paid debts. There was a range of honesty, however, even among Christians. Telling lies for good results was common: keeping bad news from aging mothers, unhooking car odometers, covering up blunders to keep grandpa from pitching a bitch. Bundling family votes for a trustee to get a road graveled, paying a smart person to take the teacher's examination in another person's name, get the license.

Young men had wild streaks. Fast driving in Model As, drinking moonshine, sparking, getting home at daylight on Sunday mornings. Sex before marriage was a sin. Wasn't anything to brag about after marriage. Men and women lived by the slogan, *"If you can't be good, be careful; if you can't be careful, name the baby after me."* Expecting meant staying in the house for a few months, visiting a relative in Toledo, getting married, or naming the man, having the law make his dad pay up, one-time-settlement, over. Even pregnant, married women hated to be seen, people looked at big bellies, we know what you've been doing. That was the only sign anyone had sex, no talking around women, among children. Men, women, lived their lives never seeing another adult naked. A blessing for some.

Photo courtesy Brenda Koontz Collection

Appalachian dudes on a Sunday afternoon. Circa 1930

had nice cars, houses, didn't carry on about it. Pride was sin. Imminent death, fear of hell, dread at separation from family, harsh judgment by God, left a cloud of melancholy over the valley. This, plus eating or starving at the whims of nature's floods, droughts. Living in houses that took in winter's wind through cracks, summer heat through tin roofs decorated with worthless lightning rods. Men were stoic. Women worried, thrived on it as a mental state, embraced it as a talisman that increased with age. If everyone in the family was well, cows giving milk, flu season passed, they worried that another steamboat on the Ohio would blow up. Many even had a form of click language like selected tribes in the far East. Tsk, tsk, tsk, tsk, sure to come out if a righteous lady of the church saw a young woman painted up, sporting a short skirt.

Photo courtesy Gallia County Historical Society

Covered bridge, flood, Gallia County, Ohio. Circa 1913.

Guyan Valley was tobacco country. Took a lot of work, but an acre brought cash money in December. Tobacco had an exquisite aroma, was pleasing to the eye when ripe with golden brilliance. Made good smoking, too. Twists for chewing. Packaged tobacco, Days Work, not made for Rockefellers, Vanderbilts. Even the preachers smoked, tailor made Luckies, Camels. Radios and seventy-eight rpm record players were sold in Crown City, Ohio, late 1920's, early 30's, on. Lyrics and tunes about great disasters, *The Sinking Of The Titanic*, morbid lyrics blended with religion, Billy Sunday's message. Charlie Waller singing *Amelia Earheart*, first lady of the air, lost, but landing in field that was fair, made so by God. Why does God let that kind of stuff happen? Was it punishment for sin? Might we be next? Carter Family music from Bristol, Virginia, sold good, loaned around. *Will The Circle Be Unbroken?, Wildwood Flower*, songs about murder, heartbreak, mothers, dead kids, jealousy, drunks, cheating played over and over again, dull needle scraping a seventy-eight on a hand-cranked Victrola. In the song, *Don't Make Me Go To Bed And I'll Be Good*, little boy died in the night, having been made to go to bed by his dad. Church songs: *Pass Me Not Oh Gentle Savior, What Would You Give In Exchange For Your Soul?* Nashville music came in on radios, Roy Acuff singing *I heard the wreck on the highway, but I*

Photo courtesy Gallia County Historical Society

Shuler's Grocery, Kyger, Ohio. Floods like this one, about 1913, were thought to be acts of God. Better roads and engineering came later

Photo courtesy Gallia County Historical Society

Calvary Baptist Church, Rio Grande, Ohio, 1956. Don't know about you, I wouldn't want to face these saints after a night of dancing, drinking.

didn't hear nobody pray. Send a quarter, get a song book through the mail. Hard times, small-time crooks, romanticized: *I'm not in your town to stay/ Said a lady old and gray, I'm just here to get my baby out of jail.* John Dillinger, killer, folk hero. Hobos begged farm owners: *May I sleep in your barn tonight, mister?/ It's so cold lying out on the ground.* Vernon Dalhart's, *Prisoner's Song*, first million selling country record: *I'll be carried to the new jail tomorrow/ Leaving my poor darling alone/ With the cold prison bars all around me/ And my head on a pillow of stone*. Sympathy evoked for downtrodden, free born men taken down by hard times. Wasn't this what Jesus said? What you do to the least, you do to me. Even doggerel written by children inside old handed down McGuffey readers was gloomy: *When this you see/ Remember me/ Although on earth I may not be/ And if the grave should be my bed/ Remember me when I am dead.* Children memorized:

My lids have long been dry, Tom,
But tears came in my eyes:
I thought of her I loved so well,
Those early broken ties.
I visited the old churchyard,
And took some flowers to strew
Upon the graves of those we loved
Just forty years ago.
(Author unknown)

And Eugene Field's *Little Boy Blue*

"Now don't you go 'till I come,"
he said,
"And don't you make any noise."
So, toddling off to his trundle bed,
He dreamt of his pretty toys;
And, as he was dreaming, an
angel song
Awakened our Little Boy Blue—
Oh, the years be many, the years
are long,
But the little toy friends are true.

Working, playing together brought comfort, security, relief from boredom. Going into town Saturdays was as much social as to pick up horse feed, sugar, lard, pay taxes. Nickel cones of ice cream, Lash LaRue westerns playing at the Marlowe, slip off to live shows, actors, painted up hussies putting on melodramas like *The Drunkard* on a showboat. Good old melodrama, but cost money, worldly pleasure, don't tell the preacher. County fairs were an exception. Once a year, families risked mingling among clowns, freaks, girlie shows, carnies. *"Step right up, see Little Egypt. She wriggles, she*

Photo courtesy Gallia County Historical Society

Johns Creek Methodist Church near Waterloo, Lawrence County, Ohio. Organized by early Wiseman settlers and their relatives and friends, it was first named Whites Chapel, later changed to Johns Creek. It was here, in this church yard, that muster days were held during the Civil War, and it was here that many men of the neighborhood volunteered for military service

shakes, she crawls on her belly like a reptile. One thin dime is all it takes. So come on in, see Little Egypt." Ladies stayed with canned goods up for ribbons. In high summer, families got together for reunions. Up to 50 people came to school grounds for a long day of visiting, eating, singing. Children ran in the groves, played hide-and-seek, crack the whip. Old folks dressed in suits, print dresses, sat in metal chairs. Men formed quartets, sang harmony. Pickers opened black cases, broke out guitars, mandolins, banjos, seeming to horse around, tune, more than rendering songs.

Election days were social. Men standing for offices stayed at the polls of their home precinct all day, shaking hands, greeting voters. Political hacks watched as people came and went, checking them off. They knew how each person voted, like a family of seven eligible, count them for our man, said to be voting right. Two or three fist-fights before the polls closed, brass knucks a weapon. A school janitor fired for not doing his duty? Well, he didn't vote right, sign he didn't do his duty. Election days were celebrated by drinking, carousing. Votes bought for a horse-quart of moonshine, a pint of Old Grand Dad. Really now, was this a lot different from a rich person giving a candidate big money legally knowing it improved the giver's chance of getting his daughter a job in the court house?

Hunting, trapping were fun for men even if kills were slim. Good hounds, men chasing foxes, coons through the night. Men tapped maples, got syrup. Cut down bee trees, salvaged honey. Beauty of nature, fall foliage, dew on honeysuckles, June sun, better than a Monet. Playing checkers, homemade board, red, yellow corn as men. King me. Pitching horse shoes: ringer five, leaner three, closest to pin, one. Working on old cars, changing spark plugs, changing oil, wires, distributors, tires, tubes. Crank it up, give it some spark. Putting up old car license plates on barn walls along side bushel baskets used as hen's nests. Richard Boston, earliest riser in the valley, tomatoes ready for market. A friend came to his house, one-in-the morning, pickup with a busted muffler, enough noise to raise the dead. Richard went out, invited his friend in for breakfast, ham, eggs, coffee, said, "Eat all you want, I've already had mine." Good food, fresh sausage from hogs, wild black raspberries topped with cream. Fruit, vegetables, year-round from the cellar. Men together, laughing, stoved up from lifting too much, still getting by. Women quilted, made dresses from feed sacks, cooked, cleaned, washed, nursed babies, read the Bible.

Schools held social affairs. Pie suppers. Young women baked pies, men bid money for them at auction. Deal was, buy pie, eat with girl, good luck after. Gimmick to draw money for new school maps. Halloween parties, cider, pumpkins. For the rowdy, destruction, cut trees, keep school busses from running Monday. Throw rotten eggs at houses. Families celebrated Christmas, Christ's birthday, special foods like wild turkey, ruffed grouse, few toys, crossword puzzles, big gifts. New Year's Eve, churches held watch meetings, sang, prayed the new year in. Women served cooked cabbage for luck. Children walked around on homemade stilts, cut from small trees.

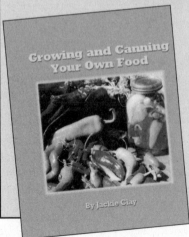

The churches rolled on, strengthened by tough times. Preachers, deacons, faithful members, mainstays in the flood plain that was Guyan Valley. Cited great disasters, deaths, privation, as God's will. End times prophesied. What if Jesus came back, you weren't ready? They couldn't stop chicken thieves, moonshiners, midnight ramblers, blackguards, rollicking times in beer joints. But you had to choose. The straight, sober life of a Christian. The crooked life of sin leading to death and eternal fire. Guilt, remorse, soaked up. People knew big cities existed, but seldom went there. Too many Germans, Poles, Italians, drinking spirits through the week, going to church on Sundays, hypocrites. Never saw or heard of hot, smoky southern honky-tonks where blacks tangled together raucous music, belief in Jesus, spared of guilt. The jazz age, flappers, prohibition, speakeasies, saloons, dirty dancing, passed Guyan Valley by. Δ

May/June 2005
Issue #93
$4.95 US
$6.50 CAN

Backwoods Home magazine

practical ideas for self-reliant living

Finding your own freedom

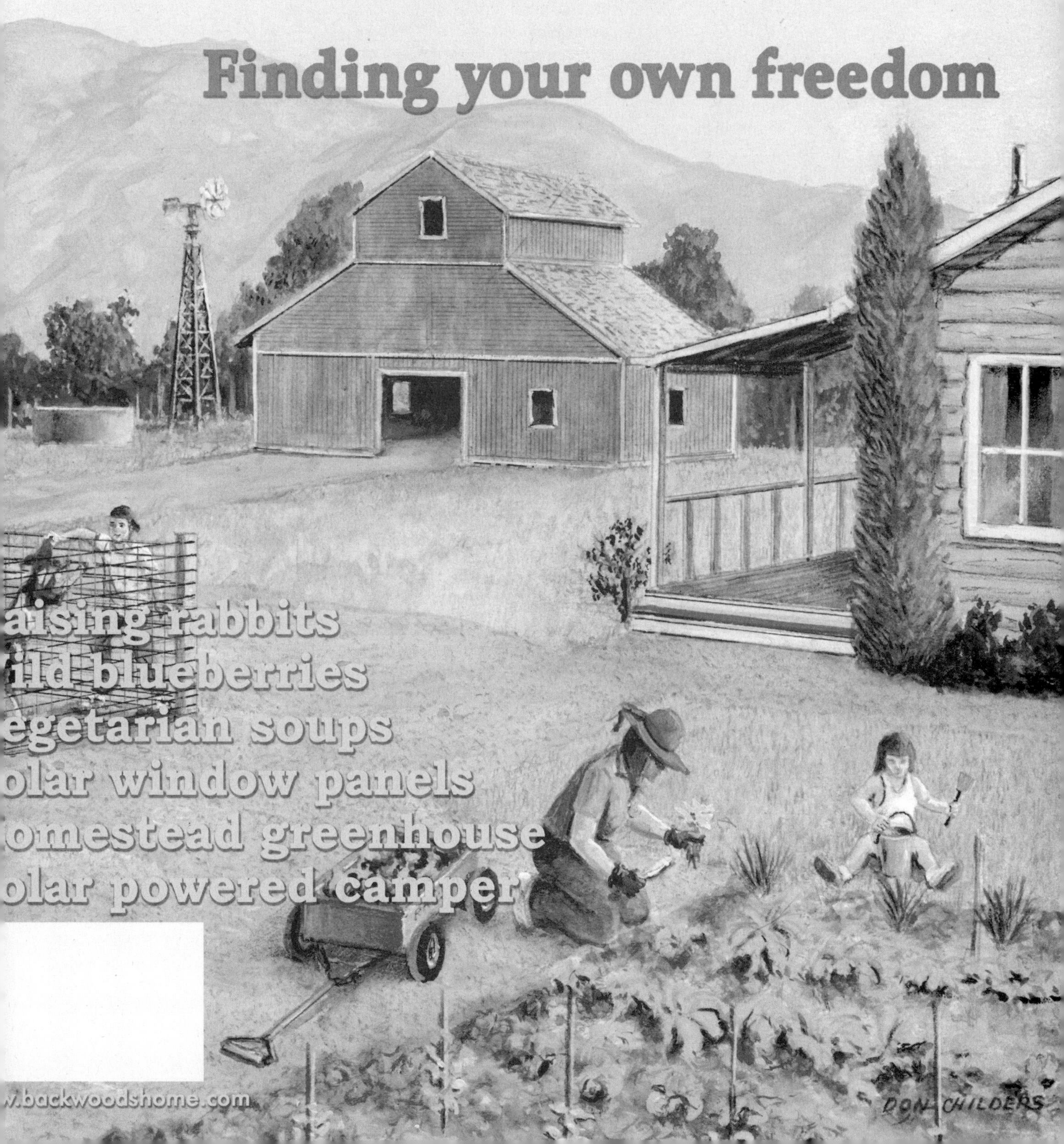

aising rabbits
ild blueberries
egetarian soups
olar window panels
omestead greenhouse
olar powered camper

.backwoodshome.com

Publisher's Note

Beginnings and endings

The world is a mixture of joy and sorrow, and so it was between issues for the *Backwoods Home* family.

The in-office atmosphere while putting this issue together was particularly enjoyable as we worked in our newly acquired building with its sumptuous spaciousness. My three young boys, Jake, 13, Rob, 12, and Sam, 10, did their usual romping through the office, and this issue they were joined by the soft murmurings of my one-year-old granddaughter, Olga Tuttle, who crawled about the office making her little sounds while her mom, my 22-year-old daughter Annie, layed out the issue on the computer.

All the staff enjoyed the usual festive family atmosphere, but they especially liked having Olga around. She's one of those babies who is full of curiosity and seems to only cry when she's hungry or taken a spill. Even though she has yet to speak her first word, she seemed to be the main deadline conversationalist with everyone else.

Associate editor Annie Tuttle takes a break from laying out the issue to hug her daughter, and newest member of the Backwoods Home Magazine family, Olga.

But then we got the call from Jackie Clay. Bob, her husband and best friend, had died suddenly. It was a sudden chill on a pleasant day, reminding us of the incredible heartbreak that can follow in the footsteps of life's most profound joys.

BHM lost a friend between issues when Bob Clay, 58, husband of our most popular writer, Jackie, died suddenly. Jackie's tribute to her husband is in this issue.

Our hearts go out to Jackie and her 14-year-old son, David, who was very close to his father. We'll do all we can to help them through this time of grief, fully aware that grief is a road that must be walked alone. Jackie has already received many letters of condolences. If you'd like to write her, please do so in care of this magazine. We will forward all letters, unopened, to her, but Jackie has already told us she is unable to answer the letters. The hole Bob's death leaves in her life is complicated by the fact she is now taking care of her aging parents, ages 88 and 93. She said she intends to complete the new home she and Bob had planned for their new northwoods homestead.

Jackie also insisted on completing her article and column for this issue. She shares her memories of Bob in a special one-page insert in her *Starting Over* series.

We are reminded too that the *Backwoods Home* family extends far beyond the Duffy and Clay households. Symbolically we hold hands with all of you whose lives have been touched and retouched by great joy and great sadness. Life is a wonderful journey that travels all roads. Olga Tuttle's new life and Bob Clay's completed one form a comforting circle of love, work, dreams, and a satisfying finality that you have lived well.

Changing your address?

So you don't miss an issue, please send your change of address to us at P.O. Box 712, Gold Beach, Oregon, or call us toll free at 1-800-835-2418. We need your old and new zip codes.
— Dave

My view

Practicing what we preach

Probably the most consistent theme this magazine has stressed in the 16 years we have been publishing is that the determined, hard working individual can take care of himself or herself. You don't need government, you don't need a support group, you don't need anyone at all holding your hand. If you're willing to do the necessary work, you can take control of your life and do anything you want. Essentially we've been selling good old fashioned common sense advice: to succeed you must simply choose a goal and work like heck until you achieve it.

So I'm proud to report that between issues we have been practicing what we have been preaching. We worked like heck for five straight weeks, seven days a week, and built a big, handsome, comfortable office for ourselves out of a 7000-square foot, 40-year-old empty building. I personally had a very exhausting but satisfying five-week workout, shedding about an inch around my waist and gaining a lot of strength by using a variety of power tools to lay floors, erect walls, and drywall. And I'm about as euphoric in my pride of accomplishment as I've ever been about a project.

Our quest for our new office began even further back, about a year ago when it became apparent we needed more office space because the magazine and its products, mainly anthologies of past issues, were growing. Our staff worked among ever increasing stacks of boxes holding the books we sell. My children even built forts in them.

So I launched an exhaustive search for a building, and ultimately found this one, the longtime home of the *Corner Drug*, a Gold Beach landmark, whose owners planned to build anew. I bought their old building, from an absentee landlord who had not been within 500 miles of Gold Beach in 20 years, before anyone even knew it was going to be for sale. And we got it at a good price because I became a determined pain in the butt to the seller and real estate brokers involved. They just wanted me out of their lives.

When the *Corner Drug* finally moved we found a building in disrepair because the absentee landlord had refused over the previous 24 years to invest a dime in its maintenance. He had even refused to sell it to the owners of the *Corner Drug*, which shows how determined I was in buying it. But in five weeks we revamped it totally. We spent $25,000 on materials and labor, but got at least $100,000 of improvement.

Here's what we did. First, we ripped out most of three decrepit bathrooms and put down new linoleum and fixtures. Then we erected walls that would define the spaces needed to publish the magazine and fill orders. I designed the spaces because 16 years had taught me exactly how

Work has begun on the old Corner Drug building...

...and five weeks later we were producing this issue.

BHM worked. Then we laid 20-foot 2 x 4s on the hard concrete floor, a ¾-inch plywood subfloor on top of them, and a wood laminate "floating floor" on top of that. The laminate floor, whose springiness was calculated to safeguard the backs of my employees and my investment in training them, was purchased at a warehouse sale at a fraction of the price it normally retails for.

We worked like the devil. I operated on the principle that you need only one real smart, knowledgeable person to honcho a building project. That was Don Van Hooser, a 65-year-old carpenter who had helped me add on to my home two years previous. He was the chief carpenter for a local contractor, but I hired him on weekends and paid him $25 an hour, more than he was getting at his regular job. Everyone else got $10 an hour, but they not only worked weekends with Don, but during the week carrying out Don's instructions under my supervision. It worked beautifully. By the time each weekend came we had completed assigned tasks and were ready for new training by Don.

Much of the work during the week was done by me and Jim Van Camp, one of the volunteers who had helped the *Corner Drug* move out. He was so effective I hired him permanently as a *BHM* staffer. In the end we built the best office we've ever had at a quarter of the cost to hire it built.

We just took *BHM's* own practical advice and worked hard and smart. And I don't mind saying that it was the best advice I ever got. ***— Dave Duffy***

Finding your own freedom

By Claire Wolfe

The letter to *Backwoods Home* pleaded:

I have long aspired to a simpler life in a quiet area where I may live as my forefathers did and support and sustain myself. I would like to buy a small farm where I could raise poultry and produce and network with like minded people for companionship and barter. The biggest question for me is the one I've never been able to glean an answer for from your publication: Where?

Where can a person go to escape the tyranny of overbearing government and brutal law enforcement? Where can a person experience the elusive liberty of days gone by? Where the hell is Hardyville anyway?

Where would someone begin researching "livability" of specific areas? I must get out of this vile, filthy, vermin ridden prison of a city within about 36 months. The farm is the ball and I have had my eye on it but the clock is ticking and I don't want to do this twice.

Signed, Miserable in Metropolis

This letter poses so many dilemmas that Dave and Company could devote multiple articles—maybe even entire issues—to finding answers.

Only one problem: After all those future issues of *BHM* had thundered off the presses, we'd still be waiting for a universally satisfactory solution to *Miserable's* puzzles.

As I interpret his letter, *Miserable* actually asks three very heavy questions. The answer to one is simple—but unsatisfying. The others we can ultimately only answer for ourselves.

The questions I hear are:

1. How can I live as my forefathers did?
2. Where can I find the most livable geographic location?
3. Where can I live in freedom?

We can toss out question one right now. We can't live as our forefathers did. Even the Amish use cellphones and have to put up with the *Internal Revenue Service.* Even ardent backwoodsmen enjoy the benefits of power tools and suffer the nuisances of the welfare state.

Dave Duffy began his simpler, more free life eight miles down a dirt road in Oregon's Siskiyou Mountains. (Issue #1) From there, he founded Backwoods Home Magazine. A freedom seeker with different needs might have said, "No thanks!" to the snow, the isolation, or Oregon's infamously strict environmental laws. But it worked for Dave and family.

We can recapture some of what we believe was pleasant about "the olden days." But the olden days were never as glorious as we imagine and we can't get them back.

The days of our forefathers imposed unimaginable work and hardship on most individuals. Those fondly imagined olden days had some very serious troubles: slavery and indentured servitude; the threat of terrible hunger after a bad harvest; war on the homefront; savage bosses, satanic factories, and seven-day work weeks; hellish penal colonies; malaria in the nation's capital; unwanted immigrants; poor sanitation and high infant mortality; women and children treated as chattel.

Gentlemen like Thomas Jefferson had leisure to ponder the great questions of life. The majority simply worked their tails off, hoped they'd have food on their tables, and died young.

For good or ill, our forefathers and their ways are dead. Try to resurrect the dead past and you know what you end up with? The cultural equivalent of a zombie flick.

Next question.

Where can I find the most livable geographic location?

Thermopolis, Wyoming, appeals to anyone who likes high, dry places, bubbling hot springs, and a blessedly laissez-faire attitude. (Issue number 85.) Wyoming is truly one of the nation's prime havens against high taxes and government brutality. Finding work can be tough, though. And when the cold wind howls, many newcomers want to run for "home."

This is a far more meaningful question and is in some ways right up *BHM*'s alley. It's also a more challenging question.

I don't mean to sound glib, but you'll find the best answer to that question where *you* find it, not where anyone else may suggest you look.

As a perfect example of what I mean, take the *Free State Project.*

Please.

Seriously, the *Free State Project (FSP)* is the first place to turn if you're seeking a preassembled wealth of information about livable locations within the U.S. It's also the first place to turn for a vivid demonstration of why one person's heaven is another person's hellhole.

The *FSP* was born in 2001 in the mind of then-grad student Jason Sorens. His notion was that if 20,000 freedom activists moved to a single low-population state, those activists could change the state's culture and political climate.

Even if you have no interest in politics and no desire to relocate for political purposes, there's great information to be gleaned from the *Free State Project's* website. If you have no Internet access at home or work, book a computer at you local library. (See sidebar for more information on this and other relocation resources.)

Members of the *FSP* spent two years compiling their wealth of info. Then in the fall of 2003, they voted to select the one future *State of the Free.*

Prior to the vote, passionate advocates for each candidate state offered facts, figures, contacts, and the voice of experience to back their favorites.

They also argued endlessly and often acrimoniously.

The state eventually chosen was New Hampshire.

And today members and former members of the *FSP* are *still* arguing acrimoniously.

Let me give you an example of why the *FSP* couldn't determine the best "livable" spot for everybody, and why nobody else can do that, either.

It became obvious well before the vote that *FSP* partisanship was split between one eastern state (New Hampshire) and three western states (Wyoming, Montana, and Idaho).

The arguments on each side were varied. The following won't even try to do them justice. But ultimately the arguments could be summed up as a giant clash of values:

New Hampshire partisans: *New Hampshire is near Boston where we can get jobs! There are too few jobs in the west!*

Western partisans: *Boston, with all its congestion, regulation, and taxation is a perfect example of what we want to get away from! Give us wide-open spaces and room to expand!*

There was more, of course. Western partisans pointed to land as little as $500 per acre. Eastern partisans said $5,000 per acre and up was no big deal if the land was more fertile and had easier water sources.

Western partisans cried, "New Hampshire has lousy weather!" Eastern partisans rolled their eyes and groused, "Look at the pot calling the kettle black!"

So the arguments go to this very day.

No one can define "livability" for another person. But the facts others have discovered and the subjective reasons others have given for their choices can help you clarify—and move toward—your own goals.

For starters, I'll offer my own 10-Point Livability List by which I'd judge any small town or rural area. Your mileage will vary. My own mileage might vary, if I were to compose this list on another day. But here's what immediately rises to the top of my mind:

1. Low land cost
2. Low cost of living

3. Wide-open spaces with lots of room to roam
4. Beautiful surroundings
5. No huge metropolitan area that dominates the entire state's politics
6. A welcoming attitude toward polite strangers
7. Reasonable access to water for irrigation, animals, and drinking
8. A positive, laissez faire attitude toward guns and gun owners
9. Respect for privacy; lack of busybodies
10. The absolutely indefinable *something* that simply says, "You've found your home!"

Hearty adventurers like the Stram family find quiet, freedom, and opportunity in Thorne Bay, Alaska. (Issue number 84.) You might find your dreams in Alaska, too. But it's a sure bet that some BHM reader looks at a photo like this and says, "Give me sunshine!" or "Give me a shopping mall within driving distance!" Our concepts of livability are as varied as we are.

It's perfectly possible that your list might not have a single element in common with mine.

It's perfectly possible that something as indefinable as a sense of "Home" could overrule every pragmatic consideration on your agenda.

That's life. It's an adventure.

Of course, it's not always a *pleasant* adventure—which brings us to the next, and even more difficult, question.

Where can I live in freedom?

I realize that *"Miserable's"* three questions are ultimately bound up into one. Being free and living like his forefathers mean much the same thing to him. Therefore a livable location must also be one where freedom reigns.

Understandable.

Unfortunately, political freedom doesn't reign anywhere on earth. You can go to wide-open Wyoming and end up running afoul of bureaucrats. Randy and Vicki Weaver had one of the world's most horrible jackboot encounters high on a ridge in rural Idaho, in what they imagined to be splendid, self-sufficient isolation.

Given that all of us face limitations on our freedom, we have to choose the kind of freedoms that most matter to us (just as we must choose the elements that constitute "livability") and seek to maximize those freedoms in our lives.

Once again, one person's heaven may be another's hell.

Acquaintances of mine recently moved to a Central American country, praising it for being more free than the U.S. However, their report included a casual account of being stopped at a checkpoint in the middle of that nation and forced to show their "papers, please!"

To them it was no big deal. Me, I crossed that country straight off my list.

Other acquaintances have "gone expat" on Caribbean islands, in Mexico, in other Central American countries, in Asia, and in Canada. They call out to their stateside friends, "Move here! Be free!"

I ask, "Can I bring my guns?"

And they respond, "Well, no."

Or they respond, "It's easy. All you have to do is a apply for a permit and fill out form XYZ ..."

Or they respond, "Just smuggle 'em in and bribe the customs officials. That's the way it's done around here!"

And I say, "No way. I ain't goin' from a place where I can own firearms in complete privacy to a place where gun owners are either permission-seekers or criminals."

Those offshore friends think I'm less free than they. And I think they're fooling themselves. And on it goes.

Although pure political freedom doesn't exist anywhere on the planet, there is one place where we can seek and find our personal maximum degree of freedom—in our own attitudes and actions.

And I hate to tell you, *"Miserable in Metropolis,"* but I don't think you're going to find freedom.

"Miserable," this stab of the reality needle isn't just meant for you. Your plea is one I've heard before—a hundred times. Maybe a thousand. I expect that Dave has also received hundreds of letters like yours.

Most freedom lovers understand and share the anguish of your cry for liberty, a peaceful life, and simple values.

If I'm going to jab you now, it's a jab I've even had to administer to myself at times.

Go back to the top and look at *"Miserable's"* letter. When I do that, several huge "reality gaps" gape before my eyes.

* *"Miserable"* wants desperately to be out of the city in 36 months and hasn't even begun researching yet.

* Instead of going to the library or the Internet, he passively awaits answers from an outside party.

* He believes freedom should be obtainable simply by going somewhere other than where his is now.

* Even after reading *BHM,* he still has one very starry-eyed vision about country life. A few chickens, a little barter, guaranteed neighborly neighbors and—bingo!—you're a Jeffersonian yeoman farmer, living the self-sufficient life according to the values of yore.

The major reason we've lost freedom is that millions of people sit idly by, trusting others to provide or protect their freedom. Almost nobody admits to being *against* freedom. They just don't care enough to do anything about keeping it.

Then it's lost and even sincere, hard-working freedom lovers don't know where to turn.

But how hard has *Miserable in Metropolis* been working toward any of his desperately professed goals?

There's no clue in his letter. The desperation and passivity say he's probably envisioning himself to be in a deep hole. Instead of trying to climb out, he's sitting in the pit crying for someone else to lift him.

But freedom doesn't arrive like an ambulance or a firetruck to save us. It doesn't get delivered to our doors in pink ribbons. Nor can we find it simply by renting a moving van.

Same with self-sufficiency. It amazes me how many people claim a desire for self-sufficiency—*when they don't seek to be sufficient within themselves.*

Find data for planning a move—on and off the Internet

The Internet is the best place to begin any search for relocation information. You'll have easy access to an abundance of statistical data. But even better, a few clicks of a mouse will also take you to photographs, discussion forums, real-estate agencies, state law codes, local business directories, and online visitor centers. It's really the way to go.

If you have no Net access, your local library almost certainly has Net-capable computers you can use.

One of the best sources of data for people who are specifically seeking freedom in their new home is the *Free State Project.*

Go to www.freestateproject.org/. Click on "Site Index." Then head for "Archives—State Data" and "Archives—State Reports." You'll be busy for many days and you might just get a lead to your dream haven.

This data focuses specifically on a double handful of low-population states. But even if you're not interested in those states, the data can lead you to other sources of information and can help you set your own priorities for selecting a future location.

If you're uneasy on the Net, then your library is still the place to begin. Ask the librarian to show you publications like these:

* *The Statistical Abstract of the United States*—A very dry, but comprehensive publication that describes the population, education, geography, economy, job picture, and other detailed characteristics of every region of the country. The *Abstract* also contains a list of other useful sources of information. (The complete *Abstract* is also online at http://www.census.gov/statab/www/)

* *USA Counties*—Another Census Bureau publication focusing on county data. This is available in both book and CD-ROM form. The CD will let you easily compare counties.

* "Best places" publications. Several magazines and organizations periodically name "best places" to live in the United States. Keep in mind that these usually focus on cities. Also remember that what's "best" for your neighbor might be pure awfulness to you. Nevertheless, these surveys can give you factual data that might lead you to the best rural area or small town *near* one of these "bests."

* *Finding and Buying Your Place in the Country* by Les and Carol Scher. *BHM* has called this the "bible" of locating and buying rural land. What more can anyone say?

* And finally, don't forget *How I Found Freedom in an Unfree World* by Harry Browne. Every freedom seeker should have it nearby at the beginning of the journey.

Backwoods Home gives volumes of information on everything from honeybees to firearms. It can certainly offer both encouragement and tools to sad city dwellers wanting out. It can help country people be more happy and successful.

But—DUH!—self-sufficiency is a do-it-yourself project!

It's a *lifelong* do-it-yourself project. Ceaseless work from now until your personal doomsday.

And so is freedom.

If you don't think and act like a free person, then you'll be unfree wherever you go.

If you *do* think and act like a free person, you'll always find a degree of personal empowerment even if your home is a prison cell.

Being free means not only taking responsibility for our own choices. It means taking initiative so that we *have* choices.

Dorothy Ainsworth built her economic freedom, literally, with the incredible determination it took to design and build her vertical-log home—then built it all over again when it burned down. (Issue numbers 27, 38, 50, and 86.) Claire Wolfe admires Dorothy Ainsworth from afar—while finding her own freedom in a tiny cabin on which she did only the "lite" finishing work. Each woman made the decision that was right for her at her point in life; neither would say that her solution was the only one for everybody.

It means we figure out what we want in life, then begin actively heading in that direction.

It means when we run into an obstacle we figure a way around it or we change our course. But we don't just shrug and wait for a bailout.

Sure, ask for a helping hand along the way. But don't expect others' hands, or weary backs, to haul you the whole distance.

One familiar obstacle every freedom lover has smacked into at one time or another is that the life we desire is so far from the life we have. Worse, what we want is far from any life that even seems possible to attain. Our ideals glow on the horizon—but the horizon always remains distant.

Miserable's dilemma seems to be a classic case of the perfect being the enemy of the good.

If you'll settle for nothing less than total gloriousness, delivered to you wrapped in the aforementioned pink ribbons, you're already lost. Enjoy those city vermin. Because either you'll never get out of the slums or you'll dash out to the country unprepared and end up running back to the comforts of shopping malls and cable TV within six months, disillusioned and probably broke.

If you must have total freedom or nothing...you'll end up with nothing.

Here's a plan for achieving our own best possible degree of both freedom and country livability. It's not a plan for achieving perfection, but it is a plan that can help us pull ourselves out of a pit of despair and into a better, freer life.

* Read Harry Browne's book, *How I Found Freedom in an Unfree World*. Although written approximately 30 years ago, there is still no better resource to help you begin your journey. Browne helps us recognize the many false assumptions that keep us from moving toward a better life. Get it. Study it. Make its attitude your own.

* Know what you want.

* Set realistic priorities and deadlines for moving toward your dream, recognizing your limited amount of time, money, skills, and the restrictions of the outside world.

* Research. Consider the costs, the benefits, and drawbacks of every backwoods or small town location that interests you.

* Adjust your goal if necessary.

* Visit the places that interest you and talk with people there. Spend as much time as you can in your chosen locations.

* And again, adjust your goal if need be as new data and new impressions come in.

* Don't reject a location because it doesn't have perfect freedom; no place has perfect freedom. Find a place that's got the best laws and least oppressive law enforcement you can. A place where you can reasonably expect people to mind their business as long as you mind yours.

On the other hand, don't ignore your "spidey-sense." If you perceive anything importantly wrong about a place you visit, you'll really, really, really perceive that wrongness after you move there.

* Once you've chosen your location, then choose your specific land or home with equal care. (See sidebar.)

* Then when you run into problems—as you absolutely, guaranteed, 100 percent will—be prepared to adjust again. And keep on keeping on.

Finally, as rural freedom seekers have already figured, one of our jobs in a free, self-sufficient life is to give as much assistance to others as we get.

Read *BHM* and glean what you can from its pages. But what you find here is a friendly hand to help you along your own chosen—and hard-earned—way. Δ

Raising rabbits on the home place

By Charles A. Sanders

One of the most efficient and nutritious animals that can be raised on the small place is the rabbit. They are particularly worth considering if you live on a small tract of land where the raising of other types of livestock is not practical.

Interestingly, Americans eat about 25 to 30 million pounds of domestically produced rabbit meat per year. All of that meat is produced in small backyard rabbitries and in the many large commercial rabbitries. The animal is well adapted to both types of production.

For our purposes, we will concentrate upon the smaller scale operation. Once you get into raising these interesting animals, you will probably find that you can develop a good homestead market for surplus rabbit meat, if you have any. Our family loves rabbit and it can be cooked into a wide variety of tasty dishes.

A good starting point for the home rabbitry is a couple of does and a buck. From there it will be easy to increase production if it fits into your plans. Two does will provide plenty of young fryers, yet not be too much of a burden to care for.

If I were starting over with rabbits, I believe that I would opt for all wire cages in which to house them. My original cage was based on the popular drawings found in many books and government publications. It is framed with wood and featured two cages under one roof. A hay manger in the middle of the small structure separated the cages.

The main reason that I would make new cages from wire only is based on my experience that combination

Here is the simple setup we used for our rabbits. The cages offer plenty of air circulation, a hardware cloth floor for cleanliness, and plenty of shade. Note the heap of nutrient-rich manure under the cages.

wood and wire cages provide too many places for urine and droppings, as well as spilled water and feed, to accumulate. In time, the buildup can create a health hazard unless it is cleaned out regularly. All-wire cages prevent the problem by eliminating areas where the buildup can occur. I believe that they are simply more sanitary. Rabbit supply catalogs and some good hardware stores carry the pliers and metal crimping sleeves that can help you turn hardware cloth and welded wire into neat and sanitary cages.

Water and food

A heavy ceramic dish makes an ideal water dish for your rabbits. Being notorious for overturning water dishes, the heavier dish should eliminate the problem. Even these dishes or any open container are easily contaminated, however. But this is not usually a problem for the small rabbit raiser who can easily provide fresh water as needed.

Another possibility is the use of the simple tube and ball or "dewdrop" waterers. These neat little devices can be bought with a heavy plastic bottle or can be attached to a plastic pop bottle. I have found that the thin soft plastic of a soda bottle, though, will collapse and not permit water to be dispensed. Whatever type of container you use, be sure to use a bottle large enough to hold a day's worth of water, or check the water often.

Feeders come in a wide variety. One of the best feeders is nearly impossible to find anymore. That was simply one of the old short coffee cans which were about four inches tall. The cans were easily attached to a small piece of board or wired

Building a rabbit cage

The major thing to consider whether constructing or purchasing a rabbit cage is to get one that is self-cleaning. No part of the floor should be solid. Diseases can be spread from dirt, moisture, and droppings remaining on these areas.

Wood is not a desirable material for cage construction. Rabbits gnaw on wood. It absorbs water and urine, making good sanitation more difficult. If wood is used at all, it should be limited to the framework. All of the inner portions such as the floor and partitions should be made of wire.

If you are building your own rabbit cages use ordinary welded wire. Wire cages are more durable than wooden cages and are less expensive in the long run. Wire cages reduce the incidence of disease because they are easier to clean and disinfect.

Many manufactured cages are available. The basic cage used in most rabbitries is 30 inches wide, 36 inches long, and 18 inches high. Most have rectangular sides (conventional style), but some have rounded tops (quonset style). Doors may be hinged at the top, sides, or bottom.

Rabbit cages are usually placed on some type of framework supported by legs. This method requires some type of cover to protect the rabbits from sun, wind, and rain.

On the next page is a plan created from information found in Mississippi State University Plan 1195. The plans illustrate the procedure for building one unit of two 30 x 36 inch wire single-tier cages. Each cage will house a medium-sized doe and litter or five to seven fryer rabbits. All of the wire for these cages except for the flooring consists of welded, 14-gauge galvanized wire with 1 x 1 or 1 x 2-inch grid openings. The floor is made of 16-gauge welded wire with ½ x ½ or ½ x 1-inch grid openings. The materials for these cages can be found at most good hardware or farm and ranch supply stores.

Construction

These cages are most easily constructed in units of two cages. Lay out the floor first by removing a 3 x 3-inch section from each corner of the flooring. Bend up a 3-inch section along each side of the floor to prevent young bunnies from falling from the cage. Attach the steel rods to the front and rear edges of the floor, using hog rings.

The partition and ends of the quonset cage are shaped using a pattern. Allow a $^5/_8$-inch section of the wires to extend beyond the pattern. Bend these wires around a No. 12 edging wire.

Position the ends and partition on the floor and fasten them using small hen-cage clips. Attach the front and back sides of the conventional cages to the bent-up flooring. Do not fasten the partition to flooring in the area where the doors will be located. Fasten sides to the partition and ends.

Lay the top of the quonset cages over the floor, ends, and partition. Fasten to the front and rear of the flooring, using small hen-cage clips spaced every 5 inches. Raise the center partition and fasten to the top. Repeat the process with each end section.

Cut the door openings in the front side of each cage. Each opening should be 2 inches smaller than the doors in height and width. File all sharp protruding wires. Attach the doors, using large hen-cage clips as hinges. Attach the No. 9 wire around the door openings, using the large-sized clips. Install the door latch to complete the cage.

The cages can be suspended from an overhead support, using six strands of No. 12 galvanized wire. Attach a wire to each corner of the individual cages for proper support.

directly to the cage wire to prevent overturning. They were just the right height for bunny feeders.

Feeders available on the market usually include a feed hopper in their design, into which may be placed several days' worth of feed. They are attached to the cage by cutting a hole in the cage wire. This places the feed trough inside the cage and the feed hopper remains conveniently outside for filling. I prefer to feed daily, so as not to allow feed to draw moisture. Some of these feeders come with a wire mesh bottom to allow the feed dust to fall through. This is an important point. Although we did not experience the problem, it seems that rabbits are pretty easily affected by inhaling this or other dust.

Breeding

Once you get your animals and introduce them to their quarters, you will need to arrange for them to begin production of offspring. True to their reputation, the bunnies are generally eager to cooperate. The does come into heat about every two weeks or so, but due to their makeup, they may actually be bred at any time. When the doe is interested, she will do a good deal of thumping with her hind feet, and rub her chin on the water or feed dish.

When getting your rabbits together, you need to remember to put the doe into the cage of the buck, not the other way around. Doe rabbits are very territorial and in putting the buck into the doe's cage, the health and safety of the buck is jeopardized, for she will give him a sound trouncing. A buck should have no problem servicing a couple of does; in fact a maximum ratio of bucks to does is about 1:10 for good breeding results.

Within minutes, the buck should complete his work, after which time the doe should be returned to her cage. It is normal for the buck to perhaps fall to the cage floor immediately after copulation. Don't be alarmed. I have found that if the doe is left with the buck for a few minutes, returned to her cage, then put back with the buck in a half hour or so, that breeding is nearly certain.

After you feel certain that the doe has been bred, it is a matter of waiting the 30 days or so for the young to be born. In the meantime, you should place a nest box within the doe's cage. Nest boxes are simple to build. Page 24 has an illustration of a good one. It can be made from inch lumber or from plywood. The measurements are approximate. Make it from what you have, but don't make it much smaller than the illustration. The doe will need some room and relative darkness for her new brood of bunnies.

At about 20 days of age, the new youngun's will be ready to clamber out of the nest box and will begin to nibble on the pelleted feed that you have for the doe. They will be ready to butcher at about 8 to 9 weeks. If you plan to keep some for breeding, they reach sexual maturity at about 6 months.

Rabbits do best where they do not get too much sunlight. This is why old garages, sheds, or pole buildings work well as rabbitries. For the small rabbit raiser, the shady side of a building will work nicely. Shade and ventilation is especially important in summer. Conversely, during winter, awnings which unroll or drop down over the sides of the cage will help to prevent drafts and retain heat.

Lift rabbits properly and never by the ears. While at the local sale barn, I have seen grown men grab rabbits by the ears and go

CONVENTIONAL STYLE

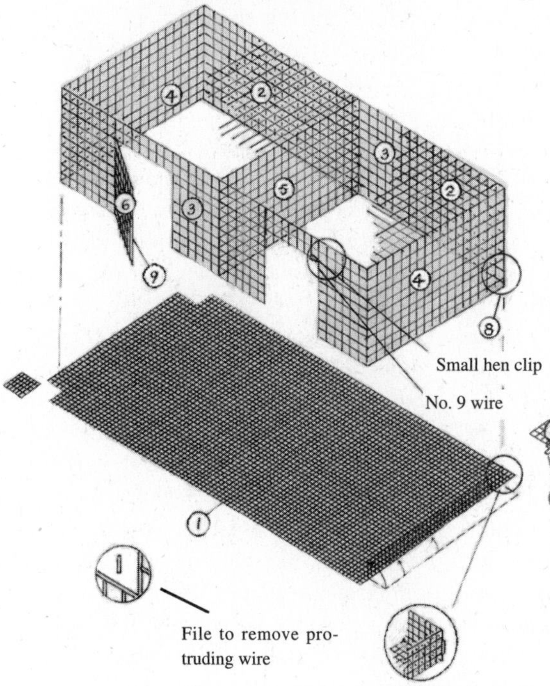

QUONSET STYLE

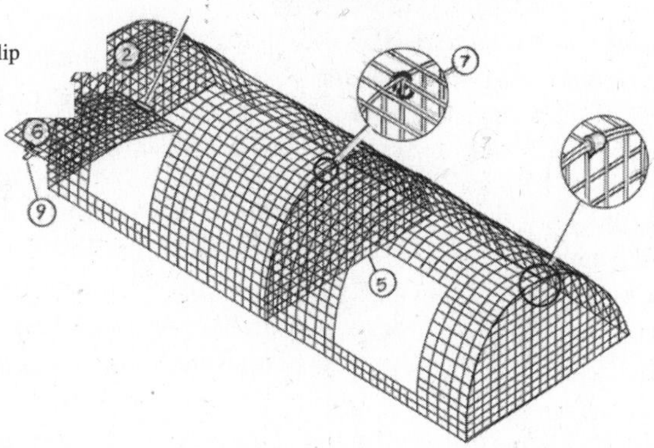

Two types of wire rabbit cages

		Conventional	Quonset
FLOOR:	(1)	1 piece of 36 x 78 in. wire mesh	1 piece of 36 x 78 in. wire
TOP:	(2)	1 piece of 30 x 72 in. wire mesh	1 piece of 48 x 72 in. wire
SIDES:	(3)	2 pieces of 15 x 72 in. wire mesh	---------
ENDS:	(4)	2 pieces of 15 x 30 in. wire mesh	2 pieces of 18 x 30 in. wire
PARTITION:	(5)	1 piece of 18 x 30 in. wire mesh	1 piece of 21 x 30 in. wire
DOORS:	(6)	2 pieces of 16 x 18 in. wire mesh	2 pieces of 18 x 20 in. wire
MISC:	(7)	----------------	3 pieces of No. 12 galvanized wire
	(8)	2 pieces of 72-in. sections of 5/16-in. steel rod for floor	2 pieces of 72-in. sections of 5/16-in. steel rod for floor
	(9)	2 door latches	2 door latches

FASTENERS: (Common to both styles)	100 small hen-cage clips 25 large hen-cage clips 30 no. 101 hog rings 2 pieces of 24-in. length, no. 9 galvanized wire

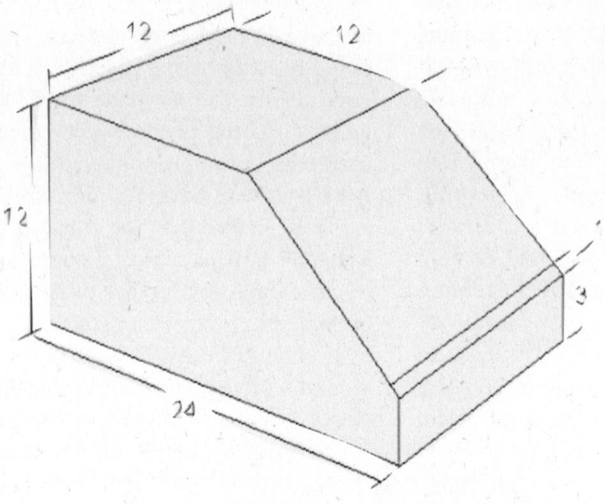

A nest box can be made easily from dimensional lumber or plywood.

toting them off. To properly pick up an adult rabbit, pick it up by the scruff of the neck and put the other hand under the rump for support. The rabbit will appear to be sitting on your support hand yet is firmly held by the scruff of its neck.

For small rabbits, grasp the loin area gently and firmly. The thumb will be on the left side and the fingers on the other. The web of your hand will be across the back. The heel of the hand will be naturally pointed towards the tail of the rabbit.

Killing and butchering

Rabbits do not have a great tenacity for life. That is to say, they are easily killed. Although it might seem unpleasant the first time around, you will quickly get accustomed to it and should be able to accomplish the chore quickly and humanely.

Perhaps the simplest method is to grasp the rabbit by the rear legs and suspend the animal so that it can be delivered a sharp blow at the base of the skull with a stout stick or similar club, or even the heel of the hand, "karate chop" fashion. I've used a short piece (16 to 18-inch length) of ¾-inch pipe or conduit on several occasions. After the rabbit flops around a bit, the head must be removed promptly so that the animal bleeds out properly. The easiest and quickest way to remove the head is merely to grasp it firmly in one hand, with the shoulders of the rabbit in the other and twist. It doesn't take a lot of effort to completely twist the head off of the carcass. If the idea of doing this does not appeal to you, then sever the skin, meat, and fiber of the neck with a sharp knife. Then grasp the head and carcass as described above and twist enough to break the spine and remove the head.

Rabbits are not difficult to skin, although I have never mastered the art of getting the hide off in one nice piece. Their hide is relatively thin and tears rather easily, so that I have never been left with any usable rabbit hides. Unless you wish to tan and use the hides yourself, this is not a big deal. Generally, rabbit hides are not very marketable unless you have a great number of them.

Once you have the critter skinned, then carefully open up the abdominal cavity with a sharp knife, cutting from the breastbone to the tail. As with any other meat animal, be careful not to puncture the entrails when you cut through the abdominal muscle layers. Once the entrails are exposed, reach up into the chest cavity and firmly grasp the organs found there. Pull them downward and keep going until you have the "guts" removed from the body. Some folks retain the liver and kidneys for later use, and leave them in the carcass. Cut or break apart the area at the anus and remove all of the vent gut.

Immediately rinse out the carcass and put it in cold water for just a few minutes or place the meat in a refrigerator. This firms up the meat and makes cutting the carcass into fry pan-sized pieces much easier.

When cutting up a fryer rabbit, you should end up with 6 or 7 pieces. Remove each rear leg at the ball joint. Similarly, at the shoulders, cut into the meat at the base of the foreleg and remove each. Next, I usually cut the trunk into two pieces, cutting it in two just below the bottom rib. If you have not done so, split the rib cage down the breastbone. I think that this opens the piece up a bit and helps it to cook more thoroughly. Once you get the hang of all this, it will go quickly and smoothly. Don't be discouraged by those first attempts that might look like you tried to gnaw the carcass into pieces. Remember, the main purpose is to make the rabbit carcass fit in a skillet. If you do that, then you are successful.

One of the best ways to prepare rabbit is also the simplest. Merely take each cut-up piece of rabbit and shake it in a bag to which has been added a quantity of well-peppered flour. With each piece thoroughly coated, place them in a skillet of hot grease and fry them until they are golden brown. Use the "leavins," that is, the remaining grease and fried flour crumbles as the beginnings of some good gravy. Keeping it hot, stir in a few tablespoons of flour, and stir with a fork until it begins to thicken. Once it gets to a thin, paste like consistency, gradually add a cup or two of milk. Keep stirring until it thickens up. If necessary, sprinkle in a bit more flour and keep stirring to keep it from getting lumpy. Once it is the consistency you like, serve it while hot, along with the fried rabbit, some hot biscuits, green beans, and mashed potatoes if you want. Δ

Ask Jackie

> If you have a question about rural living, send it in to Jackie Clay and she'll try to answer it. Address your letter to *Ask Jackie*, PO Box 712, Gold Beach, OR 97444. Questions will only be answered in this column. — Editor

Jackie Clay

How close can cabinets be to a wood cookstove?

I have read numerous books on woodstove cooking and how best to choose a cookstove. Unfortunately, there is never any information on what is the minimal safe distance for your kitchen cabinets to be from the stove. Since I am trying to build the smallest house possible, I need to know this distance so that I can finalize my house plan.

Sabrina Kuethe
Alhambra, IL

The reason no one gives distances is because they don't want to be sued. There are differences between stoves, making differences required between the stove and flammable surfaces, such as your kitchen cabinets. I've had several wood ranges in my kitchens, and will tell you what worked for me. I am not advising you to follow my experience, only telling you what worked for me.

I've never had my kitchen wood range further from the back wall than 16 inches. However, I've always used drywall, masonite, or a relatively hard-to-burn surface behind the stove. But I've never found excessive heat behind a wood range in good shape. You can run into difficulties if you have a hole or crack in the casting or metal. That hole will let a lot of heat escape. You can patch them with furnace cement.

It's a good idea to place your firebox end of the stove next to a doorway so that you have a natural space between the working end of the stove (i.e. "hot end") and anything flammable. You do not want your cabinets closer than three feet from this end of the stove.

The other end of the stove is much safer. This is especially so if you have a water reservoir on the side, further tempering the stove's heat.

I've found that you need at least three feet in front of the stove. This not only prevents cabinets from getting too hot in front of the stove, but lets you fully open the oven door. Another foot is very convenient, as you can open the door *and* walk past it, too.

Having the stove on a nonflammable surface, such as tile or brick, is safest in case hot coals should pop out when you are adding wood to the fire or when you have the side vents open for a better draft. It does happen.

— Jackie

Preserving bacon, feed for chickens, and diseases from mice

How do you preserve bacon? Is there a way to can or dry it? I would like to buy a fresh pig and it would be cut up. I planned on canning most of it. But what about ham or bacon?

A while back you mentioned that if we knew how they made laying mash, we wouldn't buy it. Is it bad for the chickens? Quite frankly, I don't have much leftovers to feed them (my husband is a big eater and loves my cooking.) In place of the mash, what should I buy instead? I plan on developing a small laying flock.

My last question is the disease you can get from mice. I always thought that mice in the country wouldn't be in people's garbage, so they wouldn't carry disease.

My dogs and cats, and even my chickens, eat the ones they catch. And we are tearing out walls and ceilings in our house. They are full of mice nests from the years and years our house was a hunting camp with no full-time residents.

Should I stop our animals from eating them? But it's okay for them to catch them, isn't it? I'm not sure what kind of mice we have. Some are gray and some are brown and they aren't very big. Most of them live in the woods and come into the house only occasionally now.

Kathy Lupole
Oxford, NY

While I have canned bacon, we usually just have our hogs butchered and hung up during quite cold fall weather. When the hams and bacon are finished smoking I hang the bacon, covered with cheesecloth, from wires in an unheated attic. Perhaps one ham is hung with it, while the rest is cut up and canned.

The unheated attic was usually about 35° F on average and the ham and bacon kept just fine until we ate it up.

The ham, I slice, debone, and slightly pan fry, then add enough water to make a broth to cover the slices in wide-mouthed canning jars. Some of the ham I dice into one-inch cubes to use in mixed dishes such as scalloped potatoes and ham or ham and beans.

I place the slices or cubes of ham in the canning jars to within an inch of the top, then pour on the hot broth, covering the meat to within an inch of the top. The jars are processed for 90 minutes at 10 pounds pressure unless you live at an altitude requiring adjustment of the pressure. Read your canning manual for instructions.

I don't feed my chickens laying mash. I don't like feeding dehydrated slaughterhouse waste products (interpret for yourself here) to birds who provide my eggs and sometimes meat. Yuck! Instead, I give them all my peelings, parings, over-the-edge fruit and vegetables, extra goat milk and whey, and any table scraps we have left. I also raise extra produce for them such as squash, carrots, apples, turnips, Swiss chard, etc. In the winter, I shake a leaf of alfalfa or clover hay onto a tarp, then pour boiling water over the leaves. This makes a nice warm chicken salad.

The disease you get from mice is Hanta virus. More correctly, this should be "the disease you can possibly get from mice." I have cleaned up huge filthy mouse messes and have not contracted the disease (yet). The virus is carried in the urine of deer mice. These are the little tannish mice with white feet and vest, large ears and eyes. They are very cute.

To be safest, wear gloves and old clothes when doing mousy cleanups. A paper face mask is also a good idea. Carry a spray bottle of diluted bleach water and dampen an area to prevent flying dust before you work on it. When finished cleaning for the day, put your clothes in a hot water wash, throw away your face mask, and take a good hot shower, washing your hair. (You'll want to do this anyway, Hanta virus or not.)

No, you do not need to prevent your dogs and cats from hunting and eating the mice. As if we could do that anyway. After awhile, the mice will decide that back in the woods is a safer place than your home.

— Jackie

Battling mice and rats, and wintering animals

I have a condo chicken coop, electric heat lamps, heated water tank to supply the hens with unfrozen water, southern facing picture windows for a great view and winter sun, and it is fully insulated. Well, it's now partly insulated. The mice have made tunnels and nests all over the walls and ceiling. I used three-inch styrofoam sheets. I thought about using the fiberglass insulation but I was told the mice liked making nests in it also. What can be used to insulate a condo chicken coop that the mice won't destroy?

Before electric was available to the farm areas, what did the farmers long ago use instead of tank heaters and electric water heaters? Straw, hay and all sorts of combustable materials are everywhere in a barn. Not to mention what the livestock could do to any kind of open flame heat source.

Our barn is over 170 years old and still has the bark on the beams. It would go up in flames and be gone in a few minutes. I had back surgery a while back and carrying buckets of water is out of the question, not to mention I didn't like that method before the back problem.

Kyle Laukus
Coloma, MI

Unfortunately, mice will dwell happily in any insulation you put in your coop, from sawdust to fiberglass. The answer is to get rid of the mice. Enter the mighty barn cat. One good cat will end your problems right now.... Or at least within a few days' time. On my first homestead, I had trouble with rats. Big ones and lots of them. They were not only in the chicken coop, but in the walls of my house. I was afraid to go to sleep at night, it was so bad. I shot one, the size of a raccoon, off my kitchen counter. (Okay so I did exaggerate a little bit, but he was huge and he about flipped me off while he was sitting there looking me in the eye.)

But someone dumped a scrawny female cat off on my driveway and as soon as she was home from the vet for a spay job, she set off to rid the farm of all rodents. In a month there was no scurry noise in my bedroom walls, no mice in the chicken coop, not even poopies on the feed and counter top.

Get a cat and treat her royally.

As for your watering problem, the old-timers housed their water tanks inside wooden boxes, lined with sawdust or hay, with an insulated lid over the top. This was opened twice a day for the animals to have access. When ice was on the top, it was broken with an ax and lifted out with a pitchfork. The tank was located in a barn aisle so the animals' warmth kept it from freezing hard.

You can copy this or you might install a frost free hydrant in or near your barn, running a buried water line down from your well. This is ideal, as you don't have to maintain a stock tank, yet you have water handy to water your animals twice a day. I also have a bad back (had a big horse come over backward into my lap when I was 18) and cannot lug water everyday. The frost free hydrant is a godsend. Just make sure it is installed over a bed of gravel, so it drains well. And buy a long enough hydrant to get the water line down below the frost line.

— Jackie

Cleaning cast iron

I have gotten some cast iron cooking utensils from my mother. The mice had gotten into them and left spots in them. How can I clean them and are they safe to use?

Leona Martel
Stratford, SD

Yes, you can clean the cast iron, provided they aren't *too* rusted. I would fill them with boiling water and let them sit until the water has cooled. Dump out that water. Then scrub with steel wool and hot water. This should remove nearly all the rust. If some remains, use fine wet-sanding sandpaper to smooth out any remaining spots. Wash with warm water and dish soap. Rinse well. Now rub vegetable oil in the pans and place in the oven on pilot or the lowest setting. You want to heat the pans, not "cook" them.

Rinse this oil out with boiling water and rub dry. Do not use dish soap. The first time you use the pans, use plenty of shortening or oil and fry something easy. It takes a little seasoning with oils to get the pans in great condition, but it can be done. And it isn't really that hard, either.

— Jackie

The many, many uses of dehydrated tomatoes

Memaw and I have dehydrated some tomatoes we can't use immediately. How do we use them?

Charlie
Salem, IN

If your tomatoes are dehydrated well, with no moisture, simply pack them in quart jars (or even gallon jars, if you have enough) and screw the lids down snugly. They will store in a cool, dark place for a long time, coming out like freshly dehydrated even after months of storage. I don't think a person can ever have too many dehydrated tomatoes. I dice them up and put 'em on pizzas, in spaghetti sauce, casseroles, lasagna, and lots more. We even snack on them (especially Sun Gold yellow tomatoes) like dried apricots.

You can rehydrate them at any time simply by placing a handful in a bowl and pouring hot water over them and allowing them to "plump up." Or you can stew them in a little water with seasonings you prefer. The end result is about like canned tomatoes only they have a richer taste.

— Jackie

How to get "real" bacon from a butchered hog

I'm getting ready to butcher a hog, and a friend wants to do it for us. It's just the last time I had unprocessed bacon it was like eating fried pork roast. What can I do to make it taste like store bacon?

Linda Royal
Chipley, FL

"Real" bacon tastes so much better than store bacon it's not funny. You just had a bad experience. What probably happened is that the bacon was heated too much during the smoking. This causes it to get soft and "runny." Bacon needs to be smoked slowly and in a relatively cool smoke. Smoking meat is an art, as are many homesteading skills. But it's something anyone can learn, especially following the lead of an experienced friend or neighbor.

— Jackie

More details on the kerosene lamp brooder

In the Jan/Feb 2004 BHM, you told how to build a kerosene lamp-heated chicken brooder.

I was not sure of the size of the box. How much room do I need for 25 chicks? We do not have electric so this is my only way to keep them warm.

Lorraine Warsop
Ewen, MI

We brooded 50 chicks in our kerosene lamp brooder. The box was 18 inches deep, 24 inches long, and a foot high. It had an attached pen on the front that was 18 inches by 4 feet. In this pen was their food and water. On a table nearby, we kept a lantern burning at night to provide light at night. This prevented them from smothering from huddling together. With the lamp, they pecked and ran around most of the time. The front of the box was hung with a piece of blanket with slits cut in it to hold in the heat, but allow the chicks to come and go at will. This brooder worked very well and we only lost one weak chick. Don't forget to have a good layer of sand on the metal bottom to prevent the chicks from getting hot feet from the lamp(s) below.

— Jackie

Homemade concrete

I once saw a show on Discovery where several hundred years ago they had made concrete out of sand, rock and burnt seashells. Although there was some erosion, the outside walls were still standing. Can you print for us a homemade recipe and the process for concrete? I have heard of using oyster shells. But would fresh water clam shells work as well?

Also, I have abused my body by a poor diet for about forty years now. Is there a homeopathic recipe to clean the accumulated poisons and bring back balance to your organs, or is that quackery?

Calvin White
Omaha, NE

Yes, you *can* make concrete from limestone (and probably your clamshells; you'll just have to experiment). My grandfather, Eddy, was a stone mason who needed to have mortar to build the family a house and barn up in Canada at the end of the Depression when money was extremely scarce. Luckily, the homestead had limestone on it and he and the neighbor set about to make their own.

First they tunneled several feet into a steep hillside, digging a hole about four feet in diameter. Then they went on top of the hill and dug a large hole (six feet by six feet by seven feet deep) down to the tunnel, making a pipe-shaped firebox and chimney. Then they filled the chimney nearly to the top with pieces of limestone.

Building a hot fire in the tunnel, they kept a roaring fire going, which sucked up through the limestone for three days and two nights. Mom says that the sight of the multi-colored flames shooting up into the night sky was truly awe inspiring.

After the three days were up, the stone had slaked and turned into a crumbly powder—lime.

This was mixed with sand to make the mortar that Grandpa used to build his house and huge barn. Most of my notes are packed somewhere in a box, stacked in a storage building in town, but I'll bet you can find the correct mix of gravel, sand, and lime somewhere without too much trouble. Or you can simply experiment. And I'll bet your clam shells could be used as well.

As to renewing your body using homeopathic methods, I really don't put much stock in this. I've talked to dozens of people who have tried many of these methods and I can't see that they really did much over time. But I do guarantee that if you begin taking care of yourself, cut out the smoking, booze, any "recreational" drugs and begin a self-reliant lifestyle (growing your own food and cooking from it, exercising daily, enjoying life) your body *will* bounce back from past abuse. *That* I have seen work time and time again.

— Jackie

Hopi Pale Grey seeds

I noticed the information in your October column on the Hopi Pale Grey seeds. I would like to ask you if this is the same as "Ancient Hopi Blue" winter squash. The Hopi Blue is a rare squash. I grew those in my garden this year and I am saving seeds from them. I only got one huge squash from each plant. They were a bluish-gray in color and a few had pinkish hues. Very long, like an oblong watermelon. I obtained the seeds and their history from a seed trader years ago. Do I have the same seeds as the Hopi Pale Grey? If I do, I will be willing to share them for an S.A.S.E. I hope my seeds are the same.

Lillian Faubus
Yellville, AR

No, Lillian, these are not the Hopi Pale Grey squash. There are several Hopi winter squash. And the thing that I love about the Hopi Pale Grey is that you get half a bushel of basketball sized pale bluish gray squash from each rank vine.

These squash are exceedingly rare now, but my friend, Shane Murphy in California, is growing out a batch this year, as I hope to as well. Shane's growing season is more dependable though, and I promise to keep readers posted on the progress of this truly great Native American squash.

— Jackie

Huckleberry recipes

Can you give me recipes for huckleberries? I have a freezer full of them. What now?

Robert Jungwirth
Outing, MN

Check out the article on blueberries in this issue for lots of ideas. Lucky you.

— Jackie

Hopi Pale Grey squash are not frost tolerant

Can you tell me how frost tolerant the Hopi Pale Grey squash plants are and how many days to harvest? Would you know how long the seeds last in storage? I've never had such rare seeds before and I'm a bit perplexed about what to do.

Becky Blue
Cedar Ridge, CA

Hopi Pale Greys are not frost tolerant, especially as baby plants, so plant them when the soil and spring temperatures are dependably warm. They tolerate slightly more cold weather when the vines are huge in the fall. In my experience, they mature in about 90 days in most climates. The seeds last a long, long time in storage. I've planted some that were 10 years old, but of course germination is safer when the seeds are younger. This is a truly rare squash. Three of the main suppliers in the U.S have quit propagating and selling this wonderful squash. It's a shame, as it's a definite favorite of ours, producing tons of squash that has outstanding flavor and keeping abilities. Raise *lots* and I'll bet you can sell seed to many other gardeners.

— Jackie

My canner won't seal

I was trying to can some fish and my pressure cooker won't seal. I don't know any other way to store it. Can you help me please?

Patty
stones@wvhome.net

I'm hoping that you are canning your fish in a *pressure canner*, as a pressure cooker really isn't meant for canning. Usually when the canner won't seal it means that the rubber seal in the lid has become stiff. Almost any good hardware store that carries home canning equipment and supplies can sell you a new seal. This is inexpensive and a quick fix for your problem.

However, sometimes the canner has become pitted or developed a nick or crack. This is not repairable and you must replace the unit.

In the meantime, you can freeze the fish in small packs until your canner is back working again. To test it before you use it again, just bring it up to pressure with no jars inside—only the required water. If it comes up to pressure with no leaking, you're back in business.

— Jackie

Keeping chickens warm in very cold weather

I would like to know how everyone else keeps about 20 chickens warm in the winter when it is 10 or more degrees below zero? You certainly can't run an electric heater with the cost of electricity. How tough are chickens?

Cindy Hills
ccrmuggs@vbe.com

Chickens are amazingly tough, provided that they are cared for properly. To keep them reasonably warm in the winter, size the coop to the number of chickens you have. With 20 chickens, you won't want a coop much larger than eight by ten feet. Keep the ceiling low, too, to hold in as much warmth as possible. If you are five feet two inches tall, make the ceiling six feet high at max (allowing for bedding building up).

Give the "girls" plenty of south facing windows to gather as much warmth from the sun as possible. Make the coop as tight as possible, yet vent through the roof for some air movement but no drafts. Make double walls, and between them either use commercial insulation or pour dry sawdust, or even staple layers of cardboard in between—anything to provide at least four inches of insulation. More in the ceiling is a good idea. Even fluffy straw in the ceiling is better than nothing when it comes to holding in warmth. Use a storm door, as you do on your house, and tack plastic over the windows during the winter for extra wind protection.

Make sure they have clean, dry bedding. This can be wood shavings, straw, or even ground corn cobs. Scattering a handful of whole corn in the bedding will make the hens dig and scratch for feed. And this will, in turn, do much to warm them up.

Choose a breed with a rose comb. That is a comb that does not stand up, but is tight to the head. Look in poultry catalogs and you'll see the difference. An upright comb will freeze quite easily. Usually this does nothing but cause the comb to turn black and fall off, but sometimes it so stresses the hen that she gets sick and dies.

Give the hens warm water twice a day when the weather is very cold.

Also provide them with a little more corn than normal to give more heating to the body. Extra calories are necessary when it is quite cold.

If you'd like to provide a little more warmth, many farmers simply run a light bulb in the coop, day and night. You'd be surprised how much warmth a 100-watt light bulb provides in an insulated coop.

My chickens are doing just fine in our goat barn this winter, provided with a small "coop in the corner" in which to roost at night in very cold weather. We've had temperatures lower than -43°F and they continue to thrive. But they do have plenty of hay for bedding, a snug barn, and several goat and sheep "heaters" as well.

— Jackie

Some cautions about castrating older bulls

At what age or weight would you not castrate a bull? I usually band newborns when they are a few days old. I have some that I have bought and wonder what chances I have of losing them if I castrate. Their weight is from 150 to 1,200 pounds.

K. Bishop
KBISHOP594@aol.com

It is certainly possible to castrate any size bull. But I would not band a larger animal. There is much danger of tetanus with a bigger animal, as the wound is larger (yes, there *is* a wound where the band cuts into the flesh, causing the testicles to become necrotic and drop off) than in a newborn calf.

I prefer to use a Burdizzo emasculator on larger animals. This pinches the cord and blood vessels, which causes the testicles to shrink and the animal to become sterile. There is no wound, no bleeding or shock. If you don't have, or can't borrow this "clamp" as it's often called, you might consider having your vet come out for those big bulls. Or butcher them as bulls. The meat is not affected by being left entire.

If you do use the clamps, *never* attempt to do both testicles at the same time. You must isolate and clamp one cord, leading to one testicle, at a time. This requires two pinches with the emasculator.

— Jackie

Crystallized sugar

I saw a recipe for Christmas apple pie and it calls for crystallized sugar. What is crystallized sugar and where can I buy it?

Mariette Gagne
Hickory, NC

Crystallized sugar is the coarse sugar that is often sprinkled onto cookies during the holidays. It is often colored, but you can find uncolored sugar, as well. Look in the baking department at your larger supermarkets or go to bakers' supply houses that carry cake baking supplies.

— Jackie

Harvesting the wild blueberries

Blueberry plants. Notice the oval leaves and the "crown" on the blossom ends.

By Jackie Clay

Few wild fruits are abundant over such a wide area as is the blueberry. Found all across most of the U.S, Canada, and Alaska, the blueberry is truly a delight to gatherers of wild foods. In areas where it does not grow, its cousin, the huckleberry, grows in abundance.

The blueberry and huckleberry are in the same family, *Ericaceae.* The low-bush blueberry is *Vaccinium augustifolium*, and the high-bush blueberry, *Vaccinium corybosum.* The black huckleberry is *Gaylussacia baccata*, and the dangleberry (also a huckleberry), *Gaylussicia frondosa.*

Luckily, the blueberry is quite easy for the beginner to identify in the wild, as very few non-edibles look anything like it. But, of course, to be absolutely safe a person should go blueberry picking with a knowledgeable person the first time.

The blueberry is a shrubby, woody-stemmed plant with oval leaves. Most varieties of wild blueberry are the short, low-bush or swamp blueberry, but one of the most wonderful blueberry harvests I've ever had in my life was a huge patch of bushes four feet tall, the wonderful high-bush blueberry. The flowers are little bells, light to dark pink, hanging in clusters along the stems of the plant. Later on, you can tell the ripening green blueberries because of their little "crown" on the blossom end of the berry. When the berries are ripe, they appear a nice bright blue, but if you rub the blue dust off, they shine a deep bluish purple. Inside are several small seeds, scarcely noticeable.

Huckleberries have seeds which are just a little larger.

Squeeze a berry, then sniff it. It will have a distinct "blueberry" fragrance. Then pop one into your mouth and taste. There is no mistaking the delightful flavor of a wild blueberry. They make those $3 a half-pint giant berries at the store taste positively bland. The wild blueberry may be small, but it is delectable.

Back in the thumb of Michigan, when I was a new homesteader many years back, I was telling an older woman in a local feed mill that I was canning blueberries I'd found in the woods up north the last weekend. She smiled a knowing smile and told me that I didn't have to go way up north for blueberries. She looked around quickly, then leaned close, giving me intimate directions to her favorite patch that she had picked for 30 years.

"I'm too old to go out there now," she said, "but I'll bet you'll just *love* this spot!" She patted my arm and turned out the door.

Well it was only two hours later when I drove my old Chevy up that dirt two-track in the woods, turned left at the old burnt stump, and followed a trail so faint that young trees grew in the middle. Then it ended, just as my new friend had said it would, and I knew I was at the right place. "Just go downhill from the turnaround," she had said, "and you'll be right in amongst them."

I had brought a small pail and an old blue water bath canner. Perhaps I was a bit over optimistic, as it held four and a half gallons, but she was adamant that I would need a *big* kettle. Down, downhill I walked, ending in a soft moss bed a foot deep. That in itself would have been wonderful, but glancing around, I saw huge old blueberry bushes, just hanging down with literally tons of fruit.

Plopping down on that soft, dry moss I started filling my little pail, milking clusters of the blue-black fruit off the drooping branches, the pail filled in less than fifteen minutes. My canning kettle was *not* too much. In fact, I filled that and went home to can them up. Hardly sleeping, dreaming, smelling, and feeling blueberries, I couldn't wait to go back for the next batch. That time, I took two canning kettles and a big turkey roasting pan. Both were filled to overflowing that day and two days after that. At night, I put them up as blueberry syrup, jam, and canned blueberries. What fun.

Not only did I spend hours out in the woods enjoying the birdsong, whisper of wind in the pines and oaks, but I brought home wonderful wild fruit and a memory that will last forever.

Where to find wild blueberries

Blueberries like disturbed areas, loving sunlight and a place to spread out. You will often find them following a fire or logging operation. They especially favor a clear-cut logging area.

The blueberry plant loves acid soil, so look for it where you find moss growing on the ground and strawberry plants in abundance.

I've found most of the best patches on sandy or gravel hillsides near low areas or woods. High bush blueberries seem to like their feet a little damper, favoring the edges of sphagnum bogs.

Aside from just asking around for blueberry picking spots, a good bet is to go in and talk to the Department of Natural Resources folks. Not all of them get into the woods, but they might be able to steer you to the right person. (Don't expect anyone to divulge their best spots, though. You'll just have to get lucky, or find your own picking heaven through walking many hours through the woods before season.)

Generally, blueberries begin to ripen in June, hit their peak in July, and struggle on until frost. Of course, this depends much on the growing season each year and the amount of rainfall. Sometimes a hard late frost or hail storm kills the blossoms, resulting in a poor picking in one area.

Wild blueberry picking tips

Unfortunately, the season in which wild blueberries are the best, the bugs are too. Ticks, chiggers, biting flies, mosquitoes, and yellow jackets also are foraging. And they seem to love berry pickers. I've found that by wearing long socks and tying my

The blueberry plant loves acid soil, so look for it where you find moss growing on the ground and raspberry plants, such as these, in abundance.

jeans shut around my ankles I don't receive so many "lower bugs'" such as ticks. I also wear long sleeves to protect my arms and a baseball hat to keep the deer flies out of my hair. By picking early in the morning, you can generally avoid most of the undesirable critters that want to snack on you.

If they are really bad, you can rub some repellent containing DEET on your cuffs and the back of your hat, including your hair. I don't recommend taking it to the field, as it is not something you'd want to use liberally. I always wash my hands well after applying it, before picking berries my family will be eating. You can also use a spray repellant that your hands do not have to touch at all.

In locales where you could run into poisonous snakes, it's a good idea to carry a walking stick and rustle around in the bushes where you plan on walking and picking. Most snakes are happy to leave when they are disturbed and you can see or hear them on the move. A rattler will usually buzz when annoyed in this way, letting you know you might want to go elsewhere to pick. I've gardened and picked berries in snake country many years, and have never yet run into a poisonous snake, but it could happen, and it is wise to be a bit cautious. Don't walk quickly through heavy bush and don't just plop down where the berries are thick. Go slow and be cautious. You'll enjoy your berrying much more that way.

Then there are the bears. Everybody asks me if I run into bears in the blueberries. Of course, bears are master wild foragers. They have to be, in order to survive. (I'd hate to weigh over 300 pounds and depend on eating blueberries to make a living.) I've often picked where I've seen sign (scat and tracks) and even bears, themselves.

But they're busy snacking and really don't pay much attention to you, as long as you are a respectful distance away. I've picked on one side of a large berry patch and had a bear filling his belly basket on the other. He paid me no more mind than if I'd been a grouse or deer.

In grizzly country (Alaska, western Canada, mountainous Montana, or Wyoming) it's a good idea to be more cautious than where you would only come across a more timid black bear in the berry patch. Grizzlies are more territorial and can be aggressive. Make a bit of noise when approaching a berry patch, then scout it out for bear sign before you begin to pick. If you see torn up ground, large piles of bear dung, and large bear tracks with the claws digging into the ground away from the toe prints, you're probably poaching in a grizz's berry patch and it would be wise to forage elsewhere.

It's also a good idea to pick in a group. More human scent and noise keeps a grizzly away in most cases. Most folks I know out west have never even seen a grizzly in all the years they have picked berries.

The picking itself is simple. As the berries hang in clusters, one just has to milk them off by rolling them between the thumb and fingers lightly, letting the ripe ones drop into a pan or small bucket. I recommend picking in a fairly small container and then dumping it into a larger one when it is full. I've never known any berry picker who hasn't, at some time or another, dumped their picking bucket. And it's just about impossible to pick up all those spilled berries

My daughter-in-law, Kelly...

...and my sister, Sue, in hog heaven on our quarter-mile-long blueberry ridge.

from the bushes and litter of the patch. It's a sad feeling, but much sadder if you just dumped a three gallon bucket.

Luckily, blueberry bushes do not have thorns, so picking is painless. I usually find a good spot and either sit or kneel and pick, pick, pick. It's sometimes tempting to look over a patch you are picking and see "over there" better berries. But when you go "over there" you always look around and see still a better spot. You can waste a lot of time jumping all over the place instead of methodically picking berries.

If you are patient, you can fill up a five-quart ice cream bucket in no time. And that's a lot of blueberry muffins, pancakes, jam, and pies. I try to only pick as many berries as I can put up in a day or two. Although blueberries do not squash, as do strawberries and raspberries, they are best preserved in good, fresh condition. And talk about easy to preserve for months to come. The blueberry is one of the easiest to put up and one of the most versatile. Unlike some wild fruits, there is no pit, no coarse seeds to deal with, and no peel to remove.

The only preparation to preserving blueberries is cleaning them of leaves, twigs, etc. An easy way I've found is to get an old window screen and prop up one end high enough that berries roll down to the bottom fairly easily. Under the bottom of the screen, place a large container, such as a turkey roaster. Then simply trickle the berries out of a pail. The leaves and other debris do not roll and hang up on the screen, while the berries roll to the bottom and fall into the pan. A friend of mine uses a towel in the same way. When there is an accumulation of debris, simply turn the screen over or shake the towel out and replace it for the next run of berries.

When they are relatively clean, rinse them in cold water, letting them bob and float about. Any remaining debris or insects can easily be picked out of the water they are in. Strain the berries dry, then pour them out in a single layer on a large cookie sheet or other shallow, large container. Go over the berries, looking for any that are shriveled, rotten, or green. That's it. You're done with the preparation and are ready to preserve your berries.

Dehydrating wild blueberries

Dehydrating wild blueberries is as simple as it gets. Because they are so small, you only have to lay them out in a single layer on cookie sheets in a gas oven with only the pilot light on or any other quite warm, dry spot. I've even used the back of our

Black bears love blueberries, but will do you no harm when treated with respect.

Suburban. Of course, I now also have a dehydrator that I use in the evenings while I work on the computer. A few hours, even once in a while, will easily dehydrate our lovely blueberries. It's a good idea to use a spatula and turn them about a time or two, when using a cookie sheet. On a window screen or dehydrator tray, there is adequate air flow and turning is not necessary.

You want your berries dried down to little hard blueberry "raisins." When dry, you can pour them into a glass jar with an airtight seal. They will keep this way nearly forever. The only enemies of dehydrated blueberries are moisture, which causes mold and insects, or rodents which will eat them. (Hmmmm, maybe I'd better include my son, David, as *he* eats them out of the jar for a snack.)

Home canning wild blueberries

Canning your wild blueberries is also as easy as it gets. They are high acid, as is all fruit, so you only have to use a water bath canner, processing them for a short time. Here's how. Simply pour your blueberries into a large kettle with just enough water to float them. Add enough sugar to taste. This can be very little or a lot, depending on your taste and needs. Heat to boiling, stirring well to mix the sugar in with the water. Don't boil long or the berries will soften. Dip out the berries and fill canning jars to within half an inch of the top of the jar. I use many, many half pint and smaller jars because I find that these small jars come in very handy for adding to my favorite batches of muffins or pancakes or else mixing with other berries for mixed berry recipes.

Blueberries often grow in clusters like grapes.

Fill the jar to within half an inch of the top of the jar with the hot syrup in which the berries were heated. Wipe the rim of the jar clean and place a hot, previously boiled lid on the jar and screw down the ring firmly tight.

Blueberries, washed and ready to can

Place jars in hot water bath canner. Make sure the hot water covers the top of the jars by at least an inch to ensure even heating. Process pints or smaller jars for 15 minutes, starting timing when the kettle reaches a rolling boil. You can use quart jars to can blueberries, processing them for 25 minutes. The quarts make a good pie or nice dessert.

Blueberry jam

When you put up blueberries, you can scarcely make enough blueberry jam. It is one of the very best jams of all. And it is very quick and easy to do, too.

The simple, old-fashioned method of making blueberry jam is to measure out equal portions, by volume, of berries and sugar into a heavy, non-aluminum kettle that is large enough to let the jam boil while thickening. And this is much higher than you'd imagine. Pour in the berries, and then add an equal amount of sugar. With a potato masher, mash the berries to create juice, stirring in the sugar, and turn up the heat. Stirring constantly, boil the jam down, watching it as it thickens. When it is thick enough, pour it into sterilized pint jars to within a quarter inch of the top. Wipe the rim of the jar clean, place a hot, previously boiled lid in place and screw down the ring firmly tight. Process in a hot water bath for 10 minutes.

Once in awhile, the jam does not set. Usually this is because you didn't wait long enough for the batch to thicken properly. This is not a problem. You have just made great blueberry pancake and ice cream syrup.

You can also make blueberry jam with less sugar, using one of the commercial pectin products available in the home canning section of your local store.

Using wild blueberries

Of course, the best way to use wild blueberries is just to eat handfuls right out of the sun-warmed patch, with the morning dew clinging to them. But there are so many other uses for blueberries. This is the main reason we try to pick lots and lots of them.

Here are a few recipes and ideas for you to start with.

Fresh blueberry cobbler

½ cup sugar
1 Tbsp. cornstarch
4 cups blueberries
1 tsp. lemon juice
1 cup flour
1 Tbsp. sugar
1½ tsp. baking powder
½ tsp. salt
3 Tbsp. shortening
½ cup milk

Heat oven to 400° F. Blend ½ cup sugar and the cornstarch in a saucepan. Stir in the blueberries and lemon juice. Cook, stirring constantly until it thickens. Boil one minute. Pour into an ungreased 2-quart casserole. Set aside.

To prepare biscuit topping, measure flour, 1 Tbsp. sugar, the baking powder, and salt into a bowl. Cut in the shortening and add the milk. Drop dough by spoonsful onto the hot fruit. Bake uncovered for 25 to 30 minutes or until the biscuit topping is golden brown. Serve warm with whipped cream. I usually reserve a handful of fresh berries to toss on top of the whipped cream.

Blueberry pancakes

3 cups flour
3 Tbsp. sugar
3 tsp. baking powder
pinch of salt
3 eggs
3 cups milk
large handful dehydrated blueberries *or* 1 cup of fresh or canned berries

Mix the flour, sugar, baking powder and salt. Beat egg yolks with milk and add to dry mixture. Whip the egg whites until stiff and fold in to the batter. Add the blueberries (drained if canned). Bake or fry on hot griddle by large spoonfuls. These are great with fresh blueberry syrup.

No time to make "from-scratch" pancakes? Toss your blueberries into your favorite batter from a mix. They're not the same, but are pretty darned good.

Fresh blueberry syrup

1 cup fresh blueberries
1 cup water
2½ cups white sugar
2 cups light corn syrup

Simmer fresh blueberries in 1 cup of water. When they are soft, add the other ingredients and bring to a boil. Simmer just long enough to blend the flavors. Serve warm over a fresh batch of blueberry pancakes and you'll earn raves, or pour this over your favorite homemade ice cream.

Blueberry muffins

1 egg
¾ cup milk
¼ cup vegetable oil
2 cups flour
⅓ cup sugar
3 tsp. baking powder
1 tsp. salt
1 cup fresh, drained canned, or ¼ cup dehydrated blueberries

Grease the bottoms of muffin tins. Beat the egg, milk, and oil together. Stir in the dry ingredients. Do not overmix. Fold in blueberries. Fill the muffin cups half full. Bake till the muffins are golden brown. Immediately remove from the pan. You can dip the tops in butter and sprinkle sugar and cinnamon over them for a fancier muffin. Serve hot with homemade butter.

Blueberry yogurt

Simply add blueberries and as much (or as little) sugar to your favorite vanilla or plain yogurt as you want, or make a parfait by dipping some fresh blueberries into a cup, adding a layer of yogurt, then more berries on top. Top with a swirl of yogurt and a few fresh blueberries for an easy, fancy snack or desert. Or sprinkle with granola and layer in fresh strawberries, too, and you have a golden arches treat at home, without the chemicals and 100 percent fresh.

Blueberry pie

For a double pie crust:
3 cups flour
1 tsp. salt
1½ cups cold shortening or lard
cold water

Cut the shortening (or lard) into the flour and salt mixture until the shortening is the size of large peas. Add just enough very cold water to make a ball that sticks together without being sticky itself. Divide in half with one half being a little larger.

On a floured surface, roll out the larger ball. Do not work the dough too much or the crust will become tough. When you think it is large enough for the bottom pie crust, turn your pie pan upside down on it for measurement. There should be at least two inches all around the edges, to allow for the depth of the pan and the lip. When it is the right size, carefully roll the dough up on your rolling pin and lay it in the pan. Do the same for the top crust, only leave it on the board. Cut two slits in the top crust. I make these slits into stems of wheat, using the end of a knife to make indents on both sides of the top of the slit for the wheat berries. It lets the steam vent from the pie and looks pretty, to boot.

The filling:
¼ cup water
2 Tbsp. cornstarch
¼ tsp. salt
1 cup sugar
4 cups fresh blueberries
3 to 4 tsp. butter to dot with

Stir the water slowly into the cornstarch, mixing as you go. Then add the salt and sugar. Before it thickens, add the berries. Cook until thickened, stirring often to prevent sticking. Cool. Pour into the cold pie crust. Dot top with the butter. Moisten the lip of bottom crust and lay on the top crust. Trim off the excess and seal by using the tines of a fork to mash the dough together all around or use the end of a table knife to make a fluted edge by shoving the dough toward the center between your thumb and first finger. Bake at 350° F until golden brown. Or you may rub butter on the top crust before baking and sprinkle with sugar and cinnamon for an extra flaky crust.

Serve warm or cool with whipped cream.

You can also use the same recipe to make tarts by cutting the pie crust around an upside down cereal bowl or mug to make the right size to tuck down into muffin cups. Then simply fill each cup and bake without a top crust. These are awesome when served hot with a dollop of whipped cream and fresh berries on top.

Taming wild blueberries

As with many wild-harvested foods, you can certainly bring home some blueberry plants to grow in your own garden. Of course, the trip into the woods at berrying time is one of the best things about picking wild blueberries, and you'll miss that if you grow your own.

Blueberries like acid soil, so you must acidify your soil unless it is already acid by nature. You can do this by adding one of the commercial garden acidifiers along your proposed blueberry row. Ask at your garden center. It is not expensive, but will have to be done each year to keep the soil pleasant for the berry bushes.

Till up the soil and remove any weeds or grass roots.

When you dig your berry bushes from the wild, be considerate. If on private property, ask the owner if you may dig a few bushes. It is not legal to dig on state or federal land, but the removal of a few bushes, dug over a large area will certainly not harm anything. (Don't tell 'em I told you that.)

With a good shovel and a cardboard box or other sturdy container, go out and carefully dig one small clump of blueberries, getting as many of the roots as possible. They are not hard to dig, as the roots are tough and fairly shallow. They are so tough that we consider them almost weeds here on our new northern Minnesota homestead, having had to pull and dig them out of our garden. Even after being tilled under five or six times, they still tried to come back.

After you've dug a clump and put them in your box, carefully sift soil and debris back into the hole and leave no trace of your digging. Then move to a different spot and dig your next bush. It's best to dig a few, then go home and plant them, without giving the roots a chance to dry out. We always think we can plant a whole bunch of plants, and end up with some being held over. Better to dig a few, plant them well, then go back another day and dig more, if needed.

Plant the clumps as deep as they grew in the wild and mulch them with three or four inches of leaves or straw. Then gently soak them in to make sure there are no air pockets in the soil around their roots.

Blueberries require no pruning and have few insect pests. Grasshoppers, though, will eat the foliage so if they're bad, sprinkle rotenone powder on the leaves to protect them from damage.

Transplanted blueberry bushes usually require at least one year to begin bearing well, so have patience. The fruit is certainly worth it. And once they start to produce, they will slowly spread and produce for a lifetime.

If you have no wild blueberries growing nearby, you can buy bushes that are "nearly wild" from many nurseries and seed companies. Just look for the smaller varieties with smaller berries for that tangy, impossible to duplicate wild blueberry taste. Good eating. Δ

Paring down for off-grid living

By Steven Gregersen

My first exposure to a home power system came when I visited the remote homestead of a retired electrical engineer. What a setup. Housed in its own little building was a diesel generator, a bank of batteries, and a control panel that looked like something designed by NASA. Outside stood a three-legged tower with an elevated platform crowded with solar panels that automatically tracked the sun. When he told me the price tag of his investment I came to two conclusions. First, he had more money than sense. Second, there was no way I'd ever be able to live off grid without reverting to a 19th century lifestyle. Well, I was half right.

That was 10 years ago. I have a lot of respect for those who have the knowledge and cash to set up a classy solar energy system. Our problem is that we are not electrical engineers nor are we financially able to build a system that can compete with the power company. We needed something simpler and cheaper. What we've learned is that with careful planning and self-discipline, it is possible to have your electrical needs met without investing thousands of dollars in a home power system. Here's how we did it.

Step one: reduce demand

When you think of electrical demand on a home power system visualize a 50-gallon barrel of water. Water is running into the barrel at the rate of five-gallons-per-minute. The barrel also has a hose attached to the bottom in which the water is running out at the rate of ten-gallons-per-minute. It doesn't take a rocket scientist to see that the water is running out twice as fast as it's going in. Obviously you're going to run out of water. To avoid that you need to (a) reduce the rate the water flows out, (b) increase the rate the water flows in, (c) put in a larger reservoir—which won't stop it from eventually running out, but it will last longer, or (d) some combination of the above.

To apply this to powering your home, think of the energy flowing in and charging your system (solar, wind, or hydro power) as the water flowing into the barrel. The storage system, which would be your batteries, is like the barrel. The amount of electricity you are using is like the water flowing out. Obviously, wind and solar energy outputs fluctuate according to the amount of sunlight or wind you have available so you're going to need batteries to store the electricity they produce. The more batteries you have, the more electricity you can store. The more or larger solar panels or wind generators you have, the more power you can produce. The problem is that batteries, solar panels, and wind generators are expensive. In addition, you're going to need an inverter to convert the electricity stored in the batteries from direct current (DC) to alternating current (AC). Good inverters are (like everything else that's good) expensive, and the larger the inverter, the more it's going to cost.

Cutting back on your electrical needs is the easiest and most economical way to save money when setting up your home power system. By cutting back on your needs you can get by with a smaller inverter, fewer batteries, and fewer or smaller solar panels or wind generators, all of which saves you money.

Take an inventory of everything on your property that uses electricity. List all electrical appliances and tools, from the water heater, the

My wife, Susan, using our energy-saving handwringer to do laundry.

Tristan enjoying nonelectric entertainment

stereo, and television, to the bulb used in the porch light.

List the number of watts the item uses. (This will be found on the tool or appliance.) Some appliances use an amp rating instead of watts. Multiply the amps by the voltage to get the number of watts needed to run the appliance. For example: our vacuum cleaner uses 12 amps. Twelve amps X 120 volts = 1440 watts. The reason you'll need to know how many watts are required is because generators and inverters are rated in watts rather than amps.

Some things may have two listings. One is the number of watts needed to start the tool or appliance. The other is the number of watts needed to run it once you get it going. Be sure to figure in the *higher* number. Your power supply must be adequate for the highest figure.

Next, decide if this is an "essential" or "nonessential" item. This is entirely subjective. If mom can't do without her hair dryer or curling iron then list it as essential. The same goes for dad. If he can't imagine life without his table saw (or hair dryer?) then it too must be listed as essential.

Some things might be considered essential even if they are seldom used. We kept our waffle iron even though we use it only occasionally.

Estimate how often you use the appliance (daily, weekly, rarely, etc.). Is the appliance "home power friendly?" For example: some televisions, VCRs, DVD players, etc., draw power even when the unit's power switch is turned off in order to maintain memory, run clocks, or energize "instant-on" circuits. If you have appliances like these you'll want to be sure that (a) the batteries never go completely dead, or (b) you have an automatic back-up system such as a generator that will kick in if your batteries get low. Of course if you don't mind the clock flashing the wrong time or waiting a bit longer for the television to come on you can put in a separate switch to completely shut off the power to the unit and end the drain on your batteries. Those multiple outlet power strips work well for this.

Overall electrical draw may or may not be a red flag in this category. A microwave may draw a lot of power but only run for a few minutes, whereas a toaster oven with the same watt rating may be in use for 30 minutes or more. Obviously the toaster oven will use a lot more power in the long run.

Are there practical, non-electric alternatives to the appliance? For example: a refrigerator or freezer may not use much electricity per hour but it's on 24 hours per day, seven days a week. That's no big deal if you're on the grid, but when you're generating your own power it can be a problem. That doesn't mean you

Electrical Appliance Worksheet

(Note: multiply volts times amps to get the watts needed to run the tool or appliance.)

Electrical Appliance	Watts Start/Run	Need Rating	Frequency Used	Home Power Friendly?	Available Alternatives	Notes or Comments
Blender	300	Low	Seldom			
Circular Saw	1080	High	Monthly			Use Generator
Computer (Desk)	200	Low	Weekly			
Computer (Lap-Top)	60	High	Daily			
Drill	400	High	Seldom			
Microwave Oven	800	Medium	Weekly			Use Generator
Mixer	125	High	Weekly			
Radial Arm Saw	1560	High	Monthly			Use Generator
Television	100	Low	Weekly	No		
Toaster	1000	High	Bi-weekly			Use Oven or Stove Top
Toaster Oven	1500	Not Needed	Seldom			
Vacuum cleaner	1440	High	Weekly			Use Generator
Waffle Iron	700	Essential	Monthly			Use Generator

Example of electrical appliance worksheet

must go without a refrigerator. There are propane and kerosene powered models that work just as well. There are multiple alternatives to electric lights as well, such as propane, kerosene, or gasoline. There are also low-wattage fluorescent lights that work quite well.

An example from our household is the toaster. We like toast but due to the high electrical draw, the toaster didn't make the move with us. However, we still have toast. We just make it in the oven.

One thing to be aware of is that some gas appliances must have electricity to operate. We once owned a gas stove that had electrically powered oven controls. No electricity? No cake or cookies.

Step two: conserve energy

This should be a basic part of everyone's routine whether on or off the grid. I can guarantee that if you go to someone's off-grid home you will not see lights left on in unoccupied rooms nor will you see a television left on with no one watching it. People tend to be wasteful when there's a sense of plenty. Use only what you need. You don't need lots of overhead lighting if you're just lounging on the couch reading. Use a reading lamp.

Other ways to conserve include using energy-efficient appliances whenever possible. Laptop computers need far less power than desk models and a 15-watt fluorescent bulb puts out the same amount of light as a 60-watt incandescent bulb. Replace high-draw items with energy efficient models as the old stuff wears out.

When you live off-grid you gain a new appreciation for the electrical power you use. Conservation becomes a way of life.

Step three: be shrewd

Don't run the vacuum cleaner, iron, clothes washer, computer, etc., at the same time. This saves you money in several ways. **First**, your inverter must be able to handle the maximum load placed upon it. If you use the vacuum cleaner and the toaster and the microwave at the same time, you'll need a 3300-watt inverter. If you run them one at a time, you can get by with a 1500-watt inverter. Quality inverters are expensive and as the output of the inverter increases so does the price. By spreading out the demand you can use a smaller inverter. **Second**, spread the power usage out over the week.

Remember the water into the 50-gallon barrel vs. the water out of the barrel? Starting with an empty barrel, if the bottom spigot is closed, the barrel will fill completely in 10 minutes with five gallons per minute pouring in. Then if the spigot is opened all the way (letting out 10 gallons per minute) it will take 10 minutes to empty it—remember, you are also putting in five gallons per minute while the spigot is open. If you drain it at only 7½ gallons per minute, it will be 20 minutes before it runs dry. That's twice as much "run time" by reducing your draw by only 25 percent. Your home power system works the same way.

When you produce more electricity than you are using, the batteries store it. The batteries allow you to use that excess power during times your system is not charging or when you're using power at a faster rate than the system is replenishing itself. Anytime you draw power out faster than you put it in you're going to run your batteries down. By spreading out the work you'll get by with fewer batteries and a smaller generating system.

So, instead of doing the wash, vacuuming, and all the other housework in one day, spread it out. Do the wash on Tuesday and Thursday, and use the vacuum on Monday and Friday. Spend the other time reading, working in the garden, walking, or doing

Costs

Being somewhat financially challenged, we've had to put our home energy system together one piece at a time. We began with an extra automotive battery and a cheap, 350-watt inverter. The only cash outlay was $40.00 for the inverter. One lesson we've learned is that you get what you pay for in inverters. The better ones are a wise investment and should probably be your first major purchase.

Our current system consists of three deep cycle batteries, a used 850-watt Trace inverter, a fast charger, and a 4,000-watt generator.

There are cheaper generators available. Ours was chosen for some of its options like an electric starter, low idle capabilities when not under a load, a heavy duty engine, low oil shut-off, and a few other things. If you have a larger inverter and a way to charge your batteries, you may not need a generator or fast charger.

As a side note, in our area most people purchased a generator before they purchased solar panels. With our northern latitude (we live in northwestern Montana) daylight is in short supply during winter and solar power is not very productive. In addition, we sometimes have weeks of cloudy skies to contend with. Generators are the only reliable way to charge batteries.

3 batteries @ $60 each	$ 180
Used 850-watt inverter	$ 200
4,000-watt generator	$ 750
Fast charger	$ 140
Total	$1270

something that doesn't require electricity.

Step four: a generator for big draw items

A 5,000-watt generator is much cheaper to purchase than a 5,000-watt inverter. When we fire up the generator we can forget about rule number three. We may charge batteries and use the electric grain mill (much faster than the hand mill) to grind enough flour and corn to last a month or more. We might also use that opportunity to iron my uniforms, run the vacuum cleaner, and/or use any high draw power tools like my shop equipment.

The generator was the last item we purchased. The only thing we needed it for was the radial arm saw, the vacuum cleaner, and cement mixer. None of these were considered essential items.

Charging batteries and running generators

We will eventually have solar panels and/or a wind generator, but for now we charge our batteries in other ways.

When I go to work I take a 10-amp charger and charge batteries there. I can charge one while I'm on my shift then leave another one on the charger overnight. When I arrive the next day I take it off and put on the next one. We also have a fast charger that we use while the generator is running. It will bring a deep cycle battery to full power in about three hours. The generator has a 10-amp charger built in so when it's running we plug another battery into it. If we're going to be on the road for a couple of hours, we take the car battery out and put in one that needs to be charged and let the vehicle's alternator charge it while we're driving.

Under normal use our three deep-cycle batteries will go for two weeks or more before we run low on power.

If you're planning on running a generator all day long, think about this: a generator that will survive continuous duty is very expensive to purchase and run. If you thought your previous electric bills were pricey, wait until you purchase gasoline, diesel, or propane to run a generator 4,380 hours a year (12 hours per day for 365 days a year). We've known people who've tried it. Not only is it expensive but the noise will not be appreciated by neighbors who moved out in the woods seeking peace and quiet. In addition, if your goal was to conserve our natural resources, running a generator for hours at a stretch will definitely defeat that purpose.

Our system has served us well and can be updated and improved as time goes on. As the batteries wear out they'll be replaced with golf cart batteries. They cost more but are worth it in the long run. Our future plans include solar panels and/or a wind generator, but that will have to wait until next year. Fortunately, our need for electricity is so low that it won't take much to keep up with the demand.

If you have the resources to build a first class system, then more power to you. For us that wasn't an option. Rather than live totally without electricity we designed a system that would meet our needs at a price we could afford. Hopefully some of the things we've done will work for you as well. Δ

Add solar power to your truck camper

By Jeffrey R. Yago, P.E., CEM

The recreational vehicle (RV) world is having a major comeback with the influx of baby-boomers. Today's travel trailers, 5th wheels, and motor coaches now include everything from satellite television and central air conditioning to built-in electric fireplaces. However, these luxury land yachts have one major disadvantage over the RV world of earlier years—they require large amounts of electrical power to operate.

Most high-end RVs can power all of their lighting and a few DC-powered appliances without an external hookup, but their limited onboard battery capacity will quickly be depleted when powering larger loads like a gas furnace fan or color television. These large RVs require a generator to power their major appliance and air conditioning loads when not plugged in at an RV park.

Dry campers, or boondockers, do not move each day from one high-tech camp ground to the next. The motorized covered-wagon pioneers of today head for the backwoods or fishing hole in smaller, less energy intensive campers. Many convert old buses into RVs or build their own truck campers. Some of you may use an enclosed truck-bed cap to protect your camping gear, build a fire for cooking and keeping warm, and set up a tent for sleeping. If you fall into this low tech camping category, your power needs will not include central air conditioning or electric hot water heating. However, you still may want to at least power several 12-volt DC lights, a laptop computer, and a radio. Even these limited power requirements can still deplete a typical RV/marine battery after only a few days. This article describes how you can build your own solar powered charging system for your camping or fishing RV/marine battery, or add a solar charger to an existing truck camper battery system.

100 watt solar module mounted on roof of truck bed cap

System sizing

Unlike my previous solar articles, I am not going to describe how to calculate battery and solar array sizes. The battery of choice for most RVers is the 12-volt deep cycle RV/marine battery, and your truck camper will probably not have the space or weight capacity for more than one.

In addition, your smaller roof area will not be able to accommodate more than one or two solar modules in the 50 to 75-watt size range. Taking this design approach, there is no need to estimate how many days

Completed battery box with top mounted battery isolator and solar charge controller

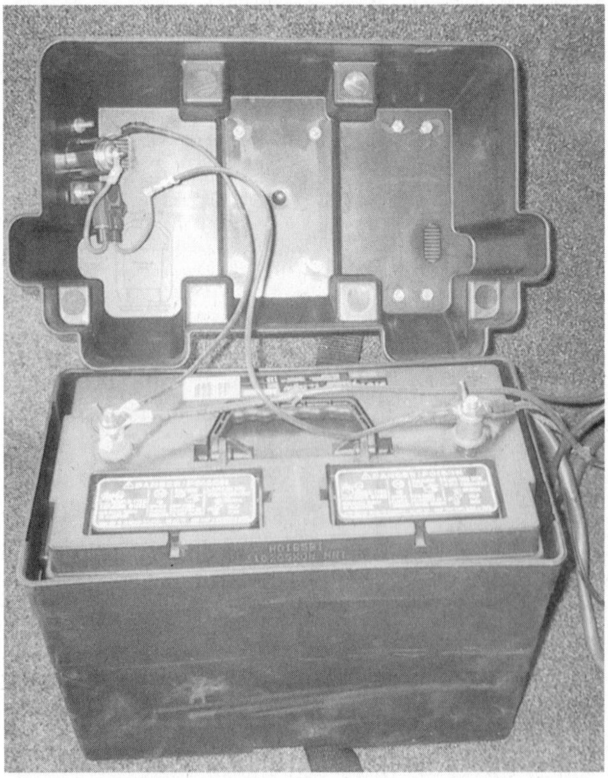

Battery and battery box. Note cigarette auxiliary power socket and in-line fuse mounted in lid.

your battery will operate during cloudy weather. If this fully discharged point is reached, you either go to bed early or fire up a generator.

Conventional dual battery charging systems

One of the first wiring issues to address is battery isolation. The RV/marine battery for your camper must be isolated from the starter battery in your truck, or you could have a very long walk after you discharge the truck starter battery from the camper.

Although we want the truck starter battery isolated from the loads being supplied from the camper's battery, we still may want both batteries charged by the same alternator. This can be easily accomplished using a battery isolator, available from most auto supply stores.

Different models are available for different truck and alternator types, but they all work the same way. They function like a check valve in a plumbing system, allowing charging current to flow out to each battery from the charging source but block a very high reverse current flow from the fully charged battery back into a fully discharged battery. The positive (+) output from the truck's alternator feeds the battery isolator, which then has a separate positive (+) connection for the truck battery, and one for the RV/marine battery.

The negative (-) leads from both batteries and the alternator are usually connected together. If your present RV battery is wired to the truck battery charging system using a battery isolator, you need to decide if you want the planned solar charger to charge both the truck battery and RV/marine battery, or just the RV/marine battery.

We want to make sure we do not alter the existing dual-battery alternator charging system, and we also need to make sure the new solar wiring does not provide a path for large discharge current flows from one battery into the other. A second battery isolator can be added to divide the solar charging current between both batteries, while still keeping the batteries isolated from each other.

Many solar charge controllers need to "see" the battery voltage in order to constantly adjust the rate of solar charging. Unfortunately, many conventional battery isolators can block the reverse battery voltage sensing of a solar charge controller, resulting in

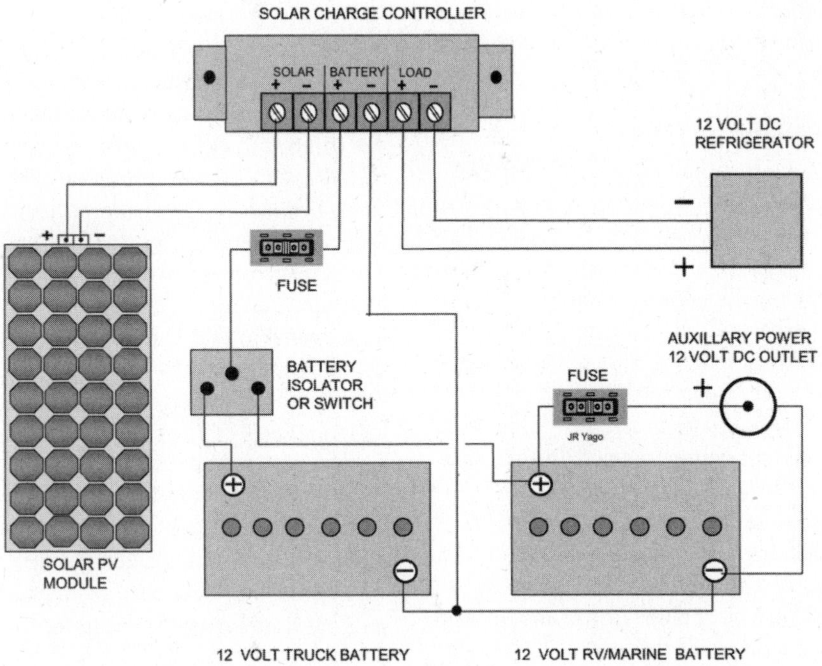

Wiring diagram #1

no solar charging taking place. The solar charge controller thinks the battery was disconnected and stops charging. If this is your situation, you either need to divert the output of the solar charge controller manually between the two separate batteries using a DC-rated three-position switch (battery 1/off/battery 2), or install two separate solar charge controllers connected to the same roof-mounted solar module.

Materials & construction

Since I wanted to keep this simple, I designed everything around off-the-shelf components. The bed cap of my truck was too small for two or more smaller solar modules, so I mounted a single Siemens 100-watt 12-volt DC module using aluminum brackets. I selected a high capacity 12-volt sealed RV/marine battery that can be found in most discount warehouse stores for under $75. These batteries will take repeated slow discharge/recharge cycling, yet are still fairly inexpensive. If you need more battery capacity, consider using two 6-volt golf cart batteries wired in series.

Unlike a conventional alternator that is only charging when the vehicle motor is running, a solar charging system is able to provide many hours of charging current every summer afternoon that it is not overcast. Unless you have a very high quality solar charge controller and perfect charge voltage setpoints, it is very easy to overcharge these batteries with a solar charger and eventually boil them dry.

It is also possible that hydrogen gas will be generated during extended charging which is explosive in high concentrations. For this reason I like to place my batteries in a rugged liquid-proof battery box with vented lid. You will need to check the water level in your battery much more often than you normally do, as even "Maintenance Free" liquid electrolyte batteries with sealed gas recombiner caps will lose water during extended charging.

I found the perfect battery box at a local marine supply store for under $20. Since these are available in several sizes, be sure to measure your battery before purchasing. I also purchased two in-line 20-amp automotive type fuses and fuse holders, and a cigarette lighter auxiliary powered socket designed for bulkhead mounting. I mounted the auxiliary power socket on the side of the lid of the battery box, which makes it easy to plug in 12-volt DC radios, portable

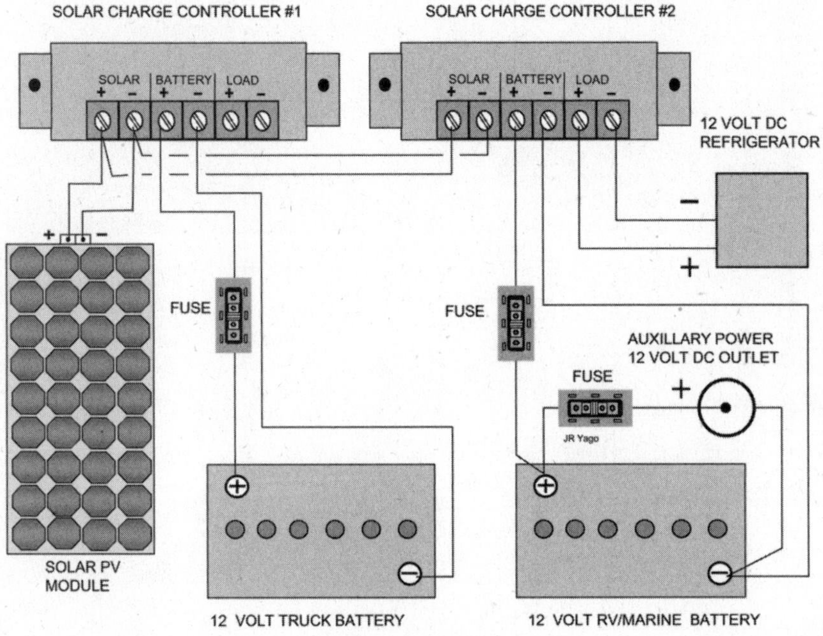

Wiring diagram #2

televisions, or laptop computer power adapters.

I purchased a 12-volt Morningstar 10-amp charge controller with built-in load control, which I mounted on the top of the battery box lid. I really like this controller, as it is very rugged and includes a temperature sensor that adjusts battery charging voltage based on ambient air temperature. I connected the "load" control terminals to my small portable 12-volt DC refrigerator.

Unlike the temporary electrical loads powered from the auxiliary socket, a refrigerator operating for extended hours can easily discharge a battery this size in less than 24 hours. The load control terminals on the charge controller will shut off power to the refrigerator if the battery voltage drops below safe limits. It will then reconnect the refrigerator after the battery is recharged.

Wiring layout

I have included two different solar battery charger wiring diagrams that you can use, depending on which battery isolation method you need. Wiring Diagram #1 shows how to charge your RV/marine battery and the truck battery using a battery isolator or a manual switch.

Wiring diagram #2 shows the same solar charging system with two separate solar charge controllers to provide the battery isolation. This keeps each battery isolated from each other. If you intend to charge only the RV/marine battery, omit the second solar charge controller.

Summary

Make sure your battery box lid is strapped down, and the battery box is properly anchored to avoid acid damage to your truck. I located my completed assembly near the front of the truck bed where it will be protected from the elements by the bed cap. There are many low cost 12-volt adapters and pocket-size inverters now available that can power almost anything that runs from a 12-volt DC battery power outlet. Although you may not need to power a wide screen television, it is still nice to take along some small 12-volt DC appliances and lights that you can operate at night without running a generator.

Keep on the look out, as we may pass each other on the camping trail one day. Δ

Solar window panels

By David Lee

New England is a SAD area. Perhaps where you are is too. SAD means *Seasonal Affective Dis-order,* a fancy way to say winter is depressing. The theory is that in winter you get so much less sunlight that it causes you to become morose and unhappy. I saw a doctor talk about this on TV so it must be true.

Happiness will return, according to the doctor, if you go to Florida or sit in front of a special light panel that radiates full spectrum light into your eyes for half an hour a day, preferably in the morning while you drink your first cup of coffee. For only $150, much less than a plane ticket to Florida, you can buy one of these special light panels and be on your way to grinning in January.

Or...you can apply a little science and some artistic carpentry to solve the problem if you have it. And while we are at it, let's take care of a couple of other jobs too. This project may be the most fun you have all winter. First, some background.

Years ago, when we bought this lot to build our home, one of its positive features was the south-facing orientation of the house site. I made the most of it. The south wall of the house is 66 feet long and contains 15 big windows, each 36 by 75 inches. And, oh my goodness, do we get solar—especially during the winter when the angle of the sun is low. It is warm and wonderful and saves us loads of money in the heating budget. That is the good part.

A window panel showing variations in decoration with tea cups, several colors of "nuggets," butter dish cover, colored glass containers, serving dish, broken platter, and Aunt Jemima bottles. The dark part of the picture is pine lumber.

The less than good parts began to show during the first winter. To get the most solar gain we had to let the sun shine right into the house. That meant the curtains were open all day, which is not so bad because it is pretty outside. However, the road parallels our south wall and is only about 100 feet away. Our house happens to be unusual and people like to stop on the road to gaze at it and often take pictures. Or maybe they confuse it with a drive-in theatre screen. Anyway, there are times when I walk around in the house wearing just my dainties and would prefer not to have people who may be harshly critical of my attire looking in on me, or my wife. But with the shades drawn we get SAD. We considered moving the road but the town disagreed.

Another nuisance was the need to pull the shades and close the curtains on 15 windows just as the sun went down each day and uncovering them each morning. I had to think of something clever.

One day while looking through a picture book of churches and cathedrals, I came upon a photograph of one of those stained glass window walls so popular in that kind of architecture. Right then the revelation came to me that I had such a wall waiting to happen.

Part of the revelation was something I recalled from my high school science classes about light. Light is made up of various energy waves recognized as colors by

View of upper section of a solar window panel showing "nuggets," small knick-knacks, glass tiles, and pieces of broken glass glued to clear glass pane. Note the cutouts in upper right and left corners. These are screened and allow sun-warmed air between panel and the permanent window to flow into the room.

the human eye. These visible colors, and some invisible ones, coming at you all at once are the full Monty of light. Or if you are going to be scientific about it, the full spectrum, that wonder cure for SAD.

When I look at a stained glass window I feel pretty cheery. It occurred to me that all those colors, in an artistic setting and lit up by sunlight, might cure SAD just as well as sitting in front of an expensive lamp. It would be way better than staring into the sun and accomplished for less money than frequent trips to Florida. I decided to build a few for our south wall.

Colored glass is one of my weaknesses. I collect it. I even spend money on it sometimes. All the neighbors save their fancy colored wine bottles for me. I get first dibs on any chic glassware that gets broken. I buy stained glass "nuggets" from the manufacturers by the pound. The point is, since I maintain a large supply of colored glass, I already had the makings for a window wall that would cure the SAD affliction.

For my first sample effort I decided to use wood as the matrix for holding the stained glass. I am suspicious of lead, the usual stuff used in stained glass art. I chose a small window and made a basic board panel with drilled holes to accommodate colored glass nuggets glued in place with clear silicone glue. This made me so blissful when the sun beamed through it that I started getting more ideas.

I brainstormed the project and came up with eight things I expected these panels to accomplish.

First was the SAD cure. I decided to use as much stained glass of every color in the spectrum as I could. Mostly I use stained glass nuggets because they come in pure colors and when the bright light shines through them they make beautiful splashes of color on the floors, walls, and furniture that slowly move around the room as the sun crosses the sky. This alone is enough to cheer up most people better than a martini.

Prisms are the most effective cheerer-uppers because they truly radiate the full spectrum of light. But they are expensive and I am way too cheap to buy very many. There are alternatives. I collect colored bottles, smash them into pieces that I glue to clear glass panes built into the window panels. I'll tell you more about this process in a few minutes.

One of the best sources for pretty glass for these projects is the kitchen…or a flea market. Cake platters, goblets, etched glass vases, butter dishes. Any sparkly glass things are usable in these window panels, even if it is broken into pieces. In my household I am only allowed to use them if they are already broken. Women are very sentimental about their special things. Sometimes, though not with my wife, it is possible to obtain these pretty glass knickknacks, unfractured, by explaining how other people could share the enjoyment of them if displayed in a window.

Did you know that the reason gemstones are so popular and expensive

Closeup of broken glass glued to plain pane of glass using clear silicone glue. This is the side of the panel facing the sun. The angles and position of the pieces refract light; the glass aids solar gain.

is because, in historic times, they were thought to heal certain ailments? They supposedly have other powers too. Just think of the power a diamond has to make a woman rich and a man poor. Each Zodiac sign has its special power gem. Maybe it is all superstition, maybe not, but imagine basking in the health-giving glow of the gemstone that suits your needs throughout each sunny day. It's got to do some good. Maybe those ancient people knew about SAD all along.

If you decide to build some of these window panels pay close attention to the colors and type of glass you use. This is the artistic, cabin fever curing, aspect of the project and quite important.

The second thing I wanted these panels to do was to give us back our privacy. Sixty to eighty percent of each panel is composed of wood and the rest is mostly translucent glass. That preserves our modesty very well, night and day, in a most intriguing way.

Third was the replacement of shades and curtains. Shades and curtains can be used with these window panels and would be useful for extra insulation on cold winter nights but we found them to be unnecessary. We do not use solar panels in all of our big windows so we still have shades and curtains on those.

The fourth requirement of these panels was to allow us to see outside. I made this happen by putting clear glass panes in the panels at just the right locations for looking out. They are not too big, about six by six inches, more or less. In the living room there are clear lookouts at eye level when standing. In the bathroom, where we have three solar window panels, I put little porthole-sized windows where I can look outside while sitting on the throne. It's very nice. The areas of the panels where I used broken or knick-knack glass does not totally block the view so we really don't miss the panoramic effect of all those big windows.

Looking into the house from outside is not as easy as you might think. Our windows are elevated somewhat and the embellishments on and in the window panel camouflages the inside of the house day and night. Looking out is easy because you can walk right up to the panel, look out through the clear places and some of the decorated places and see everything. I have gotten some good wildlife pictures because of this situation.

Our cat, Honey, sits next to a solar window panel. You are seeing it from the side that will be facing the sun. Clear panes of glass are glued (with black silicone) over cutouts and randomly drilled holes with colored glass 'nuggets' glued in. The structure of the panel is made of stained pine boards with side walls (that determine how deep the panel will set into window case) and trim pieces holding large glass panel in position.

The fifth and sixth requirements work together. I wanted these panels to be easy to clean. I also wanted them to be easy to remove and replace. Mine are held in place with simple turn locks attached to the window frame. This way I can remove the whole panel, take it outside and either hose it off, vacuum it, or use compressed air to dust it. This also allows easy access to the permanent window for washing.

If you only want to use these panels part of the year, easy removal is important. They can be stored in a shed or even outdoors for some attractive weathering. You could move them from window to window, if the sizes are the same, as are our 15 big windows. This keeps monotony, though cheery monotony, to a minimum.

This brings me to objective number seven, the most important one. I wanted these panels to be effective solar collectors. And they really are. Each panel starts out as an uninterrupted wood surface that fills the window case from side to side, top to bottom and an inch or more away from the permanent window glass. Into this surface you drill or cut holes that will be filled or covered with glass so you still have a continuous surface.

What makes this panel a solar collector relies on two things. First, cut one or two small holes about three inches in diameter, or square, or odd shaped near the bottom of the panel and one or two more, same size, near the top of the panel. Cover the holes with insect screen on the side facing the sun.

Second, stain the wood that faces the sun a dark color. I use Minwax Early American or Ebony stain. These colors make the wood warm up in the sun. The heat generated makes hot air rise between the permanent window and the panel. The bottom holes pull in cooler air from the house and warmed air flows out of the top holes. It is elegant in its simplicity.

The panels I have made are not tightly fitted into the casings. A little looseness lets some air escape around the edges but it does not matter much. The heat pours out into the room just fine. Building them with loose tolerances makes the job easier, too.

A nice bonus during the first year of using these panels is the pleasant aroma of the sap in the wood evaporating into the air of the room. I guess we could call these Aromatic Stained Glass Passive Solar-Collecting Therapy Panels, because they are. And I like pompous descriptive titles.

The eighth intention I had was for these panels to be display cases for various things. Besides the colored glass I mentioned earlier, they are a good way to show off some of those trinkets we all have in a drawer somewhere. I build little shelves onto the front of the panels so small objects such as flowerpots and incense burners can be set on them or held there with a little dab of silicone. Hooks made of wood or fancy metal hold towels, clothes, or plants.

Shelves on the other side of the panel, behind a clear glass pane, are good places to display more fragile or valuable objects, ones you want seen but not touched. My old Aunt Jemima glass bottles are preserved there until they become collectables. Anything on the sun side of the panel contributes to the solar gain. Special bottles filled with sand or pretty gravel increases collected warmth. Your Avon bottle collection would display very well in one of these panels. Fishing lures, salt and pepper shakers, Hot Wheels, coins, old jewelry, and much more can be incorporated into the structure of these window panels.

Don't hesitate to adapt these panels to your own needs and the type and size windows you have. While they are most efficient on the south side of the house, the east and west side could work, too. Northern exposure gives enough light to make these window panels effective for illumination, and they could act as interior shutters for extra insulation in winter. They could be built sturdy enough to also be security panels.

Building these panels is quite easy compared to some carpentry work. You will be building a five-sided box. The height and width of your box is the same as the window opening minus ¼ inch, ⅛ inch if you are a finish carpenter, .010" if you are a machinist. Just kidding—¼ inch is fine.

The sides of your box determine how far your panel sets into the window case. You need some space between the permanent window and the solar panel. From one to four inches is about right. Remember, you need room for displaying your goodies and a passage for the warm rising air.

The panel can be set flush with the surrounding frame of the window, indented or projecting out into the room a little. It is your decision. Make the sidewall dimensions of your panel accordingly.

Consider how to secure the solar panel to the window case. I use simple turn locks made of wood screwed to the window case to clamp them in place. Hook and eyes are another method. Carefully placed wedges may work for you. Whatever you use, make sure it is adequate to the task. My 36 by 75-inch solar panels weigh about 40 pounds with all the fru fru on them, so I make sure they are well secured.

My panels are made of #4 pine boards. The knots look good in this setting and there is extra pitch in them for that nice aroma I mentioned earlier. Now and then a knot will shrink and fall out. It is very charming. Pine is easy to drill and cut, takes stain beautifully and is reasonably priced. If you get the urge to use other species of wood or plywood, go ahead. I never got that adventurous. If I had some mahogany lying around I would be tempted to try it. I did make a panel of tempered glass with no wood once that worked out well. Assemble your "box" with nails or screws, no glue. You may want to resize or rearrange your panels someday, so making them easy to disassemble is helpful.

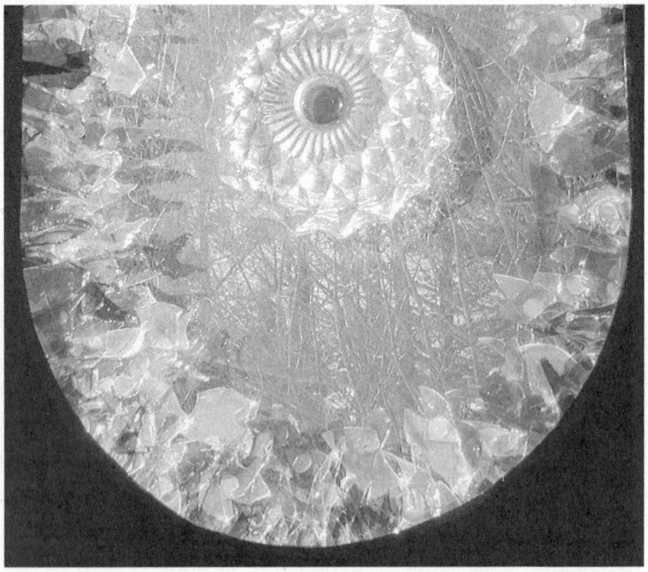

Looking through clear pane at broken glass pieces glued to clear pane and onto each other, creating a three-dimensional light catcher. Note old-fashioned heavy glass ash tray centerpiece with blue glass "nugget" in the middle.

Now comes the fun part. Gather your stained glass, clear glass, and gewgaws and buy a tube of clear and/or black silicone glue. Lay out the design that uses your supplies best and cut out the holes you need with a power drill and a hand held saber saw. Trace around any odd shaped pieces you are using and cut carefully so they fit as closely as you are skillful enough to achieve. If the fit is a little loose the silicone will fill the space. Don't forget the inlet and outlet holes for the warm air.

Where you want clear glass, cut a hole an inch or so smaller in width and height than your clear pane and glue it on the back (sun side) of the panel with silicone. Add shelves where you want them, in front or on the back of the panel. I recommend screws to attach shelves. They hold longer and better than nails.

As you build your masterpiece use a utility knife or whittling knife to cut away the square edges of drilled and cut holes. This gives the panel a distinctive rustic touch. I add an antiqued look to my panels by using a knife and I dent the wood by whacking it with various instruments including a hatchet, a ball peen hammer, a screwdriver, and a curved chisel. You can carve in your initials. Perhaps get out that wood-scorching tool you got as a kid but never used and play with it at last. I even found a use for the Dremel tool I've had for years.

Here are a couple of important things to remember. Do all the denting, cutting, drilling, dinging, scorching and carving you want before staining the wood. Do not glue in the glass and fru fru until the panel has been stained and the stain is thoroughly dry. Otherwise the silicone won't hold. I use a small paintbrush and make sure the stain liberally penetrates all the nooks and crannies of the wood. I let it set about half an hour before wiping the wood with a rag. Then I give it 24 hours to dry completely. Minwax is my stain of choice and, remember, dark colors warm up best in the sun. Wear gloves for this job if you like the color your hands are now.

Gluing the glass in place is the next step. Silicone glue works best for this job. Have a rag handy and be sure your work surface is clean. Silicone is slippery. Attach the large clear glass panes onto the back of the panel with a bead of glue. Staple screening over the back of the air inlets and outlets.

While the panel is on your workbench, with the sun-facing side up, use clear silicone to attach colored glass, and whatever amusing bric-a-brac you like, to the clear panes of glass. Look at the pictures included here for suggestions. Broken glass is a bit dangerous so, if you dislike the sight of blood, work carefully. Do not attach any broken glass or sharp things to the side of the panel that faces into the room. That would be negligent.

If you acquire some of those stained glass nuggets I keep mentioning, there is a special way to put them in. They come in stock sizes of ½, ¾, 1, 1¼ and 1½ inch. I drill holes in the wood the same size as the nugget then press them into place. Clear or black silicone applied with a toothpick around the nugget holds it in place. The sun shining through these beauties is really nice.

Take your time, let the silicone dry between work sessions and you are ready to be cheered up every sunny day to cure that cabin fever. As with any project, try a small one first to become familiar with the process and develop your skills. If you start coveting the pretty glass things in your neighbors' and in-law's cabinets then you know this project is for you.

View of the solar window panel from outside

In the sunlight these panels absorb the sun's rays and convert them into a surprising amount of heat. You will notice a nice warm breeze flowing out the top exit holes minutes after the sun hits the panels. Ordinary windows left uncovered at night, especially clear-sky nights, cool a room as effectively as they warm it during the day. These panels cool a room too but do it so inefficiently that we have not found it necessary to cover the air holes at night. I considered making little doors for the air holes but I rarely do everything I think up.

Creating these panels was one of the most enjoyable home building projects I have ever done. When I see one of those glassed-in rooms attached to some homes, often called Florida rooms, I have visions of turning it into a small stained glass cathedral. Maybe you will too. In the meantime, try one of these solar panels and see if you feel less SAD. Δ

Starting over again: Part 4

Preparing for winter, putting in a well, David's first deer, jerky, roofing the barn, plowing the trail

By Jackie Clay

Late autumn was upon us here on our new homestead in the remote northern Minnesota backwoods. And we were busily readying for the long, cold typical Minnesota winter. After all, winter is *one* reason that there is still much wilderness up here. (If it weren't for the lengthy, snowy, bitter winter and the bugs in the summer, all of our 10,000 lakes would be built up, elbow to elbow, and the woods nearly so.)

With a bare-bones homestead, there was much to do and money was tight. We worked long into the evening one day, hearing of a snow storm headed our way. All day we had picked up stray tools, fencing, building material, buckets, and anything else that the snow might bury. Often, when the first heavy snow comes, it does not melt away, but is with you until breakup in April. A tipped-over shovel or anything left unprotected simply disappears until spring.

Then there were the animals to weatherize. The partially built goat barn was nearly done, but we threw two sheets of plywood on that part of the roof that was unfinished and screwed them down for protection. Then David ran to the house for two green plastic tarps and the staple gun. By cutting one of them in half, we stretched plastic over each gable end to keep out the snow and wind and hung another down over the door. Animals can stand very cold temperatures if there are no icy drafts blowing down on them. The metal roofing would have to go on, as far as it would go, if this snow did not stay long or the storm did not come.

Working by flashlight, we stuffed straw into the unfinished openings between the rafters. And as we walked back to the house, the first snowflakes began to blow through the cold night air.

David takes the old Jeep out plowing.

We live our lives according to the weather radio, listening to it the first thing in the morning and the last thing at night. This was a habit we had developed when we lived seven miles off a road, a thousand feet higher than the continental divide, back in the Elkhorn Mountains of Montana. Being snowed in from the first of December to mid-May, our travel plans hinged heavily on the weather. The only way down the mountain during the winter was via snowmobile. And with David only a little guy, I stayed home when Bob went down to gather our mail, gas, and supplies. I can't tell you how many mornings he had planned to snowmobile down to "civilization" on a bright, sunny day when the weather radio strongly advised otherwise.

Storms can come up in less time than it takes to think about them and one needs to be prepared for what they will bring. In Montana, we simply hunkered down, brought in more wood, tightened up the livestock, and I baked bread and cookies while Bob read. And, likewise, here in Minnesota, we live our lives around the same little $12 weather radio. We feel it is foolish to disregard what *Mother Nature* is about to hurl at you.

So we continue to listen, watch the skies, and prepare. Even the wildlife prepares for storms. We have noticed that when the deer get up midday and forage hard or when our bird feeders are suddenly swarming with more customers than usual, we can expect a change for the worse in the weather. Sort of like when you look up and see a huge ring around the moon—a sure sign of changing weather with moisture.

The next morning, I opened one eye at a time, expecting solid white outside. What a surprise to learn that the storm had swung south of us at the last minute. But it was a good wake-up call to us, knowing that winter was pretty darned close upon us.

Putting in the well

So we continued to prepare. Mom and Dad wanted to contribute to our homestead, as they were now members of our backwoods family. Dad bought an old Jeep pickup truck with a rough but useable snowplow on the front and had me call a well driller. While we worked on the Jeep, getting it ready to plow the drive this winter, I hoped KO Well Drilling from Cook would get their big well rig out before the snow was too deep. We plan on hand-drilling a well off the hill down by our garden. But after talking to several knowledgeable people, we bit the bullet and called a well driller for our house well. It seems that there is a lot of granite ledge rock in the area and many wells, especially those on high ground like our home site, run right through hundreds of feet of solid rock.

Well drillers charge by the foot. In our area the going rate is $22 per foot with another $15 a foot for steel casing. Whew! But Mom and Dad were adamant. We were going to have a well.

We hadn't heard much from the company, but one bright, cold morning they called and said their truck was on the way out. I'll admit I was a little (no, make that a *lot*) scared. In Montana, we had a well driller come out and he went down 385 feet and hit only a trickle of water, basically a dry hole that took hours to fill part full with water. And we had sunk over $5,000 into that hole.

The huge red drilling truck backed into our well site that we had chosen for ease of drilling and because it was about halfway between our temporary mobile home and our new homesite. This site would enable us to run water to both homes, as well as to the goat barn, where we will put a frost-free hydrant.

They set up and began to drill. Each length of drill was 20 feet, and I stood and watched while the pile of drill pipe stacked on the side of their truck shrunk all too quickly. By noon, they had run down through 87 feet of gravel. But right after lunch, they ran into the dreaded ledge rock. (Dreaded by *me*, at any rate.) Shades of the hole we had drilled in Montana.

David finds a good fresh buck rub: white scar, sap still wet, and shreds of bark.

Well, the guys drilled and drilled, having to quit at four o'clock, down 260 feet and still nothing. The day was clear, but bitter cold. They would be back the next day.

And so they were. Well, they drilled and drilled, ending up at 325 feet. Luckily, there had been cracks in the ledge rock, and trickles of water slowly filled the well. It wasn't a super strong well, but it would more than meet our needs.

A week or so later, we had a submersible pump dropped down the well, and we were in business, netting five gallons a minute for many hours' pumping. We felt fortunate to have good water, too, as much of the well water in our area is orange with iron and minerals. (We are north of the Minnesota Iron Range, where much iron is mined.) To prevent our well pipe from freezing during the bitter cold, we drilled two eighth-inch weep holes in the plastic pipe, down 10 feet. These drain the water out of the pipe, down to below frost level, after the pump is shut off. So it is a freeze-proof well.

We had lucked out. It was still relatively snow-free. But deer hunting season was upon us. And we still had to put the sheet metal on the goat barn roof.

David's first deer

David was excited. Although he had been taught from an early age to shoot both a bow and arrow and rifle, by both Bob and me, he had to take rifle safety classes to get his first hunting license. He did that during the previous summer and received his certificate. And because he runs the woods nearly every day, he knew where the deer came and went and what they did all day. He came home one day, just before opener with the news that he'd found some good buck rubs down by our creek, quite close to his deer stand. Buck rubs are a very good indicator of deer activity, not only of bucks, but also does in the area, for if there aren't does during rutting season, there certainly won't be bucks. Those rubs are cleanly skinned smaller trees and brush, usually down about knee level. Often the ground in the area is also stamped and trashed as he goes about his ritual "fighting" poses. "Take that! And that! And if that isn't enough, I'll really rough you up!"

All summer David and his cousin, Sean, had improved the huge, old deer stand, using it for a hang out, but now the stand was going to get serious.

The first two days of deer season, David spent the entire day out in the woods. He saw many deer, but the only buck he saw provided him with only a fleeting glance, and he'd been taught for years not to shoot when there was no clear shot and not to shoot a running animal. There are too many deer to hunt to risk a poor, wounding shot.

David went out before daylight, using a flashlight to find his way. At first he hunted the woods over on state land and Potlatch timber land, keeping away from his stand. Then he decided to go to his stand about an hour before sunset. Being the anxious mom, I worked about the house, listening. Wondering. He was using my old Winchester Model 94 .30.30. It's a good gun for the woods, light and easy to carry, and dead accurate.

I was washing the dishes, watching the shadows lengthen. Wham! I heard my rifle bark. Just once. We'd taught David to wait 10 minutes after shooting a deer before going after it. (A deer that will lie down and die after being shot, might, on pure adrenaline, still run at the sight of a human. Running just a few hundred yards can make it impossible to find.) So I bundled up in my blaze orange, grabbed a flashlight and kept an ear out for another shot. Nothing.

I also waited 10 minutes, then started walking down towards the deep woods where his stand is located. On the way down, I whistled once and he yelled back. The whistle doesn't scare game, and if he'd needed to he would have whistled back. He had either clean missed or had a deer laid out.

David and his first deer. A proud moment for us all.

One look at his smiling face as he walked to meet me told the whole story. The 14-year-old had his first deer. And it was a very fat, nice forkhorn buck, too. This is our favorite age and sex to hunt. The meat is wonderfully tender and flavorful. He is also easily spared in the breeding needs of the local herd.

And I was proud of David. He'd fired one shot at about 150 yards, neatly dropping the buck with a heart shot, right in the trail. There was a lot of meat lying there ready to haul home.

By flashlight, we dressed the buck, propping his front end up on the snow so gravity would help us. Using Bob's nifty skinning knife with its razor sharp four-inch blade, I held the skin up and carefully inserted the tip into the lower abdomen, next to the scrotum. Once into the abdomen, I kept the sharp edge of the knife towards myself, guiding the blade with my fingers inside, slitting the belly from scrotum to brisket. Then with my sharp hatchet, I chopped the pelvis bone carefully between his hind legs, while David held his hind feet apart to ease the operation.

Once that was cut through, I carefully reached up into the body cavity and opened the diaphragm and reached as high up into his lower neck as I could. Very carefully, I severed the windpipe. Then I handed David my knife and began pulling the insides down and out. With gravity working for us, it did not take much touch-up work here and there with the knife before the gut pile slid out onto the snow covered ground.

We wiped out the cavity with piles of snow and loaded the buck on the sled, heading for home. There, we also rinsed out the body cavity very well with cold water, propped the cavity apart with a willow stick, and hung him on the side of our stock trailer. It is very important to clean out the body cavity, both of blood and debris, and to cool the carcass quickly. (In our yard, there are no trees large enough to hang a deer and the bears were not yet hibernating, so the stock trailer was used.)

The next day I skinned the deer and began canning the meat. I cut one hind quarter off the carcass with a sharp knife and a few strategic whacks with my little hand ax. Luckily, the meat was partially frozen, just perfect for cutting. When it is warmer, the meat does not cut nearly as well, being "sloppy" to handle.

David wanted me to make the whole deer into jerky, but I talked him into letting me can up a bunch of stew meat, as well. Yes, he does love jerky. I sliced the meat into boneless steaks, carefully trimming away any membrane, fat, and gristle. I'll admit I'm a fanatic about meat; it must be clean and nice. Every jarful.

Then, as I use stew meat in so many recipes, I diced the steaks into pieces about three quarters of an inch square. I used to put up my meat raw, to save time precooking it. But I've found out that it tastes and looks better when precooked. It is also more tender. So I got out my largest cast-iron frying pan and, using the least amount of vegetable oil possible, I stir-fried the meat until it was nicely browned. Then, adding water to cover it, I mixed in two tablespoonsful of powdered beef stock. I like this broth over venison. Even people who "hate" venison gobble down my "beef" stroganoff and other dishes.

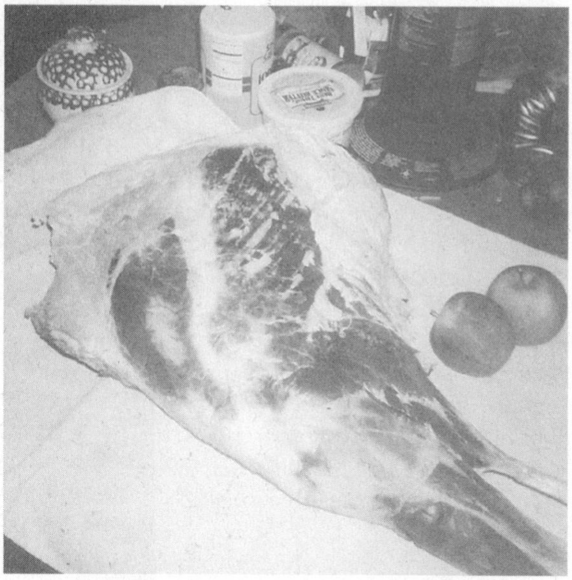

A venison haunch ready to cut up and can

Once the meat is mixed well with its broth, I dip out the meat, filling the jars to within half an inch of the top. Then I dip up enough broth to fill the jars to the same level, covering the meat. Then, after wiping the jar rim clean, I place a hot, previously boiled lid on the jar and screw down the ring firmly tight. The jars are processed, at 10 pounds pressure for 90 minutes, in my huge pressure canner. I have to laugh, because I've canned at 10 pounds pressure, at altitudes below 2,000 feet, all the way up to 14 pounds pressure way up in our Montana mountains. Now, I have to think a minute before processing.

Trimming the steaks takes time, but results in very fine canned meat.

I used to can most of my meat in quart and pint jars. But now I've learned to can very little in quarts and much more in half pint or smaller jars, as I use less meat in mixed dishes, using the meat more as a flavoring rather than the main ingredient. It's healthier and the meat goes a lot farther. You scarcely notice there's less meat, either.

Then I sliced up a backstrap to use in David's favorite jerky recipe. Most recipes say to use "cheaper" cuts for jerky, but that results in tough, stringy jerky. We like the backstrap or tenderloin better and the jerky is very tender. I slice the meat across the grain, making it more tender, yet. While some of my jerky is in the "traditional" strips, more is in little discs from the tenderloin or small end of the backstrap sliced straight across. This makes jerky rounds or chips. They are very good eating.

I slice up the meat and place it into a glass bowl. Then I add about half a cup of brown sugar, one teaspoon of garlic powder, half a cup of soy sauce, one tablespoon of onion powder, half a teaspoon of coarse black pepper, a tiny bit of roasted chili paste, and a few drops of liquid smoke. Mix the meat well with this, cover and store in the fridge overnight, then lay the pieces on a dehydrator tray and dry at about 140 degrees, until nearly dry. Turn and continue until they are stiff and leather-like. Or do as I do and hang

BOB CLAY 1946-2005

We are very much broken hearted to tell you that my husband of sixteen years and best friend, as well as David's father and best bud, died suddenly of a brain hemorrhage. The night before, Bob and David had gone to David's karate practice, the Cook High School basketball game, and come home feeling happy and well. I woke up at 2 a.m. with Bob having a seizure. He was taken by ambulance to the Cook Hospital, then airlifted to Duluth via helicopter.

Surgery was done to try to relieve the pressure in his brain, but it did no good. By 2 a.m. on the 16th of February, only 24 hours from the onset, Bob died.

He was a *Purple Heart* Vietnam veteran who suffered from the effects of Agent Orange and post-traumatic stress disorder. But to us, and those who knew him, he was a quiet, special man with a wonderful sense of humor and caring ways. We may never know how many lives he touched, but after his death we received so many cards and notes, often from people I did not know, telling how Bob had always had time to talk to them and what a great guy he was. I was surprised, as we have only been in the area for a year and didn't know that so many people even knew who we were.

During our life together, Bob always went ahead of me, breaking trail. I kidded him about it because he was part Cherokee and said the warrior always went first to scout the dangers to protect the woman. (He knew I could handle trouble as well as he could.) But he still went on ahead, stomping a trail in the snow while I padded on behind watching for tracks and nature signs.

Bob was always going ahead of me and breaking trail for me, as he is in this photo when we went out and checked some wolf tracks. He still does.

It recently occurred to me that he is still going on ahead, breaking a new trail for me to follow someday.

It was Bob's wishes that he be cremated and his ashes spread on a special place down by our creek, where we feed the birds and other wildlife. David and I will be planting a small memorial garden down there for him when the weather warms.

And yes, we will remain on the homestead and continue with the dream Bob and I had from the start. With luck, we'll get that log home dried in this summer and plant a better garden. But it would have been better with Bob there to enjoy it. We will miss him terribly.

Bob always had time for David. They were best buds.

them on a cake rack in your gas oven, using only the pilot light, and dry until done. You must place a cookie sheet under the jerky to catch the drips or you'll make a mess of your oven.

You can store the finished jerky in a canning jar, in the fridge, or in the freezer. Old-time jerky was dried much more than you'll enjoy—nearly like sticks of wood. When there is a bit of moisture left in, the way most folks like jerky today, the jerky will not last too long at room temperature and will begin to mold.

David had a quart of his new jerky gone in a week's time, but I figured he'd deserved it, bringing home the bacon, so to speak.

Roofing the barn

In between canning the deer, we hit a period of nice warm, sunny weather and got busy screwing down the sheets of green metal roofing we had stacked out next to the goat barn. As it is simply not safe walking on barn roofs that are icy and snow covered, we'd waited until the roof was clean and dry to get at it, feverishly hoping that would happen yet, before winter set in.

David got on the roof with a 12-volt power screwdriver snapped to his belt and Bob and I carefully handed up one eight-foot sheet of roofing at a time. (You *don't* want to do this with *any* wind blowing, as they want to take you sailing.) With an eighth-inch drill bit in another power driver, David quickly positioned the first piece and, while we held it from ladders below, he drilled several pilot holes to receive the roofing screws. In the past we'd tried to simply drill them in through the aluminum roofing, but it took forever before the screw would bite and pass through the metal. And you can't pound a pilot hole with a nail or punch, as it will dent the thin roofing.

The screws are driven in the top of the ribs and are screwed in tightly enough to flatten the rubber washer that comes with them somewhat, but *not* so much that the roofing is dimpled. This would allow water to pool around the screw and possibly leak.

We were able to put up three sheets the first day before our power drivers were out of battery. It sure would be nice to have extra batteries for such things. The next day, we hauled our generator out to the site and simply used a regular drill, fitted with a Phillips bit to finish the job. It was quicker and no worries about running out of battery. Just weather. It was starting to snow in earnest.

The east side of the goat barn is still sheeted but not covered with metal roofing, but as soon as the spring thaw begins that, too, will be finished.

David learns to plow

Our first major snowfall dumped over a foot on us, and we still have it on the ground, buried under several more feet. David had been practicing driving the old Jeep plow truck here and there in the yard, moving it as needed. At first, of course, he couldn't get the hang of the clutch. But because he had used Bill's tractor during the summer, it was only a few minutes before he was cruising around smoothly. I envy these country kids, learning to drive around their own land before hitting the highways. When I learned, it was driver's ed in high school and crowded roads from the first. I was terrified.

David was dying to plow our mile-long trail, and when that foot of snow fell he just about dragged Bob out into the truck for a trail run. David and the old Jeep did a great job. The trail was clear and as nice as blacktop. The smoothest our trail becomes is during the winter when the ice and snow fill all the little ruts and pockets.

The one thing he soon learned, however, is that one must plow extremely wide at first because during the winter, with more and more plowing, the trail becomes narrower and narrower. Pretty soon there's not much of a place to *put* the snow; it simply falls back onto the road. The first few times I plow, I begin plowing outward from the center of the road, then work further and further toward the woods, as you would if you were sweeping the snow off with a broom. This makes the plow banks nearly at tree line, not just off the roadway. Plowing this way leaves quite a bit of room to stack snow on subsequent snowfalls.

Another lesson I learned years back is not to create plow banks on the upwind side of the drive in areas that are clear and wind blown snow is a problem. Banks catch blowing snow, acting like a snow fence, dumping huge snow drifts across the road. It is much better to plow *only* to the downwind side. Then if drifts form, they are heaviest way off the road.

"I'll plow it out a lot wider, next winter," he said. He had learned. Another lesson he learned was *not* to race the engine when plowing on ice.

He took the truck out of the yard with the rpms up way too high one night, trying to plow deep snow, with an inch of ice underneath. I yelled and yelled, but of course he couldn't hear with the engine revved up so high. But the truck seemed to even out and down the trail he went.

But he didn't come back.

We took the Suburban out to find him, cringing to see the Jeep in the trail with the hood up and a puddle of oil under the engine. "It started making a clanging noise..." David peered into the engine compartment. "And there's this crack or something...."

Sigh. He'd blown the engine. One thing I'll say for Bob; he never raised his voice a bit. "I guess you've learned not to race an old engine, huh?" David only hung his head and nodded. Lessons are sometimes hard here in the backwoods. Δ

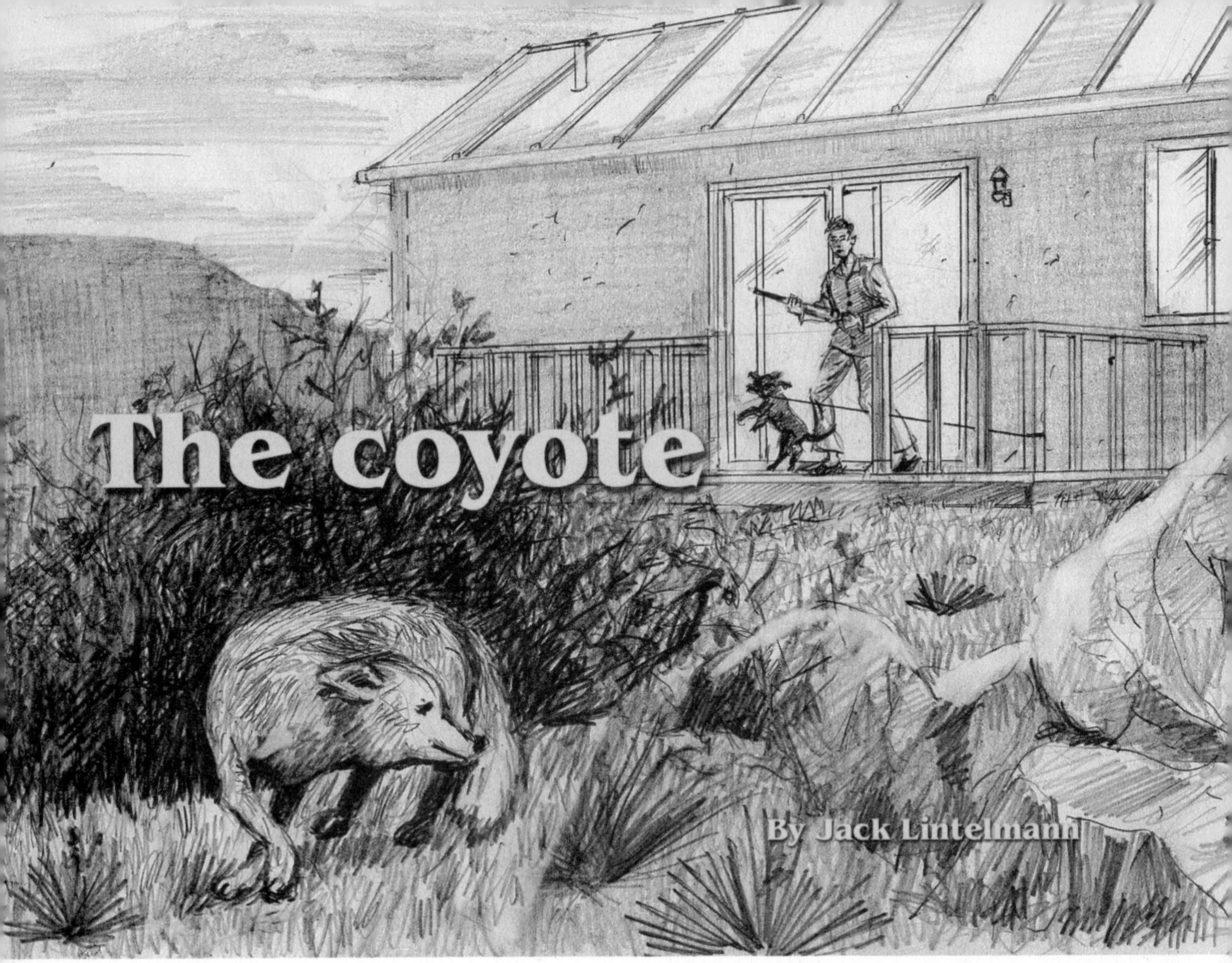

The coyote

By Jack Lintelmann

The coyote was lying just inside the fringe of sagebrush forty feet down a gentle slope from the house. He was a larger than average male, mostly gray in color with a random mixture of light and dark brown with black markings. He was almost obscured by the brushy veil, very difficult to see in the predawn light. In a short while the sun would begin to brighten the eastern sky making his position less tenable, and certainly more perilous. But, for the moment, he felt reasonably secure.

He was hunkered down flat, his hollow belly pressed against last year's crop of various dry indigenous weeds interspersed among the sage, with his legs stretched out before him. A close look would reveal the lower part of his right leg skewed and twisted at a slightly discernible angle, swollen from wrist to paw. His head was erect, the sharply pointed black-tipped ears alert. His eyes were focused on the expanse of glass across the side of the small house. Three large bay windows were fitted side by side affording a view of the panorama of river valley and canyon rimrock to the north.

Moving his head to the left the coyote could also see part of the low front porch and a large portion of the near-ground-level deck. He knew that often, soon after the lights came on in the house, the man could be seen moving around inside, and shortly thereafter let the small dog out through the front door. From time to time over the past many months he had monitored this recurring procedure during his travels up and down the valley, and he had locked away this information in his predator brain. Those were times when he had no reason to believe that one day he would need the knowledge, certainly not in such dire circumstances as was now the case. So he waited in silent desperation, harboring an acute hunger that dictated his patience. He was also mindful of the approaching daylight when he detected a faint shadow of movement behind the glass.

The man rolled over onto his stomach and lowered his arm off the bed. Even before he opened his eyes he felt the cold nose as the dog nuzzled the back of his hand. At some time during the early morning hours he thought he had heard his little pal yap once or twice, but he couldn't be sure. Oftentimes during a fitful sleep the man would hear sounds, familiar and unfamiliar, imagined and sometimes unimagined. Living in quiet solitude had done that to him. This time he decided to investigate. Before he turned on the reading lamp he looked out the bedroom window facing east. The night sky was just light enough to show that there were no strange objects or shapes on the porch or on the dusky gray flat of the deck beyond.

The kitchen and living room were combined into a large area with the rooms divided by an open see-through island. He walked through the hallway into the larger room and approached the bay windows in the darkness. A long sofa was backed up against the middle window, and when he was close, he could make out a very prominent indentation in one of the soft cushions. It was warm to the touch and he knew that his little companion had been on guard duty at her favorite observation post. He stared out into the night but could only see a few feet of bare ground leading to the sagebrush. It was too early to tell if anything unusual was out there. Still, he thought, she had seen something. He often played with the idea that because of her small size her senses, her defense mechanisms, were honed to a much sharper edge than most. He flipped on the kitchen switch, flooding both rooms with brilliant fluorescence, and walked to the door. His tiny friend was already there nervously wiggling to get out, her body language a red flag of apprehension. Could be a rabbit, the man thought, or may be a wandering farm dog, but more likely one of the many small critters of the night,

The man was also aware, as were many of his neighbors, that coyotes were becoming noticeably more aggressive during recent months. Working alone, as well as in packs, they had been patrolling ever nearer to farmhouses and adjacent outbuildings. He remembered a brief conversation he had had with the Johannson boy during a chance encounter at the mail boxes on the main road. Rolf Johannson was in his late teens, an average, hardworking farm boy. He was also a hunter when the opportunity arose, and his hostility toward coyotes was well known. He hated foxes, too, for killing his chickens, but he was passionate in his hatred for coyotes, and his bitterness had become obsessive. He blamed them for the depredation of most every other living creature in the valley, both domestic and wild, and for the depletion of upland game birds. He also blamed them for the loss of his hunting dog, although it was never proven.

During that exchange of pleasantries, young Johannson had mentioned seeing a large coyote several times crossing a section of open rangeland to the west, not far from the Johannson farm, before the animal disappeared into the long grove of Russian olive trees straddling the canal. Rolf had observed the actions of this lone animal from a distance and he told the man that someday he would try to make use of that knowledge. Unless they are disturbed, driven away, or have other reasons to change their pattern of movement, coyotes will habitually roam, following the same general routes to and from proven, and productive, hunting grounds. They are scavengers as well, and when it comes to a menu, they are not overly selective. The man had noticed that Rolf still carried the deer rifle in the window rack of his truck. It was an old military 30-06, and when it was fired, the report could be heard far and wide, easily distinguished from smaller calibers used by most farmers in the area.

So the coyote had watched and waited and although his attention had been on the front deck, he had not failed to see the shadowy movement in the dark room behind the glass, and he was not surprised when the windows and the interior of the room were suddenly awash with white light. It was his signal to move. Experience had taught him that at night, with a building lighted from inside, he was not easily observed. For reasons unknown to him, men were not able to see through the glass.

With the interior light on he felt safe to change locations. As he struggled to his feet he choked back a cry of pain caused by the pressure on his right foot. Carefully, unsteadily, he backed away and moved farther into the sage before he began a circuitous route to his left through the brush. His movement was an ungainly, three-footed hobble, painfully slow as he occasionally tested his damaged leg. He wanted to be in a position as near as possible to take the dog, yet do it with enough remaining darkness to effect a safe getaway. He was sure the small animal could be easily killed and carried off, with a little luck. But everything must work in his favor. First and foremost, the leg must hold up. His ability to put on a burst of speed was essential. The pain must be dealt with. If possible, it must be completely disregarded, at least during the initial sprint, and for that reason the shorter distance would be a great advantage. He continued on toward a heavy thicket of shrubs closer to the deck.

The coyote guessed that the outside light would be turned on before the dog came through the door. It had happened that way in the past. If his new position in the thicket was satisfactory, the porch light would not be a factor. On previous occasions, both morning and night, the light had been on but it had not been important. He had never considered the dog as a target, and on those occasions food had not been a measure of survival. Those were the days before the coyote had made the mistake that had cost him his pain and gut-gnawing hunger. He was paying a high price for a serious miscalculation.

Two days previously he had been patrolling along an irrigation ditch looking for his next meal when he had spotted a mature rock chuck in an open field of short grass. He immediately stopped and remained motionless. Certain that the chuck had not seen him, he stepped back into the tangle of undergrowth beneath the trees and continued forward within the shadows, moving closer to his prey while staying hidden as much as possible. He wanted to close the distance between himself and the boulder field at the edge of the pasture. He would have to get between the marmot and sanctuary in the lava rock, but he didn't get the chance. The rock chuck suddenly turned, sat up on its haunches, looked directly at the coyote, then, just as quickly, made a dash for the rocks.

The chuck startled the coyote with its agility and initial speed. Its bounding, lumbering gallop had proven to be deceptive, given the amount of ground the pudgy mammal covered. The coyote exploded from under the trees knowing that he would be lucky, now, to intercept the marmot before it reached the safe haven of boulders. The coyote had to cover twice the distance as that of his target. Even so, the race to the rocks ended in a dead heat.

The rock chuck reached the boulder field and was halfway into an angled passageway, almost home free, when the coyote clamped his powerful jaws into his hapless victim's lower back and pulled the doomed animal back out of the narrow slot. As he did, the chuck twisted around and in frantic anger lashed out at the nearest piece of his enemy. His chisel-like teeth gouged into the coyote's leg carving a groove, snapping a metacarpal bone. With his jaws still firmly imbedded in his prey, the coyote yanked the marmot away from his leg and in doing so ripped a tear in his own hide and tissue, exposing the bone. He flipped the chuck away from the safety of the rock. Its back had been broken and it was then easily dispatched.

The predator's hunger had been satisfied, but he had paid dearly for the last meal. The significance of his wound was soon realized with increasing pain as he limped back toward his den, bone grating on bone. That had been two days ago. He had been unable to chase down rabbits, unable to dig for gophers and ground squirrels, unable to ambush rock chucks, unable to pounce on mice: in short, he was unable to hunt and was facing starvation. He had laid in his den the rest of that day and throughout the night licking a laceration that might never heal, tending a leg bone that would never mend. Food had become the number one priority, and scavenging was an iffy business, especially in his weakened condition. Later that evening, moving slowly, he headed for the house where the man lived with the tiny dog. Better to try for a sure thing.

Unless they are disturbed, driven away, or have other reasons to change their pattern of movement, coyotes will habitually roam, following the same general routes to and from proven, and productive, hunting grounds.

The man waited at the door looking down at his little friend. His conversation with the Johannson boy was uppermost in his mind when he stooped down to scratch her ears and caress her, to calm her, and to reassure her. He surely loved the little tyke, and God help those who would do her harm. He stood and switched on the porch light, then hesitated and walked into the hallway. From a shelf in the utility closet he removed a length of lightweight chain with snap hooks on each end, and as he did he slid aside some foul weather gear and took a look at the shotgun standing in the corner, and then decided against the idea. He clipped the chain into the dog's collar and immediately felt a tug as the pooch led him out the door and across the porch. The man bent down to tether her to an eyebolt on the outer lip of the deck.

As he watched from his new vantage point in the shrubs, the coyote was alarmed at the scene unfolding before him. The outside light had brightened the porch area. That didn't concern him. He could deal with that, but the man had chained the dog to the deck. He was reminded of his near disastrous failure with the pygmy goat. The goat, too, had been tethered. He continued his silent vigilance in the bushes, sitting on his haunches, as the dog clattered across the deck toward him.

Normally, without a chain restricting her movements, the little mutt would make the short leap down onto the grass, but this time, with her hackles up, she dragged the chain to the corner of the deck and started out to the northeast, trembling, quietly whimpering. Her actions were somewhat out of character but not earth shattering. The man could hear nothing other than the dog and could not see beyond the perimeter of the porch light.

He was inwardly relieved with his decision to use the chain and he walked onto the grass to listen more carefully. As he moved around in the darkness, still in his pajamas and slippers, he could make out the broadening band of lighter sky beginning to climb above the horizon and he lingered a few minutes longer. It will soon be daylight, he thought, as he walked back to the house, and as he entered he switched off the porch light.

The moment he saw the dog with the chain rattling across the deck, the coyote knew it was all over. It was not to be. Even in his crippled and hunger-weakened condition he would have made a try for the dog, except for the chain. How could he have foreseen use of the chain? How could he carry the animal away when it was tied to the house?

The sky was becoming brighter by the minute. Visibility was improving to the point whereby the coyote had no other choice but to leave. His thoughts were focused on the dog and the front door. When he stood up, he inadvertently put an excessive amount of pressure on his leg, and he cried out in pain revealing his presence and exact location in the shrubs.

The tiny mutt, whose senses had now proved conclusively that "something was out there," began yelping like hell wouldn't have it. It was not her typical yapping, but deeper-throated, rip-roaring, bonafide barking. The clamor immediately alarmed the man. Her sudden outcry, coupled with the unusual tenor of her voice, at once elicited his pent up fear, and it angered him. Shotgun shells for the double-barrel were in the kitchen. Still in his pajamas and slippers, he quickly grabbed two of them from the drawer and rushed into the hallway. He opened the door to the utility closet, broke open the gun and stuffed the buckshot loads in as he went out the front door. Taking a line of direction from the pooch he hurried out into the sagebrush. It was light enough now to see the coyote limping toward the brow of the slope. Just beyond, it dropped sharply off at a steep angle to a neighboring farm tucked into the base of the hill.

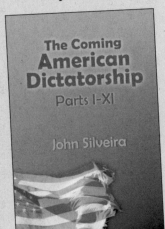

The man quickly gained enough ground on the coyote and he stopped and raised the gun. His mark was a clear silhouette outlined against the sky within easy range of the shot shells. He couldn't miss, but he didn't shoot. He was unsure of the shot pattern at that range and he had no idea how far buckshot pellets would carry in an arc over the hill. Because from his angle of sight he wasn't exactly sure where the farmhouse was, he decided not to fire. The last thing he wanted was to rattle a few .32 caliber lead balls onto his neighbor's roof, especially after delivering a wake-up call with the shotgun blast. He lowered the gun and watched the limping animal disappear from view. It would likely drop down the steep pitch, traverse the hillside above the farm, and head west toward safety in the trees. Dressed as he was, the man was not about to give chase.

His minuscule guard dog was anxiously awaiting his arrival at the house, and after he unloaded the shotgun he sat on the edge of the deck and rubbed the dog affectionately, rewarding her with words of praise. He then began to pick the foxtails out of his soft slippers as he spoke to her. He told her what had happened and that he could not see how the coyote could survive, crippled that way. She cocked her head and looked at him, trying to understand.

Later that day the two of them were walking the bank of the small irrigation ditch looking for obstructions in the stream flow, when they heard the shot. It came from in front of them, right out of the declining sun, echoing across the pasture land. They both stopped short. There was no mistaking the familiar crack and prolonged reverberations of a large caliber rifle. It's just as well, the man told the dog. Starving is a rotten way to die. Then the two friends continued on their way. Δ

Rebuilding the homestead greenhouse

By Charles A. Sanders

Way back in *Backwoods Home Magazine*, Issue #67, I wrote about building a greenhouse on our place. In the time since, that handy structure has served its purpose and then some. Last spring, it finally came time to rebuild the sun-catcher and get ready for several more years worth of growing.

Although I planned to make the new greenhouse essentially the same as its predecessor, when I started to rebuild, I made a few design changes, though this one would also be built lean-to fashion, on the side of the garage/workshop.

Initially, I decided to use a front wall that was to be a bit taller than the original. This would help in building the greenhouse's benches I had in mind and would also call for less plastic covering. Second, I used more treated lumber to cut down on rot in the damp greenhouse environment. I made the starting bench a bit shorter in length than the original. This was to make room for a chair and for placing some rubber tire growing beds during the winter. Finally, I added another used storm door at the back of the greenhouse.

I began, of course, by completely removing the old greenhouse. The lumber and other structural components were pretty much useless and were discarded. The exception was the one-inch conduit ribs I had used before. These curved galvanized tubes were already recycled from a commercial greenhouse when I built the first greenhouse. So, in effect, I was recycling recycled material for the new one. I did have

Site of the old greenhouse with the front wall of the new greenhouse

to cut off a length of pipe at the front end of each tube since I was using a taller wall in the front. This was not a problem, and was done by individually fitting each pipe in the wall, then marking and trimming it to the correct length. You can see in the illustration below just how each rib was fitted into the base wall.

The foundation consisted of short 4x4 posts set in the ground 12 feet from the wall. Treated tongue and groove 2x6s were secured to the posts to allow for some leveling which was necessary on the slight slope. On the front wall, a 2x6 plate was nailed atop the posts. Next, a treated 2x4 plate was bolted onto the exterior wall of the garage below the eaves. Holes spaced to correspond to the holes in the front base wall were bored in the wall plate prior to putting it up. As each rib was set in place and fine tuned to the correct arc, a small hole was drilled in each of the plates through the conduit, and a galvanized nail was used to secure the rib. After each rib was in place, a straight length of conduit was attached using metal screws. It was

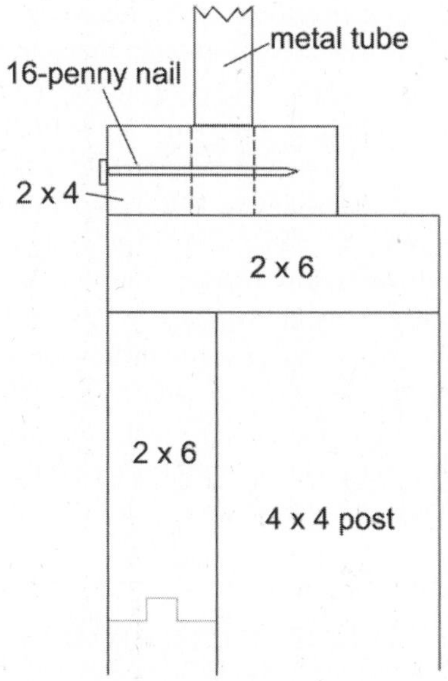

This illustration shows how the conduit tube is anchored in the front wall of the greenhouse.

run straight across the length of the greenhouse and just above head-high. This would help greatly to stabilize the ribs. It also serves as a handy place from which to suspend hanging baskets.

A treated 2x4 plate was applied along the front base wall, and holes were bored in both the top wall plate and the base plate to accommodate the conduit. Treated 4x4s were erected at each end and cut to match the angle of the end ribs. The ribs would later be drilled and nailed to the post prior to putting on the plastic covering. You can see some of these details in the illustrations and photographs.

Next, the door and window openings were framed, using measurements to accept the used door and window frames I had used before. Notice that I added a "back door" to the greenhouse this time. It is handy for accessing the compost pile.

As with our previous greenhouse, I recommend the home greenhouse builder use a material that is available from Northern Greenhouse Sales. The rugged woven plastic is designed for greenhouse use. It consists of a 7-mil woven plastic "fabric" with a 1-mil layer of solid plastic bonded to each side. The woven texture provides great resistance to ripping or tearing and the solid layers bonded to each side help greatly in the weatherproofing. Further, the whole fabric is treated to resist ultraviolet degradation, a factor that normally contributes to the short life span of plastic films in greenhouse applications.

Additionally, this time I used some tough plastic lath strip to help secure the

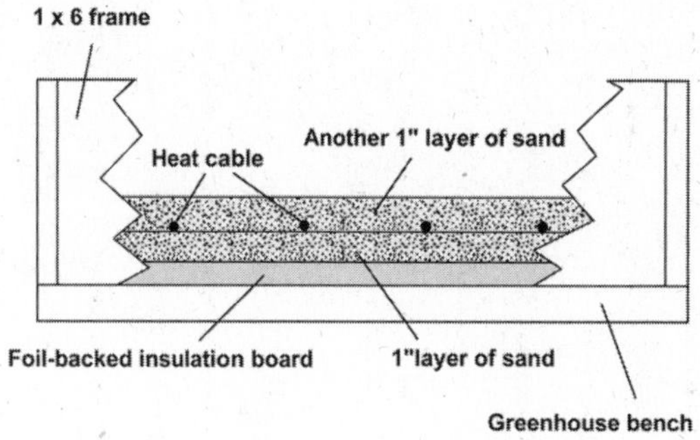

Germination bed details

plastic. The stuff comes in a 100-foot roll and works very well for keeping the greenhouse covering in place. To use the lath strips, first anchor one end with heavy staples or a roofing nail or two. Then unroll an appropriate length, stretch it snugly, and go down along its length, nailing as you go.

For more information on this rugged woven plastic covering and the rolls of plastic lath strip, contact Bob Davis at Northern Greenhouse Sales, Box 42, Neche, ND 58265.

One thing that I did on the new greenhouse bench, that I wish I hadn't, was build it with a slight drop towards the front of the bench. I thought that this would help preserve the benches by allowing excess water to run off. Well, it does just that, usually right on my shoes while I'm

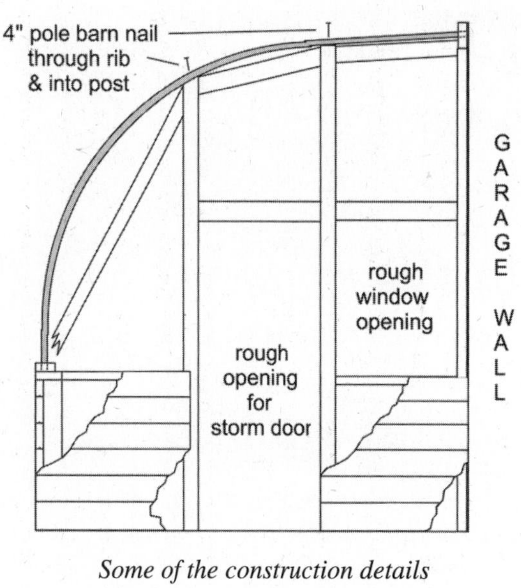

Some of the construction details

The frame of the new greenhouse with the doors installed

watering the plants. I think that just building the bench level would have been better.

The germination bed in the old greenhouse worked very well, so the replacement was based on the same design. It was constructed on the taller, work-height bench along the back wall by first framing up the sides with 1x6-inch lumber. A sheet of foil-backed foam insulation board was cut to fit the bed (made just slightly wider than the seed germination trays are long). Next, a one-inch layer of sand was spread over the foam board. An electric heat cable was arranged on the sand, and was then covered with about an inch more sand. The cable does a nice job of heating the seed trays and the sand acts as a heat sink, absorbing and distributing the heat. The thermostatically controlled heat cable maintains a good germination temperature for most varieties of vegetables we grow.

One handy thing about the location of the greenhouse is that it is attached to my garage and shop. I utilize an existing window opening, the wood stove in the garage, a window fan, and a timer to add heat to the greenhouse. Sometimes, I place a kerosene heater in the greenhouse to provide some extra heat. In most cases, however, by keeping a fire going in the garage, which I often do anyway, and timing the fan to turn on as the day begins to cool, sufficient heat is kept going into the greenhouse.

Starting plants

For starting seeds and transplants, the home greenhouse is hard to beat. We start by using some of the black plastic flats that stores and nurseries display their containers of plants in. The local grocer saved a bunch of them for us. They are great for filling with planting mix or compost and starting seeds. I attached some wooden ribs to a suitable piece of plywood, added a handle, and can quickly make rows in flats of soil mix. The planting board speeds things up when planting seeds.

After adding a handle and attaching some wooden ribs to a suitable piece of plywood, I can quickly make rows in flats of soil mix for planting seeds.

The seeds sprout quickly on the heated germination bed. Once they grow large enough to move into separate containers, they are gently lifted, one by one, and transplanted into ordinary styrofoam cups. I prepare the cups by poking two or three small holes in the bottom of each to allow water to drain. This can be done a stack at a time by shoving a long heavy wire down through the cups. A friend also saved us a large grocery sack full of used plastic yogurt cups that worked well, too. We have also used commercial-type plant containers which held six plants each. Any of these containers will work fine and I'm sure you can come up with ideas for other suitable plant cups as well. Anything from tin cans to boxes will work.

Building and working in your own small greenhouse is a very rewarding way to spend some time. It's nice to spend a cold January afternoon in shirtsleeves in an 80-degree greenhouse heated by the sun.

Remember, there are as many ways to build a greenhouse as there are homesteaders. The main thing is to use what you have or can readily obtain, adapt the structure to your own circumstances, and then use the dickens out of it. If you are working towards selling plants, you will find an eager market waiting. In any case, you will be rewarded with fresh vegetables nearly year-round, healthy and vigorous garden plants, and the satisfaction of knowing that you're another step closer to self-sufficiency. Δ

Fiddlehead ferns

great fun, healthful eating

By Linda Gabris

Fiddleheads growing in the woodlands

Spring is the time to get outdoors and enjoy the sunshine and nothing is more fun than going on an old-fashioned wild food hunt. One of Mother Nature's first and finest treats of the season are fiddlehead ferns.

Ostrich ferns (*matteuccia struthiopteris*) are more commonly known as fiddleheads because the unfurled frond of the fern resembles the finely crafted head of a fiddle.

Depending on weather, the fronds begin to appear around late April and by early May they can often be found growing in abundance on moist, fertile grounds throughout North America.

The most prospective places to hunt fiddleheads are along river and stream banks, in moist open woodlands, and at the edges of swamps and marshes.

Fiddleheads are the uncurled, deep green fronds of the graceful ostrich fern. They are at their prime for eating while young, firm and tightly curled. As the fern stalk reaches about six to eight inches in height, the frond begins to uncurl into a soft, feathery fern, losing its table appeal.

In recent years fiddleheads have become a commercial vegetable showing up in the produce departments of larger grocery stores across the country selling fresh and frozen at fairly hefty prices. If you've never seen fiddleheads before, check them out at the supermarket before hitting the trails. This will ensure you know what you're looking for.

Fiddleheads grow in clumps and should be picked in a thinning-out fashion, taking several fronds from each cluster rather than stripping the whole clump. This is how my grandmother taught me to pick and I have been harvesting from the same bountiful patches for years.

Since new roots are produced annually from the base of the current year's fronds, harvesting in this manner encourages new growth for the following season and does not harm underground rhizomes.

Some foragers use a small knife for cutting the heads but I find they break off very easily by hand—a safer method, especially for kids and healthier for the plant.

When collecting early fronds as they first emerge from the ground, work your fingers to the base and break the head from the cluster. Once fiddleheads rise on their stalks, they are much easier to gather. Just break off the fronds and leave stalks standing.

Green "wheels" with cheese

Fiddleheads with toasted sesame seeds

Oriental fiddleheads and prawns

Violin heads (teté-de-violon) with peppers and pecans

The fronds are covered with a brownish, onion-skin like coating that must be removed before eating. This can be done by shucking with your hands. After the chafe is removed, wash the fiddleheads well under cold running water to remove dirt before cooking. Finicky can rest assured that worms and bugs are seldom found on the fronds.

Always gather edible wilds away from roadsides and other areas where they might be contaminated with dust, herbicides, and pesticides. This will ensure that you are bringing home a super clean, organic vegetable for the supper table.

Caution:
Consuming raw or undercooked fiddleheads may cause 'green apple' symptoms including diarrhea, nausea, and upset stomach.

North American aboriginal people are credited with being first to cash in on the nutritional value of fiddleheads. After surviving long winters with scarce greenery, spring fiddleheads were a much needed supplement for the body, mind, and soul. They were a highly-prized medicinal plant, said to act as a natural cleansing agent ridding the body of accumulated impurities and toxins. Fiddleheads were also well respected by early settlers as one of spring's first offerings for the table.

Fiddleheads are rich in iron, potassium, niacin, riboflavin, magnesium, phosphorus, and vitamins A and C. Some folks compare them to asparagus while others say they taste like a cross between okra and broccoli. I find they are distinctive in taste and texture but if I had to liken them to anything, I'd say they taste like spring itself.

Cooked fiddleheads are delicious dotted with butter and sprinkled with fresh herbs and a splash of lemon juice or Tabasco sauce. They are well-suited for cheese, tomato, or cream sauces and add delightful color and taste to stir-fried dishes. For enlivening flavor and texture, add them to vegetable melodies, soups, stews, and casseroles. Once you try the recipes below, I'm sure that goin' fiddleheadin' will become one of your favorite spring pastimes.

Recipes

Oriental fiddleheads and prawns: Here's a healthy, delicious dinner that is truly a gourmet feast. Good news is, it's fast and super easy. Make it your meal after a fun day in the woodlands picking.

3 Tbsp. sesame oil
2 cloves minced garlic
1 sweet yellow pepper, cut into thin rings
2 cups prawns or shrimp, pan ready
1 Tbsp. fresh grated ginger
2 cups of fiddleheads, boiled until fork tender
1 package of thin Chinese or angel hair noodles (about 16 ounces)
½ cup chopped fresh tomato
minced green onion for garnish
soy sauce

Heat oil in wok. Sauté garlic until fragrant, but not brown. Add pepper rings and prawns and stir-fry about three minutes or until prawns are cooked. Lower heat, add ginger and fiddleheads, and stir-fry three minutes. Meanwhile prepare noodles according to package directions. To serve, put noodles on heated plate, arrange fiddleheads and prawns on top. Dot with tomato and garnish with green onion. Serve with soy sauce for sprinkling. Makes 4 servings.

Fiddleheads with sesame seeds: A quick and easy vegetable dish that's good warm or cold.

3 cups fiddleheads
2 Tbsp. sesame oil
1 thinly sliced hot or sweet pepper, to suit taste
1 clove minced garlic
2 tsp. lemon juice
seasoned salt and pepper to taste
¼ cup toasted sesame seeds (or slivered almonds)
lemon slices to garnish

Boil fiddleheads until fork tender. While cooking, heat oil in small skillet and sauté pepper and garlic until soft. Remove from heat and add lemon juice and seasonings. Drain the fiddleheads and toss with the oil mixture. Sprinkle with seeds and garnish with lemon.

Violin heads (tete-de-violon) with pecans and peppers:

- 3 cups fiddleheads
- 3 Tbsp. melted butter
- 1 Tbsp. lemon juice and bit of grated zest
- 1 roasted red pepper, cut into small cubes
- 1½ cups pecans

Boil fiddleheads until fork tender. Drain and put in heated dish. Drizzle with butter, sprinkle with lemon and zest, and top with roasted peppers and pecans that have been warmed in the microwave or oven.

Green "wheels" and cheese: Tender little "wheels" in creamy cheese sauce are a hit with little kids and big ones, too. This was my Grandfather's favorite fiddlehead dish.

- 4 cups fiddleheads, boiled until fork tender
- cheese sauce

To make Grandma's cheese sauce melt two tablespoons of butter in small saucepan over low heat. Add two tablespoons flour and stir until blended. Remove from the heat and gradually stir in one cup of hot milk. Return to the heat and cook until thick and smooth. Add 1½ cups grated cheddar or other cheese of choice and a drop of Worcestershire sauce. Stir until the cheese is melted. Season with salt and white pepper. Pour over hot, drained fiddleheads.

Variation: Make it a whiz dish by using processed cheese spread from a jar instead of homemade sauce.

Old-fashioned potato and fiddlehead soup:

- 4 large potatoes, peeled and diced
- 2 Tbsp. butter or oil
- 1 chopped onion
- 2 cloves minced garlic
- 2 Tbsp. flour
- 3 cups hot chicken stock
- salt and pepper to taste
- dash of cayenne
- ½ cup milk
- 2 cups fiddleheads, boiled until fork tender

Put the potatoes in soup pot in enough water to cover. Bring to boil, reduce heat and simmer until mushy, adding water if needed. Do not drain off the liquid. Using a hand masher or blender, puree until smooth then return to cooking pot. Melt the butter in a saucepan and sauté the onion and garlic until soft. Stir in the flour until blended. Slowly add the chicken stock and cook until smooth. Add the onion mixture to the potato puree and stir until well blended. Stir in the milk and add the cooked fiddleheads. Heat to almost boiling. Taste and adjust the seasonings. Serve with crusty rolls for a one-dish supper. Serves 4 to 6.

Freezing fiddleheads

All of the recipes above can be made from frozen fiddleheads. They freeze very well so you might want to put some up for winter enjoyment. Fiddleheads will last in the freezer from one season to the next. To freeze, blanch cleaned fiddleheads in boiling lightly salted water for one minute. Drain, cool, then put in airtight bags and freeze. Δ

Ayoob on Firearms

Choose your ammo...police style

One of our greatest modern gun experts, Lt. Col. Jeff Cooper, USMC, Ret., once made the observation that the bullet is more important than the gun. The gun, he explained, is merely the launcher. It is the bullet that actually does the job.

This is true for an armed citizen's home defense gun, as surely as it is for the battle weapon of one of Col. Cooper's brother Marines. Ditto for the police officer's ammunition. And ditto again for the bullet a rural American citizen uses to harvest game for the family table.

The military is bound by the codes of international warfare, going back to the Geneva Conventions and the Hague Accords, all of which predated napalm, chemical warfare, and the concept of thermonuclear war. Interestingly, the Judge Advocate General's office has already determined that these restrictions apply to declared wars between recognized nation-states, not things like the current "war on terrorism," but that's another story.

The Geneva Conventions and Hague Accords require that the bullets used not be designed to expand. Essentially, they call for full metal jacket projectiles that just punch neat, clean holes through the bodies of enemy soldiers. Ironically, in the name of human decency, virtually every state in the union forbids the use of such ammunition against deer, bear, or other big game. The reason is that it tends to result in slow death and is not humane.

In warfare, the bullet that wounds an enemy soldier becomes a greater "force multiplier" than the one that kills him. A dead soldier means one less enemy. A wounded soldier means at least three less of the enemy: one down, and two more to carry him off the field of battle.

I am sure that this makes good sense to the generals behind the lines, and the bean counters behind them. However, the soldier who is bad breath distance away from an Al-Qaeda fanatic with an AK47 doesn't just want his opposite number wounded, he wants him instantly out of the fight at the moment the bullet hits him.

At this point, both the semantics and the ethics of the matter start to become complicated. No young man fighting for his country wants, when he thinks about it, to end the life of another young man fighting for his country. However, that young man desperately wants the other young man not to kill him or one of his comrades. Therefore, the job of the bullet he launches is instant incapacitation.

This may cause death. When you get into it deep enough, you realize that the righteous combatant does not shoot to kill, he shoots to stop. A mortal wound is not enough. Many an American soldier who was mortally wounded went on to kill so many of the enemy before he ran out of blood and died that the majority of those on the sacred list who won the Congressional Medal of Honor won it posthumously. Every combat soldier who fought in heavy battle can tell you stories of enemy soldiers who, wounded unto death, still took one or more Americans with them. These men had been killed, but not *stopped*.

Massad Ayoob

In the big picture, the firearm is a tool. We *homo sapiens* are the tool-bearing mammal. We are also, ipso facto, the weapon-bearing mammal. We have become the dominant species—the alpha, the top predator if you will—because we have learned to tailor our tools to the given task.

Therefore, Logic 101 tells us, if we must tailor the tool to the task, and if the tool is the gun and we know that the gun's bullet is more important than the gun itself, why, we realize with our superior human brains that selection of ammunition is absolutely critical.

The history of law enforcement ammunition selection is a good one to study because it encompasses all four of the basic models of selection that the civilian will have available. It is from experience that common sense is born, and the police sector has that experience.

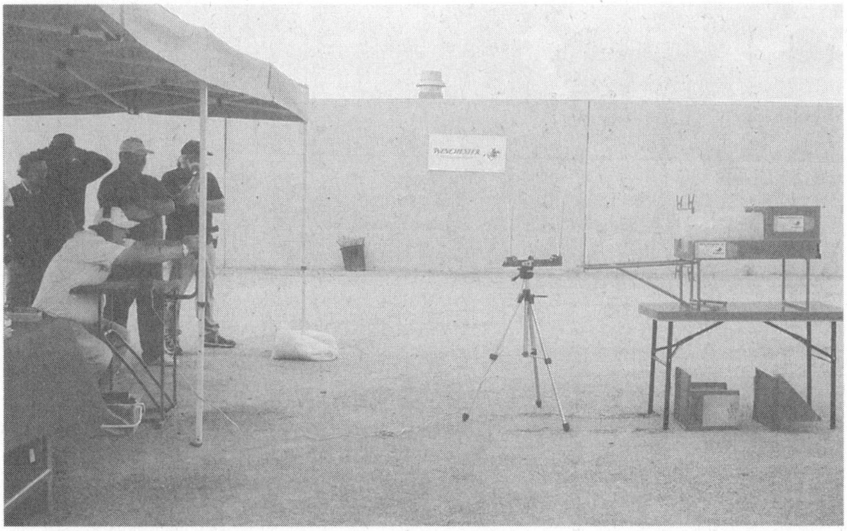

Modern ammunition testing. Paul Nowak of Winchester (left, with Springfield Armory pistol) fires over a chronograph (on tripod) which measures the bullet's velocity, and into the block of ballistic gelatin set on steel holder at right.

Four models

There are essentially four models that police used for selection of ammunition over the years. They might be described as the Traditional Model, the Advertising Model, the Laboratory Model, and the Experiential Model.

The **Traditional Model** was used for the first two thirds of the 20th Century—longer by some of the more institutionalized departments—and it failed miserably. The .38 Special revolver was the standard then, using 158-grain round-nose lead ammunition with a muzzle velocity of 755 feet per second, generating some 200 foot-pounds of energy at the muzzle.

This ammunition, from the beginning, performed dismally at its intended purpose. The rounded tip of the bullet slipped through flesh with a wedge effect, leaving behind it a dimpled channel similar to an ice pick wound. It would kill, but slowly. However, it had little "stopping effect." The round became known on the street as "the widow-maker," because you could empty your gun into your attacker and he could still make your wife a widow before he went down. Because the bullet tended to go through and through, there was great danger of striking an unseen bystander behind the intended target with the exiting projectile. Because of its low energy, this same bullet that penetrated too much on humans penetrated too little on hard barriers, such as car doors and windows, often bouncing off a felon's windshield.

In the late 1920s and the '30s, efforts were made to find something more powerful. These included the .38/44 round, simply a high velocity 158-grain .38 Special; the .38 Super Automatic from Colt, with a pointy nose 130-grain full metal jacket bullet at some 1200 foot per second, generating perhaps 420 foot-pounds of energy; and the .357 Magnum cartridge jointly introduced by Smith & Wesson (the gun) and Winchester-Western (the cartridge). In the Magnum, the 158-grain bullet was retained, but with a flat point and much greater velocity and energy.

These hotter loads were better man-stoppers if heavy bone was struck and shattered, or if the bullets hit a liquid part of the body, such as the brain or a full bladder. Otherwise, they simply zipped through the body with even more exit force than a .38 round nose, and most police chiefs banned them for fear of their corollary damage capability to bystanders.

The .38 Special round nose stayed dominant for the first two thirds of the 20th Century, simply because of tradition. "It's what we've always had." "We've always done it this way." Not until the 1960s did things get better. Lee Jurras in Shelbyville, Indiana, founded the Super Vel ammunition company and produced a line of light weight, high velocity hollow point rounds. With these, the .38 Special now had an expanding bullet that would open up or "mushroom" in the body. It delivered much more "shock effect" and was much less likely to exit. It was also much less likely to ricochet, which round nose bullets were and are infamous for doing.

Now was born the **Experiential Model**. Police departments that took

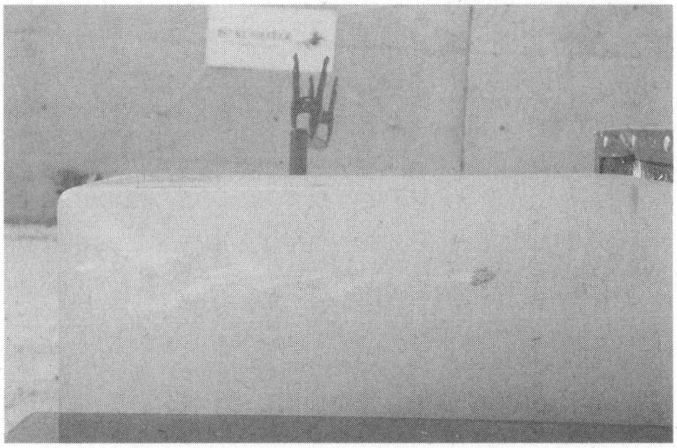

Bullet has lodged in the translucent gelatin, leaving a "wound path" clearly visible behind it. Note that damage is greatest early in the path, before resistance has slowed the bullet and reduced its energy.

the bold step of adopting the new ammo were inundated with queries from other agencies as to how it had performed. When learning of its highly satisfactory results, the inquiring agencies adopted it themselves.

With widespread adoption came more collective experience. Police had at last fallen back to their core competence—being trained investigators—and applied it to equipment selection. The result was much better ammunition and a quantum leap in both officer safety and public safety.

In the mid-1970s we saw the first large-scale application of the **Laboratory Model**. In what is now recognized as a classic example of junk science, the National Institute of Justice spent seven figures on a study to determine RII, or Relative Incapacitation Index, of handgun ammunition. Using an old formulation of ballistic gelatin as flesh simulant, the testers went on the assumption that whatever bullet created the greatest temporary cavity in the substance would deliver the greatest "stopping power" in living tissue. They then set about quantifying stopping power value, with tables that indicated the old .38 round nose might be a better stopper than the Army .45, and that a 9mm automatic with ball ammunition would be more potent than the .45. "Softnose" bullets received the same value as hollow points.

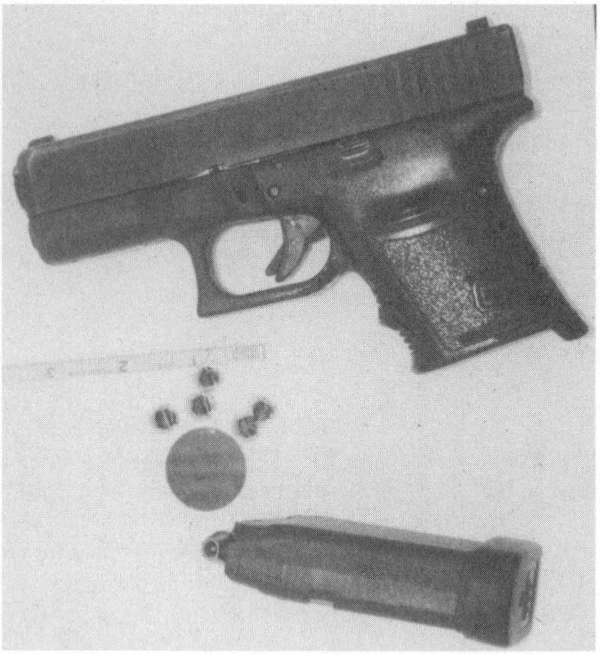

Accuracy is usually a welcome side benefit of purchasing premium ammunition. 230-grain Federal Hydra-Shok .45 Auto round has given author a $1^{3}/_{8}$" group at 25 yards with compact Glock 30 pistol.

The expensively funded study had the prestige of the U.S. Government behind it, and departments flocked to buy ammunition that rated well in the RII studies. Unfortunately, they were doomed to disappointment.

The RII results flew in the face of three quarters of a century of observed reality. The first test of junk science versus real science is, "Do the results from the laboratory correlate with known factors from the field?" If they do not, we know something went wrong in the lab. Many of the hypothetical conclusions that the RII study put forth as written in stone were in fact 180 degrees off from a large body of observed reality. That early warning signal was ignored, and the results were tragic.

Police calibers today, in order of popularity. .40 S&W is far and away the most used. .45 Auto and .357 SIG are increasing in popularity. 9mm use is waning greatly in law enforcement.

Many of the quick-expanding bullets favored by the RII study would not penetrate deeply enough into a human body to reach the vital organs of a large man from certain angles. In Michigan, a policewoman fired two light, fast .38 hollow points into a gunman's chest, and apparently believing that this had done the job, lowered her service revolver. Instead of collapsing, however, the assailant raised his gun and shot her in the head, killing her instantly. He survived to stand trial. In Miami, a bullet that had done well in the RII tests was fired into the chest of a gunman who, unfazed, then shot and killed the man who shot him and his partner, both FBI agents, and wounded several more agents before being killed by bullets in the head and neck.

This resulted in the FBI Wound Ballistics Workshop of 1988 in Quantico, Virginia. Among those present were Dr. Martin Fackler, head of wound ballistics research for the US Army's medical training center, Letterman Institute. Fackler had developed an improved ballistic

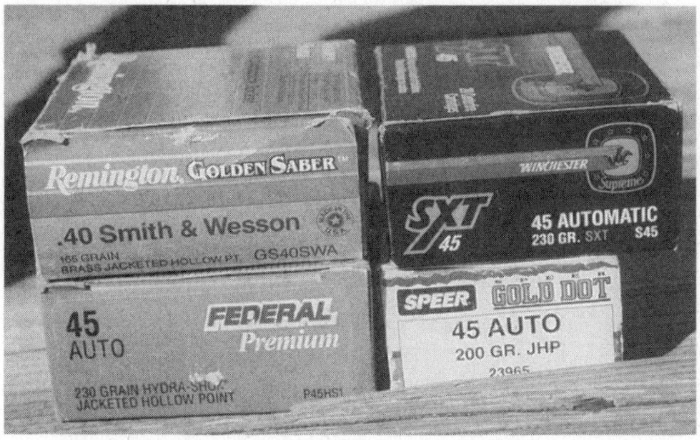

High tech bullets in premium ammunition are what most cops use today, and most hunters are going in the same direction. Top: Remington brass jacket Golden Saber, and Winchester's SXT. Below: Federal's proven .45 Hydra-Shok and Speer's popular, effective Gold Dot bullet with bonded jacket and core.

gelatin model that he had scientifically correlated to swine muscle tissue, which in turn is comparable to human muscle tissue. He hypothesized that wound depth was much more important than previously thought, and recommended ammunition that could send a bullet at least twelve inches into his ballistic gelatin.

The FBI agreed. By this point, the 9mm semiautomatic pistol had ascended to dominance over the six-shot service revolver in the police world, and the FBI adopted a heavy, slow moving 9mm bullet that weighed 147 grains and traveled at a subsonic velocity of less than 1000 feet per second.

Even this did not work terribly well. The bullet often went deep, but also frequently failed to expand reliably, and penetrated too far. Most departments that adopted it were so disappointed in the street results that they either changed ammunition or went to more powerful pistols.

Meanwhile, in a classic example of the Experiential Model, Detroit homicide detective Evan Marshall had begun a collection of thousands of police gunfight reports, and attempted to rate the stopping power of the ammunition used based on what actually happened in gunfights. He was soon joined by ballistic researcher Ed Sanow. In a separate study commissioned by the Police Marksman Association, Richard Fairburn analyzed gunfights submitted to his data base by various agencies, and his results were almost identical to those of Marshall and Sanow in identifying the best performing police handgun rounds.

Meanwhile, the **Advertising Model**—taking the manufacturer's grandiose claims for having the newest and deadliest ammo at face value—had quickly failed. Winchester's early Silvertip performed dismally in most handgun calibers, though it would later prove itself in subsequent generations of improved ammunition. Federal's Hydra-Shok series worked superbly in .45 caliber, but performed less effectively with some smaller diameter bullets. The police soon learned to trust only the Laboratory and Experiential Models, preferably in combination.

Combined models

Experience has taught police that what actually happens on the street is more important than what happens in the artificial environment of the laboratory. The 9mm round now acknowledged to work the best is a 124-grain to 127-grain high tech hollow point at a velocity of 1250 feet per second. NYPD, with some 30,000 officers carrying this type of ammo, the Speer Gold Dot +P 124-grain, is happy with the performance of its 9mm service pistols. Ditto the Orlando, Florida, Police Department, which uses the Winchester Ranger 127-grain +P+ in their standard issue 9mm SIGs.

Most other departments have gone to more powerful rounds. The .40 S&W caliber is the overwhelming top choice of police departments today, followed by the .357 SIG and the .45. Created to duplicate the best ballistics of the .357 Magnum revolver in a semiautomatic pistol, the .357 SIG spits a 125-grain jacketed hollow point at 1300 to 1400 feet per second, delivering 500-plus foot-pounds of energy. Departments which have adopted it are delighted with the performance, reporting a high frequency of one-shot stops. The Virginia State Police, who issue the .357 SIG Model P229 pistol, told me that they were particularly pleased with the number of felons who dropped and stopped fighting after receiving non-fatal wounds in non-vital parts of the body.

In .40 caliber, the original 180-grain hollow point at subsonic velocity has worked better than expected, but the star performers in .40 ammo tend to be high tech bullets

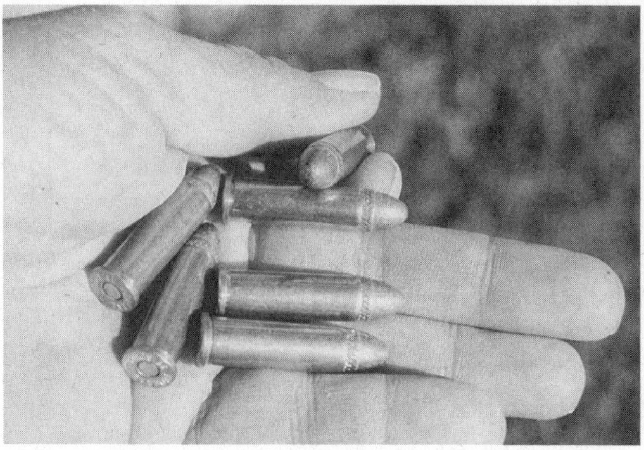

Once-traditional 158 grain round nose lead .38 Special ammunition is now recognized as obsolete, and a poor choice for anything but target shooting.

such as the Winchester SXT or Ranger T, the CCI Gold Dot, and the Remington Golden Saber with 155-grain bullets at 1200 foot-seconds or 165-grain bullets at 1140 to 1150 feet per second. Using the 165-grain Ranger in their .40 caliber Glocks, the Nashville, Tennessee, Police have amassed a long series of impressive one-shot stops.

In .45 caliber, the matured Federal Hydra-Shok design is something of a gold standard, and the Winchester SXT, Remington Golden Saber, and CCI Gold Dot also have delivered impressive performance in the field. These bullets reliably open up and get the job done. In .45 Auto, the 230-grain bullet at some 880 foot seconds has become standard in police work. Note that all of these are high-tech projectiles, what is known in the trade as "premium ammunition."

Premium ammo

High tech bullets are more expensive to manufacture. The bonded core of the Gold Dot, the interlocked bullet body and jacket of the SXT, the post in the center of a Hydra-Shok's hollow point, and the driving band that surrounds the base of a Golden Saber bullet are all more expensive to manufacture and therefore cost more.

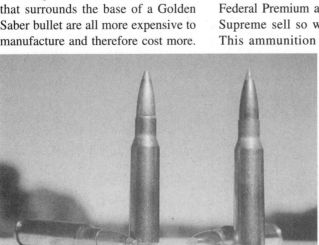

Tailor the tool to the task. Both of these hunting cartridges are .308 Winchester. The 165 grain Federal Premium at left is ideal for large deer, while the 125 grain Nosler Ballistic Tip at right is better suited for smaller animals like pronghorn antelope.

Why do police departments that buy on bid specify this premium ammunition? Because it works better, and with human life on the line, they cannot afford to economize.

America's most popular police service pistol today is this Glock 22. It holds 16 rounds of .40 S&W ammo like this Black Hills EXP, which delivers 485 foot-pounds of energy per shot.

The same is true for the hunter, to a degree. Life may not be on the line, but performance is still important. If you are shooting a small deer at relatively close range with a high-powered hunting rifle, conventional hunting ammo bought in a "value-pack" at Wal-Mart will probably be good enough. However, if you are aiming at a thousand pound moose, and winter meat for the family hinges on the bullet performing its job, it's more than worth a dollar a cartridge to have a high-performance bullet designed for this particular task.

This is why hunting rounds like the Federal Premium and the Winchester Supreme sell so well in gun shops. This ammunition is bought by the serious hunters. Their research, and the anecdotal experience of their friends who have used it in the game fields, has convinced them to pay a few dollars extra to guarantee as much as possible the best performance when there is an opportunity for only one shot and the results are critical.

In the end, the smart hunters have done exactly what the cops did. They went with the reality of what worked in the field, in a way that was quantified and given credibility in the laboratory. This approach mirrored the collective, institutionalized learning experience of law enforcement in ammunition selection.

Some call it a combination of the Experiential Model and the Laboratory Model. Some might call it Reality Based Selection Protocol.

And some just call it common sense. Δ

Salmon candy and pickles

two unique ways to enjoy your next catch

By Linda Gabris

Salmon is always a treat, but if you want to try something different, how about making pickles and candy out of the next fish that lands in your kitchen. In my house, when there are salmon pickles in the crock and a stash of salmon candy in the cupboard, everyone is happy.

Mention pickled fish and most folks think of herring. I used to, too, until a few years ago when I was introduced to a platter of pickled salmon. Traditional Old World rollmops are good but, in my opinion, newfangled salmon pickles are a whole lot better. They earn such big raves when served as an appetizer, you'll hate to confess how easy they are to make.

For the ultimate treat, salmon or Indian candy is sweet enough to pass off as dessert. Chewy salmon candy makes a satisfying snack for nibbling on while you're waiting for a nibble at your favorite fishing hole or for toting as a pocket treat to enjoy along the trail. The secret to making good candy is in the brining and basting so don't skip any steps and you'll end up with a perfect batch every time.

Sometimes I halve a hefty salmon in order to make a batch of pickles and candy from the same fish. The recipes below can be doubled or tripled to accommodate the catch.

Salmon pickles

There are two basic ways to pickle fish. One method calls for brining raw fish. The other method, which I prefer, calls for the fish to be blanched or lightly poached before putting in the crock. The latter produces a lighter-colored, milder tasting pickle.

- 3 pounds salmon fillets, skin and bones removed
- 4 cups white vinegar
- 1 cup water
- ½ cup sugar
- 2 Tbsp. pickling salt
- 4 Tbsp. mixed pickling spice
- 4 thinly sliced onions
- 1 red pepper, thinly sliced (optional)

Cut the fish into one-inch cubes. In a large skillet bring enough water to cover fish to a boil. Gently ease fish into the water and poach for one minute or until it turns from red to pink. Drain and let cool. Combine the remaining ingredients, except onion and pepper, in a saucepan and bring to boil. Simmer five minutes. Layer salmon chunks with onions and peppers in an earthen crock. If you don't have a crock, use a gallon jar or other glass container. Pour the boiling vinegar solution over the fish. Cool, cover tightly, and refrigerate for at least three days before serving. Serve salmon pickles with crisp rye crackers and a little pot of sour cream for crowning.

A platter of salmon candy makes a sweet treat.

Salmon candy

I use real maple syrup in my salmon candy recipe but you can substitute maple flavored pancake syrup, if you wish. Or you can use plain syrup and add a few drops of maple flavoring to the brine. Use maple, apple, cherry or other fruit chips for smoking the candy.

- 3 pounds of salmon fillets, skin and bones removed
- 5 cups water
- 1 cup of pickling salt
- 4 cups of brown sugar
- 1 cup maple syrup (or other)
- 1 cup liquid honey mixed with 5 tablespoons water for basting

Cut the salmon into one-inch cubes. Mix the remaining ingredients, except the honey-water mixture, in a glass bowl. Stir until the salt and sugar are dissolved then add the fish. Cover and let brine in the fridge for 24 hours. Remove the fish from brine and discard the liquid. Insert a sturdy wooden toothpick into each chunk of salmon and place on smoking rack, using a toothpick as a hanger (as shown in photo). Let the fish drip over paper or sink for 20 minutes. This air drying step helps produce a glossy finish. Smoke for six to eight hours, brushing several times with the honey mixture until glossy. If you like it moist, reduce the smoking time. For more leathery candy, go the full eight hours. When done, the toothpick will be well secured into the fish, making a handy candy stick. Store in a wooden box in a cool place. Δ

The last word

One good reason for tax reform

The other day *Backwoods Home Magazine* got a notice of a "tax increase" from the IRS. We've gotten quite a few such notices through the years. This one was for $3,802.49 including over $600 in penalties and interest charges. There was no explanation as to why this "tax increase" is due (I'm not sure we'd understand the reason even if it was explained), but the threat of more penalties was very clear.

These notices seem to come at the worst possible moments. This one not only came during this issue's deadline, but it came while the accountant we must retain to figure these things out was up to his own eyeballs in the April 15th tax filing deadline. But we couldn't deal with this notice even if we had the time because too much of tax code is incomprehensible to even the smartest of businessmen. So off to the accountant it went—at $140 an hour.

Usually, he calls us back on these matters and says, "Don't pay it. You don't owe it." Fine. Then he notifies the IRS with the reasons why it's not owed (while still billing us at $140 an hour) and it's settled. So, whether we pay the IRS or pay the accountant, we're out dough. And on the occasions we do owe it, we have to pay them both.

These tax notices cannot be ignored, even when the assessment is small, because if left unpaid, interest and penalties pile up. What starts out as a small problem becomes a big one, and when they get big enough, the IRS can take your property, take your business, and even send you to jail. So, when the small ones come in, we have to judge the size of the tax assessment, along with its interest and penalties, against the accountant's fees and determine which is smaller. If it costs less to pay the IRS than to pay the accountant, we pay the IRS, even though if past history is a track record, *we probably don't owe it.* Every one of these notices cost us money no matter what.

The cost of an incomprehensible tax code is greater than just the cost to businesses to comply. There is a national cost, as well. The amount of talent that is wasted to the nation just trying to figure out how to deal with the tax code is enormous. Men and women who should be looking for cures for cancer, creating products and manufacturing processes to make us more competitive in world markets, teaching our youth, etc., are instead committed to trying to make sense of bureaucratic nightmares.

Solutions

There have been various prescriptions for dealing with the current tax code. A flat tax, a national sales tax, or a consumption tax have been suggested and each would cure some of the problems. But each also creates its own problems. Just as an example: with a national sales tax, compliance becomes a problem. One of the things Canadians have learned with their national sales tax is that it has led to smuggling, just as states in this country have discovered that smugglers try to import cigarettes from low cigarette tax states to states with higher taxes. On top of that, one legal way to avoid a national sales tax would be for consumers to reduce spending, and many economists fear that is a recipe for a recession or worse. And if that's not bad enough, a national sales tax will make it easier for Congress to raise taxes. Other tax schemes will create other problems that are beyond the scope of this column.

What is needed, no matter what kind of tax structure we have, is a clear, concise tax code, one the average businessman can comprehend so when he (or she) gets a notice from the IRS he can understand the assessment, and if he feels it's unfair he can argue against it—without *needing* a high-priced gun to keep him solvent and out of jail. With what we have right now it's hire the high-priced experts or perish.

The costs to you

If you think this is just us whining about a personal problem that doesn't really affect you, consider this: the costs to businessmen to stay out of trouble affects us all. Like any other business, we have to pass along *all* our costs to our customers if we're to stay in business. That's higher subscription costs and higher newsstand prices to you, and higher advertising rates to our advertisers. Also, keep in mind that our suppliers including our printer, our distributor, and all their suppliers have to pass their costs on to us, and we have to pass those costs on to you, too. And it's not just us. Your groceries, your gasoline, your home, and almost everything else you buy has hidden costs as businessmen struggle to comply with the tax codes. Scott Moody, senior economist for the *Tax Foundation,* estimates that the total cost of tax compliance for all businesses in the United States runs to more than $100 billion per year. For a family of four, that comes out to over $1300 a year in hidden costs.

Despite congressional tax hearings of a few years ago, the tax code is still confusing. It still behooves us to retain experts to stay out of trouble and stay in business. But a clearer tax code, one that even you and I can understand, is something Congress could mandate right now. So why don't they? Δ

— John Silveira

Backwoods Home magazine

practical ideas for self-reliant living

July/Aug 2005
Issue #94
$4.95 US
$6.50 CAN

Special Section: Self-Reliance for Women

plus:

eautiful awnings
olar powered farm
est Coast Tsunami
abulous picnic recipes
ealthy living to avoid cancer
egetarian delights for summer

ww.backwoodshome.com

My view

Planning for a Gold Beach tsunami

For years I've known that Gold Beach, the hometown of *Backwoods Home Magazine*, was in a tsunami hazard area. They have tsunami drills at the local schools, and there are tsunami warning signs around town. In 1964 a tsunami generated by an Alaska earthquake killed 11 people in Crescent City, a mere 53 miles south of Gold Beach.

But I did not know until recently that Gold Beach, like other Northwest coastal towns, sits atop the *Cascadia Subduction Zone*, a meeting place of tectonic plates that is very similar to the subduction zone that generated the great tsunami that killed 250,000 people in Asia six months ago. The only difference, according to a *Discovery Channel* documentary, is that the *Cascadia Subduction Zone* will likely generate tsunami waves that are much bigger than the ones that devastated Asia. Where Asia experienced waves on the order of 30 or 40 feet, we will quite possibly endure waves from 50 to 100 feet.

Hence my keen interest in tsunamis that prompted John Silveira's excellent article in this issue. John and I both did research on the article so were well informed by the time we attended a local "tsunami information meeting" in Gold Beach. The 14 "experts" who constituted our local tsunami panel confirmed our research: our local subduction zone will eventually generate a quake of 8.5 to 9 on the Richter scale, which will in turn generate tsunami waves with a possible height of 50 to 100 feet, and Gold Beach residents will have between 5 and 15 minutes from the start of the quake to get to higher ground. The type of quake at our subduction zone will be fairly long lasting, from 1 to 4 minutes, which effectively cuts our escape time from the ensuing tsunami waves to 1 to 11 minutes.

I had one pressing question to ask the panel: How do my three young boys, ages 10, 12, and 13, get evacuated from the local grammar school in the event of this giant quake and tsunami? The school sits at 43 feet. In fact, how do all 500 students at the school, including the young kindergartners, get at least 50 feet above the school in that short amount of time?

So after listening for two hours to the 14 "experts" warn residents that this anticipated giant quake and tsunami were virtual certainties some day in the future, and that residents had best prepare for it now, I asked my question. Three of the experts volunteered lengthy assurances to me that the school had things under control and that the students practiced regular tsunami drills.

But the first chink in their assurances came only a few minutes later when a panel member noted that a high power electrical line ran up the hill behind the school. The hill was the prime anticipated escape route for the children. A local power company employee quickly assured everyone that Bonneville Power, the owner of the line, would automatically shut off power to that line should such a big quake occur. Besides, another panel member said, just in case the power line comes down and is still electrified, there was another escape route, behind the bus barn at the back of the school. "But the bus barn is a quarter mile away!" another panel member cautioned.

All this made me a bit nervous, of course, even though panel members assured the audience that the power line question and the alternate escape route would be thoroughly checked out. The day after the meeting I began doing my own investigating. I had been assured by "experts" in the past about various things and was often disappointed when the experts turned out to have scant knowledge backing up their assurances.

First I asked my children and some of their friends how many tsunami drills they had taken part in during the school year. "None" was the unanimous reply. The day after I questioned the children, the school did indeed hold a tsunami drill, but according to the kids they walked over to the bus barn (elevation about 60 feet), then back around the block to the school.

I then met with school officials responsible for disaster preparedness, and they insisted the school had had two tsunami drills this school year, which is still a far cry from the "regular drills" the panel of experts had talked about. But during the two drills the students had not gone up any hills that would have escaped 50 to 100 foot tsunami waves. They also did not know whether the electricity to the power line that lined the main escape route would actually be turned off in time. It was a far cry from the assurances I got at the meeting of experts. Silveira also informed *them* that a tsunami hazard map the "experts" had referred the audience to was based on a 35-foot wave.

The school decided to hold another tsunami drill, one more realistic, before the school year was finished, and they assured me they would investigate once and for all whether or not that power line along the main escape route would be rendered inactive by Bonneville Power. I will also work with them and a local Civilian Emergency Preparedness group on Cascadia quake and tsunami planning. Meanwhile I have begun making my own personal plans for my family in the event a big quake and tsunami occur while my children are at school. I've tried to ingrain in my kids how to recognize the conditions that could precede a tsunami, and how to act to save themselves. I've also struck a deal with a local minister who lives on a "safe" hill behind the school to collect my kids from the tsunami evacuation area in the event I am unable to.

There is a lesson in all this. Don't ever rely on experts for anything, especially when it comes to the safety of your family. Rely on yourself. It's the same old self-reliance story. The buck stops with you. — ***Dave Duffy***

PVC pipe

in the home, garden, farm, and workshop

By Charles A. Sanders

Perhaps one of the most important innovations in modern plumbing has been the development of polyvinyl chloride (PVC), chlorinated polyvinyl chloride (CPVC), and related plastic pipe. These materials have enabled the average homeowner or builder to become an expert in installing plumbing anywhere it is needed around the home. The versatility, durability, and simplicity of the pipes and the dozens of different types of fittings and couplings make just about any project a snap. The predominant material used in drain, waste, and vent applications, PVC pipe is also used extensively in cold-water delivery systems to or for buildings.

PVC pipe is available in a variety of lengths, diameters and pressure classes. It has a full complement of standard fittings, valves, and couplings. And it is compatible with other pipe materials, so it can be specified for either new construction or system upgrades.

It's tough stuff. It is designed and manufactured to be that way. It provides time-tested resistance to costly leakage. It is corrosion resistant and reliable. It is not a conductor of electricity, nor is it affected by excessively hard or soft water, changes in water pH or the chemical constituents found in both domestic and industrial wastewater. When used in household plumbing systems, PVC pipe resists attack by cleaners and other household chemicals. Because PVC withstands conditions that other pipe materials cannot, it frequently is selected in place of, or to replace, other pipe materials.

PVC pipe is even flexible. It can bend without breaking. Both pipe and joint assemblies withstand pressure surges and shock. PVC pipe is resistant to impact, general wear, and abrasion, providing reliable service and less costly maintenance. With all this said, one of the best qualities of PVC pipe is simply that it is easy to work with.

Bend it, shape it

Some PVC projects require the PVC pipe to be bent. Although PVC pipe does have the quality that permits it to be bent somewhat, more drastic shaping calls for other methods in which it must be temporarily softened with heat. Heating the pipe to a point where it is malleable can be accomplished in a number of ways.

1. Hot water: Dip the piece to be worked into very hot or boiling water. Allow the pipe to heat completely through. As you work the piece, repeated dunkings into the hot water may be necessary.

2. Heat lamps: An ordinary heat lamp can heat PVC pipe to workable temperatures. Allow it to get thoroughly heated and resoften as needed.

3. Heaters: I have heated pieces of PVC pipe over the burner of the kerosene heater that I use in my workshop. It quickly softened the ends of the pieces I was working. Again, reapply heat as the piece cools and hardens.

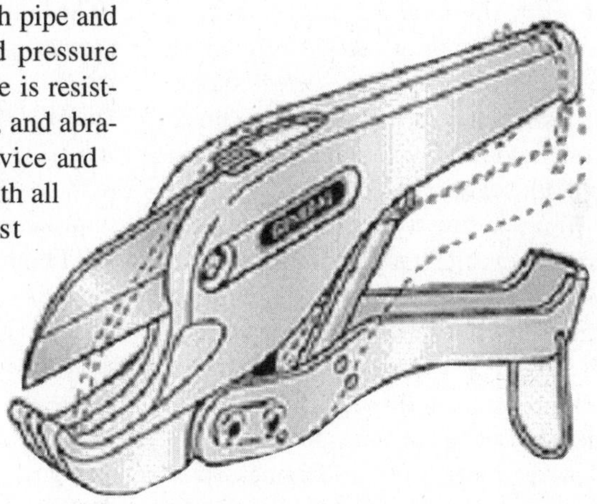

Ratcheting cutters are useful for making square cuts on PVC pipe.

Once you have the piece softened sufficiently, you can bend it, pinch it, and shape it.

Cutting and shaping

PVC pipe should be cut square with a wheeled tubing cutter or fine-toothed saw such as a hacksaw. A handy cutter that resembles hand pruners is also available. The ratcheting action makes it simple to cut pipe up to one inch in diameter. In my experience, however, it is difficult to make a precisely square cut when using these cutters. If that is important for your project, then use a saw. Otherwise, the ratcheting cutters are great for general cutting of PVC pipe.

Before gluing, pipe ends should be de-burred and wiped clean and dry, free of any oil or dirt.

Painting PVC pipe

As with any painting project, your goal is to apply a finish that is durable and wear resistant.

Prior to attempting to paint PVC, you must first give it a thorough cleaning to remove any grease, oil, or other contaminants that may be on its surface. After the surface is clean, use some fine sand paper or fine steel wool to rough the finish just enough to help the coating adhere better. Since PVC is not really designed to be painted, apply the selected coating in a small test area and check to make sure it adheres well before continuing with the entire project.

You may use a coat of primer paint to help your final finish coat adhere better. I have successfully painted many PVC items, and like anything else, find that if the item is used frequently or roughly, some touch up may be needed at some point.

As you begin to use the ideas presented in this article, as well as come up with many of your own, you will need to have a few basic tools on hand. Here's a list of the common ones needed for most of the projects discussed here:

- PVC pipe—various lengths and diameters
- PVC fittings—various assorted
- Pipe cutter
- Hacksaw
- Tape measure
- Pencils
- Pocket knife
- Sandpaper
- File
- PVC Cleaner
- PVC glue
- Drill
- Screws
- Propane torch, heat bulb, or other device to heat pipe for bending or shaping.

Row hoops at work in the early garden

Let's get started on some simple and useful PVC projects for the homestead.

Row hoops

Possibly one of the best uses for joints of ½-inch PVC pipe is to create a miniature greenhouse in your garden. The material combined with a sheet of heavy clear plastic, can make a great growing season extender in your own garden no matter how large a plot you have.

To construct your row covers, you will first need to cut twice as many 18-inch pieces of ¼-inch reinforcement rod (commonly called re-bar) as you have pieces of PVC pipe. Here on our place, I simply used light metal electric fence posts. They worked very well.

Drive one re-bar or fence post at the proper distance where you want the end of the PVC pipe to be. Continue down along either side of the row at about three or four-foot intervals. Directly across the row or seedbed, set another post. Place one end of the ½-inch pipe over one of the posts. Bend the pipe over like a hoop on an old covered wagon and slide it down over the other post. Repeat this down the row until you get the number of hoops set that you need.

Cut the plastic plenty long, so that you can gather it up and anchor it at the ends with big rocks or blocks. Allow for an extra 12 to 18 inches on either side as well. I used this extra plastic to help anchor the little structure. Simply take a piece of pipe or conduit, and utilizing a helper, hold the edge of the plastic to the pipe and roll it up over the pipe. After rolling it up a few times around the pipe, lay a block or rock on either end of the pipe to anchor the plastic.

PVC storage container

Occasionally, you may be presented with the need to store, cache, or hide items. Perhaps you wish to hide your

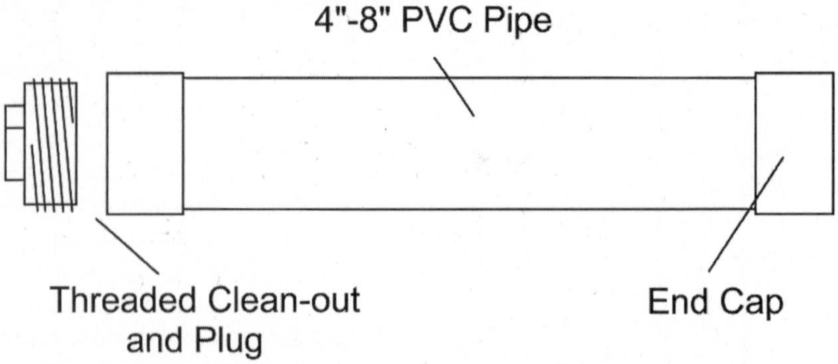

A handy storage container may be made from any size PVC pipe.

egg money in something other than a fruit jar. You may feel the need to put away a firearm and supply of ammunition. Or you may just have something of value which you would like to hide away securely from prying eyes. A simple and durable storage container may be made in a few minutes by using scraps of appropriate sized PVC pipe. All it takes is a section of pipe of the proper diameter and length for the item or items that you are wishing to store. You can

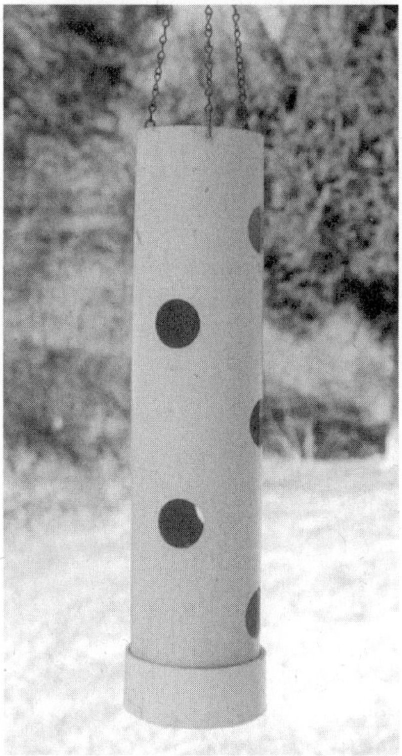

Hanging planter

make these in 4, 6, 8, 10, or even 12-inch diameter.

Glue into place an end cap on one end of the pipe. On the other end, glue into place a collar with female threads to accept the same size male screw-in plug. You are all set.

When using your storage container, you may have the need to use a desiccant to prevent damage to the stored item. This is simply and cheaply done by merely tossing into the container an old sock or other cloth bag filled with rice. The rice will serve as a suitable moisture absorber. Another thing to do is to apply a bead of silicone sealer when you thread the cap into place. This will serve as a final moisture barrier.

Here's another tip. If you choose to put your storage underground, that is, bury it vertically in a post-hole like hole, then consider this: Get a piece of black corrugated plastic drain tile in the next size larger than the PVC container you have. Dig the hole large enough to accommodate the black drain tile. Once it is in place, just drop your PVC container in. Cover with a large flat stone and cover with soil. If you are concerned about finding your storage site later, lay a piece of metal atop the stone before you cover it with earth. This will enable you to locate the site using a metal detector.

PVC hanging planter

An attractive hanging planter can be made from PVC pipe. To create your planter, first locate a piece of 4-inch PVC pipe in the length which you want your planter, something in the area of 16 to 24 inches works well.

Next, bore 1½-inch diameter holes in the pipe at points where you want plants in it. I spaced the holes staggered in rows up and down the piece of pipe; a row of three, turn the pipe 90 degrees, then a row of two. Add another row of three and another row of two turning the pipe as you go.

Next glue an end cap onto the bottom of the pipe with regular PVC cement. Near the center of the end cap, drill three or four small holes to allow for water drainage. At the top of the pipe, drill three holes of about 1/8 inch diameter at points dividing the circumference of the pipe into thirds.

To hang the planter, you may use twine, wire, chain, or whatever you have handy. I used four small S-hooks and some light chain. Equal

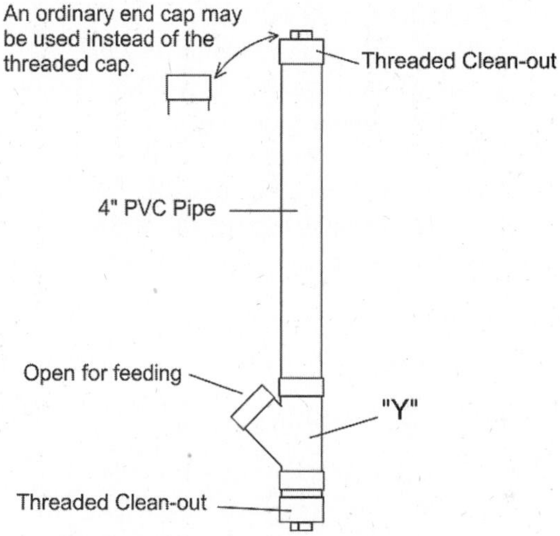

Wildlife, livestock, or pet feeder

lengths of chain (about 12 to 14 inches) were attached to the three small holes using S-hooks. The three pieces of chain were joined at the top by the fourth hook.

You can now add soil and your plants. You may also add a watering tube to the planter if you wish. Merely take a piece of ¾-inch PVC pipe about ½ to 1 inch longer than the planter and drill several small holes up and down its length. Position the small pipe in the center of the planter as you fill it with soil. You will end up with soil packed around the hollow center tube that will permit water to evenly reach all the plants in the planter.

This planter works especially well with plants such as geraniums, or other compact bushy flowers. Compact strawberries could also be planted in one of these planters.

Wildlife, livestock, or pet feeder

Using a piece of four-inch PVC pipe approximately four feet long, glue a threaded clean-out on one end. On the other end, glue a "Y." Using another short piece of pipe about five to six-inches long, glue it into the bottom end of the Y. To that, glue in place another threaded clean-out. This handy feeder can be tied or wired onto a post or tree and used to feed farm animals such as goats or sheep, or wildlife. Merely remove the top threaded cap and pour the pipe full of feed and replace the cap. To occasionally clean out the feeder, you can simply remove the bottom clean-out plug, clean the feeder out, replace the plug and refill.

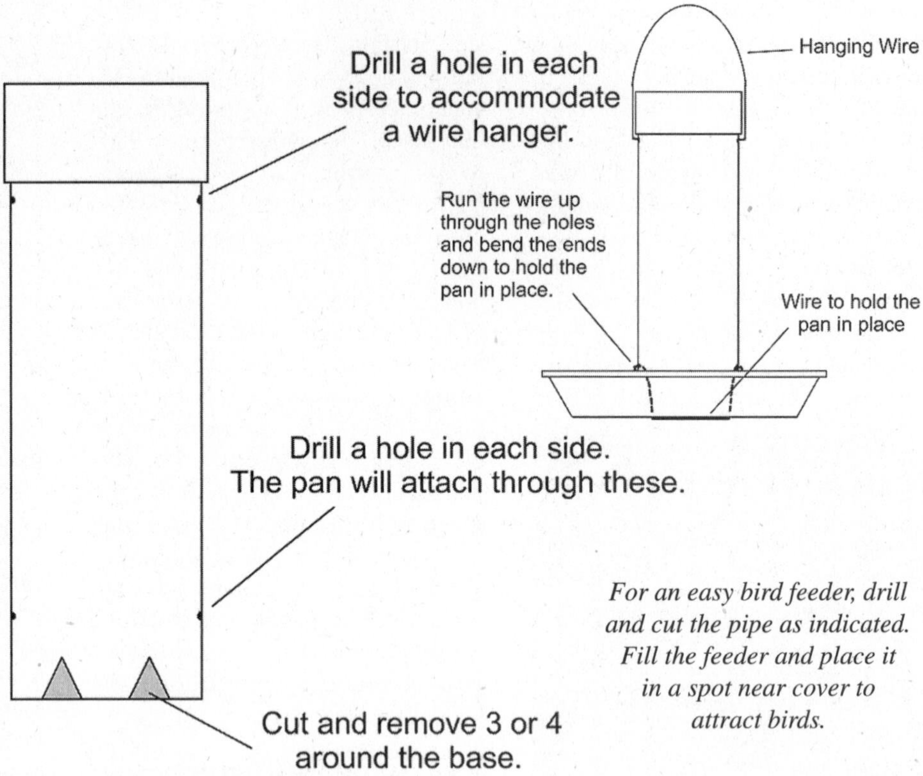
Drill a hole in each side to accommodate a wire hanger.
Hanging Wire
Run the wire up through the holes and bend the ends down to hold the pan in place.
Wire to hold the pan in place
Drill a hole in each side. The pan will attach through these.
Cut and remove 3 or 4 around the base.

For an easy bird feeder, drill and cut the pipe as indicated. Fill the feeder and place it in a spot near cover to attract birds.

Cold frame cover

I made this cover for my cold frame from one-inch PVC pipe and a few fittings. It was designed and cut to fit the area that I had to cover. I cut the pieces to fit and then put it all together without glue to make sure everything fit properly. Next, the whole thing was glued together. I added some strong greenhouse plastic by doubling the ends and attaching it with screws and washers, making sure it was pulled taut all across the frame. Then, it was simply put in place to protect the small plants in the cold frame.

Bird feeder

A simple and easy bird feeder can be made from a short piece of 4-inch PVC pipe, an end cap, some stiff wire, and an old pie pan.

First, cut your pipe in the length that you want your feeder to be; 14 to 18 inches is good. Slide the end cap onto one end of the pipe. Just below where the cap fits, drill a couple of small holes that will take a piece of wire that the feeder will be suspended by.

On the other end, saw out a few notches around the circumference of the pipe. A couple of inches up from this end, drill two more small holes.

Drill two small holes in the bottom of the pie pan at points that will line up with the last two holes you drilled in the pipe, or close to it. Now, run each end of a length of wire from the pan bottom up and through the small holes, from the inside out. Bend the ends of the wire down to securely hold the pan in place.

You can see in the illustration that the wire will hold the pan in place while the notches that you cut in the bottom of the pipe will allow bird feed to settle into the pan. It is also a good idea to drill several small holes in the pie pan to allow rainwater to drain from it.

Cut a piece of wire to use as the hanger. Bends on each end of the wire are inserted into the holes near the top of the pipe. Now just remove the end cap to fill the feeder, then hang it in a good spot near some cover. The birds will soon find it.

You may also paint the feeder as you wish, a solid color, or add some hand-painted flowers, etc.

Bird feeder post (squirrel-proof)

If you are erecting a birdhouse or feeder on a wooden post, squirrels and raccoons can become a real pest. Try this to keep the furry pilferers from climbing up the post. Simply use a section of 4-inch PVC pipe as your post. This will keep uninvited critters from helping themselves. They will not be able to climb up the slick surface of the PVC pipe.

The addition of a toilet flange at the top of the post can provide a sturdy mount for your birdhouse or feeder.

For many more ideas on using PVC Pipe around your place, look for this new book by Charles Sanders: *PVC Projects-101 Uses for PVC Pipe on the Home, Garden, Farm, and Workshop*, by Charles A. Sanders which is published by Burford Books, Springfield, NJ. Available from the *BHM* bookstore. Δ

Grid-tie solar powered farm

By Jeffrey R. Yago, P.E., CEM

Most of my past articles described solar systems that included a battery or batteries to store the collected solar energy. There are many types of solar power systems with battery backup that can be connected to the utility grid. However, technically speaking, a "grid-tie" system refers to a solar power system that transfers all of the electrical power generated directly back into the local utility grid and does not have a battery bank.

Not needing a battery bank can greatly simplify system complexity and reduce installation costs, but by code the system is not allowed to produce any power when the utility grid is down, which means a grid-tie solar system is not suitable for use as an emergency backup power system. It will, however, significantly reduce your monthly utility costs, and since there are no batteries to maintain and periodically replace, there is almost no maintenance involved with a grid-tie solar system.

System components

A grid-tie solar photovoltaic system consists of individual solar modules wired together to create a solar array, one or more inverters to convert the solar DC power to AC grid quality power, and associated switchgear and wiring.

Although almost any size solar module can be used, most grid-tie solar inverters operate at much higher voltages than a typical 12 to 48-volt battery based solar power system, which allows more solar modules to be wired into each series "string." Solar modules for grid-tie systems are usually chosen in the larger 100- to 300-watt per module size range, and usually include prewired weatherproof male and female plug connectors as shown in photo #2.

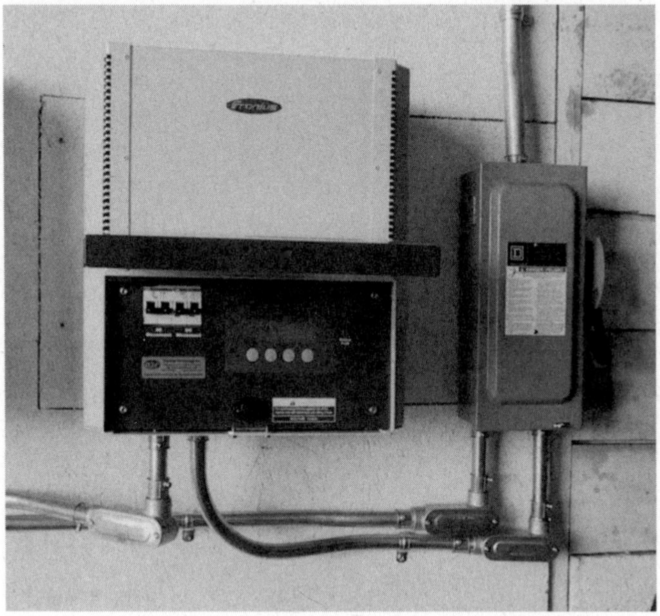

Photo 1: One of two Fronius 3-kW grid-tie inverters. Note the DC-rated safety disconnect and all high voltage wiring installed in metal conduit.

This means high voltage solar array wiring consists of just "plugging" the positive connector of one module into the negative connector of the next module until they are all connected together, with a final positive and negative connection made at the start and end of the array string. A word of caution is in order. Since most grid-tie inverters will allow 16 or more individual modules to be wired in each series string, you could easily be dealing with voltages over 340 volts DC, and this will generate a very large arc and very hazardous conditions if you do not use the proper components and wiring.

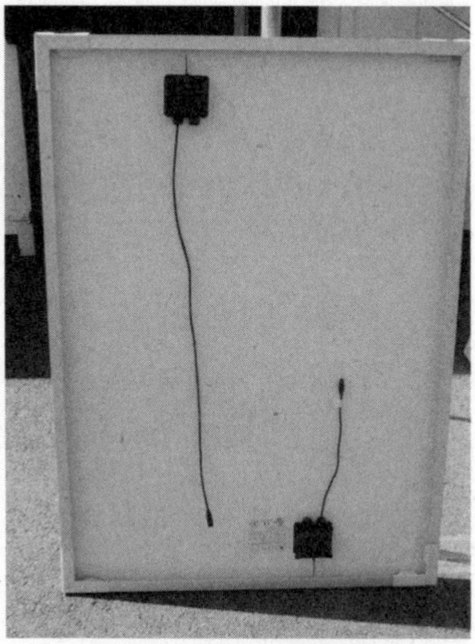

Photo 2: Back view of 165-watt solar module showing preinstalled weatherproof male and female connectors

This grid-tie project required mounting thirty-two 165 watt solar modules on a raised seam metal barn roof. Fortunately, the solar industry now provides precut mounting systems for almost any solar module mounting arrangement, and we found a design that included clamping blocks that anchored the mounting rails directly to the raised seams of the metal barn roof.

Photo 3: Solar array mounting rails and raised seam metal roof clamps

Photo 4: Start of installation of solar modules on raised mounting rails

Photo #3 shows how these adjustable high strength aluminum mounting rails and related stainless steel hardware were attached to this barn roof.

Photo #4 shows the array installation beginning with the attachment of the solar modules to the mounting rails. Since each module just "plugs" into the next, the array wiring is completed as each module is physically attached to the mounting rack.

Utility interconnection

Since you are using the local utility grid as your "battery," not all electric utilities will look kindly to sending electric power back into their utility lines and turning electric meter backwards in the process. You will need to check with your local utility company before installing a grid-tie solar power system to make sure they allow this type of interconnection.

Most states that do require their electric utilities to offer net-metering have a simple, no cost application process. Some utilities will require changing out your existing electric meter to allow them to separately record your electric flows in both directions, while a few electric utilities are still down right hostile to anyone wanting to back-feed power to the grid. Older style mechanical dial electric meters will run backwards for any reverse electrical flow and subtract from the total monthly reading, while most new electronic meters are programmed to ignore any reverse flow. There are currently 35 states that allow utility interconnection or net-metering. Although the utilities that do allow interconnection have different rate structures and billing arrangements, most will allow a monthly carry-forward credit balance, which means those summer months when you generate more power than you use will offset purchased electrical power you used later during the winter months.

Ideally you would like to have any solar electric power sold at the same rate that you purchase electricity. This is called net-metering since you are just paying the difference between what you use and what you produce. However, some utilities only pay a very low rate for the solar power they purchase even though it is being supplied during their afternoon peak load period when their high demand generation costs are much higher.

Utilities operating in states that do allow net-metering usually require your system to include a manual disconnect switch located next to the electric meter so they can "lock-out" the solar power grid connection when they are doing any maintenance on the nearby power lines. Since utility linemen will always earth ground and disable any power lines before they start working, and will most likely not even know if you are located near their repair location, it is doubtful that this switch will ever be actually used. Utilities will also require that you provide documentation that your inverter meets UL 1741, IEEE 929, and NEC Art. 690 code requirements, which ensure the inverter will automatically disconnect from the utility line anytime the grid is not energized.

Photo #6 shows our completed 5,280 watt installation on the south-facing roof of the barn. This system will generate almost all of the power needs of this hay barn, which

Photo 5: Utility required emergency solar disconnect located next to utility meter

Photo 6: Completed solar array on south facing barn roof

includes a repair shop, carpentry shop, and small office.

Although the simplicity of a grid-tie system makes it easy for a do-it-yourselfer to install, if you are not an experienced electrician, I strongly recommend hiring a professional due to the very high voltages involved with these systems. A list of professionally trained and certified solar photovoltaic installation professionals located in each state can be found on the Internet under the North American Board of Certified Energy Practitioners, (NABCEP).

On a final note, although solar power system costs for the same size system will be competitive from state to state, different utility rates, local tax credits, and state rebate or buy-down programs offered in some states and not others can make this either a really good investment or a very poor one. Be sure to find out what utility rates and incentive programs are available in your area before making your final purchasing decision. Δ

Useful references

NABCEP Certified Solar Installers:
www.nabcep.org

List of states allowing interconnection:
www.dsireusa.org

Fronius grid-tie inverters:
www.fronius.com

Solar mounting rail systems:
www.directpower.com

Subduction Zone Tsunami

津波

What the residents of the Pacific Northwest have to fear

By John Silveira

I was sitting in my cubicle poring over a map of the Oregon coast—actually, just that part of the coast that is Gold Beach where *Backwoods Home Magazine* is located. Suddenly, I heard a voice behind me ask, "What map is that, John?"

I just about jumped out of my skin. I turned around and there, standing over me, was O.E. MacDougal, our poker playing friend from southern California. He was holding a grocery bag in his left arm.

"Sorry, I didn't mean to startle you," he said.

"It's okay," I said, "I'm just jumpy."

He nodded "I forgot."

"Tsunami Hazard Map of the Gold Beach Area, Curry County, Oregon," he read from the top of the map. "Are you expecting a tsunami?"

"Well, sort of. I mean, I've been told one will happen sooner or later."

"It will!" he said.

I looked at him. That kind of certainty from Mac was unsettling. "You really think so?"

"Well, this area is one big subduction zone, and you know the old saying, 'It's not a matter of *if*, but *when*.'

"Really!" I said.

"One of the things that's certain from the geological record," Mac went on, "is that there have been plenty of tsunamis, or tidal waves, on this coast before and you can bet that there'll be more. And the odds are pretty good that it will be a big one, possibly much bigger than the one that hit Asia the day after Christmas six months ago. That was caused by an earthquake on a similar subduction zone. The Asia tidal waves killed 250,000 people."

"You're using both terms, Mac. Is there a difference between a tsunami and a tidal wave?" Dave asked. Dave Duffy, the publisher of *BHM*, had just walked in.

"Hi, Dave. Good to see you," Mac said shaking Dave's hand.

"No difference," he continued. "They're also called seismic sea waves, and sometimes they're called names I'd never say in front of small children or my mother. But that's only when they're barreling down on you."

"How do you like the new office?" Dave asked.

"I like it."

"Want a tour?"

"Sure."

"What's in the grocery bag?" Dave asked.

"I told Ilene I'd make lunch. You guys hungry?" Mac asked.

"Sure," Dave and I said in unison.

"Well, I am too, and lunch is what's in the bag, so let me fix it, then we'll take the tour."

We led Mac from my cubicle to the lunchroom.

He placed his bag on one of the counters and proceeded to go to work.

"What are you making for us this time?" Dave asked.

"Sort of a fish salad."

"Your own recipe?"

"Yeah. I'm sure I'm not the first person to come up with this idea, but I'd never seen one before.

"So, what's with the interest in tsunamis?" he asked.

"I want John to write something about them," Dave said. "I watched a TV program on the *Discovery Channel* that stated our Pacific Northwest coastline has a very similar subduction zone to the one that spawned the tsunami waves in Asia. They said it could happen here."

"It has and it could," Mac said. "In fact, it will happen here." He started to shred some lettuce.

"That's what the program said; it's only a matter of when. Mac, what do you know about tsunamis?"

"Well, most tsunamis are caused by earthquakes and that's what's most likely to cause a big one here. But earthquakes aren't the only cause. The next leading causes are submarine landslides, then volcanoes, and least often they're caused by impacts from celestial bodies—like the one that finished off the dinosaurs. That one probably sent a tsunami clear across the Florida peninsula."

The Cascadia Subduction Zone

"But here the chief danger is *tsunamigenic earthquakes*—they're the earthquakes that most often cause tsunamis. They occur at what are called subduction zones."

"Just *what is* a subduction zone?" I asked.

"It's where one of the tectonic plates that makes up the surface of the earth is moving under another one, as opposed to the plates sliding past each other horizontally, as they do in much of Southern California. You have the *Cascadia Subduction Zone* here, and it may be one of the worst in the world when it comes to its potential to spawn a tsunami."

"How would it happen?" I asked.

"At a subduction zone, when the fault between two tectonic plates finally breaks, the plate on one side of the fault bounces up while the plate on the other side often sinks. When this occurs under the ocean it creates a huge 'paddle effect' that moves an enormous amount of water creating a tsunami."

"How big could the tsunami be?" Dave asked.

"There are no hard and fast rules for the sizes tsunamis come in. An earthquake-generated tsunami is usually about 30 feet high. But it's possible a really large earthquake, like one along a major subduction zone such as you have here along your coast, or one that's accompanied by underwater landslides, could cause a tsunami that's 50 to 100 feet high. That's much bigger than the ones that hit Asia. They're unusual, but some geologists feel that could be in the future of the Pacific Northwest coastline because of the severity of the *Cascadia Subduction Zone.*

An East Coast tsunami?

"However, they can be even bigger than that. There are scientists who believe a volcanic eruption in the Canary Islands, off the shore of West Africa, could lead to the collapse of the western flank of the Cumbre Vieja volcano on the island of La Palma. It would create a landslide

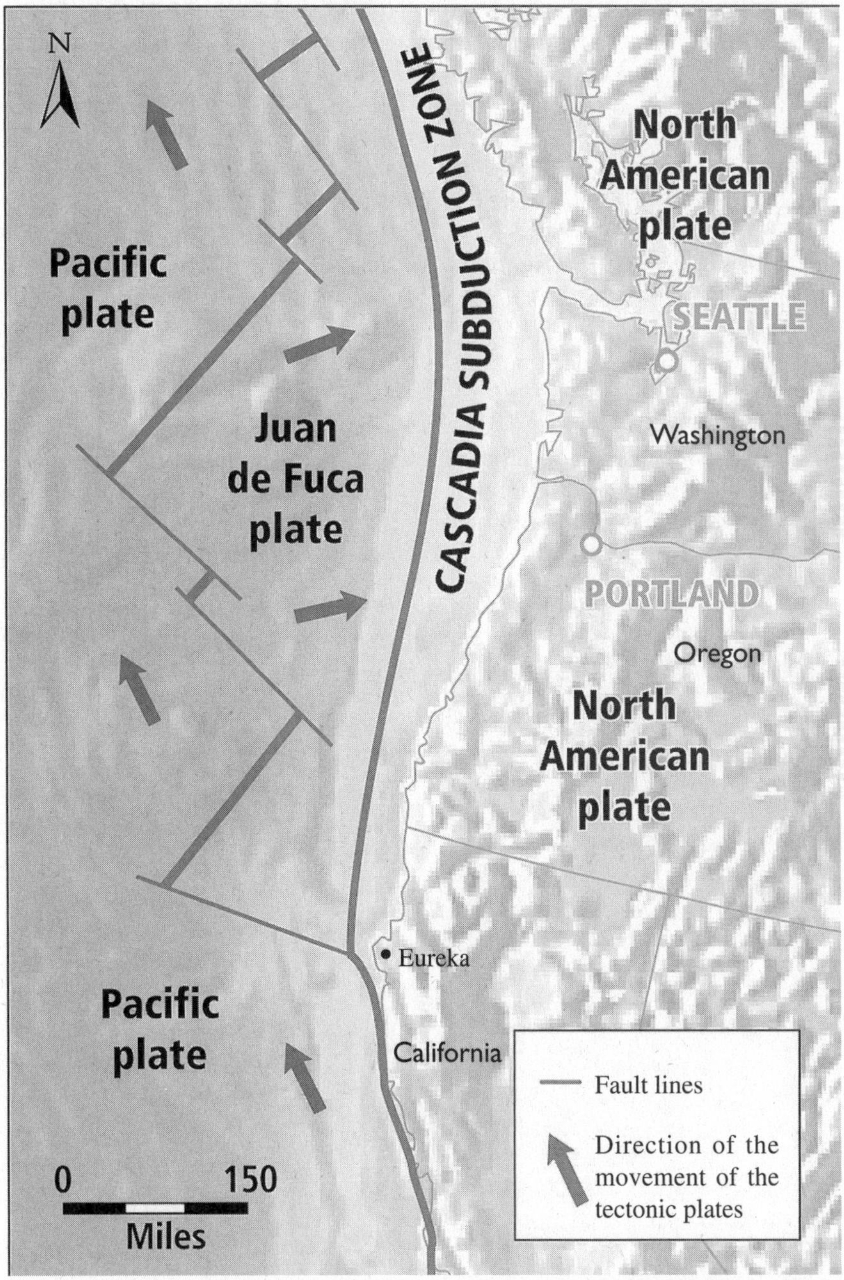

Courtesy U.S. Geological Survey

Where the Juan de Fuca and North American tectonic plates meet they are locked together and form the Cascadia Subduction Zone. Periodically, the plates break apart creating earthquakes capable of generating tsunamis.

that would drop as much as 125 cubic miles of rock into the Atlantic Ocean and create a tsunami at least 150 feet high—and perhaps as much as 300 feet high—that would hit the East Coast from Florida to Maine."

"What would a tsunami like that do?" I asked.

"It would wash inland for miles and cause trillions of dollars in destruction. But the good news is that it would take nine hours before it reached Boston, New York, and other places along the East Coast, allowing plenty of time for warning. The bad news is that there's no in-place warning system or evacuation plan for the Atlantic seaboard so it's likely there would still be a huge loss of life."

"This sounds like science fiction," Dave said.

"It's not. Two of the scientists who have written about it are Dr. Steven Ward of the University of California and Dr. Simon Day of the Benfield Greig Hazard Research Center at University College London."

"How likely is such an event?" Dave asked.

"It's one of those things that no one knows for sure. Volcano prediction is still in its infancy. But sonar mappings of the seabed off the islands have revealed deposits from a dozen or so large collapses that occurred there in the past. So we know it *can and does* happen there, just like it *can and did* happen here."

"Can we get back to the West Coast?" I asked.

Mac was slicing mushrooms. "Okay," Mac said. "A subduction zone like you have here is much different than the faults you have in, say, Southern California, where the fault lines generally move parallel to each other. When the tectonic plates just slide past each other, horizontally, they usually don't create tsunamis. But in a subduction zone, the tectonic plates move over and under each other, and when the earth under the ocean moves up or down like that *suddenly*, it moves an incredible amount of water that creates a tsunami. And it is also possible that the shaking from one of those kinds of earthquakes could cause an underwater landslide, and that in itself can cause a huge displacement of water that creates a tsunami."

"Can you give me an analogy of all this tectonic plate movement stuff?" I asked.

"Imagine the surface of the earth is like a soft boiled egg whose shell is rife with cracks," Mac said. "Some of the pieces of the shell are big while others are small. But unlike an egg, where the pieces stick to the egg, the earth's shell—the tectonic plates—floats on top of nearly molten rock deep inside the earth. That's where

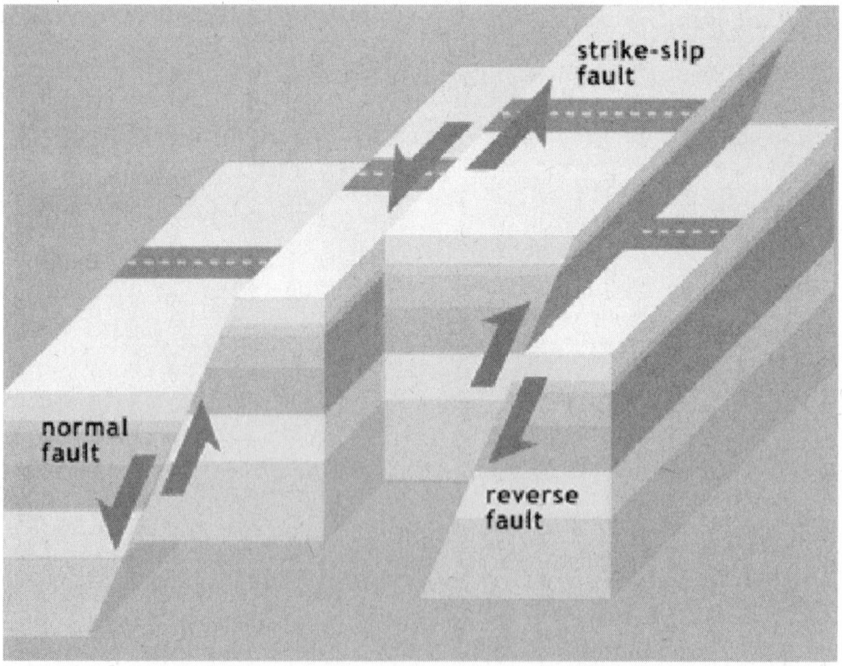

The three basic fault types: the normal fault, where one plate drops down relative to another; the strike-slip fault, where the plates meet evenly and slip horizontally past each other; and the reverse fault, where one plate is thrust up over another. When under water, it is the normal and reverse faults that create the kind of water displacement that can cause tsunamis.

Why they're called

tsunamis

They used to be called tidal waves, but the powers that be don't want to use that term any longer because they fear people will think they're caused by tides, when they're not. But it's not likely the term tidal wave was invented because people thought they were caused by tides. It was invented because the waves seemed to rear up from nothing in the deep ocean and manifest themselves in tidal zones—areas where the ocean and the land meet.

So we've replaced it with the Japanese word *tsunami* which, in Japanese, means harbor wave.

Does that mean the Japanese thought the waves were caused by harbors? No. They used it because the waves seem to rise up from nothing and do their worst damage in harbors. But I guess the theory is that if we use a foreign word, no one will question what it means.

we are, living on these pieces of shell that are literally floating on this nearly molten rock. Some float past each other like barges floating on a river, but others crash head-on, with one trying to go under the other."

"And where they're trying to go over and under each other is called a subduction zone," Dave said.

"That's right. Earthquakes occur because all the plates, whether they're moving horizontally against each other or trying to move over and under each other, tend to hang up on each other along their edges. Meanwhile, the motion of the nearly molten rock beneath tries to keep them moving. The forces that are trying to move them start to accumulate. Eventually, those forces get so strong that something has to give, and the fault literally breaks, and when all that energy is released, *wham!* That's your earthquake. And here along the Pacific Northwest coast, that's the likely trigger for your tsunami."

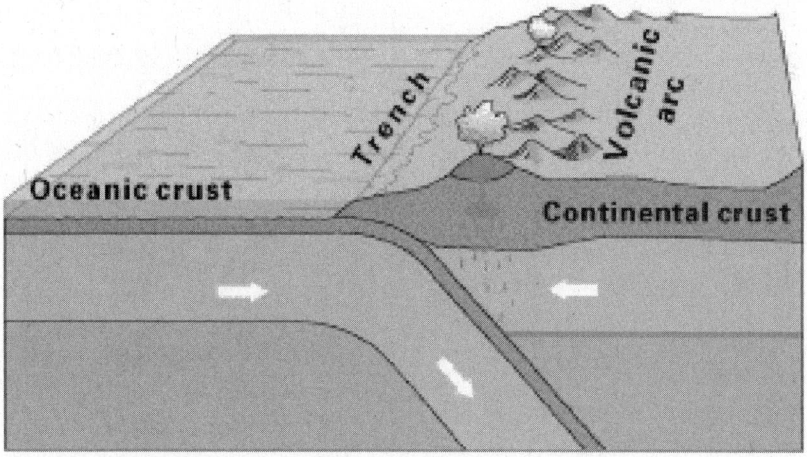

A cross-section illustrating what the Cascadia subduction zone looks like. Where the Juan de Fuca (left) and North American tectonic plates (right) collide, the dense rock that underlies the ocean tries to go under the lighter continental crust. Where the plates collide a subduction zone is formed. The movement of the plates doesn't go smoothly and they hang up on each other forming a "fault." As pressure builds up, the continental plate, including part that is submerged, buckles upward while the oceanic plate bends downward. When the pressure becomes too much, the fault breaks creating an earthquake. Meanwhile, with the pressure gone, the continental plate suddenly sinks lower while the oceanic plate springs up. The up and down actions displace billions of tons of water that create a tsunami.

"How powerful can they get? Is there a limit to an earthquake's size?" I asked.

"There appears to be. The reason you won't see too many quakes that go much over a 9.5 on the Richter scale is because the rocks just can't hold much more energy without breaking. The largest recorded earthquake in history was the 9.5 Chilean earthquake of 1960. It's possible that one could be a little larger, but there's a limit, somewhere. Maybe it's 10, maybe it's a little higher."

"Exactly what is the Richter?" I asked.

He was cutting up a red bell pepper, and paused as if to search his memory. "It's a scale of measurement invented by two guys, Charles Richter and Beno Gutenberg, for quantifying the magnitude of earthquakes."

The Richter Scale

"But how do the numbers on the scale work?" Dave asked. "I mean, it doesn't seem like there should be much of a difference between an earthquake that's a 4 on the Richter scale and one that's a 7. Yet, there is."

"It's a logarithmic scale," Mac replied, "and first you've got to understand what a logarithmic scale is.

"Using what's called a *common logarithm*, the number 10 is represented by the number 1, the number 100 by the number 2, the number 1,000 by the number 3..."

"It sounds like powers of 10," Dave said. "10 to the first power is equal to 10, 10 to the second power is 100, 10 to the third power is 1000."

"You've got it," Mac said. "So, when you go from an earthquake that's measured as a 4 on the Richter scale to one that's a 5, the one that's a 5 is 10 times more powerful than the one that's a 4."

Dave said, "So if you go from a 4 to a 7, it's three powers of 10 making a 7..." He paused for a second and mumbled under his breath, "...10 times 10 times 10 ...

"1000 times more powerful than a 4," he said out loud.

"Right," Mac said.

"So when you're talking about a 9, that's gotta be one *huge* earthquake," Dave said.

"It's a monster," Mac replied.

"It's 100,000 times greater than a 4," Dave said.

"That's right," Mac replied.

"Another mystery cleared up," Dave said. "But I have another question. Is there a nuclear bomb equivalent to the Richter scale? I mean, they're always comparing volcanic explosions and hurricanes to atom bombs."

"Sort of. The Richter scale measures the intensity of a quake. But how much energy is released depends on both the intensity and how long the quake lasts.

"Typically, a 5 on the Richter scale releases about 1½ times as much energy as the atom bomb dropped on Nagasaki. A 6 on the scale is like a one-megaton bomb or about 50 Nagasaki bombs exploding.

"Each whole number increase on the Richter scale translates into about 30 times more energy released.

"The Northridge, California, earthquake of 1994 was a 6.7." He picked up the calculator. "Figure it released about as much energy as a five-megaton bomb, or about 500 Nagasaki bombs."

"Wow!" was all I could say.

"What about the San Francisco earthquake of 1906?" Dave asked.

"That's a tough one," Mac said. "The traditional number assigned to it is 8.25, though it may have been smaller, but we'll go with 8.25."

He pushed a few keys on the calculator. "It released the energy of some 95,000 Nagasaki bombs going off in the ground under the city."

"The numbers are becoming incomprehensible," I said.

"They are," Mac agreed.

"What about the quake in Indonesia?" Dave asked. "I understand that was about a 9.3."

Using the calculator again, he said, "It was like more than three million of those bombs going off in one place. But keep in mind, these are just rough figures."

"Yeah, but it gives me an appreciation for just how powerful earthquakes can be," Dave said.

Mac was now putting a variety of seasonings on the salad.

"Here's another thing about tsunamis. Although the dangerous ones are the ones that are caused by earthquakes at subduction zones, there are some other factors. For example, the more shallow they are, the bigger they are. The really dangerous ones are those generated by earthquakes centered 30 miles or less below the earth's surface, in an ocean, near a subduction zone, and with a magnitude of 8.5 or greater. And they're even worse if they also cause an underwater landslide.

"You said landslides are the second most common cause of tsunamis," Dave said.

Mac put the salad in the refrigerator, then started seasoning a piece of red snapper as we watched. "That's right."

"I presume a landslide causes a tsunami just by creating an almost instantaneous displacement of water," Dave said.

"That's exactly how they do it."

"And it's possible they could get as big as 300 feet high, like the one that could come out of the Canary Islands?" Dave asked.

"Bigger. The highest tsunami on record was caused by a landslide in Lituya Bay in Alaska in 1958. The landslide itself was triggered by an earthquake, but the tsunami was caused by the earth that slid off a mountain and fell into the bay."

"How big was it?" I asked.

"It depends on how you measure it. Some say it was 1720 feet high."

"Yikes!" I said. "That's like a third of a mile high."

"But...the 1720 feet was actually how high it ran up on the mountain on the other side of the bay. The wall of water itself, as it crossed the bay, was anywhere from 150 to 500 feet high. No one knows for sure. We have eyewitness accounts from two of the three fishing boats that were in the bay at the time."

"What about the third boat?" I asked.

"The crew drowned when their boat capsized."

"The other two boats rode out the tsunami?" Dave asked.

"It was a miracle," Mac responded.

"Why didn't it create damage further away? Like across the ocean?" I asked.

A homeschooling project

Comparing earthquakes with a calculator

You can readily use a common calculator to compare the magnitudes of earthquakes, as long as the calculator has an *exponent key*, usually designated as x^y. (The calculator included in Microsoft's Windows operating system has such a calculator. When you access it, turn on the *scientific* view.) For every whole number increase on the Richter scale, the increase in the magnitude is tenfold. So, when comparing a 7 on the Richter scale to one that measures 5:

- enter 10 in the calculator and press the exponent key
- in your head subtract 5 from 7...it's 2
- enter 2 in the calculator
- press the "=" key...you'll get 100

This also works for fractional numbers. To compare the Northridge, California, earthquake of 1994 (a 6.7 on the Richter scale) with the Indonesian quake of 2004 (a 9.3):

- enter 10 in the calculator and press the exponent key
- in your head subtract 6.7 from 9.3...it's 2.6
- enter 2.6 in the calculator
- press the "=" key...you'll get 398.1...with a whole bunch of other trailing numbers

So, the Indonesian earthquake was about 400 times greater in magnitude than the Northridge quake.

"Even though it was high, it was only a few miles wide. When it left the bay and entered into the vastness of the open ocean, it dissipated rapidly.

"On the other hand, an earthquake-generated tsunami is going to start out at least as long as the fault that creates it—the one in Sumatra was some 750 miles long. Waves that broad don't dissipate quickly."

"Is there any danger to us here, on the West Coast of the United States, from landslide-generated tsunamis?" I asked.

He put some olive oil and sesame oil in a skillet he had heating, then added the fish. "There can be. Earthquakes can cause landslides along any of the continental shelves that lie off our coasts. The earthquake wouldn't even have to be that severe. All it would have to do is trigger a large underwater slide and the resultant displacement of seawater could cause a catastrophic tsunami that would be out of proportion to the magnitude of the quake.

"For example, there's a fear that, though the faults in Southern California are not the type that directly cause tsunamis, they may be capable of producing a landslide off the continental shelf that runs along the coast there. And that could cause a massive tsunami that would send a wall of water into Los Angeles and other cities along the coast like Long Beach, Malibu, Oxnard, and Ventura.

"Worse, since the edge of the continental shelf on the West Coast is so close to the shore, the wave could take as little as one minute to rush onto the beaches."

"It would be on top of people before they even had a chance to think about it," Dave said as Mac turned the fish over.

"And you said volcanoes can also cause tsunamis," I said.

"Underwater volcanoes can cause them either by an explosion where the pyroclastic flow explodes into the water, by landslides, or by collapses of an underwater caldera.

"The eruption of Krakatoa in 1883, though above sea level, caused a landslide that generated a 100-foot tsunami that swept up onto the coasts of Java and Sumatra and killed some 34,000 people."

"What's a pyroclastic flow?" I asked.

"Do you recall seeing sequences of photos from Mt. St. Helens when it erupted? Remember seeing an explosive cloud of ash, dust, and gasses that sped across the landscape?"

"Yes," I said. "*National Geographic* did quite a spread on it."

"That's pyroclastic flow. It would expand like an A-bomb going off underwater."

"What's a caldera collapse?" I asked.

"The caldera is the volcanic crater. Sometimes during an eruption, the caldera collapses. This happens both above and below sea level. But when it happens below sea level, the almost instantaneous displacement of a huge amount of water can generate a tsunami. When it happens above sea level, it can cause a landslide that falls into the ocean.

"It's also thought that an explosive volcano could expose enough hot magma to cause an underwater explosion as the seawater rapidly turns into steam. This actually has a name; it's called a phreatic explosion.

Dave said, "You said the biggest tsunamis of all can be created by..."

"...meteors," Mac said. "It's suspected that a comet or an asteroid could cause a tsunami that's both high, like those that can be generated by landslides or caldera collapses, and massive like those created at faults. Some scientists estimate that the asteroid that is thought to have driven the dinosaurs into extinction, when it created the Chicxulub crater in the Gulf of Mexico, sent a 400-foot tsunami that was miles thick into the Florida peninsula. It may well have swept all the way to the Atlantic. Incidentally, today there is no point of land in the entire state of Florida that's over 345 feet in height."

"So, if that happened again..." I asked.

"There'd be no high ground to run to."

He turned the fish over one more time and it was done. He took it out of the pan and let it cool.

"So, are we in any real danger here in Oregon?" Dave asked.

Mac smiled without humor. "The Cascadia Subduction Zone is a fault that lies about 20 to 100 miles off the northwest coast. It's real close here, in southwestern Oregon. It's about 680 miles long and runs from roughly Cape Mendocino, in California, to Vancouver Island in Canada's British Columbia.

"A *major* break in the fault along the Cascadia Subduction Zone would cause the sea floor on one side of the fault to bounce some 20 feet, maybe more, while the other side sunk, and this will create huge ocean waves, some of which will rush into shore here. You'll have less than 30 minutes to get out of their way. Actually, I heard one geologist say that here, in southwestern Oregon, you may have as little as five minutes."

"Will the quake itself be a big one?" Dave asked.

"Possibly as big or bigger than the one they had the day after this last Christmas in Indonesia. It'll last about five minutes, and if the whole fault goes it's likely to be a 9 or better on the Richter scale. So, when the shaking stops, be ready to head for higher ground. The waves will be hitting the shore before you know it."

"Five minutes of shaking and the waves may get to shore in five minutes?" I asked. "Do you mean the shaking may stop just as the tsunami hits?"

Mac nodded with a sardonic smile. "It's possible."

"And did you say 'waves'?" Dave asked. "*Plural*? As in *more than one*?"

"Yes. I should have said it earlier. Tsunamis are actually trains of waves. There could be four, five, maybe more. And they'll be anywhere from 15 minutes to an hour apart. And there's no way to know ahead of time which ones will be the biggest. Worse, if there are major aftershocks in the days following the first quake, they may be accompanied by even more tsunamis."

"I guess our consolation is that we'll at least get some warning of the approaching tsunami from the shaking caused by the earthquake itself," I said.

"Most likely, but that's not a certainty either. Sometimes, an earthquake may not feel like much to those on land because so much of the energy released is absorbed by the seawater. In that case, with the ocean absorbing most of the energy, the resulting tsunami can still be huge even though the ground doesn't seem to have been shaken much at all. It's thought that that's what happened in Nicaragua in 1992. The earthquake was generated at a subduction zone, like the one you have here off the coast, but it was barely felt by people on land. However, it was followed by a tsunami that surprised everyone and was catastrophic."

"And, from what you said, a minor earthquake could cause an underwater landslide off our coast, and that could spawn a tsunami too," Dave said as if in deep thought.

"Right."

"Good grief," I said. "Do you know how much trouble I'm going to have sleeping tonight? I only live a few hundred yards from the beach."

"Move," Mac said.

Dave laughed. Then he said, "So we should head for high ground with even a tiny earthquake."

"If you live on the coast, you should really consider it."

History of Cascadia fault

"Have there been big quakes here before?" I asked.

"We know from the geologic records that earthquakes have taken place along the Cascadia fault, irregularly, about every 500 to 600 years, for the last 10,000 years."

"What do you mean 'irregularly'? Dave asked.

"It's not a 500 or 600-year 'cycle,' it's an average. They run from about 100 years apart to about 1,000 years apart. And each was accompanied by tsunamis that swept ashore."

"How can the geologists tell there've been earthquakes here in the distant past, when there's no written history about them?" I asked.

"What they're doing is radiocarbon dating of organic material in the layers of sand, called turbidites, that come from underwater landslides the earthquakes cause. From that they know there have been about 20 major earthquake events off the coast here just in the last 10,000 years."

"When was the last big one?" Dave asked.

"On January 26, 1700, the whole 680-mile Cascadia fault let go. There were no writers in this part of North America at that time chronicling the event, though there are legends of that quake that come down through the local tribes. Then, a few years ago, geologists in Japan informed their counterparts here in North America that there had been a quake of at least 8.5 magnitude, and probably greater than a 9, that occurred the evening of January 26, 1700. They know the date because the Japanese have kept records of tsunamis since the 1500s and one hit their shores January 27, 1700, with waves more than 15 feet high. American geologists studying tree rings knew an earthquake had happened around that time. Suddenly they had the exact date. Estimates are that the first waves took about 10 hours to get from here to Japan, a distant of about 5,000 miles."

"That's like 500 miles an hour," I said.

He took the salad out of the refrigerator and broke up the cooled fish into it. Then he added some olive oil and vinegar dressing. He was thinking.

"It's done," he said.

We scooped some of his salad out into plates and tasted it.

"Holy cow," Dave said. "This is good."

"Let's go back to the office," Dave said.

Just then, Ilene, Dave's wife and the magazine's business manager and managing editor, came into the kitchen.

"It's ready," Mac said to her.

"Good, I've been waiting," she said as we left.

Back in the editorial part of the magazine I said, "So, the only tsunami danger to the East Coast is one coming from the Canaries, right?"

"Relatively speaking, they're in less danger. Some 75 percent of all tsunamis take place here in the Pacific. But on the East Coast, they're still in danger from tsunamis from other sources. One is the Mid-Atlantic Ridge, a chain of underwater mountains that runs up the middle of the Atlantic Ocean. It's seismically active making it another possible source of underwater landslides that could trigger tsunamis that could endanger North and South America, Europe, and Africa. And there's the danger of landslides off the edge of the continental shelf there.

"There's also a subduction zone in the Caribbean Sea. Earthquakes that originate there could trigger tsunamis along the Atlantic and Gulf coasts. In 1946, an earthquake-generated tsunami killed at least 1800 people in the Dominican Republic.

"There's the potential for tsunamis that comes to us from Europe. A tsunami generated by the great

Lisbon earthquake of 1755 reached across the Atlantic and was felt in the Caribbean Islands and even the northeastern coast of South America. But, for some reason, there's no record of it hitting the Atlantic Coast of what was to become the United States."

"Why wouldn't it have hit here?" Dave asked.

"I don't think anyone knows. But it may have been something as simple as the Mid-Atlantic Ridge I just talked about. It reaches all the way from the Arctic Ocean to the southern tip of Africa, and in some spots it's above sea level. The ridge may serve as a barrier in some places, or even a mirror of sorts, reflecting most of the tsunami back to Europe. If you look at the Azores, they rest on an underwater plateau and are in a line between the part of Europe where Lisbon is located and the East Coast of the United States. So that plateau may have blocked most of it; if a small amount of the tsunami reached here, it may not have been enough for chroniclers of the time to have made note of it. But that's just speculation on my part."

"So, where we are in the Pacific Northwest, particularly here in Gold Beach, what kind of danger are we in?"

"Danger is a relative term. On any given day, your chances of dying in an auto accident or any one of scores of other ways is greater than your danger of getting killed by a tsunami. That said, a tsunami is still going to strike here."

Tsunami from afar

"It could come from a distant source, or one right off your coast."

"How far can the ones that form across the Pacific reach?" Dave asked.

"The Chilean earthquake of 1960 sent a tsunami from the southern hemisphere to the northern hemisphere that reached Hawaii after 15 hours where it killed 61 people. It continued on and reached Japan after 22 hours where it killed twice that number."

"That fast?" I asked.

"Figure a tsunami travels at 450 to 600 miles per hour in deep water—about as fast as many commercial jetliners."

"How will we know if one's coming from far away?" I asked. "It's not like we're going to feel an earthquake in China."

"There's now a tsunami warning system in the Pacific. If a tsunami originated from Asia or Alaska, we'd know it and have hours in which to evacuate to high ground."

"But that's not the one we're really worried about, is it?" Dave said.

"No. With the Cascadia Subduction Zone just some 20 to 100 miles off your coast, you may be an eyewitness to the largest tsunami in recorded history. It could be as big as 100 feet."

"Yikes!" I exclaimed.

"What happens when it hits the shore?" I asked.

"It'll stop just long enough to ask directions to your house," Dave said.

Mac laughed and I have to admit, I did, too.

"It will slow down," Mac said. "When a tsunami enters shallow water, it slows down, but it also gets higher."

He looked at Dave and laughed again. He shook his head. "Ask for directions to John's house," he muttered under his breath. Then he continued. "A tsunami wave that is a few inches to a few feet high in the deep ocean can get to 50 feet high, or even higher, when it hits the beach. No longer doing 600 miles an hour, it's now going about 30 miles per hour. You'll never outrun it without a humungous head start."

"Why do they get so high near shore?" I asked.

"In deep water, these waves reach from the top of the ocean to the ocean floor. In mid-ocean they may be just a few inches or feet higher than the ocean's surface. But when they come into shallow water, all that displaced water—a column of water that may reach 12,000 feet from the ocean's surface to its bottom—gets funneled into a smaller and smaller space. That huge column represents energy.

Mac's fish salad

Salad basis:

Iceberg lettuce, shredded
Tomatoes, sliced
Cucumber, peeled and sliced
Red bell pepper, cut in small strips
Mushrooms, sliced
Avocado, sliced
Garlic powder
Onion powder
Black pepper, freshly ground
Salt to taste
Oil and vinegar dressing

* * * * * * * * * *

Fish:

Italian seasoning
Garlic powder
Onion powder
Salt to taste
Black pepper, freshly ground
Cayenne pepper to taste
Olive oil
Sesame oil (optional, but good)

1. Put the veggie stuff for the salad in a large mixing bowl.
2. Put the seasonings on the veggies and toss. (**Don't** put the dressing on yet.)
3. Put the bowl in the refrigerator until you finish preparing the fish.
4. Coat the fish with the seasonings and sauté in the olive oil (with a touch of sesame oil in it).
5. When the fish is done, break up into bite-size or smaller pieces.
6. Take the salad from the refrigerator and add the fish to the salad.
7. Add the dressing and toss again.

When the energy is compressed, the wave correspondingly expands."

"How far are you above sea level, John?" Dave asked.

Fleeing a tsunami

I didn't answer. "So," I said, "if the Cascadia fault goes, the evacuation must be essentially complete within just a few minutes."

"Well..." Mac paused, "...possibly a little bit sooner. It depends on how the wave comes in. Significant inundation can begin well before the peak of the wave hits."

"I guess I'll just hop in my car and scoot," I said.

Mac smiled that humorless smile again. "I don't mean to rain on your parade," he said, "but one of the problems is that if the tsunami is caused by a major earthquake in the Cascadia fault—one that's an 8.5 or bigger—it'll drop buildings, power poles, and live power lines onto the road. It may also make driving difficult enough to cause accidents that block the roads. But, more so, it's pretty likely that it will tear up the roads so badly that you won't be able to drive away from it. Driving is likely to be out of the question."

"So you may have to leave on foot and literally run for your life," Dave said.

"Run for high ground," Mac said.

"Oh, that's cheery," I said. "Now I've got to find out where the high ground is in my neighborhood."

Dave suddenly looked up at the ceiling as if thinking. "You know," he began, "I remember seeing something on TV about how tsunamis are preceded by a big outrush of water from the beaches. Sometimes it moves out so fast that it leaves fish flopping in the mud."

"Any time you see the water rush out to sea, exposing seabed you've never seen before, you can bet it's coming back in as a tsunami," Mac said. "So you've got to get to high ground immediately. It may be the only warning you'll get.

"But not every tsunami is preceded by the water going out. So if you feel the ground shaking or you hear a tsunami alert, and you're not already on high ground, get there as fast as you can. Don't wait to see what the ocean's doing."

"What determines whether or not the water rushes out or not?" I asked.

"The side of the fault you're on. In a subduction zone, when the fault breaks, one side will suddenly sink and the other side will bounce up. The wave radiating from the side that sinks will start out as a trough or a 'negative' wave. If it's headed for the shore, the tsunami will start with the water rushing out to sea. When the trough hits the shore it's called *down-draw*. The outrushing of water may be your only warning that the wave's crest is coming in right behind it. Usually, the continental side of a subduction zone will get the trough first because it's the side that's been buckling up, and now it will suddenly sink.

"The wave generated on the other side of the fault will start out as a crest, or a 'positive' wave. When the crest hits the shore it's called *run-up*. Other than the quake itself, there will be no warning except for the arrival of a wall of water."

"Which one do you think will arrive here in Gold Beach first?" I asked.

"From the looks of it, it'll be a negative wave."

"So, the water will rush out, first," Dave said.

"That's the way it looks," Mac replied. "Then it will be followed by a massive wall of water."

"Won't the quake itself kill most of the people?" I asked.

"Maybe not. In the recent earthquake in Asia, most of the people who died were killed by the tsunami spawned by the quake. The same could happen here, with most deaths by tsunami instead of earthquake."

"Let's say the quake happens," Dave began. "If the highest wave we can expect to see from one generated out here on the Cascadia Subduction Zone is a 100-footer, is anyone above 100 feet elevation safe? I mean, does John just have to figure out where there's a point near his house that's 100 feet above sea level and go there if there's a quake?"

"No. That may not be enough. There are other factors that figure in. For example, the topography of the land below the waterline can change a wave's height. Underwater canyons can channel the wave—it's called 'focusing'—and a wave that should be just 30 feet high may get focused and come ashore as a 60- or 100-foot wave. And, of course, that means that other spots on the shore would necessarily receive smaller waves.

"It's one of the things about coastal cities: more often than not they're founded where there are good harbors formed by underwater canyons. Those canyons can focus the wave.

"Another thing that can change the appearance of a tsunami are changes to the tectonic plate you're standing on. When this Cascadia Subduction Zone gives, this side of the fault is expected to sink anywhere from two to eight feet, so a tsunami, regardless of its height, is going to appear to be higher just because the land will have sunk."

"Does that mean parts of the coastline here are going to be underwater after the quake?" Dave asked.

"Most likely."

"For how long?"

"Until more pressure builds up and buckles the plate again, bending it up."

"The airport here in Gold Beach is just above sea level," Dave said. "So, for all intents and purposes, it *could* be underwater for years after a major earthquake."

"If this shore falls far enough, it will."

"How far inland can a wave go?" I asked.

"Depending on the size of the wave and local geography—like how flat the area is that gets hit—a large tsunami could wash anywhere from a few hundred yards to a couple of miles inland.

"On the other hand, because tsunamis will also wash up rivers, river cities several miles from the ocean can be struck by tsunamis. It would depend on how the wave hit the river and the geographical factors.

"It's worth noting that the tsunami from the 1964 Alaskan earthquake was detected 100 miles up the Columbia River. Not that it did damage that far upriver, just that it was detected there."

"Is there any way to know how far the waves might go locally?" I asked.

"If you put 'Oregon tsunami maps' in an Internet search engine it'll take you right to a website that has the historic tsunami inundation boundary. But keep in mind, you may be looking at old maps with inundation boundaries expected for a 30-foot or so wave. Right now, for the Northwest, they're preparing maps for larger waves. They should be up on the web soon. Nonetheless, until they do put them up, the maps they're publishing now show elevation contour lines that are useful in trying to guess the boundary of larger waves."

"Well, now that I know I may not be able to drive away at the first signs of shaking, I'm out of my house and up the hill at the end of my street," I said.

"No you're not," Mac said. "If the whole fault lets go, the ground is going to move with .7g acceleration."

"What's that mean?" I asked.

"Well, 'g' is the acceleration of gravity, 32 feet per second per second; .7g is about 22 or 23 feet per second per second. In other words, the ground will be moving back and forth underneath you with about three quarters the acceleration of gravity. And everything—your house, the roads, the trees—will be going back and forth with it. So, don't bet on being able to stand, much less run, for several minutes. That means the furniture in your house is going to start moving around. So, if you've taken refuge under a table, hold on to it and try to move with it; otherwise your cover is going to slide away and you can get hit by falling objects."

"How should you prepare?" Dave asked.

"First, keep you glasses near your bed. I know that sounds dumb, but you don't want to be looking for them when the shaking starts. I'd keep them where you can find them in the dark.

"Second, keep shoes next to your bed, too. When the big one hits, things will be falling and windows will be breaking. You won't want to get up and be stepping on glass in your bare feet, especially if the power has gone out and it's the middle of the night.

"You should also have a survival plan that includes food and fresh water to last you at least several days. If the Cascadia fault goes, rescue workers may be tied up in the bigger cities. In the little town of Gold Beach and in its rural surroundings, people could be isolated for weeks. You should also have something like a three-day survival pack you can grab. You should have a medical kit. You should also have one for your car, just in case you can drive away."

"We've had stuff like that in the magazine," Dave said.

"And keep in mind, wherever you go, every foot farther from the shore, and every foot higher in elevation, helps.

"What's the likelihood of another earthquake here, in the Cascadia Subduction Zone?" Dave asked.

"It depends on how much time into the future you're talking. I can say, with virtual certainty, there's going to be another one *someday*, but the scientists who do this stuff figure that in the next 50 years there's a 10 to 20 percent chance you'll have a big one here. The further into the future you figure this, the more likely one will occur.

"But seismology is an inexact science. Scientists are trying to find some way of predicting or forecasting them. At this point, there are certain things they expect to see before the Cascadia fault does go, and right now they're not seeing many of them."

Just then, Ilene passed through the office. "Mac, that's the best salad I've ever had."

"Thank you," he responded.

"I want the recipe."

I'll write it down," he said, and she left.

"I think I'll have some soup," Dave said. Δ

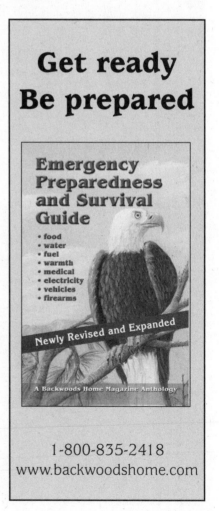

Make shade when the sun shines

Above and below, awnings on the main house

By Dorothy Ainsworth

While others are basking in the sun, and loving it, I run for the shade. I know there would be no life at all without that huge ball of hydrogen fusion radiating down on us, but after being scorched a few times, my motto is: *"Use it but diffuse it."* Sunlight and heat, over time, will oxidize, vaporize, and brutalize everything it blares down on that isn't protected.

After building my vertical-log home and piano studio a few years ago, (see *BHM* issues #27 & #86) I've been watching the logs on their southern faces dry, crack, and bleach out in spite of restaining them regularly. Last summer I decided to protect them from the direct rays of the sun, once and for all, with nice big awnings.

Like most DIY projects, I started out with a little research. I looked on the internet for sample fabrics and custom-made-awnings and their prices. I entered the dimensions and styles I wanted for the main house and optimistically clicked on "quote." $4000 popped up—$1000 in materials and $3000 in labor. Gulp! Excuse me while I gasp for air. I earn $8.50 an hour as a prep-cook making chicken shish-kabobs. I figured out I would have to make 10,000 shish-kabobs to *have* the job done, or 2,500 to do it myself. Either way it's a lot of

Above: *View from my loft bedroom—nice diffused light in the morning sun.*
Left: *The same awning, as viewed from the outside.*

"skewering," but 2,500 was the number I was willing to make for shade.

Fortunately, I know the "awning guy" here in town, and he agreed to order the special weather resistant awning fabric I needed (Sunbrella), at cost plus 10%. He has plenty of business from people who *want* a professional job and *can* pay for labor, so he was kind enough to help out this do-it-yourselfer. Note: You can expect to pay $12 to $20 a yard for fabric.

I don't have a welder or a tubing bender, so I turned to what I'm familiar with for the awning frames: pipe construction. It doesn't take a lot of skill to use a couple of pipe wrenches together. That's why they call 'em "monkey wrenches." (Well, cousins to monkey wrenches for you tool purists.) I also know how to use a sewing machine, so I was all set to tackle the project.

Here's how I did it

"I measured and measured and fussed and fussed, but in spite of mistakes, I never once cussed!" It's one thing to see an awning already up on a house and say, "Oh, no biggie; that looks easy," and quite another to wave your wobbly tape measure around in thin air trying to get exact measurements, especially in a breeze.

I had drawn the basic layout on paper first, so I filled in the measurements as I took them. The math in the layout stage has to be extremely accurate—adding up the lengths of all the tees and nipples and unions that go in-between the long pipe pieces, and the elbows that go on the ends. In my case, all those fittings and pipes, when screwed tightly together, had to total exactly 19 feet. After much deliberation and preplanning I finally completed my pipe order and took it to the hardware store where they cut and threaded the various lengths of ½-inch galvanized pipe on the list. I bought the fittings at the same time and couldn't wait to get home to assemble the frame flat on the deck to make sure it ended up as a rectangle instead of a

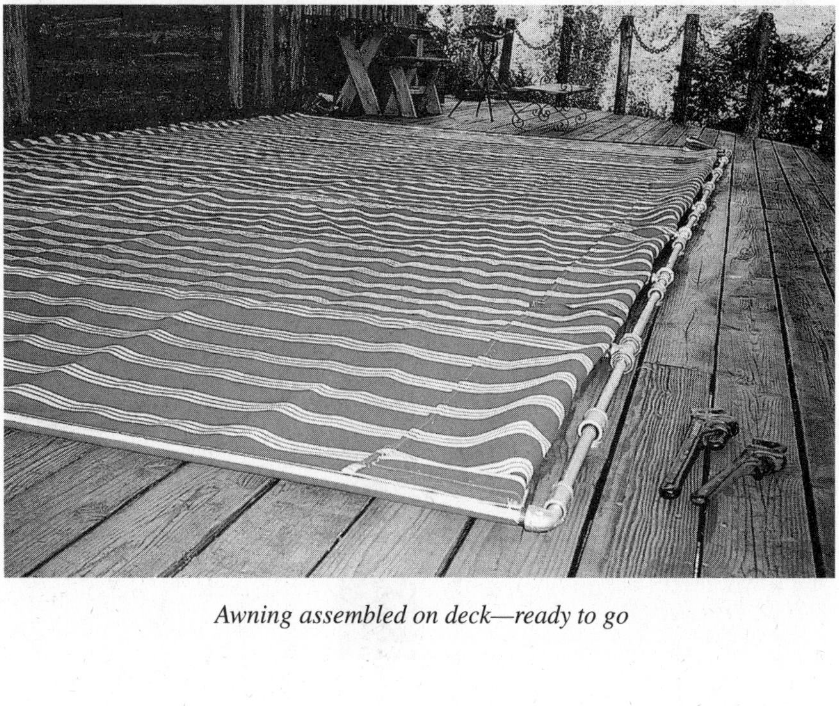

Awning assembled on deck—ready to go

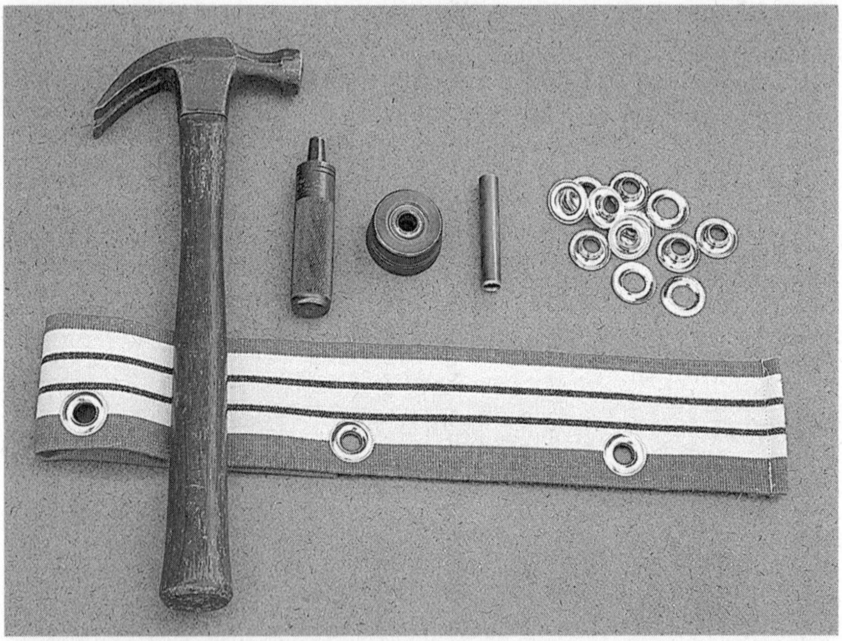

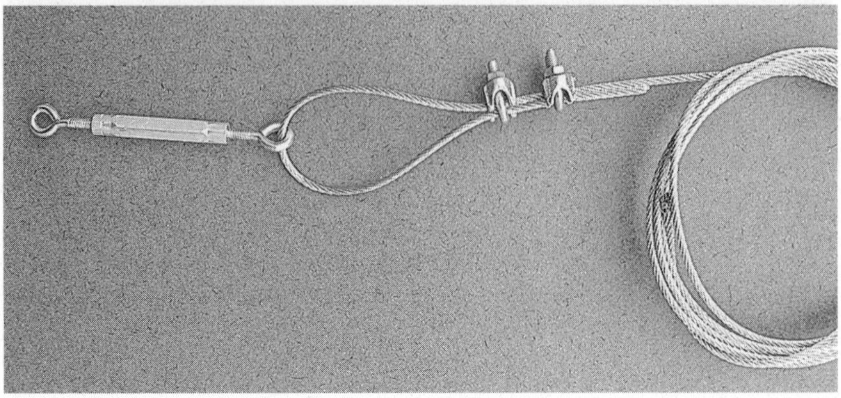

parallelogram or rhomboid. Miraculously it did. Note: ½-inch pipe costs about 75 cents a foot, and pipe fittings are amazingly cheap.

A rude awakening about pipe-construction of a closed rectangle is the way it *has* to go together in the proper sequence or you end up unscrewing a pipe that you just screwed in. That's why God made "unions" (see photo). They allow you to screw "righty-tighty" without simultaneously unscrewing "lefty loosey." It's not as complicated as it sounds on paper; it's completely logical *after* you unwittingly do it wrong. In fact, it's almost worth the laugh when you catch yourself saying, "What the...?" But the important thing to remember here is that every rectangular or square or triangular section of the frame has to have its *own* union.

My assembled frame was a grid of rectangles made from two 19-foot pipes linked together by nine 12-foot pipes perpendicular to the 19-footers, and was now ready to receive its covering.

It was time to cut the fabric to fit the frame. Standard awning fabric is 47½ inches wide (I don't know why they don't just make it 48 inches) and my awning had to be 12 by 19 feet, so some head scratching ensued (like a monkey again). There were some other considerations too. My fabric had stripes, so they would have to go in the right direction. There would be a series of long narrow pockets, 4 inches wide, sewn 24 inches apart on the underside of the awning, to hold each cross-pipe of the frame. The cross-pipes have to be close together (18 to 24 inches) or the awning fabric will sag in between, no matter how tight you try to stretch it. You have to keep in mind the wind-flapping, rain-pooling, and snow-loading your awning will have to endure over time.

I proceeded cautiously, more measuring...more scratching. I finally got brave enough to cut six 13-foot lengths off my 40-yard roll of fabric,

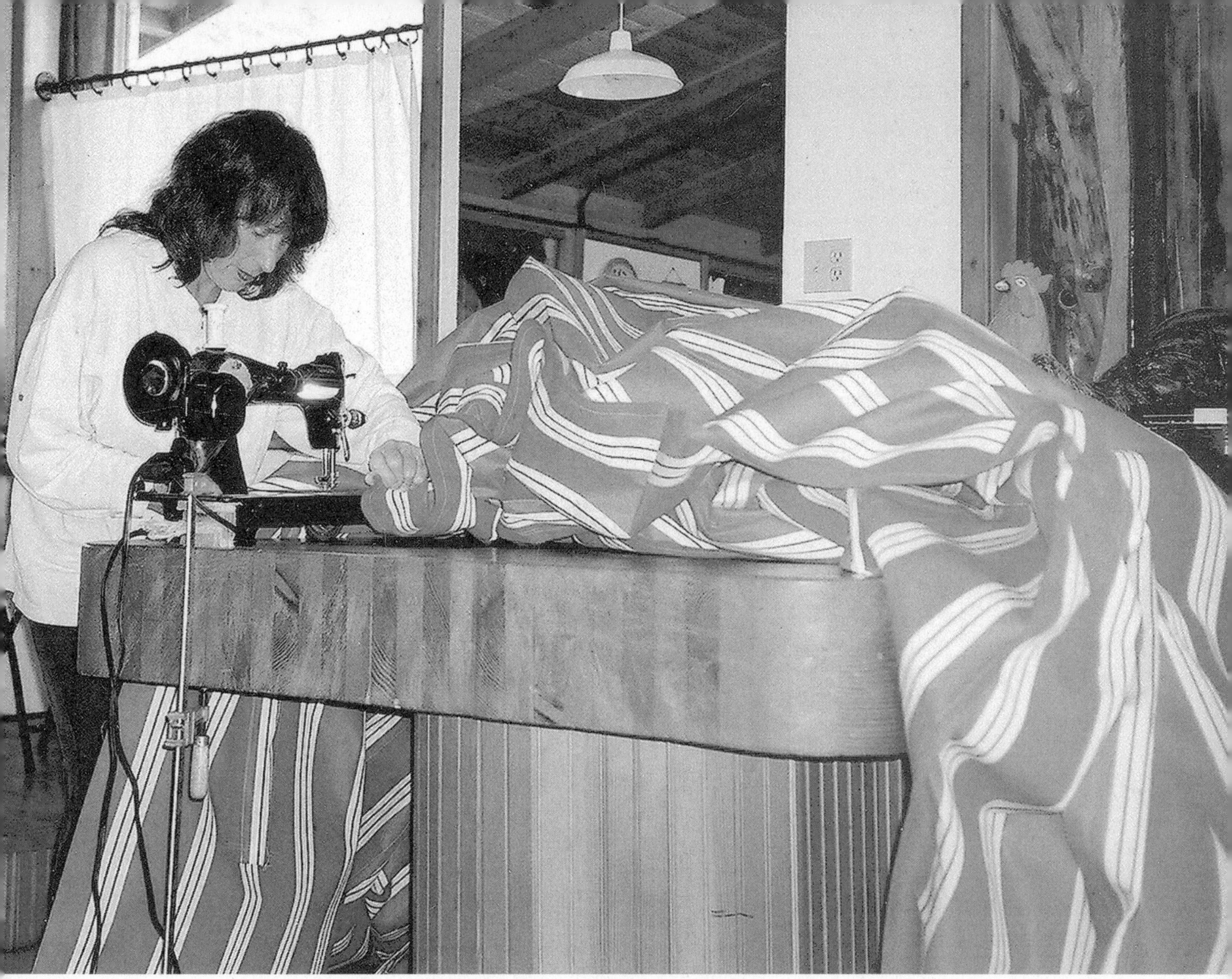

Dorothy at work sewing away.

allowing the extra footage for seams and end flaps. It's wise to think ahead before you get scissors-happy, or you'll be very UN-happy ordering more fabric. Important tip: Cut with "pinking shears" so the edges won't fray.

I sewed only two of the 13-foot by 47½-inch pieces together at a time *lengthwise*, then laid them out on the frame to mark where the long pocket strips had to go. While sewing the long strips on, I took great care to provide some slack space for the pipe to fit in, by bunching up the fabric as I went along to create a "tunnel" the entire length of each strip. (See photo.) If you sew the strips on *flat*, when you push the round pipe in, it'll pull and pucker everything out of shape.

The reason I didn't sew *all* the 13-foot lengths together first and *then* sew the strips on is because it would make the awning too huge and cumbersome to work with. When you are sewing an awning on a small sewing machine, the sequence of putting it together is very important. After all the pocket strips are sewed on, then you sew the sections together, and then hem the entire perimeter of the giant rectangle. Note: It's important to use 100% polyester thread because it is more weather resistant than cotton.

Since I have an old 1940s Singer sewing machine that sits on top of my dining table, I clamped it securely to the table with a bar clamp so it wouldn't skate around as I guided yards and yards of fabric under the needle. Projects like this make going to the fitness center entirely unnecessary.

I gathered up the huge awning (300 square feet of fabric) and wrestled it outside to the deck to "try it on." That required taking the frame apart (in place) and inserting each 12-foot long pipe into its respective pocket (tunnel), then screwing it all tightly back together again. (Tightening the fittings by straining two pipe wrenches against each other is another great workout.)

Everything fit beautifully, so I danced a little jig on the deck (high on oxygen), before tackling the actual installation of the awning on the house. But while it was still flat on the deck I sprayed two coats of invisible silicone water repellent on the fabric to make it even more weather resistant than it naturally is.

The assembly would first be raised straight up, flat against the house, then fastened along its 19-foot edge to a horizontal beam above the picture windows...16 feet up. I got a couple of husky friends to lift it vertically and hold it there while I climbed up a ladder and screwed clamps around the pipe and to the beam at two-foot intervals. The U-shaped clamps allowed the 19-foot pipe assembly to rotate in the "cradles" as we pivoted the awning out and propped it up on four supporting pipes.

The pipe-legs were screwed into tees already installed 5 feet apart in the outer 19-foot pipe, 12 feet above our heads. I had used ¾ x ¾ x ½-inch tees so I could slip the ¾-inch holes onto the horizontal ½-pipe and rotate the tees at any angle I needed. Then the ½-threaded hole of each tee was used to receive a leg. I screwed a pipe flange onto the bottom of each supporting pipe-leg and fastened the flanges to the deck with hefty #12 screws.

The lengths of the vertical legs determined the pitch of the awning. I wanted a 4-foot drop in the 12-foot run—steep enough for good sun protection and rain run-off, but not too steep to block the view.

Sewing the trim on the "scalloped" edge. Note: it's not too difficult because all the fabric is on the left side.

Everything went well and my sigh of relief echoed across the canyon. The hardest part was over.

The next step was to make the triangular pieces to close in the sides of the awning. For now it was just a big wing hovering over the south-facing deck. A triangle on each side would provide more shade east and west, and help stabilize the awning.

I had planned in advance how I would attach the two triangular frames to the house and to the outer corners of the awning. I had installed 90-degree "street ells" on all four ends of *both* 19-foot pipe assemblies to receive the horizontal pipes of the right triangles. (Street ells have male threads on one end and female threads on the other.) The right triangle itself was formed with a 90-degree elbow connecting the two legs. The vertical leg was screwed into a tee that was "waiting for it" in the 19-foot horizontal pipe on the house.

After a test run, I took the triangular frames back down and made their respective awnings to fit, then put them back up. The "dress rehearsal" went well so I attached them permanently to the house with a pipe flange on the horizontal leg, and U-clamps on the vertical leg. The "hypotenuse" edge of the fabric was "pipeless" but had a two-inch-wide industrial-strength Velcro strip sewed on it that mated to a flap I had pre-sewn on the main awning.

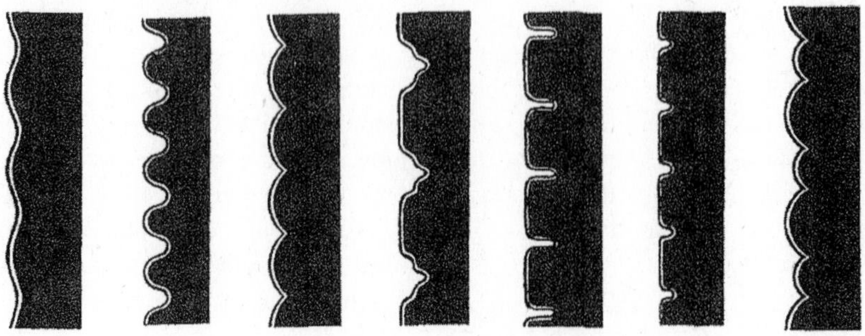

Sample valance (trim) styles.

Finishing touches

I live on a windy hilltop, so I set about to make sure the awning would not "rack" and turn into a giant parallelogram in a strong wind, or worse yet, a pretzel. I fastened two large Xs, made from 1/8-inch aircraft cable and closed-eye turnbuckles, to the underside of the awning frame (diagonally corner to corner). The two 10 by 13-foot Xs, pulled taut by tightening the turnbuckles, keep the awning braced for a hurricane. Caution: If you live in a windy area, this step is absolutely necessary. (See the close-up photo of turnbuckle assembly.)

After successfully completing the large front deck awning, I made two small box-type awnings for the side windows, also out of pipes. Then I decided to put an awning over the loft-deck on the back of the house. After finishing that one, I went completely awning-crazy—being only mildly awning-crazy to begin with. I bought 50 more yards of awning material from the awning man, and made awnings for the piano studio's deck, south-facing windows, and entranceway. Even my shop will eventually get the "awning treatment."

The nine awnings I've made so far have cost a total of $2000, *one-fourth* the cost of having them custom-made. They have increased the value of my house and studio, but what's most important is that they have increased my enjoyment and quality of everyday life.

It was well worth the 5,000 shish-kabobs I ultimately had to make to pay for all nine of them.

Closing thoughts

I don't think there's a house alive that wouldn't look better with an awning or two. Depending on the architectural style of one's home and the setting and the type of awning, they can add a whimsical "holiday" look (festive and inviting), a European or Mediterranean look, a classic look, a quaint and charming look, or a modern and stylized look, just to name a few.

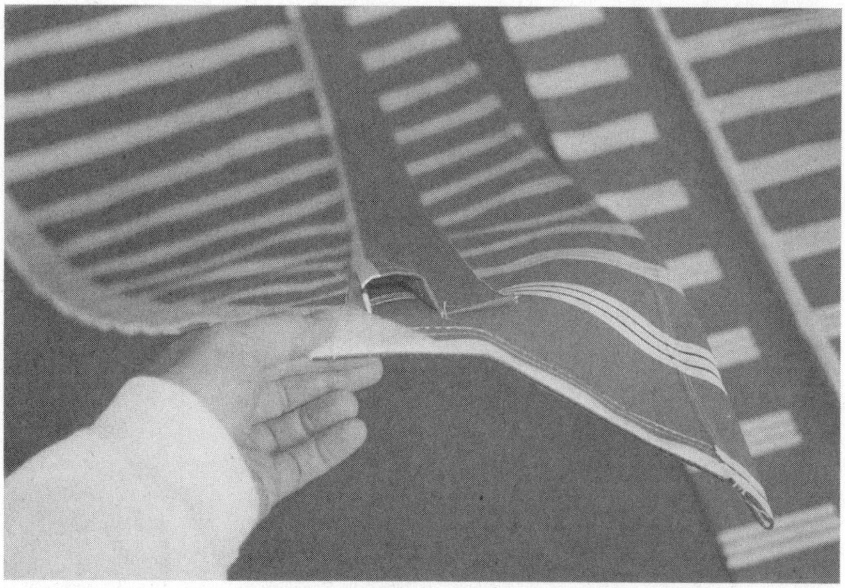

"Tunnel" created with strips of fabric sewn on to receive pipes. With this method, the awning and pipes must be preassembled on the deck.

Awnings appear to increase the size of a home, and give it a well-groomed, cared-for attractiveness. They prevent birds from flying into picture windows and help insulate the glass from heat and cold, but best of all—they offer delicious shade. You can go out on your deck when it's raining or snowing—or stay IN. At least you have the *choice* when you have an awning. You can thumb your nose at Mother Nature when it starts to sprinkle during your preplanned BBQ, and not a drop of water lands on the sizzling steaks (or tofu-burgers).

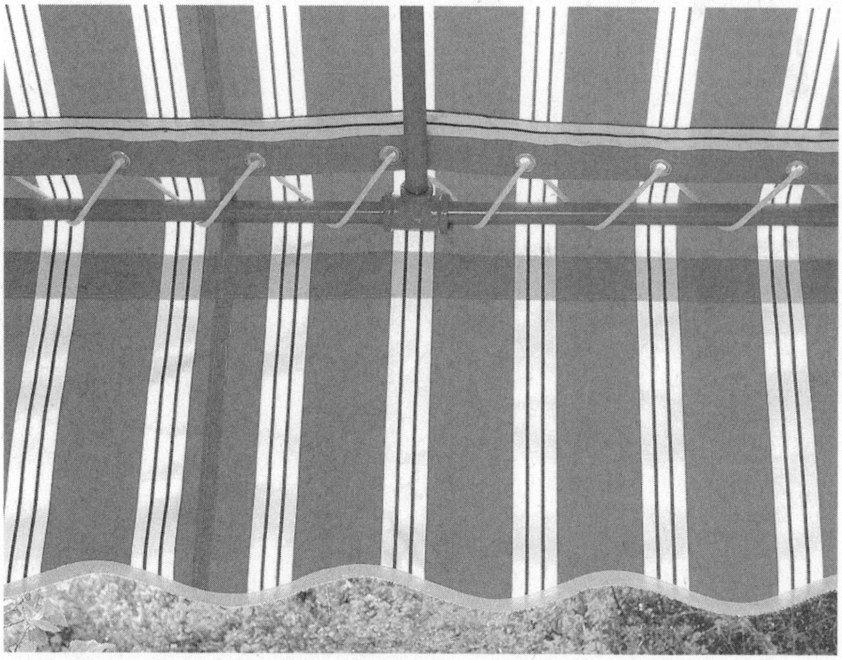

Lashing the awning to the pipes, instead of sewing tunnels for the pipes to go in, is easier because the awning goes on top of the frame and is then lashed down.

The bare frame of the piano studio awning

Another serendipitous use of an awning is for a photo shoot. The diffused and reflected light under its canopy is perfect for taking pictures of friends and relatives who come to visit. You can also temporarily close in the sides of the awning with gauzy material or bamboo curtains or whatever you like for added privacy and shade. Simply hang fabric between the vertical pipes and secure it to the legs with handy spring clamps. Your once-exposed deck could also be a nice sheltered place to "camp-out" on a warm summer night.

Visualize *your* home with awnings. Take a photo of your house and draw awnings on it to see if you like the look. Even small "visor-type" awnings over the windows dress up a home and are easy to make.

There are many ways to build awning frames, but I found that playing with pipe fittings is a whole realm of creativity unto itself. It's a world of adult tinker toys and there seems to be no end to the possibilities of practical things one can build with pipes. They are strong and versatile, come in many sizes, and if galvanized or copper, are almost weatherproof. I recently made curtain rods for a motor home out of gleaming copper pipe and bronze fittings and they looked so beautiful that it was a shame to cover them up with curtains.

The piano studio, all decked out

After building the frames, you can get as wild and creative as you like with fabric and trim. Your choice of awning colors and style of valances (trim) can be an extension of your personality—like choosing a bright colorful tie or scarf to go with a conservative suit. (See illustration of valance styles)

Making awnings is fun and only requires a few tools: two pipe wrenches, a sewing machine, a pair of scissors, a tape measure, screwdriver, hammer, and a grommet tool. It helps to have a high pain threshold, a little brawn, a little brain, and a little money, but that goes without saying for *any* construction project. If you have none of the first two, then you need *lots* of money.

Next time you walk out onto your porch of deck bathed in bright sunlight and have to scrunch your eyes into little slits like "Squint Eastwood," *do* something about it. Go ahead, make your day. Make an awning. Δ

Starting over again

without a man

By Jackie Clay

Little did I know that when I began this series, telling of our family's building a brand new homestead in the wild woodlands of northern Minnesota, that the title "Starting over again" was to soon be doubly true for me. For on February 16th, I lost my husband, Bob, and would be starting my own life over again.

There is still family about me at home. I have my youngest son, David, as well as Mom, who is 89, and Dad, 93. But there is this huge emptiness in my life now. How many times I see something beautiful and turn to tell Bob, who has always been there. And there is just the wind.

This is my first experience with a close death. It is not an easy experience. One moment Bob and David are chatting happily, bantering about tonight's karate practice and only a few hours later I wake up with Bob, next to me in bed, drenched in sweat, having a seizure, and vomiting. I feel his spirit left him then, for he never responded to anything thereafter. Not the ambulance crew, the doctors, or even David and me.

Massive brain hemorrhage. It sounds like something that couldn't possibly happen to a middle-aged man who is in relatively good health. No injury, no warning, just this.

And my husband and best friend laid in the hospital bed 24 hours later with a ventilator doing his breathing for him, and enough intravenous tubes running into his veins to make me wonder how they could possibly find room to stuff them all into his arms. The specialist had done surgery, removing a piece of skull to try to reduce the tremendous pressure in his brain from the bleeding, but he doggedly held absolutely no hope of any type of recovery.

Just another woman seeking a self-reliant lifestyle

photo credit: David Clay

I numbly stood and felt his words strike my heart. How could this be?

I held Bob's hand and talked to him for 24 hours, desperately watching the heart monitor, blood pressure, and oxygen readings. I prayed, I hoped, and waited. Sometimes his hand seemed to squeeze mine and I hoped even more. But deep down, I knew. I knew.

We had had the talks about not wanting to be kept alive by artificial means, ventilators and tubes, when there is no hope of recovery. But talk is easy. The decision was the most horrific one of my life. I fought it hard. I am not a quitter. But finally, the swelling in Bob's brain pressed so hard that it ruptured the brain stem. The doctor bluntly said he was now brain dead.

Even then, I held Bob's hand and hoped for a miracle. My oldest son, Bill, and his wife, Kelly, had come to be with us and had brought David down the two-hour drive to see his dad. Even earlier, I knew. But in those long dark hours of the night, I fought the decision and hoped. He no longer squeezed my hand and I knew Bob was not coming home.

I made the decision, feeling like a traitor. A murderer. And began to cry for the first time since it had all begun. They sent for a chaplain so I would not be alone when he died, and I cried as they removed the tubes and ventilator. We prayed, I held his hand, and cried like I've never cried before. He went from me quickly and peacefully, but it did not help.

I relive the day every night still.

Surprisingly, most folks' response, other than shock and sadness, of course, is questioning me as to what we will do now. I suppose they expect me to fold up the homestead, pack up my 14-year-old son and elderly parents, and move to town. Why, I just can't guess. Perhaps it's the old gender prejudice that says a woman just "can't make it out in the woods" without a man.

But I already know that's so much a lie that it's obscene. Self-reliance is not just for men, you know. We women can be quite efficient at it too! In fact, continuing onward with our new homestead is the one thing that keeps me going after such a tragedy. Of course, it's easier and a whole lot more satisfying to have your husband share it with you, but the truth is the way of life is just that. It's a path, a way. And all you have to do is put one foot in front of the other every day and you find yourself on the way. Even if you are alone again doing it.

But, thank God, I am not "alone," even though sometimes I feel lonely, hollow to the heart. I have my youngest son, David, with me, my folks at home and other family within a couple of hours' driving time away. And I do have a great family and wonderful friends and neighbors, even though we're just newcomers to this area.

So what's to become of us? Simply, we are going on. Oldest son, Bill, came up with an old dozer he'd bought and cleared a good road out to our house site. By the grace of God, Bob had just been awarded 100% disability from the Veteran's Administration for his Agent Orange-induced health problems, which was retroactive to when his claim had begun years ago. Just two weeks before he died, we received a lump sum check, which Bob wanted to use to buy a 1960s Volkswagen and have a small log house roughed in by a local company. As we were caring for my folks (Mom in a wheelchair and Dad on a walker), we just couldn't go into the woods for cutting logs to build the way we had planned.

Bill dozing off an old slash pile for another garden.

It seemed as if it was meant to be. So we have our house in process. We'll still have to do a lion's share of the work, as Bob's check did little more than buy the basement and logs, stacked. But it will give us a good start.

Mom enjoying her birthday (89th) with young tomatoes and peppers. Life goes on.

The dozer also cleared my garden spot and opened up another spot of rich wood's dirt next to the old mobile home we're living in temporarily. So I'm clearing gardens, picking rocks and old logs, sorting seeds, and planting flats of vegetables.

I guess it helps that I was divorced in prior life, having kids at home to raise. You soon develop a forward going spirit and learn ways of doing things, even though you are a "woman alone." Yes. That did help with this time of aloneness. But then, it's not really aloneness, at all. Having David to be there and help me is great. He was raised on wilderness homesteads for most of his life and was totally immersed in all aspects of it, right from birth. This young man is not your typical 14-year-old. He has developed real skills, from building, gardening, hunting, tractor driving, to logging and more. Bob is not here, but David fills in when he is not in school.

My son, Bill, who also grew up "doing," is a great supporter and advisor. He provided many, many suggestions on our house plan, in order to get the most living out of a small house, and to make it work well for us. He and his wife, Kelly, have visited often, sometimes bringing equipment and supplies, which helps boost my sad times.

And our neighbors and friends keep popping in with saws and hammers in hand asking what project they can help me with today. It is so nice of them I can scarcely thank them enough.

At 58, I've learned a lot. I've had to. So may I offer a little of what I've learned to other women traveling down the self-reliant living path without a man at their side?

Start small & make a list

First of all, I've learned *not* to try to do everything at once. Getting a big flock of poultry, many dairy goats, cattle, sheep and horses, building housing for them (and you), fencing, working up a large garden, and canning all of it just won't work. Add the caregiving necessary for children (or elderly parents) and the time window narrows even more.

It is awfully tempting to instantly become self-reliant by overestimating our abilities. You look at that great piece of land, just lying there waiting, and you itch to *do it*. But it just doesn't happen all at once, even with the constant help of a man.

I've learned to start small. Then work as you can, each day, toward a final goal. If you're a list-maker, by all means make a list of your goals on a dry-erase board tacked in a prominent place. Use an outline form with your basic goals, such as BIG GARDEN, then the goals broken down into priority "bites" toward that goal, through the years ahead. For instance:

Big garden

Make six 12 by 4-foot raised beds:

- Place railroad ties on ground.
- Fill beds with rich compost and rotted manure.
- Plant the beds.

Or:

Rent, borrow, or pay someone to till garden spot.

Clear and till a 25 by 50-foot garden spot:

- Pull grass roots.
- Pick rocks and rotted wood off garden.
- Plant easy-to-grow crops on the new land.

Next: Make eight more raise beds, 20- by 4-feet each.

Or:

- Buy good used rototiller. (Or new, if I can.)
- Till up another larger section for next year's garden.
- Fence garden spots to keep deer and other varmints out.
- Build portable panels for trellising peas, pole beans, and other climbers to make more use of existing garden.
- Build a small greenhouse so I can start my own vegetable and flower plants.

Once you have the list, you can cross off each task as you get it done. This gives a visual, which is of immense importance. Especially when you are having a down day.

These lists should include nearly everything you hope or need to accomplish. Do not erase the tasks as you accomplish them, but cross them out or check them off in **RED**. It is a great morale booster!

Enlist folks to help you when appropriate. I say "when appropriate" because it is very necessary not to fall into the habit of using people. When someone offers help, honestly and enthusiastically, accept with true gratitude. If you need help, call out to friends, family, or neighbors. However, make that a "once in awhile" event, not frequently. You *can* do so much more than you think you can if you just keep at it and learn new skills. I learned to sweat-solder copper pipes over the phone with my Dad after my pipes froze and broke in the basement. It took a few calls and a little experimenting, but I can now solder with the best of them.

Remember that there are books and magazine articles available to teach you those new skills, too. When you see there's something a bit scary and new coming up on your list, do your research before you start. It's not so scary, after all. I've stumbled my way through so many "new" ventures that I laugh to even try to count them. And everything came out pretty much fine anyway.

Our friends and neighbors have been great. Here, Tom Richardson helps us start our new 10x10 greenhouse to grow garden plants.

Even your young children will enjoy being included in new projects. David was pounding nails in our kitchen addition when he was two years old and simply loved it. There are many, many appropriate tasks you can share with children. It makes all of you feel a part of the homesteading family. If there are no children, you can still share your homesteading life with interested neighbors, friends, or family. Self-reliance is not living a hermit's life. Although I would be perfectly happy living in an isolated chunk of interior Alaska, it's also great to share with others.

When to hire or barter a job done

If there are big jobs that are simply too much for you due to time, physical constraints, or other constraints, pay someone to do it for you. There are always folks around who pick up spare cash by hauling gravel, doing odd job carpentry, bulldozer or backhoe work. It is dumb to spend two weeks shoveling a ditch by hand when your neighbor would be tickled to do it with his tractor for $25. Time is so valuable on the homestead. In that same week, I could build a greenhouse, fence a goat pasture, *and* can two turkeys. Of course, this is providing you have $25. I've been broke, too, not having a dollar, let alone $25. I would still use the equipment to dig the ditch, bartering for the operation. For instance, trading two days' of my labor doing fence repair in his cow pasture, or trading vegetable plants for his garden (I built the greenhouse, remember), or taking his kids to music lessons for a week. Get creative and save your back and time.

In New Mexico, to give you an example, I bartered with our neighbor, Earl Beard, to help on his ranch, branding, vaccinating, and castrating calves one spring, in exchange for him bringing his tractor and post hole auger over to dig half a mile's worth of fence post holes. I spent two days at the Beard ranch, working cattle, and had the holes dug that would have taken me all summer to do by hand. Time is valuable on the homestead.

Stay out of debt

Finances are a bear for most women attempting self-reliant living. In

David and I pulled nails from scrounged lumber and made greenhouse tables from it. Free is best!

today's world, charging seems to be a way of life. Buy a new car for monthly payments, buy a house with nothing down, have credit cards galore. It is a trap, and a huge number of people fall right into it and can't escape. It is deadly.

To become self-reliant, you *must* escape debt as much as humanly possible. This takes a huge amount of self control, plus a huge amount of anger at what these "helpful" people and companies are really doing to you. All you need to do is to figure up just how much you will actually pay for that new car or new home with "low down payments and low monthly payments' or what your credit cards are *actually* costing you and you'll see red. I guarantee it!

Every day, I fight to chop down any debt. I have no credit cards. Our land is paid for in full. There are no loans, nor will I get one. Helpful folks have encouraged me to mortgage our 80 acres in order to have our new log cabin finished this summer. But, no. I don't feel comfortable getting back into that same tub of debt that I escaped from long ago. Who knows what the future may bring? My own illness or injury? Economic crash in this country? A terrorist attack disrupting daily living? We'll get the house finished. Maybe not this year, but it will get finished and I won't owe for its building.

Another thing that has helped me is to make a list of more expensive items you need to make your homestead work more productive or easier on you, in a prioritized format. For instance:

- Snowplow truck
- *Troy-Bilt* rototiller
- Tractor with front end loader
- Lumber for small barn

Then, as you get a larger chunk of cash such as an income tax return, or

After a trip to the dump, Dad's car is full of lumber.

a lump sum payment such as from insurance or summer job, plunk it down on the item on top of the list. I worked for a firefighter for the Department of Natural Resources for a couple of years during the summer fire season and used this lump sum check for such purchases. If you don't use such cash it will just be frittered away, leaving you with nothing to show for it. Get your priorities in order or you'll end up with a few meals eaten out, a few new clothes (that you could have bought for next to nothing at thrift shops), while not much has changed on your homestead.

Sitting out in our yard right now are a 16-foot stock trailer, a riding lawn mower that doubles as a homestead tractor, a 4x4 ATV, a snowmobile for winter access in bad weather, a big pile of rough-sawn lumber, the 30' travel trailer we lived in on our new homestead, and a Troybilt tiller. All of these were bought using large lump sum windfalls of cash. (No, they didn't all come at once. The stock trailer is twenty years old!) This method works for getting you ahead. Slowly, but surely.

Likewise, I try to make one or two large purchases every month or so, as my money allows. Again, I use a list of priorities. This includes bulk foods for my storage pantry, fencing, garden supplies, or whatever. To do this, I scrimp like heck on other things, but it slowly allows me to get ahead. Last year I bought half of the metal roofing for the goat barn, steel fence posts, and enough wire for two strands around the horse pasture. Last winter I bought two rolls of field fencing and several bundles of steel posts for our goat barn, 300 pounds of flour for the pantry, and a case of canning jar lids.

Some things I buy when they are on sale, of course. Other things I simply buy because I know I will eventually need them and can now afford them. Then there is the alternative shopping I do, which saves tons of cash. Every time I get our local shopper paper, I quickly read through it for great buys in homesteading supplies. You'd be surprised what I've found: fencing for little or nothing, lumber, you name it.

Dumpster diving

Every time I go to the local dump, I check out the demolition dumpsters. I've come away with truck-loads of 4 by 8 sheets of plywood, wafer board, lumber, windows, and more. True, the wood was full of nails in many instances, but we pulled the nails and saved over half of them to use. If you don't have a dump that allows recycling of building material, run a small ad in your shopper: "Wanted, building materials, free or very cheap."

Likewise, I almost never buy clothes for myself or my son at even Wal-Mart. I've shopped at the Goodwill half-off days, the Salvation Army, yard sales, and especially at our Hospital Auxiliary Thrift Store on Bag Days where you can get a grocery sack, stuffed plumb full, for $2. And this store has donations from large income vacationers, so labels read Levi, L.L. Bean, etc. Most are hardly used or even brand new.

Every dollar I save on food (which we grow much of on the homestead), clothing, and living expenses, I can sock in on our homestead. By making investments in the homestead, I can increase our standard of living as well as safety margin, should world events take a dive.

If you'll look back, you'll see that none of this requires a man. Nothing against a man, you understand. I loved my husband of 16 years. But self-reliant living does not require a man's presence.

Tools for heavy work

There are a lot of helpful tools a woman homesteader will find nearly indispensable. Not all are expensive, but all of them will make life much easier. A simple moving dolly works for many more jobs than carrying boxes into a moving truck. I've used one to stack bales of hay or sacks of feed so I could pull it to the goat barn. And I've also used a truck dolly to haul cement blocks, flagstone, railroad ties, garbage cans, etc. Yes, I do have a bad back (had a horse rear over backward into my lap when I was seventeen), but life doesn't stop because of body weaknesses.

Me, tilling the old slash pile garden
photo credit: David Clay

A garden cart with large wheels works even better than a moving dolly. The large wheels roll easier over rough terrain. And to load heavy objects, you just tip the cart on its nose and roll your load onto the cart. I've even hauled my 17-foot canoe on the garden cart by strapping the bow onto the cart with nylon ratchet straps and simply lifting the stern a bit and steering it around, pushing it ahead of me. Piece of cake! This also works with larger timbers, logs, and railroad ties.

A power driver, which is a battery operated drill/screwdriver, is *so* handy on the homestead, especially when you're doing it alone. By using screws instead of nails, you can change things around even after you've fastened lumber together—without tearing up boards as you can when pulling nails. For instance, we've just built a 10 by 10-foot greenhouse onto the back of our temporary mobile home. It's too nice to just leave there when we move into our new log home, so it is built entirely with screws so it can easily be disassembled and moved to the house. There it will become a permanent fixture.

I'm not selling rototillers, but there are two of them I really would hate to do without. One is my big 8-hp Troy-Bilt Horse, which is a hard working, heavy duty rear-tined tiller. This is my second; I wore out the first with 15 years of very serious gardening, including a three-acre market garden. Being a rear-tined tiller, it takes away most of the jump and hard to handle pounding a front tined tiller dishes out. Women, especially, will love this factor. I know I do. Yes, you can actually walk quietly next to the tiller, just like the picture in the advertisement shows. (Be advised, though, that is when your garden has been worked up well, with most of the stones, heavy sod chunks, and branches taken off.)

My other tiller is a little 20-pound Mantis. This little guy is *not* a wimp. It is like tilling with a very mad weasel. I use it for in between my plants, to till raised beds, and to till small beds around the buildings. I also use it to dig tree holes and short ditches. You just walk it into the place you want to dig and pull backward slightly. By repeating this, you dig deeper and deeper. Then I shovel the loose dirt out of the hole and dig some more. You can dig a big fruit tree hole in about 10 minutes. Or you can bury an electric conduit, water line, or make an irrigation canal in the same way.

A riding lawn mower may seem to be a foo-foo tool, but I've used one for years, not only to mow extensive lawn (from which I save my grass clippings for the animals and for compost), but to use as a garden tractor. I've hauled rock on our bad driveway with one pulling a small trailer. And I've hauled hay, compost, manure, mulch brush, and more. I've also dragged the driveway, using a wood pallet, to smooth out ruts. I've spread grass seed on the pasture, hauled water to animals and potatoes out to the field. Of course, I've also used one to haul garden harvest into the house and to back into the aisle of the goat barn to clean pens.

A good pair of loppers (long handled pruners) is a good tool to have around too. I not only use mine to prune shrubs and trees, but also to cut small saplings to use as bean poles, trellises, etc., and to snip off corn stalks after they have finished producing so I can feed them to the animals. They also whack off prickly thistles, briars, and vines on the edges of your garden and saplings that want to grow in your pastures.

David is a big help digging rocks and cheering me up, too.

When you're feeling blue

You get the picture. A willing spirit and a few good tools will do much. But what about the times you feel so down, like you're the only woman in the world homesteading alone. We all have those times, especially when things are going wrong. The truck broke down, the hail got the garden, your relative says you're nuts for living like you do.

Get out and get some support. For me, this is a talk with friends who live a similar lifestyle, reading a few good magazines such as *BHM* or *Countryside*. Make an effort to find other women who live relatively close to you so you can visit with them on your down days. They'll probably do the same, using you to boost their spirits when they droop. No homesteading women close by? Get pen pals, phone pals. But friends who are also homesteading under similar circumstances! When you're alone, you don't want to hear about how so and so's wonderful husband just built her a fabulous goat barn or fenced in her garden while she was shopping. You're already having a bad day. You don't need to be kicked too.

Time is the hardest aspect for single women trying to develop a self-reliant lifestyle. In the real world, we must have some kind of income to survive, but when we work a full-time job, it's awfully hard to drive home and homestead too. But it can actually be therapy for most of us. I did it for years, and was usually very glad to come home and dig in the garden or visit with my livestock.

Just know that a woman seeking a self-reliant lifestyle is far from alone. There are thousands of us out there. But we aren't the "norm." We are more unique. We feel the call, the challenge. And we respond with dreams and the vigor to make them happen.

Sometime maybe some big hearted guy with homesteading dreams will again walk beside me, listening to me point out the spring's first new wild flowers, will hold up the other end of the board, and will cuddle with me at night. But for now, my dreams of self-reliant living are still there and I'm working like heck to make them happen. Δ

David helps me finish the greenhouse.

Females and firearms

By Massad Ayoob

History is replete with lone women and single moms who've had to manage in the backwoods, and have often moved there by choice. Not surprisingly, most of them have discovered why firearms are all but indispensable to this lifestyle.

The fact of it is, though, most firearms are built by men, for men. The woman's typically shorter stature, shorter arms, and proportionally smaller hands and shorter fingers are key elements that you need to take into account. With long guns, rifles, and shotguns, there is also the element of recoil to be dealt with: having less musculature in the chest and shoulder area, pound for pound their bone structure is more vulnerable to painful "kick."

A matter of fit

Guns are like clothes: style is secondary to fit. The element of fit-to-user that is most important with a rifle or shotgun is the dimension of "pull." This is the measurement from the trigger area to the butt of the gun where it rests against the shoulder (or the "shoulder pocket," the cleft between the deltoid muscle and the pectoral muscle). A good rule of thumb is that if you crook your shooting arm 90 degrees, the butt of the unloaded gun should comfortably be at the inside of the elbow resting against the upper arm with the finger comfortably positioned on the trigger.

If a woman can't reach the trigger comfortably from this position, the gun is too long for her. To hold it properly from a standing position, she'll have to cantilever her shoulders backward. This will cause the muzzle to jump much higher when the gun goes off, and will drive her shoulders much farther back when any substantial recoil hits. That's an extremely awkward way to shoot. It will slow down her ability to track a moving target, and it will greatly reduce her ability to deliver accurate rapid fire. It will also make shooting much less fun and much more difficult overall.

If one gun is to be used by multiple people, it is best to have it fitted for the smallest statured person who is likely to wield it. It is no trick for a man (or a woman) to handle a gun with too short a stock; simply pull it in tight and everything will still work. But it is close to impossible to do your best shooting with a gun that is too long for you, no matter what your gender.

How short should the stock be? Fit it specifically to the shooter. In the 8/2/2004 issue of *Shotgun News*, Paul Mazan wrote about fitting shotguns to his 4'11" wife. A Winchester pump "with a 12½-inch length of pull, a 19-inch barrel, and a 1-inch Decelerator Recoil Pad" was part of the answer, and a gas-operated 20-gauge auto took care of the rest. "To accommodate that short a stock on her Remington 1100 Lightweight, and add a 1-inch recoil pad, I cut the stock off to 11½ inches and found that it was necessary to inlet about 3/8 inch of the return spring guide into the recoil pad," Mazan wrote.

With a handgun, the most important element of fit is the dimension called trigger reach. Hold the unloaded gun firmly in the hand with the web high on the back strap of the revolver's grip frame, and high enough to be pressing against the grip tang of the semiautomatic pistol. Make sure the barrel of the gun is in line with the long bones of the forearm. From here, the shooter should be able to get at least the tip of the finger on the trigger without having to shift her grasp. Better yet is a fit where the pad of the fingertip (i.e., the center of the fingerprint) can sit flat across the trigger. If the handgun has a fairly heavy trigger pull, such as a double action design, a trigger reach short enough to allow

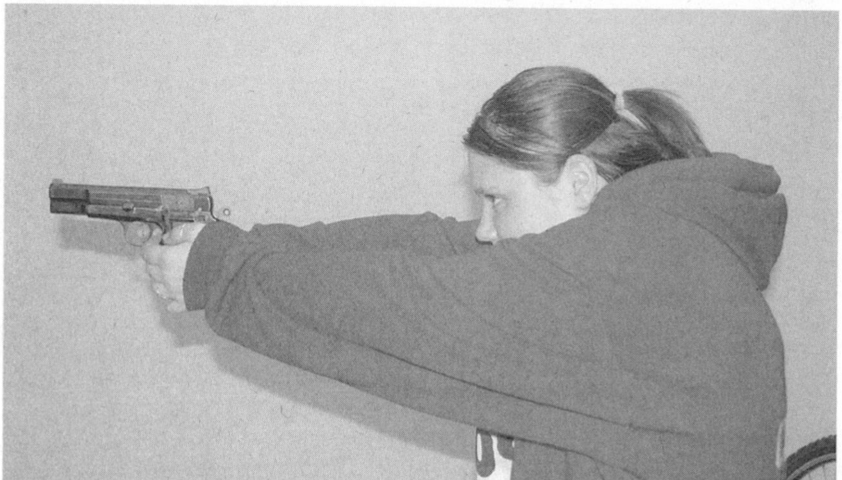

Courtney Kemp, already an accomplished shooter at 14, stands 4'8" with proportional size hands, but easily handles Browning Hi-Power 9mm pistol.

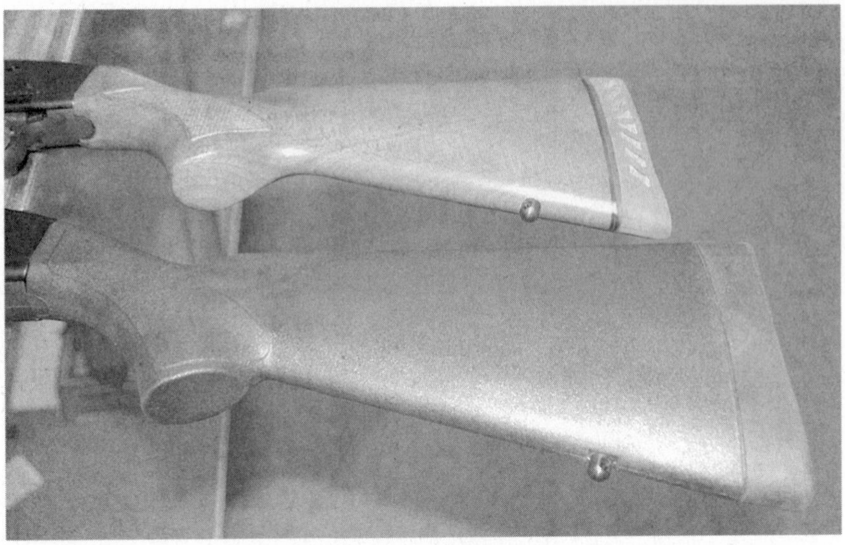

The importance of getting a "youth stock" for smaller statured shooters. Black synthetic shotgun stock in foreground is "standard adult male" size; many women will be more comfortable with shorter wood "youth stock" behind it. Both shotguns are Mossberg Model 500 pump guns.

the palmar crease of the distal joint of the index finger to be centered on the trigger is the best fit of all.

The matter of recoil

We've noted that the skeleto-muscular support structure of the female is not ideally compatible with a shotgun or rifle's powerful recoil into the shoulder. There are several ways to deal with this.

One is a cushiony recoil pad made out of something like Sorbothane, or the new pads with impact-absorbing medical gel pioneered by the Italian shotgun manufacturer Benelli. Bear in mind that such pads will be thick. Their thickness adds length to the stock, and must be factored into the "gun fit" equation. It may take the ministrations of a gunsmith to get the pull dimension short enough with the extra-soft recoil pad in place.

Another avenue is high-tech stock designs. Some even have spring-loaded impact absorption devices built into the stocks themselves. I've found that mercury recoil reducers built into the stock can work well; the Harrt's Recoil Reducer is one proven brand. It may take a professional, or a very handy amateur, to cut away the inside of the stock to perfectly install it, however.

"Back-boring" the barrel can also reduce recoil. Explained with perhaps a touch of oversimplification, back-boring means that the taper inside the barrel is lengthened and made less steep, which reduces the force with which the shotgun's pellets are suddenly constricted at high pressure, and under Newton's law, commensurately reduces the rearward reaction (recoil) which inevitably accompanies any action.

Various other approaches can be taken from the muzzle end. My friend Al Greco (www.alscustom.com) at Al's Custom, a gunsmithy in Freedom, Pennsylvania, makes an extraordinarily effective shotgun recoil reducer that he calls "the bird cage" because the tubular, ventilated device adds a bit of bulk at the business end. Less protrusive is the MagnaPort system developed by my old friend Larry Kelly at MagnaPort, Inc. in Mt. Clemens, Michigan. Now in the competent hands of Larry's son Ken, the company reduces muzzle jump by using electron discharge machining (EDM) to mill ventilating ports into the upper portion off the barrel just behind the muzzle. Expanding gases from burning gunpowder jet upwards through the ports, propelling the muzzle downward and largely countering the front end's tendency to leap up when the shotgun is discharged.

If the budget allows, multiple recoil reduction devices can be applied at once. Mike LaRocca at LaRocca Gun Works in Worcester, Massachusetts, has built two tricked out shotguns for me. Both are Remington gas-operated semiautomatics, a type of mechanism that reduces recoil in and of itself by bleeding off some of those burning gases to operate the action, which

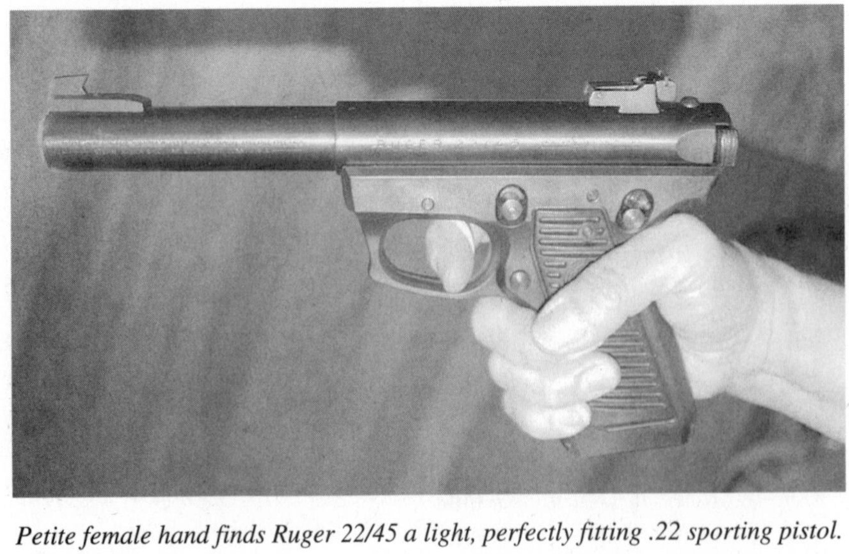

Petite female hand finds Ruger 22/45 a light, perfectly fitting .22 sporting pistol.

siphons them away from the recoil force they would otherwise contribute to. My 12-gauge LaRocca has a Sorbothane pad, mercury recoil reducers in the stock, and MagnaPorting, and kicks as softly as a 20-gauge. The 20-gauge he did for me has the same good stuff, plus a bird cage up front, and it in turn recoils no more than a pistol caliber carbine...which is to say, very little indeed.

For rifles as opposed to shotguns, most of the same recoil reduction technology can be employed. A muzzle brake, which reduces recoil at the expense of a louder, sharper gunshot report, can be particularly effective on high-powered rifles. So can the MagnaPort concept, and so can new-tech recoil pads. Back-boring, of course, is a technology that cannot be applied to a rifle, which fires a single solid bullet instead of a compressible cluster of relatively small pellets. For some reason, rifle stocks with recoil reduction designs don't seem to have caught on so well as shotgun stocks of that type.

Marsha Rath (carrying 1911 pistol, left), manager of Midwest Sporting Goods in Lyons, IL, fits 5'0" Gail Pepin with a short-stocked Mossberg shotgun. It's worth going out of your way to find a female gun shop person to help the female shooter pick a gun: deeper understanding, more credibility.

If recoil is a problem for the shooter of either gender, there is also the option of going to something a little lower in power. A mild 20-gauge shotgun will often do everything the user needs a shotgun to do; why put up with nearly twice the recoil, in the bigger 12-gauge, if that's the case? Similarly, in rifles, it may be that a mild 7X57 Mauser cartridge, a .30-30, or even a .243 will be powerful enough for the tasks the owner needs accomplished, and if that's so, why should the shooter put up with a .30-06 or even a .300 Magnum, which kicks her around a helluva lot more and in return only gives her superfluous power that she doesn't really need?

With handguns, it's not always practical to do some of the things that

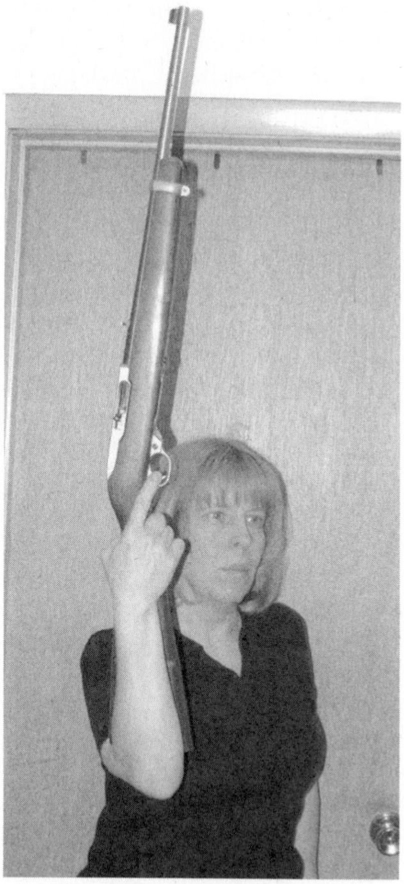

Gail Pepin shows how to check "pull." With finger on trigger of empty long gun, crook arm as shown. If butt comfortably touches inside of elbow crease, length is right. This standard Ruger 10/22 rifle fits her fine.

make sense on rifles and shotguns. Add-on recoil compensators that extend from the muzzle may be very efficient, but are disproportionately bulky on a short holster gun as opposed to a long shoulder gun, and are more likely to be deemed impractical by shooters in the field. MagnaPort and other systems that vent burning powder gases upward to work are very efficient and practical on long guns, because those jets of hot gas are safely forward of the eyes. In emergencies involving man and beast alike, the short "belt-gun" may be fired so close to the shooter's body that the vented gases send their burning flame and particulate matter up toward the shooter's eyes, which are often unprotected in any environment but the shooting range.

With handguns even more than long guns, the most sensible way to make the gun more comfortable to shoot is to choose one in a less powerful caliber. A 9mm semiautomatic kicks less than a .45 of the same type. A .38 Special revolver kicks less than a larger caliber or a Magnum version with full power ammo. A .44 Magnum will fire less powerful .44 Special and .44 Russian ammunition and still deliver a respectable level of power, but with much less recoil than Magnum rounds.

Marsha Rath demonstrates a tricked-out Beretta Storm 9mm carbine, a light, easy-handling gun for the smaller statured.

Proven choices

Shotguns? As noted earlier, gas-operated shotguns have the softest recoil. The Remington Model 11-87 in 12-gauge and Model 1100 in 20-gauge are among my personal favorites in this regard. The Winchester Super-X semiautomatic is another excellent choice. Both are amenable to add-on recoil reduction technology, as are many other shotguns. Remember that women's upper body strength (in most cases) will be somewhat less than a male's of similar height and weight, and a shotgun that is light up front may be easier and more positive to swing on moving targets. The lively, slim Model 1100 Special Field 20-gauge from Remington, with its short 21-inch barrel, is particularly suitable for the smaller, more slender shooter.

Rifles? Something compact and not too heavy up front may likewise be appreciated by the female shooter, A lot of female hunters have, like Jackie Clay, learned to like a compact lever action carbine in .30-30 Winchester or .35 Remington caliber because of their combination of light weight, mild recoil, good balance, and fast action. The Winchester '94 (in .30-30 and .44 Magnum) and the Marlin 336 (in .30-30 or .35 Remington) are both excellent, long-proven choices. Each is available with a barrel as short as 16 inches, which is less heavy up front than the standard length gun. In a bolt action, Ruger, Remington, Savage, Winchester, and other makers offer compact youth models with short stocks and short barrels in a wide variety of calibers.

What used to be incorrectly called an "assault rifle" in some quarters—a semiautomatic rifle in a military caliber, capable of taking large capacity magazines—is now known in some quarters as a "sport utility rifle." Many outdoor people have found that their heavy-duty construction ideally suits them to the bouncing and constant vibrations inflicted upon any piece of equipment routinely carried on a snowmobile, all-terrain vehicle, tractor, or farm pickup. Another pleasing attribute from the perspective of the female shooter is that these guns often have shorter buttstocks than typical American sporting rifles. The military-style guns have to fit smaller-statured members of the service, and also need to be short enough at the rear end to work well for someone wearing heavy armor and arctic combat uniforms. This means that their pull dimension is frequently more suitable to a petite woman.

The AR15 rifle in particular can be had with a telescoping stock. These three- and even four-position units are easily adjusted for someone with short arms. Forbidden for a decade by the ill conceived "assault weapons ban," these stocks are now legal to buy and retrofit to existing rifles, or on new guns.

In **handguns**, because so many are intentionally made small and flat for concealment purposes, it is easier than ever to find one whose "handle" has about the right girth for even the most petite female hand. Some handguns are more amenable to smaller hands than others. In revolvers, Ruger's compact SP101 has an ideal "trigger reach" for shorter fingers. For sporting as opposed to self-defense purposes, single action "frontier style" revolvers intended for sport have triggers set more to the rear than most revolvers of more modern design, and a number of women are happy with them.

In the list of popular and affordable semi-automatic pistols, some stand out as being better suited to the average-size female hand, which is thinner in width and much shorter in the fingers than the average size male hand. In a single action semiautomatic, two outstanding choices are the 1911 pistol in calibers ranging from 9mm to .45, and the 9mm and .40 caliber Browning Hi-Power. The 1911 is available with a short reach trigger that ideally suits short fingers, and even in .45 caliber, the gun doesn't kick nearly as much as legend says. The Hi-Power has similarly excellent fit characteristics, and also does not have objectionable recoil.

The more recently designed Glock pistol has met with much favor from female shooters. Its polymer frame seems to soak up recoil. For those with very small hands, experts like Robbie Barrkman at Robar Industries, Rick Devoid in New Hampshire (www.tarnhelm.com), and Dane Burns in Washington can slim down the Glock's already manageable frame to an even smaller circumference, greatly improving trigger reach. The single most popular Glock among the most skillful female shooters I know is the 9mm Glock 19, a compact pistol that can hold 16 cartridges when fully loaded. Springfield Armory's XD pistol is another modern design with a very forgiving trigger reach, and generally undersells the Glock slightly. In more traditional double action auto pistol designs, Smith & Wesson's Model 3913 compact 9mm is quite popular among experienced handgunning women, and is available as a .40 caliber with one less round in the magazine, the Model 4040. SIG-Sauer offers a double action auto of similar size, the P239, in calibers 9mm, .40 S&W, and .357 SIG.

Female shooters' advantages

We've spent a good deal of this space discussing women's disadvantages in the world of the gun: firearms sized for men, disparity in upper body strength and hand size, and so on. It's past time for us to talk about some of the advantages the female of our species has on her side when the guns come out.

Concentration. Any seasoned shooter will tell you that becoming a top gun is far more mental than physical. Most teachers will also tell you that girls often have more powers of concentration than boys, and longer attention spans. Moreover, being "immune to testosterone poisoning," they take instruction better in "macho" disciplines and therefore learn faster, as a rule.

Flexibility. Sisters tend to be more flexible than brothers. If a male and a female are the same height, as a rule of thumb she will have about 30% more flexibility in the pelvic axis than he, and she will have a lower center of gravity. This means that she can more easily take cover behind smaller objects in a combat situation, and better maintain her balance in circumstances where they both have to move rapidly in confined quarters.

As women have repeatedly shown, beating men for national rifle championships, this lets them better adapt to shooting from positions like sitting.

Fine motor dexterity. It is common knowledge that most women have greater fine motor skill capability than most men. Manipulating a trigger is, without question, a fine motor skill. This gives the wife one inherent marksmanship advantage over the husband. We have known for

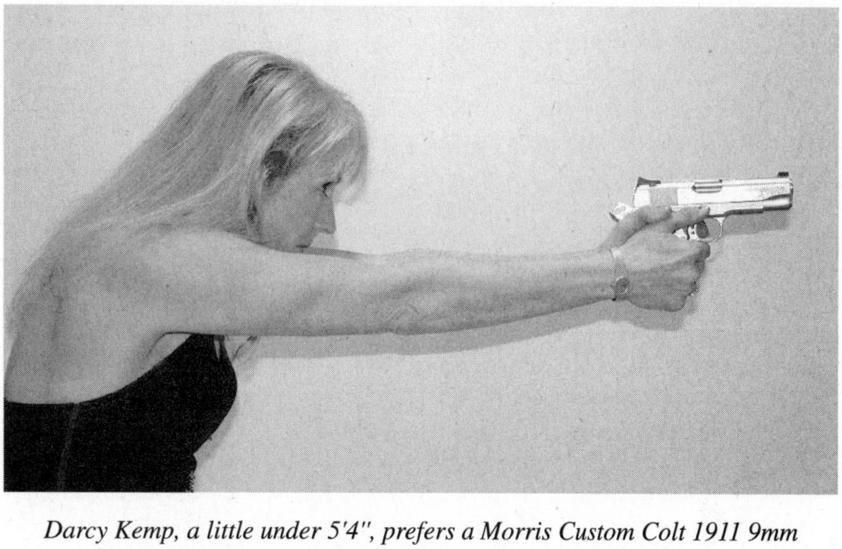

Darcy Kemp, a little under 5'4", prefers a Morris Custom Colt 1911 9mm automatic with short-reach trigger. Fit is perfect.

Jessica Pinkston, a slender 5'4", has no trouble adapting to standard stock of Rock River AR15 rifle. Someone with shorter arms might work better with multi-point adjustable collapsing stock, now legal to purchase again.

a long, long time that under stress, fine motor skills degrade precipitously. The more of that capability you have to start with, the more you'll still have when the "stress flood" hits you, all other things being equal.

Stress Response. Stress hits us all in different ways, in different circumstances. Music teachers and drama teachers call it performance anxiety. Competitive target shooters call it match nerves. Hunters call it buck fever. Cops and soldiers call it pucker factor. At the risk of oversimplification, the word "stress" covers it all.

At Lethal Force Institute over the last two and a half decades, we've done a great deal of research on this, sometimes simply monitoring the students' vital signs as they went through demanding interactive "force on force" role-play scenarios, and sometimes actually hooking them up to telemetry. We've seen heartbeat increase to the level of life-threatening tachycardia with little or no actual physical exertion, and normal blood pressures soaring to 220/110 under the same circumstances. And we've noticed something else.

As a rule, the female students seemed to handle this type of stress better than the males. Their vital signs escalated more slowly in the same situations, and tended to plateau sooner. I have come to believe that most stereotyped "hysterical" behavior (a male-coined term, by the way) has its roots in cultural predispositioning. If little boys had been raised to be dependent, and told by their culture that they were expected to act hysterically in certain situations, they might jump up on a chair and scream when a mouse entered the kitchen. Little girls who are raised to be independent and resourceful don't act hysterically, nor do those who have consciously gotten past such old-fashioned cultural expectations. We have seen some extraordinary feats of arms in combat by women of the American armed services in Iraq, and by women of the domestic police service on the streets of the United States. There is every reason for this to be the norm, not the exception.

The firearm is among the most male-oriented icons in this society. The irony is that in the 20th Century, women's advances in male oriented job markets, from construction to law enforcement, have written a history of using mechanical equipment to compensate for any lack of physical size or upper body strength. The gun, that little piece of mechanical equipment known since the 19th Century as "The Equalizer," has played a large part in this. More and more American women are recognizing that, which is why we are seeing more and more of them buying guns, applying for permits to carry concealed firearms, and purchasing hunting licenses. It's not about stereotyped, obsolete gender role models anymore.

One of my daughters put it better than I could. When asked why she owned guns and enjoyed shooting—and beating males in shooting matches—she answered in a single word: "Empowerment." Δ

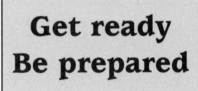

Self-reliance for women

— surviving a biochemical attack

By Kelly McCarthy

(This is the first in a series of self-reliance articles by Kelly McCarthy. McCarthy was publisher and editor of *Self-Reliance for Women* but decided to end publication of that journal and give her 700-name subscriber base to *BHM* so we can fulfill unexpired subscriptions. — Editor)

Three and a half years ago, on the morning of September 11th to be exact, I was just ending a White House tour with my husband, children, and four friends from overseas. We were evacuated, along with all White House staff, into Lafayette Square in central DC. The security guards who had been clad in suits on our arrival were now wearing Kevlar, and there were men with SAMs on the roof. We were being shouted at, "This is not a drill. Clear the area." We drove home past the smoking Pentagon.

We all changed that day. Suddenly we began to look at things differently. I know I did. Is that a briefcase or a bomb? Would the kids know where to go if I couldn't get to them? What would I do if a biochem cloud were coming my way? What is a hemorrhagic fever? How do I purify ground water? Does powdered milk go bad?

At home I started to prepare for whatever life could throw at me, whether it's a terrorist attack, freak weather incident, fire, mugging, or an outbreak of disease. I don't live in the backwoods. I'm guessing that people out in the countryside are better prepared than we suburbanites. After all, if you're following Jackie Clay you must have canned fruit and veggies out the wazoo! You're probably all tooled up with big guns, solar power, artesian wells, and more wood than you can shake a stick at. Well, where I live, in Northern Virginia, the neighborhood would pretty much grind to a halt if *Trader Joe's* shut down.

So I set out to make alternative arrangements in case the world gets complicated, or just goes to hell. And why *Self-Reliance for Women*? Because women think differently, that's why. We're big on "what if?" questions. We like to be prepared. We like to have back-up plans. And we're more than likely to be the ones that have to organize food, sanitation, and morale during an emergency. I want to know I'll have enough calories stored away to cope with a super volcano erupting, enough fuel options to cook food in a power outage, alternative solutions for water purification, many ways to light and warm my home—whatever happens.

> **Why *Self-Reliance for Women*?**
> Because women think differently, that's why. We're big on "what if?" questions. We like to be prepared. We like to have back-up plans. And we're more than likely to be the ones that have to organize food, sanitation, and morale during an emergency.

As I write this, a review of the government's first response plans have just been judged woefully inadequate. Well, duh! Did we really think they'd get it right? Just look at the flu vaccine fandango. If they can't get enough shots out into the community to protect our old and young folk against a predictable annual problem, how good will they be when there's a real emergency?

So, since 2001 I have been collecting all sorts of information that might help me to protect my family and friends in an emergency. As I live 12 miles downwind of the Capitol, one of my big concerns is a biological terrorist attack.

A bioterrorist attack

Bioterrorism is the intentional use of biological agents, or germs, to cause illness. Biological agents include viruses, bacteria, fungi, and toxins from living organisms that have illness-producing effects on people, plants, or livestock. Toxins are poisons produced by living organisms and their synthetic equivalents. The effects of a biological agent disseminated in a public place may not be known immediately because of the delay between exposure and onset of illness. Those most likely to identify the symptoms of such attacks are the primary care physicians. School nurses or teachers may be the first to detect an illness from a biological attack in children. Among the biological agents of greatest concern are: anthrax, smallpox, plague, and botulism. A biological agent may be introduced to the system through the skin, or by ingestion or inhalation.

It makes no sense to me that we aren't all offered an inoculation against smallpox. I for one would opt to have it. It is a terrible disease, with a 20-30% fatality rate, that scars and blinds its victims. It is highly contagious and we all know that vials of a lethal strain went missing with the break-up of the Soviet Union. How long before it ends up in terrorist hands—if it isn't there already? Vaccination takes a couple of seconds to perform (I know, I've had two). It's a slightly uncomfortable scratch, and its effects last ten years. A 1968 study conducted in the United States involving over 14 million vaccinated people resulted in just nine deaths from all age groups and levels of immunity. Yet family doctors are not allowed near the government's stockpile of vaccine. Surely, if most of the nation were vaccinated, the potential threat from releasing smallpox into our population would become irrelevant?

And remember, all the powers of Homeland Security couldn't track down the Capitol Hill anthrax mailer. Three years later and we're still waiting for an arrest. And this was finely milled, highly distinctive pharmaceutical grade anthrax produced in a place where people require high-level clearance—not some naturally occurring anthrax that came in from a field.

My advice: Stay home. Don't touch your mail or newspapers. Wait it out. Avoid contact with other people and things they may have touched. During any type of bio attack, everyone should wash their hands frequently; avoid close proximity to an infected (or potentially infected) person. Isolate potentially exposed family members. If one member absolutely has to come and go, they should live separately from the others. Make sure you are thorough with cleansing; bleach surfaces, sinks, taps, toilets, etc. Boil-wash clothing that an infected person may have touched in disinfectant/bleach and soap. Avoid touching your eyes. These basic hygiene practices will greatly increase your chances of avoiding infection. Make sure you have weeks of supplies—not days, as FEMA suggests. I recommend having at least a month's supply of essentials. I always aim for at least two months. I'll share my list of supplies and how to calculate the basic requirements that your family would need to survive in a later column.

Some biochem weapons are spread through human contact. Remember to drain standing water as it attracts mosquitoes, which can be disease carriers. Keep your house clean so that it doesn't attract disease-infested flies, rats, and other creatures. You may even have to bury your dead. This isn't as straightforward as you'd imagine, so I hope to cover this some other time.

Consider your own psychological state. Do not underestimate this. To endure a major biological attack you may have to cope with:

- The death of family members and close family friends.
- The disappearance of reassuring and familiar rituals and people. No store visits, maybe no TV or radio, certainly very different TV and radio. No sport to play or watch, no daily papers, customers or deliveries, or group worship.

In crisis situations, interestingly enough, it often seems that those who survive are those who don't give in to despair. In order to prepare yourself psychologically for any type of disaster, there are several steps you can take:

- Fear and despair are contagious; discuss the impact of a possible attack (calmly) with your family. Do not panic them, just present the situation as realistically as possible and get them involved with possible solutions. Advance planning solidarity and mutual aims will help you to work as a unit.
- Put together two comprehensive emergency packs. One in case of evacuation, the other for "sheltering in place."
- In your emergency pack include something diverting such as a game (a set of cards, a board game). No matter how dire the situation, human beings need to be able to switch off occasionally.

Fitness

It might seem obvious, but the people most likely to survive a bio attack are those who are fit and healthy in the first place. If you have no health regime, ignore exercise, smoke and drink excessively and are either significantly over or under weight, then you are more likely to become a victim of a deliberately induced contagion. Even if you suffer from a medical condition such as diabetes, or asthma, the fitter you are the more likely you are to survive.

Communications

Keeping in touch with the outside world will be important. We are used to 24/7 news. However, most modern forms of communication rely on a regular power supply, which cannot be guaranteed in an emergency. An exception is the clockwork radio, now used widely all over the world where power supplies are erratic or absent.

For cell phones, there is a device that makes it possible for you to recharge your cell battery without main power. Called the SideWinder, you attach it to your phone via a cord that comes with it, and turn the crank, much like you would on an old-fashioned pencil sharpener. Two minutes of cranking creates about six minutes of talk time and significantly more time in standby minutes. If the SideWinder is cranked without being attached to a phone, it produces a small, white light, bright enough to read by. Turn the crank for 30 seconds and you will get five minutes of light. It costs around $25 and it's guaranteed for life.

As for TV viewing, if the TV networks are broadcasting you might not get to see them if your signal comes in via satellite or cable. Consider a portable battery TV such as fans use at football games, or an AC/DC TV

Sources

Clockwork radio
http://winduppradio.com/trevor.htm

SideWinder charger
http://store.sundancesolar.com/sicephch.html
http://www.cgets.com/item--Sidewinder-Cell-Phone-Charger--sidewinder

Potomac Emergency Escape Mask
http://tricon-env.com/potomac.htm
http://www.ioffer.com/i/Potomac-Emergency-Escape-Mask-3625259

with a "rabbit ears" aerial that plugs into the cigarette lighter in your car. Relatively cheap and easy to run, these devices have proved their worth and it might be an idea to invest in one.

Backwoods bioterror

Maybe you didn't know it but deer mice, cotton and rice rats and white-footed mice carry the potentially deadly Hantavirus. This causes a disease known as Hantavirus Pulmonary Syndrome (HPS), a very dangerous hemorrhagic fever. Although it is on the list of potential biochemical weapons, it is also becoming a reality in barns across America. Victims become infected by inhaling infected mice droppings, urine, or saliva in dust/aerosol form, often when sweeping or moving hay around. It is not spread through humans. Symptoms can take up to five weeks to appear and include a fever, muscle aches, nausea, and vomiting.

After these initial flu-like symptoms, victims experience shortness of breath and have coughing fits. The final stages of HPS disease include internal bleeding and breathing failure. Over 50% of reported cases of HPS have resulted in death. Although there aren't many cases, it's wise to keep your homestead rodent-free, as this disease appears to be on the increase in the US. Hantavirus can be killed by bleach, household disinfectant and UV rays, but you must be careful not to stir up the dust. The virus can live for two to three days at normal room temperature. If you have been exposed to rodent infestations and display any symptoms described above, see your doctor immediately.

Of course the big problem with biological threats, whether naturally occurring or from terrorists, is that either you are unaware a substance is being dispersed or you have very little time to react to it. However, there is a practical aid now available. It is a mask, small enough to fit easily inside a purse or briefcase and can be put on in six seconds. It filters out smoke and its related gases, tear gas as well as biological and chemical agents including anthrax, smallpox, sarin and cyanide. It's called the Potomac Emergency Escape Mask. At around $125 it's the perfect accessory for alert commuters in at-risk cities—and people with mice in the barn.

I hope in future columns I'm able to bring you some new ideas and solutions for dealing with emergencies. I also hope to share some of the things I do to teach myself how to deal with day-to-day threats such as personal assault and general stupidity. And I hope I can explain some of the self-reliant—and often contrarian—thinking that goes with it. Δ

Self-reliance is a mindset

~ A woman's opinion ~

By Dorothy Ainsworth

Self-reliance is a mindset. If you have it, you are on your way to independence. If you don't, it would be in your best interest to develop it. It requires a conscious effort of replacing an "I need help" attitude to an "I can do it myself" attitude.

I was lucky; I acquired it at an early age by default. I grew up in a large family with no money for anything but the barest necessities. If we wanted something extra, we had to work at an outside job to get it. We didn't resent that reality; it was a given. There was no sense of "entitlement" in our family. We were raised with the philosophy that nobody owed us anything.

An example of the self-reliant mindset already in place at 5 years old is illustrated by my first day of school. I got on the bus with my brothers and sisters and felt happy and proud that I was all grown up and on my way to school—until my older sister left me off at my classroom and disappeared. I loved the learning part that day, but it was over-shadowed by being worried sick about how I was going to find my way home (5 miles away). It never occurred to me that I could actually ask for help to find the right bus at the end of the day. I truly believed it was solely up to me to figure it out, and if I didn't, I would be spending the night in the dark parking lot.

The sense of abandonment I felt was seared into my brain and probably contributed to the life-long desire for security I still have. But strangely enough, I handled my problem that day by exhausting all options possible before crying for help. I did manage to get on the right bus and I remembered feeling really good about finding it "all by myself!"

Therein lies the silver-lining of self-reliance. When you achieve even a

modicum of it, you feel really good about yourself.

There are degrees of self-reliance, and even a little bit is better than none, but let's assume your goal is "extreme self-reliance", like mine was: Move to a small town, buy 5-10 acres in the country, build a house, have your own water supply and septic system, and possibly be off the grid for your electricity. Have a few chickens, assorted dogs and cats, and a nice garden. Work at a job you like (ideal) or one you don't like (survival), and simplify your life to the point that you can spend every extra cent for developing your property.

I still drive an old truck, buy my clothes at Goodwill, eat plain healthful food, and don't give a hoot about what anybody thinks. That's another mindset to achieve—freedom from the shackles of convention. When you become a landowner and you start actually achieving your goals in tiny steps, and you can visualize the end result, all of a sudden it really doesn't matter if your hair is messed up and you have dried caulk under your fingernails. You'll be on a roll. You'll have more important things on your mind, like survival.

Obviously there are some personal requirements for becoming self-reliant: You have to want it badly, and you'll have to be in pretty good shape. You'll end up in excellent shape, but you should be fairly healthy to begin with. It helps to dream big and visualize what you want because that's what keeps you going, but focusing your energy on the task at hand is what makes it happen. Have a plan and a list of priorities and start transforming wishful thinking into labor.

You are smarter and more capable than you think. You can't learn if you don't try. If a task looks daunting, get started anyway. Take it one tiny step at a time. Dream big but take baby steps. Write down a plan. List your priorities. Number them. Start in. You want to design your own house? Go downtown and buy graph paper and a ruler. Go to the library or magazine rack and look at house plans. Ideas will snowball. The mind does funny things when you give it a problem. It keeps on working overtime. In fact, you can't shut it off. It's important to get started with something tangible. Make a model. You'll see there's no big mystery to putting a house together. The sum total always looks bigger than the parts...but a house is just one board put up at a time. My house was one log at a time.

To achieve self-sufficiency, you have to delay gratification. The only instant satisfaction you're likely to get for a while will come in tiny increments like hammering a nail in straight and cutting right on the line with the saw.

Each little job is an end in itself, but a stepping stone to the next level. You'll be living in the moment, but working like hell for the future. Some of those moments won't be happy, but they'll always be meaningful. Real happiness is found in the everyday struggles and the little peak experiences you can glean out of them. Hsun-Tzu said: "If there is no dull and determined effort, there will be no brilliant achievement." I don't know who in the heck Hsun-Tzu was or even how to pronounce his name, but he was a wise man. Progress happens in tiny increments. And when you are the one doing the work, each little accomplishment is a big deal.

Sometimes you have to do what doesn't come naturally.

People who read my articles and see the house I built call me a "Gutsy Lady." That couldn't be further from the truth. I'm actually quite wimpy and hesitant to try new things, but if I want something passionately enough, my drive over-rides my fear. Years ago I raced motorcycles because we had a motorcycle shop and my husband wanted me and the kids involved. I am not by nature an aggressive competitive female and I was terrified at first, but so motivated to please my husband that I donned my leathers and "skidshoe" every weekend and actually got good enough to win some flat-track races, even against men. I'm telling you this story just in case you are a woman who can't even imagine doing something like that. I couldn't either, until I tried.

I had been raised with traditional 1950's values where the woman is the caregiver....she makes dinner, makes the kids, and makes her husband happy. That's all fine if you aren't sacrificing your very soul to do it. My marriage turned out to be so one-sided that I eventually had to get out.

If I could break free to develop my potential and become self-reliant, anybody can. At 30 I was a divorced woman with two kids to support on waitress earnings and no child support. And I was a "girlie-girl" and a "fraidy cat" to boot. But there was one thing I was never afraid of—**work, hard tortuous work!** I believed fervently that I could create what I wanted by myself, within realistic financial and physical capabilities, and I didn't care how long it took. I didn't get started until I was 38, and now, 24 years later, I'm still working at it.

No one is confident about everything, certainly not me. I learned by mistakes and failures (Darn! I cut that board ½" too short!). I had YEARS of "oops" and "darns!" I learned that if you can accept your mistakes, it will free you up to take more risks. Trying until you get it right is how most people learn things. Perfectionism = procrastination and paralysis. You have to cut yourself some slack (just don't cut yourself!) A job done reasonably well is good enough!

Every time you are confronted with a new task that requires learning a new skill, hit the books! That's how I learned everything I know, by reading and practicing.

Even if you have money, do it yourself. The actor, Harrison Ford, repairs his own fences and makes furniture in his shop. There's a reason for this. It's profoundly satisfying. There is no shortcut to get that feeling, and no substitute for it.

If you do have plenty of money, and can hire everything done, and buy all the goods and supplies needed to survive in your home and possibly your custom-made bomb shelter, remember this old saying: "The real measure of a person's character isn't how well he or she does in bad times, but how well he or she keeps striving in good times."

If you are lucky enough to have a wonderful mate, you can still become incredibly self-reliant if you make a conscious effort to do so. To this day I tend to let a man take over if there's one around. It's biology and conditioning. It's also nice to have "manpower." Men are a lot stronger. But if you find yourself single and alone you can manage anyway.

My niece is a single mom who sent me an email recently telling how she moved a washer and dryer up some steps and into her house all by herself. She said: "When you don't have might, you tend to use your wits!" She proved there is more than one way to solve a problem.

Self-reliance is learned. It's a process of acquiring the knowledge and skills necessary to enable you to take calculated risks and achieve your goals even if you don't have a partner. When you have tools and know how to use them, everything seems possible! And, you know what? It IS! Δ

A view of self-reliance

from a more timid perspective
~ A woman's opinion ~

By Claire Wolfe

My fellow *Backwoods Home* writer Jackie Clay is a domestic wonder woman who can do anything from can kumquats to butcher an elk.

Not me. Unh uh. No way. Making blackberry jam once a year is the extent of my culinary heroism. My mainstay recipes often begin, "Take one can of Campbell's Cream of Mushroom soup..."

My fellow *Backwoods Home* writer Dorothy Ainsworth is a super woman who can build an elaborate log home almost single-handed—then build it all over again when it burns down.

Me? Well, I'm real handy with drywall. And I can tile a floor. Or hammer together a deck or a footbridge. But don't get me up there on that roof, hoisting a 250-pound beam over a 20-foot drop. Sorry. Not my job.

In fact, I tend to receive each issue of *BHM* with a mix of delight and abashed inadequacy. Wow! Lookit these cool ideas! And Geez, what am I doing among all these hearty pioneer types? I live in fear that my fellow backwoodsians will find out I'm a complete fraud, a refugee from the suburbs who brought way too many suburban assumptions with her when she took to the woods.

So what's my role out here in the backwoods? I contemplate. I sit and stare out at the landscape and I do what writers do: think until my brains feel like they're going to leak out my ears. It's a lot easier to do that in rural silence than it is amid the noise of the city.

Even though there are plenty of demands on a person's time here in the hills (when the wind blows a tree down on your shed or the blackberry brambles threaten to form an impenetrable wall across your driveway, you pay attention), somehow country tasks and country demands seem less demanding than such city chores as sitting in traffic or painting over the latest displays of gang graffiti. Out here, I can work with my hands and think at the same time—a writer's delight.

To work with wood or stone or earth is somehow healthier than to work with computers or plastics (even though I realize all those forms of work are necessary—and without my computer I wouldn't be here talking with you about the virtues of wood, stone, and earth).

So even though I'm a wuss compared with Jackie or Dorothy, I'm still one more member of the big, quiet backwoods family.

I can't remember a time when I didn't want to get out of the city and into the woods. I always had the longing. But like millions of other people, my livelihood depended on the city. And my habits were with the city. It's always so much easier to stay where you are than to change, even when you're pretty sure the change would be for the better.

If I were to look back on the one moment that prompted me, finally, to get out, it would be the moment I looked down from the upstairs window of my town house to see members of the homeowners' committee peering—once again—into my postage-stamp sized backyard, tsk-tsking to each other and scrawling my latest infraction on their clipboards.

That might have been the time they reported that my trellis was two inches higher than my fence (a no-no). It might have been the time they noted that I hadn't gotten their approval before buying my porch swing. It might have been the time they threatened to take legal action because the potted plants next to my back door were not on the association's approved list.

Whichever time it was, it was the time I'd had enough. Within a year or two, I'd found a way out. And ever since then, my neighbors have been more like real neighbors, even when they've been a mile away instead of near enough to measure my flowerpots.

I may never be a rural superwoman, but I know a good neighbor when I see one. And I like 'em even better when I don't see 'em every time I step out my door.

There are as many motives for living the backwoods life as there are people who choose to live the life. And there are as many ways of being a backwoods home person as there are backwoods people.

Editor Dave Duffy made an observation when we first discussed this article. He said that while he believed most readers of *BHM* were women, more men than women had the big dream of moving to the backwoods.

It's always risky to generalize, especially in these days of stereotype-busting, but I think it's always been true: More men than women dream of picking up and wandering off to the unknown, of taking risks, of being self-sufficient, of living on their own, of marching to that different drummer that nobody else can hear.

In many ways, the migration to the American west was a man's dream, on which women were pulled along, often reluctantly. And the same thing may be true for families who leave the city for hard, spare, rural lives today.

We glorify the resourceful pioneer mother and wife of yore, baby in one arm, rifle in the other hand, child clinging to her skirts as she saves a calf from marauding wolves. We try to forget the same woman, confined to an isolated homestead without friends or neighbors, depressed and homesick, going suicidally mad in the howling winds.

The rural life today is seldom ever so harsh. Yet it still appeals more to those who like to challenge themselves, to those who can patch it and fix it and do for themselves. It's a dream for those who glory in the image of the rugged mountain man, trapper, or fully self-sufficient Jeffersonian farmer. And that dream still has more testosterone than estrogen.

Today, more and more women launch themselves into great adventures, glowing with competence and willingness to give the unknown their best shot. Yet millions of us remain "nesters" in our hearts, no matter how busy and active our lives. Our nest remains wherever home and family are—which, these days, is usually in city or suburb.

Even today, if you wander down lonely tracks out in the desert, or wend your way into steep, wooded Kentucky "hollers," wherever you find people living alone in primitive conditions, they're more likely to be men than women.

At times I admit I've wondered what I'm doing out here. It's taken me far longer to develop a real country attitude than it took me to get out into the country. In fact, I expect to be working on my country living skills until the day I die—helped along, but also at times intimidated by, the superhero backwoodspersons of *BHM*.

And you know, I have a sneaking suspicion there are a lot more people like me, out there in *BHM* land. I have friends, for instance—*BHM* subscribers—who recently moved 10 miles off-grid and plunged whole-hog into the self-powered life. But by golly, they'll still make a 100-mile round-trip impulse trek when the Chinese-food munchies strike them. (A habit with which I can really identify.) And they have no interest in making do or doing without. Their country life runs on hard work—but done only with the newest and best supplies from a chain store.

It occurs to me that one reason women have traditionally been reluctant to leave the city for the backwoods or the prairies is that for many it's simply been more of the same—housework, childcare, and cooking as usual. Only harder. (Or at least it appears harder to someone who's always lived within five miles of a shopping mall.)

But there's something interesting about my fellow sisters. No one else seems to remark upon it, but that I've noticed again and again. Once we decide to embark on an adventurous life or step out of secure territory to take a strong stand on something, we often go to the max.

For instance, I'm a libertarian and a gun-rights activist. Most libertarians and most gun-rights activists are men. Bless 'em all. (Or most of 'em, anyway.) We women here are fewer in number. But when I look around, I see male activists who cross the spectrum from mild-mannered compromisers to the most hard-core, no-nonsense, no-compromise positions. The women? Nearly all are on the, "Liberty or death" side of things. And I'm talking about, "Stay out of the way of my liberty or else."

Your mileage may vary. But while suburbs are no doubt filled with women who don't share their husbands' dreams of getting away to the woods, the woods are also filled with hard-core Jackie Clays and Dorothy Ainsworths.

Today, when women's lives are so much more than they once were, the backwoods also beckon as one more form of adventure and personal challenge.

We may still hesitate before making the leap. But once we get to the backwoods, we find everything here. New experiences. Challenges to body and mind. Neighbors who know how to tend their own business—but still help us when needed. Chances to get closer to our families. Opportunities to socialize in ways that are more meaningful than chatting over lattes at Starbucks. The chance to taste a bit of the life of, and gain some insights into, the sister-mother women of the past.

Not to mention the sheer joy of looking out a window on a foggy morning like this one, gazing over a peaceful landscape, sipping a cup of tea, and simply enjoying being here. Δ

Lifestyle and cancer

By Gary F. Arnet

"Why me?" is a common response when someone is diagnosed with cancer. "What could I have done to prevent it?"

Cancer is a complex disease that can be from inherited genes, exposure to cancer-causing factors, or a combination of both. It is not always possible to determine why any one person develops cancer, however certain factors are known that put people at greater risk.

Cancer is the second leading cause of death in the United States, following heart disease. Almost 23 percent of Americans who died in 2002 died of cancer, about 557,270 people, while heart disease was the cause of death for 28 percent. Both diseases are largely preventable through lifestyle changes and early detection.

According to the American Cancer Association, about one-third of all women and one-half of all men in the United States will develop some form of cancer over their lifetimes. These range from relatively minor skin cancers to more aggressive lung, breast, prostate, and colorectal cancers that cause most cancer deaths. Many cancers are preventable through changes in lifestyle, such as stopping smoking, eating healthier, avoiding excess sun, and increasing physical exercise.

What is cancer?

Normal cells of the body grow, divide to form new cells, and die in a predictable pattern. During youth, cells divide more rapidly allowing for growth of a child into an adult. Once development is complete, cells divide only to repair injuries or replace worn out cells.

Cancer develops when cells in a part of the body begin to grow out of control. The normally dividing cells lose their control mechanism and continue to divide and make many more cells than the body needs. Cells are controlled by their DNA, the genetic blueprint that directs all of their activities. Damage to DNA by substances such as chemicals, viruses, and other environmental substances, called carcinogens, causes normal cells to become cancerous.

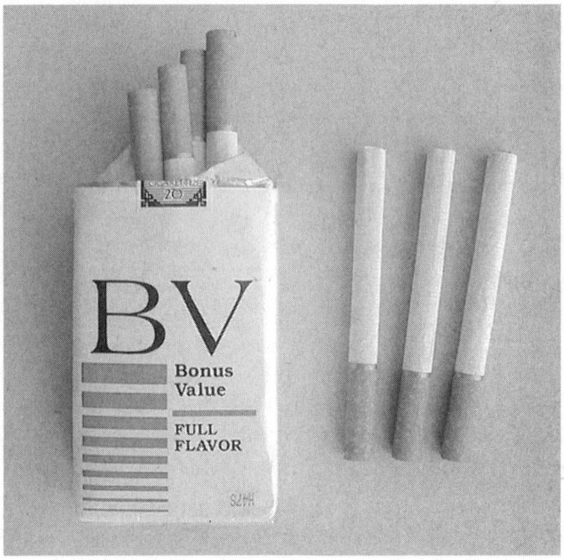

Forty-five million Americans smoke and almost half who continue will die of a smoking related disease. Smoking is the most preventable cause of cancer.

Once most cancer cells start growing, they form a mass of cells called a tumor. As tumors get larger, small groups of cancer cells can invade nearby blood vessels or lymph vessels where they are carried by the bloodstream to distance locations in the body where they establish new sites of the tumor. This is called metastasis.

Cancers of different types of cells react very differently. Some are very aggressive, growing fast and tending to metastasize rapidly. Others grow slower and tend to stay localized in the area they develop. The type treatment and its success depend on the type of cancer. One type of skin cancer called a basal cell carcinoma can grow for years and never metastasize, while another called a malignant melanoma will metastasize very quickly.

Our lifestyle causes much of the cancer that occurs. Damage to the DNA generally requires exposure to carcinogens and mutations of the genetic material of the cell. Avoiding exposure to these carcinogens can prevent many cancers that occur.

Prevention

Just because a person is exposed to a carcinogen does not mean they will develop cancer. Some carcinogens require high levels of exposure or years of exposure to cause cancer. The individual's genetic makeup also is a factor in determining if the carcinogen will cause cancer. So much is not yet known about why some individuals are susceptible to cancer from certain carcinogens while others are not.

Known carcinogens include certain chemicals, radiation, and certain viruses. Where you work, what you eat, and your lifestyle can all affect the risk of developing cancer. The most common preventable causes of cancer include smoking, sun exposure, environmental and occupational risks, diet, and exercise.

Tobacco

Despite years of public education, 45 million Americans continue to smoke and almost a half of those who continue to do so will die of smoking-related disease, including cancer. Of the 4,000 known chemicals in tobacco, more than 60 are known to be carcinogens.

Smoking is the number one cause of cancer and accounts for about 30 percent of all deaths from cancer. It is directly responsible for cancer of the lung, mouth, throat, larynx, and esophagus and increases the risk of other cancers including bladder, liver, pancreas, and colon cancer. Smokeless tobacco, such as chewing tobacco or snuff, is not a safe alternative to smoking, as it also causes cancer.

In addition, smoking is a major factor in lung disease, high blood pressure, and heart disease.

Quitting smoking is the number one thing a person can do to lower their risk of cancer and to improve health and quality of life. Anyone who has tried knows it is difficult. Nicotine is as addictive as cocaine or heroin and the body becomes both physically and mentally dependent.

Help is available to those who want to quit, however. Medicines to help the nicotine withdrawal, a change in personal habits, and emotional support are the key. A person wanting to quit should talk to their doctor or find a smoking cessation program often offered by local hospitals or organizations such as the American Cancer Society, American Lung Association, or the American Heart Association. All can be located in a local phone book or online.

Sun exposure

Exposure to ultraviolet (UV) radiation has been shown to cause mutation of the DNA of skin cells, causing skin cancer. We are constantly exposed to ultraviolet radiation from the sun and from indoor lighting from fluorescent and tungsten-halogen light fixtures. It is thought that we will be exposed to even greater amounts in the future as the ozone is depleted from our atmosphere. Tanning booths are a huge source of UV radiation and should be avoided.

Short-term exposure to UV radiation can cause sunburn, while long-term exposure is associated with aging of the skin, cataracts of the eyes, and skin cancer. With more than one million skin cancers diagnosed each year, skin cancer is the most common type of cancer. More skin cancers occur per year in the United States than most other types of cancer combined.

Basal cell carcinoma and squamous cell carcinoma are types of skin cancer that are generally curable with surgery if detected early. Melanoma is the third type of skin cancer and is more dangerous since it is very aggressive and tends to metastasize early. It occurs most frequently on the legs of fair-skinned women and the chest or back of fair-skinned men. It is curable if detected in early stages, but is often fatal once it has metastasized. Melanoma is of concern because it often affects young adults and because its occurrence is dramatically on the rise.

Exposure to sun accumulates over the years and limiting exposure is the key to preventing skin cancers. Obviously, it is not possible or wise to avoid the outdoors, so we must do things to prevent the sun from damaging the skin. This should start as children and adolescents and continue into adulthood.

Ultraviolet radiation is greatest between 10 a.m. and 4 p.m., so this is the prime time to minimize exposure by avoiding the direct sun or by protecting oneself. Snow, the beach, and water reflect sunlight, increasing the exposure to UV radiation.

Preventing overexposure to sun is recommended by wearing clothing such as long pants, long-sleeved shirts, long skirts, and hats with a broad brim to shade the face and neck. Fabrics that are tightly woven protect better than loosely woven material. Lightweight fabrics that are tested to be sun-protective are becoming more available. Eyes should be protected from the sun by wearing sunglasses that block 100% of UVA and UVB radiation.

Sunscreens available as lotions, creams, and gels give some protection against UV radiation. Products used should be labeled "broad spectrum" (effective against both UVA and UVB radiation) and have a SPF of 15 or greater. The SPF represents the level of protection against sunburn, the larger the number the more protection. Some cosmetics also contain sunscreen.

Diet and exercise

It is commonly accepted that diet can affect the chance of having cancer, either by avoiding foods that cause cancer or by selecting foods that protect against cancer. The National Cancer Institute, American Cancer Society, and U.S. Department of Agriculture all have similar dietary recommendations that may help prevent cancer. These are very close to the American Heart Association's dietary recommendations for the prevention of heart disease.

While the recommendations may be right, the fact is that it is very difficult to do accurate scientific studies on the diet and cancer. Cancer takes years to develop and it is difficult to accurately monitor the diet of thousands of people over decades of life. The definite scientific proof of what foods to eat and what to avoid is just not available.

That said, the recommendations are based on informed observations by scientists and make sense. There are no radical ideas recommended, with most being no different than what our

Smokeless tobacco, such as snuff, also causes cancer and is not a safe alternative to smoking.

grandmothers would have told us to eat.

Some chemicals in our diet are proven to cause cancer, although they are rare in the United States. Aflotoxins are a chemical produced by a common mold found on contaminated foods in parts of the world, including Africa and East Asia. They are known to cause liver cancer.

Concern has been raised in the United States over the possibility of cancer due to food additives, nitrites as preservatives, and pesticide contamination of foods. The American Cancer Society reports that to date none of these have been proven to cause cancer.

Pesticides are used widely in agriculture. In high doses, some pesticides have been shown to cause cancer in industrial or agricultural workers, but low doses found in some foods have not been shown to cause cancer. In fact, many plants produce natural pesticides. People who eat more fruits and vegetables, even if they have pesticide residue, have a lower rate of cancer than people who don't.

Are organic or "certified pesticide residue free" foods safer to eat? We really don't know. Based on the fact that high doses of pesticides can cause cancer, one would think so, but there is no scientific research to confirm that the small amount of pesticides that may be found in foods is a health or cancer concern.

Certain diets are known to help reduce the risk of cancer, including diets with increased fiber, decreased fat, foods rich in vitamin A and vitamin C, and diets that include cruciferous vegetables (broccoli, cabbage, kale, turnip, mustard, etc.)

Studies clearly show there is a significant decrease in colorectal cancer with an increase in fiber in the diet. Colorectal cancer is very rare in countries with a high fiber diet and one of the more common cancers in the United States and other developed countries.

The reason for the decrease in cancer is not completely known. It could be components in the fiber, such as non-digestible cellulose, some substance that is in the fruits and vegetables that make up much dietary fiber, or the fact that fiber increases the speed at which food goes through the intestines so they are exposed to carcinogens in the feces for a shorter time. Whatever the reason, increased

Classifying ultraviolet radiation

Ultraviolet (UV) light given off by the sun is divided into three categories, based on the wavelength.

UVC - 100 to 290 nm
UVB - 290 to 320 nm
UVA - 320 to 400 nm

A healthy diet containing at least 5 servings of fruits and vegetables a day is recommended to help prevent cancer. Fruits and vegetables provide fiber and vitamins A and C. Cruciferous vegetables, such as broccoli and cauliflower, protect against colon cancer.

fiber in the diet does decrease the risk of colorectal cancer.

Fat in the diet has been found to be a factor in the development of colorectal, prostate, and other types of cancer. Obesity has been found to be a risk for other cancers, including breast cancer. Individuals who are 25 percent or more overweight are more likely to develop some type of cancer. In laboratory animals, decreasing the calories eaten reduces the rate of cancer.

As with fiber, the exact reason is not known. It may be the fat itself, total dietary calories, or obesity that causes the increased cancer risk. It is known that fat cells produce a small amount of estrogen, a female hormone associated with increased breast cancer.

Some research suggests that it might be the type of fat rather than the total amount in a diet that is responsible for the increased risk. Reducing the amount of saturated fat by choosing lean meats, low-fat dairy products, and by using olive oil or canola oil instead of butter or lard may reduce the risk of cancer and has been proven to reduce the risk of heart disease.

Skin cancer is the most common type of cancer. Sunscreens with an SPF of 15 or greater should be routinely used. Some cosmetics contain sunscreen.

Obesity is a risk for cancer as well as a risk for heart disease and diabetes. Losing weight through a combination of diet and exercise is a good idea. Like quitting smoking, losing weight is not easy, but is important. Exercise is associated with decreased rates of cancer, probably due to decreasing obesity.

Foods rich in vitamin A or its related compound, beta-carotene, such as milk, green leafy vegetables, and yellow fruits and vegetables appear to reduce many types of cancer including lung, prostate, and colorectal. The reason is not understood but may be due to antioxidant properties. But high doses of beta-carotene, given in the form of supplements, has been found in some studies to actually increase the risk of lung cancer in smokers.

Eating fruits and vegetables rich in vitamin C has been shown to reduce the rates of certain cancers including those of the mouth, lung, and breast, although when taken as a dietary supplement it has little effect on risk of cancer. One study has shown that reducing fat intake and increasing consumption of foods containing vitamin C reduced breast cancer risk by 25 percent.

As with many other foods, the reason why vitamin C works is unclear. It is suspected it could be because vitamin C acts as an antioxidant and free radical scavenger (oxygen-free radicals damage DNA).

Cabbage, cauliflower, broccoli, Brussel sprouts, kale, and turnips are cruciferous vegetables that reduce the risk of cancer. They contain a sulfur compound that inhibits the growth of some cancers, including colon cancer.

American Cancer Society Recommendations on Diet and Exercise:

- Eat five or more servings of vegetables and fruits each day
- Choose whole grains instead of refined grains and sugars
- Limit consumption of red meats, especially those high in fat
- Maintain a healthy weight
- Exercise 30 minutes a day, five days a week
- Limit consumption of alcoholic beverages

It is recommended by the American Cancer Society that the drinking of alcohol be limited, if done at all. This is based on studies that show an increase in cancer of the mouth and esophagus among those who drink, especially if combined with smoking. Drinking three to four glasses of wine per day has been shown to increase risk of breast cancer.

There is clear evidence that the dietary recommendations above may help prevent some types of cancer and will help prevent heart disease and diabetes. Yet, despite decades of recommendations for healthy eating, only a minority of Americans eat a healthy diet.

Environmental and occupational risks

Chemical and environmental exposure to carcinogens can also cause cancer. Some of the many chemicals known to cause cancer include asbestos, benzene, uranium, lead, and radon. Workers in industries using carcinogenic materials should use protective measures recommended by

OSHA and other safety recommendations to avoid exposure.

Radon is an odorless, colorless gas which is a breakdown product of naturally occurring uranium in the soil. It seeps up from the ground and is found everywhere. Outdoors it causes no risk; however, high concentrations have been found in some homes. Exposure to high levels for some time can cause cancer of the lungs. The US Surgeon General has stated that radon is the second leading cause of lung cancer, following smoking, and recommends radon levels in houses be checked. If high levels are present, venting systems can be installed to reduce exposure.

Early detection

Prevention of cancer through changes in lifestyle is certainly the best option when possible. When cancer does occur, detecting it early is the key to successful treatment. Many cancers are nearly 100 percent curable when treated early, but nearly always fatal if they have metastasized.

Early detection includes recognizing symptoms, performing self-exams, and having regular check-ups with a doctor. Special screening tests for some cancers are available to detect cancer early before symptoms appear. The age and frequency they are used depends on a person's risk for a particular type of cancer.

Recommendations from the American Cancer Society for early detection of cancer include the following:

- For breast cancer, monthly breast self-exams, clinical exam during checkups, and annual mammograms starting at age 40.
- Colorectal cancer can be screened for with fecal occult blood tests as part of checkups and with colonoscopy or similar tests starting at age 50.
- PSA blood test and digital rectal exams are recommended for men over 50 to screen for prostate cancer.
- Screening for cervical cancer is recommended during checkups.

For more information on recognizing symptoms, performing self-exams, and for recommendations on screening tests, contact your local American Cancer Society office or visit their website at www.cancer.org.

Many cancers are due to our lifestyle and environment. A healthy lifestyle and early detection are important factors preventing or successfully treating cancer.

Note: All cancer statistics used in the article were obtained from the American Cancer Society. Δ

Ask Jackie

If you have a question about rural living, send it in to Jackie Clay and she'll try to answer it. Address your letter to *Ask Jackie*, PO Box 712, Gold Beach, OR 97444. Questions will only be answered in this column. — Editor

A gray sourdough film and my "falling" bread

Why is a gray film forming on top of my sourdough pot? I've had them for years, and this is a new problem. Is it mildew? Is the seal on the lid of the pot not tight enough? Is it because I am now trying white winter wheat? Is it because I have a plastic bowl? Those are the only things that I am doing differently. What's going on?

Also, I had a loaf of rye bread fall in the oven. I looked it up, and the book said if it falls it's because it rose too fast. Another book said not to let it rise too fast or it would fall. How am I supposed to keep it from rising too fast? Speak to it harshly?

Thanks for your words on Alaska. It is incredibly beautiful, a land of fire and earthquake, volcanoes and glaciers, boom and bust. It is not for the faint hearted. I came here 39 years ago, at the age of 35, with a small girl and all my bridges burned behind me. I've been through a lot, but never regretted coming here.

Evalyn Preblich
Anchorage, AK

I'd guess that the gray film is probably a type of mold. Like good things, like the yeast we capture for our sourdough, mold spores can float around and begin a colony in nearly any warm damp spot. Unfortunately, the best solution is to dump that batch of sourdough (hoping you don't have personal attachements to it), and start anew with a sterile bowl or pot.

Now you have a good talk to that bread! The way to keep it from rising too fast is to let it rise in a slightly cooler spot than you did before. I've had bread fall because I was canning that day and the kitchen was warmer than it usually is when I bake bread. No big problem. ***—Jackie***

Breeding ducks

I have a wonderful flock of Muscovy ducks that I started raising last year. My question is about breeding. Is it a good idea to introduce "new blood" to prevent inbreeding. Or is it a problem? Should I obtain new birds from outside the flock occasionally?

Jack

Yes, it is a good idea to introduce a new male from outside the flock from time to time. This goes for almost any breed of bird. The easiest ways are to simply trade males with a neighbor or give your drake to someone and buy a younger male from a different bloodline.

— Jackie

Potatoes in containers

Can you grow sweet potatoes or regular potatoes on a deck/balcony in a bag or trash can?

wolf and cat
wolf_tracker@hotmail.com

Jackie Clay

Yes. Not only will they produce well, but they look attractive as well. For your sweet potatoes, you can either choose a bush sweet potato or vining type. On a deck you might perhaps prefer a bush plant, where sweet potato vines could trail beautifully down from a balcony. The leaves on both of these varieties are attractive.

Simply drill a few holes in the bottom of a large container, such as your plastic trash can, for adequate drainage, then fill with good rotted compost or garden soil. Even commercial potting mix will work, but will cost more of course. Snug your plant in the center of the soil and cover it with about two inches of the dirt. Then water well but don't drench the container.

Irish potatoes are even more fun. To grow these, fill your container ½ full, then place the seed potato chunk with at least three eyes with the eyes up in the soil. Cover it by two inches and water. When the plant is a few inches tall, again bury it with soil. Keep this up until your container is full. Irish potatoes grow tubers along the stems, not from the roots. So the more you encourage stem growth and cover the stems, the more potatoes you will harvest. This is one reason you need to hill your potatoes in the garden. The more times you hill them, the better your harvest will be.

While your plants are growing, keep them watered, but never have the soil soggy or you can rot your plants. **—Jackie**

Butchering 12 pigs in high heat a bad idea

We slaughtered 12 pigs yesterday morning and hung them overnight. This morning we will be doing the cutting and wrapping. Yesterday's temp reached almost 79 degrees but pretty windy. We hung the split sides in our pole barn to firm up overnight. The temps overnight stayed in the mid 60s. Is their any concern that the meat may be compromised due to the temps? We are located in rural Kansas.

Chris Needham
cneedham@industrial-chrome.com

Why did you butcher 12 hogs when it was going to be so warm is the question that comes to my mind first off. I much prefer to wait until a very cool day, even freezing. And I never butcher more than one or two animals at once, as I don't have the help to get them taken care of and cut up in a timely manner.

Freshly butchered meat needs to be cooled down pronto. This can be done by rinsing well with cold water or even wiping out with snow if water is unavailable. In warmer weather, filling the body cavity with ice and covering the carcass to hold in the cold helps keep it cool.

Pork, being so fatty, tends to sour quickly when not cooled properly. I sure hate to tell you to throw away 12 pigs' worth of meat, but I really wouldn't want to come to a roast pork dinner when you were serving one of them.

—Jackie

Keeping homemade pickles crispy

Is there any way to keep your homemade pickles crispy. My mother makes mustard pickles but they sometimes don't stay crispy like the ones in the store.

Sherry Sigler
ssigler@tidewater.net

The best way to keep pickles crisp is not to boil them too long before you waterbath them. A very old time pickle maker told me this secret, and since I really watch my timing, my pickles are always nice and crisp. No, I do not add alum or lime to my pickles to make them crisp. They are just naturally crisp by themselves.

Another thing that will help you make crisp pickles is to pick your produce in the cool morning and immediately wash and process your pickles. And when it says to soak the cukes or beans in ice water, it means just that. Keep those veggies cold and crisp as long as possible. But don't over-chill them, either, by putting them in the freezer for awhile or pouring ice over them. These things will result in limp pickles too.

—Jackie

Buy a big enough canner

I am purchasing a pressure canner for my son for a birthday present at his request. He said I should write to you and ask that you recommend a few brands. I did see a Presto on the net but did not wish to get it if it is not going to last. Price was about $90. Can you give me some help?

Debbie
patron@cuyahoga.lib.oh.us

Presto is a good brand of canner. Many are in use that are over 50 years old. Personally, I prefer a gasketless canner so that you do not have to change gaskets through the years. Unfortunately, these canners cost a little more to purchase. I believe Mirro makes a line of these canners. It really doesn't matter which brand you choose, but be sure you get a large enough canner. Some folks have been fooled into buying a small "pressure cooker/canner," which doesn't even hold quart jars and makes home canning a nightmare. Get your son a larger canner that will hold at least five quart jars and he will be eternally grateful.

—Jackie

Searching for Hopi Pale Grey squash seeds

It seems that I've been looking forever for Hopi Pale Grey Squash seeds. I tried the sources you listed but they don't have them either. I even tried a seed exchange.

Joe Herzog
bigfish344@hotmail.com

It seems that the wonderful Hopi Pale Grey squash is on the verge of extinction, when just two years ago several seed houses carried plentiful seed for it. This just goes to show you how quickly you can lose an old open pollinated variety that has been around for centuries. Over a hundred disappeared just this last year. Forever. That's scary to me. Diversity is the framework of our food. And that is folding very, very fast. Just look at the seeds on your local seed racks. I've been watching, and nearly every rack, regardless of the company, has about the same varieties. To make matters more depressing, these are not the best of the best. Many are mediocre.

This year, I cannot find one good American source of Hopi Pale Grey squash. My good friend, Shane Murphy, in Santa Cruz, CA, is growing out a crop this year and should have seeds to sell next year. I will also be growing HPGs this year, but Shane has a much better growing season and his crop might be more reliable. Shane grows for Seed Dreams and you might contact Tessa Gowans, Curator, P.O. Box 106, Port Townsend, WA 98368 or e-mail Gowantoseed@yahoo.com to find out how things are going and to get on a list for seeds this fall.

—Jackie

Canning milk

We will be getting a milk cow soon and are excited to use the milk for butter, cheese, etc. I would also like to can some. But I just can't find out how long to process it. Because of the acidity, I believe the only way to successfully can it would be in a pressure canner. Could you please help me?

Dianna
diannaew@earthlink.net

Milk is easy to can, but it does not come out like raw milk. It is fine to cook with, but it sort of caramelizes and gets thicker. Milk is higher in acid than one might think, containing lactic acid. So you can either pressure can it or process it in a water bath canner. To pressure can the milk, cool your fresh, strained milk, then pour it into clean jars. Leave half an inch of room at the top of the jar. Place a hot, previously boiled lid on the jar and screw down the ring firmly tight. Process in a pressure canner for 10 minutes, at 10 pounds pressure (unless you live at an altitude, requiring adjustment; see your canning manual for directions).

To water bath process your milk, simply place the jars in your hot water bath canner and process for 60 minutes, counting from the time the kettle comes to a rolling boil.

—Jackie

Low maintenance, edible landscaping

I am 61 years old. I live in a small town in SD. I have 3 lots. I have tried to find some one on Match.com with no luck. So I am asking you if you could give me some advice as to how to do the landscaping and gardening that would take the least care. I would like to do as much landscaping as edible as possible. The lowest maintenance as possible. Now that I have asked the impossible, thank you for any help you can give.

Leona Martel
South Dakota

No, Leona, you have not! I totally love the idea of edible landscaping. I fell in love with it when my grandmother landscaped her Detroit double lot with food. I grazed through those trees, vines, and shrubs all summer long.

Most folks have shrubs and trees in their yard for shade and beauty. Why not plant shrubs and trees that also give you food? Instead of a plain old hedge for privacy or a windbreak, why not plant a hedge of food? Hansens bush cherries and hazelnuts make a great hedge and will give you more than beauty. Likewise, instead of planting a flowering crab in the front yard, why not plant a North Star pie cherry? This wonderful, hardy pie cherry has beautiful blossoms in the early spring, and gorgeous red cherries later on.

Clematis vines are pretty to look at, with their colorful flowers, but how about planting a clematis and a grape vine next to each other so that you have food for your soul and your pantry as well?

Foundation plantings are often green shrubs intermixed with flowers. Why not plant several bushes that bear food in there, instead? There are pretty blueberry bushes, dwarf fruit trees, current bushes, highbush cranberries, and more that have not only flowers but food on them as well.

And don't forget ground covers. Today you can buy bog cranberries that don't need a bog. These creepers do well in a partially shaded flower bed edge. Next Thanksgiving you could be eating your own cranberry sauce.

Then there are hardy kiwis, plums (shrubby tree), quinces, semi-dwarf apples, nuts, strawberries and so many more. It is surprising how many foods you can grow right in your yard, replacing unproductive landscaping for a very full harvest.

—Jackie

Preserving bread, growing lentils, and plastic eating squirrels

One of the local specialty bakeries gives away day-old bread for free once a week at the college I attend. It's good bread, no preservatives, baked fresh every morning. Is there any way of preserving bread, other than freezing it? Is it worth the trouble? I can get all I can carry for free, but I won't be attending this school much longer, and I'd like to take advantage of this bounty while I can.

Secondly, I've never seen lentils advertised in any seed catalogs. What kind of plant are they? How are they grown? Are they difficult to grow and harvest?

Thirdly, have you had any experience with plastic-eating squirrels in your area? The ones around here eat anything that isn't moving, and seem especially fond of plastic and fiberglass. They've chewed on tires, plastic flower pots, milk crates, etc. They ate an entire hose reel. They even got under the hood of my dad's truck and ate his distributor cap. Is this something that's been happening for decades, and we just noticed it, or is this new? Any idea what causes this behavior? Or how widespread it might be?

Thank you for your time and help!

Melanie Rehbein
lil_vader@hotmail.com

There really isn't any practical way to preserve bread, other than to freeze it.

Lentils aren't commonly grown in the garden as they are small and "too much trouble" for most gardeners to harvest. They have small pods with only a couple of seeds in each one. But they are easy to grow, and if you'd like to try them, Native Seeds/SEARCH has seed for you to try. Their Address is 526 N. Fourth Ave., Tucson AZ 85705 or www.nativeseeds.org.

Yes, I know squirrels chew plastic. I'm not sure that they actually eat the plastic. Chewing is just what squirrels do. And there is just more plastic around today for them to chew on. Years back, hose reels were made of metal, flower pots of clay and distributor caps bakelite or some such material. The more plastic, the more squirrels, the more chewing.

Our squirrels have enough natural predators to keep them in check, so the chewing doesn't become obnoxious. Get rid of the predators, and the squirrels run amok. Sort of like people, huh?

—Jackie

Smelly coffee grounds

I spread out used coffee grounds in a container and dried them and when they were dry I put them in a larger container...and now it all smells moldy. I know they were dry when I put them in, but anyway my questions are:

1. Are the coffee grounds that smell moldy of no use anymore?

2. Is there any way to reverse the smell of the mold?

3. If they get moldy, how could they help in a garden?

4. How do I prevent this in the future?

What a waste of all that I have collected.

LittleLorelai@cs.com

Yes, you can use those moldy, smelling coffee grounds. Just work them into your compost pile and soon they'll be nice black garden gold. And the smell will be magically gone, just like the smell of garbage you composted.

To avoid the mold, dry the grounds on a cookie sheet in the oven with just the pilot on or in a sunny window. Be sure to stir them once or twice during the process so they are totally dry. Even the slightest bit of moisture will result in mold.

But if you're having trouble drying them or storing them in an airtight container to avoid moisture, why not just spread out your grounds in your compost pile in the garden, as you collect them? It only takes a few seconds to work them in and you're done. Even in the winter, you can simply pour them into a spot to be worked up when the area thaws in the spring.

—Jackie

Pressure canning stock

I just got through making 30 quarts of vegetable stock that I use as a green supplement. It's made from kale, carrots, garlic, onions, celery, seaweed, and pure water.

I combine ½ cup vegetable stock with ½ cup chicken stock and drink daily. It really helps with bone aches, arthritis, and muscular aches. When I combine it with the chicken stock it's like taking a one a day vitamin. It energizes me for the day. And no more bone aches for this gal.

To preserve the stock I either freeze it or pour the boiling stock into quart jars and seal, then I store the quarts of stock in the fridge until needed. But it takes up a lot of space in my refrigerator.

Would it destroy a lot of the useful nutrients if I chose to pressure cook my vegetable stocks? I've always heard bad things about pressure canning and how destructive pressure canning can be. Is this true? Do I need to pressure can my stock or just give it a hot water bath?

I would like to have my refrigerator space back.

Cesca
cesca@alwaysonnetworks.com

If I felt that pressure canning was destructive in any way, I wouldn't spend so much time and energy doing it. When you use fresh ingredients and follow the directions for the time and pressure, you retain most of the nutrients available.

No, you cannot water bath process any vegetable or meat product. These are low acid foods and to do so is very dangerous. I realize many people have and will do this, but it is still dangerous. I would try pressure canning a few jars of your stock and see if you like the results. **—Jackie**

Sept/Oct 2005
Issue #95
$4.95 US
$6.50 CAN

Backwoods Home magazine

practical ideas for self-reliant living

GOLD PANNING

Kinder goats
Solar batteries
Making sausage
Gather rose hips
Starting over: Part 6
Put your garden to bed

w.backwoodshome.com

My view

Sgt. Jim Duffy — an ordinary hero

My brother, Jim, died between issues. It was an expected death, as Jim suffered from lung cancer. My oldest brother, Bill, had called with the news in the middle of the night. He asked me to do Jim's eulogy at the wake.

Jim was a Marine Corps veteran who served two tours of duty in Vietnam. He was an American hero in my eyes who had endured four decades of combat-induced mental turmoil. We would honor him with a Marine Corps color guard and flag-draped coffin, and taps would be blown at his internment at the Veterans National Cemetery of Massachusetts in Bourne.

In the eulogy I told the story of a young man who had fought bravely in battle for his country, suffered greatly in civilian life in the aftermath, yet who had retained his sense of humor through it all. Jim talked little about combat, but he liked to tell one story in particular that took place at night near Khe Sang during a ferocious battle marines fought against a surrounding force of Viet Cong and North Vietnamese Regulars.

As Jim relates it: "I was a bit nervous. We knew the VC were all around us. I had a funny feeling, like something was near me. Then all of a sudden the bushes moved, and I just opened up and sprayed everything." He laughed every time he told the punch line: "The next morning I discovered I had killed the CO's dog; they had to hide me for three days because he wanted to *kill* me."

After the war Jim never found his footing in civilian life. Like so many other vets, he drifted from job to job, found solace in alcohol and isolation, and never quite recovered. He died after years in half-way houses and finally in a nursing home. By the end, at the age of 63—a mere 23 months older than me—he was a wreck of a man, both mentally and physically.

After the phone call came from Bill, I slumped into a chair, almost relieved that Jim's ordeal was finally over. But the image that filled my mind was not that of an exhausted, defeated man, but that of Jim as a high school football hero. It was at Franklin Field in Dorchester, Mass. Jim and I were playing for *Cathedral High*, he as the big defensive end and I as a utility quarterback waiting on the sidelines. *Mission High* was marching toward our endzone with the help of a short pass off both our ends. The coach called a time-out.

"We've got to stop that pass," coach said. Then he looked straight at my big brother: "Jim, try to get a jump on that pass and see if you can pick it off!" Coach had confidence in Jim's ability. We all did; he was good.

A few plays later, at our 10-yard-line, Jim leaped to his left as soon as the ball was snapped. Sure enough, *Mission's* quarterback had called that short pass again, but he saw Jim too late as he released the ball toward his own tight end at our goal line. Jim picked it off at the 5-yard-line to avert the touchdown.

U.S. Marine Corps Sgt. Walter James (Jim) Duffy, Jr, served two tours of duty in Vietnam in the early 60s. He's shown here at age 21 after graduating boot camp.

I was elated. We lost the game, but it didn't matter. My brother, Jim, was a hero. Even his response to my congratulations after the game was typical of Jim: " Yeah, so they beat us by only 33 points this time instead of their usual 40."

It was only a few years after that that Jim found himself surrounded by the Viet Cong near Khe Sang, and I think that was the beginning of the end for him. The tall, handsome end with the quick, self-effacing wit might as well have died on the battlefield, thus averting four decades of wandering, confusion, and misery.

During his final years, his brothers, Bill, Hugh, and I, made many trips to Boston to visit with him at the Don Orione Nursing Home in East Boston. Often the talk centered on our youth growing up. We were ordinary kids from Boston's Irish ghetto, *Southie*, and we had wonderful youthful memories of fun and daring exploits.

I look at my own three sons now and I see my brothers and me years ago. Carefree youths. All playing one sport or another at school. Our adult lives and dreams and girlfriends all still in the future. My oldest son, Jake, is about to enter high school. He's becoming a big tall, handsome boy, just like my brother, Jim. He even has some of Jim's youthful mannerisms: the tossing of his head to the side, the quiet disposition, the well-timed self-effacing one-liner. What's to become of him? Will he too go off to war after high school?

Jim's service at the national cemetery was wonderful. The taps, held long by the bugler, drifted over the beautiful cemetery. On one knee a Marine presented the flag to Bill, the oldest brother: "Sir, the President of the United States, the Commandant of the Marine Corps, and the American people present this flag to you in honor of your loved one's faithful and honorable service to God and country."

The tears flowed. It was a proper goodbye to an ordinary hero. ***— Dave Duffy***

David enjoys the potato harvest after the first killing frost.

Put your garden to bed for the winter

By Jackie Clay

During the crispy fall afternoons, we listen often and intently to the weather forecasts. "It's going to be clear tonight," I'd tell my late husband, Bob, and my son, David. "It could frost...." So we cover everything that is not frost hardy. Everything that we can, that is. The rows and rows of sweet corn, beans, and potatoes will have to tough it out. We just don't have enough "cover" to cover them. We drag out the huge plastic tarps we've salvaged from the throw away bin at a truss mill, blue and green cheapy tarps, old clear plastic, feed sacks, rugs, old blankets, saddle blankets, buckets, and anything that will protect our precious tomatoes, peppers, and melons. Working until after dark sometimes, we desperately tuck our plants in for the night. We drag into the house, knowing we've done everything we can. Sometimes it frosts, other times we get lucky and the Frost Fairies bypass our patchworked and ugly garden for easier targets.

The process is repeated several times each fall. Often the first frost comes early, leaving a good bit of

Indian summer behind it. This adds weeks to the growing season at the peak of production. We *don't* want that first frost to cut us off early. And since we eat what we grow, this is vital to our family.

But as the autumn colors bloom about us, those chilly nights become sharper and the air clearer until the weather radio doesn't warn of frosts. It calls for a freeze. This differs from a frost in that you can't simply cover your plants to protect them as you can for frost. With a frost, anything you are able to cover will *usually* survive and go on to produce. So when we hear the dreaded "F" word, we pull out all the stops and gather what we can, for after the freeze most of your garden is nothing more than soggy, drooping black vines full of frozen, useless vegetables.

We pick all of the tomatoes and peppers of any size. Even the egg-sized fully green tomatoes will be used for relish, green tomato pie (look up my "fake" apple pie recipe in Issue #77, Sept/Oct 2002), dill green tomato pickles, and more. I pick the tomatoes carefully, sorting them by ripeness. The red-ripe ones together, the yellow-orange ones together, and so on down to the rock-hard little green guys. The reason for this is that the tomatoes will easily and swiftly finish ripening in the house with no special help. I don't put them in a sunny window, wrap them with newspaper or anything. I just sort 'em and stack the pails, kettles, boxes, and baskets in rows in any warm place I can: the kitchen floor, the pantry, or even on my son David's lower, unused bunk bed.

Me in early winter garden, harvesting the last carrots before the ground freezes. They ignore frost and light freezes. (Bob Clay photo)

Likewise, all the beans are picked along with any ripe melons. Melons don't ripen much indoors, so it isn't a good idea to harvest little ones. They will only rot. Every cuke of any size is picked, from tiny pickler to salad slicers. Even a light freeze will kill the plants even when covered, leaving the fruits of the vine soft and unusable. Squash and pumpkins are loaded into the garden cart and toted into the goat barn. They will survive lighter frosts, uncovered, but the freeze will make them soft and they will quickly rot. Every ear of sweet corn is picked and brought in to process as soon as I can. Corn doesn't take freezing well, and sometimes a light frost will "burn" the plants, leaving the corn leaves first dark, then yellow brown on the edges.

After such a frost, or before a freeze, the corn must be quickly picked and processed to keep it sweet and tender. Even a couple of days on the dead stalk will often result in tough corn with little sweetness or corn taste.

We work like dogs, knowing that this is about it for our biggest part of the harvest. The onions, carrots, and potatoes are safe from all but a dreadfully hard freeze. The cabbage family, including broccoli, cauliflower, and Brussels sprouts are fairly safe, but we always cover the cauliflower and broccoli, just to be sure, as a sharp freeze can damage these crops.

Even after a good freeze, it seems like there are some "hangers on" in the garden, some green tomatoes that survive under the now black vines to go ahead and begin to ripen, a few bits of this and that, so we still watch the garden and harvest what we can.

But finally, it's about done. The root crops are dug, the cabbage, broccoli, and late onions are harvested, and the garden stands tattered and worn. After a season's hard work, culminating in the mad pre-freeze harvest, we are ready to rest a bit.

But this is not to say we are done gardening for the year. For it's time to put the garden to bed for the winter.

Get rid of dead plants

Most of the "ugly" in the garden now is jutting, broken, black and brown dead plants, looking used and sad. Some gardeners simply till under all of the garden plants. Of course this is a simple fix to the problem, and it does add some organic material to the soil. But there are times that this is not the best idea. First of all, think about any insect problems you have had in your garden this year. Many of these nasty pests breed and stash their eggs in the stems and roots of the very plants they infested.

How about cukes that had white powdery spots on leaves, or beans whose vines yellowed and wilted? Or tomato vines that had yellow spots, black dots, or wilted and died? These are all signs of diseased plants. To simply till them under just about guarantees that you'll have the problem again next year—and probably worse.

What I do is gather any such plants into a pile in the center of the garden and burn them on a safe day, usually when it has snowed. I make sure that every corn stalk, every vine is burned to white ash, even if I have to add some light dry brush for fuel. Let corn ear worm eggs or powdery mildew survive *that*!

Another time to either compost or burn heavy garden waste is when you live in the dry climates, such as we had in New Mexico. There, I opted to chop and compost my corn stalks because it took years for such heavy material to finally rot away. And unrotted, it tangled tiller tines and was a possible home for garden insect pests.

FREEZE IN FORECAST! Bob and David madly begin picking everything the cold will harm: cukes, tomatoes, squash, pumpkins, peppers, corn.

Don't worry that you will waste this material because the ash generated from burning it is a good addition to your garden, being high in potash. In fact, we liberally sprinkle our ash from the wood kitchen range across the garden each year.

Add organic material

Before you till that garden plot the last time in the fall, add as much organic material as you can. I doubt that it is possible to add too much, if the material is right. You *don't* want to put a foot of raw manure without bedding onto the garden. If you do, your next year's garden will appear fantastic, but your crops will be huge plants and vines, and little fruit due to the high nitrogen content of the raw manure.

Instead, use at least partially rotted manure with a decent amount of straw or sawdust bedding mixed with it. This will provide plenty of organic fertilizer, and the straw or sawdust bedding will help tame the excess nitrogen and add extremely valuable compost to improve the tilth of the soil.

Another easily added natural material that will do this is bushels and bushels of leaves. If you don't have enough leaves of your own, gather bags of them from the curb in your town. I used to have a "leaf route," which was simply a lot of town folks who loved to have me stop once a week and throw their bags of leaves into my truck to use on the gardens instead of paying to have the trash haulers take them away. It was a simple word-of-mouth thing. In the late summer, I just told a few people on a few streets that I needed more leaves for my garden and would happily pick them up. By the time the first flush of leaves hit the ground, I had a list of 15 people who wanted me to stop regularly. And that doubled as other neighbors saw what was going on. It seemed that even town people were tickled to see their leaves go to a good use.

You can spread a foot of leaves on your garden, then either wait for a good rain to mat them down or water the garden well. When it dries enough to till, run the tiller through them until they are chopped up and buried. Then you can wait a few days and do it again. The leaves rot very quickly, and it's amazing how many leaves you can work in each fall. (Plus, you have garbage bags enough for your trash all winter.)

With your strawy manure, dump six or eight inches over the garden area and till that in well. You can add another layer, as you did with the leaves, *except* on the area where you will plant your potatoes next spring. If you get this area too rich in nitrogen, your potatoes will be quite prone to scab, making them unappetizing as well as lower producing.

Want a "different" soil amendment that is also free for the taking? You folks who live in the country can go talk to your local grain elevator (not feed store) manager. Ask him if they haul away screenings. Screenings are grain hulls, bits and pieces of husk, straw, and leaves, as well as broken bits and pieces of grain, left over after corn, oats, and other grains are run through a screen to clean them for market. Sometimes there are even piles of wet or sour grain that has spilled when trucks are unloaded. Tell him that you are looking for this to add to your garden soil. In grain producing areas, truckloads are often available *free*. Watch out for concentrated weed or other seeds in screenings, as you can easily "seed in" a great patch of weeds. Once in a while you'll see lots of seeds in screenings. Feed these to your chickens or soak them well in an old trough to sour them, then dump them in your compost pile to rot.

My first homestead was located only two miles from a small town with a large grain elevator. They were thrilled to be able to have their dump trucks haul their "refuse" to my place, just to get rid of it. I had so much that I had to hire a fellow with a small bulldozer to come and work the mountains of rotting grain into the ground of my garden and pasture.

It sure smelled high that fall. But when spring came, it had all rotted and turned my garden from a sandy piece of worthless ground to heaven on earth. I tilled the ground and found it deep and black, crumbling behind my tiller like we've all dreamed of. It was so productive that my first year was unbelievable. And when I wanted

The first unexpected frost paints cuke vines a pretty silver. By afternoon they will be black and droopy, stone dead.

to fish in the river across the road, I could literally take a stick, poke it into the ground and flip out enough worms to fill a soup can in a couple of minutes. That's God's truth.

Likewise, my first garden in Minnesota, back in 1972, was on solid red clay, down eight feet or more. I had to plow with a tractor to get my root crops out of the ground. It was that hard. Now *that* wouldn't do. So I borrowed a manure spreader and spent two weeks hauling a mountain of old black cow manure from beside the old barn right out onto the garden. Everyone said I'd "burn" the garden plants right up. But I remembered the results of the grain screenings and figured that *anything* was better than that red clay.

Turns out that I was right. The next year's garden was *much* better, and the carrots could be dug, not plowed up at harvest. But every year, for the next 15, I hauled many loads of strawy manure out there and worked it in. And, of course, the truckloads of bagged leaves. When I left, the soil was black, crumbly, and you could not dig deep enough to get down to red clay without a backhoe.

Should you be in an area where the soil is acid, it's also a good idea to sprinkle lime over the garden as you work in this material. Acid soil is found where you see wild strawberries, wild blueberries, and moss growing across the ground. Of course, it's best to take a simple soil test to find out exactly how acid or alkaline your soil is, for most plants like a fairly neutral soil to thrive in.

Enlarging your present garden

Fall is the best time to enlarge your garden for next year. This gives time for the sod and plants that you've tilled under to rot, making tilling and planting next spring much, much easier. Haul away any logs and large debris. Dig any stumps that you can. (Don't let a few that remain daunt you, though. Just plant around them and cover them with small compost piles to help them rot quicker.)

Like your main garden plot, till it in, digging out as many weed and brush roots as possible to help avoid weed problems next year. Then work in as much organic material as you can, such as strawy manure, compost, or leaves. This will quietly rot during the winter, making the soil happy and healthy.

Do you need to fence your garden? Fall is the perfect time to get this done, before the rush and craziness at planting time. Deer need at least a six-foot fence, with another foot or more of top wires above that. Rabbits *usually* will keep out of 2"x 4" wire, but I've stood in the garden and watched an adult cottontail scurry through it. Heavy-duty chicken wire is safer. I've had good luck with 6-foot high 2"x 4" welded wire with a two-foot bunny and ground squirrel chicken wire run around on the outside of the welded wire. This pretty well keeps out everything but chipmunks and birds.

How about trellises for grape vines, hardy kiwis, and so forth? If these are in your plans, this is a good time to get them placed in the ground. That way they will be firmly set long before you plant your vines in the spring.

By now, your garden is wonderfully cleaned up, fed, groomed, and tucked into bed for the winter. The new fence is up and you *and* your garden are ready for a good winter's rest. I sometimes believe that God gave us winter so we would be forced to take it easy for awhile. Walk out and pat those wonderful beds before it snows and tell them to have a great winter.

Before you know it, you'll be getting those seed catalogs in the mail and you'll get the fever again. It happens to me every single year. Δ

Working in a truck load of rotted strawy horse manure into our fall garden. (Bob Clay photo)

GOLD PANNING

for fun and profit

By Gail Butler

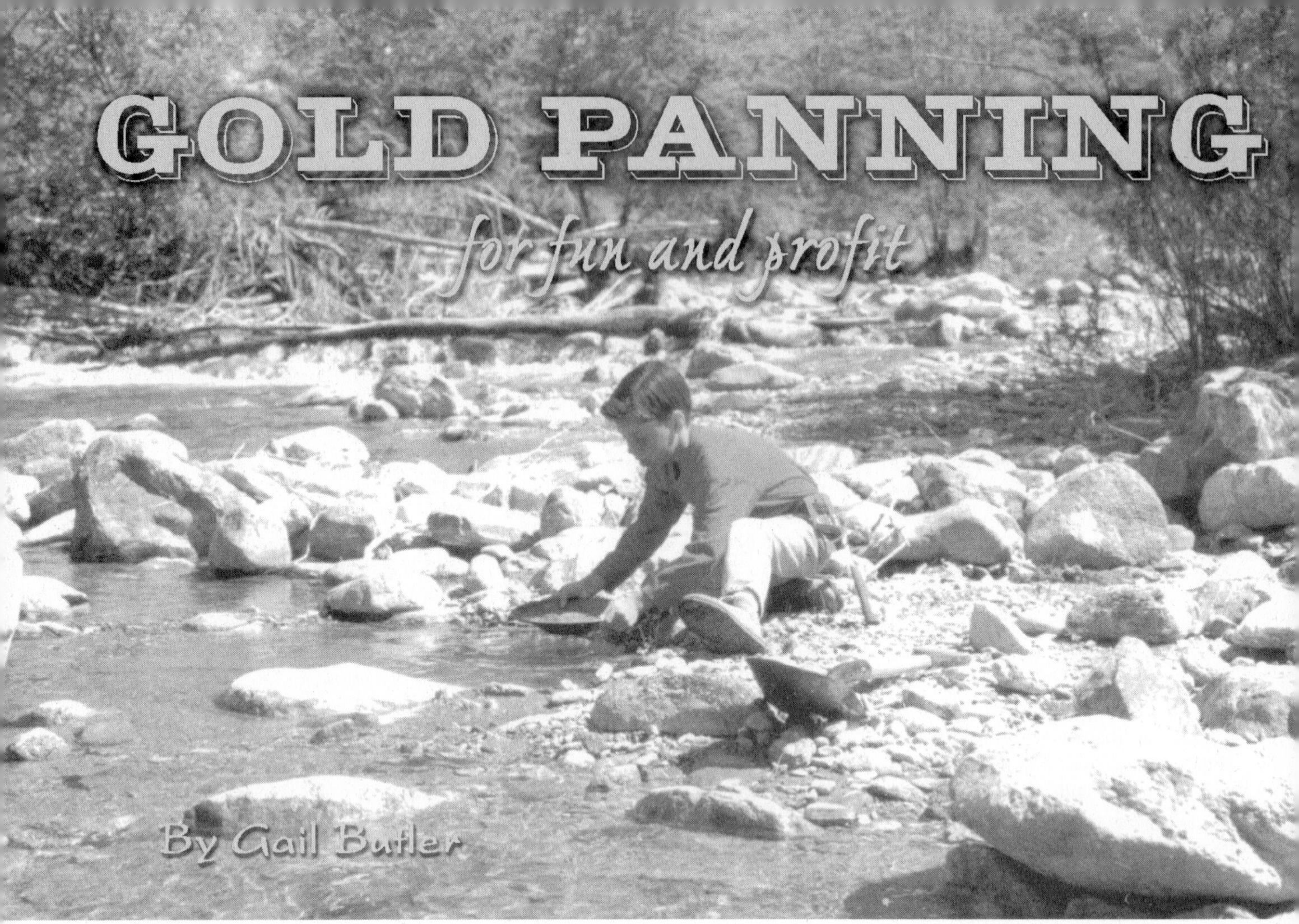

Want to earn a little extra income and enjoy the outdoors in the process? Then pack yourself a lunch and a gold pan and head to the nearest gold-bearing stream, creek, or river in your area. With gold at $437 per ounce as of this writing, it's a good time to begin planning your own gold panning expedition.

As the economy weakens—a trend presently driven by high fuel prices—the monetary value of gold generally rises making prospecting for it a more popular and profitable venture. Also, the 2004-2005 drought-breaking snows and rainstorms that inundated most of the nation have insured ample spring runoff guaranteed to churn up and replenish old gold deposits for several seasons yet to come. This replenishing process brings gold flakes and nuggets down from higher elevations via runoff from snowmelt, concentrating them in pockets nearer the ground surface within easy reach of the gold panner.

When to go

Many gold prospectors head creekside in early spring in order to be among the first to sample banks for deposits of gold. However, many years of successful gold prospecting has taught me that it is more profitable to wait until late summer and into autumn for the best success. Also, in autumn most vacationers have returned to work so that I have the river essentially to myself should I happen upon a rich little gold deposit.

Creeks and rivers carry a majority of gold where currents are strongest and deepest. Springtime creeks may be so turbulent from one bank to the other that the prospector hasn't a safe spot to pan. Also, the majority of gold deposits are as yet underwater and unavailable. Bedrock crevices, the richest sources of easy-to-reach gold, generally remain underwater until mid to late summer. In late summer and fall, creeks have shrunk considerably, leaving boulders and bedrock crevices exposed for easy prospecting.

Springtime can be a dangerous season to be near rain-swollen creeks and rivers. Water levels fluctuate radically and can rise a couple of feet in minutes without warning. A sudden slip on wet rocks can send a person tumbling into brutally turbulent white water. This is an especially bad time to take young children along.

Getting equipped

Much of what you need in the way of equipment may be found in your own garage and kitchen, with perhaps the exception of a gold pan. Most hardware stores sell them if you don't already own one. The best size pans for most people are those 10, 12, 16, or 18 inches in diameter. Women and children are generally more comfortable with pans in the 10- or 12-inch range.

You'll also need a shovel and a gardening trowel, an old paintbrush, a long screwdriver, a fine-tipped, narrow artist's brush, and a small water-filled bottle with a secure cap. An old metal spoon is useful for scooping gold-bearing gravel from narrow crevices in exposed bedrock. Tweezers make picking large flakes and small nuggets out of your pan easier, so add them to your prospecting pack too. Pack a picnic lunch, add a few libations to quench your thirst, and you are ready to go gold prospecting by yourself, with friends, or with the family. If you go by yourself, be sure to tell someone where you are going and when you expect to return.

Panning for gold is an activity that can be enjoyed by anyone regardless of age. Most children take to it quite naturally. Gold panning is not strenuous and can be enjoyed by those with age-related or physical handicaps. Most of the process takes place sitting down, kneeling, or squatting. As long as you can get down to the water's edge you can pan for gold. In many areas it is possible to drive right to river's edge.

Where the gold is

Gold deposits are continually eroding out and being washed into creeks and streams. During spring runoff this process is accelerated. Gold is still found along the same watercourses where it was found in the past.

I have been a gold prospector for nearly 30 years and have consistently found profitable amounts of gold in well-known gold areas. In California's historic Mother Lode region, along Highway 49, a friend and I once recovered over four ounces of gold. The area we prospected was along the Yuba River where it passes through a public campground. This popular campsite is visited each year by hundreds of vacationers. Yet, we dug under some blackberry brambles and found gold that had been accumulating, undisturbed, for many years. If you are willing to do a bit of creative digging in spots others tend to shun, such as under thorny blackberries, you too can find and recover the gold others have overlooked.

Places where gold has been found historically are easily located with a bit of research at the library or on the Internet. Talk to the old-timers. They can tell you a great deal about an area, offering insight and sometimes even firsthand experience. Areas with gold history continue to be profitable, especially after a season of higher-than-average runoff.

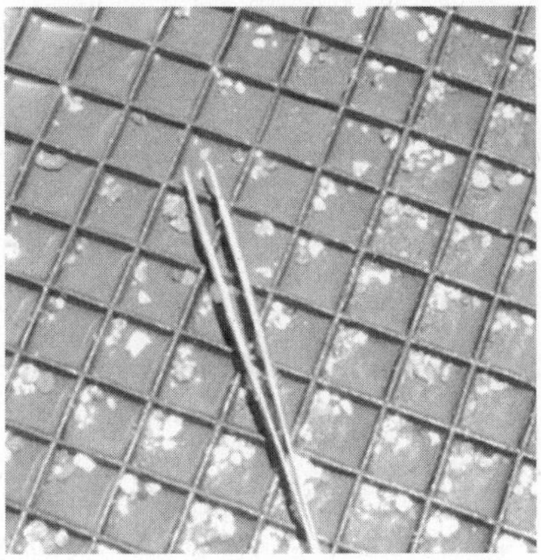

Adding rubber matting to your sluice acts as a trap for nuggets and gold allowing for easy spotting and removal with tweezers. To get matting with gold-trapping pockets like those depicted in this photo, search auto wrecking yards for old VW vans.

Gold settles in predictable places along a watercourse due to its specific gravity, which is, technically speaking, the weight of gold in comparison to an equal volume of water.

What this means, simply, is that gold is very dense—the densest thing, relatively speaking, that will end up in your pan. Therefore, during the gold panning process you will easily be able to pan away rocks, gravel, sand, metal particles, fishing weights, buckshot—just about anything else barring the occasional platinum nugget—and retain all the gold in your pan down to the smallest speck. Gold in your pan will be safely tucked from view beneath a layer of black sand. Swirl aside the black sand and golden flakes and nuggets reveal themselves.

An important secret to keep in mind when prospecting is that gold will settle out anyplace along a watercourse where water slows down. Look for physical features and objects that cause water flow to fluctuate. Bends in the river, trunks of trees, roots of grasses and bushes, sand bars, rocks, boulders, and derelict automobiles all cause water to slow down or alter its course. As a result, gold ceases to move with the current and begins to settle. Gold tends to accumulate and concentrate in quantity in these types of places over the course of one or several seasons. Concentrations of gold are what prospectors look for. Panning up and down the river in these types of places is what prospecting is all about. Doing so will indicate to you where, along a river's bank, gold concentrations are highest. A few hours spent prospecting will yield the greatest profits as you work the spots where you've test-panned the most "color" (gold).

Another important secret is that more gold will generally be found under gravel on the downstream side of any rock, boulder, or other object that impedes the natural current.

A third secret is that water levels change drastically throughout any season. In spring, water coming down from the mountains and hills will raise a creek's water level dramatically. In late fall a watercourse may shrink to a mere trickle. Being able to project where water flowed and what objects impeded the flow at any time throughout the season will enable you to find gold in places others don't think to look.

Technique

Gold panning is easy. There are just two basic motions although techniques vary slightly from prospector to prospector. The old-timers used frying pans, metal pie plates, or tin cups if a pan wasn't handy. So can you if you can't find or borrow one.

Locate a likely looking spot along the river where you suspect gold has settled. Dig up some of this gravel and put it into your pan. A trowel is useful for removing gold-bearing gravel from tight spots between tree roots or boulders. Fill your pan half to three-quarters full. Gently immerse the pan in water in an area where the current is slow and won't whisk away the pan's contents. Allow the pan to fill with water. Stir and knead the contents with your hands making sure everything is well saturated. Lift your pan from the water, keeping it level, and begin to swirl it gently in a counterclockwise motion being careful not to let the contents slosh out. Use one or both hands, whichever is most comfortable.

As you circulate the pan the process of gold settling to the bottom begins. Rocks and gravel begin to surface and ride atop the pan's contents. Next, dip your pan at a slight angle and partially submerge it. With a backward and forward motion allow water to gently sluice off the top layers of dirt, rock, and gravel. Don't be too cautious. You can pan off rocks as big as one inch in diameter and not worry about losing gold. As your confidence grows you will soon be able to pan down to black sand in a matter of moments.

As the bulk of the pan's contents begin to gravitate closer to its lip bring it back to level, remove it from the water and repeat the counterclockwise motion. This movement allows water in the pan to assist additional gravel to rise to the surface. Gold then resettles in the crease where the sides of the pan meet the bottom.

Panning can yield this pan full of gold flakes and nuggets.

Basically, gold panning is the sequential repetition of two simple movements—the circular counterclockwise motion and the angled sluicing motion—until you have greatly reduced the pan's contents with only a few layers of black sand remaining. At this stage it is a simple matter to swirl aside the black sand to expose any flakes or nuggets. Process several pans full from each location where you suspect gold may have concentrated. If you don't get anything or only a few flakes, move on to the next likely site. Make a mental note which sites along the bank yielded the most gold. Go back and work these exclusively.

To remove fine gold from your pan, use a fine-tipped artist's brush to scoop up as many flakes as the brush will hold and transfer them to your water-filled bottle. As soon as the brush touches the water in the bottle,the gold will drop off plummeting to the bottom. Use your tweezers for removing larger flakes and any small, flat nuggets. Bigger nuggets can be picked out with your fingers. Securely cap your bottle and put it in a safe spot where it won't roll into the river or get broken. A front shirt pocket, securely buttoned, is a safe spot to keep your bottle. I once lost three-quarters of an ounce of gold when I bent over and my bottle rolled from my unbuttoned pocket into the fast-moving current of the Yuba River.

Bedrock crevices

Crevices in bedrock trap gold in quantity as it moves along the bottom of the creek bed. One of the most profitable panning methods is to extract and pan the tightly packed gravel of bedrock crevices. Many a gold panner has extracted more gold in a day from exposed bedrock crevices than a team of divers operating an expensive gold dredging device. In the autumn more crevices are left high and dry as water levels shrink in streams and creeks.

Digging, brushing, and scraping gravel from narrow bedrock crevices is where a spoon, a paintbrush, and screwdriver come in handy. Because gold eventually sinks to the bottom of a crevice, be sure to empty it completely of gravel, sand, and the clay-like substance found at the bottom. Break up clay with your fingers and rinse it into your gold pan to release any embedded gold.

Fool's gold

How can you be sure that what you are finding is really gold? There are a few simple tests you can perform. Subject the suspected gold to the edge of a pocketknife. If it shatters or separates into flakes it is either iron pyrite or mica. Real gold will flatten or dent. It won't shatter.

Both iron pyrite and mica display a brassy color in the sun, but when shaded by your hand or hat tend to fade in color or "brown out." Real gold is a warm, golden yellow and retains its color even in shade. Iron pyrites crystallize in cubes while mica resembles fish scales.

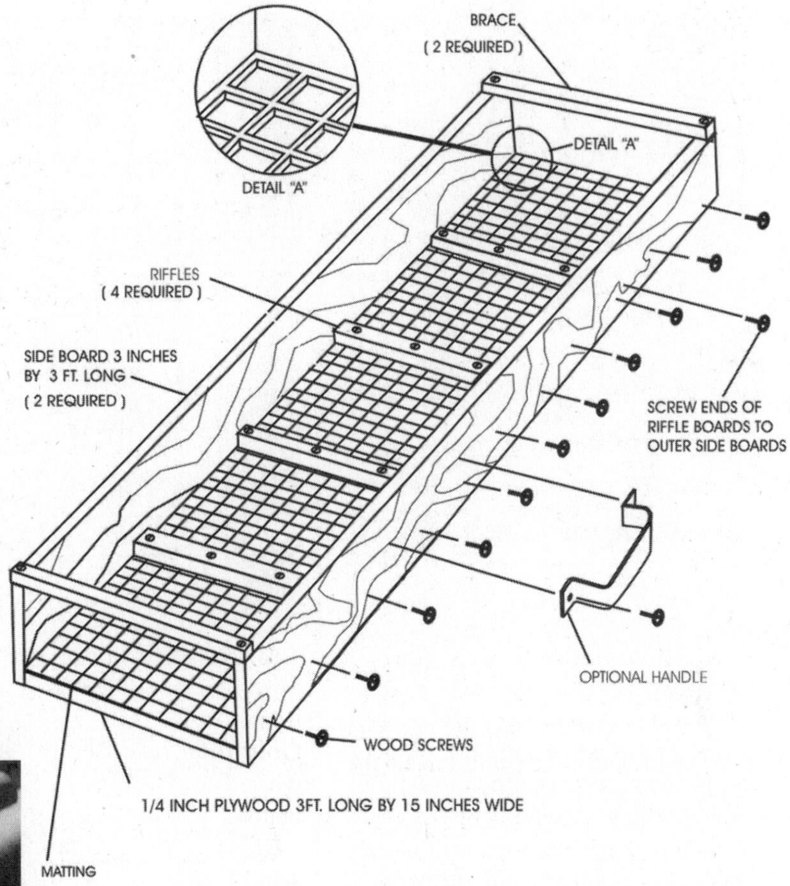

Both iron pyrite and mica display a brassy color in the sun, but when shaded by your hand or hat tend to fade in color or "brown out." Real gold is a warm, golden yellow, and retains its color even in shade.

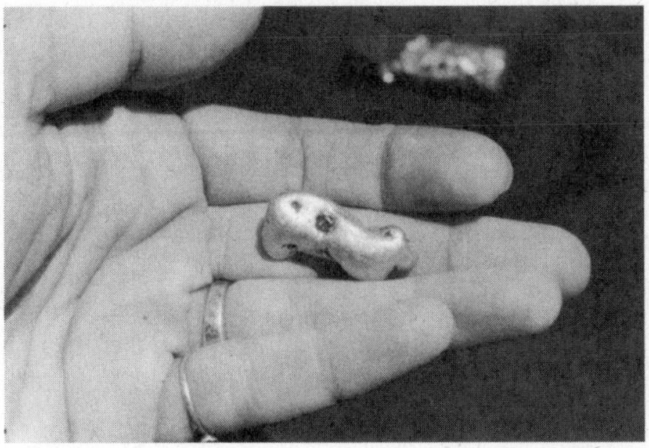

Other tools

Besides *panning* for gold, there are other techniques you may want to consider. The next logical step after mastering the art of panning is sluicing for gold. The old adage, "The more gold-bearing dirt you move, the more gold you get," remains true. A **sluice** will process many times more gold-bearing gravel than a pan.

Drywashers, as the name implies, process gold-bearing gravel from waterless desert washes. You'll need to tote a few gallons of water to pan the gold-bearing "concentrates" the drywasher produces.

For those with diving experience, **dredges** can be used to recover gold from deep riverbed crevices. Dredges tend to be the most expensive gold recovery devices and are the target of most anti-prospecting legislation. Dredges require permits in most areas and can only be used May through October. However, dredging season may vary from area to area so be sure to check with the governing land agency—usually the Bureau of Land Management (BLM) or Forest Service.

Build your own sluice

After learning the art of gold panning, most beginning prospectors want a technique for processing more gravel, faster, in order to recover greater quantities of gold. A sluice box is the usual first choice.

The author pours screened gravel into a sluice.

A manufactured 10-inch wide, 3-foot long sluice can cost $60 or more. While this cost is reasonable when compared to the cost of other types of gold recovery equipment—usually amounting to hundreds of dollars—building your own sluice will reduce your expenditure to only a few dollars in materials.

For many years I used a sluice I fabricated from wood and rubber matting. It was much easier to clean than those mass-manufactured sluices with expanded metal screening, riffle beds, and outdoor carpet pieces which must be disassembled and reassembled each time you need to clean it out every hour or so. My homemade sluice proved to be very sturdy and long lasting. After many years of seasonal use, I eventually sold it to a co-worker.

Required materials

To make your own sluice from wood, stay true to the measurements of manufactured sluices that are 10 inches wide and 3 feet long for ease of portability. These measurements also allow your homemade sluice to slip into a five-gallon plastic bucket for removal of your gold concentrates.

To construct a wooden sluice you'll need:

1. A piece of ¼-inch plywood that is three feet long by 15½ inches wide
2. A package of ¾-inch Phillips flat-head wood screws
3. A tube of waterproof marine/auto silicon adhesive
4. Four pieces of ½-inch-thick oak or other hardwood cut to 9¼ inches long (to form the riffles)
5. Ribbed rubber matting cut to 9½ inches wide by 32 inches long
6. Optional garage door handle and nuts and bolts to attach it
7. Also optional, two ¼-inch thick, 10-inch long by 1- to 2-inch wide strips of plywood for use as stabilizing bars

Using a circular saw, cut two 3-inch-wide, 3-foot-long strips off your piece of plywood. These will form the sides of your sluice box. This should leave you with a piece that is 9½ inches wide by 3 feet long for the sluice bed. Also, cut the riffles to size. You can, if you wish, have the lumberyard cut the wood for you. If you want to install the optional stabilizing bars, you can usually find plywood scraps at the lumberyard at no cost. You might even have unused plywood stored in a garage or shed, reducing your materials costs to practically nothing.

With the adhesive, glue one of the side pieces along the sawn edge of the sluice bed so that it is perpendicular to the sluice bed, forming a neat 90-degree angle. In this case the adhesive is used more for sealing and waterproofing than adhering the two pieces of wood together. Using wood screws, secure the side to the edge of the sluice bed every couple of inches all along its three-foot length. Be sure that the cut edge of the sluice bed meets the bottom of the side piece evenly before screwing the two together. Attach the other side to the opposite edge of the sluice bed in the same manner.

Eight inches in from either end of the sluice bed, glue in one of the four riffle pieces horizontally across the sluice bed. Secure each end of the riffle to the inner sides with a screw drilled in through the outer sides. Secure each riffle to the sluice bed with three additional screws evenly spaced along its top. Apply the other two riffles in the same manner, spacing them eight inches apart. Seal any tiny gaps between the sides and the riffle ends with the adhesive/sealer.

Run a thin bead of the adhesive to seal the edges of each riffle to the sluice bed so that sand and small pieces of gravel and gold do not slip beneath during use. Rubbing alcohol will remove adhesive from your fingers and clean up any excess on other surfaces. Secure the optional plywood braces as shown in the diagram at this time.

After the adhesive dries (usually 24 hours is sufficient), sand any rough or splintery edges, then apply several coats of marine varnish, letting each coat dry before applying the next. This will prevent the wood surfaces from swelling and warping from prolonged contact with water. Let the varnish dry thoroughly according to the manufacturer's directions.

Measure the space between the riffles, and use a carpet knife or utility knife to cut the rubber matting to fit between the riffles and onto the sluice bed's "head" and "tail." Glue down the matting pieces, sealing any small gaps with the silicon adhesive. Matting that protrudes beyond the head or tail of the sluice should be trimmed away with a utility knife. It doesn't matter whether the matting is ribbed, ridged, or "pocketed." The matting I prefer is found by rummaging through the backs of old VW buses I find in junkyards. Pull out and flip over the mat and its bottom side reveals rubberized squares—the perfect nugget trap. Ribbed matting may be found on measure-and-cut rolls at hardware stores. You might even have an old rubber porch mat you can put to a new use. Tire tread is an option I haven't tried. It might work well if it isn't bald.

If desired, you can drill a couple of holes in one side of the sluice and attach a garage door handle to make your sluice easy to carry as you would a suitcase. Seal around the nuts and bolts with the marine/auto adhesive.

Before using your sluice the first time, let the varnish and adhesive cure for about one week.

Using your sluice

There are some factors to consider when setting up your homemade sluice to recover gold. These concern depth and velocity of water flow through the sluice and the angle at which to set it in the river for maximum gold recovery.

While this may sound complicated, it isn't. An easy rule to remember is that water must cover and be able to move the largest single object that will pass through the sluice. If you screen your gravel (as most prospectors do) using a ½-inch mesh screen, the largest object moving through the sluice will be slightly less than ½ inch in diameter. Rocks of this size, if your sluice is set at the proper angle and depth, should move easily through and items with a higher specific gravity, such as iron-rich gravel, gold, black sand, and mineral-rich pebbles will settle behind the downstream side of the riffles.

Screening gravel for the sluice using a homemade classifying screen

A simple test to determine depth and angle is to set your sluice into the current near creek's edge so two or more inches of water pass over the sluice bed. Secure the sluice in place using some boulders wedged against its sides. A wide flat boulder can be laid across the sides to weight it down. You'll want the upstream end, or sluice head, slightly higher than the tail end.

Drop in a shovel full of gravel containing three or four BBs. The BBs serve to mimic gold in your test. Much of the gravel should pass through the sluice leaving the BBs caught by the riffles or matting along with any iron-rich sand and mineralized stones. Ideally, your BBs should stop in the upper third to one half of your sluice.

If the BBs pass clear through or end up behind the lower riffle, flatten the angle of the sluice and/or erect a simple wing dam of boulders to slow

Preparing to pan gravel from a desert dry wash in Southern California

water flow before it reaches the sluice head.

If the gravel and BBs fail to move, you'll need to raise the sluice head's angle a bit and create a chute of boulders to angle a greater volume of water toward the sluice head. In the case that additional water cannot be channeled to the sluice you may have to relocate it until proper angle and depth of flow can be achieved. With a bit of practice you will soon be able to "eyeball" the proper angle and flow conditions without the need to use BBs.

In the case of insufficient water flow in a creek, as may occur at summer's end or during drought conditions, the sluice can be set up on shore and water poured over it to process gold. This is more work but when in a good gold area will be well worth it.

I once had to do this in Northern California's gold country because the river was in a perilous flood stage and would have swept my sluice, not to mention myself, away. The 1½ ounces of gold I recovered that afternoon made the extra work of bucketing water worth the time and effort.

With your sluice angled properly and with adequate water moving through, gravel, gold, minerals, and sand will be classified within the sluice according to the specific gravity of each of those components.

Occasionally pyrite cubes and gems, such as garnets, will lodge behind the riffles and in the ridges of the rubber matting. Depending on the area you are prospecting, you may even recover a rare diamond.

Classifying gravel

Most prospectors build or buy a classifying screen to set over a five-gallon plastic bucket. A homemade classifying screen consists of two simple wooden frames with ½-inch screen secured between. Each shovel full of gravel is then dumped onto the screen. The screen is shaken or agitated so gold and smaller than ½-inch stones fall through the screen into the bucket. Always check the screen before dumping off rocks for gold nuggets larger than ½-inch in size. And, don't dump rocks on a spot you later want to dig for gold.

A nice gold nugget can be mounted in a plastic locket and worn or sold.

Screening your gold-bearing gravel before pouring it into the sluice serves several purposes. The first is that you'll move more gold-bearing gravel by eliminating the bulk and weight of large stones. Second, your sluice will last longer and function more efficiently by eliminating rocks that would gouge and flatten the riffles. Also, the bulk of rocks landing and settling in the sluice tend to interfere with the efficient classifying of material and gold by altering the manner in which water moves through the sluice.

Avoid dumping the entire bucket of gravel into the sluice at once. Use a measured shaking motion or slowly and steadily pour the gravel into the sluice head, watching to see if the water flow is accepting and processing the gravel evenly.

Seeing the gold

The rubber matting you installed in the sluice bed will allow you to take a visual check for large flakes and nuggets of gold without having to raise the sluice and pan its contents. Large pieces of gold will settle into the upper portions of the sluice while fines are buried under mineralized sand and gravel in the lower end. Keep a long pair of tweezers handy to remove large flakes and nuggets. If you try to remove gold with your fingers, you'll alter the flow of water and cause the gold to skip away further down the sluice bed.

After running several buckets of gravel through your sluice, you'll notice that material is beginning to fill the spaces between the riffles. When it begins to reach the top of the riffles, it is time to take up the sluice and clean it.

Carefully remove the sluice, keeping it as level as possible so that gravel (and gold) in the lower end doesn't fall out. Upend the sluice, tail first, into a five-gallon plastic bucket. You can use a gold pan or another five-gallon bucket to rinse material from the sluice into the bucket it sits in. When the sluice has been thoroughly washed of material, remove it from the bucket and set it back into the water, re-anchoring with boulders. Now its time to pan your concentrates.

Slowly pour the gravel and water contents of the bucket into a gold pan until the pan is half to two-thirds full. Be careful that your gold-bearing material doesn't overflow the edges of your gold pan. Usually a sluice will process enough gravel for three or four pannings.

Here is a secret: The gravel remaining in the bucket for the last panning will contain the most gold. Knowing this, you may want to let your partners pan the first few pans, reserving the last one for yourself. Your partners will soon catch on and want the last panning for themselves. Traditionally, at the end of each day's prospecting, all gold recovered is equally divided among all partners. It all comes out even in the end regardless of who gets the richest dregs in the bucket.

Thoroughly rinse any remaining material clinging to the sides of the bucket into your gold pan for the last panning. Small bits of gold and black sand tend to stick to the bottom and sides of the bucket. Tossing a handful or two of water up into the bucket dislodges anything that remains. Be sure the bucket is upended over a gold pan so that your rinsings fall into the pan.

With this easy-to-build sluice you'll have an efficient, inexpensive, and easily transported gold recovery system that will allow you to process profitable amounts of gold all season long for many seasons to come.

Summing up

Due to increasingly negative legislation, sluicing, drywashing, and even panning may be subject to restrictions or require a permit in some areas. Be sure to check before heading out.

Environmentalists often confuse recreational prospecting with commercial mining and are continually attempting to get legislation passed that limits, even prohibits, gold prospecting in particular areas they want to "protect." A normal spring runoff will erase all traces (holes) left from gold panning, sluicing, and dredging operations of the previous season. Recreational gold prospecting is not the threat to the environment that it is sometimes depicted.

Most private claims are posted with "no trespassing" signs. Be sure to respect them and stay out. Some prospectors have been known to enforce their mineral rights claim with a shotgun.

If you find a rich gold area on public lands, you can stake a mining claim if it is presently unclaimed or has gone inactive due to failure to file required assessment work papers. You can request a packet from the BLM detailing the claim process that also includes a variety of claim forms. Mining claim forms may be purchased at stationery stores that sell forms for deeds and wills.

You are not subject to taxation by the IRS for any gold you find until you sell it. Gold nuggets can be bartered for goods and services. It is still possible to purchase groceries at some general stores in Northern California and Alaska with native gold. Your gold will be weighed to determine value, and you can shop accordingly. Your native gold will usually contain a minor amount of silver or copper alloys and will not be worth quite as much as the current market price of refined gold. Do keep in mind that gold nuggets are often worth more than current gold prices because each, like a fingerprint, is unique and has "specimen" value. Use your accumulated gold flakes to shop. Save your nuggets to sell to jewelers.

You may decide to make your own gold nugget jewelry to wear or give as gifts if you have basic jewelry soldering skills. Nuggets may be backed with black velvet and secured in clear plastic lockets if you have no jewelry-making expertise.

If you have little success locating gold on one side of the river, try the other side. Gold can move and reconcentrate from year to year. If you've had success in a particular location one year but strike out the next, try different spots up and downstream from your former "glory hole."

Gold prospecting is a fun and profitable form of recreation on its own but may be incorporated into other types of outdoor activities such as fishing, hunting, and hiking.

Gold is found in about half of the states comprising the continental United States. Books outlining "how" and "where" may be purchased at rock and gem shows, gun shows, on the Internet, in bookstores, at gold prospecting supply shops, and checked out from the library. My book, *Recreational Gold Prospecting for Fun and Profit*, outlines basic, intermediate, and advanced prospecting techniques and where to shop for equipment. It also contains a list of prospecting clubs and enumerates known gold-bearing sites.

Edward Abbey, author of *Desert Solitaire* wrote, "Once bitten by the golden lure you become a prospector for life, condemned, doomed, exalted!" It is possible that the first time you see "color" in your pan you too may be bitten by the gold bug. It happened to me. It could happen to you. Δ

Resources

Rock & Gem Magazine
P.O. Box 6925
Ventura, CA 93006
www.rockngem.com
805-644-3824
623-327-3525

Gold Prospectors Association of America
P.O. Box 891509
Temecula, CA 92589
www.goldprospectors.org
951-699-4749
1-800-551-9707

Gather rose hips for health

By Gail Butler

Vitamin C-rich rose hips can be found in dried form in most health food stores, but why not gather your own? You'll save money and you'll know where they came from and the conditions in which they grew. Furthermore, you'll be adding to your own self-sufficiency by locating and gathering a nutrient-dense food source to nourish yourself and your family.

Growing along the main irrigation canal in the small farming community where I live are hedgerows of wild roses. In spring they produce lovely pink blossoms. As the petals fade, a green hip, or hypanthium, begins to swell at each blossom's base. From mid-September into October when they are fully red and ripe, and before frost tinges their foliage with autumn color making the hips harder to see, I gather bagfuls for making soup, wine, syrup, jelly, and tea.

If you live, as I do, in a temperature zone that's too cold to grow citrus fruit, rose hips are an excellent alternative food source of Vitamin C. All roses are edible, but we are most familiar with the rose's tasty cousins—fruits such as plums, apples, blackberries, and raspberries—all of which have small, rose-like white or pink flowers before setting fruit. A rose hip is merely the fruit of the rose plant.

Unlike their popular fruiting cousins, rose hips don't have much flesh beneath their skins. Instead, they are filled with tiny seeds covered with silky hairs. The skin of the hip, often tasting like an apple, is where most of the food value and nutrition lies.

Most wild roses will have four- or five-petal blossoms that are either white, yellow, or pink. Five-petal pink blossoms cover the wild roses in my area in spring.

Nutritional powerhouses

Known mostly for beauty in the garden and as a floral declaration of love, roses don't usually come to mind when we think of either food or nutrition. Yet, all parts of the rose, and especially the hips, are storehouses of Vitamin C and other important nutrients.

Compare the nutritional content of oranges to rose hips and you will find that rose hips contain 25 percent more iron, 20 to 40 percent more Vitamin C (depending upon variety), 25 times the Vitamin A, and 28 percent more calcium.

In addition, rose hips are a rich source of bioflavanoids, pectin, Vitamin E, selenium, manganese, and the B-complex vitamins. Rose hips also contain trace amounts of magnesium, potassium, sulfur and silicon.

Finding and gathering rose hips

Wild roses grow throughout the world. There are literally thousands of varieties worldwide and most have been part of the human diet. In fact, it is difficult to find an area of the world or a temperature zone—barring parts of the Antarctic and the Sahara Desert—where wild roses don't grow.

We can also look to our own gardens. The domesticated roses we find there are rich in nutrients. Look for

Rosa rugosa that develops many large, bright red hips that look and taste like small apples. Rugosa roses are found in most nurseries and plant catalogs. *Rosa gallica*, a native of the Middle East no longer found in the wild but available from nurseries and plant catalogs, is a favored old garden rose. It will grace your garden with beauty and scent and your table with nutritious foods and beverages. Even the well-loved "hybrid tea" roses produce edible hips, although not as prolifically as their wild and semi-domesticated garden cousins.

Many enthusiastic gardeners never see the development of colorful hips because as soon as blossoms fade they are snipped off to tidy up the garden. Blossoms must be left on the plant to naturally fade and fall for hips to develop.

The most abundant source of Vitamin C-rich rose hips is from wild hedgerows and thickets. Here hips can be gathered in ample quantities for cooking and storing. You'd have to grow a vast number of garden-variety roses to get a sufficient quantity of hips for use all year long. As most roses have thorns, gloves are helpful although not essential when gathering hips.

Rose hips as food

Once you locate your rose hip source there still remains the question of turning them into something we deem not only edible, but tasty too. Rose hips can be made into a variety of appetizing, healthy dishes. Turned into jelly, syrup, and wine, they make delightful gifts.

Rose hips may be used fresh or dried. To dry them, discard any with discoloration then rinse in cold water, pat dry, and spread on a wax paper-lined cookie sheet. It takes a couple of weeks for them to dry. They will be darker in color, hard, and semi-wrinkly. Rub off any stems or remaining blossom ends. Pour them into jars for storage in a dark pantry or cupboard.

Dry rose hips on an old cookie sheet for a couple of weeks until completely dry. When ready to store, they should be darker than their fresh counterparts, hard, and semi-wrinkly.

One of my favorite ways to use rose hips is to brew them into tea. For tea they may be used fresh or dried. For fresh brewing, steep a tablespoon or two of clean hips in a cup of boiling water for about 10 minutes. Sweeten with honey and enjoy. To make a tea of dried hips, use only two teaspoons to one cup of boiling water and steep for 10 to 15 minutes.

My favorite syrup for pancakes, waffles, and vanilla ice cream is made from freshly gathered rose hips. Rinse and pat dry the hips and place them in a saucepan. Barely cover with water and bring to a boil. Lower the heat and simmer until soft, about 10 to 15 minutes. Cool and strain the mixture, pressing the liquid off the hips gently with the back of a spoon, being careful not to break them open and release the seeds. If this happens, merely strain the seeds out. The resulting liquid may be frozen in batches for future

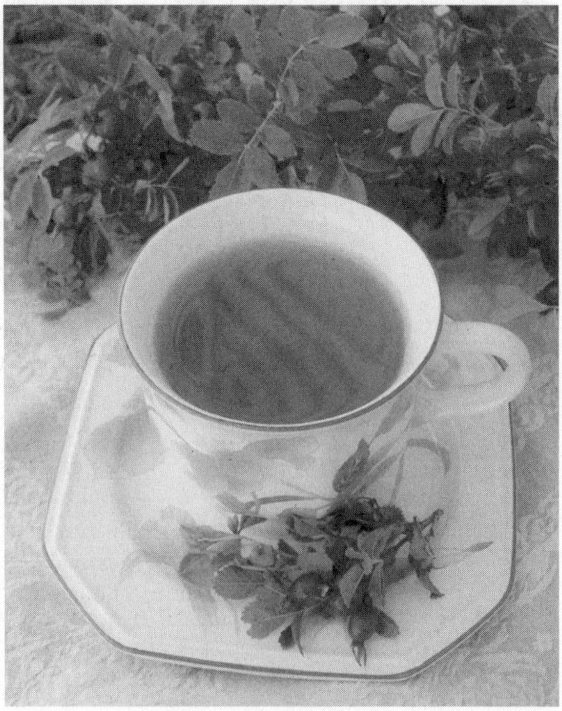

Rose hip tea is a tasty, nutritious beverage that can be made from fresh or dried hips. This cup was made from freshly gathered wild rose hips.

In late summer, rose hips ripen to bright red and are ready for gathering.

use in soup or jelly, or turned into tasty syrup. The solids left over from straining can be fed to chickens or tossed onto the compost pile.

To make rose hip syrup, add one part honey to two parts of the heated, strained liquid. Stir to dissolve the honey and refrigerate. After refrigeration, the syrup will thicken slightly. Rose hip syrup will keep in the refrigerator for about two weeks. Reheat the syrup for use on pancakes and waffles. Use it warm or cold to top vanilla ice cream.

Heated syrup may be canned by pouring it into hot, sterile jars and processing in a boiling water bath for 15 minutes. For every 1,000 feet above an elevation of 5,000 feet, add one minute to the processing time.

For a refreshing spring tonic punch, simmer rhubarb in rose hip syrup until soft. Strain and adjust sweetening as needed. Chill, and pour over ice for a refreshing, healthful libation to clear out the winter cobwebs. Add a sprig of fresh spearmint or lemon balm as garnish. Rose hip syrup may be used to sweeten and flavor herbal or black teas, as well.

A favorite dish of the Swedish is **rose hip soup.** They literally consume rose hips by the tons each year. To make approximately four servings you'll need:

- 3 cups of freshly made or thawed unsweetened rose hip liquid
- 2 Tbsp. honey
- 2 Tbsp. lemon juice
- 2 tsp. corn starch
- 4 Tbsp. sour cream or yogurt as a garnish
- minced mint

In a saucepan, heat the liquid and add the honey and lemon juice. Remove ½ cup of the heated mixture. Into this, whisk the cornstarch until smooth. Add the cornstarch mixture back into the pan and bring to a high simmer, stirring, until the mixture bubbles and thickens. Add a dollop of sour cream or yogurt to each serving, topping with minced fresh mint, if desired.

If you make your own wine, the following recipe for **rose hip wine** is one of the healthiest and most lovely in color. You'll need:

- 4 pounds of fresh rose hips
- 3 pounds of sugar
- 1 gallon boiling water
- 1 tsp. black tea
- 1 tsp. baker's or wine yeast

Rinse and drain the hips. Place them in a primary fermenting vessel such as a clean food-grade plastic bucket that has a tight-fitting lid.

After a hard frost, autumn color makes the hips harder to see.

Pour in one gallon of boiling water. Add the teaspoon of tea and all the sugar, stirring to dissolve the sugar. Let the mixture sit tightly covered for 24 hours. Add one teaspoon of baker's or wine yeast and let the mixture ferment for seven days, covered, stirring once per day with a clean spoon.

Strain off the rose hips and pour the liquid into a one-gallon glass jug (an old wine jug works great) and fit with a fermentation lock or balloon. If you use a balloon, be sure to release the gases occasionally or it will burst. Place the jug in a warm spot until fermentation ceases. Siphon (rack) the liquid off of the yeast solids into a clean glass jug and refit with the fermentation lock or balloon.

Racking will usually reactivate fermentation for a short time. When fermentation ceases completely for several weeks, siphon the wine into clean wine bottles. Cork the bottles securely or use wine bottles with screw-on tops and store in a cool spot for six months or longer. There will usually be a glass or two of wine left after bottling. This you can enjoy right away.

Precautions

Wherever you gather rose hips, be sure they have not been treated with herbicides or pesticides. If wild roses grow on your property or you gather from your garden roses, you can manage them to your satisfaction.

Wild roses, despite their beauty and usefulness as perimeter plantings, food, and wildlife habitats, are considered by many to be a nuisance. They do spread by suckering, and a single plant will become a thicket eventually. If you have enough property to sustain several thickets where they can grow without interfering with your other operations, you will have an ample source of nutritious hips to nourish yourself and your family throughout the year. Δ

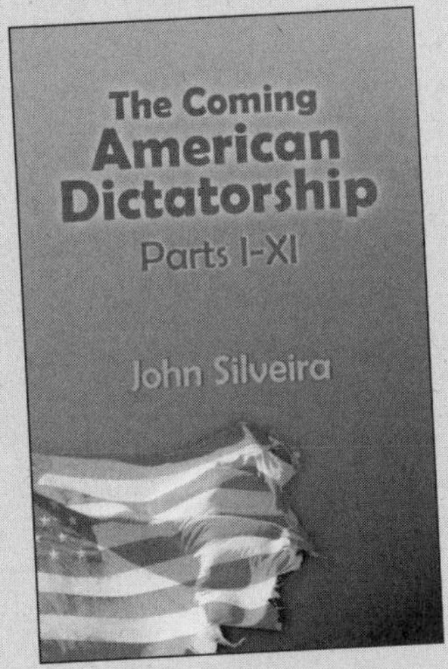

6

Starting Over

By Jackie Clay

One thing I've learned is never, NEVER to say "What else can happen?" when things go bad. As if losing my husband, Bob, in February was not enough, I was told that tiny pea-sized lump on my elbow was cancer. Cancer! Me. How could that be? We live pretty darned healthy; I never smoked, drank, or did drugs. I take care in the sun, eat home-raised food as much as I can, and exercise by walking miles a day, digging, sawing, pounding, and all that goes with a homestead. So in addition to spring's normal hustle and bustle, I began a grueling schedule of first a radical surgery on my elbow (a nine-inch incision for a pea-sized bump!), radiation, and chemotherapy. Luckily, the pea was my only spot, which brought great relief; the elbow is easier to treat than lungs, liver, and a lot of other places.

In our little greenhouse we started hundreds of plants.

But with bad things, there are always the good. Throughout all of this, I was planting seeds, tilling the garden, and watching our new house take shape.

David fills Walls o' Water around the tomatoes.

Starting seeds

In our little 10'x10' greenhouse, I was able to start a huge array of plants for our gardens. Not only did I start several varieties of early season tomatoes, including Early Cascade, Early Goliath, Oregon Spring, Sun Gold, Lemon Boy, and a new hanging basket tomato called Tumbler, but I also started broccoli, peppers, watermelon, muskmelon, cucumbers, and my wonderful Hopi Pale Grey squash that is now nearly extinct. Of course, I also started hundreds of different flowers to cheer up the place. Food feeds your body; flowers feed your soul.

Setting out tomatoes

By raising your own plants from seed carefully chosen for the attributes that matter most to you, a garden is much more successful than if you go to the garden center or discount store to buy your plants. A tomato is not the same as any other tomato. Some are very good tasting and extremely productive, and some (the ones often seen in stores) are just cheap to grow. Some require 100 days or more after transplanting to set a crop of tomatoes, while others only take 52 days. In a cold-season area, those 100 day tomatoes just won't make a crop.

Likewise, choosing seeds for your garden requires a bit of study. I need varieties that produce very heavily so I am able to can them, ones that taste great, and are early to produce.

I've learned that in cold-season gardening, you can raise watermelon, muskmelon, and squash if you start them indoors like you do tomatoes and peppers. I plant three seeds in a foam drinking glass and write the variety on the side. Then I place the cups, with a small hole punched in the bottom, in an old roasting pan. This keeps them from tipping over and allows excess water to drain from the cups to water the roots later on. I've used peat pots, but the foam cups work much better. Perhaps it is extra insulation on the roots, keeping them nice and warm on cool nights.

By planting the peppers in early March and the tomatoes in mid-March, they are ready to go into Walls'o Water in early May here, when normally you wouldn't plant them outside, unprotected, until mid-June. We nearly always get a VERY cold night right about June 15th.

I plant the tomatoes and peppers in deep plastic trays that a friend collected for me. Mine are actually discarded sterile containers that held instruments and materials for surgery. They're about four inches deep and grow wonderful roots. Smaller containers are easy to handle and will raise all the plants the normal gardener could wish to grow, letting you separate the different varieties with ease.

In my containers, I plant between eight and ten tomato or pepper seeds, spaced carefully so as not to waste seed. Nearly all of them germinate. By starting the seeds in trays, you do not have to transplant later on into a larger container.

I always place my containers of planted seeds, which I've watered with very warm water, in a plastic bag to conserve moisture. This is usually a bread bag but can also be any small plastic bag, twisted shut. These are then placed in a high, warm spot. I'm always careful to check the containers every day after planting because sometimes those seeds that aren't supposed to germinate for a week to ten days pop up in two or three. If you don't check and get them into the light as soon as they sprout, they will become leggy and delicate and never amount to much.

The basement goes up.

As we have no heat in the greenhouse, I was carrying plants out in the morning and back inside in the afternoon for several weeks. At first there were only tomatoes, peppers, and geraniums. But by the time it was safe to leave them out there all night, I was really glad to stop hauling dozens and dozens of flats of plants twice a day.

Our new home

About this time, construction on our new log house began. Our mile-long trail through the woods was still muddy from spring breakup, but we had worked hard on it last summer and even the biggest trucks were able to get in. We decided to use a good local log builder to do the basic shell. Bob and I had always done everything ourselves and I felt like I was wimping out by letting someone else do the grunt work, but it couldn't be helped. This was the only alternative that would let us have our small home, especially after Bob died and my bump exploded my life. I couldn't work with one arm in a sling and stitches up and down my arm.

So the only choice was to have a not-quite-dried-in shell. When you buy from a log builder, there are many ways to go. You can just buy

The logs came numbered for ease of construction.

David helps lay caulking tape on the tongues of the logs.

the logs, have them delivered, and stack 'em on your own foundation and sub floor. I couldn't even do that. (Well, I probably could have, but Mom and Dad would not have been able to enjoy living in it, as it would have taken years.) You can also have the foundation contracted out, along with the sub floor, then have the logs stacked by the log builder. By the grace of God, we had just enough money from Bob's retroactive VA disability payment to have the logs,

Log builder Mark Carlson helps the logs into place with a maul.

including the ridge pole and rafters, stacked on the sub floor and the roof boards nailed on. On top of those, we stapled Typar roof wrap, a woven waterproof material that will last longer than tarpaper.

Of course, many people have the house dried-in by the log builder. This means the roof is finished with insulation and shingles or metal roofing, and windows and doors are also installed. But we can handle this, with help from friends and family.

Be careful when shopping for a log home kit. You need to find out exactly what is included. Some kits only include the logs for the walls. Others include the walls, rafters, loft floor, roof, insulation, windows, doors, and trim. You can't just pick the cheapest kit, thinking that all are the same; they're definitely not. Ask lots of questions.

With the brute work done for us, there will be plenty for me and David to do. And I wouldn't have it any other way or the house would never seem truly ours. This summer, David has grown up. At fourteen, he's a young man, not a kid any more. Not because it's been forced on him by the death of his dad, or by me making him do work I can't do. He's just pitched in where there is a need. And in doing so, he's won the respect of every man who's worked on the new house.

David first helped the masons lay up the block for the basement, mix and wheel cement, learning new skills every day. Then he worked in the rain all morning Saturday with the carpenter to lay the plywood sub floor. (Luckily, our friends Paul and Marcia showed up just after it began raining. I think the carpenter would have quit because of the rain, but together, they got the job done.)

We were really under the gun, since the logs were going to be delivered first thing Monday morning, and they were going to be stacked onto the sub floor. Luckily, Voyageur Log Homes has a crew that stacks logs and they have a big crane. This enabled them to lift pallet loads of logs directly off the trailers onto strategic locations on the sub floor. Not only did this keep the logs extremely clean but it let them stack the logs right where they would be working, saving much time and labor.

When you buy logs and plan on laying them up yourself, you usually are responsible for unloading the logs off the truck or trailer yourself. This entails either renting an all-terrain fork lift, a small crane, or using a tractor with a loader. You also need to know that the driver of the log truck will wait a specified time, then you will be paying him "overtime" for waiting for you to unload. Have help and work quickly.

It's best to stack logs on your slab or sub floor, but if that can't be done, at least have a deep bed of fresh straw to stack them on and plenty of tarps to cover them later, as logs weather quickly and get dirty even faster.

The logs usually come numbered or lettered if you buy a kit that is precut. Stack all like logs together to find them easily when you put up the walls. You don't want to move piles of very heavy logs, searching for "log 12S."

The same day our logs were delivered, construction began on the walls. Scarcely were the logs unloaded when the half log ends were screwed over a foam sill seal with long log screws and the first full logs laid snugly over them. Voyageur Log Homes uses a notched corner and a full two tongue and grooves on each log. Caulking tape is fastened to the tops of both tongues, all the way down the log's surface, then the next log is settled tightly down onto it, with its grooves sliding snugly over the tongues. There is no chance of air leakage.

We've always done log work with a Swedish cope, where the top log is grooved broadly to fit down over the top of the one below. But Voyageur's system is extremely air tight and quick to go up.

David quickly began helping Mark Carlson, the log builder, and his helper. Three men build much faster than two. David is a good workman. He began taping the caulking down on the logs, and was soon hooking logs with tongs for the crane to lift in place, carrying shorter logs, and helping set them into place.

The first day, the walls were half up, and by evening of the second day, they were done. I was amazed. Even our log chicken coop had taken Bob and me all spring to build.

But I did notice many similarities in construction. We, too, used a heavy maul to "help" the logs fit into place tightly. Where we used long spikes, counter sunk two inches to allow for settling of the logs, Mark used Oly log screws, also countersunk to allow for settling. No log building is ever built that has no settling, and I've seen many that were nearly ruined when builders did not allow for it.

For instance, over every door and window you must leave a space so that when the building settles it does not bind, jam, or hang up on them. Stairs to a loft or upstairs must be slotted to let them slide an inch or two as the home settles through the months. Kitchen cabinets need to be fastened firmly to one log, with a slot or other allowance made for the logs to compress without being held by the cabinets. (I've seen ugly log damage from bowing and twisting caused by a single piece of 1" x 4" trim in the wrong place to allow settling.)

A log going into place

Last of all that day, the large, full-length log was hoisted into place as a collar tie, spanning the width of the house. This will prevent the long log walls from bowing outward years from now. It also greatly strengthens the entire home from snow loads and fierce winds.

When it came time to set the log rafters, on day three, Mark quickly manufactured a jig out of a few scraps of lumber. This jig was screwed to the flat top of each rafter, and his chainsaw slid neatly along the angled piece of 12"x12". This gave him an exact angled cut for each and every rafter with no monkeying

The higher the walls went, the harder the work to get them layed up.

around or climbing on the ridge pole to precariously cut rafters way up in the air.

The rafters were then lag screwed together and raised up onto the walls with the crane. Pretty slick! And pretty soon all the rafters were in place and the ridge pole was easily raised up under them with the crane. One by one, the pairs of rafters were straightened and lag bolted securely to the ridge pole. And soon, all that remained was to add a pair of large support posts under it.

Under the lower end of the post is a steel plate foot with a heavy steel threaded rod and nut. The rod fits into a hole on the bottom of the post and the nut with its heavy washer can be turned down as the house slowly settles. This keeps the collar tie beam and ridge pole nice and level.

We were truly sad when it came time for Mark to leave. He had become family and was truly a joy to work with, cheerful, and happy to share log building tips.

The next day, while I went in for minor surgery to have my chemotherapy "port" installed below my collar bone, the carpenters arrived to nail down the 2" x 6" tongue-and-groove roof boards. As the lead carpenter was "all business," David didn't get to help much, but he acted as a go-fer and still managed to learn a lot.

By the time I got home, the roof was done and they were stapling down the roof wrap. Amazing. None of this was cheap, and knowing that hurt my severely Scotch blood, but I was glad to see our house standing there, looking like a house.

We had planned to make a small partial basement under one end for a water handling area and place to store my canned goods and garden harvest. The rest of the house would be on cement piers to save money. But it turned out that for $1,800 more I could have a full basement. I gave the nod, and I have never been sorry. It added so much useable room to the little house that it's not believable.

There will be a small wood storage room for the wood stove in the basement, the water handling area with a place for the wringer washer, ample space for my canned goods and root cellar, a place to store all those boxes in storage right now, and even a small corner that David has claimed for "his" game room. I certainly can't deny him that.

I am so grateful for what we have, but I still feel that I didn't sweat enough to deserve it. I only wish Bob could be here to enjoy it with us.

The wall is almost finished.

Bigger, better gardens

While the construction was going on, I worked on the gardens. My son, Bill, more than doubled the size of our "lower" garden with his bulldozer.

Before I had surgery, I tilled the house garden next to the mobile home, then David gave it another tilling before I began to plant. One end was very rocky and he used a crowbar to dig out rocks as he worked. I was pretty much useless after my surgery, but after it was tilled, I slowly brought out a few plants and planted them or a package of seeds and gritted my teeth while I dragged furrows to plant them. Definitely this was the slowest I've ever planted a garden in my life.

The good thing is that it makes me appreciate everything so much more. The tiny steps forward, the sunsets, the wildflowers, the fragrance of spring turning to summer in the northwoods, the birdsong in the growing pines around us, my family. Everything. We all take life too much for granted.

Because our house garden is not large, I've planted things in square-foot style, for the most part. For instance, I planted my sweet corn in a sixteen foot by four foot bed, with seeds every six inches, all ways. Then, to hopefully deter the ground squirrels who dug up my corn seeds when the plants were six inches tall, I surrounded the bed with discarded window screens from the dump. So far the corn is up, and the little buggers are staying away.

Likewise, I've set in a four foot by six foot patch of broccoli, with the

The jig makes it easy for Mark to cut the top angles for the rafters.

plants a little over a foot apart; squash, watermelons, and muskmelons in another bed. To further save space, I used an extra sixteen-foot stock panel fastened to steel T posts from the dump as a trellis for cucumbers and pole beans. I planted a dozen foam cups of cucumber plants, complete with climbing tendrils started, along one end of the trellis and a double row of Cherokee Trail of Tears pole beans (our favorite) on the other end, on both sides of the fence. These are beans that Cherokee women sewed into their skirt hems and carried in their pockets during the awful forced march from their homes in the south to Oklahoma "Indian Territory." There are few beans that taste as good.

When you don't have a lot of space, it's a good idea to garden up, so I am trellising anything that I can. Watermelons and muskmelons don't climb, but can be gently tied and encouraged to sort of climb on pieces of fence wire stapled to pole garden panels.

Because this new garden, which last spring was a pile of rotted logs, is oddly shaped, I have tucked other vegetables in at different spots; green peppers in a four foot by four foot bed, yellow Romano beans in another, a row of Provider bush beans along the tomato patch, a little tiny row of radishes here and a few odd seeds of this and that all over. That little garden is jam packed with edibles. And it is on the highest piece of ground we have. It is safe from all but the most dangerous cold, as cold is like water, flowing down to lower ground first.

Like I said, everything in the garden took so long this year because of all the running around we must do and the lack of normal energy and strength on my part. But we got both gardens in, albeit a bit later than usual.

The new "big" lower garden is now planted with three hundred-foot rows

The rafters go into place. Note the lag bolts in the top, ready to screw into the ridge pole later that day.

of potatoes, two of Yukon gold, and another of Norkota russet, which keeps very well. The Yukon gold we simply laid on the tilled bare ground and covered with old straw from around the trailer this winter. The plants will grow nicely, free of weeds, and when harvest time comes all you have to do is fork off the straw and pick up the clean potatoes. I even sneak around the plants and harvest a few new potatoes after the vines bloom to have with creamed fresh peas and bacon crumbles. This is always an awesome meal.

David and I also planted three hundred white and yellow onion sets, two long rows of carrots, and two rows of Provider bush green beans.

We really need to get this garden fenced. The deer won't bother it until fall, but then they will harvest it for us unless we do.

Because of all the rain and unseasonable heat here this spring and early summer, everything is growing like mad, including all our bountiful wild fruit. I've seldom seen blueberries and wild raspberries so large and plentiful. This year I'll be canning plenty of fruit and jam, plus doing a whole lot of berry dehydrating. I can't wait! Δ

The roof goes on, four days from sub-floor to house.

Marlin 336:
The other classic backwoods home deer rifle

By Massad Ayoob

Veteran hunter and gun dealer Jeff Boss demonstrates the excellent handling of the lever action Marlin carbine, unusually accurate for a rifle of this type.

In the March/April 2005 issue of *Backwoods Home Magazine,* this space was devoted to the "Winchester '94: the Classic Backwoods Home Deer Rifle." And you know, even when I was writing that paean to the lever-action .30-30 that sold over five million units since the year 1894, I knew that I'd have to follow up with an article on the other such deer rifle, Marlin's Model 336.

Marlin introduced their Model 1893 rifle in the eponymous year, initially in old black powder calibers like the .32-40 and .38-55, but soon chambered for the .30-30 Winchester round. Some 900,000 of these guns were made between then and 1935, when the company replaced it with their sleeker Model 36. Where Winchester emphasized a lean, mean straight-stock design with a slim, spare fore-end, the Marlin had a pistol grip style stock with its lever loop bent accordingly, and a fuller fore-end. These attributes were carried into the newer gun, destined to be their longest-lived deer rifle: the Model 336, introduced in 1948 and still Marlin's most popular hunting rifle.

Useful, inexpensive accessories include lightweight fabric carry sling and elastic butt cuff for spare cartridges. Telescopic sight is easy to mount on a Marlin 336, enhancing both accuracy and hunter safety.

The rest, as the saying goes, is history. At the SHOT Show—it stands for Shooting, Hunting, and Outdoor Trade, the largest trade show in the firearms industry—in Las Vegas in January, 2005, I had the privilege of looking over a handsomely engraved rifle that was Marlin's four millionth Model 336.

From the early days, the Marlin's solid frame with ejection to the right side (instead of out the top of the mechanism, as with the Winchester) was one of its distinguishing features. This continued with the Model 336 and its many variations. As telescopic sights became more popular among American outdoorsmen, this became a key advantage. The top-ejecting Winchester would have its mechanism blocked by a telescopic sight in its usual position atop the rifle's frame. This led to all manner of adaptations. With the stock Marlin, a hunter could simply attach an ordinary scope on an ordinary mount in the traditional position.

The 336 was a stronger rifle than the Model 36 that preceded it, not only in terms of more modern metallurgy but because of its rugged and simple round bolt mechanism that rolled smoothly inside the receiver, or frame. There are many who believe it was, from the beginning, a stronger rifle than the Model '94 Winchester to which the Marlin played Avis opposite Hertz. Slightly heavier, in part because of its action design and partly because its more generous stock design simply had more wood on both ends, it was never weighed more than a pound over its Winchester equivalent of the same barrel length and caliber, and the difference was often even less than that, depending on the density of the wood.

Most, if not all Model 336 rifles were produced with the company's trademark Micro-Groove™ rifling. Marlin's thesis was that many shallow grooves in the barrel would stabilize a bullet better than a few deeper ones. Whether this is truly the case remains about a two-beer debate in the shooting club bar after the guns are put away. Personally, I've always found the Marlin to be a little more accurate than the equivalent Winchester, but by so small a margin as to be inconsequential. (Whether a quarter inch or even half an inch better accuracy at a hundred yards matters in a woods rifle is another two-beer debate.)

What no one argues is that the Marlin is much easier to take apart for maintenance and repair than the Winchester. As a youngster, I was frustrated that I needed my dad's help to get my Model 1894 back together, but when I got my first Model 336 as a junior high school student, I was delighted to discover how simple its takedown and reassembly were. Simply back out the screw that holds the lever to the receiver, and everything slides out nicely for cleaning and lubrication—and more important, goes back together almost as easily. In a backwoods environment, this can be the most decisive advantage of all.

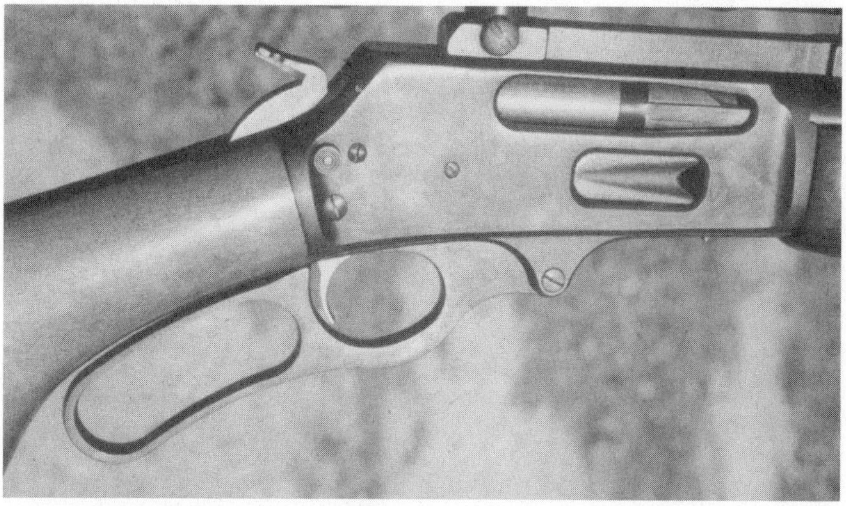

Key Marlin features: side ejection port, traditional loading gate, crossbolt (push button) safety, and extended hammer for easier cocking.

When I discussed the matter of relative ease of scope mounting in the Winchester '94 article in the March/April issue of *BHM*, I wrote, "...and the telescope's magnification is a safety factor in that it helps the woodsman identify the target." This did not set well with reader John B. Williamson of Spokane, who wrote, "I'm sure Mr. Ayoob didn't mean it the way it sounded. The telescope's magnification is a safety factor in that it helps [a] woodsman identify the target. You NEVER, NEVER use the scope to identify a target unless you know it is a 4-legged animal, not a 2-legged one. If in doubt use binoculars. If you notice as soon as someone sight(s) thru a scope their finger is inside the trigger guard usually resting on the trigger."

When scanning the woods, Mr. Williamson is 100% correct: if you use your telescopic sight as a spyglass, you are pointing a loaded rifle at everything you look at, which may include other hunters. Get caught doing that, and you face a range of

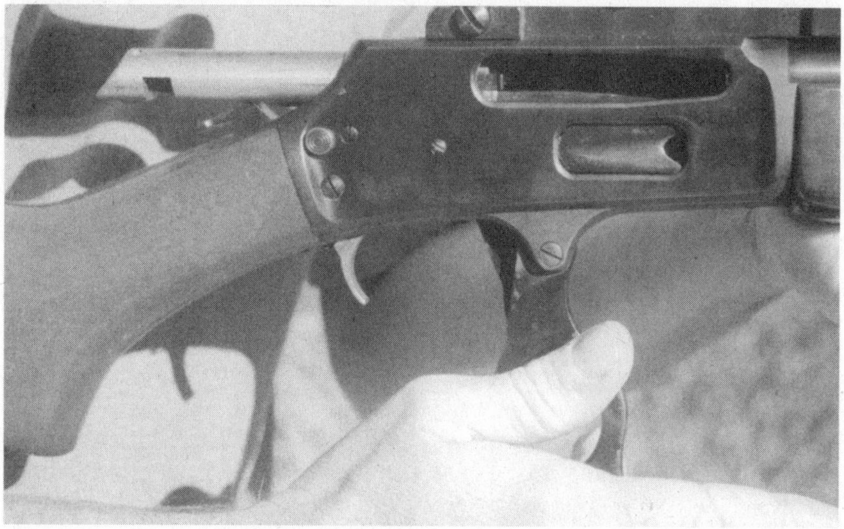

The smooth, low effort operation of the 336's lever is one of its good points.

3rd from bottom is the 336M in stainless steel. Just below it is the pistol-caliber Marlin Model 1894, with distinctly shorter action.

results that can be tragedy at the worst end of the scale, loss of your hunting license at the lighter end, and a charge of felony aggravated assault (pointing a lethal weapon at another person) in the middle.

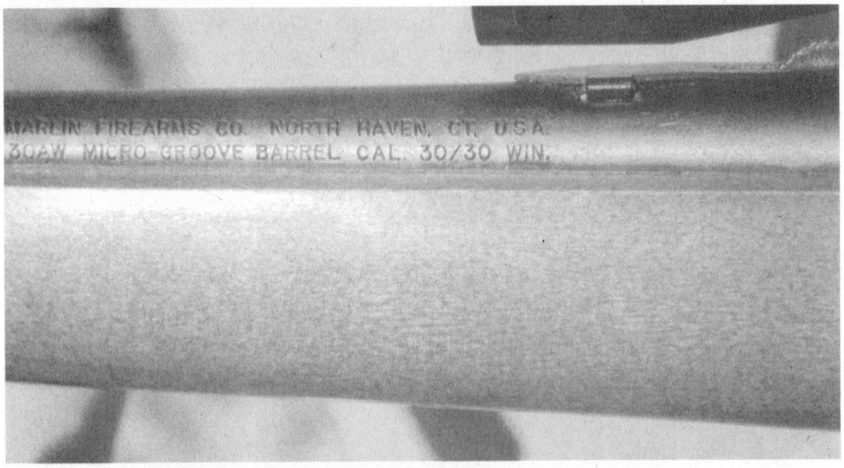

This Model 30AW is the low priced version of the Model 336, still with the accurate Micro-Groove ™ rifling and in the most popular caliber, .30-30. Nondescript wood is cheap but functional.

By "identify the target," what I mean is a last-second verification that what you are aiming at is in fact a game animal. The scope can tell you if that white flash you saw with your naked eye in the shadows of the forest was the deer's tail, or a man's handkerchief. On the lower end of the scale, it can also tell you whether you really saw a buck's antlers, or an off-limits doe standing amid some antler-like branches.

As a younger man, I hunted with iron sights on Winchester and Marlin alike. I was confident of my sharp eyes; the scope broke up the classic lines of the rifle and made it more awkward to carry all day; and in thick woods, I knew I'd be encountering Bambi at short range anyway. Today, older and wiser and dimmer of eye, I prefer magnifying optics on most of my hunting rifles, and still consider it a safety feature.

Over the years, the Marlin 336 has been made in many calibers. As with the Winchester '94, the .30-30 has been overwhelmingly the most popular. However, I've seen a very few in .32 Special. It was made for several years in .219 Zipper, a light varmint cartridge that spat a 56 grain hollow point at 3110 feet per second. However, varmint hunters wanted super-accurate bolt action rifles, not light weight lever guns, and the 336 never caught on in this caliber. The 336 was also produced in the more powerful .375 Winchester cartridge, which never became popular either.

No, the round that made a difference was Marlin's second most popular in this rifle: caliber .35 Remington. Remington created this cartridge in 1906 for their then-revolutionary Model 8 semiautomatic hunting rifle, and in 1952, Marlin began chambering the Model 336 for it. Throwing a 200 grain soft point bullet at 2210 feet per second, it generated 2170 foot-pounds of energy. With a 170 grain bullet at about the same speed, the .30-30 comes up short by comparison with only 1860 foot-pounds of energy.

In the early '50s, Marlin advertised this as the "brush-busting .35," though today we know from exhaustive testing that virtually no bullet can go through heavy brush without being deflected. However, as an active deer hunter in my younger days, I noticed that the .35 seemed to take down white-tails with distinctly more authority than the more popular .30-30. Noted Henry M. Stebbins, one of the great rifle authorities during that period in American firearms history, "...the 336 was not planned as a mountain rifle. Adding the .35 Rem to its lineup made it one of the best-liked rifles for those who want considerably more than .30-30 power, but not high velocity or flat trajectory." (1)

When I started junior high school my deer rifle was a long-barrel

Winchester '94, caliber .38-55. It was heavy and kind of clunky with its 26" barrel, and achingly old-fashioned with its crescent butt plate and all. Kids don't like old-fashioned things, so I saved up for a new Bambi-buster. I wanted a short barrel carbine that was light and handy, and was already habituated to the lever action, so the choice pretty much came down to Marlin and Winchester.

I was quite taken by what seemed like a smoother action in the Model 336. The Winchester required a little bump at the far end of the lever stroke to lift the cartridge carrier, or it wouldn't chamber the round. The Marlin had no such idiosyncrasy, and working its action it seemed lighter and smoother and arguably even faster.

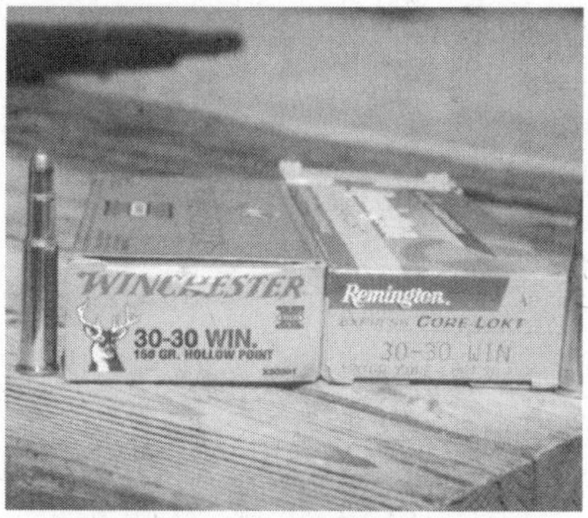

.30-30 is the traditional caliber for a Marlin 336, but this rifle has been chambered for many other cartridges.

For a bit more "fire," the .35 Remington caliber has been offered in the 336 since 1952. Author is partial to this 200 grain Winchester Power Point round.

It also felt better in my hands than the Winchester with its slim, straight wood. The aforementioned Henry Stebbins explained this subjective characteristic well. "Design makes the 336 a handy rifle for the timber," he wrote. "Forefinger and thumb fall naturally on trigger and hammer, the firing hand sends the lever out and back readily if the stock is short enough for the woods-hunter who uses it, and grip and forestock are big enough to make shooting comfortable and to give sure command of the rifle. If the forestock seems too wide to a short-fingered shooter—and it might, even on the slimmed down Texan carbine with straight grip and full magazine—he could taper it just ahead of the receiver. Then it would suit him in carrying. The comb and pistol grip stand well back, and if you wear heavy gloves against the cold you'll be glad that they do." (2)

My dad and I found a used Model 336 in excellent condition at Stan Sprague's gun shop in Hooksett, NH. It was the SC model, with 20" carbine barrel and 2/3 length magazine. The action worked smooth as glass, and the previous owner had installed an aperture sight. Best of all, it was chambered for .35 Remington. Dad bought it for me for about $65. I unscrewed the aperture in the peep sight so I could aim through a larger opening, a 19th Century deer hunter's trick that Jeff Cooper re-popularized in the late 20th Century as the "ghost ring" sight concept, and I was good to go.

That was my deer rifle for most of my teen years, and I loved it. It helped me learn a lot of things, one of them being that if you busted your butt to get "all-A" report cards in school, the teachers of the early '60s would be lenient if you played hooky for most of deer season.

By age 16, I had switched from traditional stalking to the deer drive method. This involves a group of men moving loudly through the woods and "pushing" the deer ahead of them toward a line of "standers," riflemen taking their turn as shooters. As a stalker, I had loaded my lever action in the morning and unloaded it at night when I came out of the woods, and levering the rounds out of the gun once a day was hardly a chore. In driving, however, we were in and out of pickup trucks several times a day, which of course involved carefully unloading the rifle before you got into the truck and reloading after you debarked again. Jacking rounds through a lever action several times a day got to be a pain in the butt, and it chewed up the cartridges at the rims and noses, which could later compromise both feeding and accuracy. I noticed that most of the adults I hunted with had box magazine rifles, usually the Remington Model 742 semi-automatic or Model 760 slide action, or less often, the Winchester Model 100 autoloading .308. These were much handier to unload and reload. Trying all of them, I found the Winchester 100 the more accurate, and in my hands the better balanced, being somewhat less muzzle heavy. After a couple of years, I traded the sweet little Marlin .35 for a Winchester Model 100 .308.

I have that Model 100 still, and many good memories come with it. However, I wish I had saved up longer so I could have bought it outright and kept the Marlin as well. The more powerful .308 Winchester cartridge didn't drop a deer a darn bit faster than a 200 grain .35 Remington slug, and even though the Model 100 could group in an inch and a half at a hundred yards then and now, it was not a whit more accurate than my old Marlin 336 SC. A lot of memories went with that Marlin, and I regret my decision to trade it in.

As my life went on, I got away from hunting for many years, and though I went back to it, I never did so with the ardor I had applied to the sport in my youth. I didn't get another Marlin Model 336 until my 40s, and it was sort of by accident.

I owned an apartment building, and one of my tenants apologized for being short on the rent. He paid me with his deer rifle, a 336 Marlin .30-30 with a K2.5 Weaver telescopic sight. The rifle was clean on the inside, rough and weather worn on the surface, and somehow the scope looked funny. Upon examination, I realized that the previous owner had mounted it incorrectly, turned a quarter of the way over onto one side. In effect, the windage knob now corrected for elevation, and the elevation adjustment knob now controlled the windage. When I stopped laughing, I decided to take it to the range to see how this had affected point of aim/point of impact before I remounted it correctly.

I picked up one of those Federal brand 24-round value packs of generic soft nose hunting ammunition at Wal-Mart, and headed to the gun club. Jacking the first round into the chamber, I was reminded of the smooth action I had come to love so long ago on my Marlin .35. I put the crosshairs on the bullseye and began shooting, noticing that the mild .30-30 round's recoil was softer than I remembered the .35's having been.

With only two and a half power scope magnification, I couldn't quite see the group downrange, so I set the empty rifle on the bench and walked to the target. The little .30-30 had not only shot dead center where it was aimed, but had put every shot into a group that measured only an inch and a quarter, center to center on the farthest-apart bullet holes.

I decided to leave the little Marlin exactly as it was.

There are nearly as many Marlins as Winchesters still serving rural American families, with close to ten million specimens produced by the two companies combined. More than that, if you count models other than the Winchester '94 and the Marlin 336. Many of them are marked with other names. Marlin produced them under the "J.C. Higgins" brand for Sears, Roebuck; under the "Western Field" brand for Montgomery Ward; and if memory serves, under the "Revelation" brand for Western Auto Stores. There may have been others. The "trade brand" guns may have birch instead of walnut stocks, and less fancy blue finishes, but underneath they're all the same good rifle.

In the year 2000, Marlin introduced the Model 336 M, in stainless steel. This makes particularly good sense in hostile weather environments. They have also, in the last few years, offered these rifles with camouflage stocks.

Marlin's crushingly powerful Model 444 in caliber .444 Marlin and Model 1895 in .45-70 are popular for close range hunting of moose and large bear. Both are built on the Model 336 mechanism, though not catalogued as part of the 336 series. Where Winchester offers its pistol caliber lever guns on the rifle-length Model 94 frame, Marlin chooses to use a smaller action, which they call Model 1894, in calibers like .357 Magnum and .44 Magnum. The latter is particularly handy for close range deer hunting. In cowboy action shooting matches, what is generally perceived as the smoother action of the Marlin has made it the overwhelming choice of the winners over the Winchester, at least in the matches I've been to.

Like Winchester, Marlin felt the need to put a cross-bolt safety onto the rifles many years ago, to render them drop-safe when carried with a cartridge in the chamber. With either brand, most professionals are now more comfortable carrying them with the chamber empty, and levering a round out of the magazine and into the launch tube only when intending to fire immediately. Lowering the hammer onto a live round can be tricky. Reader Williamson, a retired hunter education instructor, notes, "Nine out of every ten students drop the hammer on the firing pin as their finger slips off the hammer." It's safer to just leave the chamber empty.

Remember that the telescopic sight gives a safety factor of last-instant confirmation of target verification, as well as more accuracy for most people, and that most Marlins are easier to equip with scopes than most Winchester lever actions. The rest of it is a matter of personal preference.

The Marlin Model 336 and the Winchester Model 94 are both classic American rifles, their histories inextricably linked with the traditions of rural America. Owning either is owning a piece of genuine Americana. If it's that difficult to choose between them, do what I've done, and put one of each in your gun safe.

(1) Stebbins, Henry M., "Rifles: A Modern Encyclopedia," Harrisburg, PA: The Stackpole Company, 1958, P. 120.

(2) Ibid. Δ

The care & feeding of solar batteries

By Jeffrey R. Yago, P.E., CEM

I have been receiving many questions from readers and visitors to the *BHM* web site concerning deep discharge solar batteries. These questions include: How do they work? Which type is best? How long will they last? Are they dangerous? Do they require maintenance? Can they be located outside? How low can they be discharged? How do you clean them?

There are all kinds of batteries, using all kinds of materials. Battery technology is rapidly advancing to increase power density and reduce weight for everything from cell phones to electric vehicles. Unfortunately, this usually requires more toxic materials and a much higher cost. When it comes to choosing a battery for an off-grid solar home or back-up emergency power system, we usually are not that concerned with battery size or weight. We just want a battery that can be quickly charged, then supply power slowly for one or more days, and last six or more years. With all this battery research, it is still hard to beat the lowly deep-cycle lead-acid battery for this type of solar system performance and low cost.

Rack-mounted solar gel-cell sealed batteries

Since any battery is stored chemical energy, perhaps a brief review of basic battery construction and the chemical to energy conversion process is in order.

Solar battery types

If you want to avoid all battery maintenance, you can purchase sealed "gel" or absorbed glass-matt (AGM) type lead-acid batteries. These have the sulfuric acid converted to a jelly-like consistency, or absorbed in a sponge blanket surrounding the individual lead plates, with the entire battery sealed at the factory. They can be mounted in any direction and are used in solar applications that cannot receive regular maintenance, like solar-powered street lights and remote cell phone towers. Since sealed batteries do not need regular maintenance, they can be stacked closely together.

Unfortunately, maintenance-free lead-acid batteries have a much higher price tag without gaining any more amp-hour capacity than an equal-sized open lead-acid battery. A sealed battery is also very sensitive to charging voltage, and even a slight overcharge can release hydrogen gas and cause rapid battery heating and permanent damage. A sealed battery cannot be equalize charged, since any release of hydrogen gas through the safety pressure relief valve cannot be replaced, so the battery will soon dry out. This usually results in a much shorter life for sealed batteries.

Most off-grid solar and battery back-up systems use an open-cap deep-discharge liquid lead-acid battery. The battery bank will be a group of individual 2 or 6-volt deep cycle batteries wired together to provide a higher system voltage. For small systems, the "L-16" size traction battery is the battery of choice. It has the same base size as a golf cart battery, but is taller and much heavier. It was originally designed to power battery floor sweepers, fork trucks, and mining cars, and is very ruggedly constructed. It is also available at most battery distributors for a reasonable price, and can have up to six-years of useful life for most solar applications.

If handling and transporting a heavy battery is not a problem for you, larger solar applications can use a "tray" battery. This battery is made up of very tall 2-volt cells, pre-wired into a 12, 24, or 48-volt configuration and housed in a metal box, like the 24-volt tray battery pictured. With individual tray batteries weighing up to a ton, many installers prefer using individual cells and make the battery interconnects after the individual cells are moved to the job site. Although difficult to handle, the tray battery's cells are very tall, providing lots of room at the top for reserve electrolyte, and lots of space at the bottom for flaked off sulfates. The industrial tray battery will last longer than the smaller 6-volt batteries, and an 8 to 12-year life is possible with proper maintenance.

Battery chemistry

Lead-acid batteries can be divided into two basic subcategories: lead-antimony and lead-calcium. Since pure lead would be too soft to form the battery plates, several other materials are added to improve plate strength and charge performance. When antimony is combined to make the lead plate stronger, it also improves how low the battery can be repeatedly discharged without damage.

Many deep-cycle lead-antimony batteries can withstand a daily discharge down to 20% remaining charge without any damage. Since lead-antimony plates release much more hydrogen than other battery types, this battery will require more watering and have more out-gassing during the charging process.

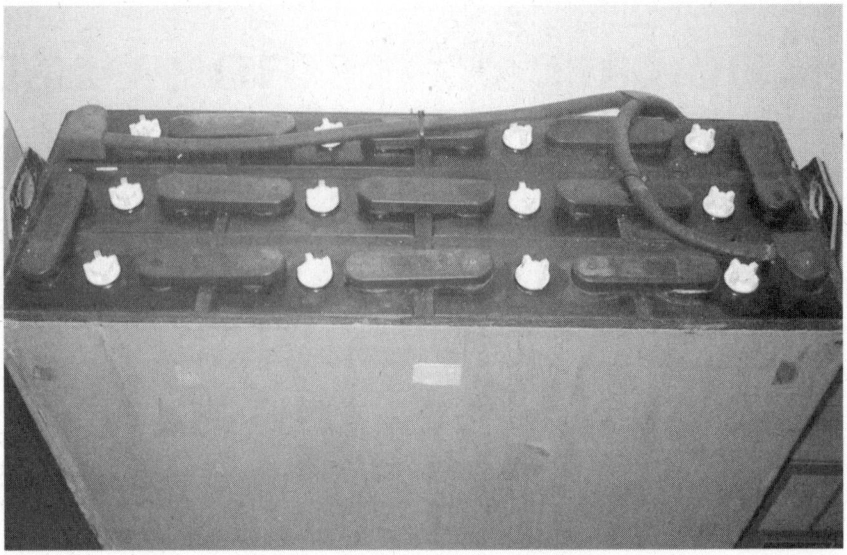

24-volt industrial tray solar battery

When calcium is added to a pure lead plate, this also improves plate strength, but this battery type will have a much lower rate of water loss. This battery is usually referred to as "maintenance-free," and may include sealed cell caps designed to recombine the vented hydrogen and oxygen gasses back into water during the charging process. A car battery is an example of a lead-calcium battery. Before deciding that a lead-calcium battery is right for your needs, please note that for the same size battery, a lead-antimony battery can store up to three times the amp-hours of a lead-calcium battery, because the lead-calcium (low maintenance) battery cannot be repeatedly discharged below 75% full (25 percent used) without damage.

For those of you who still remember high school chemistry, the positive (+) lead plate is covered with a paste of lead dioxide (PbO^2). The negative (-) lead plate is called "sponge" lead (Pb). Both are fairly soft, and are formed into a waffle shape to increase the amount of surface area exposed to the sulfuric acid (H^2SO^4). The plates are separated from physical contact by a porous spacer or fiberglass matt.

During discharge, oxygen molecules (O^2) from the positive plate combine with hydrogen molecules (H^2) from the acid to form water (H^2O). The now free sulfate molecule (SO^4) in the acid then combines with the lead in the positive plate to form lead sulfate ($PbSO^4$).

On the nearby negative plate, the lead in the plate also combines with the free sulfate molecules (SO^4) to form lead sulfate ($PbSO^4$). This discharge process causes the acid to become diluted when the battery is fully discharged, due to the chemical conversion of acid molecules into water molecules.

In fact, a battery that is 75 percent discharged can freeze at no colder than 3 degrees due to this change in acid concentration. However, a fully charged liquid lead-acid battery will not freeze until 70 degrees below zero. Always try to locate a battery where it will not exceed 90 degrees, or fall below 50 degrees, with 77 degrees the ideal temperature for maximum battery performance. Battery efficiency and length of service will drop significantly outside these temperature limits.

During battery charging, a reverse chemical process takes place, as the negative lead plate, now covered with lead sulfate ($PbSO^4$), separates back out into lead (Pb), and the sulfate molecule (SO^4) is released back to combine with hydrogen in the water (H^2O) to reform sulfuric acid (H^2SO^4). The positive lead plate recombines with the left over oxygen molecule in the water releasing hydrogen gas. This is the out-gassing of hydrogen that takes place near the end of every charging cycle, as the battery reaches its fully charged state. At this point a good quality battery charger will "sense" the battery is almost fully recharged, and switch to a small "float" charge to limit out-gassing and water loss.

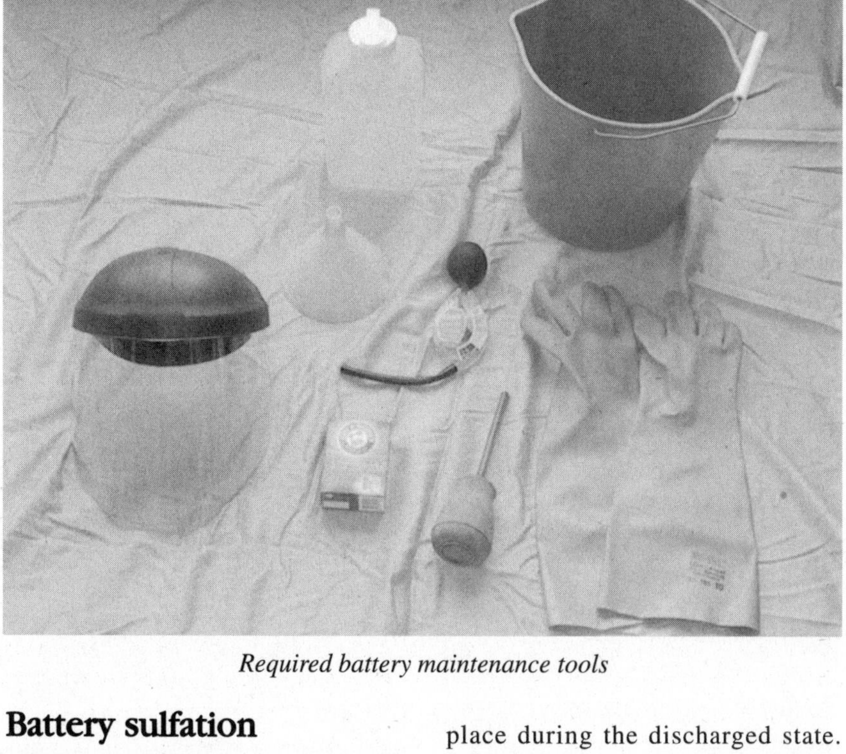

Required battery maintenance tools

Battery sulfation

Battery sulfation is the normal process of small sulfate crystals (SO^4) forming on the surface of the lead plates during the discharge process. If a lead-acid battery is not fully recharged, or if left in a discharged state for a long period, these sulfate crystals will begin to "grow" on the lead plates, just like as a child you grew salt or sugar crystals in an evaporating pan on the window sill.

If allowed to grow larger, these sulfate crystals will "insulate" a larger and larger surface area of the lead plate from the acid, and physically expand against the soft lead plates which can cause permanent deformation. Large sulfate crystals can also "flake off" the plates and pile up at the bottom of the battery cells. If the battery casing has limited space under the plates, they can actually pile high enough to short out the separate (+) and (-) plates. The higher the ambient air temperature, the faster this sulfate building process will take place during the discharged state. Below 60 percent remaining charge, this sulfating process increases dramatically.

Unfortunately, the portion of the lead plates that are now heavily coated with sulfate cannot be completely cleaned of the sulfate during battery charging, although there are some "pulse-type" battery chargers that can correct some of the damage. Sometimes repeated over-charging can partially remove the sulfate buildup, but once the initial damage is done, the battery will never reach its original state again. If you want to avoid battery sulfation from reducing the exposed plate area and charge capacity of your batteries, do not let it start in the first place. Keep all batteries topped off with distilled water and fully charged.

Battery care and feeding

To keep your solar or emergency power lead-acid battery at peak performance, you will need some basic tools and supplies.

Batteries need water to replenish the constant water loss during each charging cycle as hydrogen gas is released, and only distilled water should be used. You do not want to add "hard" water or water having dissolved solids which can increase this sulfate problem even more.

Before handling battery caps, adding water, or checking individual cells, you need to protect yourself from potential acid spills, splashes, or hydrogen gas ignition.

A full face shield and chemical-resistant heavy-rubber gloves are an absolute must. Do not use those thin throwaway gloves which can tear very easily on sharp corners, and will start to disintegrate when in contact with acid.

You will need a good quality specific gravity electrolyte tester, which is the only accurate way to measure and compare the state of charge of each individual cell. You will also need a squeeze-bulb battery filler which allows removal of acid from an overfilled cell. Never remove liquid from one cell and place in another. Regardless of size, each cell of a lead-acid battery at 77°F will have a specific gravity of 1.260 when 100

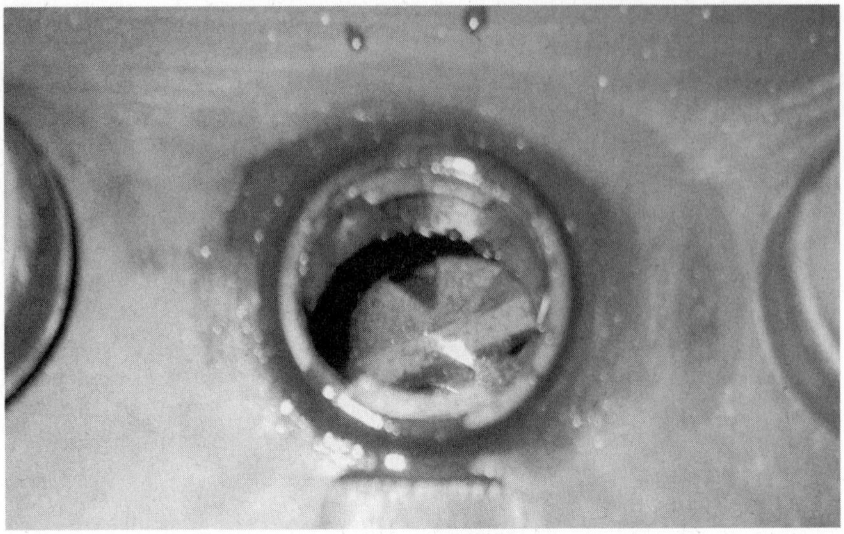

Looking into a lead-acid battery with the cap removed

percent fully charged, and a reading of 1.150 when the battery has dropped below 25 percent remaining charge. Notice this is a very small change in readings, for a large change in charge. If the readings are taken when the temperature is below 77°F, the specific gravity will read artificially high. When the temperature is above 77°F, the specific gravity will read artificially low. Better quality battery testers will include a thermometer and reading adjustment table.

Use a good quality acid resistant nylon plastic funnel when adding water to any battery cell. You may need to cut off the long tube end to obtain a larger bottom opening that fits better in the short opening space.

When you look into a lead-acid battery cell with the cap removed, you should see liquid covering all metal surfaces of the cells. If you can see a dry lead surface, the cell has a very low liquid acid level and probably is building up sulfate. Distilled water should be added until just below the bottom of the "ring" or dip tube that extends down from the cap. Over-filling will cause the acid to bubble out of the cells during charging, when the battery temperature increases and there is a discharge of hydrogen gas.

You should periodically check several individual battery cells before and after charging. Be sure to note any cell with a specific gravity that is lower than the other cells. Do not take readings just after adding distilled water, as it will be "floating" on the top surface and cause an incorrect reading. I prefer to add distilled water just before starting an equalization charge, which causes good mixing of the added water and acid. I then check again after the equalize charge is complete.

On larger systems, some homeowners use a pre-printed form to record these readings, which are usually taken every three months. This will provide an early indication of any problem or downward trend. If you only sample a few cells each time, be sure to always take your readings from the same cells, and be sure the cells near the end and center of each row of batteries are included, as these will be more representative of the other cells. I have noticed the cells closest to the end of string load connection posts seen to loose the most

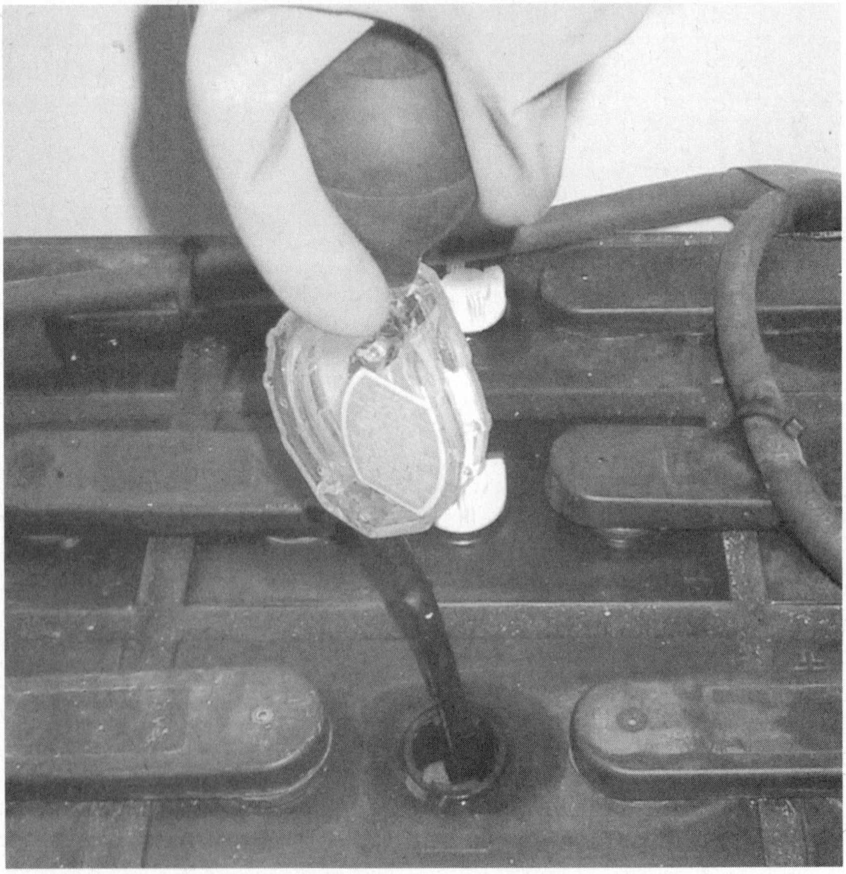

Checking battery electrolyte

water. I like to check my battery bank at the change of seasons to help remind me when three months have passed. This is noted on all calendars and mentioned in the news as the first day of spring, summer, fall, and winter.

Equalize charging

Your off-grid or battery back-up power system will use either a solar charge controller, a generator powered inverter, or grid powered charger to keep your battery bank fully charged. However, this day-to-day charging is only replacing the amount of amp-hours that were removed during the last discharge period. Over time and multiple charge/discharge cycles, each individual battery cell will begin to have a different charge level due to minor differences in cell construction and acid concentration.

Eventually, the cell that has the lowest charge capacity will limit the ability of a battery charger to fully recharge all other battery cells that are connected in series with the lowest cell. This condition is usually reached every three to four months in new batteries, but older batteries will need water more often and will require a shorter period between equalize charges. Increased water loss is an early indication of battery aging.

To make the equalize-charging process easier, your battery charger or inverter should have an "equalize" charge mode. This switch or program setpoint temporarily overrides the normal "float" charge voltage of the battery charger, which allows battery charging to continue. In a short period, the fully charged cells will start to "boil off" excess hydrogen gas as the water (H^2O) in the acid begins to be converted into hydrogen gas and oxygen.

The battery also starts to heat up and the heavy acid near the bottom of the battery cell starts to mix with the lighter water near the top of the cell. Finally, the lowest charged cells reach their fully charged level and the process is ended. Although different battery sizes and charger amp-ratings will determine the actual time required, a typical equalize charge usually lasts two hours longer after the battery has reached its initial full charge voltage.

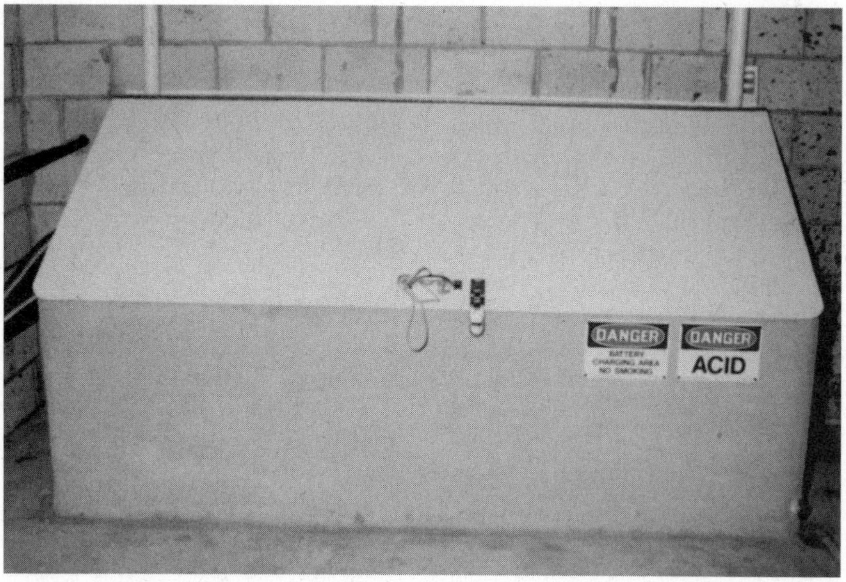

Air-tight insulated battery box with PVC air vents to the outside

What about hydrogen?

I am not going to diminish the danger of a battery explosion, but it is also not like the large fireballs in a Hollywood special effects movie either. I have been next to industrial batteries when they exploded and I assure you the sound alone will take five-years off your life. However, unless the hydrogen gas has completely filled up a large room in very high concentrations, there should be no fireball. Most of the battery explosions I witnessed were like a flash, lasting only a fraction of a second, with no smoke or burning parts. Regardless, the real danger is large pieces of acid-covered plastic battery case "shrapnel" flying through the air. This most likely will not cause a fire, but it sure can put your eye out, burn your skin, and permanently damage surrounding surfaces.

Although it may be theoretically possible, I have not heard of any battery "exploding" while supplying power to a load or sitting on the shelf and not being charged. It is also rare for any battery to explode during normal charging, as long as it is in a well ventilated area. The greatest danger is that point when the battery is almost fully charged, but the charger is still operating, or when an equalize-charge is in process and a large quantity of hydrogen gas is being generated.

Hydrogen gas in the air "tastes" salty when you breathe it. It reminds me of being near the ocean, and this is a good indicator that more ventilation is needed. If the battery room is well ventilated, these gases will eventually dissipate and will no longer be concentrated enough to present any danger.

However, if the battery is in a small room or battery enclosure with limited or no means of air ventilation, the hydrogen gas can reach a dangerous level of concentration. Hydrogen gas is only explosive when in high concentrations, which can form near the battery room ceiling or top of a battery enclosure. Note the two PVC vent pipes at the top of the custom built battery box in the photo this page.

Any small spark or nearby flame can cause concentrated hydrogen gas to ignite. It will then travel down through the battery cap vents like a lit fuse on a cannon, where the explosive force of the ignited hydrogen gas in the closed cell cannot escape, resulting in flying battery parts. In one of the larger battery explosions I witnessed, a battery on an electric fork truck exploded after being on charge all day. A tiny spark from a worker's hand grinder over 30-feet away ignited the concentrated hydrogen gas that had formed around and inside the battery at the end of a long charge cycle.

I recently had to replace a sealed 12-volt RV/Marine battery in a trailer, when it exploded and tossed acid and plastic parts in all directions. A tiny "trickle" charger had been left on for several months at the same time the battery was not supplying any loads, which eventually "boiled" the battery dry. It appears the continued charging caused the battery plates to short out or heat up, which ignited the surrounding hydrogen gas. Although there was no fire, it was a real mess to clean up and the acid permanently blackened and softened the surrounding wood walls and floor.

Periodic battery cleanup

Lead-acid batteries contain sulfuric acid which is very corrosive. If you splash it on your clothes, the threads will eventually dissolve everywhere it made contact. If it gets on wood building materials it will damage the wood. If it gets on concrete, it will damage the concrete. I have already addressed the danger to your eyes and skin.

In addition to normal acid spills and drips during the adding of distilled water, long term battery charging also causes an acid "mist" to settle on the top of the batteries and battery cables, causing corrosion and poor electrical contact at the terminal connections. This surface condition can also allow small electrical currents to flow between the battery terminals, which increase standby charge loss.

Since any acid and "base" forms water and a salt when combined, battery acid can be neutralized when in contact with baking soda (a strong base). I like to mix a bucket of warm water with a half box of baking soda, and wipe all batteries and cables with a cotton rag dripping with the solution. Be sure you do this with all the battery caps tightly secure, as you never want any of the solution to drain down into the battery cells. This solution should always be nearby to control any spills or accidental splashes of battery acid onto skin or clothes.

Battery myths

Storing a battery on a bare concrete floor will "drain" away the charge. No, a concrete floor surface is usually much colder than a higher wooden garage bench. Placing a battery on a cold concrete floor lowers the battery's state of charge due to the lower temperature.

You can use a car battery for solar applications. No, car batteries have very thin lead plates to reduce vehicle weight, and will quickly fail after only a few deep discharge cycles.

Old lead-acid battery technology is wasteful and contaminates landfills with hazardous wastes. No, lead-acid batteries carry a high refundable cash deposit to ensure the old battery will be exchanged, and almost every part of the old battery will be 100 percent recycled into new batteries.

Conclusions

This article is not intended to scare a potential solar system buyer. It is however, intended to give everyone a healthy appreciation of how to take care of and work safely around a lead-acid battery bank. These batteries are still the easiest and lowest cost way to store the excess energy from a solar array, wind generator, or hydro turbine, and with regular maintenance, a lead-acid battery will provide many years of safe and trouble-free service.

Jeff Yago is a licensed professional engineer and certified energy manager with over 25-years experience in the energy conservation field. He is also certified by the North American Board of Certified Energy Practitioners as a licensed solar installer and a licensed journeyman electrician. He has extensive solar thermal and solar photovoltaic system design experience and has authored numerous articles and texts. Δ

Kinder goats
a small breed for milk and meat

By Kathleen Sanderson

I have had dairy goats for most of the last 20 years or so and have raised almost every standard breed. But when my grandmother, my youngest daughter, and I moved to a bare one-acre lot near Klamath Falls, Oregon, I decided it was time to look at the smaller breeds. We wouldn't have room for pasture, so all feed would have to be purchased. Smaller goats eat less than their full-sized counterparts, and so would cost less to keep. I would be able to keep more of them in a smaller area. Also, as I get older, the advantages of smaller animals to care for become more and more obvious.

Pygmies were immediately ruled out because our primary need was milk and, while pygmies can be milked, they are really not dairy goats. I looked into Nigerian Dwarfs, but they are still somewhat in the exotic category and seem to be more expensive than the standard breeds. When I read about Kinder goats (pronounced with a short 'i' sound, as in the German word for children), I knew I'd found what we were looking for. A new breed, started only about 20 years ago, they are dual-purpose, good for both milk and meat, and approximately in the middle between their Pygmy and Nubian ancestors in size.

There are enough breeders already, so that Kinders have their own classes in some goat shows making them fairly available almost anywhere. It is also possible to start your own line of Kinders by crossing a registered Pygmy buck with a registered purebred Nubian doe.

I chose to find a breeder, as we are limited on the number of animals we can keep on such a small place. I looked through the breeders listed at the Kinder Goat Breeders Association (KGBA) website, and found someone fairy close to home.

Dawn Leaming has been raising Kinders for a number of years, and after several e-mails, my daughter and I made the six-hour trip down to her place near Nevada City, California, on a hot July day. We came home through a raging thunderstorm with a five-year-old milker, twin doe kids, a little buck, and a wether to keep him company.

The kids were still on bottles, and settled in quickly, but Mazola, the milker, was heartbroken at being separated from her pen-mates, and bawled loudly for hours on end at first. She still thinks I ought to live in the goat pen with her, and cries when I go back up to the house. But the noise doesn't last very long—and thankfully, our neighbors seemed more amused than bothered by the racket.

However, I learned my lesson. If I purchase an adult doe again, I will also purchase one of her pen-mates, if possible.

Mazola, one of the author's Kinder does. She has been recently milked, but you can still see that she has decent sized teats for milking.

I was really surprised at how quickly Mazola decided I was her friend. Within days (after some struggles at milking time, as I was *not* the person who was "supposed" to be milking her) she was nuzzling up to me while I gave the babies their bottles. These are very friendly, affectionate goats

Thunder, the brown and white buck, and Lightning, the wether who keeps him company. Goats are herd animals and don't do well if kept alone.

and really not all that noisy once they've settled in.

High quality milk

So far, I haven't found any serious downside to these little goats. Oh, if I take up goat-packing, they might not be able to carry as much as the big guys, and they don't give as much milk in sheer quantity as some larger does, but what they do give is the best quality milk I've ever had. The butterfat is high, ranging from around 5½ to over 7 percent. Milk solids are also high, making for excellent cheese yields. A gallon of milk from one of the larger breeds of goat, or from a cow, will usually yield around a pound to a pound and a half of cheese, but a gallon of Kinder milk will yield about twice that.

The flavor of the milk is excellent, and it seems to have good keeping quality. Of course, it's really important to follow good dairy practice in cleaning your equipment, so you don't end up with milkstone deposits. I only have one milker right now, and she peaked at two quarts a day and was holding steady months later at a little over a quart a day, so I haven't had a lot of surplus milk to play with yet, but I have made kefir cheese and some yogurt.

I keep two jars of kefir going all the time and have found that a couple of jars of kefir, let sit for 24 hours in a clean muslin cloth, makes a nice sour soft cheese that is excellent with some herbs and garlic powder added to it.

The yogurt made from Kinder milk is also excellent. It isn't quite as thick as store-bought, which has all kinds of thickeners added to it, but it is thicker than the yogurt I'd made in the past from Alpine or Nubian milk.

When I got Nubians for the first time several years ago, I thought their milk was much better than the milk of the other breeds of goats I'd raised. But the Kinder milk is even better than the Nubian milk was and it has seemed to keep its quality clear through the lactation, even with the stress of moving to a new home and several feed changes.

My little doe gives enough milk for us for kefir and a little cheese, but many Kinder does give three or four quarts of milk a day right through their lactation. There are a few Kinder does who average over a gallon of milk a day.

Now, I realize that many Alpines, Saanans, Toggs, LaManchas, and Nubians give much more milk than that. There are standard-breed goats who average over two gallons of milk a day, and some record breakers that give a lot more than that. This is good if you are selling milk, or have some other use for it. You can use goat milk as an addition to the feed of many other animals. However, I'm a very practical person, and I don't want to be feeding animals who are producing more than we can use. Goats that give two or three quarts of rich milk each day are very practical animals for most people.

Breed year-round

One advantage Kinders have is that they will breed year-round. The Northern European breeds of goats are all seasonal breeders, but goats from the tropics, such as the Nubians and Pygmies, will breed at any time of the year. This means that you can breed one doe to kid in the spring and milk through the summer, fall, and early winter. Then breed the other doe in April or May for a winter supply of milk. They'll overlap a little bit, but you can make cheese with the surplus. It's always nice to have a home supply of milk. However, you should plan your breeding so you don't have kids being born during really cold weather.

Easy-milking teats

As I started looking for goats to buy, I was concerned about teat size. I knew that Pygmies normally have small teats and are no fun to milk. Some of the Nubians I'd had were quite easy to milk, but there were a couple of them with tiny teats. I have a little arthritis and have carpal tunnel in both wrists, so easy milking was important for me to look for.

Thankfully, Dawn Leaming is breeding for easy-milking goats. Mazola is very easy to milk with her hand-sized teats, and the doe kids,

Lark and Linnet, already look like they will have easy-to-grasp teats when they come into milk in a year or so. My low milk pail with a half-moon cover fits nicely under Mazola's udder. From what I've heard, owners of Pygmies and Nigerians sometimes have trouble getting a milk pail underneath their little goats.

Good meat animals

Kinders are also useful meat animals. I haven't butchered any of mine yet, but people who do butcher surplus animals are reporting dress out percentages of 60 percent or higher. A six-to-eight month old kid weighing 50 pounds should dress out to 30 pounds. A 14-month-old wether weighing 80 pounds should dress out to about 50 pounds, a dressing percentage of nearly 63 percent.

I plan to save and tan the hides and feed the offal to my dog as part of a "natural" diet for him. So there will be very little waste of any kind.

Having some experience with butchering larger animals such as moose and caribou from my years living in Alaska, I know that when butchering time does come here, I'll be thankful these guys aren't huge.

Since Kinder does have a high kidding percentage—with whole herds averaging 300 percent or higher, and individual does often having quads, quints, or even sextuplets—and the kids have a very high rate of growth (often as high as Boer kids), you can see that the potential for meat production from Kinders is very high. One 115-pound doe can easily produce 150 pounds of meat, or more, in 14 months. And by the time you butcher the first batch, she'll have kidded again and be raising another batch of kids.

Two or three Kinder does, some poultry, and maybe a few meat rabbits can easily provide all the dairy products, meat, and eggs most families can use, all on a very small piece of land.

Feed efficiency

Their feed efficiency is good, also. They can milk as well as their Nubian ancestors, but because they are smaller-bodied, they need less feed. Mazola was getting fat while eating grass hay and about two pounds of grain a day, and giving two quarts of milk a day. I had to cut her grain by half to keep her from getting too fat. Now I'm feeding the does alfalfa pellets, about half a pound of COB (corn, oats, and barley mixed with molasses) each, and a handful of sunflower seeds each day, and they are all in good flesh, even well into the winter.

They are also getting a loose salt/mineral mix (I'm using one meant for cattle, as goats need more copper than sheep do), and a supplement meant for horses that contains selenium and Vitamin E. Some breeders use Purina Goat Chow, but my goats are doing well on COB, and I know what's in the COB.

Hardy and long-lived

In addition to all their other advantages, Kinders seem to be hardy, healthy, and long-lived. Pat Showalter, of Zederkamm Kinders in Snohomish, Washington, had one of her original Kinder does born in 1986, still going strong in 2001 at age 15. They also don't seem to need their hooves trimmed quite as often as some breeds, though this important chore still can't be neglected. If they are going to stay productive for as long as possible, they need sound legs, and letting their hooves get overgrown can damage their legs.

Easier to fence

Another advantage is that it is easier to fence them. The consensus among breeders is that, while once in a great while a Kinder will be a fence-jumper (and this usually stops after they kid for the first time), very

The Costco carport goat shelter. Fencing is "combi" cattle panels, which have smaller holes at the bottom.

Linnet (left) and her twin sister, Lark, trying to see what I'm doing, and Mazola, watching the buck's antics next door. Notice how broad-chested these girls are.

few will jump out of a cattle panel fence. I use combi cattle panels turned upside down for my goat pens, so the smaller holes are at the bottom. This keeps young kids from escaping, usually. I cut out a section of wire in each pen, so the goats could reach through to their water buckets on the outside of the pens, where the water stays cleaner, and the buckets are less likely to get knocked over.

My two doe kids discovered that when the water got low in the buckets, they could knock them over and then squeeze through the holes. The smaller of the twins can still do this, so I have to watch her when I'm cleaning and refilling their water bucket. She doesn't go anyplace, and right now there isn't anything she can damage while she's out, but pretty soon I'll be planting the garden again, so I hope she outgrows the hole quickly.

Of all the breeds of goats I've had over the years, Kinders are proving to be my favorite by far, and I plan to never be without at least a few of them around.

Resources

For more information, including milk records and a list of some Kinder goat breeders, go to: www.kindergoats.com.

There is also a Yahoogroups list for people who have, or are interested in, Kinder goats at: http://groups.yahoo.com/group/KinderGoats/?yguid=109437082. There are over one hundred members, and a lot of good advice and information from people with years of experience. It's also a good place to find breeders who aren't listed on the association website.

The following recipes are taken from *Goats Produce Too, The Udder Real Thing, Volume 2,* by Mary Jane Toth, 2833 N. Lewis Road, Coleman, Michigan 48618.

Plain goat milk yogurt

2 qts. goat milk
1 cup powdered milk (optional, and not really necessary with Kinder goat milk)
2 tsp. plain cultured yogurt
clean canning jars, pint or quart

Warm milk to 115 degrees. Stir in powdered milk if desired. Add 2 tsp. of cultured yogurt. Mix well and pour into clean jars. Place filled jars into a roaster or kettle. Fill the roaster or pan with hot tap water up to the neck of the jars. Cover and set in a warm place to incubate for 6-8 hours. Do not disturb during incubation. Yogurt will thicken when ready. When making plain yogurt, save some to use as a culture for your next batch. Keep refrigerated.

French style chevre

5 qts. whole goat milk
½ cup cultured buttermilk
2 Tbsp. diluted rennet (dilution = 3 drops liquid rennet into ⅓ cup cool water. Do not use rennet tablets from the grocery store.)

Warm milk to 80 degrees. Stir in buttermilk. Mix well. Add 2 Tbsp. of diluted rennet mixture. Stir well and cover. Let set at room temperature for 8-12 hours. Cheese is ready to drain when it looks like thickened yogurt. Curds may have a thin layer of whey floating on top.

Only use muslin cheesecloth (not the gauzy stuff called cheesecloth) or pillowcase cloth to drain. Line a large bowl or pan with cloth. Pour curds into center of cloth. Gather up corners of cloth and hang to drain 6-8 hours.

When dripping has stopped, cheese is ready. It should be the consistency of cream cheese. To speed up draining, scrape the sides of the bag towards the center several times during the draining process.

This cheese is soft and mild. It can be seasoned with a variety of herbs or spices. Or, use it as a substitute for cream cheese in other recipes. The cheese keeps well, refrigerated, for two weeks.

Freeze unseasoned, in one pound packages. Keeps well frozen for 6 months. Do not freeze seasoned cheeses. Herbs and spices will lose their potency and flavor. Thaw at room temperature. Season after thawing. (One pound = two cups)

Wrap well before freezing, or use heavy freezer bags. Δ

Making sausage

By Linda Gabris

While most folks in my neck of the woods are busy barbecuing during the last leg of summer, my thoughts are wistfully drifting to autumn and the brand new hunting season it's about to bring. It's round about this time of year when lingering whiffs of smoke whet my appetite for a feed of delicious homemade sausages, and I can't think of a better time to free-up the freezer in anticipation of another lucky season. Turning game meats or domestic buys that are about to expire their prime frozen shelf life into an array of spicy, mouthwatering sausages is an excellent way of putting old trophies to good use.

Sausage making is a rewarding Old World craft that has been made easy by modern day contraptions like electric meat grinders, kitchen scales, portable smokehouses, and the wonderful convenience of readily available casings, premixed cures, and seasoning kits.

There are two main categories of sausages—fresh and cured. Fresh types must be cooked prior to eating and are usually commercially sold in casings but when made at home are often formed into patties and conveniently fried like traditional hamburgers. Fresh sausages will keep in the refrigerator for up to about a week, after which time they must be frozen for safe keeping.

Cured sausages are drier types made out of meat that has been cured by methods used for centuries as practical ways of preserving meat before days of refrigeration. Such methods include the use of salt, fermentation, drying, and smoking which renders sausages that will keep indefinitely when hung at pantry temperature.

One of the most confusing aspects of sausage making is the topic of cures. In earlier times, meat was cured with plain table salt and some old diehards like myself still use heirloom recipes with success. However, novice home sausage makers today have the option of using premixed cures and binder mixes that contain sodium nitrite, a chemical agent that safeguards against the growth of organisms that can cause sausages to go bad. Commercial cures can be bought at meat shops, larger grocery stores, and from sausage making suppliers. Using such mixes will take the mystery out of curing and ensure success, especially for beginners.

The basic ingredient for tasty sausages is good meat. Now that doesn't mean that you have to grind up choice cuts like sirloin or top round, which I find are usually long gone by the time my sausage making season rolls around, but you must use meat that is in good condition. If your cuts are starting to show signs of frost bite, be sure to trim it off and discard. Properly wrapped meat will last for

Ready for the casings

up to two years in the deep freeze, but I like to use mine up before it has a chance to get nipped.

Since I find the less desirable cuts are always the last to go, these are what gets made into my sausages. Trimmings from ribs, meat off shanks, flanks, stew, and ground are ideal choices for sausages, and you can use moose, deer, beef, pork, or mix and match any game or domestic meats you wish.

In the olden days, traditional or natural casings (obtained from pork, sheep, or calf intestines) had to be hand cleaned after the animal was slaughtered, and this, I can vouch, is no easy task. Today, gut casings can be bought salted or brined and need only to be soaked to remove salt before using. They are most commonly obtained from pork and sold by the "hank," which is a bundle that will do about a hundred pounds of sausages, but you should be able to buy a half or quarter pack. Leftovers can be salted back down and saved over and over for future use, so don't fret if you have to buy more than you think you are going to need for one recipe.

I prefer pig casings for my sausages, but there are other choices like collagen casings, which are made out of a secondary layer of cattle hide, and man-made casings made out of cellulose, muslin, or other synthetic, non-edible materials. Casings come in various sizes to accommodate pepperoni-to-bologna sized sausages and can be bought at butcher shops or from specialty suppliers.

Because game meats are very lean and good sausages must contain some fat content, it is necessary to add pork or beef fat when using game or lean meats in sausage recipes. I find fat trimmed from pork butt is a good pick, and ratios can vary according to liking and type of sausage, anywhere from one third to fifty percent fat. Trial and error is the only way to perfect sausages to suit your own taste.

There are two ways of adding spices. One is to spice the cubes of meat before grinding, which allows the spices to be ground evenly into meat. The other is to add spices to meat after it has been ground and work it through with hands. I follow the second method. Either way, the spices must be evenly distributed.

Getting started

First and foremost, keep a clean, cool workplace. Assemble everything needed and have scalding water ready for rinsing tools. Meat must be thoroughly thawed before making into sausages so take it out of the freezer beforehand. Once thawed, keep in refrigerator until ready to use. Weigh on kitchen scale. Cut meat into cubes that will fit into the funnel of your grinder. Grind and refrigerate or hold over ice. I usually work in 25-pound batches, but when making a proven sausage you fancy, you can double up if you wish.

Spicy fresh sausages: This is a basic recipe for fresh sausages that must be cooked before eating. They will keep refrigerated for up to about a week and then must be frozen for safekeeping.

20 pounds lean meat (moose, deer, beef, or mix and match…using what's available in your freezer)
5 pounds pork fat (if you want moister, juicer sausages, increase fat and decrease lean accordingly)
½ cup salt
8 Tbsp. fresh-ground black pepper
6 tsp. cayenne pepper (more, less, or none to suit taste; I like mine hot)
3 Tbsp. rubbed sage
2 Tbsp. ground thyme
3 tsp. marjoram
7 Tbsp. garlic granules or garlic powder
optional spices: nutmeg, ginger, mace or anything that tickles your fancy. A tip on spicing: after adding suggested amount, fry a marble-sized ball of meat and taste. Adjust seasoning, if needed.
about 12 to 15 yards of natural sausage casings (or omit casing and form into patties with hands)

Cut lean meat and fat into workable cubes and grind coarsely using recommended plate for your grinder. Mix seasoning together in bowl and sprinkle evenly over meat. Using hands, lightly but thoroughly work spices through meat. Regrind through a finer sausage plate. Form sausage meat into patties or stuff into casings. If using natural, salted down casings, rinse under cold running water to remove all traces of salt. Follow package directions for other types of casings.

Slide casing onto stuffing nozzle, tie knot at end of casing, and push sausage meat through the hopper according to your manual, twisting into 6-inch links or desired length. Put the sausages into the refrigerator and allow to meld for at least eight hours before cooking. These sausages must be frozen after about a week in the fridge, but they're so good they'll be gone before you know it.

Cased sausages can be fried, baked, barbecued, or broiled. Patties can be served burger fashion or crumbled and used in spaghetti or lasagna sauce, chili-con-carne, pizza topping, or any recipe calling for spicy ground meat.

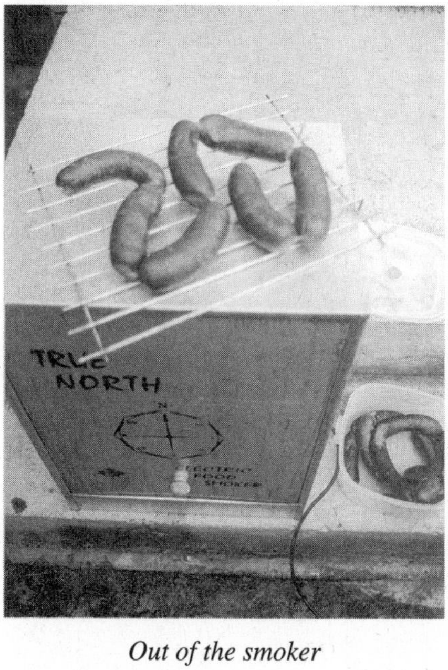

Out of the smoker

Hungarian-style sausage supper

Smoked trophy sausages:

- 20 pounds lean meat (again, use what you have available)
- 5 pounds pork or beef fat (I prefer pork fat as it doesn't overpower)
- 1 cup of salt
- ½ cup sugar
- 7 Tbsp. fresh-ground black pepper
- 8 Tbsp. garlic granules or powder
- 4 Tbsp. crushed chili peppers or cayenne (more or less to suit taste)
- 14 Tbsp. sweet paprika
- 2 Tbsp. ground mustard seed
- 3 Tbsp. coriander seed
- 3 tsp. ground cardamom
- about 12 to 15 yards of natural casings

Cut the meat and fat into workable cubes and grind coarsely. Mix the remaining ingredients, except casings, and sprinkle over the meat. Mix by hand until well distributed. Regrind through a medium-sized sausage plate. Stuff into prepared casings, as above. Allow to cure under refrigeration for 24 hours. Put in the smokehouse and smoke according to your manual. Immediately after removing from the smoker, shower the sausages with cold water to cool them down. These sausages will keep indefinitely when hung at cool pantry temperature, but it is advisable to keep them under refrigeration for long-term storage.

Hungarian-style sausages:

- 1 Tbsp. oil
- 3 or 4 coils of spicy smoked sausages, cut into ¼-inch slices
- 3 chopped onions
- 1 chopped green pepper
- 2 or 3 finely chopped hot chili peppers
- 2 gloves minced garlic
- 1 Tbsp. sweet red paprika
- salt, pepper
- 3 chopped tomatoes
- 1 cup water

Heat the oil in a skillet. Lightly brown the sausage. Add the onions, peppers, and garlic and sauté until the vegetables are soft. Add the paprika, salt, and pepper. Stir until the paprika is absorbed. Add the tomatoes and about one cup of water. Cover and simmer over low heat for 20 minutes. Serve with crusty bread or fluffy rice. This goes great with a glass of red wine—Egri Bikaver from Hungary is my pick. Δ

Build a component water system

By David Lee

I want to show you a home water system that can become so complicated you need a Ph.D. in Industrial Arts to build the whole contraption in all its glory.

I'll start with the simplest version, adding layers of complexity as we proceed. If you did well in high school shop class or have mastered your DVD remote control, most of this will make sense to you.

If you are not on your way to the recipe section of the magazine by now, let's begin with why it might be worth the trouble to take on this project.

After air, water is the most important element we need in order to stay alive. It must be clean and plentiful for good physical health and hygiene. Water is also an important part of the third most essential life element: beer—or for some people: food.

Having a constant supply of fresh clean water is a benefit shared by only a small percentage of the population of the world, and we who have it should be very grateful. I know I am.

Municipal water systems serving large groups of people are well maintained and the purity is monitored. They are the Mercedes Benzes of water systems. If you are fortunate enough to be connected to one of these be doubly grateful. This article is intended for people who have their own dug or drilled wells. These folks must take responsibility for their own systems and here is where the Component Water System becomes useful.

The system I describe here supplies water to your home all the time, even when the lights go out. One of its versions can provide running water to homes off the grid more efficiently and conveniently than other methods.

I read somewhere that beer was originally invented to replace undrinkable water. That was brilliant! We won't be creating anything that dazzling here, though water purity is very important. I will also explain methods of treating your water supply without super expensive equipment.

Refer to the schematic drawings included in this article for help in understanding the text. They do not cover all the details but give lots of clues.

Location

Your first decision is the location of the water storage tanks. They must be elevated above the highest faucet or fixture so gravity can let it flow through the pipes.

An attic is the most logical place. A specially built shelf on a wall in an upstairs room will work too.

I recommend a minimum of three food grade 55-gallon plastic drums for water tanks. More are better but since each full drum is similar in weight to a sumo wrestler you must take into account the structural support required for these tanks up there over your head.

Position them inside a sturdy box, with a plywood floor and three or four-inch high sidewalls, that is located over a load-bearing wall. Line the box with waterproof material to protect your ceilings from escaped moisture. The box liner is there to catch condensation or accidental overflow from the water tanks. A child's wading pool could also be used for this. As a precaution, rig a drainpipe to the overflow container and route it to the out-

Insulated cabinet built as high as possible in the home. In this case it is an unheated room. The cabinet and passageway for the waterline are insulated with 2" styrofoam, as are the panels which enclose the cabinet.

Three 55-gallon food grade tanks built into an insulated cabinet. Insulated panels will enclose the tanks.

doors. This will protect your home from water damage in case anything goes wrong.

These drums are three feet high and need another foot of clearance above them for pipes and other equipment. The more room the better.

If you are nervous about supporting the drums you can build sturdy bookcases, closets or shelves against the support wall and ceiling under the tanks for extra strength. Most homes have potential locations for a project like this in their attics with the addition of some structural support below.

Let's review. You have built a shallow box in the attic that is attached to everything around it, is over a strong wall, has a waterproof lining with a drain, and enough room in and over it for at least three 55-gallon plastic drums. Or else you have a very sturdy, reinforced shelf as high on the wall as possible in the uppermost room in your home with clearance above and drainage under the tanks.

The tanks could be placed in more than one location in the attic, allowing for more storage barrels. Just be sure they are all on the same level. I have been tempted to use one of those farm-sized water tanks for a project like this. If you can do so, go ahead. Just be aware that water weighs 8.35 pounds per gallon and build accordingly.

Now that we have three or more well supported tanks installed as high in the home as possible, refer to the drawings. Run a water line of one-inch black plastic pipe from the well pump up to the tanks and right down to the bottom of each one, using tees and elbows as shown. Include a one-way valve in the waterline above the pump and a tee above that to supply the house water system.

At this point you have a simple gravity-fed water system. A manual switch for the well pump allows you to fill the tanks and gravity sends the water down to your fixtures as needed. As long as your piping is tight and

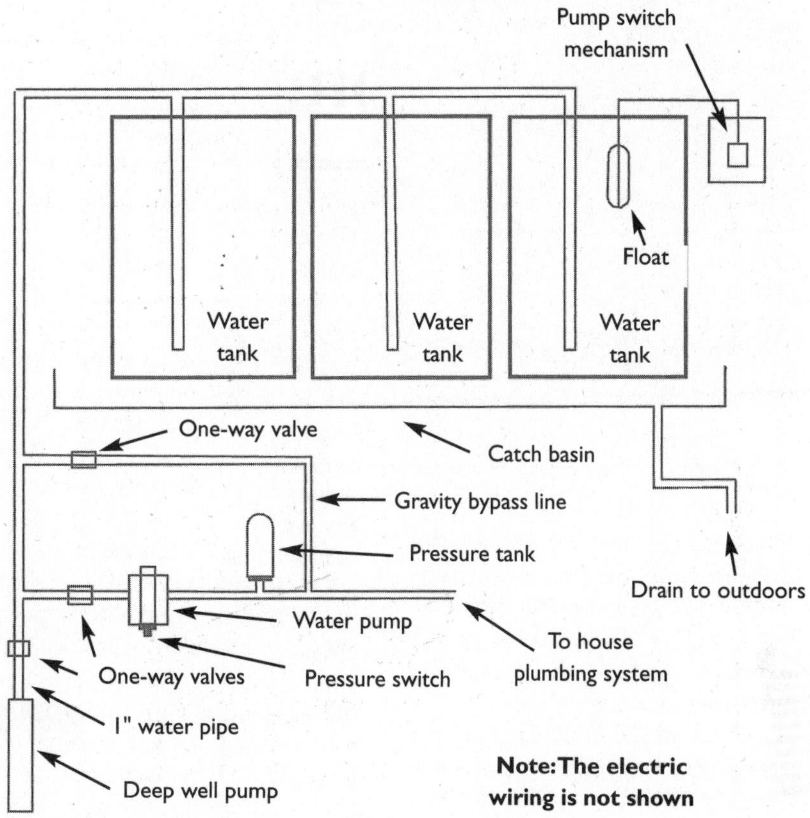

Schematic diagram of component water system. (Not drawn to scale.)

reaches the bottom of each container, filling the tanks creates the siphon to get all the water back out of each tank during use. If you live off-grid, this system along with a generator sized to run the well pump offers a convenient way to have running water for days between refills.

Automating a little bit

If you have full-time electric service, the next step is to make the refilling of the water tanks automatic. Refer to the drawings that show two Rube Goldberg devices for operating a 220 or 115-volt switch, depending on the type of well pump you have.

No matter how many of these systems I've built I never do two the same because there are so many ways to accomplish it. You can start with a 3/8-inch wooden dowel epoxied into an empty two-litre soft drink bottle as a float (see drawings). The dowel is flexibly attached to a lever arm pivoting on a nail on a board solidly mounted on a wall stud near the water tanks. This gives you an adjustable (by relocating the pivot hole) range of motion for the lever arm as the water level rises and falls in the water tanks. How you convert the movement of the lever arm to operate the electric well switch is the challenge.

When planning this operation, make sure the water and electricity will never meet. For this job be careful and clever, or seek help from someone skilled in the art of linkage design.

Increasing water pressure

Now you have an automatic gravity-fed water system. Unless your

220-volt switch attached to mounting board. Moving the left end of the metal arm turns the switch on and off. One of many versions.

home is an old church and your water tanks are up in the belfry, gravity is not going to give you that satisfying high-pressure shower some people like. So let's add another component and fix that.

Go back to the drawing. Find the tee (T1) that supplies the house plumbing system and notice the one-way valve, water pump and pressure tank included in it. The pump, usually called a "shallow well pump," is not very expensive. It comes with its own built-in pressure switch and can be plugged into a regular wall outlet. Put it all together according to directions on the water pump package and in my illustration, including all necessary tees, elbows, clamps, etc.

The pump draws its water from the storage tanks, pressurizes it with the pressure tank, then delivers it to the home's plumbing with enough pounds of pressure to impress anyone. What more could a plumbing junkie ask for? Well there *is* one more thing.

If the power goes out

If the power goes out you will appreciate having a line bypass the water pump, which we just discussed, so gravity will take over and supply water until electric service is restored or the tanks go dry. Check the drawing and notice where this bypass line with its one-way valve is installed. Now you have an automatic water supply system to keep you in water even during electric outages.

Well, that wasn't so complex, was it?

Before we continue, I want to point out another benefit to this system. A deep well pump is an expensive machine. The installation or replacement of it costs a lot of money for labor and materials. It works under very harsh conditions at the end of a long electric cable using ever more expensive electricity. On top of that, it is expected to pump its little heart out by squeezing a rubber bladder of air until it produces 65 pounds of pressure against the water in your pipes and hot water tank. It must do this many times each day. That is a lot of hard thankless work.

In this component system, the deep well pump just pushes water through the feeder pipe, a much easier task. This means the pump will have a longer service life. Or it may mean you can use a 1/3-horsepower pump rather than a ½-horsepower pump, saving money on the purchase price and the cost of electricity to run it.

That second water pump has a pretty easy time of it too. It gets a head start on pressurizing the system because the water coming to it is already under gravity pressure. It does not have to suck its water up from a well somewhere so it lasts longer than usual, too. Plus, it can be located in your cozy home rather than out in a clammy old well house.

If you already have a plumbing system in your home it is relatively easy to add new parts to convert to this upgrade. The latest one I did cost about $275 for the tanks, secondary water pump and miscellaneous parts. Everything else was there.

Removing pollutants

If you are not yet satisfied with how easy this job has been, let's add some

Plastic water pipe connected and installed in tanks. Pipes must reach to the bottom of each tank to maintain syphon. Note cutouts in tank tops for venting, also styrofoam wall insulation.

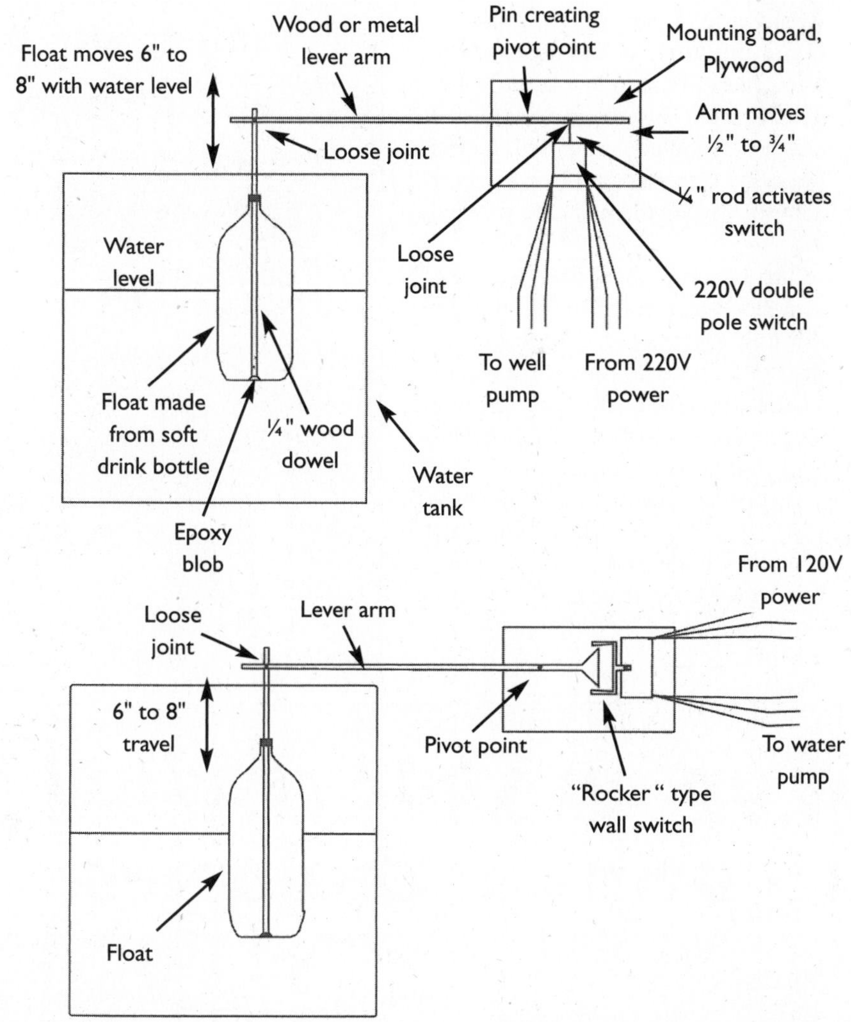

In the top illustration, float movement operates a 220-volt switch through linkage attached to mounting board. In the bottom illustration float movement operates a 120-volt rocker-type switch through the lever arm. (Not drawn to scale.)

bells and whistles. Having a water storage tank under your control is advantageous for several reasons.

Water right out of the ground often brings along some undesirable gases, solids, and maybe even biological specimens. We once lived in a place with so much limestone in the water that people who drank it straight eventually became their own tombstones. Our storage tank allowed the minerals to settle to the bottom before the water went into our supply pipes. Even though I had to clean out a one to two inch layer of mineral sand every six months it was better than clogging up dozens of filter elements per year. If our whole water system had been pressurized from pump to faucet it would not have been possible to separate the solids from the water without great difficulty.

Water, dozens or hundreds of feet down in the earth, is under pressure and contains gasses which are collected by the deep well pump, kept under pressure, and delivered straight to your faucets. When you turn that water loose, out come the gases. The ones you can smell are not the only ones invading your living quarters.

Here in New England, we have a problem with a gas called radon. It is down there deep in the granite. It rises from the water table, through the waterline, and when the faucet is turned on, out comes a puff of this radioactive gas. However, if the water is pumped into an open-topped holding tank, the gas escapes and can be vented to the outside of your home, thus reducing your chances of glowing in the dark after drinking a glass of water.

Products that treat household water supplies are a multi-billion dollar business. The equipment is expensive, costly to install, requires regular maintenance, and lots of replacement products. The major reason for this is because treating water that is under pressure is very difficult. It requires technically complicated machinery. Just go on the internet and google "water treatment." Be prepared for a shock. A reverse osmosis unit for just one cold-water faucet costs $750. Then it must be installed and recharged periodically. You would need a second mortgage for a whole house unit.

Aerating your water

Now back to our story. Another good thing you can do with this system is aerate your water to further dissipate gasses and freshen its taste. Install a fish tank bubbler in one or more of your water storage tanks. Plug it into a timer and set it to run several hours during the night when there is less water going through the system so you start each day with fresh aerated water for your coffee.

If you suspect bacteria is in your water, you have two remedies. First is to add a little bleach to your tanks from time to time. A couple tablespoons per 55 gallons every few months or so will keep it sanitary.

The second option is to shine an ultraviolet light into the water in your tanks. This could be set on a timer to run a few hours a day. Of course the sun is also a source of ultraviolet light so you could arrange for it to shine on your water, but that is probably too much trouble. Ultraviolet light helps annihilate harmful microbes.

So, rather than buy reverse osmosis units, chlorine injectors, various filters, and other pricey gadgets you can keep your water fresh and clean by yourself for a reasonable amount of time and money by converting your present water system to this one.

More details

Before I go, here are a few more details to consider. You may have to build your storage tanks into a little insulated room of their own if you live where it gets cold enough to freeze the water in the tanks or the water lines to them. My latest installation is built into a sort of insulated closet and includes a small electric heater on a thermostat. It may never come on but it's there in case we need it.

During above-freezing weather, vent the "water room" to the outdoors through a screened opening to let gasses as well as moisture vapor escape. Too much damp air can cause other problems in your attic or wherever your tanks are located.

That is the good news: a component water system you control. The only bad news is that now you have one less excuse to drink beer. Δ

Time to strike ~~black bear~~ off the food blacklist

By Linda Gabris

There's no denying that when it comes to meat, most North American hunters rate members of the venison family a cut above the rest. Venison is deeply rooted in our heritage and few folks I know today would shun a tender deer cutlet or a spicy bowl of moose stew. Yet, invite those same guests to sit down to a supper of bear and you'll be surprised at how fast they've gotta run. Black bear are intelligent, alert animals that offer one heck of a challenging hunt and an ample amount of good meat to boot. In some parts of the country spring bear hunting is more popular than fall bear and some hunters swear that nothing makes better eating than an early spring bear that has spent the winter months sleeping off excess fat.

Other bear hunters vouch for the fact than an autumn bear nicely fatted up for hibernation is hard to beat. Over many years of hunting bear, I've been privileged to dine on both spring and autumn trophies and find they are equally delicious in their own right. When my pantry is running low on fat supply for baking, I'll go for a fall bear with an abundance of snowy white fat that renders down into supreme pastry lard. On the other hand, if it's a pelt to throw over the back of my rocking chair that I'm hankering for, a spring bear from an area where spring hunting is legal will give me both a well-groomed rug and good eating. Here are a few of my all-time favorite recipes for bear. Try them, and you'll see that a supper of bear is indeed the grand finale to a great hunt.

Marinated black bear roast with wild blueberry sauce

Marinated black bear roast with wild blueberry sauce

Nothing complements a bear roast like a tangy sweet sauce made from wild blueberries. However, if you do not have a bear roast in the larder, you can use any venison meat in this recipe. It's also a great way to dress up a plain, lesser choice cut of beef.

First, prepare the marinade. My husband threw this recipe together years ago and it is one of our favorites for use with game meats as it instills delightful aroma and flavor. It makes a good soak for venison meats, but is especially well-suited for bear. Be versatile and add any spice or seasoning you fancy.

Sam's special game meat marinade:

2 cups red wine (I use homemade blueberry wine from our cellar, but any rich red will do)
½ cup liquid honey
2 tablespoons virgin olive oil
½ cup vinegar (you can use apple cider, malt, or flavored vinegar)
2 crushed, dried hot peppers or a pinch of crushed chilies
6 or 7 minced cloves of garlic (more or less to suit taste)
a few strips of chopped, sweet red pepper
1 chopped onion
sprig of fresh or dried sage
2 teaspoons salt

Mix all ingredients in an earthen or glass bowl big enough to accommodate the meat. Trim a bear roast—rump, blade, or ham—of excess fat, leaving enough on to flavor meat. Marinade and refrigerate for several hours, turning occasionally. Discard marinade and place meat in a tightly covered pan. Roast at 350° F for 2 to 3 hours, depending on size, until completely fork-tender all the way through, or until a meat thermometer registers 185° in center of roast.

NOTE: It is extremely important to cook bear (like pork) thoroughly. (See sidebar about Trichinosis.) When meat is done, remove from pan, wrap in several folds of heavy tinfoil, and allow to rest while preparing blueberry sauce.

Wild blueberry sauce:

- ¾ cup sugar
- 2 tablespoons red wine vinegar
- ¾ cup port or water
- 3 tablespoons cornstarch mixed into enough water to dissolve
- 2 cups blueberries (if you don't have a stash of wild blueberries, then store-bought tame ones will do)

Put first three ingredients in small saucepan and bring to a boil. Reduce heat and simmer for five minutes. Blend in cornstarch mixture and stir gently over low heat until thickened and clear. Fold in berries and heat through—not too long or the berries will burst. Drizzle over thinly sliced roast bear or serve on the side. Plain or wild rice makes a great side-dish and a glass of red wine tops the meal off in gourmet style.

Best ever bear steaks

Here's a recipe that also does justice to any venison meat or tougher cuts of beef.

- 3 or 4 boneless bear round steaks, trimmed of fat
- 2 tablespoons olive oil
- 2 tablespoons cider vinegar
- 4 cloves crushed garlic
- ½ teaspoon mixed peppercorns, pounded in mortar with pestle until fine
- 6 juniper berries, crushed
- 1 thinly sliced onion
- 2 tablespoons butter, bacon grease, or other suitable frying fat

Rub bear steaks on both sides with olive oil. Sprinkle with vinegar. Mix garlic, peppercorns, and juniper berries and rub into meat. Spread top with onion. Cover tightly and let stand for a couple of hour in fridge. Pat steaks dry with paper towel, removing most of the seasonings and discarding along with the onion. Melt grease in heavy bottom skillet, I find that cast-iron works very well as it holds and distributes heat evenly. Over high heat brown quickly on both sides. Reduce heat, cover, and cook until well done. Season with salt and pepper. Sautéed wild mushrooms such as fresh or dried morels or any store-bought mushrooms makes a delightful topping.

Best ever bear steaks

Hungarian bear stew

Try this recipe with deer or moose meat for wonderful variety. It is also a very popular dish in Hungary when made with pork stewing meat.

- 2 pounds boneless bear
- 4 tablespoons flour that has been seasoned with 1 teaspoon seasoned salt and ½ teaspoon freshly ground black pepper
- 3 tablespoons butter, shortening or oil
- 3 large chopped onions
- 4 cloves minced garlic
- 1 red sweet pepper, chopped fine
- 3 tablespoons sweet paprika (Hungarian paprika is superior, but use what you have)
- pinch of caraway seeds
- 2 cups beef stock (can be made from cubes) or water
- 1 cup sour cream (optional)

Cut bear into 1 inch cubes. Put seasoned flour into a paper bag and add meat, shaking until each piece is evenly coated. Melt butter in saucepan and when hot, add meat. Sauté turning constantly until meat is lightly browned. Add onions, garlic and red pepper. Stir until onions turn soft. Add paprika and stir over low hear until paprika is absorbed. Do not let it burn. Add caraway seeds and broth or water. Bring to boil, cover, reduce heat and simmer for 1 hour or until meat is fork tender. Before serving, 1 cup of sour cream can be stirred into the stew and heated gently

Black bear are intelligent, alert animals that offer a challenging hunt and an ample amount of good meat.

before removing from stove. Or you can pass a little pot of sour cream around the table for dabbing onto the stew. Delicious when served atop homemade egg noodles.

Homemade egg noodles:

Nothing goes with Hungarian bear stew better than a side-dish of hearty homemade egg noodles.

2 cups flour
pinch of salt
2 eggs

Put flour and salt into bowl. Break in eggs and using a fork, work through the flour. This dough must be very yellow and hard. If the flour will not bind, add just enough water to gather it up. Using floured hand work the dough until smooth. Pinch off portions and roll into long fingers about the diameter of a dime. Working with a sharp knife, cut though into thin 'dimes' and let air dry for about an hour. Just before serving time, drop the egg noodles into rapidly boiling, lightly salted water and cook for 4 minutes. Drain. Toss noodles with fresh or dried parsley.

What is Trichinosis?

Trichinosis is a disease caused by the presence of parasitic roundworms, known as trichinae which live in the intestines of a wide variety of animals. In commercial meats, this parasite is most commonly found in pork.

How is it transmitted?

Trichinosis is transmitted to human by eating the undercooked flesh of infected animals. Most human infections are caused by eating undercooked pork and game. Since bear, like pork has the tendency to carry trichinosis, it is a meat that must be handled with the same precautions as pork-never served rare.

How can one prevent infection?

Since trichinae larvae are invisible to the eye when present in meat, it is impossible to detect it by mere inspection. The easiest way to ensure that susceptible meat such as pork and bear are safe for consumption is by cooking them thoroughly. Heat destroys the organisms, so any meat suspected of being infested should always be cooked until well done. A bear roast is ready when the interior temperature has reached 185 degrees Fahrenheit on a meat thermometer in the center or when the meat is fork tender to the bone. Since freezing is also known to help kill trichinae, a stay in the freezer before using is good practice. Δ

The benefits of mulching

By Raymond Nones

When I established my present vegetable garden I wanted to start it off right. First, the area was double dug with plenty of organic material being incorporated. This gave me nice fluffed up soft plots. Next they were painstakingly raked into fine smooth seedbeds. Then to finish off, a layer of fine compost was evenly spread over all before sowing. As soon as the seeds germinated the plants grew beautifully.

But as the season went by, I watched in dismay as large areas of exposed soil was pounded into a hard concrete like surface by hammering rains. It didn't take a genius to figure out that this was not good.

A later careful check of all of the crops revealed that the low growing leafy vegetables that are planted closely had not suffered to any great extent. Their overlapping leaves protected the soil, keeping it soft and absorbent.

The crops most affected were the tall growing vegetables, like fava beans, which are spaced much further apart and don't have enough leafy growth in their early stages to give any meaningful cover of the bare soil between plants.

Simple two-by-eight-foot panels of poultry wire are used to keep the shredded leaves in place over the winter.

Softening the blows

Since the alternative to bare soil is covered soil, I decided to try mulching. One half of all of the fava bean rows were covered with a shredded leaf mulch and the other half was left uncovered. As the rains came it quickly became clear which half was faring better.

In the covered half the mulch dissipated the energy of the driving raindrops as the soil underneath remained pliable and absorbent.

In contrast, the exposed half was rapidly compacted when pelted by the falling water. It gradually lost much of its ability to soak up new water. Frequent cultivations were necessary to reopen the surface. Needless to say, I now mulch the rows of all of the tall growing, widely spaced crops.

Mulches also help to keep soil-borne disease spores from splashing up on foliage, infecting the plants. In the case of tomatoes this is especially important since several of their most common diseases are spread this way. To take advantage of this preventative measure, once the soil has warmed up I spread a two to three-inch shredded leaf mulch over the entire area under my tomato plants.

Using a leaf mulch & the "no dig" method

Encouraged by the positive effect of mulching, I decided to try a "no dig" method at the end of the season. I garden in four by eight-foot framed raised beds. In the fall, instead of turning over the earth as is usually done, the beds were simply stripped of all crop residues, given a shallow cultivation with a rake, and covered with four inches of shredded leaf mulch.

Rectangular panels made of poultry wire framed with furring strips were placed over the leaves to keep them from being displaced by winds or marauding squirrels. They were then left through winter.

The following spring when the shredded leaves were removed, I was amazed at how moist, mellow, and friable the soil was as a result of being under that thick mulch for the winter months. I've used this practice ever since.

Mulches not only contribute to the fertility of earth but also create a healthy soil structure with water holding capacity being greatly improved. In addition, organic material is added to the soil by earthworms and other microorganisms that chew up the mulch. The decomposition process slowly releases nutrient elements in a form naturally usable by plants.

Mulching saves water, and it suppresses weeds

A big benefit of mulches is the reduction of water evaporation from the soil surface. This is an important advantage as plants thrive when an even soil moisture is maintained.

Wide fluctuations between dry and wet soil can seriously retard root growth. Not only will the plants do better with mulches, but you will also benefit by receiving lower water bills.

Concerning weeds, every time the soil surface is broken more weed seeds are brought up. The more you cultivate the more weeds you will have to contend with. But mulching eliminates the need for cultivation.

Large plastic bags are the most practical way to collect and store leaves.

Shredded leaves

Many materials can be used as mulch; the list is long and varied. But the substance most readily available to the backyard gardener is tree leaves. However, leaves must be shredded; otherwise they will pack together and become a barrier between the rainfall and the soil.

Large plastic bags are the most practical method of collecting and storing them. What's more, in many areas residents are told to bag leaves and put them out curbside for collection by the sanitation department. If you live near such a community, all you have to do is ride around and pick them up from the curb. Only one caution: Just because something looks like a bag full of leaves doesn't always mean that it is. In fact, some people mix in a lot of trash with their leaves.

When fava beans have grown to about four or five inches, the author puts down a mulch.

Shredding can be done by piling them up near a wall or fence and running them over with a power lawn mower. The wall or fence will contain them, making gathering easy. Another way is to put a small amount of leaves in a garbage can and shred using a string weed whipper.

Shredded leaves have earned their place in my garden. There is nothing else so readily available that can provide their benefits. Leaves can hold roughly up to 80 percent of the nutrients that a tree soaks up during the growing season. When they decay on the earth, all those nutrients are returned to the soil. Tree leaves are a rich source of organic matter for your garden. Use them not only as mulches but also as a major ingredient in the compost pile.

Some guidelines

While the benefits of mulches are many, not all crops should be mulched. Mulching also would not be advisable where seasons are extremely short or in very wet gardens where slug and disease problems could be worsened. Here are a few guidelines:

- Wait until the vegetable seeds germinate and plants are at least an inch or two higher than the thickness of the mulch you are going to use before putting down the shredded leaves. Early in the season, don't rush; let the ground warm up first.
- It is important that the soil is open and moist before covering. Always lightly cultivate, and if dry, water the area before proceeding.
- Low growing leafy vegetables don't need to be mulched if they're closely sown. The overlapping of their leaves as they grow will shade the soil in between, inhibiting weed

Garlic planted in the fall grows up through the shredded leaves the following spring. Then most of the mulch is removed slowly, leaving a thin layer to hold in moisture.

growth and maintaining moisture. If conventional wide spacing is used, mulching will save you a lot of work, as it will eliminate the need for any further cultivating.

• Although mulch will impede new weed germination and growth, generally it won't help with established weeds unless it is so extremely thick as to be impractical. The weeds have to be pulled before any mulching is done.

• Do not tightly pack around plant stems as this could cause rotting. It is advisable to leave a little "breathing room" or spaces around stems, especially if there are slugs around.

• Depth of shredded leaf mulches depends on the situation. In the fall I put my garden to sleep using a four-inch blanket to cover the bare ground. During the growing season the thicknesses range from less than a half inch up to a maximum of three inches. Just remember that the soil underneath needs to breathe and that water has to be able to seep through. Don't go too deep. Any thick mulches should be "fluffed up" with your hands or a tool once in a while.

• Using mulch to over winter a vegetable presents different problems. The goal here is insulation; the vegetables have to be protected from the cold by a thick layer. As a general rule build up and surround these crops with a cozy sweater of shredded leaves in late fall. Leave the tops showing until lower temperatures become frequent. Then cover completely. Over-wintering a crop is not easy; sometimes you need a little luck.

(Raymond Nones is a retired graphic artist, lifelong home gardener, and author of the book *Modular Vegetable Gardening; The Three Module Home Vegetable Garden.*) Δ

Ask Jackie

If you have a question about rural living, send it in to Jackie Clay and she'll try to answer it. Address your letter to *Ask Jackie*, PO Box 712, Gold Beach, OR 97444. Questions will only be answered in this column. — Editor

Jackie Clay

First of all, I would like to say a HUGE thank you to my Backwoods Home family, both staff and readers, for the outpouring of kindness following Bob's death. Know that it really helped ease the pain and loneliness. God bless every one of you.

Growing apples, peaches in northern Minnesota

I just got my hands on a back issue of Backwoods Home Magazine and read your article on the Pole apple trees and container trees. Where can I get my hands on a couple of these?

I do not know how to get in touch with Stark Brothers, and I would dearly love to have a dwarf apple tree....and peach tree! Although I live in the north on the Minnesota border I am sure with proper care I could grow them. Peaches sound wonderful.

Mary Ellen Cooper
Grand Marais, Minnesota

Stark Brothers's address is P.O. Box 1800, Louisiana, MO 63353, or online at www.starkbros.com. Another source for container trees is Miller Nurseries, 5060 West Lake Road, Canandiagua, NY 14424. Miller

Nurseries carries a few more cold climate trees and plants, more adaptable to northern Minnesota.

Remember, though, to grow peaches in Grand Marais, you will have to bring them into a cool basement or lightly heated garage after they have had a few weeks of cold, but not severe cold temperatures. I grew peaches on a dwarf tree in my large year-round greenhouse here in Minnesota to the amazement of my doubting neighbors. It can be done!

Know that you can also grow "regular" apples way up north. Get super hardy varieties such as Fireside, Harlson, Sweet Sixteen, or Harlred. Then plant them well in an area where they are protected from severe winds in the winter. Be sure to wrap the trunk up higher than snow level so that voles, mice, rabbits, and other critters won't girdle the tree in the winter. I lost a whole orchard one year before I learned to do this. It was an unhappy experience. I would also fence the tree in well with tall wire to keep deer and moose from munching on the twigs (or the whole tree!) which may kill the fledgling tree.

— Jackie

When you grow a good crop, put up all you can

I would like to know how long my home canned beach plum jelly can safely be kept on the shelf?

Pam Hall
PammerHall@aol.com

How about forever? Honestly, Pam, most all home canned food, especially jams and jellies, can remain wholesome and great tasting for years and years on your pantry shelves. This is the reason that when I have a bounty of a certain food, I can all I can possibly put up, because in some years some things just don't make a crop. This allows you to build up a solid storage pantry. Some folks tell me, "Oh I only canned 20 pints of green beans and gave away the rest. We only eat a few jars every year, anyway." Phooey! Maybe next year the beans will freeze, be eaten by pests, or whatever. When I have the opportunity, I put up all I can.

— Jackie

Preserving yellow crook-neck squash for frying

What is the best way to preserve yellow crook-neck squash for frying? Seems that everything we have tried caused them to have a bad taste when cooked. I live in North Georgia and grow them in the summer until the beetles and worms kill the plants. If you have a cure for these pests, I would like to know that also.

Gary Williams
gw1248@alltel.net

To preserve your summer squash for frying, pick the smaller ones with very tiny seeds, for it seems to be the seeds in larger squash that causes off tastes. Slice them up in half-inch thick slices. Pack them into a jar to within an inch of the top, add a teaspoon of salt, if desired, then fill the jar to within an inch of the top with boiling water. Process pints for 30 minutes and quarts for 35 minutes in a pressure canner, at 10 pounds pressure unless you live at an altitude above 2,000 feet. If so, consult your canning manual for pressure adjustment.

Usually, you can keep the squash beetles at bay by dusting the entire plant with rotenone powder when you see the first bugs on the plant. Or you can cover the entire plant with a lightweight row cover, weighting it down well all the way around to prevent the bugs from getting on the plant.

If your trouble is squash vine borer, which is a white maggot-like larva about an inch long which drills into the vine causing it to wilt and die, you can also cover the plant from late June to early August, which is when the moths lay their eggs on the squash plant. Or spray the vines with a biologic insecticide weekly during the time from when the vines begin to grow large to harvest. You can get some good "green" ideas from gardens alive!, 5100 Schenley Place, Lawrenceburg, Indiana 47025 or www.GardensAlive.com. You can learn a lot about diseases and pests of garden plants and find out how you can combat them naturally.

— Jackie

Canning lentil soup without getting lentils mushy

I am new to the canning world and have a question on canning lentils. I have invented my own recipe for a hot lentil soup and was wondering what are the rules, if any, for canning lentils. I have been sending my home canned goodies overseas and know my honey would greatly appreciate any advice you have.

Rhiannon Oyster
Colorado

When canning any mixed product, such as soups and stews, process the jar in a pressure canner for the length of time required for the ingredient in the recipe that requires the longest processing time. If you have meat in your lentil soup, process it for 90 minutes. If just the lentils, an hour will do. Bring your soup to a boil, then fill your jars and process. Don't fully cook the soup first or your lentils will get mushy when canned.

—Jackie

Agricultural lime, cow corn, and corn flour

Isn't agricultural lime not good for human consumption? I really enjoyed reading Issue No. 64. I had actually used Google to try to find that kind of information. But it's still not very clear how to make "limed corn flour."

I am living in India for a long term basis and would like to figure out how to do this for our people here. Here are a few questions:

1. What is "agricultural lime?" I don't know if there is such a thing in India or not.

2. "Cow corn" is what? Does ordinary corn on the cob work? Does boiling it and boiling it make it puffy into hominy?

I'm missing a lot of information here, but the goal is to produce some limed corn flour for tortilla (etc.), making.

Donal L. W. Thompson, India
donallthompson@mail.com

Agricultural lime is the natural lime that is spread on farm fields to neutralize acid soil. I sure wouldn't eat it or mix it with a recipe. But when you make hominy, after the corn is soaked in the boiling lime water and the skins come off the kernels, you rinse the corn well, which removes all but traces of the lime. In some old, traditional recipes, you soak the corn in boiling water with lye added. I much prefer the milder lime.

After the corn is "hominy," you then dry it well on a cookie sheet, bed sheet, or even boards, stirring it a few times to keep it drying evenly. When it is very dry and hard, grind it in any grain mill. Old time Indians and Mexicans used stones to grind this corn flour. Once it is ground, store in an airtight container and use within a few months or it may go rancid.

"Cow corn" is simply farm field corn that is harvested for animal food. You want a larger kernel hard corn for corn flour as in the initial hominy making process. It takes too long to process small kernel corn, although it can be done. Yes, boiling it in the lime water makes it puffy and when the "skin" is removed from the kernels it is then hominy. I've heard that some old timers removed the skins by boiling the kernels in plain water, then pounding them with a blunt stick in a wooden trough. But I've never done this, myself.

—Jackie

Discolored canned fruit, making elderberry jelly

Last year I canned up a bunch of pears that I got for free from a woman who didn't have the time.

The first batch I canned cold packed in pint jars; the rest I hot packed after realizing how much they shrink during heating, again in pint jars. Most of them look wonderful, but the jars from the first batch that I cold packed are discolored on top. The seals are intact, but the contents are browned on top. The rest (hot packed) did not do this.

What did I do wrong?

Also I have an abundance of elderberries. Do you have any recipes for them? They grow all over the place around where I live here in Michigan.

Lee Robertson
Webberville, Michigan

You didn't do anything wrong. When you cold pack many food items, the fruit tends to float to the top. When you leave the needed headspace or air space at the top of the jar, this air can darken some foods, such as your pears, or shrivel the pickles that are out of the brine. This food is unappetizing to look at, but is not "bad." I simply take a fork and remove the ugly food and go on and use the rest. For pretty food that packs better in the jars, hot pack the food. I'll admit that when I'm in a hurry, I just jam the cold food into the jar and get it into the canner. If I get a few bits of ugly food, I just remove it before serving it.

Elderberries are wonderful! I like them as they not only taste great, but are quick and easy to pick in their large fruit bunches. I dehydrate elderberries, just like blueberries, using them by the handful in muffins and pancakes. Some folks might not like this use, as they are a fruit with a larger seed than some. We don't mind, though.

You can make elderberry jelly, which is real tasty. To do this, you'll need only a few ingredients.

Elderberry jelly

3½ cups elderberry juice from about 3½ lbs. fruit
apple juice (optional)
½ cup lemon juice
7½ cups sugar
1 pkg. powdered fruit pectin

Wash and remove large stems from elderberries. Place in large kettle with a tiny bit of water to begin juicing. Crush berries. Cover and simmer for 15 minutes, stirring once in a while. Strain through jelly bag.

Measure juice. If you don't have quite enough, add apple juice. Add lemon juice and pour into a large kettle.

Heat, adding sugar, and bring to a boil, stirring constantly to prevent scorching.

Add pectin. Bring to a full rolling boil and boil hard 1 minute. Remove from heat and skim off foam.

Pour into hot sterilized jars to within 1/8" of top. Wipe jar rim clean and place hot, previously boiled lids on, screwing the ring down firmly tight. Process in boiling water bath for 5 minutes.

Or you can home can the elderberries. This softens the seeds up quite a bit. But some people still don't like them this way. We do. Here's how to do it:

Wash, stem, and pick through the elderberries. Drain berries. Place in a large sauce pan with half a cup of sugar for each quart of berries. Cover and heat, shaking the pan to prevent berries from sticking to the bottom of the pan and scorching. Simmer for a few minutes.

Pack berries into hot sterilized jars to within ½" of the top and process for 15 minutes in a boiling water bath. These are great in pies, muffins, or over ice cream. Add a few chopped nuts and no one will notice the seeds. To make a pie, simply use a blueberry recipe and you're in business. Lucky you.

— Jackie

Eliminating mosquitoes from a home cistern

I have a cistern that is mostly situated under my house. I use this cistern to water my plants as well as to supply my fish pond with good clean water. My problem is that when I open the lid the mosquitoes come pouring out. My father passed away 2½ years ago from West Nile so this is really a concern of mine. The only suggestion I have received for eliminating the mosquitoes is to pour bleach in the cistern, and I don't feel like this is a good solution. Do you have any suggestion?

Kathy Kinn
kmkinn@thewavz.com

Sure, Kathy. For mosquitoes there is an easy fix. Many companies now carry Mosquito Dunks or No-Squito, which are bioinsecticides containing bt, an organism fatal to mosquito larvae but harmless to humans, fish, plants, or birds. Simply pop the appropriate number into your cistern (depends on square feet of water surface) and you're mosquito free! These really work well. The company, gardens alive!, 5100 Schenley Place, Lawrenceburg, Indiana 47025, carries No-Squito. Many home centers and garden supply houses carry Mosquito Dunks. Bleach may be okay for bacteria, but these work much better (and have no smell!) in your cistern.

—Jackie

Diatomaceous Earth to control soft-bodied pests

Have you ever heard of "Diatomaceous Earth?" The website described it as "consists of the broken up shells of tiny critters, called diatoms, that lived long ago and died in groups so massive that they can, today, be mined and bulldozed."

Apparently you use it as a pest control. I guess it slices the insects so they dehydrate. I am asking because I am looking for other ways to control ants and other insect pests. I would think it would kill good insects such as ladybugs. I am looking for alternatives because we have a new puppy.

Becky and Vinny Del Signore
Atkinson, New Hampshire

Yes, Diatomaceous Earth works well for soft-bodied insect control. Many people simply dust their pets once a week with it for flea control. It also works well for ants in most instances, and is extremely safe for all concerned. This seems to work quite well unless the pests are extremely bad. In this instance, I believe I'd use a 1% rotenone dust. This is also a safe natural insecticide, but more speedy in its effectiveness. I've also used this for ants, sprinkling a little where they gather or enter the house. Once they crawl through it, they don't return.

— Jackie

A salt water bath gets bugs out of blackberries

How can I get those really tiny bugs out of freshly picked blackberries? I've soaked them in vinegar water or salted water, but some still survive. After I've drained the berries and inspect them, I still see some bugs. Help!

Shirley Hebert
shirleyhebert@yahoo.com

One thing that may help you is to pick your berries in the early morning. These berries are usually much more free of insects than ones picked later in the day. Then soak them, a quart or so at a time, in cold water with a little salt in it. Use enough water to totally cover the berries, weighting them down with a plate if necessary. In 10 minutes, drain the berries and rinse them gently. You should not find insects. And if you do, they taste the same as the berries anyhow. Eat 'em and enjoy. (Just kidding, Shirley. The little guys should be gone.)

— Jackie

Buying Hopi Blue seed by the pound for beer

I was wondering if you knew where I could get purple or very dark blue corn seeds by the pound. I called Native Seeds Search in Tucson. They have a Hopi Blue and Navajo Blue I was interested in, but they told me they just don't have the volume of seeds necessary to sell it by the pound. I do not have the room in my city backyard to grow it myself.

I brew my own beer and was told if you use colored corn you will get colored beer. My daughter (age 14 now) had made a song she called "Roses in Purple" and I was going to brew a purple tinted beer and call it the "Purple Rose." By the way do you drink at all? The internet searches I've done will sell me purple corn by the 50 count for around $2.75.That could get a little pricey to get a pound of it.

Mitch Keiper
Glendale, Arizona

No, Mitch, I don't drink at all. I had the misfortune to be married, years back, to an alcoholic husband and drinking is a big turn-off to me today as it was then.

Jungs sells Hopi Blue seed by the pound. Not cheap, but available. Their address is 335 S. High St., Randolph, Wisconsin 53957, or www.jungseed.com.

— Jackie

Black Chokeberry used primarily to attract birds

I live in England in the UK and I've bought a chokeberry bush from a garden center. I don't know anything about them. Could you tell me if the berries are edible. The bush is only small yet, so there aren't any berries on it. I would be grateful if you could tell me a few things about them.

June Lindop, England
penandjay@ntlworld.com

The fruit of the black chokeberry (note: this is not the same shrub as chokecherry), Aronia melanocarpa, is edible and sometimes used for juicing and jelly making. But it is principally used for colorful fall colors and attracting birds to your garden. To make sure your shrub is Aronia melanocarpa, or black chokeberry, consult your local botanist.

— Jackie

Suggestions so your bread won't turn to glue

Hello! I was given several copies of Backwoods Home Magazine, and I really enjoyed them. One issue had your bread on the cover. I used to make my bread in a breadmaker but I will spare you the gory details as to why I stopped, but I was inspired to start again—but from scratch. Well, I tried your basic white bread recipe faithfully for at least a week. It was a scary thing. It was like glue. My sons really got a good laugh. Finally I got out a recipe book and tried another recipe, and it was so nice to have it work out. I am in Alabama, do you think the altitude makes that much of a difference? Do you have any suggestions? It was like it was too much water, but if I added enough flour to work it, it became a hard rock. I am determined to make it work, now that I have made bread successfully with another recipe.

Patty Martens, Alabama
Patriciamartens@bellsouth.net

I'm really sorry that my bread recipe didn't work for you. I've never had it fail. I re-read the recipe to make sure someone didn't make an error in printing it along the way, but it's what I use. I never have used a bread machine, so that may have had something to do with it, but I don't think so, due to the consistency you described (glue?). Okay, let's figure out your problem so you have confidence in me again. First, was your yeast fresh? Did you mix it with lukewarm water and a bit of honey to get it growing? Old yeast will result in bread that will not rise and very hot water will kill yeast. This is why I mix hot water with the shortening, salt, honey, and 5 cups of flour, ***then*** let it cool to lukewarm before I add the yeast and the rest of the flour.

If your dough seems sticky, add more flour, a little at a time, as you knead the dough. Don't add so much that the dough becomes stiff. It should be "alive" and workable.

My guess is that your yeast was old or the water too hot and it killed it. Did you buy new yeast to make your successful recipe? You want fresh yeast, moderate temperatures to keep it alive and a bit of honey to feed it so that it rises well. With lively yeast, even "glue" will rise—it's called "sponge."

— Jackie

Do you long for SOS? Here's how to make it

I'm a veteran and miss the creamed beef they served at breakfast. Do you have a recipe and is there a way to freeze it so I can just warm it up?

NUPHOENIX@aol.com

So you actually ***miss*** SOS (sh-t on a shingle) do you? Well, okay. I really like it too. So we're strange. To make a batch, get a jar of dried beef at the grocery store. (You'll find it in the section where Spam is.) Then at home make a simple white sauce like this:

Melt 2 Tbsp. margarine or butter in a saucepan and stir in 2 Tbsp. flour. Then add 2 cups milk and heat until it is moderately thick. Stir in as much of the dried beef as you wish. Heat gently, adding more milk if needed. You can make a double batch if you want and pour half into a plastic freezer container, cool, then freeze. To reheat, either microwave or add to a saucepan with a little milk. Stir while gently heating.

Serve over toast for your "shingle" and enjoy the memories!

— Jackie

Canning meat in ½ pints

In Issue #93 you talk about canning meat (deer) in ½ pints or smaller. I had contacted the extension office about doing just that and they told me not to can that way. I live alone and can't use a pint of meat at one time. If you would tell me how to convert meat canning to ½ pints or smaller I would be eternally grateful.

Chalice Call
Soda Springs, Idaho

You've ***got*** to be kidding! Since when is canning in smaller jars ***more*** dangerous than in pints? Smaller jars allow more thorough heating of the meat than even pints, so should be much safer, not to mention more convenient. It seems that the extension offices are trying to get us to quit canning at home. MMmmmm. I don't like the sound of that, but have figured it was coming for years now.

Just make sure you process the jars for 90 minutes at the same pressure you would your pints where you live.

— Jackie

Saving squash seeds, harvesting cowpeas

I would like to know how to save seeds from winter squash. I tried last year and the results were not good. I washed the seeds and let them air dry on towels in my kitchen. After they seemed crispy dry, I packed them in mason jars for storage. I later noticed that they had molded, and I had to throw them all away. Can you tell me where I went wrong?

Also, I know many readers are interested in the Hopi Pale Gray squash. I too am looking for seeds. Is there any suppliers now who sell them? I have tried seed savers exchange and many others to no avail.

Finally, what is the best way to harvest cowpeas in the dry stage? I am trying them this year but have no experience with any beans.

Vanessa Riffenburg
Palmdale, California

Saving squash seeds is easy, but as you found out if they are not dry enough they will mold during storage. To save the seeds, just remove them from the squash and place on a cookie sheet in a dry area such as on top of your fridge. Stir them with your hand once a day to ensure even drying. In a few days, they will be dry enough to store. (Better to leave them a couple of extra days, as it won't hurt anything.) Store in an airtight jar.

I'm ***so*** sorry that seeds from the Hopi Pale Grey squash have become unavailable this year. It just goes to show you how quickly a great vegetable variety can become extinct. It's really scary and so few people seem to care. I have a small patch of these wonderful squash in my garden, and if they make a crop (baring hail, freezing etc.) I will give seeds to anyone who wants them. I'll let you all know in the fall. My good friend Shane Murphy in Santa Cruz, California, is also growing out a good bunch of these squash and his small seed house, *Seed Dreams*, may also have seeds for next year's gardens.

To harvest cowpeas, simply wait until the pods mature and dry. When they are dry, pile them in a basket and crush the pods with your hands, freeing the seeds. Then rake off the pods with your fingers and shake the basket. This helps separate the pieces of vine and pod from the seeds. On a windy day, gently pour the basket into another on the ground, letting the wind carry off any chaff. A few pours later, you will have clean cowpeas. Like the squash seeds, make sure they are very dry and then store for use.

— Jackie

Battling bugs like ticks & cooking with propane

I plan to build a home on 50 acres of mostly pasture and hayfields, with a little fringe of woods and a couple of ponds. The worst thing about my future location are the tick (and chiggers, I'm told, tho' I haven't run into those yet). I can deal with just about every other kind of critter, but really ***hate*** *those little blood suckers! Do you have any suggestions for a strategy to combat them? I plan to keep the grass trimmed near the house, and use long sleeves and bug juice when in the woods or fields, but am reluctant to use powerful pesticides because of small domestic/wild animals, the potential to contaminate well/pond water, etc. Is there such a thing as an organic solution? I do a body check every night, but on my last trip one apparently hid in my clothes until I returned home and I found it when showering nearly a week later (it wasn't attached that long, just took that long to latch onto me).*

The other debate I'm having with myself is in regard to cooking methods. There is electrical power to the property, and most folks use that, or propane. Here in the suburbs, I cook with natural gas and like the control it gives me, though I did grow up with an electric stove at home and could adapt back if needed. What I'm unsure about is propane. I'm sure it's safe or so many people and appliances wouldn't use it, but it makes me really nervous. Here, I have a special valve that will shut off the gas in case of an earthquake. Do you know if there is anything similar for propane? What if someone decided to take a pot shot at my propane tank? The thought of a huge propane tank exploding just outside my door doesn't make me feel warm and fuzzy. What would you see as the pros and cons of propane vs. electric, and would you recommend one over the other, or something else entirely?

Sally Hamilton
San Dimas, California

One great way to help get rid of ticks is to have a small flock of guinea hens running loose. They gobble up many of these annoying little critters during their daily forays about the place. Keeping the grass trimmed and the brush down around the house and outbuildings will also greatly help.

You might try using Avon's ***Skin So Soft*** or another of the copy cat products. Not only do they keep your skin nice, but they repel ticks and other blood suckers. We live in the best bug country in the country, having mosquitoes, black flies, sand flies, noseeums, ticks, deer flies, and horse flies so big you could about saddle 'em. But we coexist with them by timing our outside activities, using jeans and long sleeves, bug spray, and hats.

For me, propane or wood is the way to go for cooking. I have cooked with electric stoves and absolutely hated them. Yes, you can shut off your propane tank with a valve in case of emergencies. And as for someone shooting and exploding your tank, I, personally, have never heard of that happening. For that matter, they could shoot you inside your house. That, I've heard of! By accident of course! Stuff happens, but I wouldn't worry about it enough to cook with electric stoves.

Of course, during the winter I feel that a wood kitchen range is definitely the way to go. I've had both propane kitchen range and wood ranges in my homes. The propane is for the hot months and wood for the rest of the time. Not only does the wood cook better, but it heats your house at the same time. And it provides a cozy warm place to congregate too.

— Jackie

Getting rid of the slime & smell of pack rat urine

About 3 years ago my husband and I purchased 20 acres in Oregon, with a small A-frame cabin on it. We want to restore the cabin to make it livable. But the only real problem other than no water is that people had gone in it and left the doors open and let the pack rats in. The pack rats got up on the top of the loft and urinated on the floor where it dripped down on to a beautiful rough cut old beam and down to the main floor. My question is how can we get the syrup type urine off the wood and the terrible smell out, without ruining the wood? We also want to know, when we do find a way to clean it how can we keep ourselves safe from the toxic smell and from breathing it into our lungs and getting sick.

[We tried to have a well dug and didn't hit] any water after 300 ft.—it set us back a spell. Is there any way to find the right spot for us to dig a well? We had a local witch the spot where we dug but no luck there. Is there any other inexpensive way to try to find the right spot where we will hit water? My husband wanted so bad to move back to Oregon (his home state) but it always seems to be such a setback on how to get started, and a loss of funds from failures. Please help us get back to basics.

Elizabeth Stewart
Fallon, Nevada

Ah, the lovely fragrance of pack rat urine! It's the stuff the West was made of. Just kidding. But I've been in ***so many*** old, abandoned cabins and barns in the West that were inhabited by these "cute" varmints. (Actually they ***are*** cute, looking like chinchillas!) But their potty habits leave much to be desired.

Yes, you can get rid of the smell, but it will take lots of work. First, shovel out all the nests and clutter, being sure to wear a good ventilator so you don't breathe in anything bad. Then scrape off as much of the yellow gook that you can. A hoe works pretty good for that. Heat a wash tub of water to boiling on a camp stove or outdoor grill, whatever you have. Mix half a cup of bleach with a bucket of very hot water and add a half cup of laundry detergent. Start at the top of the mess and slop your water on and scrub with a broom, mopping up as you go with old towels used as a mop. Of course you will want to use rubber gloves. When this has been done, use another solution of "pet odor control" detergent available at most large stores, mixed with hot water again. Usually you can leave this right on to soak into the wood. This almost always gets rid of the smell.

Work your way from the top of the house down to the crawl space or basement. In a crawl space, remove the nests/messes, and spray on your pet odor solution.

But the trick to pack rat removal is removing the critters once and for all. This usually involves shooting or trapping them. Rat poison doesn't often work as they carry it off and store it for later food they may or may not use. When you are living there, the pack rats will be more easily deterred, especially if you have a good cat or dog to help.

As to the water, I feel for you. When we lived in Montana, we had a well driller go down 385 feet in solid rock and never hit water of consequence—only a trickle. No. If I knew any way to "guarantee" water, we would certainly have done it. I'd certainly contact a geologist with knowledge of your area and see where he recommends drilling next.

We hauled water in a 350-gallon poly tank in the back of our pickup for four years. It wasn't such a big deal, and we got very good at water conservation.

— Jackie

Using rancid olive oil; baking on a wood stove

I have some olive oil that is rancid and I'm hoping there is a way I can use it as lamp oil or whatever so as not to waste it?

Even though our winter is almost over, I'm wondering if there's some sort of contraption that can be placed atop a wood burning stove to use as an oven for baking. Perhaps you have recipes modified for a wood burning stove.

Chris Celeste
Cedar City, Utah

In the old days, folks would simply pour a little oil in a small dish, twist a bit of cotton fabric into a wick and shove it into the large holes of a button to hold it erect in the oil. This made a basic oil lamp. Today, you can buy candle wicks with a metal tab to eliminate the fabric and button. Or you can use the oil to make soap, rub on your dry skin as you would lotion, or even wipe it on the cooking surface of your wood kitchen range to make it glow nice and black beautifully. Simply wipe it on a warm stove and keep a low fire for half an hour.

Yes, there are neat little sheet metal ovens made as "camp ovens," which can go right on a wood stove or even a Coleman camp stove. They can be bought at many sporting goods stores or via mail order from several well known companies. They are not large, but will bake a small loaf of bread, a batch of biscuits, or roast a chicken.

You don't have to modify recipes for a wood kitchen range; they all turn out well just as they are. And even if you cook on a wood heating stove, most recipes only require a good heavy pot or frying pan and you're in business.

— Jackie

Backwoods Home magazine

practical ideas for self-reliant living

Nov/Dec 2005
Issue #96
$4.95
$6.50 CAN

Build a tower onto your house

Fuel efficient cars
Hearty winter soups
Sensible preparedness
Grow shiitake mushrooms

www.backwoodshome.com

Towers

Eight-foot by eight-foot tower with balustrades containing a Component Water System, a meditation room, and a bathroom. It was built within the footprint of the existing home.

by David Lee

Your home is your castle and a castle worth the name needs a tower. A tower may not, at first, seem like a very practical project until you consider all the things a tower can do for you and your castle. It is perfect for paper airplane test flights, UFO watching and, during hard times, artillery spotting, plus other uses we will get to later.

By tower, I mean a structure at least three, and preferably four, stories tall. Beyond that height is in skyscraper territory, a whole other type of engineering. Local building codes will confine your enthusiasm for height, too. The actual dimensions of your

This is an example of a 12-sided full-featured tower with a roof along with its little brother. The small tower covers a water wellhead, contains an electric outlet, and controls yard lighting (under the eaves) with a motion sensor switch. It is about nine feet tall, two feet in diameter, and it has a secret door.

This tower houses a yard light, covers the water well, and protects the water pump from cold while allowing easy access for maintenance.

tower should fit the purposes you have for it, but generally a well-proportioned tower is three to four times taller than it is wide. It could be a stand-alone structure but is more useful and stronger if built onto your home as an addition.

Before discussing construction let's consider the uses for a minimum sized tower 8-foot square and 34-foot tall. This gives you four rooms totaling 256 square feet and a 64-square-foot roof top all built on a 64-square-foot concrete foundation. An 8' x 8' room is just right for an entry area, staircase, kitchen or kitchen annex, a pantry, bathroom, hot tub room, a sauna, utility room, a furnace room, a screened porch, an office, a computer room, library, TV room, music listening room, a hobby room, a closet, dressing room, or a small bedroom.

The top of the tower with a balustrade (that is a castle word meaning good solid railing) around its perimeter is a feature not available on homes for the commoners. From up there you can enjoy the view of your realm and several of your neighbors' realms. It is a special place to hold conversations, star gaze (with or without a telescope), sleep out, or get a suntan in privacy. By some ecclesiastical sort of coincidence the first visitors we entertained on the top deck of my latest tower were Jehovah Witness friends of ours and they never once mentioned *Watchtower*, though it looks very much like the one on their magazine. If you don't quite have the best vista from down below, a tower may improve your view and your property value, plus bring you closer to Heaven.

The top of your tower is an excellent place to set up your TV or other type antennas and satellite dishes. The extra height gives you a head start on reception and you have easy access to the equipment for servicing from a safe platform that minimizes the chance of your wife collecting your life insurance. As another safety measure, be sure to mount a lightning rod up there, too. By now you probably have some good ideas of your own for a tower, so let's build one.

Anyone who can manage the erection of a 34-foot tower gets a lot of respect, and it all starts from a solid pair of bases. One is the foundation and the other is the structure you are building against. Since the tower is tall enough to be affected by wind, it needs to be strong as a unit, well anchored to the ground, and solidly connected to your house.

First, build the foundation. I am partial to poured concrete slab foundations for more reasons than I can deal with here, but for the 8-foot square tower an 8-inch thick slab requires about one and one half cubic yards of concrete. This is a bit less than the ready mix companies want to deliver but well within the capabilities of three or four friends judiciously fortified with beer for a few hours.

Before the arrival of your work partiers, dig out an 8-foot square by 8-inch to 10-inch deep hole. Build an 8-foot square form with treated 2x10-inch lumber that will be left in place with the concrete. Make the form level and square. Place a 6-mil plastic vapor barrier in the bottom of the form. Install 8-foot lengths of ½" rebar in a grid pattern plugged into holes that have been drilled 16" apart along the horizontal centerlines of the form lumber. Add 6" reinforcing mesh wired to the rebar for good measure. Drive nails or screws partially into the inside walls of your form (without distorting it) for more cohesion of the form to concrete. If there are clever things you want to add to the project, like plastic tubing to protect electric wiring or plumbing pipes or secret hiding places, put them in at this time. Now buy beer, buy bags of concrete mix, invite friends, mix, pour, and smooth out the concrete to the top of your leveled and square form.

Torch lights on motion sensors light up the garden and front lawn when visitors, human or animal, arrive at night. A radio tuned to a talk show can be plugged into the light circuit to scare away garden raiders. The light shuts off after a few minutes.

You may have special considerations to contend with when building the foundation. If you live in deep frost country, you may want piers below your foundation down to below the frost line or to bedrock. You may want to insulate the slab with foam board underneath. Lord knows why, but you may want a full basement under your tower. Think about and plan all this before you start.

I avoided the whole foundation necessity by building one of my towers in the footprint of the existing house. I added structural elements

If you really enjoy tower building, then here is a house for you.

inside the house under the tower location to support the extra weight and stresses I expected, then went through the roof and built on up.

Most towers will be built against another building. Check the existing wall for level and plumb and plan to outmaneuver any inconsistencies. Rearrange the surface of the wall and cut roof eaves to accommodate the tower connection. It is imperative to bond the tower to the structure of the house not with just a few nails or screws, but bolts or other heavy-duty connections between tower framing and house framing.

It may be necessary to add a little dormer to the building to prevent rain from running down the house roof directly against the tower wall, which would create leak problems in the future. This dormer could be built in such a way that it becomes a walkway from the tower to the house rooftop. I am sure you can think of reasons why that would be a good thing.

Build the tower strong. I use 2x6 framing on 24-inch centers and 2x8 or 2x10 floor joists on 16-inch centers. Use a single bottom plate and double top plates on each level to support the weight. Picture each level as a strong, rugged cube.

The first two stories of your tower go up pretty fast using conventional methods involving ladders. Above that I have a technique that lets me build from inside the tower. I precut all my frame members, pull the pieces up with a rope, and assemble a wall on the floor of the deck, stand it up, nail it in place, and brace it. Do the same with the other walls. Be sure to thoroughly connect all walls to each other and the floor and joists.

Here is the difference. Instead of attaching a whole sheet of plywood to the wall way up there, I nail on a half sheet cut the long way and positioned horizontally. This way I can reach down over the outside of the wall and easily nail or screw the panel in place.

As you can see in the pictures, I am partial to shake siding on my building projects, and this method allows me to attach the shakes as I build. Put on a circumference of 2-foot high plywood, add building paper, and attach shakes or whatever is your preference. Then add another 2-foot section, overlapping the building paper and siding to prevent water infiltration. You could continue to build on up until the air is too thin to breathe.

Getting materials to the upper reaches of a tower is done with rope and an assistant on the ground. Five-gallon buckets are handy for small stuff and shakes. To ease the lifting a little, I build a V-shaped trough of 2x8 framing lumber long enough to make a steep ramp to the floor I am working on. The buckets slide up this trough easier than lifting them straight up from the ground. You can see one of these in the photo of the tower under construction.

Finish off the interior walls and ceilings with the usual vapor barrier, insulation, drywall, and whatever so the tower rooms that access the rooms in your house complement each other. For the upper rooms a different possibility exists.

Insulate the walls with regular fiberglass. Staple on a 6-mil polyurethane vapor barrier as done in regular construction. Now, instead of drywall or other hard paneling, add a layer of something soft. I suggest canvas, or cloth of most any kind. I have even used plastic tarps for wall covering. The green ones are surprisingly pleasant. Staple the fabric to the wall studs and cover the seams with wood trim. Attach Michael Angelo cloth prints to the ceiling. For classiness, what more could you ask?

These materials are much easier to carry to the upper rooms than panels and are simple to apply. If you decide to redecorate, just remove the wood trim and staple on another layer of fabric. A little bonus offered by cloth walls is static electricity. Just rub your hand across the wall and paper sticks to it. Artists love that.

Rooms with soft walls tend to be very quiet. They are perfect for meditation, music appreciation, and sleeping. Here is a tip. Adding extra insulation to the walls gives the finished cloth wall a puffy quilt-like look and feel. This arrangement makes your tower room special, sort of girlie, but what can you do? Now that you know this, perhaps other rooms in your home could also benefit from this technique.

The top of your tower needs a waterproof floor. In a previous article I showed how to install such a floor with rolled roofing and paint. See the "Forever floor" article in *Backwoods Home Magazine's* Issue 92. The interior floors of your tower can be covered as you please, but the Forever Floor gets them waterproofed as soon as they are built and prevents rain saturation during construction.

The top of your tower also needs your choice of crowning glory. It could be just a flat top. It could be a flat top with a balustrade (pretentious railing) around it. For the most joyous use of the tower, this is it. I build my top floor out over the walls of my tower a foot on each side. This allows water to run off through openings left in the bottom of the balustrades without dribbling down the tower walls. It also gives more room up there for the crowds who come for the tower top experience.

I make the balustrade (if I use this word one more time, I will finally remember how to spell it) the same as the walls, using 2x6 frames with plywood and shakes, but I also add a cap rail with Forever Floor surfacing about a foot wide and skirted with painted boards. See the pictures for details. This gives visitors a feeling of

Here is a tower home with half timber walls and plenty of balconies designed as a series of "cubes."

A tower under construction. The wall is ready for another 2x8 foot plywood panel and more shakes. Note the V-shaped trough for hauling up materials.

safety. Don't try to fool them. Build the balustrade about waist high. Use every building technique you know and one or two more to make it strong and solid. For some reason certain people fantasize about jumping off towers. This should not be encouraged or accommodated.

If you are the extrovert high achiever type, you could put a roof on your tower. Build it in sections, and stack the sections like a wedding cake. Use screws for this work. Screws hold better and can be removed without destroying your work in case disassembly is needed sometime. Use the "work from inside" method during construction and especially when installing the roofing. The last piece can be a "plug" secured from inside. Plug is an ugly word but the top of the plug could be a fancy light, or a weather vane, or your family flag. There are so many possibilities for a tower top I will only say look at the pictures here and have a new appreciation for buildings you see in your travels, especially churches.

Access to the rooms on the first and probably second story of your tower will be regular doorways. I build ladders up the wall that access trap doors to the upper rooms and rooftop deck. This is the easiest construction method and wastes the least amount of floor space. If you are not heating the upper rooms, the trap doors can effectively shut them off from the rest of the house. Be sure the trap doors are built large enough to accommodate whatever you intend to put up there. I read in an old storybook that a measurement of Rapunzel's girth requires a trap door opening of about 20 inches square. Bigger may be better in your tower. You be the judge.

You can install regular windows in your tower walls. For the lower stories they work fine. You can match the other windows in your home if you like and they are easily reached for cleaning. I have found it a good idea to use a different method for the higher rooms. I frame an opening and use a wood-framed screen and/or a pane of tempered or plate glass as an insert held in with simple wood turn locks. This allows easy cleaning and the opening makes getting things up to the room, with a rope from outside, easier than up through the trap doors.

I have also used wood panels in these openings (called wind eyes in the really old castle days), especially in winter. Use weather stripping with these inserts. Drywall screws attaching the wood turn locks can be adjusted loose for summer and tight for winter.

Now that you understand the basics for construction and finishing a square tower, let's consider options. I like to build round or multisided towers. See the pictures. It is a little more complicated.... Okay, a lot more complicated, because you need to bone up on your high school geometry and be an experienced builder, but the construction has its advantages. Each wall frame is built like a ladder and is smaller and lighter than a whole square wall frame. After two walls are connected, the structure is self-bracing. A round tower gives less resistance to the wind while being inherently stronger because of its geometrical structure. If I were to build a stand-alone tower, it would have to be round, or as mine are, twelve-sided.

When I build one of my round castle homes I build the side tower first, or most of it anyway. This gives me some tool storage space that is out of the weather early in the construction process, but more importantly, I get the permanent electric service installed on the tower and hooked up right away. This saves the expense and inconvenience of setting up, taking down, and paying for temporary service. I even get telephone service attached about the same time. The rest of the building process is much easier with power so near and the bonus of ordering pizza right from the work site.

This tower also has the waterline from the well or other water service brought into it. This allows the waterline to supply the beginnings of my Component Water System. (See *BHM's* Issue #95.) I pump water into storage containers located in the top room of the tower and have a gravity-fed hose during construction—very handy for mason work and the occasional hosing down of sweaty workers. The rest of the water system gets built in at a more convenient time.

Tower top work. Here the balustrade is being built. Note overhang and window/vent openings in the wall.

Combining a tower project and a Component Water System addition for your home is a possibility if you are ambitious and well caffeinated.

I have a pet peeve about chimneys stuck on the outside of houses. You see scads of them everywhere. They are made of brick or stone and service a big fireplace inside the house. They are usually pretty but monumentally inefficient. The mass of stone, brick, and mortar heats up in summer, warming the home and then it freezes in winter, cooling the house. Does that seem sensible?

Well, a tower to the rescue. Build an insulated tower around that outdoor chimney. Then when you have a fire in the fireplace, you have a masonry mass that warms up and holds the heat in the house via the tower rather than wasting it outside. In summer that big mass would not warm up in the sun, but takes on the temperature of the ground it sits on and helps cool the house. If that big outside chimney is there to get attention, imagine what a tower will do for you. You get those benefits in addition to added living space.

A greenhouse tower?

Towers have other potential uses. Imagine one mostly of glass with a circular staircase and the treads doubling as plant pot shelves right out to the walls; in other words, a greenhouse. A 12-foot diameter by 24-foot high tower has enough volume for a fair-sized indoor garden that gets more sun than other designs and fewer bugs.

A tower has ventilation advantages over an earthbound greenhouse. Heat tends to rise rather forcefully in a tower. If allowed to escape through a vent at the top there is enough "pull" to draw air from the rest of your home, thus helping to cool it. In winter it can contribute significant warmth to your house just by opening the greenhouse tower to your home during the day. Even if your winters

Tower top details. A corner bench helps strengthen the structure. A shelf for convenience. On the left is a hatch leading to the rooms below. The floor of the tower top is an example of the Forever Floor. (See BHM's Issue #92.) It is painted a dark color to encourage melting of snow in winter, and the drain is on the north side to catch the sun's heat.

are too cold to grow plants, the tower greenhouse will often be a pleasant place to visit on a sunny day.

Towers can be about any size. I recommend a minimum of 8 square feet for a four-sided one and about 10 feet in diameter minimum for a twelve-sided one. These sizes use materials most efficiently. But you can go bigger. Or you can build something smaller, which still qualifies as a tower.

I like to build yard light towers that double as wellhead covers and contain a protected electrical outlet for using power tools in the yard. A motion detector on the built-in light creates a nice safe welcome when arriving home at night. Some examples of this type of tower are pictured here. One tower I did over a wellhead contained the water pump, protected from the cold by insulated walls, and a 100-watt light bulb on a thermostat switch for warming the water pipes on really cold nights. Since electric wire has to come along with the water pipe to the wellhead, adding another couple of wires to accommodate these devices in the tower is easy. I always lay some in just for such projects. A slab of concrete around the wellhead makes a very good foundation for the yard light tower.

To stimulate your enthusiasm & get you started, bring home a couple of those big spools that wire came on from the electric company, an 8- or 16-foot steel pipe that fits the hole in the spools, some tongue and groove lumber, rope, and nails and see if you can build a round tower. Kids will love you. Parents, maybe not so much. Don't ask me how I know.

My tower building experiences have been very satisfying. However, here in ultra-conservative New England my towers have earned me a reputation among the locals. They have ace you. Parents, maybe not so much. Don't ask me how I know.

My tower building experiences have been very satisfying. However, here in ultra-conservative New England my towers have earned me a reputation among the locals. They have accused me of visiting California once too often. Δ

10 country do's and don'ts

By Julie Crist

When we moved from the city to the mountains, I kept my eyes open and my mouth shut and and paid very close attention to other people's botchery. Personally, I'd really rather watch someone else screw up than have to do it myself. But of course, there's no free lunch, and so we added our own blunders to my ever-growing list. What follows are 10 lessons from my "now I know better" collection. Perhaps these lessons learned will ease your transition from the city to wilderness.

1. Know thyselves. If you are a couple who bickers over which way to hang the toilet paper roll, don't buy raw land.

The path from raw land to indoor plumbing is fraught with hundreds, if not thousands, of decisions. If you can't pull as a team over the little things, how will your relationship survive decisions like where to sink a well (that one can be worth, oh, $20,000), where to put the kitchen, do we buy or rent equipment, do we build a log house or glue it up out of egg cartons?

We have several guys (one of our neighbors included) sitting around our county amidst their half-finished projects all by themselves because the little woman couldn't handle it and ran off mid-construction. On the other hand, we have another neighbor couple who knew that they weren't cut out for the house building process. They bought undeveloped land and put a manufactured home on it. Save your marriage (or whatever) and buy a house.

2. Know thy neighbors. You may be under the false impression that since you are moving from more crowded to less crowded conditions that you will have more privacy and that neighbors matter less. Au contraire.

When looking at rural property, you will find yourself driving down many a dirt road. If there is more than one home on that road, it is a neighborhood, like it or not. Look closely at the homes and residents on that road. If your house catches on fire or you hack your leg off with a chainsaw, do you think you can depend on them to help?

When I was searching the great wilderness for our dream property, I drove down some rural roads that actually triggered the theme from Deliverance in the back of my brain. Filthy, malnourished children standing there picking their noses and glaring at you as you drive by is a bad sign. Find some excuse to go chat up some of the neighbors before you buy. Introduce yourself and ask them how bad the winters are, what advice do they have for new folks, did they marry their sister, whatever, just get a feel for the folks you may have to trust with your life and property.

3. Know thy driveway. I rarely see this subject discussed, but in the sticks, the length of your driveway can make or break the whole experience.

There is a house on our road that has seen three occupant changes in the 4 years we've been here. It is a cute, well-landscaped little place with a very short driveway. That means the house is quite close to the DIRT road. When people drive on the dirt road in the summer, the residents of the house, who might be outside enjoying their beautiful yard, get DUSTED. The dust gets everywhere—it covers their cars, it coats their garden, and it creeps into the house, too. Those folks spend their summers in a huff every time someone drives by their house. They make what I call "The Indy Report" to anyone who will listen, "So and so drives fifty miles an hour past our place, blah blah blah."

On the other hand, our driveway is a winding 700 feet long. We can't even see the road. We love it. But we also live at about 3000 feet and see a lot of snow all winter. This is OK with us because we have good plowing gear and 4-wheel-drive cars.

It also cost big money to put gravel on that much driveway, which is necessary in our area if you want to use your driveway year-round. We have a neighbor who has been out here for years who had to park at the end of his driveway half the year due to the snow and mud until just last year when he got a 4-wheel drive. A long driveway is great for privacy and air quality, but if you actually want to use it, it will cost you.

4. Don't share. If you are in such a hurry to move that the only way you can afford it is to "go in on" some property with another buyer, don't. Americans are lousy candidates for this type of financing arrangement. You may think you are a cooperative, easy-going person until Uncle Wilbur decides to clear-cut five acres so he can raise yaks. If that never happens, great, but the rest of the time the other guy usually wants out at some point, forcing you to come up with the rest of the payment or lose your home and all the work you've put into it. I have a collection of local horror stories to that tune.

5. Kill some trees. We are tree-huggers who moved to the woods. As we wandered around gawking at all the pretty trees, we decided where to build our first building, a 24 x 40-foot shop. By now, we were one with the trees and couldn't bear to part with any of them, so we sited our shop where we could take out the fewest trees.

The trees were happy but we soon saw that the approach to the garage door was too steep to be practical. And we eventually ended up taking out the trees behind the building to cut a road to the well site anyway. So we could have moved the shop back 12 feet or so to a more level spot in the first place. But here we are with an 800-square-foot building in basically the wrong place. So put your buildings where you want them and just plant a few more trees.

6. Do the wave. In the city, avoiding eye contact can be a survival skill. Congeniality can get you shot, or at the very least, panhandled.

Not so in the country. Out here, the wave is the primary social currency. Wave at everybody, whether you know them or not. If you see a guy standing by the road holding an axe dripping with blood, smile and wave cheerily. He might be butchering a deer and may choose to share some with you. You could be making meth in your basement, but as long as you wave and look friendly, people will think you are a good Joe.

If you don't wave, you could be Mother Theresa and everyone will think you are making meth in your basement. Which leads me to . . . .

7. You will earn a reputation. The reputation is a quaint concept that no longer applies to the concrete jungle. You can be any kind of scuzzball you want in the city and no one cares. In fact, some people think it's cool and they'll probably give you your own TV show.

Out here, you will earn a reputation whether you are a hermit who only comes out once every five years or the mayor. You can care about it or not, but if you ever want to do business, or anything else for that matter, your reputation will precede you, so consider how you want to be known. Be aware that anything you say will be held against you and it will also be spread all over town. And it is not cool to be a scuzzball in the country.

8. Guns are part of the culture. Guns are loud. In rural America, people have guns and they shoot them. You may no longer have freeway noise in your bedroom, but it could sound like the Battle of Gettysburg in hunting season.

One of the newer residents on our road is a pacifist-tree-hugger-gun-hater. The next neighbor up from her is an NRA instructor who also tests guns for the pawn shop he works in. Friction is not even the word here. But the problem is that Mr. Guns has every right to shoot all day and night if he wants to on his own land. That's probably why he lives here. And my guess is the more Ms. Tree Hugger complains about the shooting, the more shooting will happen. If you can't live with that concept in a rural area, you might be happier either in town, where everyone needs a toilet paper permit to you-know-what, or on a road with (shudder) codes and covenants. At least you know then that your neighbor won't be raising hogs on the property line and shooting them at three in the morning.

9. Pets—the good, the bad, and the ugly. Out here in the hinterlands the term pet food has a whole different meaning. Sure, it's great to live someplace where Fifi can run free, but just remember, so do the Fifi eaters. Let's face it, most of us city transplants grew up on a TV diet of articulate, well-dressed animals. But in reality, cougars, coyotes, bears, and even large predatory birds are all on the lookout for a nice fat Fido or clueless cat to snack on. While the thought of Yogi Bear pick-a-nicking on my cat is too gruesome an image for me to entertain, I've been here long enough to know that the risk is part of the natural life of animals. On the one hand, letting our cats in at night seems to be extending their lives and on the other, I'm sure the victims they drag home had families and jobs, too.

And on that same general topic, we had a new guy move into the neighborhood with his own personal pack of about six dogs. He thinks it's a good idea to let them all run free. Here's a little tip: Those dogs are not out at the neighbors having tea. Dogs that pack up, chase down wildlife and other people's animals, just shoot them dead. I support that. Actually, I support shooting the owner, but one solution's legal and the other isn't.

10. Electricity is not a fact of life. It is the luck of the draw.

We provincials, especially we of the woodlands, are the recipients of periodic phone and power interruptions. Trees fall on lines, aliens sever them with anti-matter beams. The utilities can even go out for no apparent reason in the middle of summer. Maybe it's just a drill. If you have big, full freezers and no backup, you will be having one hell of a steak feed that night.

We personally are off the grid, so we know when the power is out by the generator noise that resonates through our canyon. Kind of like living near a raceway. Of course, I still lose the phone at times, or it often sounds like someone's crackling cellophane while I'm trying to talk. In the winter when we've had six gloomy days in a row, we have to run the generator ourselves. It all evens out.

So spare yourself the trouble and learn the above lessons from these pages, not when you are sitting on your porch, owing the bank $200,000 or so, cursing your neighbors for actually driving their cars on the road past your house. Δ

Teaching the joy of reading

By Amy Peare

Most parents want to see their children well equipped to succeed in life, and homesteaders are no different in that regard. Many homesteaders choose this lifestyle to give their children a better chance at a wholesome start. Another tool we can give our children is the love of books. Reading strengthens minds and hearts, and widens horizons.

While some kids have a predisposition for reading, others need constant encouragement to read. This encouragement is not a difficult thing to implement in your family. It takes only a half an hour a day, or more if you wish.

First of all, show your kids reading is important to you. This is not something that you can simply tell them. They must see you reading for enjoyment and information purposes.

Second, limit the T.V. you let them watch. Television is passive entertainment. Kids can't interact with the television. They are being bottle-fed their information and entertainment, and it is difficult, if not impossible, to sift out the good from the bad in that form. We keep our television in our shed, only watching it on special occasions.

Third, make books available. Buy books for birthdays and Christmas, or whatever holidays your family celebrates. Buy books as rewards for good behavior or good report cards, or any other time a gift is appropriate. Books are wonderful entertainment,

less expensive than a movie or video game or the latest do-everything-for-you toy. If money is tight, make frequent trips to the library and utilize the inter-library loan system.

Fourth, read to your kids daily for at least 20 minutes. Find books that are fun and interesting to both you and your children. Not only does this encourage your children to read, it creates a stronger bond between you. Some of my fondest childhood memories are of my mother reading to my sisters and me.

Fifth, encourage your kids to read on their own. If they have a question, look up the answer together and have your child read it out loud to you. If your child is bored or ill, give them an adventure novel.

I will probably not get agreement from every parent who reads this article on this point, but if your kids want to stay up late reading, let them. If they share a room with others, let them have a flashlight or a small book light so they don't disturb their siblings, but sometimes it is good to get through the exciting bits of a story in one sitting.

Now that you have the steps of encouragement, finding the books is the next step. It is very important that the right books are chosen, but it isn't difficult with the tens of thousands of great books out there on every subject!

First, talk to your children about their interests. Very small children usually love what their parents or those close to them are interested in. So if you love animals, picture books on animals will be a good start, especially as you are more likely to be more animated in your reading to them. (Quick note here—do the funny voices. Kids LOVE it, and there is no one there to hear but them. Don't be embarrassed, just go with it.) Older kids will be able to articulate their own developing interests, and you can go from there.

Second, talk to your librarian or bookseller if you are unsure what to choose. They can guide you to the best books within your child's interests, both new books and the classics. For older children, the Newbery award winning books and ALA notables are a great place to start. These books are usually the best of the best.

Third, assess your child's reading level. You don't usually give a novel to an eight year old, but every child is unique, and what may be appropriate for one child may not be for another. Don't be afraid to buy a twelve year old a picture book if they are not ready for a novel, but don't hold back your eight year old if he is ready for a novel. Pushing a child too far and too fast or holding them back from what they are capable of are equally frustrating for a child. Let them set their own pace when it comes to reading, since you are striving to teach them the enjoyment of books.

Fourth, review your child's books yourself before allowing the kids to read them. Some young adult and even middle grade books have themes that your child may not be emotionally ready for, and many books may run against your family's religious beliefs.

Fifth, discuss the books your children read. This will help you to assess their changing reading level, to see if they are comprehending their reading, and to let them know you care about their reading interests.

Sixth, don't be concerned if your child fixates on a single author. Kids do that and so do many adults. They may have found a style of writing that resonates with them or subject matter that is stirring. Usually, once a kid has read everything by that author, they will move on to another. In my own life, I have fixated on different authors at different times, starting with Tolkien, moving on to C.S. Lewis, Robin McKinley, and so on down the line. As long as the writing is good, you have nothing to worry about.

The books in our home reflect who we are as people. My husband and I have many books on the various practical arts associated with homesteading, but we also have a deep love for science fiction and fantasy, as well as classic books from Dickens to Plato and most everything in between. Our children's books are a similar mix, chosen carefully to help them develop strong minds and still have fun.

A small sampling of the books we have may help you choose some to get your own family going. I highly recommend the books listed below.

Picture Books for Young Children: *Wool Gathering: A Sheep Family Reunion* by Lisa Wheeler. This is a book of short, humorous poems about a family of sheep.

Iron Horses and Covered Wagons and *Bumpy Trails* by Verla Kay. These books are written in cryptic rhyme and the subject matter is carefully researched by the author. Verla Kay has many picture books out, all on American History themes, and are a must have for any homeschooler's library.

When Moon Fell Down by Linda Smith. This is a sweet bedtime book for young children. Also, part of the proceeds raised by the sale of the book go to benefit breast cancer research in memory of the author.

Another favorite bedtime story is *Bear Snores On* by Karma Wilson.

The Three Little Puppies and *The Big, Bad Flea* by Ted Lish, illustrated by Charles Jordan, is a unique retelling of the *Three Little Pigs* story and will have you laughing out loud. Plus, Charles has cleverly hidden six elves within the book's illustrations, which are fun to try to find.

For older children—*See Saw Girl, The Kite Fighters, A Single Shard,* and *When My Name was Keoko* by Linda Sue Park, are all lovely novels about Korean children throughout history. *A Single Shard* was 2002's Newbery winner.

The Folk Keeper by Frannie Billingsley, a children's fantasy novel that was so exquisitely written, it blew me away. If you like Celtic myth, this is a great book.

Rain is Not My Indian Name by Cynthia Letich Smith is a book about a young girl struggling with her heritage and the death of a close friend. This book could lead older kids into thoughtful discussion about the issues it handles.

Dahling If You Love Me Would You Please, Please Smile by Ruksahna Khan, another book of a child struggling with who she is in society. This book can be an eye opener on what it is to be a Muslim in a society that doesn't understand, but that isn't the total focus of the book. It is a fun read, too.

Lloyd Alexander's many books are much loved here. These include the *Prydain Chronicles*, the *Vesper Holly* series, and many, many more titles.

If I were to try to list all our favorite children's books here, it would be a book in and of itself, but hopefully this will give those who need it a good start on finding something to spark your kids' interests. Enjoy your books. Δ

Ayoob on Firearms

SOCOM-16: This rugged descendant of the military's renowned M-14 may be the ultimate "ranch rifle."

Introduced in the mid-1950s, the M14 rifle became the darling of a generation of American fighting men. It was the lineal descendant of the M-1 Garand of WWII and Korea, which General George Patton himself had called "the best battle implement ever devised by man." The Garand's .30/06 cartridge had been shortened slightly to fit it. The 7.62mm NATO, known as the .308 Winchester in its commercial rendering, lost only a little power by comparison. Not enough that any game animal or enemy soldier struck with one or the other would know the difference. A little bit lighter, the M14 held a detachable, quick reloading box magazine of twenty rounds. By comparison, the Garand had carried but eight, and was awkward to reload with its proprietary en bloc magazine.

This is the rifle American troops originally took to Vietnam. Every battle veteran of that period in the conflict that I've discussed it with remembers that rifle fondly. The USA's transition to the M16 occurred during that war. Many were the soldiers who did everything they could to keep their original M14 instead of turning it in for the untested, small caliber "black plastic rifle."

Fast forward. Today in Iraq—and particularly Afghanistan, where long-range encounters are often the norm—the M14 is highly prized. Retained by the military for special purposes in small quantities (such as the XM21 semiautomatic sniper rifle) the guns are being issued again, and the services are reportedly scouring the armories for old M14s to be sent back into the fray. Gun expert John Farnam reports that new M14s are being ordered by the government for this purpose.

When the military declared the M14 to be obsolete, a great many civilian rifle enthusiasts disagreed, as did so many combat vets. Springfield Armory, Inc. answered the demand many years ago by gearing up to produce a "civilian M14," known as the M1A. While the military M14 had the capacity to be selective fire, with a removable 180-degree switch at the right rear of the receiver that could turn the gun to full automatic (machine gun) mode, the M1A was semiautomatic exclusively, allowing only one shot per pull of the trigger. The standard model followed the military rifle in being fitted with a 22" barrel.

The SOCOM-16, named in homage to our military's Special Operations Command, is in essence a very short-barreled M14. The numerical part of its designation comes from its barrel length. The minimum legal length for a rifle barrel under the rules of the Bureau of Alcohol, Tobacco, Firearms and Explosives, is sixteen inches. The barrel length of the SOCOM-16 is sixteen and a quarter inches, allowing a quarter inch "fudge factor." The gas operation system has been altered accordingly.

The key to the system is a short recoil compensator developed in-house. Working via both gas ports and an expansion chamber, it is the most efficient of its size that I have ever seen, including the much-heralded Soviet AK47 system.

A complaint against the powerful M14 was that its recoil was too great for the average soldier or shooter, pushing him backward and lifting the muzzle upward after each shot. The exhaust ports of this "muzzle brake" send burning gunpowder gases upward, channeling their power to force the muzzle down against the recoil impetus. The expansion chamber works as the fireball of expanding gases comes forward out of the muzzle. The bullet passes through a larger than bore diameter hole in the front of the brake unmolested, but the expanding fireball hits the circular steel wall around the bullet opening and pushes the rifle forward, countering the rearward recoil impulse.

Massad Ayoob

The result is, quite simply, the softest-shooting .308 rifle I have encountered in my career. We shot the SOCOM-16 next to that staple of the backwoods home, the Winchester Model 94 .30-30 lever action carbine. The .30-30 spits a sedate 170-grain bullet at only 2200 feet per second, and is known for its milder recoil. However, in the SOCOM-16, the much more powerful .308 round has distinctly lighter "kick," thanks to the effectiveness of the recoil compensation mechanism.

New purposes for the SOCOM-16

CQB (close quarter battle) was the primary mission parameter of the short barrel M14. However, it is superbly applicable to numerous purposes stateside.

It's a hunting rifle. Many people have used these military-style semiautomatic rifles for hunting. In 1987, when I hunted Africa for the first time, I took three rifles along. One was the traditional .375 Holland & Holland Magnum, in a Steyr-Mannlicher M-ST deluxe sporting rifle, with which I shot large antelope such as kudu and gemsbok. One was the .458 Magnum "elephant gun," in this case a Ruger Model 77, which I took because the huge and dangerous Cape Buffalo was on the hunting menu. And I also took a Springfield Armory M1A, the M21 "sniper" model. For hunting, I simply removed the M1A's magazine and turned it into a single shot to conform with South African big game hunting rules, which prohibit semiautomatics capable of sustained fire. With it, I shot a springbok at some 350 yards in the Kalahari Desert.

Cops love this rifle, here being tested by a member of the Suwannee County (Florida) Sheriff's SWAT team.

Nicholas Reese, the 16-year-old son of Springfield Armory executive Dennis Reese, used the little SOCOM-16 rifle last year to bag a thousand-pound elk. A single 165-grain .308 bullet fired from a hundred yards did the job. Springfield Armory offers a short magazine to suit the gun for American hunting rules, which generally limit a semiautomatic hunting rifle to a five-shot cartridge capacity.

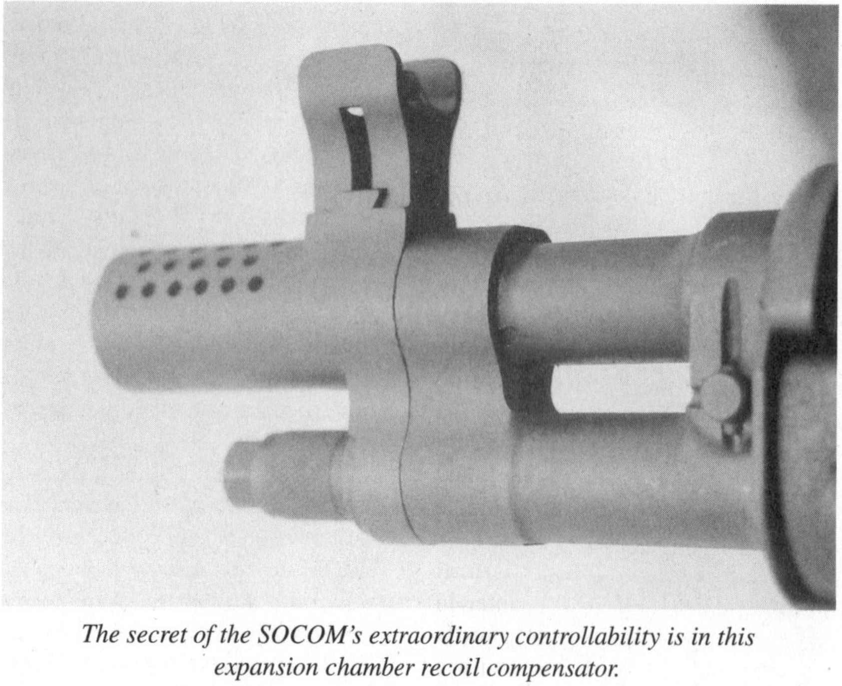

The secret of the SOCOM's extraordinary controllability is in this expansion chamber recoil compensator.

It's a ranch rifle. A short, heavily-constructed semiautomatic rifle is a handy thing indeed for backwoods living. Ruger's Mini-14 in caliber .223 and identical Mini-30 in caliber 7.62X39 mm are available in a model Ruger calls the Ranch Rifle and have become popular for that stated purpose. Both the .223 and the 7.62X39 are much less powerful than the .308 Winchester round fired by the SOCOM-16.

The rugged design of a military auto rifle suits it well to carry in a rack on a farm vehicle. The ATV, the tractor, and even Jeep CJ-5 and the farm pickup when used off-road, can impart sustained and sometimes violent vibrations to anyone and anything on board. Some carbines have become notorious for breaking down, going out of adjustment, cracking their stocks, or otherwise failing to stand up to this constant pounding.

The M1A SOCOM-16, on the other hand, was expressly designed to spend its life in a much more rugged version of that environment: aboard armored personnel carriers and battle helicopters. It will stand the gaff.

A ranch rifle is sometimes called upon to be used against large bears, or large livestock that has "gone amok." A .223 is altogether too light a cartridge for that application, and a 7.62X39mm is marginal. The .308 Winchester cartridge of the SOCOM-16 is adequate to the task when the proper ammunition is used.

Finally, the ranch rifle may be called upon for home defense. Given its CQB design parameters, the M1A SOCOM-16 from Springfield Armory is uniquely well suited to that task.

It's a sport shooting rifle. The SOCOM-16 is not built for the refined accuracy of Springfield Armory's target rifle versions of the M1A, and its recoil compensator disqualifies it from use in NRA's Distinguished-series events in formal High Power Rifle competition. The recoil reduction device is seen as giving its user an unfair competitive advantage. (For serious business, of course, anything that gives you an "unfair advantage" is probably a good thing.) However, there are a number of arenas in which this gun can compete.

The USPSA (United States Practical Shooting Association) endorses three-gun competition around the country in which each contestant fires rifle, pistol, and shotgun. Some go the lightweight route: 9mm pistol, 12-gauge auto shotgun tricked out with recoil reduction devices, and .223 caliber AR15. Some go the "hard-core" route: .45 automatic, 12-gauge pump gun, and .308 auto rifle. Among the latter is an old friend of mine, who swore he was going to adopt the SOCOM-16 as his competition rifle after firing it for the first time.

Famed military rifle authority David K. Fortier test-fires the SOCOM-16. He fell in love with it.

Ayoob fires the MIA SOCOM-16 with the company's own "scout scope" in San Diego. This one has a 10-round magazine.

Some regions have pin-shooting matches, where the targets are heavy regulation bowling pins. It's a competitive shooter's version of the old plinker's gig, shooting soda cans off a fence. In the rifle events, you need a powerful gun to get the job done, and a fast gun. The SOCOM-16 would be ideal.

My buddy Jon Strayer, a rural dweller and competitive shooter in North Florida, regularly shoots monthly auto rifle matches with a local "carbine club." On a recent Saturday, he shot my SOCOM-16 and was so impressed with it that he went to his gun dealer the following Monday morning and ordered one. It just came in, and this coming Sunday as I write this, while I'm out of town, he's going to be shooting his SOCOM-16 against the AR15s at the tournament.

If I was going to be in town, I'd be right beside him, shooting mine.

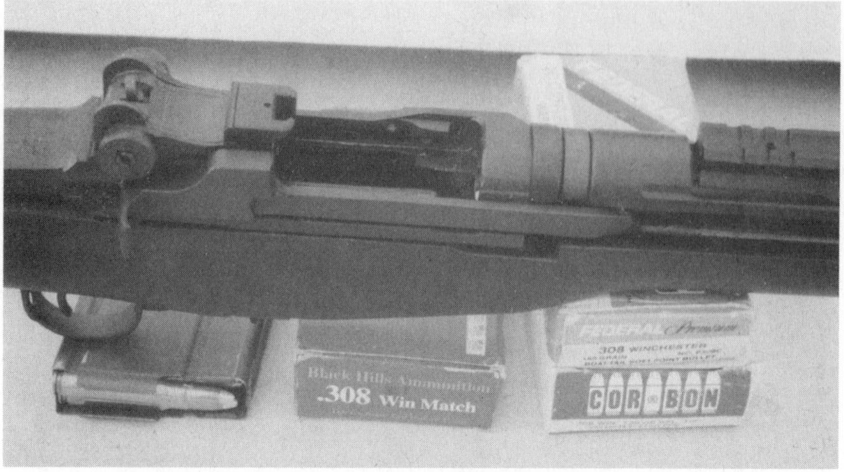

These were the three .308 loads Ayoob chronographed to determine velocity loss from short barrel. It wasn't enough to worry about.

Shooting characteristics

The sturdy little SOCOM-16 weighs 8.9 pounds, but with its short barrel the gun's center of balance is farther back than you'd expect. The weight centers comfortably between the rifleman's hands, giving him more leverage to steady it when it is at the shoulder. Whether aiming from a standing offhand position or just carrying it, the rifle "feels much lighter than it is."

Of course, the more cartridges it is loaded with, the heavier it is. There are four magazine capacity options for the M1A, which takes all M14 military surplus rifle magazines. These mags are reasonably affordable and exist in such great numbers that they were readily available even during the onerous decade-long "high capacity magazine ban," which is thankfully over now.

We mentioned the short magazine that complies with sport hunting rules. Check with your local conservation officer to make sure, but in most jurisdictions you're not limited to that when carrying an all-purpose rifle on your own property. Springfield Armory still produces the 10-round magazine they came up with when that was the maximum allowed under the ban. It's a useful thing to have, protruding only a short distance under the belly of the rifle. If the quarry is a marauding bear or the bad-tempered cow you've decided to put down, 10 rounds should be ample, and it's lighter to carry.

The standard 20-round magazine, however, is eminently practical. To make sure it locks into the gun easily with the bolt forward, load it with only 18 or 19 rounds. In carry without a sling, I hold the rifle just ahead of the locked-in magazine, muzzle down; it balances nicely and comfortably that way. From a prone position, the bottom of this magazine stabilized on the ground makes a wonderfully effective "unipod" to steady the rifle. The old shibboleth that the magazine touching a hard surface will cause the rifle to jam is just bunk. Try it yourself and see.

There is also a 30-round magazine advertised in some of the gun publications. I've never tried one. However, history and experience tell me that aftermarket magazines generally do not work well in autoloading firearms, with a very few exceptions.

The SOCOM-16 delivers good practical accuracy. Shooting with just the iron sights—a rugged, wing-protected post front sight, and a generous adjustable rear aperture sight—it has given me 100-yard groups of under two inches with the best ammunition. The gun comes with a Picatinny rail mounted ahead of the action for a long eye relief telescopic sight, the kind Jeff Cooper popularized as the "scout scope," or a red dot type optical sight. I've also found that the Insight M6 and M6X combined white light and laser sight unit can mount here. With the laser beam "dialed in," it gave coarse but acceptable night-shooting accuracy at "house to barn" distance.

However, its key attribute in addition to the wonderful handling afforded by its short overall length is its reduced recoil, which gives the shooter a tremendous ability to deliver accurate fire very quickly. At seven yards, 100-pound Terri Strayer was able to empty a 20-shot magazine into the "kill zone" of a silhouette target in four or five seconds.

Power

With a rifle whose barrel is as short as the SOCOM-16's, an experienced rifleman always has one important question. "How much velocity is it going to lose?"

The shorter a rifle's barrel is, the less powerful it tends to be. This is because it is propelled by the expansion of gases formed as the gunpowder rapidly burns, and the longer the barrel, the more opportunity there is for those gases to develop additional pressure inside the barrel's bore to propel the bullet faster. The faster the bullet, assuming identical bullets, the more energy it delivers at impact. Junior high school physics 101.

Some calibers are more sensitive to this than others. A number of professional riflemen bemoan the massive switch from the 20-inch barrel M16A2 rifle to the 14-inch barrel M4 for our troops in Iraq and Afghanistan. To be sure, these shorter assault rifles handle more easily coming out of Humvees and other vehicles, but there is a significant loss of stopping power in the 5.56mm NATO

(.223) round when 30 percent of its bore length is taken away. This is one reason our troops are complaining about the poor terminal ballistics performance of their primary combat rifle.

The .308 is so much more powerful than the .223 that it literally has energy to spare. Lethal Force Institute staff instructor Steve Denney and I took the M14 to my range with a chronograph to measure bullet speed. Black Hills Match .308 with the 168-grain Sierra Match King bullet, a boat-tail hollow point polycoated to reduce friction drag, is one of the gold standards of rifle ammunition accuracy. It averaged 2,478 feet per second. 2680 foot-seconds is the velocity generally listed for a 168-grain Match .308 load out of a full-length rifle barrel.

Federal Premium 165-grain boat-tail soft point, my favorite all around hunting load in the caliber, averaged 2,544 seconds. The manuals specify a 2700 foot second velocity for this round out of a full-length rifle barrel. The loss had been 156 foot-seconds.

The 125-grain Nosler boat-tail Ballistic Tip is a .308 bullet geared for lighter creatures: coyotes, pronghorn antelope, or violent erect bipeds. Its average velocity was 2,844 feet per second. The Cor-Bon 125-grain .308 load was advertised as delivering 3150 feet per second. It had lost 306 foot seconds. That was a velocity loss of just under 10%.

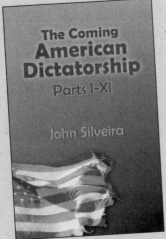

For comparison, the .300 Savage cartridge, introduced in 1920, was one of the more popular deer and bear hunting calibers when I was young, and is still frequently encountered in rural America. The .300 Savage is to the .308 Winchester as a .308 round from the SOCOM-16 is to one fired from a Springfield Armory M1A with full length 22-inch barrel.

Conclusion

The SOCOM-16 is an extraordinary rifle, and the team at Springfield Armory is to be congratulated for translating this excellent concept into functional reality. I have now seen well over a thousand rounds go downrange from SOCOM-16s, and I have yet to see one of these rifles jam.

"Built for business," the SOCOM-16 is expensive (in the $1800 range) but as a purpose-built rifle that fulfills multiple functions, it's worth every penny. Short, handy, powerful, and controllable, it is probably the ultimate "ranch rifle" and it gets my vote for "the gun of the year." Δ

Preparing for home EVACUATION

By Kelly McCarthy

Hands up! Who thinks the government will come to their rescue in an emergency?

The awful events unfolding in the aftermath of Hurricane Katrina truly demonstrate the importance of self-reliance. Outside of a war zone, I can't recall a time that so graphically demonstrates the need for all of us to have basic survival skills. And to supplement them, we should have basic survival tools.

Preparation is the key to all disaster planning, whether it's on a big scale for FEMA or on a small scale for your family.

Preparation means sitting down and facing the problems that threaten your home and family, and second-guessing the consequences. You know best what threats you face. Mostly it depends on where you live. The main risks in the USA are fire, flood, earthquake, hurricane, tornado, civil unrest, or terrorist attack. To prepare for one or more of these disasters means getting your family together and going through their roles in a potential disaster. Together you must prepare for the worst case: evacuating from your home knowing you won't be back anytime soon, if at all.

Imagine what you would most need if you lost everything. You know it isn't your photo album, much as you'd want it. You'd need your life's documentation and the basics to survive.

I have photocopied or scanned all of the documents listed in the box to the right (updated them every six months) and mailed a copy in a registered envelope to my sister-in-law in Massachusetts, more than 400 miles away. I keep a copy in a lockbox here, too. And in a grab-bag by the door there's another copy, in a plastic Ziploc along with $200 in cash, much of it in small bills, ready to leave with me. To be honest, I'd like to have more in cash but that's as much as I can tie up. In an emergency, $200 is way better than nothing. If there's an outage, credit cards don't work, greenbacks do.

A modern way to save your details is to scan your documents and save them in a web storage account such as gmail or mac.com offer. Then you can access them via the internet when you are safe. This is a great alternative for the photo album, too.

As for your survival needs, you have to use your commonsense. I know that *BHM* readers are way ahead of the curve when it comes to self-reliance, so I'll just help by suggesting things that I believe you should have ready to go in an evacuation situation. Remember that your survival needs, in order are: shelter, water, fire, food, and sanitation.

Getting out

Everyone should know the role they have to play in the last few minutes before you clear out. Of course, if it's a fire that started in your home rather than a forest fire that you know is bearing down on you, there is no time. You just get everyone out and rely upon your

Kelly McCarthy

The paperwork

To speed up the process of returning to normal in the event of a catastrophe, you're going to need a photocopy or other record of your:

- family's social security numbers
- bank and savings account details
- insurance policies
- health plan cards
- passports or military IDs
- contact numbers for your credit cards
- mortgage and deeds
- emergency phone numbers of family, friends, health professionals
- medical records with relevant shots, operations, allergies, etc.
- animal health records for pets or farm animals
- current prescriptions

documents and the kindness of others to rebuild your life.

For disasters where you have a little more warning, your family should each know their role. Set yourself a target of being able of get out in less than 20 minutes. Assign tasks such as: Mom gets the emergency rations; Bobby gets the pets; Jane grabs the bedding and clothes; Dad gets the car, fuel, gun, etc. If you are not all at home, you should pre-plan for where you will meet up. Everyone should memorize an out-of-state phone number that will become your Command Center if you are separated. Use a relative or friend. Local numbers get jammed in a big disaster.

To speed things up, be ready. Every home should have a number of emergency grab-bags, from a fanny-pack size to a car-trunk size packed with items you will need to survive until you reach your final destination. (See *BHM*'s *Emergency Preparedness and Survival Guide*.) Agree upon your destination in advance, and make sure your friends and family members know your plans. They will raise the alert if you don't arrive at your destination. You may be lucky enough to have another property, but most of us don't. Maybe you'll head for relatives. I don't have many relatives and I wouldn't want to descend upon them in any case, so our disaster escape plan is centered on heading for a place to camp. All our camping gear is in one place ready to get thrown in the back of the minivan. That's my job. The kids know where all the emergency food and water is, and it's their job to get that in the van. We all grab basic outdoors clothes and toiletries. My husband will lock down the house and stow the fishing gear and a few pre-packed tools. We grab the pets, their food and leashes, and we're gone.

You probably have emergency items such as a first-aid kit, shovel, flares, flashlight, tow rope, empty fuel can, etc., in your car already. If you don't, you're mad.

If you're very organized and have children, I suggest they all have a small backpack ready with their precious small items and things to entertain them. They will want to grab all their toys; they can't. Have them pack a bag ready to grab and go. It is a way of making them start to plan in advance and to realize what is important. Their backpacks will be useful if you get into a bad situation where you must abandon your car and carry essentials such as food and water over land. It's also something you can pack if they're not home. It's one less thing to distract you.

Lastly, grab all the oil, tinned and dried goods, and jugs of water or juice that are in your pantry and throw them in your car. (If you're on foot, take a couple of meals' worth of high-energy protein food such as corned beef or oily fish, and rice or pasta.) Don't forget the pet food. If there's time, take the bedding off your beds or grab sleeping bags. Now go!

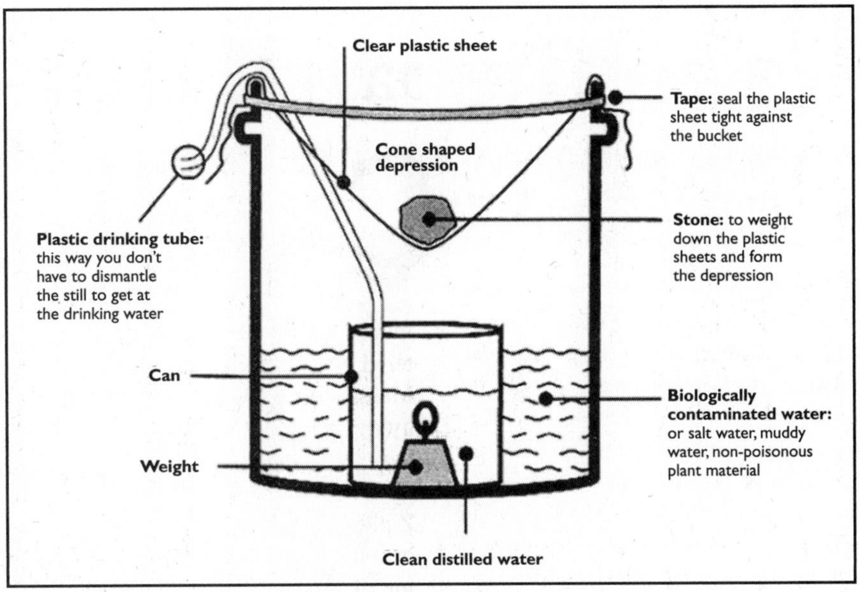

A 5-gallon bucket solar still can be used to distill contaminated water and make it potable.

Solar still

A solar still is a way of taking contaminated water and distilling it for drinking use. It does not work if there are chemicals such as gasoline present in the water, but it will make urine, seawater, and muddy creek or river water clean and potable. The version pictured on this page uses a five-gallon bucket. You can use the same method by digging a hole in the ground. It is particularly good on a dried-up riverbed. As you can see, the contaminated water evaporates, condenses on the plastic sheet and drips back into the can from where it can be sucked up. You will not get water from dry, desert ground unless you seed a dry hole by, say, urinating in it or putting in non-poisonous plant material. Don't forget this needs direct sunlight to work. It's good for up to a gallon a day. If you're nervous about drinking it, use the iodine crystals. Δ

Take the chill out of winter
grain soups, wild bird soups, and super sippers

By Linda Gabris

From its tantalizing aroma to its hearty, healthy ingredients, nothing takes the chill out of winter like a bowl of soup. Here's a few recipes of grain soups and game bird soups that will keep your family warm and healthy this season, and probably keep your relatives and neighbors visiting you all winter long. At the end of the article I've included some deliciously healthy "hot drink" concoctions.

A perfect pick of grains for old-fashioned grain soups. Jars, left to right: millet, rye kernels, oat flakes, wheat berries; far left, white rice; in scoop, pearl barley.

Grain soups

When it comes to soups, some of my most cherished recipes are those that were handed down to me by my grandmother who excelled at making delicious, hearty soups out of an array of common, inexpensive grains.

"If you've got a handful of grain," Grandma'd wink as she heated up her big cast iron soup pot on top of the crackling wood stove, "you've got fixin's for great soup..."

Since my grandparents relied upon being self-sufficient, especially in wintertime, it was important for them to have the pantry and root cellar well-stocked before cold weather struck. After putting up bounty from their huge garden and stowing away Mother Nature's offerings from backyard woodlands, there was never any fear of going hungry in the event of being snowbound for months. Along with other necessities like salt and sugar, sacks of grains topped their list of staples that were ordered from town each fall.

Even though, unlike Grandmother, I have year-round access to grocery stores, I still take great comfort in stocking my cupboard with an assortment of grains for making old-fashioned winter soups whenever the urge arises.

I admit that I don't buy grain by the bushel as Grandma did, but I do have enough on hand at any given time to throw together a delicious, nutritious supper soup. Over the years I've even added a few new grains to my soup pot like millet and brown rice that grandmother never had the luxury of using, likely because they were harder to come by or dearer than locally grown or more common picks like wheat, oats, corn, barley, rye, and plain white rice.

When buying grain, always try to choose organically grown, which is the best for boosting good health. Once home with your purchase, store grains in tightly covered containers on a cool pantry shelf.

The fascinating thing about grains is that they contain all the basic nutrients needed for good health. They provide significant amounts of protein, complex carbohydrates, vitamins, minerals, fiber, and are low in fat and contain no cholesterol.

Grandma used to quip after giving thanks for our daily bread, that it was not so much the bread we were praising, but rather the precious grains from which it was baked.

When making soups, keep in mind that grains absorb liquids and swell greatly upon cooking. Most types, especially millet and barley, can increase up to four times their original size so do not add more than the recipe calls for unless you purposely want a thicker soup—too much and you'll end up with porridge.

All the grains are interchangeable, so no two soups ever have to be the same. And in my house, no two ever are! You can even mix and match grains for exciting variety. And don't forget that grains can serve as a healthy, filling substitute for noodles in almost any soup.

The biggest secret to super soup is in dry roasting the grain before adding it to the pot. This produces nutty aroma and rich broth. To roast grains, heat a heavy-bottomed skillet until a drop of water sizzles. Like Grandma, I find that nothing beats cast iron for roasting grain as it holds and distributes heat evenly.

Rinse grain in cold water. Let drip dry in sieve, then pat dry on paper towels. This removes any grit that might be present and gets rid of some of the excess starch, especially in rice.

Empty the grain into the pan and stir constantly with a wooden spoon until roasted as directed in each recipe. Do not over-roast as this can cause a burnt taste.

When the grain is ready, empty it into the soup pot and proceed. Go ahead and let your creative juices flow. Here are a few recipes to help get you rolling.

Old-fashioned oatmeal and onion soup

Vegetable stock from scraps:

Some soup recipes call for vegetable stock. You can use vegetable bouillon or cubes if you wish, but making your own stock from scratch is so much better, not to mention easy and economical.

I keep a special container in my fridge that catches all of my veggie discards like fleshy onion and potato peelings, outer cabbage leaves and heart, carrot and parsnip scrapings, turnip trims, celery leaves, stripped parsley stems, pepper pulp, and seeds and other bits that'll yield flavor in my stock pot. Just remember to scour veggies while still whole.

To make stock, empty scraps into pot and add about a quart of water, bring to boil, reduce heat and simmer covered until every last vitamin, mineral, and drop of flavor has been extracted.

Season with salt, pepper, and any spice or herb that tickles your fancy. Strain and discard scraps. Once prepared, stock can be cooled, then frozen for safe keeping. Simple soups can be made by adding roasted grains to stock and simmering until tender.

Wheat berry and squash soup. Try this soup with any squash and any grain.

Tip: The more carrot scraps you use, the richer the stock will be, both in flavor and color.

Oatmeal and onion soup:

Here's a fragrant, filling soup that's supper in itself. The recipe can be doubled, if you wish.

3 Tbsp. large oat flakes
1 Tbsp. vegetable oil
4 large, finely chopped onions
2 cloves minced garlic
3 grated carrots
6 cups vegetable stock
pinch of dried basil

Toast oat flakes, stirring constantly until they are golden. Empty from pan and set aside. Put oil in skillet. Add onions and garlic, sauté until onions are soft. Empty into soup pot and add remaining ingredients, except oats. Bring to a boil, reduce heat and simmer covered 15 minutes. Sprinkle oats into soup and simmer, uncovered, another 5 minutes. Taste and adjust seasoning.

Wheat berry and squash soup:

Grandpa grew an array of squash in his backyard garden, enough to fill the root cellar to last all winter long. You can use butternut, pumpkin, or any squash you fancy. This is an interesting soup—tender wheat berries swimming in smooth puréed squash. Also great when made with rye kernels, barley, rice, or millet.

½ cup wheat berries (or ½ cup rye kernels, ¼ cup barley or rice, or 2 Tbsp. millet)
1 butternut or other medium-sized squash, peeled and cubed
water
4 cups vegetable stock

Toast wheat (or rye) kernels until they start to "pop." (Barley, rice, or millet until golden.) Set aside. Put squash into pot with just enough lightly salted water to cover, bring to boil, reduce heat, and simmer until soft. Puree until smooth. Add vegetable stock and wheat kernels. Simmer until kernels are tender. Taste and adjust seasoning. Garnish with parsley.

Lizzy's oriental rice soup:

Grandma had hundreds of ancient rice soup recipes in her collection. Here's a new-fangled version that beats them all. By the way, it's named after me.

All the fixins you need for Lizzy's oriental rice soup

Lizzy's oriental rice soup

½ cup rice
6 cups water
6 dried shiitake mushrooms, broken into pieces (fibrous stalk removed and saved for adding to stocks or bouquet garni for boost of flavor)
¾ cup sliced celery
2 sliced carrots
½ cup each of cauliflower and broccoli flowerets
½ cup red, yellow and/or green peppers, coarsely chopped
3 Tbsp. of soy sauce or enough to turn soup rich brown
few drops of sesame oil
1 small hot pepper or drop of chili oil (optional)

Toast rice until evenly golden. Set aside. Put water into soup pot and add shiitakes. Bring to boil, reduce heat, cover, and simmer until mushrooms bits are plump. Add rice and simmer 10 minutes. Add remaining ingredients (and any other veggies you fancy) and simmer until vegetables are tender, but not soft. Taste and adjust seasoning. Garnish with finely sliced green onion.

Old World corn chowder:

In the fall after corn was harvested, Grandma'd peel dozens of ears, tie them together by the husks, and hang them to dry in the attic. This is the corn she'd use to make her delicious corn chowder. I've updated the recipe using store-bought or home-canned corn, which produces great chowder—almost as good as Gram's. When making chowder from fresh corn, it can be cut from the cob and roasted in a 475° F oven under broiler until golden. This produces rich golden chowder.

1 quart canned corn or about 4 cups
3 cups vegetable stock
4 Tbsp. fine cornmeal blended into 1 cup soy milk (more or less depending on how thick you like your chowder)

Old World corn chowder is especially good when made out of home-canned corn and your very own vegetable stock, seasoned to suit your taste.

Old World corn chowder

Empty corn and juice into soup pot and add stock. Bring to boil, reduce heat, and simmer 5 minutes. Add soy milk mixture and heat, stirring constantly until thick and smooth. Season with salt and pepper. Garnish with a pinch of basil or a snip of chives. Serve with corn cakes on the side for dunking.

Golden corn cakes:

Put 1½ cups of flour in large bowl. Add 1½ cups yellow cornmeal, 3 tsp. baking powder, 3 Tbsp. sugar, 2 Tbsp. vegetable oil, and enough water to bind. Heat heavy skillet and lightly oil. Drop batter by spoonful and fry cakes until golden on both sides.

Super game bird soups

Game birds make delicious soups, and since they do not have as much body fat as domestic fowl they produce healthier fill for the tureen.

Here are two tasty supper soups calling for two super game birds. Although domestic birds can be substituted in either recipe (chicken for grouse and tame duck in place of wild), you'll earn bigger raves from a bagged bird.

Parsley-speckled grouse soup with egg-drops:

This recipe produces a savory, golden broth that's loaded with tender chunks of grouse breasts and hearty noodles, which are known in European cuisine as egg-drops. Fragrant fresh parsley is what gives the soup such a wonderful burst of flavor, so strive to use the fresh plant in place of dried herb.

4 grouse breasts
sprig of thyme and 1 bay leaf
1 bundle fresh parsley
2 leeks, sliced thin
1 minced onion
2 stalks diced celery
1 cup of dried mixed soup vegetables
½ tsp. basil
3 Tbsp. powered or instant chicken stock

Remove the breast meat from the bone by running a sharp knife down each side of the breastbone until meat is freed. Put breast bones into small pot and cover with water. Add thyme and bay leaf. Cover and bring to a boil. Skim off foam. Reduce heat and simmer one hour.

Meanwhile, cut breast meat into soup-sized chunks and put into pot along with remaining ingredients. Add 6 cups of water. Bring to a boil, cover, reduce heat, and simmer 2 hours or until meat is tender. When bones are done, remove from heat and strain broth into soup. Pick meat off bones and add to soup before discarding. Add salt and pepper to taste.

Egg-drops:

Egg-drops have more body than traditional soup noodles so they do not go soggy in leftover soup.

Put 1 cup of flour and a pinch of salt in a bowl. Stir in 2 eggs. Flour hands and work the dough into a firm ball. If too hard, add a drop of water. If too soft, add more flour. Pinch off golf ball sized pieces of dough, and with floured hands on floured surface, roll into "pencils." Put in fridge and allow to harden for 5 minutes. Using a sharp knife, cut into dime-sized slices. Drop into boiling grouse soup and simmer 2 minutes before serving.

Chinese duck soup:

This soup kills two birds with one stone. Since it only calls for duck broth, you can serve the delicious soup for a starter and enjoy crispy duck pieces as the main course.

1 whole duck
¼ cup soy sauce
2 Tbsp. oyster sauce
1 tsp. sesame oil
4 dried shiitake mushrooms, broken into small pieces
1 tsp. fresh grated ginger
4 sprigs chopped cilantro
vegetables—thinly sliced leeks or green onion, celery cut diagonally, chopped red and green peppers, whole snow peas, water chestnuts, baby corn, broccoli, cauliflower, or vegetables of choice cut into spoon-sized pieces

Grouse breasts, de-boned for parsley-speckled grouse soup

Making "egg drops" for the parsley-speckled grouse soup

If you like chunky soup, use lots of veggies; for thinner soup use less.

Poke duck breast full of holes with fork to allow grease to escape. Put whole duck (and giblets, if you've saved them) in large pot. Cover with water, bring to boil, reduce heat, and simmer covered for 2 hours, or until tender but not falling apart.

Remove duck from broth. Put broth in fridge to cool. Cut duck into serving-sized pieces. They are now ready for crisping in the oven. Bake at 350° F for one hour before serving. The duck can be basted with plum, orange, or other sauce while baking.

When broth has cooled, skim the hardened fat and discard or save for other use. Put broth and chopped giblets into pot and heat to boiling. Add remaining ingredients. Reduce heat and simmer 4 minutes. Do not let vegetables go limp. Season with salt and pepper.

Hot drinks

Every day all winter long my Grandmother kept a huge kettle of water simmering on the back of her old McClary wood stove that sat in the corner of the kitchen, and whenever a bundled caller entered with frosty brows and numb fingers, Grandma was ready to offer them a steaming hot drink for sipping.

"You never know when a frozen soul might happen along..." she'd wink, always eager for company. Grandma was quick to treat her guests to a delightful drink knowing darn well it would draw them back time and again.

I relish company as much as my grandparents did and, like Grandma, I believe that a knock on the kitchen door is the answer to a whistlin' kettle.

Although I still depend on Grandma's old recipes like honeyed mint, clover, and raspberry teas to warm the heart and soul, throughout the years I have added some exciting new drinks to my recipe files.

Unlike my grandmother who depended wholly on her garden and the woodlands surrounding our backyard to fill the tea tins on her pantry shelves, I am fortunate to have nearby supermarkets and specialty shops where I can purchase imported herbs, exotic spices, and other wonderful worldly things to steep and simmer into healthy, delicious drinks said to be good for whatever ails you.

Here are a few old fashioned super hot drinks and some newfangled creations that are guaranteed to take the chill out of winter and add warmth to all your friendships.

Peppy ginger tea:

Ginger tea has been used for centuries as a healthy drink administered to reduce fever and treat various everyday stomach complaints. It is reported to be good for improving poor circulation and stimulating appetite. When brewing as treatment for numb hands and feet after a skating or sledding party, add a generous pinch of cayenne pepper, which is also reported as being good for getting the "blood moving." I find that a little cup of ginger tea in the morning is a great way to start the day.

4 cups water
4 Tbsp. fresh ginger, scrubbed and grated. Some folks peel ginger, I don't.
honey to sweeten
pinch or more cayenne pepper

Adjust cayenne according to your tolerance of heat. When I have a stuffy head or am feeling symptoms of cold or flu, I increase the cayenne as it helps break up congestion. For company tea, you may wish to go very light on cayenne or omit it altogether, especially if serving to the younger set.

Bring water to rolling boil. Add ginger and cayenne. Reduce heat and simmer 15 minutes. Add enough honey to sweeten. Strain into Chinese-sized tea cups. Makes four standard cups or about eight demitasse portions.

Spicy Chai tea:

I was introduced to Chai—rhymes with "pie"—a few years ago and it has become one of my favorite hot drinks. There are many variations of this specialty tea that has its roots in India, and one of the best ways of

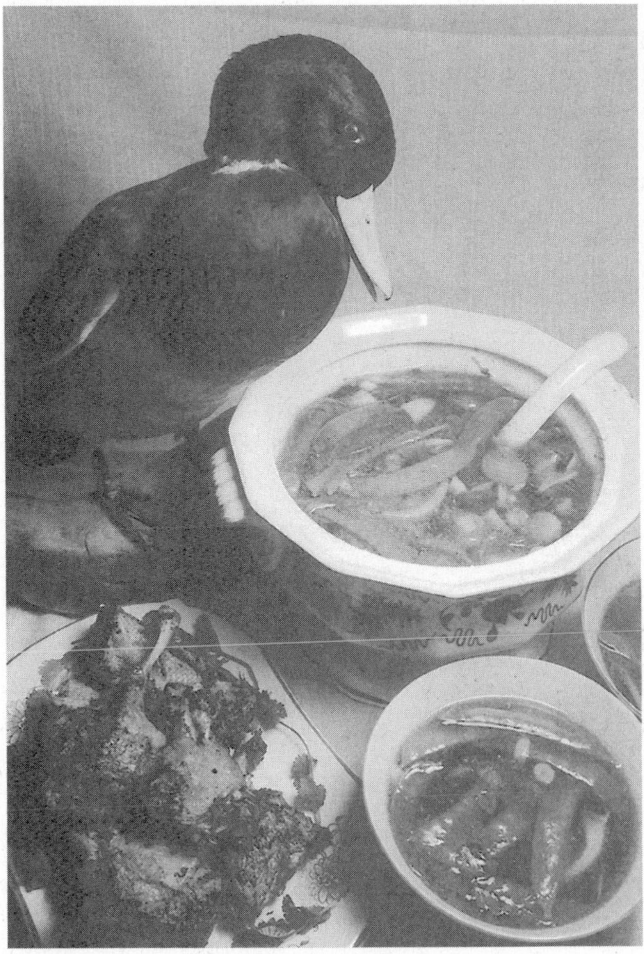

Chinese duck soup

Parsley-speckled grouse soup

Peppy ginger tea—good for taking the chill out of winter.

Fixins for spicy Chai tea

Cloudy day hot apple cider

achieving the perfect cup is to experiment until you come up with a brew that suits your own taste to a tee. Aromatic Chai tea is reported to be an excellent natural digestive aid, helping to relieve heartburn and gas. Nothing fills the house with sweeter aroma than a pot of simmering Chai.

- 6 cups water
- ½ Tbsp. ground cardamom. You can buy whole cardamom seed pods or ground powder. I buy the pods and grind with a pestle and mortar for utmost flavor.
- 1 Tbsp. fresh, chopped ginger
- 8 whole cloves, bruised
- ¼ tsp. whole black peppercorns
- 1 stick cinnamon bark, broken in four pieces
- 1 nutmeg pod, coarsely pounded (or ½ tsp. ground)
- 4 Tbsp. loose black tea leaves or 5 quality tea bags
- 1 cup warmed soy milk (I make my own soy milk out of soy beans, but if you wish, you can use whole, 2%, or skim milk)
- honey or maple syrup to sweeten

Combine water, spices, and tea in a saucepan and bring to a slow boil. Reduce heat and simmer 8 minutes. Strain into a preheated teapot and let settle 3 minutes.

Pour into cups, leaving room for the warm milk and sweeten as desired. Makes 6 servings.

Note: To perk up winter houseplants, water with leftover cold Chai. It'll also scent the room and take the moldy smell out of old earth.

Cloudy day hot apple cider:

My Grandmother made her own cider vinegar and administered a cup of hot cider for whatever ailed you. Apple cider vinegar dates back thousands of years as being a natural cure-all. It is said to have germ-fighting powers that can rid the body of impurities. Putting its healthful benefits aside, this makes an eye-opening

All you need for a pot of bone-warming miso

Simple, saucy soy drink...so good!

drink that'll warm you all the way down to your toes.

6 cups water
4 Tbsp. homemade or good quality apple cider vinegar
1 tart apple studded with cloves
¾ cup dark brown sugar or to taste (honey, maple syrup, or white sugar can be used)
½ lemon, thinly sliced

Put all ingredients into kettle and bring to a boil. Reduce heat and simmer 20 minutes. Strain through sieve, forcing apple pulp through. Put back in kettle and heat to boiling. Let settle before pouring. Serves 6. This recipe can be halved or doubled, letting one apple do the trick.

Bone-warming miso:

Miso is a miracle creation dating back about 1200 years to the Japanese Nara era and is credited with earning Japanese people longevity and good health. It is a hearty, salty paste that is made out of fermented soy beans and is rich in protein, lecithin, glutamic acid, vitamin B, and various microorganisms that aid digestion and promote general well-being. You can buy various types, including rice miso and wheat miso, at specialty and health food stores. If you haven't tried miso, then you don't know what your missin'.

4 cups boiling water
4 Tbsp. light or dark miso
generous pinch of fresh ground black pepper
pinch garlic powder
pinch celery salt
¼ tsp. black pepper
green onion stir stick

Boil water. Blend in the miso, stirring until dissolved. Add seasonings. Pour into mugs and add green onion stir stick. This drink is so nutritional and good you can call it lunch. In fact, if that drop-in company stays till lunchtime, why not throw in some cubed tofu, vegetables (cauliflower, broccoli, shredded cabbage, celery, carrot, snow peas, or whatever else you have in your crisper) and call it lunch. They'll be pleasantly impressed by your fine hospitality. Serves 4.

Simple, saucy soy drink:

So good, so easy, so perfect when you crave a hot drink with body and flair. This is another drink that can be "veggied-up" into super soup. The recipe below makes one dipper-sized serving but you can double, triple, or do a whole soup pot full. This is a great warmer-upper to serve after a day on the slopes.

1½ cup water
2 Tbsp. soy sauce
½ tsp. sesame oil
few drops hot pepper sauce
pinch fresh grated ginger
finely sliced green onion for garnish

Boil water in dipper. Blend in remaining ingredients. Simmer 2 minutes. You can serve this in a cup or Chinese soup bowl. Δ

make your own nut butters

By Sylvia Gist

When almond butter replaced peanut butter in my diet (on doctor's orders), I discovered I really liked the almond better. And it opened my eyes to the world of "other" nut butters. I also discovered they were quite expensive. I was lucky if I found a 10 ounce jar of almond butter for less than $4.00, a luxury compared to even the 100% natural peanut butter. So I did some experimenting and came up with my own recipe for almond butter that satisfied me. The same process can be used for other nuts.

To make almond butter, I use a cookie sheet or jelly roll pan to dry roast the nuts since I prefer them roasted. I also use my food processor. I have used a blender, but it took longer, required more scraping the nuts off the sides, and I had to add more oil to get a decent butter. A rubber spatula and a jar to store the butter in complete the required equipment.

Ingredients are simply a couple cups of the desired nuts and a little bit of olive oil. I buy larger bags of raw almonds, throw them in the freezer, and take them out as I need them. I prefer to start with raw nuts and do my own roasting. That way, I get freshly roasted nuts with nothing added. If I need to add oil, I prefer to use extra virgin olive oil.

The actual process of making the butter is not difficult. I put two cups of nuts on the baking sheet and pop them into a preheated oven to roast at 350 degrees, leave them there for several minutes, then remove the pan and stir. I return the pan to the oven and roast for a few minutes more, watching the color of the nuts, striving for a toasted, but not burnt, look. How long before the nuts burn? That depends upon the oven and the pan. My Air-bake pan requires a longer time than a thin baking sheet. The thin sheet can take 8 minutes or less. Just watch the nuts the first time to get an idea how long they need to bake in your oven with your pan. Once you make a batch of burnt almond butter, you will be motivated to watch the time.

Almonds ready for roasting

After toasting the nuts, I allow them to cool before dumping them into the processor. Since my food processor has just one speed, I flip the switch and watch the nuts bang wildly and loudly against the sides of the container. Gradually they get chopped up finer and finer. If particles build up on the sides of the container, stop and scrape them down with a rubber spatula. Continue processing until it begins to ball up. You may have to break up the ball, but it is most important to be patient. Sometimes the ball will bang around for a while before it begins to break down and look creamy. It takes several minutes.

It is during this time when it is balled up that I add some oil. I will add a teaspoon of oil and run the processor some more. If the butter is creamy enough without it, I omit the oil. I have never added more than 3 teaspoons of oil to the 2 cups of nuts. It is important to be patient and give the processor a chance to make the butter. Toward the end, more oil can be added if you like it creamier. If chunky style is desired, just roast a few extra nuts, chop, and stir into the finished butter.

While it is possible to make peanut butter in this same manner, I don't bother, because I can buy excellent peanut butter at a reasonable price. There are so many other possibilities for nut butters. Below are some notes about different ones that I have tried.

A jar of fresh almond butter

Almond butter. Since almonds are more reasonably priced and easier to digest, I make this type of butter more frequently than any of the others. Raw almond butter can be found in the health food stores and some people prefer the raw kind. You simply process the nuts without roasting. Two cups of raw almonds, processed with a minimum of oil, will fill a 10 ounce jar. If you are roasting them, throw a few extra nuts on the baking sheet for a warm snack when you take the pan out of the oven. They are quite tasty.

Cashew butter. Cashews are more expensive (where I shop), so I buy the least expensive raw white pieces and roast them. They brown much faster than almonds (hardly seven minutes on the Air-bake pan), so be vigilant or they burn and taste terrible. Cashews are softer than almonds and grind up quicker too. While cashew butter can be made without oil, it is fairly dry, so add some oil for a creamy smooth butter. This butter tastes more like peanut butter than any of the others I've made, but yet slightly different.

Raw pecan butter. Raw pecan butter is the easiest to make. No roasting. Pecans are soft so they process quickly and make a very smooth butter.

Hazelnut butter. Hazelnut butter is available at health food stores, so I tried to make some. Unfortunately, I roasted them a tad too much and the butter had a twangy taste. Since hazelnuts are quite expensive, I haven't tried it again.

Since I add no preservatives, these nut butters can become rancid. I always store mine in the refrigerator and try to use them up within a month or so.

Each of the nut butters tastes a bit different, so each can be used differently. I like the almond butter on a sandwich with apple butter or jam. Some are best on a cracker of one kind or another. I eat whole grain rye crackers, which always taste better with some kind of nut butter. Any of these improve the taste of a rice cake, too. One of my cookbooks uses these odd nut butters quite a lot; they seem to work well in cookies and quick breads.

If you like experimenting, check a health food store for their variety of nut butters, buy the appropriate nuts, roast (or not), and make the butter yourself. It isn't hard. Δ

Shiitake mushrooms

"good health" you can grow yourself

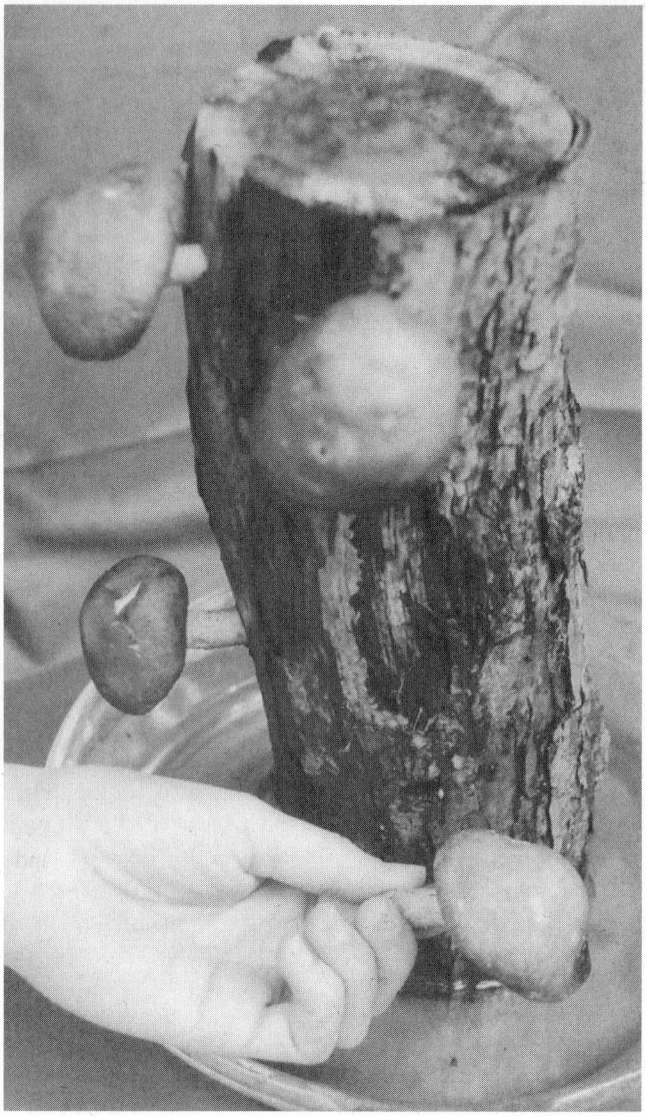

Harvesting shiitake mushrooms off your own log is a rewarding hobby.

By Linda Gabris

There's a familiar old saying about mushrooms making meals marvelous but when it comes to the delectable shiitake, here's a pick that goes way beyond the call of duty. Aside from being top choice for the pan, the healthful benefits of eating shiitake mushrooms make them even more to marvel over.

Shiitake (*Lentinus edodes* belonging to the *Tricholomataceae* family) is a forest mushroom native to Japan, China and Korea. The Japanese name, shiitake (shee-tah-kay) is derived from "shii" meaning the shiia or oak tree on which they grow and "take" meaning mushroom. In China, shiitake is known as hsaing ku, which means fragrant mushroom.

Shiitakes are deeply rooted in Asian history with the first mention of them dating back to 199AD when natives of Kyushu presented the emperor with a gift of the prized woodland gathering. During the Ming Dynasty (1368-1644), the mushrooms were considered the "elixir of life" and were a reserved pick to be enjoyed only by the emperor and his family.

Ancient Oriental healers prescribed shiitake for a host of ailments including cold, flu, sinus, headache, measles, worms, constipation, hemorrhoids, gout, liver disorders, nutritional deficiencies, poor circulation, and sexual dysfunction. The healthful fungi has held its ground in the medicinal world for thousands of years and many modern day herbalists still recommend shiitake as treatment for the above complaints.

Even though Asian people have been cashing in on the medicinal benefits of shiitakes for almost as far back as history dates, it is only in more current times that the Western World has taken a closer look at the mushroom as being useful for lowering cholesterol, treating high blood pressure, cancer, heart disease, AIDS, herpes, and other viral infections.

Research has shown that shiitake mushrooms contain an amino acid called eritadenine, which is noted for lowering cholesterol. Findings indicated that adding shiitake to one's diet helped lower blood cholesterol levels by almost 50 percent, especially in cases where high-cholesterol foods were eaten simultaneously with the mushroom.

A remarkable substance known as beta glucan, a form of natural sugar that has powerful immune-boosting and anti-cancer properties, is derived from yeast cells of shiitake. Extensive research since the 1940s has shown that beta glucan not only helps the

Shiitake omelette—a hearty breakfast

body fight off invaders but also works as an anti-oxidant.

Beta glucan is marketed as a nutritional supplement in parts of North America, Europe, and in Asia where it is being used in hospitals in conjunction with cancer treatments to slow the growth of tumors and decrease common side effects of treatments.

Today shiitakes are the second most cultivated mushroom in the world (the button mushroom is first). Japan is the largest producer, growing about 80% of the world's supply. Shiitakes are one of the most popular sources of protein in Asian diets and are often accredited with longevity, vitality, and sound mind.

I had my first memorable taste years ago when I discovered some delightfully chewy brown morsels in a bowl of wonton soup at a Chinese restaurant. After coaxing the secret out of a tight-lipped chef, I was pointed in the direction of shiitakes and became hooked on their unique, smoky flavor and meaty texture.

Back when I started indulging in the exotic mushrooms, they were, as far as my budget was concerned, a pricey condiment that usually had to be hunted down in specialty shops that catered to gourmet cooking. Most of the mushrooms I unearthed were sold dried by the ounce and I remember paying dearly for my addiction! Nowadays, I'm happy to report, they are more affordable and much easier to come by in both fresh and dried state.

Along with their growing popularity, shiitake mushrooms have sprung a host of new names including Chinese Black, Oriental Black, Black Forest, and Golden Oak mushroom. Regardless of tag, the taste is unmistakable and once you've sunk your teeth into a full-bodied shiitake, you'll have no problem identifying one upon a future encounter.

With their protein-rich reputation and pleasing steak-like texture, it's easy to see why shiitakes are popular with vegetarians and have become a number one alternative for those trying to trim down or cut meat from their diet. I find they make a very satisfying substitute for meat on pizzas, in soups, stews, rice and couscous dishes, and when added to an omelet,

Healthy shiitake stir-fry

Shiitake tea known throughout the world as the drink of good health

make a delightfully healthy stand-in for a traditional steak and egg breakfast.

Aside from being a rich source of protein, shiitakes supply niacin, riboflavin, thiamin, potassium, and iron, and are a good source of vitamins A, B, C, and when used in their sun-dried form, provide a valuable dose of Vitamin D, found in very few foods. They contain more than 50 different enzymes, including pepsin that aids digestion, and asparaginase, which is a substance that has been used to treat childhood leukemia.

Adding shiitakes to one's diet is easy these days since they are readily available in larger supermarkets everywhere, and now mushrooms lovers can have a whole lot of fun growing their own at home. To me, nothing is more rewarding than harvesting fresh mushrooms right off my own log.

There are a number of suppliers across the country that sell commercial shiitake logs that are drilled with holes in which mushroom "spawn" has been implanted. All you have to do to grow your own is buy a log and follow the easy directions from the supplier. From start-up time to harvesting, your first feed of homegrown shiitakes is only a matter of weeks. And your log will serve you time and time again.

If your log produces more shiitakes than you can use, or if you find a super buy at the grocery store, you can dry your surplus by stringing and hanging. Fishing line or uncolored thread works great for this purpose. When mushrooms are dried, unstring and store in a paper bag on the pantry shelf where they will keep indefinitely.

Fresh shiitakes can be used in place of button or other mushrooms in almost any recipe. They are delicious grilled, fried, creamed, or added to stir-frys. One of my favorite quickie suppers calls for a handful of shiitake mushrooms sautéed in a dab of butter (or olive oil) until golden, then served atop a thick slice of garlic toast. As far as I'm concerned, this is just like having a hot steak sandwich without the fuss and muss of meat.

Dried shiitakes can be broken up and added to soups, stews, sauces or any dish calling for mushrooms. Shiitake stalks, especially those from dried mushrooms, should be removed before cooking as they are rather tough and fibrous. They can be saved up and added to stock, tucked into a bouquet garni or steeped into comforting, soothing teas, then discarded.

To use dried shiitakes in place of fresh mushrooms, just soak whole or broken up pieces in enough boiling water to cover for about 20 minutes or until they plump back up. They are now ready to use in place of fresh-pick and will yield a chewier texture I find most appealing. Save the soaking water to add to gravy or soup or better yet, sit down and enjoy it as a nourishing drink.

Although shiitake supplements can be bought at health food stores in gelcap forms, powders, extracts, tinctures, and tea preparations, I find it so much more rewarding to derive the healthy benefits of shiitakes by enjoying them right at the table on my plate or in a cup. As with any such preparation, if you do opt to use shiitake supplements to treat a particular ailment, talk to your doctor first.

As far as eating shiitake mushrooms for sheer pleasure—indulge until your heart is content! You'll find that shiitakes really do make meals more marvelous—not to mention, healthy.

Try the following recipes for great eating.

Shiitake omelette

Here's a hearty omelette that sheds a new light on the old steak and egg breakfast. Serves two, but recipe can be halved, doubled or tripled as needed.

3 fresh shiitake caps, sliced ¼-inch thick (or 3 caps broken into fours, soaked in boiling water until plump, then patted dry on paper towels)
2 large eggs
½ Tbsp. cream
2 leaves of fresh minced basil (or pinch of dried)
½ Tbsp. butter (or vegetable oil)
salt and pepper to taste

Separate eggs. With a whisk, beat whites until stiff but not dry. Add basil to yolks, then beat, adding cream until thick and smooth. Gently fold whites into yolks.

Heat butter in heavy skillet (cast iron works very well) until sizzling. Sauté mushrooms on both sides until golden. Pour prepared eggs over top of mushrooms and cook until omelette has set. Turn gently and cook other side. Slide onto heated plate. Season with salt and pepper.

Super healthy shiitake stir-fry

Nothing is healthier than a stir-fry supper, except for one that's done up with meaty shiitake mushrooms in place of traditional beef. This recipe does not follow strict measurements as the whole fun of stir-frying is in creating a dish to suit your own liking to a tee. If you love your platter loaded with snow peas, so be it.

- 1½ Tbsp. vegetable oil
- ½ Tbsp. sesame oil
- ½ Tbsp. fresh grated ginger
- 2 cloves minced garlic
- 8 fresh shiitake mushrooms sliced ¼-inch thick (or dried caps prepared as above)
- about 4 or 5 cups vegetables of choice cut into stir-fry fashion: onion, cauliflower, broccoli, celery, carrot, green pepper, red or yellow pepper, snow peas, green beans, water chestnuts, baby corn, or any other veggie you fancy
- 2 Tbsp. soy sauce

Heat oils in wok over medium heat. Add ginger and garlic and sauté until aroma is released, only a few seconds. Add shiitake mushrooms and stir with a wooden spoon for about one minute. Add prepared vegetables and stir-fry, tossing with wooden spoon until fork tender. Add soy sauce and stir until evenly coated. Serve sprinkled with toasted sesame seeds, if you wish. Goes great with steamed rice. Serves 4

Shiitake soup with rice vermicelli

- 4 cups water
- 4 dried shiitake mushroom caps, broken into small pieces
- 1 Tbsp. soy sauce
- 1 Tbsp. red chili oil (adjust to your tolerance of heat)
- 1 tsp. garlic powder
- 1 small, thinly sliced onion
- ½ stalk celery, sliced thin
- 2 Tbsp. finely chopped sweet yellow, red, or green peppers
- seasoned salt and black pepper to taste
- 1 cup of rice vermicelli (broken into soup-sized pieces) cooked according to package directions, then rinsed under cold water

Put water in soup pot and bring to boil. Add mushrooms. Reduce heat, cover, and cook 5 minutes. Add remaining ingredients, except salt and pepper, and simmer until vegetables are soft, about 8 minutes. Add seasoned salt and pepper to taste. Stir in the rice vermicelli, and heat to boiling.

Makes 4 to 6 servings, but recipes can be halved or doubled as needed.

Shiitake tea

This satisfying tea is especially good for those with high blood pressure or high levels of blood cholesterol. Shiitake tea is a perfect drink for taking the edge off hunger pains and is excellent medicine for breaking up a cold and soothing sore muscles that often accompany flu. It can help relieve headache and stuffiness and is good for calming the nerves. A cup of shiitake tea is bound to pick you up every time.

For medicinal use:

- 2 dried shiitake mushroom caps, broken into bits
- 1 cup water

Put shiitake pieces into small kettle with water and bring to a boil. Reduce heat, cover, and simmer 30 minutes. Strain (save bits for supper) and administer in a Chinese-sized teacup. Makes enough for 4 doses to take several hours apart. Sip hot.

For pleasure drinking:

Use one mushroom cap per cup of water as above. In Japan, it's customary to add a pinch of sea salt to the pot. When serving, make sure that each cup gets a fair share of shiitake bits and a cocktail fork or toothpick for fishing them out. Δ

Burghul

The noblest food achieved by wheat

By Habeeb Salloum

The hot Saskatchewan July wind made us uncomfortable as my brother and myself went searching for wood scraps in the surrounding treeless prairie land. This was an important yearly task for us children in the age-old method of producing our yearly supply of burghul. We had to find enough wood to be able to boil two bushels of wheat until the kernels were cooked. For this we needed all the fire material we could find.

However, finding the wood for cooking was only the first task in the making of burghul. After the wheat was well done, it had to be spread on white sheets in the sun to eliminate the moisture. When the kernels were bone-dry we took the cooked product to our neighbor for chopping. Back home, we removed the loose parts of the bran by winnowing the crushed, cooked, wheat in the never-ending Saskatchewan wind. The burghul was then again placed in the sun until it became well dried.

Of course, as children we never looked forward to our burghul making day. It was a time of backbreaking work—a period, if possible, to be avoided. How many times we children wished we were like our neighbors who did not know that burghul even existed.

In our modern times, this method of making burghul, which is called in the lands where it is a staple 'the noblest food achieved by wheat', is only a historic memory. In North America and, almost all other countries where it is consumed, this first-rate wheat product is produced by machines and electrically controlled ovens. A housewife can purchase burghul from any Middle Eastern store, some health food outlets and in a good number of supermarkets in large cities.

This very versatile food, also known as bulgar, bulgor or bulgour, is believed to have been first eaten in the Euphrates Valley as far back as 5000 B.C. From that era in antiquity until our times, it has been on the daily menu of the peoples of the Middle Eastern. In parts of Europe and North America, it has been only in the last few decades that burghul has become known to some extent by a segment of the population. Introduced by the Armenians, Syrians and other nationals from the Middle East, this delightful product of wheat is slowly becoming known among the general public in the western world.

In the last few years vegetarian and other health conscious people have become convinced that burghul is an excellent health food. Research and experiences have proven to the health conscious diners that this cereal has very few equals in food value. The cooking of the wheat preserves most of the nutrients, even when some of the bran is removed after the grain is crushed. The calcium, carbohydrates, iron, phosphorous, potassium, vitamin B, and protein content are almost all retained. These are not lost even when burghul is stored for a long period of time. The cereal can be kept for years without loss of food value and any other type of deterioration.

Unexcelled as a nourishing eatable, burghul has more food energy than corn meal; more iron than rice; less fat than uncooked wheat; six times more calcium than corn meal and three times more than rice; and more vitamins than barley, corn meal or rice.

Simple to prepare, this ancient food is an inexpensive, natural, wholesome

Burghul and chickpea salad

and a succulent versatile cereal. Often utilized as a replacement for rice, it is cooked in the same fashion as that grain, taking about 20 minutes to cook. Used in all types of dishes, it can be employed in every course and every meal of the day.

Burghul can be purchased in bulk or packaged. It comes in three sizes: coarse, medium and fine. The coarse is utilized in pottage dishes; the medium as an ingredient in salads; and the fine as a main component in vegetarian and other meat patties or as a breakfast cereal and as a principal element in some desserts.

One of the most preferred foods found in the Middle East, this wheat product is becoming familiar to a good number of housewives in other parts of the world. Easy to prepare and very delectable and nourishing, it is truly the noblest food achieved by wheat.

From the countless burghul dishes we have selected these few for the uninitiated who wish to travel the culinary world of this healthy eatable.

Burghul and egg soup:

Serves 6 to 8
4 Tbsp. cooking oil
½ pound ground meat, lamb or beef
1 medium sized onion, finely chopped
2 cloves garlic, crushed
2 Tbsp. finely chopped fresh coriander leaves
1 small hot pepper, finely chopped
½ cup coarse burghul, rinsed
4 Tbsp. tomato paste
2 tsp. salt
½ tsp. pepper
¼ tsp. allspice
8 cups water
2 eggs, beaten
4 Tbsp. lemon juice
2 Tbsp. finely chopped fresh mint

In a saucepan, heat oil, then sauté meat over medium heat for 5 minutes. Add onion, garlic, coriander leaves and hot pepper, then stir-fry for a further 10 minutes. Stir in the burghul and stir-fry for another 2 minutes, then add tomato paste, salt, pepper, allspice and water and bring to a boil. Cover and cook over medium heat for 40 minutes, then stir in eggs, lemon juice and mint and serve immediately.

Burghul pottage:

Serves 4
4 Tbsp. butter
½ pound beef or lamb, cut into very small pieces
2 medium sized onions, finely chopped
2 cloves garlic, crushed
1 small hot pepper, very finely chopped
1 cup coarse burghul, rinsed
2 ½ cups water
¾ tsp. salt
¼ tsp. pepper
¼ tsp. cumin

In a frying pan, melt butter, then sauté meat over medium heat until it begins to brown. Add onions, garlic and hot pepper, then stir-fry for further 10 minutes. Add burghul, then stir-fry for another 3 minutes. Stir in remaining ingredients and bring to a boil, then cover and cook over medium/low heat for 20 minutes. Shut off heat and stir, then allow to cook in own steam for further 30 minutes. Serve hot.

Basic burghul:

Serves 4
4 Tbsp. butter
1 cup coarse burghul, rinsed
2 ¼ cups water
½ tsp. salt
¼ tsp. pepper

In a frying pan, melt the butter, then sauté burghul over medium heat for 3 minutes.

Stir in the remaining ingredients and bring to a boil, then cover and cook over medium/low heat for 20 minutes. Shut off heat and stir, then re-cover and allow to cook in own steam for a further 30 minutes. Serve as a side or main dish.

Burghul and chickpea salad:

Serves 6 to 8
½ cup medium burghul, soaked for 10 minutes in warm water, then drained by pressing water out through a strainer
2 cups cooked chickpeas
2 cups finely chopped parsley
1 cucumber 6 to 8 inches long, peeled and finely chopped
1 large tomato, diced into 1/2 inch cubes
½ cup finely chopped green onions
4 Tbsp. finely chopped fresh mint leaves
4 Tbsp. olive oil
4 Tbsp. lemon juice
¾ tsp. salt
½ tsp. pepper
⅛ tsp. cayenne

In a salad bowl, place burghul and all vegetables, then thoroughly mix and set aside.

In a small bowl, combine the remaining ingredients, then pour over the vegetables and toss just before serving.

Burghul and pineapple pudding:

Serves 8 to10
1 cup fine burghul, soaked for 10 minutes in warm water, then drained by pressing water out through a strainer
1 can crushed pineapple (19 oz. 540 ml.)
1 ½ cups milk
½ cup brown sugar
2 eggs, beaten
4 Tbsp. butter
1 tsp. vanilla
½ tsp. cinnamon

In a casserole, place all ingredients, then thoroughly mix. Bake uncovered in a 350° F preheated oven for 1 hour or until the top turns golden brown, then serve hot.

Burghul and cabbage salad:

Serves 6 to 8
½ cup medium burghul, soaked for 10 minutes in warm water, then drained by pressing water out through a strainer
3 cups finely shredded cabbage
2 medium sized tomatoes, diced into ½ inch cubes
½ cup finely chopped green onions
2 Tbsp. finely chopped fresh coriander leaves
4 Tbsp. finely chopped fresh coriander leaves
3 Tbsp. olive oil
3 Tbsp. lemon juice
1 tsp. salt
½ tsp. pepper

In a salad bowl, place burghul and all vegetables, then thoroughly mix and set aside.

In a small bowl, mix remaining ingredients, then pour over vegetables and toss just before serving.

Burghul with fish fillet:

Serves 4 to 6
5 Tbsp. butter
1 pound fish fillet (any kind), cut into 1 inch cubes
1medium sized onion, chopped
2 cloves garlic, crushed
1 cup coarse burghul, rinsed
2 ½ cups water
1 tsp. oregano
1 tsp. salt
½ tsp. pepper
¼ tsp. allspice
$^1/_8$ tsp. cayenne

In a frying pan, melt 4 tablespoons of the butter, then sauté fish cubes over medium heat for 4 to 6 minutes, turning them over once. Remove cubes, then set aside to drain.

Add the remaining 1 tablespoon of butter, then add onion and garlic and stir-fry over medium heat for 10 minutes. Add burghul, then stir-fry for a further 2 minutes. Stir in remaining ingredients and bring to boil, then place fish cubes evenly over the top and cover.

Cook over medium/low heat for 20 minutes, then shut off the heat and allow to cook in own steam for another 30 minutes. Serve hot.

Middle Eastern meat pie:

Serves 6 to 8

In the Middle East this dish is called kubbah and is considered the king of all food. It is prepared in numerous ways. However, versions of this recipe are the most common.

1 ¾ pounds lean beef or lamb
1 cup fine burghul, soaked for 10 minutes in warm water, then drained by pressing out the water through a strainer.
1 tsp. dried mint
½ tsp. allspice
½ tsp. cumin
2 cups finely chopped onions
2 tsp. salt
1 tsp. pepper
2 Tbsp. butter
4 Tbsp. pine nuts
4 Tbsp. cooking oil

Place 1 ½ pounds of the meat in a food processor and process well, then add the burghul, mint, allspice, cumin, and 1 cup of the onions, 1 ½ teaspoon of the salt and ¾ teaspoon of the pepper, then process into a paste and set aside.

In a frying pan, melt butter, then sauté remaining ground meat over medium heat for 8 minutes. Add pine nuts, and the remaining onions, salt and pepper, then stir-fry for a further 5 minutes and set aside.

Divide the paste into two equal portions, then flatten one portion evenly in a greased 8 by 10 to 13 inch pan. Spread frying pan contents evenly over top, then flatten remaining portion of paste evenly over top. Cut into about 2 by 2 inch squares, then sprinkle oil over top. Bake in a 350° F preheated oven for 40 minutes or until the pie turns golden brown, then serve hot or cold. Δ

Build a top-bar beehive

By Jarrett D. Kelly

One of the most satisfying pleasures of living the country life is meeting your own needs by your own labors. Many modern homesteaders plant a large garden, raise meat animals, and gather the morning eggs and fresh-squeezed milk. But to many, raising honeybees is not seriously considered. This is a shame, seeing how easy and rewarding it is to stock the pantry shelves with all the honey you could possibly want.

To many the idea of beekeeping includes images of numerous hive parts, tediously constructing frames then carefully installing wax foundation in those frames. Each time the beekeeper wishes to inspect his hive, he must lift off the honey supers, which can be very heavy to get the bees below. This is very disruptive to the bees and can often be painful for the beekeeper as well. There is a significant financial investment required in most cases to purchase the hives, frames, foundation, smoker, bee suit, etc. It is not difficult to spend several hundred dollars before even seeing the first bee.

There is an easier way. The modern hive most people imagine is the Langstroth style hive, designed by Rev. Lorenzo L. Langstroth of Pennsylvania in 1851. This style hive has been developed to maximize honey production for a larger profit. There is nothing wrong with this system. It is perfectly suited for commercial apiaries, but for the beekeeper with just a few hives, there is an easier way.

Before Langstroth designed his hives, bees were kept in a wide range of hives. Some were very complex and ornate, designed more for the beekeeper's pleasure than the bees themselves. The majority of them however were very simple. Straw baskets, empty crates, hollow logs and other devices were used primarily. The trouble with many of these systems is that in order to harvest the honey, the bees must be driven from their hive or killed. As you can imagine, this is a very disruptive method of beekeeping. In most areas, it is now illegal to keep bees in this way since the combs are inaccessible and cannot be properly inspected for disease.

So the beekeeper today must house their bees in hives where every comb can be examined individually. Usually this means a Langstroth hive. But another, easier option is a top-bar hive. This hive is simply an enclosure with individual bars across the top on which the bees build their comb. The bars can be lifted up and out and inspected, then replaced. There are no heavy, honey-laden supers to be lifted and moved. Bees in a top-bar hive are typically more mild-mannered. Honey production is usually lower than in a Langstroth hive, but a couple of hives can easily produce enough honey for the beekeeper and all his friends and neighbors.

Finished top bar beehive

Construction details

Some beekeepers choose to build their own Langstroth hives, and if you are a handy woodworker, this can be done successfully. However, there are a number of measurements that must be accurate in order for the finished hive to be easily worked. Compared to building a Langstroth hive, it is a pretty simple procedure to construct a top-bar hive.

The body of the hive is simply a sloped box. Top-bar hives have been made from an amazing variety of things. Old whiskey barrels, 55 gallon drums, packing crates, even old

Constructing the top-bar beehive

Bee's eye view of entrance

refrigerators have all been used successfully. However, most top-bar beekeepers prefer to build their own hives to their own specifications. A complete hive, ready for bees, can be made for next to nothing, using materials most likely already available on the homestead. Plywood and "one-by" lumber are the most common building materials and all dimensions given here assume ¾" thick material is being used.

To determine the size of your hives, you must first decide how long your top-bars will be. Bars are typically between 15" and 24". The shorter bars are easier to work and might prevent trouble for a novice beekeeper. Since they are shorter, there is less comb built on them, making them lighter and less prone to comb failure. Longer bars can hold more comb, but that also makes them heavier. The dimensions given here are for 19¼" bars. For shorter or longer bars, adjustments must be made.

The sides of a top-bar hive are usually slanted at an angle. This makes the top of the hive wider than the bottom. This is done to minimize the amount of attachments the bees make to the sides of the hive. A colony of bees will build comb on the top and sides of their hives, but they don't build comb on the floor. By slanting the sides, bees tend to consider them as part of the floor and do not normally attach comb to them. There will be some attachments, but these are usually few and easily removed. A common angle for the sides is about 120°. To obtain this angle, we will cut the two ends of the hive first.

If you are using boards, you will have to put them together before marking the ends of the hive. If using plywood, simply mark the measurements and cut. Cut two of these end pieces, set one aside, and remove $1^5/_8$" from the smaller end of one. This will create an entrance for the bees when the hive is complete.

A $^3/_{16}$" wide spacer must be added to the inside face of each end in order to create the proper bee-space against the ends of the hive. Cut a piece $^3/_{16}$" x ¾" and glue it to the top edge of each end. Use a couple of small finishing nails to hold them in place as they dry, or use small spring clamps. After they are dry, trim them flush on the ends.

The bottom board is 6" wide at the bottom. This can be just a flat board, but by beveling the sides to match the

Waxing the spline

ends, a better-looking hive is created. Cut a 30° angle on both sides of the bottom. This bottom board is 48" long. This will give the bees a landing board just in front of the entrance.

Now that you have two ends and a bottom, the sides can be cut to fit. A 30° bevel can be cut into the top and bottom of the sidepieces in order to keep everything snug and tight fitting, but that is not absolutely necessary. The bees usually cover any gaps or spaces once inside, but again, a nicer looking hive can be had with a little more effort. Each face of the side should be $12^{5}/_{16}$" wide.

The number of bars you desire determines the length of the sides. Thirty-two bars is a good number for both the bees and the beekeeper. You can use more bars if you wish, but I wouldn't suggest using fewer. A healthy colony can easily fill up a hive this size, but if you make it much smaller, they might get cramped. This will cause them to stop producing honey, and could even encourage your bees to look for another home! For thirty-two bars $1^{3}/_{8}$" wide, and the $^{3}/_{16}$" spacers, the sides should be a total of $44^{9}/_{16}$" long.

The final two pieces to cut are used to prevent the top-bars from sliding out of position. These can be cut a little longer than the hive and used for handles if you wish. For this hive, I have used 2" wide strips of ¾" plywood 56" long.

Now it is time to put it all together. Using screws or nails, attach the sides to the ends. They should fit just under the $^{3}/_{16}$" spacers on the ends, leaving a ¾" space for the bottom. Use just four screws to attach the back end. This will allow you to open the entire back of the hive if you need to in the future. When the sides are attached, fit the bottom board on so that it butts against the back end, leaving a 'porch' in front of the entrance for the bees to land on before entering. The last step here is to attach the handles to the outside and flush with the top of the end pieces. Leave an equal length beyond each end piece to use as handles. Make sure these are securely attached; they might have to bear the entire weight of a hive full of bees and honey! That's all there is to it.

Top bar with brood comb

The top-bars

Bees naturally build their comb with enough space between them to allow them to work. In order to lift the combs out easily and inspect them, you want the bees to build the combs in the center of your bars so you're not lifting two sections of comb with one bar, or vice-versa. A width of $1^{3}/_{8}$" gives the bees sufficient space and makes inspecting the combs easier on the beekeeper. The hive in these diagrams uses 32 bars, $1^{3}/_{8}$" wide. These are easily ripped

Hive body with completed roof frame

Covering the roof

from "one-by" lumber to the correct width. With just a little more work, the bars can be cut from 2x4" studs 8' long: two studs will give you 32 bars. Some beekeepers with more experience make the brood area and the honey storage area different widths, but $1^3/_8$" is suitable for both, and I find it easier to keep everything the same dimensions.

Unfortunately, just putting a bar on top will not necessarily lead them to build in the center of the bar. For this reason, a guide of some sort is usually built into the top-bar. A saw kerf can be cut down the exact center of the bar, and a thin wooden spline glued in the groove. The spline should be about ¼" high and about 16" long. If the spline extends all the way to the sides of the hive, the bees will attach them to the hive, making managing the hive more difficult.

The spline should be brushed or dipped in melted beeswax to encourage the bees to center their comb. Be careful not to spill the melted wax where you don't want the bees to build comb. They seem to follow the scent of the wax and build wherever it is. These bars are the most complicated part of the hive, and must be done correctly—this the where the bees will attach their combs.

Lay the bars on top of the hive. They should fit in a recess and should not move too easily. If the last bar is too tight, simply tap a few times on the inside of the end boards to make just a little more room. You don't want them sliding back and forth, but you don't want them wedged in tight either.

Topping it off

You will need a lid to cover the hive. You can use the minimalist approach and use just a piece of plywood big enough to cover, or a piece of tin. These will work amazingly well for their simplicity. However, you've gone this far to build a beautiful home for your bees, and with just a little more trouble you can top it off with style. We have built a peaked roof for several reasons. Firstly, a peaked roof sheds rainwater easily. Secondly, the air space between the tops of the bars and the bottom of the roof helps to regulate the temperature of the hive below. Thirdly, I think it just looks better.

It is an easy matter to construct the roof's framework. Cut two gable ends. [See figure 6] Cut four pieces of lumber 46¼" long and 3" wide and attach these to the gable ends. Two should form the peak and the other two should be attached to form the eaves (see photo of completed roof frame). A brace should be cut with the same angle as the peak and attached in the middle for extra support. The ends of this frame should rest lightly on the hive. This roof can be covered with tin, cedar shakes, or any other roofing material available, however it is not advised to use asphalt shingles, as these will make an extremely heavy roof. The only critical requirement for the roof covering is that it needs to be light in color; using a dark roof might cause the hive to overheat in the summer sun.

We have used pieces of ¾" thick lumber to make the roof. These have been cut 13" long to allow for a short overhang. Twelve pieces $4^{1}/_{8}$" wide for each side fit perfectly. The corners have been dog-eared to spruce up what would be an otherwise plain roof. Tarpaper is used under these 'shingles' to prevent water from seeping through the cracks into the hive below. Two strips cut at a 30° angle are attached to the top to finish off the roof. [See figure 8] The entire roof is then painted to match the hive body.

A couple of holes drilled in the gable ends and covered with screening will allow ventilation and keep the "attic space" from overheating. In cold weather, an old pillow stuffed under the roof will help insulate the hive.

The finishing touches

A coat of good exterior paint will make the hive last much longer than leaving it unfinished. It is important to use a light color to reflect the sun's heat. White is traditional, but not required. It is possible here to let your creativity shine! It is not recommended to paint the interior of the hive; leave the inside unfinished.

The entrance to the hive should be ¾" high by about 6" long. This is perfect for a strong colony, but might bee too large for a new swarm or

Hive schematics

Hive front and back

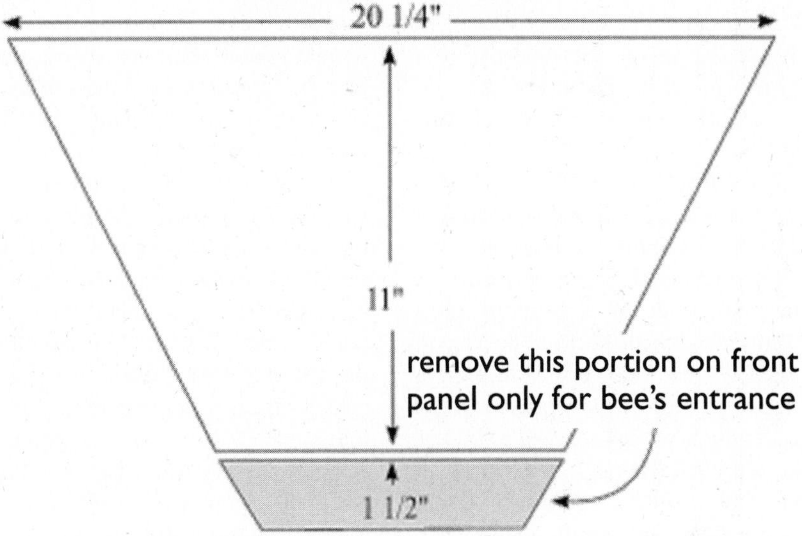

Top-Bar Details

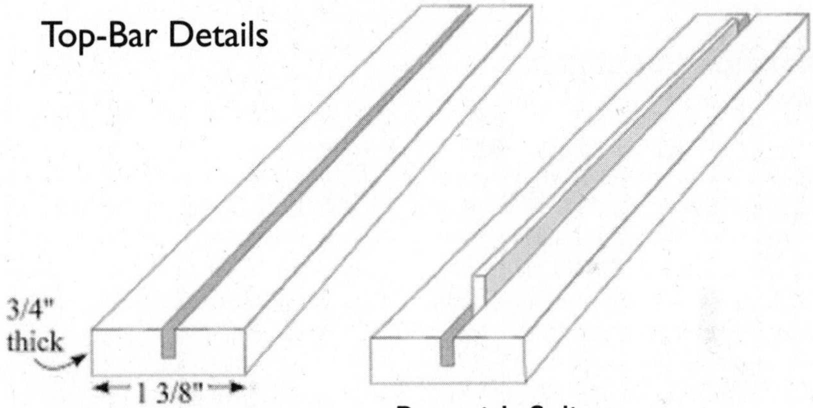

Bar with Saw Kerf

Bar with Spline

Roof Gable Dimensions

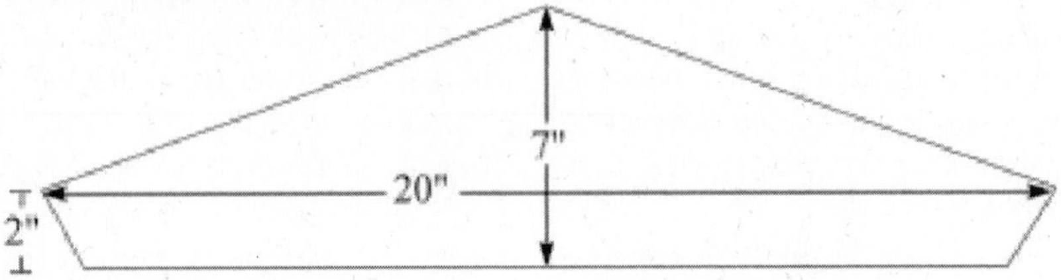

Entrance Reducer

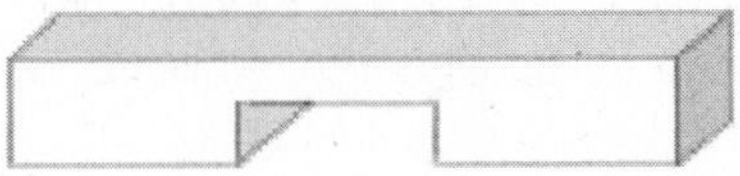

Additional resources:
Beekeeping for Dummies by Howland Blackiston
ABC and XYZ of Bee Culture by A.I. Root
Internet Resources:
Beesource - www.beesource.com

purchased package to defend. It is a good idea to make an entrance reducer to fit in this opening. A piece ¾" x ¾" x 7" long with an opening about 2" long and ½" high fits perfect. [See figure 9] After the hive gains strength, this reducer can be removed, giving the bees the full entrance.

Sometimes, it is helpful to temporarily make the hive smaller for the bees, or to divide the hive into two compartments. It is not necessary in the beginning, but as you get more experienced with keeping bees, you might want a follower board. This is simply a piece of plywood, cut to fit inside the hive and attached to one of the top bars. This can be inserted in place of one of the top bars. It should fit the sides and bottom of the hive snugly to prevent bees from moving around it.

Managing the top-bar hive

Ideally, the hive should be placed in an area that receives sun in the morning and shade in the heat of the day. A stand can be built to raise the hive off the ground. This will also bring the bars up to a more comfortable working level. For our hive, a post was buried in the ground and cut off at a comfortable height. A platform was attached to this post with braces for added support. The hive can be screwed in place from underneath the stand to prevent it from accidentally falling over, yet it can still easily be removed in case a move becomes necessary. A top-bar hive is top-heavy and a sturdy stand to prevent it from falling is crucial.

In many places where top-bar hives are traditional, they are hung from a sturdy overhanging limb. Eyebolts can be attached to the hive, two per end, and a strong chain used to hang it. Whether hanging, or building a stand, it is crucial that the bars be level. Bees use their sense of gravity to build their combs level and a tilted hive will be harder to manage.

Once the bees are installed in the hive, management is pretty straightforward. Bees in a top-bar hive will normally build their brood nest at the front of the hive near the entrance, and store their honey behind that. The most important task early on is to make sure the combs are being built straight. They should be built along the wax-coated splines. You should be able to gently lift the bars straight up and out to inspect them. If they are not straight, you will likely damage them trying to pull them out. Simply pushing them into shape is usually all that is needed to correct a problem early on. If you find that they have attached a comb to the side, you can easily cut it loose with a sharp, serrated knife. You want to cut from the bottom of the attachment up. Cutting down or sideways might tear the comb off of the bar. New comb is very delicate and soft and can easily be broken.

Since the entire weight of the comb is supported by the top-bar only, not having a frame surrounding the entire comb, you want to be very careful with them, especially when they are fresh. You cannot twist a comb or lay it flat—it will break from the bar. Beginning top-bar beekeepers will probably break off a few combs as they get accustomed to working them. If it is a good-sized comb with brood in it, you can try to tie it back on the bar with wide shoelaces. The bees should reattach it to the bar and repair any damage. If it is small or filled primarily with nectar or honey, eat it. It is amazing how fast bees can make new combs. Taking your time and being gentle is of utmost importance with a top-bar hive.

The reason for it all

All of this is done so that the bees will be comfortable and safe in their new home. A colony of bees will gladly show their appreciation by providing you with a bountiful harvest of golden honey. Depending on your preferences, you can harvest comb honey, or liquid honey.

The simplest method of harvesting your honey is to take comb honey. Pull out the bars of honeycomb and cut out good, clean sections that will fit whatever container you choose to store your honey. You can then replace the bars or use the rest of the comb for liquid honey. If you replace the bars, the bees will quickly repair the cut section and use the remaining honey for their winter stores.

Harvesting liquid honey is little more than pulling out the bars with honeycomb, brushing off the bees, and cutting the comb off, leaving about ½" on the bar. This comb is dropped into a clean bucket then crushed thoroughly. This crushing releases the honey from the comb. The crushed comb and liquid honey should now be strained and poured into jars. The now empty bars are placed back in the hive for the next harvest.

The wax can then be melted very slowly to remove a little more honey. This will separate from the melted wax and can easily be poured off. The wax can then be cleaned. Good quality beeswax is a valuable crop, sometimes bringing more per pound than the honey. It might be possible to find a buyer for your beeswax. Or you could use it for countless other projects, maybe constructing another top-bar hive.

There are many aspects to keeping bees that are not mentioned here. These are not difficult, but they are necessary. A good understanding of beekeeping is necessary to keep your bees healthy and productive. There are a number of good books and websites available on the subject. Δ

Frostbite

Don't flirt with this sneaky danger

By Tom and Joanne O'Toole

Frostbite can be defined, in its most severe stage, as when your fingers and toes freeze and have to be cut off because of gangrene. Wow, talk about drastic. Well, this *is* the extreme, but it can happen.

Being frostbitten is serious and can happen even when the actual temperature is above freezing. Wind chill or rapid movement through cold air (skiing, snowmobiling, and the like) can create a freezing effect on exposed skin, and the result is frostbite.

This condition occurs when body tissue is injured by exposure to intense cold for a period of time, and circulation slows or stops. Usually the fingers, toes, and ears are first affected, but the nose, cheeks, hands, and feet are also susceptible to frostbite. This is accelerated if the body parts are wet (or even moist) and nothing is done to re-warm them and restore circulation.

If the condition is allowed to persist for any length of time, ice crystals can actually form in the cells of the tissue.

At the first sign of this condition, get out of the cold, drink something hot, and slowly warm the affected areas with tepid (not hot) water. Frostbitten flesh should *not* be rubbed, as was the suggestion in the past. However, in order to improve the circulation, the temperature of the affected tissue must rise.

In severe cases of frostbite, victims will develop blisters on the frostbitten areas. Do not break the blisters. In this state, the skin will probably appear gray or white, and the need for medical assistance is immediate. Gangrene can result. This is when a victim has the potential of irreversible damage that can lead to amputation.

In the case of severe frostbite, the "immersion method" of treatment is the most effective. Place the affected extremity in water maintained at slightly more than 100 degrees Fahrenheit. This should continue until the affected area is completely thawed and normal color returns. The thawing period will usually bring teeth-clenching pain and severe tingling. However, elevating the affected area can help reduce these sensations until the circulation has been restored.

The sooner the warming process is started for a frostbite victim, the less chance of permanent damage being done. Actually, as soon as any frostbite symptom occurs, seek medical attention if at all possible.

Of course, this is easier said than done if you are out in the elements. That's when you seek cover under an evergreen tree and build a warming fire.

For any of us who might have had a mild case of frostbite to the ears and fingers—at any time in our lives—the burning and itching sensations have a tendency to recur when these same areas are again subjected to the cold (or even heat). Ear and finger exposure to intense cold is painful (we speak from experience).

There are more or less three stages of frostbite. The first is a redness of the skin, along with pain and a stinging sensation. The second is when numbness sets in. The last and most dangerous stage is when the tissue itself begins to freeze.

You don't avoid frostbite; you prevent it. Common sense is the key. Frostbite should not be taken lightly.

Layer your winter clothing, and make sure your ears are covered. You can work wonders with ear muffs and a scarf. In below-freezing weather, shield your cheeks and nose as well.

To protect your fingers, make sure you have good gloves or mittens. The tips of the fingers are usually the first to feel the burning sensation of frostbite.

Warm, dry socks are needed to insulate your toes and feet, and make sure your footwear is waterproof.

When selecting your clothing, remember wool is the only fabric that keeps you warm even when it's wet.

Whenever venturing into situations where the danger of cold and frostbite exists, there are four essential items to bring along: Always carry an extra pair of gloves, an extra pair of warm socks, a ski mask, and a supply of waterproof matches or a dependable lighter. Building a warming fire could save a life. These items could be invaluable in staving off the possibility of frostbite if you find yourself in the wrong outdoor situation.

However, a little hot chocolate on a wintry day might be a good idea even if you aren't suffering frostbite. Δ

Starting over part 7

By Jackie Clay

Summer has been a little crazy here on our new homestead, but rewarding nevertheless. The first wild geese are arriving from the north and the white tailed deer fawns are losing their spots. It seems like spring was just yesterday, but I guess that's how it gets when you are busy.

With me undergoing radiation and chemotherapy in Hibbing, nearly 30 miles away, (all for a pea sized bump on my elbow), it seemed like I was getting nothing done. My mind was tearing away with things to get done and my body was saying, "Go away, I want to lie down!" I couldn't believe I was taking two long naps every day.

But with my son, David, pitching in on a lot of my chores and other work, friends (especially Tom, the carpenter who I hired to help on the house one afternoon a week), and my son, Bill, coming up weekends, things have progressed.

Bill has been established on his homestead for over five years now, and having built a big, gorgeous log home, he's been there, done that, and has accumulated a lot of

Bill takes Donny's crawler down through the front yard.

Tom begins laying the floor.

necessary tools and equipment, not to mention experience.

Early this summer, not only did Bill show up one Sunday morning, but he also brought his father-in-law, Donny. And behind Bill's truck was a flatbed trailer hauling Donny's little John Deere dozer. Our new log home was in severe need of backfilling so we could safely get in and out, without walking a plank over an 8-foot deep, 10-foot wide "moat," and Donny had volunteered to bring his crawler and help Bill fill the moat and grade the yard.

With time out for lunch and very few breaks, they changed our new, rough yard into something we can work with. The 12-foot high mountains of gravel turned into a gently sloping front yard. With Bill on his Ford tractor and Donny on his crawler, they pushed dirt, graded, and designed. I could only sit on our four-wheeler, with my chin on the handle bars, watching and answering questions as they came up. Finally, Donny's back gave out (he'd had surgery last winter), and Bill jumped on the crawler and David took over the tractor, using the back blade to help grade the yard.

Donny is an artist with his crawler and likes things nice, so after a break for his back he mounted up again. By late afternoon they had graded an entrance for a walk-in basement, a level front and side yard, and the moat was only a memory. Now it was easy to get into the house to work on the inside. Thanks guys.

Work begins inside

Because I was so tired from my treatments, I couldn't handle a hammer or a saw, so my job was trying to keep things flowing. Tom came every Saturday afternoon to do his carpentry magic, so I tried to keep ahead of him, rounding up materials he would need, making sure the generator was full of gas and at the house before he came, and making plans for what I needed him to do most.

Because he is more experienced at building than I am, many of my plans were tentative and changed as the day progressed. One of these was the use of some 3x10-inch beams Tom found at a local sawmill to use as floor joists for the upstairs. Logs would have cost three times as much and these huge beams were rough sawn, strong, and fit in with our logs just right.

After framing the walls downstairs with rough cut lumber, Tom began fitting the beams into the logs. All the time we were building, we had to keep in mind the settling of the log walls. Every time you build with logs, no matter how dry they are, they *will* settle.

We were told to expect from two to three inches of settling in our log walls, so Tom couldn't simply spike the partition walls to the logs. Two options were to cut a notch into the log walls to receive a 2x4, which will let the logs slip down it as they settle, or to cut slots in the upright 2x6 that framed the partition wall so the spikes could slip downward as the logs settled, yet keep the wall in place. We chose this second option.

Likewise, Tom knew the log walls would settle, so initially the beams were set two inches high on the outside walls, which would keep the floor level as the house settled.

To set the beams into the wall, he and David snapped a chalk line from one corner of the house to the other, marking where the bottom of the notches to receive the beams would be. Then Tom marked out the sides and top of the hole and cut the sides with a carefully held circular saw. Using a three-inch hole bore, he drilled out a set of three or four holes. In a few minutes, working with hammer and chisel, he had a perfect notch.

They were so tight in most cases that he and David had to use a maul and block of wood (to protect the end of the beam) to drive the beam into the log.

The other end of the beam rested on a stoutly constructed 2x6-inch bearing wall, with the beams coming directly over upright studs.

One Saturday they got half of the house done, and the next, they nearly finished. It was slower the second

Saturday because they had to frame around the stairwell to the upstairs.

The next Saturday afternoon, Tom finished our beams and he and David constructed the stairs going up to the bedrooms. The treads were made of the old planks we had used to walk across our "moat." They were cracked, but Tom suggested temporary treads until the construction phase was past because the stairway is the first thing you see when you enter the house, and he didn't want them all dinged and scratched.

As it turned out, this was a good idea because all the tools and materials going up and down those stairs did result in dropped boards and many dents in the treads. When we finish, we'll replace the treads with nicer lumber.

During that week, Tom ordered the lumber for our upstairs floor. I chose to go with 2x6-inch tongue and groove spruce, planed on both sides. It was relatively expensive, but it would allow us to use the underneath as a ceiling in the downstairs rooms and the finished floor for the upstairs bedrooms for David and me. There would be no additional costs for drywall ceilings downstairs or flooring and underlayment for the upstairs. This ended up to be cheaper by far than doing it the "traditional" way, using rough-cut 1-inch lumber or plywood. Neither of these is cheap today. An added bonus is that because the 2x6s are tongue and groove, it stiffens up a floor quite a bit. It looks great, too.

It was an exciting day when we came home to find that the lumber truck had been here and the delivery men had stacked the piles of lumber neatly upstairs, where they were going to be used. This was a huge labor saver for us, and there was no extra charge.

When Saturday rolled around, Tom showed up with his huge red work truck full of tools and began hauling out saws, power miters and air nailer, etc. Slowly at first (it is hard working with no room at the eaves), but faster and faster, the flooring was laid. The lumber was in 14-foot and 16-foot lengths. Tom varied the cuts to save every inch of material he could, and staggered the butt joints so that no adjoining runs of flooring had butts on the same floor joist. This makes a stronger and much more attractive job.

David caught grazing in the tomatoes

I had always nailed tongue and groove lumber by hand and was amazed at how fast a job Tom's air nailer did. I learned a neat trick, too. Inevitably, you get a bowed piece of flooring. I had always nailed a block onto the floor joist and used a pry bar to force it into place so it could be nailed. Tom has a better way. He cut a five inch or so scrap of 2x6-inch flooring on a diagonal. One piece he nailed with several nails to the floor joist, a few inches from the last board, then he set the loose wedge into the space and drove it in with his hammer, firmly securing the floor board into place. Then, with two hands free, he could take his time and nail the flooring into place. It only took him a few seconds to drive the temporary wedge out and remove the nailed mate. Of course, he saved this and reused it, time after time.

The first day he laid two thirds of the flooring. It took more cutting and fitting around the stairwell. I can't tell you how nice it looks, and what a boost it gave to our sense of "home."

David and I sat out there the next day, enjoying the view from the gable end that was still open and unsheeted, planning how the bedrooms would go.

The next weekend when Tom showed up, I mentioned I couldn't wait to install two windows I picked up for the gable ends. (This end faces west, where our wind and rain usually come from.) Currently the window openings were covered over with the Green Guard wrap that also protected the wafer board on the gable end.

In less than half an hour, he and David had the windows carried up, unwrapped, and installed.

And on they went with the flooring. David was the generator man. When Tom needed power for the saw, it was "David! Power!" and David would dash down and crank over the generator. Tom would measure and saw a pile of flooring and then tell David to "Kill it!" This saved gas, and made it much nicer to work in quiet.

With the floor finally done and the windows in one end, we could see the light at the end of the tunnel. With a lot of hard work, we just might be able to get moved into our new house by this winter.

Tom and David continued working Saturday afternoons and got the east gable end framed and sheeted. I was able to pick up three Marvin windows at the local lumber yard for half price. I can only afford to buy a window or two a month, but slowly, slowly, the windows are stacking up and going in.

My son, Bill, said that when Tom finished the partition walls upstairs and the east gable end, he would come up and run the wiring. (He learned this skill by reading and re-reading a book on wiring, then wired his entire log home. Yes, it passed inspection.) So for three Saturdays, Tom and David worked at framing in the upstairs knee walls, closets, partition walls, and door openings. Time and again, Tom or I had neat ideas and we changed our initial plans, gaining storage, ease of flow, and useable floor space. It's a small house, but will live big. (I keep looking for ideas in log home magazines and am horrified at the size of most of them. Who needs a 7,000 square foot log home to visit for a few weeks a year? I sure don't want to clean four bathrooms.)

My dad's 94th birthday fell on August 16 and my nephew, Sean's, was the day before, so we planned a big birthday party in the new house. Bill and Kelly came up on the Sunday before, bearing bags of junction and receptacle boxes, coils of wiring, and tools, not to mention a small gas grill, food, and birthday presents. The week before, Bill had instructed David to pre-drill holes in the upright studs to thread the wiring through, so the wiring would go quickly.

A rare Hopi Pale Grey squash growing in our house garden

We took Mom and Dad in wheelchairs out to the house, and Bill and David carried them up the temporary steps and gave them the tour, even upstairs in the bedrooms. Then he set up his handy little grill and grilled the best hot dogs I've ever eaten.

My sister, Sue, and her son, Sean, were coming up the next day. Unbeknownst to Dad, my youngest sister, Deb, was driving up from southern Michigan for the party. It's been several months since my parents have seen Deb, so we knew Dad would be thrilled.

After lunch, Bill and David set about running wiring. It went so fast that by the time Kelly and Bill had to go, the wiring was all finished.

We were then ready to begin sheetrocking. My not-so-favorite task. Luckily, I had finished with my radiation treatments, and finally I was able to do something.

The next day Bill caught a ride north with my sisters and nephew and again we partied, complete with cake and more presents for Dad. My youngest sister thought we were completely nuts for building a log house; she insisted we'd be better off with a modular home. It'd be easier, quicker and less work. Yes, but I hate them and would rather build something that made me feel good about it. (Remember, if your family and friends think you're crazy for trying to live your lifestyle, you're not alone.)

The garden lives

While we were building and I was going through constant treatments, the gardens got little care. In fact, some of my tomatoes were not staked until they were four feet tall—some of them never did get staked. The watering was first done by heaven, as it rained nearly every day in the spring and early summer. Then the rain stopped and we went into drought for the rest of the summer.

We have a submersible pump in our well that puts out only about 3 gallons a minute, so it won't run a sprinkler, even way downhill from the well. To water the gardens, we pump water into our big 350-gallon poly storage tank next to the well. Then we hook up our gas water pump to pump the water onto the gardens. To get one inch of water on the gardens, it takes half a tank on each one.

Because we were so busy, the lower garden didn't seem to get watered when it should; I didn't even go down there because I was so tired. Finally, I decided we'd better water it and see if we could save anything. I had visions of dead, dried potato vines, deer-eaten onions and green beans, and brown tomato plants. So we hooked up the pump and walked down the hill.

I stopped in shock, literally. The garden looked terrific and it had only been watered twice that summer, with temperatures soaring to 100 degrees. The entire garden was green and growing. I had blooming potato vines taller than knee high, nice onions, green beans knee high and wide, and tomatoes loaded with green tomatoes and blossoms. It seems the angels had been watering for me.

So we soaked the garden with 350 gallons of water and went home with a thankful heart.

The gardens have continued to grow, despite the weeds, infrequent waterings, and nibbling wildlife.

Back to canning

A neighbor gave us two "out-of-date" spiral cut store hams she had bought as part of a case load deal, as well as several packs of frozen chicken. For the first time in a year, I hauled out the huge canner, hunted up clean, empty pint canning jars, and started canning meat. It felt good to be useful again.

I cut up the best of the ham and packed it loosely into the jars, leaving an inch of headroom. The rest I either diced up or packed in large chunks to use to flavor such things as baked beans, casseroles, or soups. Then I poured boiling water over the meat to within an inch of the top of the jars. After wiping the rim clean, I put on hot, previously boiled lids and screwed down the rings firmly tight.

These jars I processed in the pressure canner for 90 minutes. Every single one sealed nicely, leaving me to do the chicken.

This was a bit fussier, as I first boiled the chicken to get it off the bone. When it was cool, I de-boned all the chicken thighs, drumsticks, and wings. The bones and skin I put back into the stew pot with the broth to reboil. I added more water and seasonings: salt, celery seed, sage, powdered onion, and black pepper. While I cut and packed the chicken in pint and half-pint jars, I simmered the bones, skin, and miscellaneous discarded chicken. When all the jars were packed to within an inch of the top, I poured the broth through a strainer and discarded the bone pile into a dog-proof container to go in the trash. I dipped the broth out and filled each jar to within an inch of the top, then carefully wiped each jar rim. Chicken broth contains fat, which sometimes prevents lids from sealing.

Then, like the ham, I put hot, previously boiled lids on the jars and screwed the lids down snugly. The leftover broth was poured in the jars plain and the jars sealed as above. I processed the jars for 75 minutes at 10 pounds pressure.

All in all, I ended up with 36 ham meals and 18 chicken meals. This includes jars that were pint or half pint. Sometimes you only need a little meat for flavoring, and other times you need more as a major ingredient in a meal.

Two weeks later David and I picked our first string beans to put up. I

David is happy with our first crop of green beans in the neglected big garden.

planted several types of beans and we picked yellow Romano, green Romano, and Provider, ending up with a huge basketful to can. In fact, there were about three times more than I thought we'd have.

I love doing green beans, as they are so easy to can, and they quickly fill the jars with one vegetable that just about everyone in the world loves.

I sat on the sofa and cut off the stem ends and cut the beans into a big bowl. The work went fast, as the beans were so good—we'd only just picked them minutes ago.

When I was done, I set jar lids to boil, as well as a saucepan full of water to boil to pour on the beans in the jars. While this was going on, I filled the jars of beans to within an inch of the top, packing them down tightly. Raw packed fruits and vegetables float, leaving juice or water on the bottom of the jar; I could avoid this by hot packing them, but the raw pack is faster and I just wanted to get them put up.

By this time, the water was boiling in both pans; I turned off the jar lid pan's heat and began dipping water out of the pot to pour over the beans. (I added a teaspoonful of salt to each jar to enhance the flavor. It is not necessary.) Each jar was filled to within an inch of the top with water, then the rims wiped clean.

Sealing the jars was easier still. A hot lid was placed on each jar and I screwed down the rings fairly tightly. They were processed in the canner for 20 minutes at 10 pounds pressure. The time seemed to fly and they were done. Our first batch of Minnesota-grown green beans amounted to a dozen pints—a great start, and the garden is only getting better.

Right now, I have another batch of beans ready to put up, more than a bushel of tomatoes, red-ripe and luscious on the vines, and the potatoes...oh my! Just yesterday, David and I pulled back the straw from our Yukon gold potatoes to peek, and looking back at us was a fist-sized yellow-gold potato all clean and shiny. And the vines have not even started to die down. We should have a terrific crop of 'taters to store in our new root cellar under the stairs of the new house.

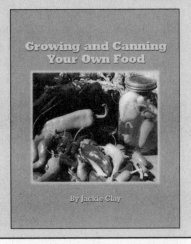

After a spring and summer of pain and exhaustion, things are definitely looking up. But that's the way life is—continuous cycles of hard and easy, joy and sorrow. I can honestly say that I'm glad we're finally on the upswing now. I'm ready to walk the wooded paths and delight in nature again. Δ

Ask Jackie

Jackie Clay

If you have a question about rural living, send it in to Jackie Clay and she'll try to answer it. Address your letter to *Ask Jackie*, PO Box 712, Gold Beach, OR 97444. Questions will only be answered in this column. — Editor

Finding wild rice seeds

I would like to know where to get wild rice seeds. Can I obtain them from a natural food store?

Norm
jmcgrogan@tlb.sympatico.ca

The only wild rice you can plant is raw, natural wild rice. The wild rice you buy in stores, even natural food stores, is parched before storing or eating. This kills the seeds' ability to germinate.

Some sources of wild rice: Triple Brook Farm, 37 Middle Rd., South Hampton, MA 01073 or www.triplebrookfarm.com; Natural Food Institute, P.O. Box 185, WMB, Dudley, MA 01570; and Wildlife Nurseries, (920) 231-3780, or P.O. Box 2724, Oshkosh, WI 54902.

— Jackie

Growing great tomatoes

I hate the "low acid" red fruit they pass off as tomatoes nowadays. They all taste like they were picked way too early or are hot house raised. I heard there is something you can add to the soil to give them some punch. Any idea what it is? Also, raising tomatoes here in Texas can be a challenge. Any hints on what to do to insure a good harvest?

Nancy Blevins
Mesquite, Texas

You don't have to add some magic ingredient to your soil to get tomatoes that taste like tomatoes should. Just buy tomato seed from some of the older varieties that are high in acid. If you want to drive yourself nuts, send for a catalog from Totally Tomatoes, Pinetree Garden Seeds, Baker Creek Heirloom Seeds, or Tomato Growers' Supply. These companies list literally hundreds of tomatoes, including dozens of older, heritage tomatoes that do, indeed, taste great.

The addresses for these companies are: Totally Tomatoes, 334 West Stroud Street, Randolph, WI 53956; Tomato Growers Supply Company, P.O. Box 60015, Ft. Myers, FL 33906; Baker Creek Heirloom Seeds, 2278 Baker Creek Rd., Mansfield, MO 65704; Pinetree Garden Seeds, P.O. Box 300, New Gloucester, ME 04260.

It really makes a huge difference when you choose and grow your own varieties, instead of buying whatever tomato plants are available at the local garden centers and stores. These are often just so-so varieties, not suited well to the home gardens in your own area.

Start your seeds 12 weeks or more before it is safe to set them in the garden, unprotected from frost and cold winds. Then set them out even a month before your last spring frost is due, under the protection of Wall'o Waters (www.wallowater.com, 801-972-1770). These are water-filled tubes, connected to make a plastic tipi to surround your baby plants. Not only do they protect against frost and freezing, but also wind, which is hard on tender plants in much of Texas and the rest of the southwest. I gardened in New Mexico for six years and have a healthy respect for the hardship wind has on garden plants.

Once your plants are in, be sure to mulch them well to conserve soil moisture and provide protection against weeds. If you mulch with straw first, then top it off after the plants begin to set fruit with well rotted manure, you will also provide natural fertilizer when the plants need it most. Don't fertilize too much, though, before they set fruit or the plants will grow huge and will produce poorly. Nitrogen boosts plant growth.

If garden dryness is a problem in your area, consider using a drip irrigation system. This is easy to fashion, sort of like playing with Tinker Toys. It conserves water while giving each plant enough water to grow and produce well. If you water using the usual overhead sprinklers, the plants are often sheltering the soil beneath them, keeping the roots dry while the leaves are soaking.

You *can* grow great tasting tomatoes at home that will bring back memories of Grandma's garden, no matter where you live.

— Jackie

Tomato sauce disaster

I just wanted to make some tomato sauce. I have a Victorio food mill, and I ran a bunch of my tomatoes through it, mostly Romas. I got about a gallon of juice/pulp. I cooked it down to about 2½ quarts and added

an onion, garlic, some basil, and about a tablespoon of sugar. I put it in the fridge in a plastic bowl for 2 days, then got it out to use to go over some ravioli for dinner. I tasted it and it was so acidic it about ate my taste buds off! So, I got a bright idea, and decided to neutralize some of that acid and stirred in a tablespoon or so of baking soda. The chemical reaction was stunning. I hurriedly transferred the expanding pink froth to a bigger pot; after stirring about 45 minutes, it was sauce again. I went for a taste and about spit it out. It was sweeter than syrup. I had to throw all my work into the compost pile, and a swarm of flies followed me the whole way. Why was my sauce so inedibly acidic? What does one do to reduce the acidity without totally removing it?

Also, I heard that you can't get parts for my food mill anymore. Is this true? It's a model 200 I bought new in 1995.

Debbie Trimble
Silex, Missouri

I have to chuckle. Here you have trouble with tomatoes that taste *too* acid, where Nancy, in the previous letter, can't get tomatoes that are acid enough. But all aside, this is perfectly common. Tomatoes *should* be acid. But for your tastebuds' sake, let's find out what to do about your tomato sauce so you can enjoy it. First of all, did you boil down your sauce in an aluminum or cast iron pot? Both of these will make a tomato sauce that is terribly metallic in taste, which tastes acid to the max. Cook it down in a stainless steel or heavy enameled pot.

Then when you season it for your sauce, add your spices and enough brown sugar for your family's taste. (A tablespoon of sugar in 2½ quarts probably won't be enough.) Taste it as you go. I'd guess you'd want about two tablespoons or possibly more. You can use the baking soda, but use much less than you did before. Half a teaspoonful is about right for your 2½ quarts. However, some people don't like the taste of this sauce as much as they do that with sugar added.

I don't think getting parts for your Victorio Strainer is much of a problem. They are still sold in current catalogs, including the different screens available for them. I would write to the company if you need a certain part. I've had mine for 15 years' worth of hard use, and never needed a single part; they are pretty sturdy.

— Jackie

Canning tomato sauce

I tried using a vacuum sealer for a batch of sauce I made. What a mistake. It didn't seal tight enough and of course I had to throw it all out. How long do you need to 'bath' the larger [24 oz] jars? I've never tried doing my sauce but I would like to avoid using so much freezer space.

Sharon Baker
Surprise, Arizona

Canning tomato sauce is so easy. I can't imagine doing anything else with it. And once it's canned, it lasts for years right on your pantry shelf with no more fuss.

To can your sauce, simply pour your seasoned sauce (taste it first!) into warm, clean quart jars, wipe the rim of the jar clean with a warm, damp cloth, then place hot, previously boiled new lids on the jars, tightening down the rings firmly tight. Process them in a boiling water bath canner, with the water at least an inch over the tops of the jars for 40 minutes, unless you live at an altitude which requires longer processing. Check your canning manual for instructions if you live at an altitude over 1,000 feet above sea level.

When the time is up, remove the jars from the canner and place on a dry folded bath towel to cool. *Do not* touch the jars until they are cool. Do not re-tighten the rings, poke at the center of the lids, or wipe off anything from the jar tops until they are cool to the touch. When they are cool, usually overnight or for several hours, you may remove the rings and wash the jars to remove any sticky or mineral residue from your boiling water. This will not cause them to unseal. You remove the rings, because they can sometimes cause the lids to rust.

— Jackie

Canning smoked salmon

I don't have a smoker to smoke my salmon, however I want the smoked flavor and was wondering if I could just add liquid smoke to my fresh salmon that I want to can? If I can do this how much would I add to a pint jar?

Any information on how to can salmon would be very helpful to me.

Beulah Fern
Lostine, Oregon

No, this will not give you the results you want. The liquid smoke might (or might not!) give you the flavor you want, but it won't give you the dry texture you will crave in your faux smoked salmon. If you can't afford a smoker (and they are getting cheaper and cheaper), you can simply build your own out of any container that will hold smoke. I built mine out of an old clothes dryer cabinet.

A simple rack can be fashioned out of wires strung across the inside top of the metal cabinet, barrel, or whatever your "smoker cabinet" consists of. You can hang pieces of fish on heavy wire hooks or lay them across the wires to smoke.

My smoking unit consisted of an old hot plate with an old cast iron frying pan on top of it. I set it on low and tossed a couple handfuls of hardwood chips in the frying pan and shut the door. You can use fruit wood, such as apple, cherry, or pear, if you have it, or whatever local wood is available from mesquite to birch or alder.

You will have to keep adding the wood chips as they char away. You don't want a hot smoke, only a smoky smoke.

— Jackie

Don't use a water bath to can green beans

I am in dire need of a good recipe for canning green beans using the hot bath method. Someone has given me green beans and I really need a good recipe.

Maxine Reed
Lakeland, Tennessee

Sorry, Maxine, you cannot *safely* can beans in a hot water bath canner unless they are pickled. Beans are low acid, as are all vegetables, meat, and fish. Because they are a low acid food, this means that under certain conditions, dangerous bacteria such as Clostridium botulinum could be canned right along with your beans. This bacteria grows everywhere, from your soil to your countertops.

The spores, which are the dormant form of this bacteria, are not deadly, but when they are canned with your water bathed beans they are not killed and can live to produce a very deadly toxin that is not killed at 212 degrees, which is the temperature of your boiling water bath. They *are* killed when they are subjected to the 240 degrees in your pressure canner (10 pounds pressure).

Now, I know, and have been told countless times, that folks used to water bath their green beans, and still do. This is true. But it's too dangerous to do, and I simply won't do it, nor will I advise anyone to do it either. People can go years eating water bathed beans and other low acid foods, and then suddenly hit a jar that is toxic. It's like playing Russian Roulette. I won't play; and I hope you won't either.

— Jackie

Is using railroad ties for veggie boxes safe?

The train company in my area has refurbished all of the railroad ties with new ones, so they have all their used ties available for the taking. I am interested in using railroad ties for my vegetable boxes. Are they safe to use?

Mary
mgpriemer@yahoo.com

Lucky you! I have to pay $8 a piece for my railroad ties! Yes, they're safe to use, much safer than the green, treated landscaping timbers available at building centers and stores throughout the country. Most of these treated timbers contain arsenic, which can and does leach out into your garden!

These used railroad ties are creosoted, but after years the creosote is leached and weakened. Enough is left to smell and protect them from rotting, but not enough to cause gardeners much concern. Of course it's better to use untreated materials, such as logs from the woods or cement blocks. But the ties work well. I have used them for years, not only for raised beds but to anchor hoop house bottoms and as a foundation for small buildings such as chicken houses and goat sheds.

— Jackie

Shelling and canning pecans

I have pecans—all that we want—for free. I was wondering how I can store them so that they will not go bad without freezing them. Also, can you turn these into pecan peanut butter? And if you can turn these into pecan peanut butter, can you can it? If you can put them in canning jars how would I go about it?

Glenda Gay
Hartselle, Alabama

Boy are you lucky! Pecans are *so good!* One year, while we lived in New Mexico, our neighbor lady traveled to her son's place down in the southern part of the state and came home with a burlap sack full of pecans. We spent the winter, on and off, yacking in her kitchen, cracking pecans, and picking out nutmeats. Then I brought my share home and canned them. They are really good this way, and now, six years later, they are still good, not rancid. And they are super easy to can, too.

The easiest method I've found for shelling pecans is the nifty little lever action nut cracker that is sold in many garden catalogs. My neighbor had one of these, and they really did a nice job, leaving most of the nutmeats in halves.

Once shelled, spread the nutmeats out on a cookie sheet and put them in the oven at 275 degrees. You want to toast them, but not brown them. You will stir them once or twice until they are just right. (Taste 'em!)

To can them, you fill the jars to within half an inch of the top, then place a hot, previously boiled, *dry* lid on the jars, screwing down the ring firmly tight. (Do not add water!) Process them either for 10 minutes at 5 pounds pressure in a pressure canner or 20 minutes in a water bath canner. This method works for all nutmeats that I can think of.

The pecans will keep quite a while in their shell without going rancid, so there isn't a huge rush in getting them put up.

— Jackie

A head of fresh dill

I have a few pickle recipes that call for a "head of fresh dill." I was wondering what that is. Is it the entire sprig or half. I'm making dill pickles and the recipe isn't exact as to the head of dill.

Julie Argo
Argojules@aol.com

The "head" of dill is the entire seed head of a dill plant. But this can vary with the vitality of the plant. Generally a head of dill is about three to four inches in diameter, having a bounty of green seeds. Stronger dill flavor is had by using the same size head, having dried seeds. If your plants have smaller heads, simply use more of them. I often put one of these smaller heads on the bottom of the jar and another on top, with a small dried red pepper on top of that, for zing. Good pickling!

— Jackie

Pickling garlic

I am looking for a good recipe to pickle garlic. I have searched my canning books and there isn't one recipe in any of them.

Becky Adams
Caraway, Arkasas

Simply peel the individual cloves of garlic, then soak them overnight in a brine of ½ cup salt to a gallon of cold water. Weight down the cloves so they remain under the brine. In the morning, rinse the cloves well with fresh water. To four quarts of garlic cloves, you will need 8 cups white vinegar, 2 cups sugar and ¼ cup pickling spices (optional). Tie pickling spices in a cloth bag and add to vinegar and sugar in a large pot. Bring to a boil and simmer 10 minutes.

Pack garlic cloves in sterilized, hot pint jars to within an inch of the top. Remove spice bag from simmering pot and pour boiling syrup over garlic cloves, filling to within ½" of top of jar. Wipe jar rim and place hot, previously boiled new jar lid on jar and tighten ring down firmly tight. Process in hot water bath for 10 minutes. If you like hotter garlic, you may add one or two dried hot peppers to each jar before putting the boiling syrup on.

— Jackie

Freezing okra

I live in Northern Alabama and have been planting a garden for all my life. I love canning and putting food in the freezer. I have a problem, I cannot find a way to put up okra so it does not taste like freezer burned, or can it to fry. If you could pass one on to me I would be ever so thankful. I have tried freezing it battered, whole, cooked and just about every way I can find. I guess I am no good at the okra thing. Just that my family loves it and my rugrats (grandkids) want it all year.

Janet James
Rogersville, Alabama

The best way I've found to preserve okra is to slice the young pods, then bread or batter the slices and fry them *just until* the breading is beginning to brown a light golden color. Then drain on a paper towel and place on a cookie sheet in a single layer. Put this in your freezer just until the slices are barely frozen.

Now pick off the sheet and pack into freezer bags. Zip them shut, all but for one tiny corner and roll the bag gently to get nearly all the air out, then shut the bag. When you want to use the okra, barely thaw enough to use and fry it without oil (there's enough on the okra in most cases), or with just a little. I think this tastes almost as good as fresh.

— Jackie

Powdered eggs

I have been trying to find where I can purchase powdered eggs. When I was a little girl the government gave out powdered eggs and cheese to some folks of Native American descent and some underprivileged folks. I'm sure we fell in both those categories but I was really too young to tell that my life wasn't as "normal" as anyone else's. One of my best childhood memories is my mother cooking a big breakfast after getting a new supply of powdered eggs and cheese. It was a taste that I can remember to this date. I now have grown children and would like to buy powdered eggs and let them and my grandchild have a taste.

Brenda Davis
Columbia, Tennessee

I buy powdered eggs from Emergency Essentials, a company in Utah that specializes in foods and supplies to stock up in case of emergencies. Not only do they have different types of powdered eggs, but powdered cheese, margarine, and a whole lot more. Their address is: Emergency Essentials, 362 S. Commerce Loop, Suite B. Orem, UT 84058, or www.BePrepared.com

— Jackie

Frozen yellow milk

I was wondering if you could tell me why milk turns yellow when you freeze it and back to white when it defrosts. It was a question from my seven year old.

Susan Liimatainen
sueiscorny@hotmail.com

I think it's the difference in the freezing of the butterfat in the milk. I've noticed that when you freeze skim milk, it freezes white, but if you freeze whole milk it does turn a bit yellowish, like homemade vanilla ice cream. The fat freezes at a lower temperature than does the "watery" part of the milk, like when the ice cubes in the freezer are frozen but the ice cream is a little soft. When you thaw the milk, the butterfat melts and is again part of the milk, losing the yellow color.

— Jackie

Getting lanolin from sheep

I have searched and searched online for an answer to my question. I hope that you can either answer my question or direct me to someone who

can. I have just sheared a very large sheep and he (he has been cut) had a couple of years' growth of beautiful gray wool. I would like to harvest the lanolin from this wool. How do I do it? I thought of soaking it in hot water and hopefully the lanolin would rise to the top....I'm not sure what to do and don't want to lose that valuable stuff. I enjoy your column and my prayers have been with your family since the loss of your dear husband.

Tamara Bock
Tulare, California

To extract lanolin from sheep wool, all you have to do is to boil the wool. The oil that rises to the top of the tub is lanolin. Skim it off, then reheat it to make it thin and strain it through a cheese cloth to remove impurities. You can best boil the wool in large galvanized wash tubs or half metal barrels over an outdoor fire. Some lanolin will rise from wool soaked in quite hot water, although not as much as when you boil it. When you boil wool, it sometimes shrinks and is ruined for spinning. But the wool that has been left on sheep for two years is often not clean enough for spinning because it requires a tremendous amount of work washing and carding to remove the dirt, hay chaff, and pasture seeds. So this may be a good year to make your homemade lanolin!

— Jackie

Safe canning

All of Jackie Clay's articles always say you must use a pressure canner. Me and my wife have been canning meat, vegetables, jam, you name it and have never used a pressure canner. We have canned food sitting on the shelves from three years ago that Jackie says you must pressure cook. I have hams and bacon hanging in the smoke house that I will can this fall. I can deer meat and sausage patties, cantaloupe. No pressure canner. Now I know Jackie is a good writer and I love her articles. Is she afraid of liability or was she just never told the Amish or old way.

Michael Ettinger
Beavertown, Pennsylvannia

You bet I know the old Amish (and other old-timer) way. Would I can meat, vegetables, and poultry without a pressure canner? NO WAY! Jam, pickles, tomato products, fruit and other high acid foods, of course.

No, I'm not afraid of being sued. I'm deadly afraid that one of my cherished readers might eat a jar of green beans, venison, or whatever that is seasoned with botulism toxin. It is not a common thing, especially if you boil your food for 15 minutes before you eat it, but it can kill you or one of your children.

Many of my Amish friends use a pressure canner, as well as the good old water bath for fruit and high acid foods. It only makes good sense. There is *no reason not to use the pressure canner.* It is not expensive, especially if you buy a good used one. It is easy to use. It works well. *And* it home cans food *safely.*

(Just because you've never had a house fire, would you let your kids play with matches?)

— Jackie

Canning dry milk?

I just read in BWH Issue #94 your description of how to can fresh milk. Do you know if it's possible to can reconstituted non-fat dry milk? I have ***tons*** *of it.*

Pat Crowder
Holyhoke, Colorado

I wouldn't bother reconstituting dry milk in order to can it. Canned milk is not really that good, except in cooking. The dry milk lasts a long, long time in air-tight jars or even in the original boxes and doesn't take up canning jars better used for something else. Nor do they take up much room on a pantry shelf. Maybe you need to begin using the oldest milk, in order to rotate your stock. Use it in puddings, cream pies, ice milk, and custards. You can even make cheeses out of it if you want.

— Jackie

Hopi Pale Grey squash

We had obtained some seed for Hopi Pale Grey Squash last year and planted some this spring. I must say that they certainly spread through the garden. We now have some fruits on the plants, one of which is larger than a football. Our question is when do we know when to harvest the vegetable? Would you be interested in the seeds? I would be more than happy to give you some after they are harvested and dried.

Bernadette Burch
Mechanicsburg, Pennsylvania

Because these squash are so rare, I would wait until they are as big as they will get before a frost hits and kills the vines. I would even protect the vines as long as you can to allow the squash to mature. When they are mature, most are about the size of a basketball, and the seeds will have a hard shell. I was sent some seeds by my friend Shane Murphy of Seed Dreams in California. He, too, is growing out a crop of Hopi Pale Greys for seed. I don't need seed, but very much appreciate the offer! I plan on giving any readers a few seeds from any squash that I have that reach maturity. It's a horse race now; the squash look great, but fall freezes are just around the corner!

— Jackie

Keeping kraut lighter

How can I keep my cabbage from turning brown when canning kraut? I pack into jars, add salt, water, and let that ferment for about seven days then hot water bath. The kraut is always good but turns a little dark. I enjoy all of your articles and wonder how you have time to answer ques-

tions with such a busy lifestyle (living simple is not so simple).

T. Rose
Princeton, West Virginia

Sauerkraut processed directly in the jars does tend to turn a little dark. It helps to keep the jars in a very dark place. Some folks even wrap the jars with newspaper to keep the light away. Kraut that is fermented in crocks, then canned is usually lighter in color.

Sometimes deadline comes too soon, I'll admit! Like this month, with me finishing up those nasty cancer treatments (the alternative didn't sound good to me, either), trying to get the new log house ready to move into before winter, and (finally) canning our garden like crazy. Sometimes I wish I were twins. Triplets?

— ***Jackie***

Sweet pickle relish

I would like to use some of the surplus cucumbers to make a relish. Do you have a recipe?

Wade Blevins
Elkins, Arkansas

Sure, I have a recipe for cucumber relish. Several, in fact, but here's one of my favorites.

Sweet Pickle Relish

- 8 medium cukes
- 4 medium onions
- 2 cups chopped green peppers
- 2 cups chopped red bell peppers
- ½ cup salt
- 7 cups sugar
- 2 Tbsp. celery seed
- 2 Tbsp. mustard seed
- 4 cups vinegar

Chop all vegetables and place in large bowl. Cover with salt and cold water. Let stand, covered, for two hours. Drain and rinse. Combine sugar, vinegar, and spices in a large pan and bring to a boil. Add drained vegetables and simmer 10 minutes. Pack hot relish into hot pint or half pint jars, leaving ¼ inch of head room. Remove any air bubbles by running a hot knife down inside jar. Wipe jar rim clean. Place hot, previously boiled new lid on jar and screw down the ring firmly tight. Process in hot water bath for 10 minutes. Remove quickly and cool on folded dry towel. Do not overboil.

— ***Jackie***

Canning beets

I would like to can beets without using a pressure canner, as I don't have one and would like to do some beets without pickling them.

Sharon McIntosh
Riply, New York

Sorry Sharon, you just can't safely can beets, without pickling them, in a boiling water bath canner. Like green beans (and all vegetables), beets are a low acid food and must be pressure canned in order to be safe from deadly botulism toxin. You can pick up a good used pressure canner at many yard sales, flea markets, and so on, complete with manuals in many cases. I have one I bought for $5 at the Salvation Army. It is a good idea to take the canner in to your local extension office to have the pressure gauge tested for accuracy. This is usually a free service.

— ***Jackie***

Saving pepper seeds

How do you prepare the seeds in a green pepper for planting and growing the next season?

Jerry Csokasy
Hamburg, Michigan

First of all, make sure your bell pepper is not a hybrid. Hybrids will grow a plant and usually produce fruit, but it will not be the same as the parent plant. Sometimes this is okay, and sometimes it makes for inferior vegetables.

Let your pepper ripen on the bush, which means it will turn (depending on variety) brilliant candy apple red and then slightly soften and wrinkle. When it reaches this stage, the seeds are mature. They will be large and fairly hard to the touch.

Remove the seeds and lay them out on a cookie sheet to dry, stirring them every day until they are very dry. Then dry them a couple more days. Mold is the enemy of seed savers. Any dampness remaining in the seeds and they will mold and this will end the germination ability of the seeds.

Once they are very dry, place them in an envelope and place that in a sealed container until spring. That's all there is to it. I should mention that seed saving is *fun* and addicting!

— ***Jackie***

Getting rid of loco weed

We recently took over the family ranchland. The area that should be good grazing is heavily infested with locoweed. There's probably 60+ acres of the stuff, too much to dig by hand. In with the loco is native grass, sage, and wildflowers.

We are reluctant to use chemicals to get rid of the loco, and would only want to as a last resort.

Do you have any suggestions to rid us of this evil weed? Can one keep mowing it down and it would eventually die off? We can't burn it due to the risk of forest fires. It's toxic to goats so we can't use them for weed control. If we must go chemical what would you recommend for the least long-term effects. There is a stream on the property.

Walt van Bielert and
Debbie Myers
Bailey, Colorado

Locoweed is a tough customer but it can be whipped with hard work. We had a good sized patch on our New Mexico ranch and after three years it was gone. I don't think mowing will get it. I tried and seemed to get nowhere. I finally had to resort to using a backpack sprayer loaded with Roundup. I didn't like using it, but I liked having our stock get in the loco even less. As you know, loco weed is addicting to livestock and will eventually make them sick with diarrhea and the staggers and kill them.

I divided the patch into quarters, and in the spring when the loco was getting going I began spraying the individual plants. Yes, it was a lot of work. And yes, the patch was very large. But every day I would walk the pasture, advancing on the nasty weeds.

Of course the Roundup didn't kill all the loco. I had to re-walk the pasture three times that spring, all before it began to bloom and make seed. But after the first trip, much was dead and a lot more was yellowed and unhealthy looking.

The next spring, I did it again, picking up many new-seeded young plants (which killed out on the first spraying.) There were also some not-so-healthy older plants, as well. But that did in the loco.

You can also use a mounted spray tank with booms and spray the whole works at a time from the seat of a tractor or ATV, but that will kill everything—grass, wildflowers, and all. I didn't want to do that because we lived on the high plains where it is dry and the native grasses take a long time to regrow after being totally killed out. And I do like the wildflowers.

— Jackie

Ice dams on roofs

By Tom Kovach

In areas of the country that experience cold weather and snow, ice dams, or ice buildup on roof eaves, can be a common and troublesome problem.

There can be a number of causes for ice dams. In most cases, ice dams begin inside the house when heated air leaks up into the unheated attic. In the winter, the roof above the unheated attic is cold. When warm air leaks into the unheated attic, it creates warm areas on the roof, which in turn cause the snow on the exterior of the roof to melt. The melting snow moves down the roof slope until it reaches the cold overhang, where it refreezes.

This continues, causing ice to build up along the eaves and form a dam. Eventually this dam forces the water to back up under the shingles and sometimes into the ceiling or wall inside the home. In addition to the damage to the roof, ice dams can cause structural framing members to decay, metal fasteners to corrode, and mold and mildew to form in attics and on wall surfaces.

The pathways through which heated indoor air moves into the attic are called attic bypasses. To reduce ice dams, attic bypasses should be eliminated. If a new home is being built, these attic bypasses are eliminated or prevented as the home is constructed.

Here is a list of common sources of attic bypasses that should be sealed:

- Penetrations in the building envelope for electrical and telecommunication equipment.
- All exterior joints that may be a source of air intrusion.
- Lighting fixtures, including recessed lights and wire penetrations.
- All plumbing and heating penetrations (including chimneys, flue pipes, and ducting)
- Attic hatches
- Balloon-framed walls and walls that span both heated and unheated spaces, such as in split level homes
- Dropped ceilings over bathtubs, closets and cabinets, and kitchen soffits
- Other areas where walls are not completely sealed at the attic, such as stairway walls and interior partition walls

Other common sources of attic bypasses are:

- Electrical boxes and fan housings (such as exhaust fans)
- Kneewell construction in story-and-a-half houses

Other factors can create warm roofs, including roof design. Roofs with large surface areas exposed to the sun and having small run-off areas are prone to ice buildup. A classic example is a roof with several gables or dormers. Very heavy snowfall can also create problems. A foot or more of snow on a roof, combined with warm winter temperatures, can warm the roof and result in snow melt and ice on eaves. Leaking or disconnected heating ducts that pass through the attic also can result in a warm roof.

Once you have ice dams, for any of these reasons, don't try removing the ice by chopping. This could seriously damage your roof. Instead, use a sidewalk snow melt product or roof steamer to remove the ice. If you're replacing a roof, install an ice and water membrane along the roof and valleys and perimeter. Δ

Hibernation

By Tom and Joanne O'Toole

It's an annual practice of a large cross-section of wildlife to spend part of the cold season in a semi or generally dormant state. It is often a matter of life or death. It becomes necessary to be in a state of suspended animation to pass the winter.

For the warm-blooded (those that produce their own heat), there are any number of options. Many species of birds take flight, heading south for the winter to spend the cold months where the weather is better and a food supply is plentiful.

Deer, elk, antelope, and other such animals seem to take winter in stride but change their eating habits and home ranges to survive the elements.

However, there are many other of their warm-blooded, stay-at-home brethren that escape the winter by simply sleeping it away. Of those that do this, there are basically two types: true hibernators and those that only aestivate.

Getting ready for the long sleep is an important time and animals do so instinctively. They try to put on as much fat as possible in the fall, especially the critical "brown fat." This brown fat is found across the back and shoulders of hibernating animals, close to the organs. This special fat has a certain quality that delivers fast energy to animals coming out of their snoozing state.

True hibernators undergo extreme metabolic changes when they crawl into their winter beds. Body temperature plummets dramatically, the heartbeat slows, organ activity is at a low ebb, and breathing comes almost to a standstill. There is no growth during this quiet state. Creatures in true hibernation are perhaps closer to death than they are to sleep. It would be nearly impossible to rouse some wildlife in this deep state.

Woodchucks, ground squirrels, and bats are among the true hibernators. Yet, some of these get up every few weeks for a snack and to relieve themselves.

With their life support functions turned down for the winter, hibernating animals expend very little energy, and some require no food other than what they have stored up for this annual cycle. Some studies claim hibernation helps animals live longer.

Scientists confess to still being a bit mystified by how hibernation really works. Found in the blood of hibernating animals is a special substance called HIT (Hibernation Inducement Trigger). If blood is taken from a hibernating ground squirrel in the winter and injected into an active squirrel in the spring, the active animal goes into hibernation.

How the urge to hibernate happens every fall, how HIT develops, and how other bodily functions change so dramatically is not clearly known.

By contrast, warm-blooded wildlife like bears, groundhogs, raccoons, opossums, skunks, chipmunks, and some squirrels do not hibernate in the true sense. Rather, they "aestivate," meaning they survive the winter by having a cozy den, enjoying long periods of intermittent sleep, but also being active when circumstances require it.

These "light sleepers" make it through the winter largely because they have eaten heavily during the late summer and fall, and have put on layers of body fat that become their food supply. Other creatures have a food supply stored alongside them in their dens and use it during waking periods to maintain the life-sustaining energy they need.

These creatures do breathe a little slower, and their body temperature drops a few degrees, but these winter naps are often interrupted by opportunities to forage. If you were to touch an aestivating animal (not a good idea), it would react defensively, albeit sluggish at first.

Once in their dens, most cold-blooded creatures (those whose internal temperatures are regulated by the temperature of their environment and cannot warm themselves) enter a state of dormancy in which their biological functions slow dramatically.

They enter this inactive period about the same time as the first frost and aren't seen again until the spring sun brings the promise of summer. Occasionally brief warm spells draw them out, but this can be a fatal decision.

Frogs dig deep into the muck of a pond's muddy bottom. Some frogs and turtles actually freeze in blocks of ice, and when thawed out in the spring, resume their normal activity. Some snakes slither into burrows made by others or coil up in crevices to escape the ensuing cold, while others gather in close contact in sheltered places. Insects might spend the winter under tree bark or deep beneath the leafy litter of the forest floor.

These and other cold-blooded critters that remain in a cold region in the winter have no options. They must become dormant or die.

True hibernators or not, all animals that den-up for the winter come waddling out in the spring anxious for their first real meal in a long time. Δ

The last word

Let prisoners get high on marijuana

Anyone who reads this column knows I don't think drugs should be illegal. I'm not saying I want to take them, because I don't. I'm just saying that what you want to do with your own body is your own business and not the state's nor your neighbor's. The primary reason the United States imprisons a greater proportion of its own citizens than any other is because of drug laws. Make most, if not all, drugs legal and the prisons will empty out. In fact, the price of drugs will plunge so far that you won't have to steal to buy an "eighth" of weed any more than you have to rob or burgle to buy a six-pack of beer.

Speaking of prisons, I've been watching documentaries on *The History Channel, National Geographic,* and others about American prisons and prisoners. Prisons are very violent places. I wouldn't want to be in one, not as a guard, not as an inmate. Then it suddenly dawned on me what the solution to prison violence could be: Let those who are incarcerated smoke marijuana, as in weed, pot, grass, maryjane, cannabis, etc. Let 'em smoke as much as they want. All day! Twenty years? Hey, do the time calmly. What do we care. Let 'em grow it in their cells.

What would a prison full of pot smokers be like? As many others have pointed out, when some guy's about to rob a bank, beat his wife, or steal a car, the drug he's going to take is a drink of alcohol, not a puff of pot. A puff of pot and all the plans go up in smoke. Stoners I've known want to socialize, not victimize. Inmates will be sitting around "zoning"—moving slowly, talking slowly. Many will just want to sleep.

The story of Clyde, the poker player

When I was young and playing lots of poker, drunks were tolerated in the game as long as they didn't slow it down. Drunks lost their money. But stoners? I hated them at the table. They couldn't lose their money fast enough to make up for the time they wasted. All they wanted to do was talk, socialize, or stare off into space. They couldn't focus on the business at hand. Everything slowed down. I figured in the games I ran, hands were dealt at about 20 to 30 hands per hour. More hands meant more money for me. But one stoner in the game slowed it to about seven hands an hour—one hand every 8½ minutes. It killed my hourly earnings.

One guy who frequented our game often showed up stoned. Each time the action came around to him he had to have everything explained to him again.

"Your bet, Clyde ....Clyde, your bet ...CLYDE!"

"Huh?"

"Your bet."

Who's in?"

John Silveira

I'd patiently explain to him what each player had done before him—who had checked, bet, called, folded, or raised. He'd stare at his hand for several seconds, examine his cards carefully, then he'd ask, "What's the game?"

I'd tell him.

"Who bet?"

Again, I'd go through who had checked, bet, called, folded, or raised. He'd call, then resume socializing or staring.

There'd be cards drawn, or another stud card dealt, or a community card flopped, and then the next betting round of the hand began. The action would get back to him, and I'd say, "Clyde, your bet ...Clyde ...CLYDE!"

"What's up, man?"

"The bet's to you."

He'd look around the table. "Who bet?"

I'd take a deep breath and go through the entire process once more. I'd even have to tell him, again, what the game was. Too many games of seven stud, with all of its betting rounds, made for a long night.

The downside is fat prisoners

In a poker game a guy like Clyde, when stoned, is exasperating. But if I were a prison guard, a warden, or especially if I were a fellow prisoner, that's what I'd want around me or occupying the next cell—guys like Clyde. Nice, slow inmates afflicted with logorrhea.

The downside? About the only things I can think of is that prisoners would exercise less, eat more, and gain weight. So what! The food bill would be going up on far fewer inmates. And gang warfare? Stoners aren't violent. Most would just want to socialize and satisfy the maryjane-induced munchies.

I know someone's going to say people will be committing crimes just to go to jail for the free weed. But I don't believe it. I don't know anyone who'd willingly go to prison, with the exception of some who have already been in so long that they're capable of nothing other than institutionalized lives. And even if there are some, don't worry. As I said, decriminalize drugs and there will be plenty of room for the few who think a nice way to spend what remains of their three score and ten is in a six-by-eight concrete condo.

You think I'm joking? Irresponsible? Insane? I'm not.

Legalize marijuana and we'll empty our prisons, and those violent people who do end up there will be more docile, making the prisons safer for both inmates and guards.

But for the love of Pete, whatever we do, let's keep it illegal to smoke the stuff at poker games. Δ